# Mastering Hyper-V® 2012 R2 with System Center and Windows Azure™

# Mastering Hyper-V® 2012 R2 with System Center and Windows Azure™

John Savill

Acquisitions Editor: Mariann Barsolo
Development Editor: Kim Beaudet
Technical Editor: Sean Deuby
Production Editor: Rebecca Anderson
Copy Editors: Judy Flynn and Kim Wimpsett
Editorial Manager: Pete Gaughan
Vice President and Executive Group Publisher: Richard Swadley
Associate Publisher: Chris Webb
Book Designers: Maureen Forys, Happenstance Type-O-Rama; Judy Fung
Proofreader: Rebecca Rider
Indexer: Robert Swanson
Project Coordinator, Cover: Todd Klemme
Cover Designer: Wiley
Cover Image: ©Getty Images, Inc./ColorBlind Images

Dear Reader,

Thank you for choosing *Mastering Hyper-V 2012 R2 with System Center and Windows Azure*. This book is part of a family of premium-quality Sybex books, all of which are written by outstanding authors who combine practical experience with a gift for teaching.

Sybex was founded in 1976. More than 30 years later, we're still committed to producing consistently exceptional books. With each of our titles, we're working hard to set a new standard for the industry. From the paper we print on, to the authors we work with, our goal is to bring you the best books available.

I hope you see all that reflected in these pages. I'd be very interested to hear your comments and get your feedback on how we're doing. Feel free to let me know what you think about this or any other Sybex book by sending me an email at contactus@wiley.com. If you think you've found a technical error in this book, please visit http://sybex.custhelp.com. Customer feedback is critical to our efforts at Sybex.

Best regards,

Chris Webb
Associate Publisher, Sybex

For my wife, Julie, and my children, Kevin, Abby, and Ben. My everythings.

# Acknowledgments

I could not have written this book without the help and support of many people. First, I need to thank my wife, Julie, for putting up with me for the last six months being busier than usual and for picking up the slack as always—and for always supporting the crazy things I want to do. My children, Kevin, Abby, and Ben, always make all the work worthwhile and can turn the worst, most tiring day into a good one with a smile and a laugh. Thanks to my parents for raising me to have the mindset and work ethic that enables me to accomplish the many things I do while maintaining some sense of humor.

Of course the book wouldn't be possible at all without the Wiley team: Mariann Barsolo, the acquisitions editor; the developmental editor, Kim Beaudet; the production editor, Rebecca Anderson; the copyeditors, Judy Flynn and Kim Wimpsett; and the proofreader, Rebecca Rider. Thanks also to my technical editor and friend, Sean Deuby.

Many people have helped me over the years with encouragement and technical knowledge, and this book is the sum of that. The following people helped with specific aspects of this book, and I want to thank them and give them the credit they deserve for helping make this book as good as possible (and if I've missed anyone, I'm truly sorry): Aashish Ramdas, Ben Armstrong, Charley Wen, Corey Sanders, Don Stanwyck, Elden Christensen, Gabriel Silva, Gavriella Schuster, Jake Oshins, Jeff Woolsey, John Howard, Jose Barreto, Kevin Holman, Kevin Saye, Matt McSpirit, Michael Gray, Michael Leworthy, Mike Schutz, Patrick Lang, Paul Kimbel, Scott Willwerth, Stephen Stair, Steve Linehan, Steven Ekren, and Vijay Tandra Sistla.

# About the Author

 **John Savill** is a technical specialist who focuses on Microsoft core infrastructure technologies including Windows, Hyper-V, System Center, and anything that does something cool. He has been working with Microsoft technologies for 20 years and is the creator of the highly popular NTFAQ.com website and a senior contributing editor for *Windows IT Pro* magazine. He has written five previous books covering Windows and advanced Active Directory architecture. When he is not writing books, he regularly writes magazine articles and white papers; creates a large number of technology videos, which are available on his YouTube channel, `http://www.youtube.com/ntfaqguy`; and regularly presents online and at industry leading events, including TechEd and Windows Connections. When he was writing this book, he had just completed running his annual online John Savill Master Class, which was even bigger and more successful than last year, and he is busy creating a John Savill Hyper-V Master Class, which will include two days of in-depth Hyper-V goodness.

Outside of technology, John enjoys teaching and training in martial arts (including Krav Maga and Jiu-Jitsu), spending time with his family, and participating in any kind of event that involves running in mud, crawling under electrified barbed wire, running from zombies, and generally pushing limits. While writing this book, John was training for the January 2014 Walt Disney World Dopey Challenge, which consists of running a 5K on Thursday, a 10K on Friday, a half marathon on Saturday, and then a full marathon on Sunday. The logic behind the name is that you would have to be dopey to do it, but after completing the Goofy Challenge in 2013—which consisted of the half-marathon and marathon portions—it seemed silly not take it a step further with the new Dopey event that was unveiled for 2014. As John's friend and technical editor Sean says, he does it for the bling ☺.

John tries to update his blog at `www.savilltech.com/blog` with the latest news of what he is working on.

# Contents at a Glance

*Introduction* . . . . . . . . . . . . . . . . . . . . . . . . . . . . . . . . . . . . . . . . . . . . . . . . . . . . . . . . . . . . . . . . . . . . . . . . . . . . . . . . . . . . *xix*

Chapter 1 • Introduction to Virtualization and Microsoft Solutions . . . . . . . . . . . . . . 1

Chapter 2 • Virtual Machine Resource Fundamentals . . . . . . . . . . . . . . . . . . . . . . . . . 35

Chapter 3 • Virtual Networking . . . . . . . . . . . . . . . . . . . . . . . . . . . . . . . . . . . . . . . . 75

Chapter 4 • Storage Configurations . . . . . . . . . . . . . . . . . . . . . . . . . . . . . . . . . . . . . 153

Chapter 5 • Managing Hyper-V . . . . . . . . . . . . . . . . . . . . . . . . . . . . . . . . . . . . . . . . 195

Chapter 6 • Maintaining a Hyper-V Environment. . . . . . . . . . . . . . . . . . . . . . . . . . . . 243

Chapter 7 • Failover Clustering and Migration Technologies . . . . . . . . . . . . . . . . . . . 273

Chapter 8 • Hyper-V Replica and Cloud Orchestration . . . . . . . . . . . . . . . . . . . . . . . 339

Chapter 9 • Implementing the Private Cloud and SCVMM. . . . . . . . . . . . . . . . . . . . . 369

Chapter 10 • Remote Desktop Services . . . . . . . . . . . . . . . . . . . . . . . . . . . . . . . . . . . 407

Chapter 11 • Windows Azure IaaS and Storage . . . . . . . . . . . . . . . . . . . . . . . . . . . . . 441

Chapter 12 • Bringing It All Together with a Best-of-Breed Cloud Solution . . . . . . . 491

Chapter 13 • The Hyper-V Decoder Ring for the VMware Administrator . . . . . . . . 503

Appendix • The Bottom Line. . . . . . . . . . . . . . . . . . . . . . . . . . . . . . . . . . . . . . . . . . 519

*Index* . . . . . . . . . . . . . . . . . . . . . . . . . . . . . . . . . . . . . . . . . . . . . . . . . . . . . . . . . . . . . . . . . . . . . . . . . . . . . . *531*

# Contents

Introduction . . . . . . . . . . . . . . . . . . . . . . . . . . . . . . . . . . . . . . . . . . . . . . . . . . . . . . . . . . . . . .*xix*

**Chapter 1 • Introduction to Virtualization and
Microsoft Solutions** . . . . . . . . . . . . . . . . . . . . . . . . . . . . . . . . . . . . . . . . . . .**1**
The Evolution of the Datacenter. . . . . . . . . . . . . . . . . . . . . . . . . . . . . . . . . . . . . . . 1
   One Box, One Operating System . . . . . . . . . . . . . . . . . . . . . . . . . . . . . . . . . . . . . 1
   How Virtualization Has Changed the Way Companies Work
     and Its Key Values . . . . . . . . . . . . . . . . . . . . . . . . . . . . . . . . . . . . . . . . . . . . . . . 5
History of Hyper-V . . . . . . . . . . . . . . . . . . . . . . . . . . . . . . . . . . . . . . . . . . . . . . . . . . 10
   Windows Server 2008 Hyper-V Features . . . . . . . . . . . . . . . . . . . . . . . . . . . . . . 12
   Windows Server 2008 R2 Changes. . . . . . . . . . . . . . . . . . . . . . . . . . . . . . . . . . . . 13
   Windows Server 2008 R2 Service Pack 1. . . . . . . . . . . . . . . . . . . . . . . . . . . . . . . 15
   Windows Server 2012 Hyper-V Changes . . . . . . . . . . . . . . . . . . . . . . . . . . . . . . 16
   Windows Server 2012 R2 . . . . . . . . . . . . . . . . . . . . . . . . . . . . . . . . . . . . . . . . . . . 21
Licensing of Hyper-V. . . . . . . . . . . . . . . . . . . . . . . . . . . . . . . . . . . . . . . . . . . . . . . . 23
   One Operating System (Well, Two, but Really One) . . . . . . . . . . . . . . . . . . . . . 24
   Choosing the Version of Hyper-V . . . . . . . . . . . . . . . . . . . . . . . . . . . . . . . . . . . 26
The Role of System Center with Hyper-V . . . . . . . . . . . . . . . . . . . . . . . . . . . . . . . 27
   System Center Configuration Manager. . . . . . . . . . . . . . . . . . . . . . . . . . . . . . . . 28
   System Center Virtual Machine Manager and App Controller. . . . . . . . . . . . . . 28
   System Center Operations Manager . . . . . . . . . . . . . . . . . . . . . . . . . . . . . . . . . . 28
   System Center Data Protection Manager . . . . . . . . . . . . . . . . . . . . . . . . . . . . . . 29
   System Center Service Manager. . . . . . . . . . . . . . . . . . . . . . . . . . . . . . . . . . . . . . 29
   System Center Orchestrator . . . . . . . . . . . . . . . . . . . . . . . . . . . . . . . . . . . . . . . . 30
Clouds and Services. . . . . . . . . . . . . . . . . . . . . . . . . . . . . . . . . . . . . . . . . . . . . . . . . 30
The Bottom Line. . . . . . . . . . . . . . . . . . . . . . . . . . . . . . . . . . . . . . . . . . . . . . . . . . . . 32

**Chapter 2 • Virtual Machine Resource Fundamentals** . . . . . . . . . . . . . . . . .**35**
Understanding VMBus . . . . . . . . . . . . . . . . . . . . . . . . . . . . . . . . . . . . . . . . . . . . . . 35
The Anatomy of a Virtual Machine . . . . . . . . . . . . . . . . . . . . . . . . . . . . . . . . . . . . 38
   Generation 1 Virtual Machine . . . . . . . . . . . . . . . . . . . . . . . . . . . . . . . . . . . . . . . 39
   Generation 2 Virtual Machine . . . . . . . . . . . . . . . . . . . . . . . . . . . . . . . . . . . . . . . 44
Processor Resources. . . . . . . . . . . . . . . . . . . . . . . . . . . . . . . . . . . . . . . . . . . . . . . . . 47
   Virtual Processor to Logical Processor Scheduling . . . . . . . . . . . . . . . . . . . . . . 49
   Processor Assignment . . . . . . . . . . . . . . . . . . . . . . . . . . . . . . . . . . . . . . . . . . . . . 52
   NUMA Support. . . . . . . . . . . . . . . . . . . . . . . . . . . . . . . . . . . . . . . . . . . . . . . . . . . 57
Memory Resources. . . . . . . . . . . . . . . . . . . . . . . . . . . . . . . . . . . . . . . . . . . . . . . . . . 60
Virtual Storage . . . . . . . . . . . . . . . . . . . . . . . . . . . . . . . . . . . . . . . . . . . . . . . . . . . . . 67
   VHD . . . . . . . . . . . . . . . . . . . . . . . . . . . . . . . . . . . . . . . . . . . . . . . . . . . . . . . . . . . . 67
   VHDX . . . . . . . . . . . . . . . . . . . . . . . . . . . . . . . . . . . . . . . . . . . . . . . . . . . . . . . . . . 69

Creating a Virtual Hard Disk . . . . . . . . . . . . . . . . . . . . . . . . . . . . . . . . . . . . . . . . . . . 70
Pass-Through Storage . . . . . . . . . . . . . . . . . . . . . . . . . . . . . . . . . . . . . . . . . . . . . . . . . 72
The Bottom Line . . . . . . . . . . . . . . . . . . . . . . . . . . . . . . . . . . . . . . . . . . . . . . . . . . . . . . 72

**Chapter 3 • Virtual Networking . . . . . . . . . . . . . . . . . . . . . . . . . . . . . . . . . 75**
Virtual Switch Fundamentals . . . . . . . . . . . . . . . . . . . . . . . . . . . . . . . . . . . . . . . . . . . 75
Three Types of Virtual Switch . . . . . . . . . . . . . . . . . . . . . . . . . . . . . . . . . . . . . . . . . 75
Creating a Virtual Switch . . . . . . . . . . . . . . . . . . . . . . . . . . . . . . . . . . . . . . . . . . . . 78
Extensible Switch . . . . . . . . . . . . . . . . . . . . . . . . . . . . . . . . . . . . . . . . . . . . . . . . . . . . 80
VLANs and PVLANS . . . . . . . . . . . . . . . . . . . . . . . . . . . . . . . . . . . . . . . . . . . . . . . . . 83
Understanding VLANs . . . . . . . . . . . . . . . . . . . . . . . . . . . . . . . . . . . . . . . . . . . . . . 83
VLANs and Hyper-V . . . . . . . . . . . . . . . . . . . . . . . . . . . . . . . . . . . . . . . . . . . . . . . 86
PVLANs . . . . . . . . . . . . . . . . . . . . . . . . . . . . . . . . . . . . . . . . . . . . . . . . . . . . . . . . . 87
How SCVMM Simplifies Networking with Hyper-V . . . . . . . . . . . . . . . . . . . . . . . 91
SCVMM Networking Architecture . . . . . . . . . . . . . . . . . . . . . . . . . . . . . . . . . . . . 92
Deploying Networking with SCVMM 2012 R2 . . . . . . . . . . . . . . . . . . . . . . . . . . 97
Network Virtualization . . . . . . . . . . . . . . . . . . . . . . . . . . . . . . . . . . . . . . . . . . . . . . 112
Network Virtualization Overview . . . . . . . . . . . . . . . . . . . . . . . . . . . . . . . . . . . . 112
Implementing Network Virtualization . . . . . . . . . . . . . . . . . . . . . . . . . . . . . . . . 117
Useful Network Virtualization Commands . . . . . . . . . . . . . . . . . . . . . . . . . . . . . 119
Network Virtualization Gateway . . . . . . . . . . . . . . . . . . . . . . . . . . . . . . . . . . . . . 124
Summary . . . . . . . . . . . . . . . . . . . . . . . . . . . . . . . . . . . . . . . . . . . . . . . . . . . . . . . . 131
VMQ, RSS, and SR-IOV . . . . . . . . . . . . . . . . . . . . . . . . . . . . . . . . . . . . . . . . . . . . . 132
SR-IOV . . . . . . . . . . . . . . . . . . . . . . . . . . . . . . . . . . . . . . . . . . . . . . . . . . . . . . . . . . 132
DVMQ . . . . . . . . . . . . . . . . . . . . . . . . . . . . . . . . . . . . . . . . . . . . . . . . . . . . . . . . . . 136
RSS and vRSS . . . . . . . . . . . . . . . . . . . . . . . . . . . . . . . . . . . . . . . . . . . . . . . . . . . . 138
NIC Teaming . . . . . . . . . . . . . . . . . . . . . . . . . . . . . . . . . . . . . . . . . . . . . . . . . . . . . . 141
Host Virtual Adapters and Types of Networks Needed in a Hyper-V Host . . . . . . . . 143
Types of Guest Network Adapters . . . . . . . . . . . . . . . . . . . . . . . . . . . . . . . . . . . . . 147
Monitoring Virtual Traffic . . . . . . . . . . . . . . . . . . . . . . . . . . . . . . . . . . . . . . . . . . . . 150
The Bottom Line . . . . . . . . . . . . . . . . . . . . . . . . . . . . . . . . . . . . . . . . . . . . . . . . . . . . 152

**Chapter 4 • Storage Configurations . . . . . . . . . . . . . . . . . . . . . . . . . . . . 153**
Storage Fundamentals and VHDX . . . . . . . . . . . . . . . . . . . . . . . . . . . . . . . . . . . . . 153
Types of Controllers . . . . . . . . . . . . . . . . . . . . . . . . . . . . . . . . . . . . . . . . . . . . . . . 156
Common VHDX Maintenance Actions . . . . . . . . . . . . . . . . . . . . . . . . . . . . . . . . . 157
Performing Dynamic VHDX Resize . . . . . . . . . . . . . . . . . . . . . . . . . . . . . . . . . . 159
Storage Spaces and Windows as a Storage Solution . . . . . . . . . . . . . . . . . . . . . . . 160
Server Message Block (SMB) Usage . . . . . . . . . . . . . . . . . . . . . . . . . . . . . . . . . . . . 166
SMB Technologies . . . . . . . . . . . . . . . . . . . . . . . . . . . . . . . . . . . . . . . . . . . . . . . . . 166
Using SMB for Hyper-V Storage . . . . . . . . . . . . . . . . . . . . . . . . . . . . . . . . . . . . . 172
iSCSI with Hyper-V . . . . . . . . . . . . . . . . . . . . . . . . . . . . . . . . . . . . . . . . . . . . . . . . . 173
Using the Windows iSCSI Target . . . . . . . . . . . . . . . . . . . . . . . . . . . . . . . . . . . . . 175
Using the Windows iSCSI Initiator . . . . . . . . . . . . . . . . . . . . . . . . . . . . . . . . . . . 177
Considerations for Using iSCSI . . . . . . . . . . . . . . . . . . . . . . . . . . . . . . . . . . . . . . 178

Understanding Virtual Fibre Channel . . . . . . . . . . . . . . . . . . . . . . . . . . . . . . . . . . . . . 178
Leveraging Shared VHDX . . . . . . . . . . . . . . . . . . . . . . . . . . . . . . . . . . . . . . . . . . . . . . 186
Data Deduplication and Hyper-V . . . . . . . . . . . . . . . . . . . . . . . . . . . . . . . . . . . . . . . . 188
Storage Quality of Service . . . . . . . . . . . . . . . . . . . . . . . . . . . . . . . . . . . . . . . . . . . . . 189
SAN Storage and SCVMM . . . . . . . . . . . . . . . . . . . . . . . . . . . . . . . . . . . . . . . . . . . . . 191
The Bottom Line. . . . . . . . . . . . . . . . . . . . . . . . . . . . . . . . . . . . . . . . . . . . . . . . . . . . . 193

**Chapter 5 • Managing Hyper-V** . . . . . . . . . . . . . . . . . . . . . . . . . . . . . . . . . . . . **195**
Installing Hyper-V. . . . . . . . . . . . . . . . . . . . . . . . . . . . . . . . . . . . . . . . . . . . . . . . . . . 195
    Using Configuration Levels . . . . . . . . . . . . . . . . . . . . . . . . . . . . . . . . . . . . . . . . . 197
    Enabling the Hyper-V Role . . . . . . . . . . . . . . . . . . . . . . . . . . . . . . . . . . . . . . . . . . 198
    Actions after Installation of Hyper-V . . . . . . . . . . . . . . . . . . . . . . . . . . . . . . . . . 200
    Deploying Hyper-V Servers with SCVMM . . . . . . . . . . . . . . . . . . . . . . . . . . . . . 202
Hyper-V Management Tools. . . . . . . . . . . . . . . . . . . . . . . . . . . . . . . . . . . . . . . . . . . . 203
    Using Hyper-V Manager . . . . . . . . . . . . . . . . . . . . . . . . . . . . . . . . . . . . . . . . . . . 205
    Core Actions Using PowerShell . . . . . . . . . . . . . . . . . . . . . . . . . . . . . . . . . . . . . 210
Securing the Hyper-V Server . . . . . . . . . . . . . . . . . . . . . . . . . . . . . . . . . . . . . . . . . . 214
Creating and Managing a Virtual Machine. . . . . . . . . . . . . . . . . . . . . . . . . . . . . . . . 214
Creating and Using Hyper-V Templates . . . . . . . . . . . . . . . . . . . . . . . . . . . . . . . . . 219
Hyper-V Integration Services and Supported Operating Systems . . . . . . . . . . . . . . 229
Migrating Physical Servers and Virtual Machines to Hyper-V Virtual Machines . . . 233
Upgrading and Migrating from Previous Versions . . . . . . . . . . . . . . . . . . . . . . . . . . 236
    Stand-Alone Hosts . . . . . . . . . . . . . . . . . . . . . . . . . . . . . . . . . . . . . . . . . . . . . . . 237
    Clusters. . . . . . . . . . . . . . . . . . . . . . . . . . . . . . . . . . . . . . . . . . . . . . . . . . . . . . . . 237
The Bottom Line. . . . . . . . . . . . . . . . . . . . . . . . . . . . . . . . . . . . . . . . . . . . . . . . . . . . 241

**Chapter 6 • Maintaining a Hyper-V Environment. . . . . . . . . . . . . . . . . . . . 243**
Patch Planning and Implementation . . . . . . . . . . . . . . . . . . . . . . . . . . . . . . . . . . . . 243
    Leveraging WSUS. . . . . . . . . . . . . . . . . . . . . . . . . . . . . . . . . . . . . . . . . . . . . . . . 244
    Patching Hyper-V Clusters . . . . . . . . . . . . . . . . . . . . . . . . . . . . . . . . . . . . . . . . . 245
Malware Configurations. . . . . . . . . . . . . . . . . . . . . . . . . . . . . . . . . . . . . . . . . . . . . . 248
Backup Planning . . . . . . . . . . . . . . . . . . . . . . . . . . . . . . . . . . . . . . . . . . . . . . . . . . . 249
Defragmentation with Hyper-V. . . . . . . . . . . . . . . . . . . . . . . . . . . . . . . . . . . . . . . . 252
Using Checkpoints. . . . . . . . . . . . . . . . . . . . . . . . . . . . . . . . . . . . . . . . . . . . . . . . . . 254
Using Service Templates . . . . . . . . . . . . . . . . . . . . . . . . . . . . . . . . . . . . . . . . . . . . . 258
Performance Tuning and Monitoring with Hyper-V. . . . . . . . . . . . . . . . . . . . . . . . . 261
    Resource Metering . . . . . . . . . . . . . . . . . . . . . . . . . . . . . . . . . . . . . . . . . . . . . . . 265
    Monitoring. . . . . . . . . . . . . . . . . . . . . . . . . . . . . . . . . . . . . . . . . . . . . . . . . . . . . . 270
The Bottom Line. . . . . . . . . . . . . . . . . . . . . . . . . . . . . . . . . . . . . . . . . . . . . . . . . . . . 271

**Chapter 7 • Failover Clustering and Migration Technologies . . . . . . . . . 273**
Failover Clustering Basics. . . . . . . . . . . . . . . . . . . . . . . . . . . . . . . . . . . . . . . . . . . . . 273
Understanding Quorum and Why It's Important. . . . . . . . . . . . . . . . . . . . . . . . . . . . 275
    Quorum Basics . . . . . . . . . . . . . . . . . . . . . . . . . . . . . . . . . . . . . . . . . . . . . . . . . . 276
    Modifying Cluster Vote Configuration. . . . . . . . . . . . . . . . . . . . . . . . . . . . . . . . . 282

Advanced Quorum Options and Forcing Quorums. . . . . . . . . . . . . . . . . . . . . . . . 284
Geographically Distributed Clusters. . . . . . . . . . . . . . . . . . . . . . . . . . . . . . . . 286
Why Use Clustering with Hyper-V?. . . . . . . . . . . . . . . . . . . . . . . . . . . . . . . . . . . 287
Service Monitoring. . . . . . . . . . . . . . . . . . . . . . . . . . . . . . . . . . . . . . . . . . . . 288
Protected Network . . . . . . . . . . . . . . . . . . . . . . . . . . . . . . . . . . . . . . . . . . . . 291
Cluster-Aware Updating . . . . . . . . . . . . . . . . . . . . . . . . . . . . . . . . . . . . . . . 291
Where to Implement High Availability. . . . . . . . . . . . . . . . . . . . . . . . . . . . . 292
Configuring a Hyper-V Cluster. . . . . . . . . . . . . . . . . . . . . . . . . . . . . . . . . . . . . 295
Cluster Network Requirements and Configurations . . . . . . . . . . . . . . . . . . 296
Performing Cluster Validation . . . . . . . . . . . . . . . . . . . . . . . . . . . . . . . . . . . 303
Creating a Cluster. . . . . . . . . . . . . . . . . . . . . . . . . . . . . . . . . . . . . . . . . . . . . 306
Creating Clusters with SCVMM . . . . . . . . . . . . . . . . . . . . . . . . . . . . . . . . . . . . 307
Using Cluster Shared Volumes . . . . . . . . . . . . . . . . . . . . . . . . . . . . . . . . . . . . 310
Making a Virtual Machine a Clustered Virtual Machine . . . . . . . . . . . . . . . . . 314
Live Migration . . . . . . . . . . . . . . . . . . . . . . . . . . . . . . . . . . . . . . . . . . . . . . . . . 316
Windows Server 2012 Live Migration Enhancements . . . . . . . . . . . . . . . . . 320
Live Storage Move. . . . . . . . . . . . . . . . . . . . . . . . . . . . . . . . . . . . . . . . . . . . 321
Shared Nothing Live Migration. . . . . . . . . . . . . . . . . . . . . . . . . . . . . . . . . . 326
Configuring Constrained Delegation . . . . . . . . . . . . . . . . . . . . . . . . . . . . . 328
Initiating Simultaneous Migrations Using PowerShell . . . . . . . . . . . . . . . . 330
Windows Server 2012 R2 Live Migration Enhancements. . . . . . . . . . . . . . . 330
Dynamic Optimization and Resource Balancing. . . . . . . . . . . . . . . . . . . . . . . 332
The Bottom Line. . . . . . . . . . . . . . . . . . . . . . . . . . . . . . . . . . . . . . . . . . . . . . . . 336

**Chapter 8 • Hyper-V Replica and Cloud Orchestration. . . . . . . . . . . . . . . 339**
The Need for Disaster Recovery and DR Basics . . . . . . . . . . . . . . . . . . . . . . . . 339
Asynchronous vs. Synchronous Replication. . . . . . . . . . . . . . . . . . . . . . . . . . . 341
Introduction to Hyper-V Replica. . . . . . . . . . . . . . . . . . . . . . . . . . . . . . . . . . . . 342
Enabling Hyper-V Replica . . . . . . . . . . . . . . . . . . . . . . . . . . . . . . . . . . . . . . . . 344
Configuring Hyper-V Replica . . . . . . . . . . . . . . . . . . . . . . . . . . . . . . . . . . . . . . 346
Using Hyper-V Replica Broker. . . . . . . . . . . . . . . . . . . . . . . . . . . . . . . . . . . . . 352
Performing Hyper-V Replica Failover . . . . . . . . . . . . . . . . . . . . . . . . . . . . . . . 353
Sizing a Hyper-V Replica Solution . . . . . . . . . . . . . . . . . . . . . . . . . . . . . . . . . . 359
Using Hyper-V Replica Cloud Orchestration for Automated Failover . . . . . . . . 361
Overview of Hyper-V Recovery Manager . . . . . . . . . . . . . . . . . . . . . . . . . . 362
Getting Started with HRM . . . . . . . . . . . . . . . . . . . . . . . . . . . . . . . . . . . . . . 363
Architecting the Right Disaster Recovery Solution . . . . . . . . . . . . . . . . . . . . . 367
The Bottom Line. . . . . . . . . . . . . . . . . . . . . . . . . . . . . . . . . . . . . . . . . . . . . . . . 368

**Chapter 9 • Implementing the Private Cloud and SCVMM. . . . . . . . . . . . 369**
The Benefits of the Private Cloud . . . . . . . . . . . . . . . . . . . . . . . . . . . . . . . . . . . 369
Private Cloud Components. . . . . . . . . . . . . . . . . . . . . . . . . . . . . . . . . . . . . . . . 374

SCVMM Fundamentals. . . . . . . . . . . . . . . . . . . . . . . . . . . . . . . . . . . . . . . . . . . . . . 376
    Installation. . . . . . . . . . . . . . . . . . . . . . . . . . . . . . . . . . . . . . . . . . . . . . . . . . . 377
    SCVMM Management Console . . . . . . . . . . . . . . . . . . . . . . . . . . . . . . . . . . . 379
    Libraries . . . . . . . . . . . . . . . . . . . . . . . . . . . . . . . . . . . . . . . . . . . . . . . . . . . . . 382
Creating a Private Cloud Using System Center Virtual Machine Manager. . . . . . . . 386
Granting Users Access to the Private Cloud with App Controller. . . . . . . . . . . . . . . 393
    Installation and Initial Configuration. . . . . . . . . . . . . . . . . . . . . . . . . . . . . . 394
    User Interaction with App Controller . . . . . . . . . . . . . . . . . . . . . . . . . . . . . . 396
Enabling Workflows and Advanced Private Cloud Concepts
  Using Service Manager and Orchestrator . . . . . . . . . . . . . . . . . . . . . . . . . . . . . 399
How the Rest of System Center Fits into Your Private Cloud Architecture . . . . . . . . 402
The Bottom Line. . . . . . . . . . . . . . . . . . . . . . . . . . . . . . . . . . . . . . . . . . . . . . . . . . . . 405

**Chapter 10 • Remote Desktop Services. . . . . . . . . . . . . . . . . . . . . . . . . . . 407**
Remote Desktop Services and Bring Your Own Device . . . . . . . . . . . . . . . . . . . . . . 407
Microsoft Desktop and Session Virtualization Technologies. . . . . . . . . . . . . . . . . . . 411
    RD Web Access . . . . . . . . . . . . . . . . . . . . . . . . . . . . . . . . . . . . . . . . . . . . . . . 413
    RD Connection Broker. . . . . . . . . . . . . . . . . . . . . . . . . . . . . . . . . . . . . . . . . . 414
    RD Virtualization Host . . . . . . . . . . . . . . . . . . . . . . . . . . . . . . . . . . . . . . . . . 415
    RD Gateway . . . . . . . . . . . . . . . . . . . . . . . . . . . . . . . . . . . . . . . . . . . . . . . . . . 415
Requirements for a Complete Desktop Virtualization Solution . . . . . . . . . . . . . . . . 416
Creating the VDI Template. . . . . . . . . . . . . . . . . . . . . . . . . . . . . . . . . . . . . . . . . . . . 420
Deploying a New VDI Collection Using Scenario-Based Deployment. . . . . . . . . . . . 423
Using RemoteFX. . . . . . . . . . . . . . . . . . . . . . . . . . . . . . . . . . . . . . . . . . . . . . . . . . . . 429
Remote Desktop Protocol Capabilities . . . . . . . . . . . . . . . . . . . . . . . . . . . . . . . . . . . 433
Choosing the Right Desktop Virtualization Technology . . . . . . . . . . . . . . . . . . . . . 436
The Bottom Line. . . . . . . . . . . . . . . . . . . . . . . . . . . . . . . . . . . . . . . . . . . . . . . . . . . . 439

**Chapter 11 • Windows Azure IaaS and Storage . . . . . . . . . . . . . . . . . . . . . 441**
Understanding Public Cloud "as a Service" . . . . . . . . . . . . . . . . . . . . . . . . . . . . . . . 441
When Public Cloud Services Are the Best Solution . . . . . . . . . . . . . . . . . . . . . . . . . 443
Windows Azure 101. . . . . . . . . . . . . . . . . . . . . . . . . . . . . . . . . . . . . . . . . . . . . . . . . . 447
    Windows Azure Compute. . . . . . . . . . . . . . . . . . . . . . . . . . . . . . . . . . . . . . . . 447
    Windows Azure Data Services. . . . . . . . . . . . . . . . . . . . . . . . . . . . . . . . . . . . 449
    Windows Azure App Services . . . . . . . . . . . . . . . . . . . . . . . . . . . . . . . . . . . . 450
    Windows Azure Network . . . . . . . . . . . . . . . . . . . . . . . . . . . . . . . . . . . . . . . 451
Capabilities of Azure IaaS and How It Is Purchased . . . . . . . . . . . . . . . . . . . . . . . . 451
Creating Virtual Machines in Azure IaaS . . . . . . . . . . . . . . . . . . . . . . . . . . . . . . . . . 460
    Managing with PowerShell. . . . . . . . . . . . . . . . . . . . . . . . . . . . . . . . . . . . . . . 471
Windows Azure Virtual Networks. . . . . . . . . . . . . . . . . . . . . . . . . . . . . . . . . . . . . . . 474
Linking On-Premises Networks with Azure IaaS . . . . . . . . . . . . . . . . . . . . . . . . . . . 483

Migrating Virtual Machines between Hyper-V and Azure IaaS . . . . . . . . . . . . . . . . . 486
Leveraging Azure Storage . . . . . . . . . . . . . . . . . . . . . . . . . . . . . . . . . . . . . . . . 487
The Bottom Line . . . . . . . . . . . . . . . . . . . . . . . . . . . . . . . . . . . . . . . . . . . . . . 490

**Chapter 12 • Bringing It All Together with
a Best-of-Breed Cloud Solution** . . . . . . . . . . . . . . . . . . . . . . . . . . . . **491**
Which Is the Right Technology To Choose? . . . . . . . . . . . . . . . . . . . . . . . . . . . . . 491
  Consider the Public Cloud. . . . . . . . . . . . . . . . . . . . . . . . . . . . . . . . . . . . . 492
  Decide If a Server Workload Should Be Virtualized. . . . . . . . . . . . . . . . . . . . . . . 496
  Do I Want a Private Cloud? . . . . . . . . . . . . . . . . . . . . . . . . . . . . . . . . . . . . 498
Enabling Single Pane of Glass Management . . . . . . . . . . . . . . . . . . . . . . . . . . . . 499
The Bottom Line . . . . . . . . . . . . . . . . . . . . . . . . . . . . . . . . . . . . . . . . . . . . . . 501

**Chapter 13 • The Hyper-V Decoder Ring for
the VMware Administrator** . . . . . . . . . . . . . . . . . . . . . . . . . . . . . . . **503**
Overview of the VMware Solution and Key Differences from Hyper-V . . . . . . . . . . 503
Translating Key VMware Technologies and Actions to Hyper-V . . . . . . . . . . . . . . . 506
  Translations . . . . . . . . . . . . . . . . . . . . . . . . . . . . . . . . . . . . . . . . . . . . . 506
  Most Common Misconceptions . . . . . . . . . . . . . . . . . . . . . . . . . . . . . . . . . 511
Converting VMware Skills to Hyper-V and System Center . . . . . . . . . . . . . . . . . . 514
Migrating from VMware to Hyper-V . . . . . . . . . . . . . . . . . . . . . . . . . . . . . . . . 515
The Bottom Line . . . . . . . . . . . . . . . . . . . . . . . . . . . . . . . . . . . . . . . . . . . . . . 517

**Appendix • The Bottom Line** . . . . . . . . . . . . . . . . . . . . . . . . . . . . . . . . . **519**
Chapter 1: Introduction to Virtualization and Microsoft Solutions. . . . . . . . . . . . . . 519
Chapter 2: Virtual Machine Resource Fundamentals . . . . . . . . . . . . . . . . . . . . . . 520
Chapter 3: Virtual Networking . . . . . . . . . . . . . . . . . . . . . . . . . . . . . . . . . . . . 521
Chapter 4: Storage Configurations . . . . . . . . . . . . . . . . . . . . . . . . . . . . . . . . . 522
Chapter 5: Managing Hyper-V. . . . . . . . . . . . . . . . . . . . . . . . . . . . . . . . . . . . 522
Chapter 6: Maintaining a Hyper-V Environment. . . . . . . . . . . . . . . . . . . . . . . . . 523
Chapter 7: Failover Clustering and Migration Technologies . . . . . . . . . . . . . . . . . . 524
Chapter 8: Hyper-V Replica and Cloud Orchestration. . . . . . . . . . . . . . . . . . . . . . 525
Chapter 9: Implementing the Private Cloud and SCVMM . . . . . . . . . . . . . . . . . . . 526
Chapter 10: Remote Desktop Services. . . . . . . . . . . . . . . . . . . . . . . . . . . . . . . 526
Chapter 11: Windows Azure IaaS and Storage . . . . . . . . . . . . . . . . . . . . . . . . . . 527
Chapter 12: Bringing It All Together with a Best-of-Breed Cloud Solution . . . . . . . . . 528
Chapter 13: The Hyper-V Decoder Ring for the VMware Administrator. . . . . . . . . . . 529

Index . . . . . . . . . . . . . . . . . . . . . . . . . . . . . . . . . . . . . . . . . . . . . . . . . . . . . . 531

# Introduction

The book you are holding is the result of 20 years of experience in the IT world and over 15 years of virtualization experience that started with VMware and includes Virtual PC and now Hyper-V. My goal for this book is simple: to help you become knowledgeable and effective when it comes to architecting and managing a Hyper-V–based virtual environment. This means understanding how Hyper-V works and its capabilities, but it also means knowing when to leverage other technologies to provide the most complete and optimal solution. That means leveraging System Center and Windows Azure, which I also cover because they relate to Hyper-V. I also dive into some key technologies of Windows Server where they bring benefit to Hyper-V.

Hyper-V is now a mature and widely adopted virtualization solution. It is one of only two x86 server virtualization solutions in Gartner's leader quadrant, and in addition to being used by many of the largest companies in the world, it powers Windows Azure, which is one of the largest cloud services in the world.

Hyper-V is a role of Windows Server, and if you are a Windows administrator, you will find Hyper-V management fairly intuitive, but there are still many key areas that require attention. I have structured this book to cover the key principles of virtualization and the resources you will manage with Hyper-V before I actually cover installing and configuring Hyper-V itself and then move on to advanced topics such as high availability, replication, private cloud, and more.

I am a strong believer in learning by doing, and I therefore highly encourage you to try out all the technologies and principles I cover in this book. You don't need a huge lab environment, and for most of the topics, you could use a single machine with Windows Server installed on it and 8 GB of memory to enable a few virtual machines to run concurrently. Ideally though, having at least two servers will help with the replication and high availability concepts. Sometimes in this book you'll see step-by-step instructions to guide you through a process, sometimes I will link to an external source that already has a good step-by-step guide, and sometimes I will link to videos I have posted to ensure maximum understanding.

I have created an application that is available in the Windows Store, Mastering Hyper-V. It provides easy access to the external links, videos, and code samples I use in this book. As you read each chapter check out the application to find related content. The application can be downloaded from `http://www.savilltech.com/mhv`. Using the Windows Store allows me to also update it over time as required. Please get this application as I will use it to add additional videos based on reader feedback that are not referenced in the main text and include additional information where required.

## Who Should Read This Book

I am making certain assumptions regarding the reader:

◆ You have basic Windows Server knowledge and can install Windows Server.

◆ You have basic knowledge of what PowerShell is.

◆ You have access to a Hyper-V server to enable test implementation of the many covered technologies.

This book is intended for anyone who wants to learn Hyper-V. If you have a basic knowledge of virtualization or a competing technology such as VMware, that will help but is not a requirement. I start off with a foundational understanding of each technology and then build on that to cover more advanced topics and configurations. If you are an architect, a consultant, an administrator, or really anyone who just wants better knowledge of Hyper-V, this book is for you.

There are many times I go into advanced topics that may seem over your head. In those cases, don't worry. Focus on the preceding elements you understand, and implement and test them to solidify your understanding. Then when you feel comfortable, come back to the more advanced topics. They will seem far simpler once your understanding of the foundational principles are solidified.

## What's Inside

Here is a glance at what's in each chapter.

**Chapter 1, "Introduction to Virtualization and Microsoft Solutions,"** focuses on the core value proposition of virtualization and how the datacenter has evolved. It covers the key changes and capabilities of Hyper-V in addition to the role System Center plays in a Hyper-V environment. I will cover the types of cloud services available and how Hyper-V forms the foundation of private cloud solutions.

**Chapter 2, "Virtual Machine Resource Fundamentals,"** covers the core resources of a virtual machine, specifically architecture (generation 1 and generation 2 virtual machines), processor, and memory. You will learn about advanced configurations to enable many types of operating system support along with best practices for resource planning.

**Chapter 3, "Virtual Networking,"** covers one of the most complicated aspects of virtualization, especially when using the new network virtualization capabilities in Hyper-V. This chapter covers the key networking concepts, how to architect virtual networks, and how to configure them. I'll also cover networking using System Center Virtual Machine Manager (SCVMM) and how to design and implement network virtualization.

**Chapter 4, "Storage Configurations,"** covers the storage options for Hyper-V environments, including the VHD and VHDX formats plus capabilities in Windows Server 2012 R2 that help manage direct attached storage. You will learn about storage technologies for virtual machines such as iSCSI, Virtual Fibre Channel, and shared VHDX; their relative advantages; and also the storage migration and resize functions.

**Chapter 5, "Managing Hyper-V,"** walks through the installation of and best practices for managing Hyper-V. The basics of configuring virtual machines, installing operating systems, and using the Hyper-V Integration Services are all covered. Strategies for migrating from other hypervisors, physical servers, and other versions of Hyper-V are explored.

**Chapter 6, "Maintaining a Hyper-V Environment,"** focuses on the tasks required to keep Hyper-V healthy after you've installed it, which includes patching, malware protection, backup, and monitoring. Key actions such as taking checkpoints of virtual machines, setting up service templates, and performance tuning are covered.

**Chapter 7, "Failover Clustering and Migration Technologies,"** covers making Hyper-V highly available using failover clustering and will include a deep dive into exactly what makes a cluster tick, specifically when running Hyper-V. Key migration technologies such as Live Migration, Shared Nothing Live Migration, and Storage Migration are explored in addition to configurations related to mobility outside of a cluster and placement optimization for virtual machines.

**Chapter 8, "Hyper-V Replica and Cloud Orchestration,"** shifts from high availability to a requirement of many organizations today, providing disaster recovery protection in the event of losing an entire site. This chapter looks at the options for disaster recovery, including leveraging Hyper-V Replica and orchestrating failovers with Windows Azure in the event of a disaster.

**Chapter 9, "Implementing the Private Cloud and SCVMM,"** shows the many benefits of the Microsoft stack to organizations beyond just virtualization. This chapter explores the key benefits and what a private cloud using Microsoft technologies actually looks like. Key components and functional areas, including the actual end user experience and how you can leverage all of System Center for different levels of private cloud capability, are all covered.

**Chapter 10, "Remote Desktop Services,"** shifts the focus to another type of virtualization, virtualizing the end user experience, which is a critical capability for most organizations. Virtual desktop infrastructure is becoming a bigger component of the user environment. This chapter looks at the different types of desktop virtualization available with Remote Desktop Services with a focus on capabilities that are enabled by Hyper-V, such as advanced graphical capabilities with RemoteFX.

**Chapter 11, "Windows Azure IaaS and Storage,"** explores the capabilities of one of the biggest public cloud services in the world, which is powered by Hyper-V. This chapter will cover the fundamentals of Windows Azure and how to create virtual machines in Windows Azure. The chapter will also cover the networking options available both within Windows Azure and to connect to your on-premises network. I will examine the migration of virtual machines and how to leverage Windows Azure Storage. Ways to provide a seamless management experience will be explored.

**Chapter 12, "Bringing It All Together with a Best-of-Breed Cloud Solution,"** brings together all the different technologies and options to help architect a best-of-breed virtualization and cloud solution.

**Chapter 13, "The Hyper-V Decoder Ring for the VMware Administrator,"** focuses on converting skills for VMware to their Hyper-V equivalent. This chapter also focuses on migration approaches and ways to translate skills.

**NOTE** Don't forget to download the companion Windows Store application, Mastering Hyper-V, from http://www.savilltech.com/mhv.

## The Mastering Series

The Mastering series from Sybex provides outstanding instruction for readers with intermediate and advanced skills, in the form of top-notch training and development for those already working in their field and clear, serious education for those aspiring to become pros. Every Mastering book includes the following elements:

- Skill-based instruction, with chapters organized around real tasks rather than abstract concepts or subjects

- Self-review test questions, so you can be certain you're equipped to do the job right

## How to Contact the Author

I welcome feedback from you about this book or about books you'd like to see from me in the future. You can reach me by writing to john@savilltech.com. For more information about my work, visit my website at www.savilltech.com.

Sybex strives to keep you supplied with the latest tools and information you need for your work. Please check the Sybex website at www.sybex.com/go/masteringhyperv2012r2, where we'll post additional content and updates that supplement this book should the need arise.

# Chapter 1

# Introduction to Virtualization and Microsoft Solutions

This chapter lays the foundation for the core fabric concepts and technologies discussed throughout not just this first part but also for the entire book. Virtualization has radically changed the layout and operation of a datacenter, and this datacenter evolution and its benefits are explored.

Microsoft's solution for virtualization is its Hyper-V technology, which is a core part of Windows Server and is also available in the form of a free stand-alone hypervisor. The virtualization layer is only part of the solution. Management is just as critical, and in today's world, the public cloud is also a consideration, and so a seamless management story with compatibility between your on- and off-premises resources provides the model implementation.

In this chapter, you will learn to

♦ Articulate the key value propositions of virtualization

♦ Understand the differences in functionality between the different versions of Hyper-V

♦ Differentiate between the types of cloud services and when each type is best utilized

## The Evolution of the Datacenter

There are many texts available that go into large amounts of detail about the history of datacenters, but that is not the goal of the following sections. Instead, I am going to take you through the key changes I have seen in my 20 years of working in and consulting about datacenter infrastructure. This brief look at the evolution of datacenters will help you understand the challenges of the past, why virtualization has become such a key component of every modern datacenter, and why there is still room for improvement.

### One Box, One Operating System

Datacenters as recent as 10 years ago were all architected in a similar way. These huge rooms with very expensive cabling and air conditioning were home to hundreds if not thousands of servers. Some of these servers were mainframes, but the majority were regular servers (although today the difference between a mainframe and a powerful regular server is blurring), and while the processor architecture running in these servers may have been different—for example, some were x86 based, some Alpha, some MIPS, some SPARC—each server ran an operating system (OS) such as Windows, Linux, or OpenVMS. Some OSs supported different processor architectures while others were limited to a specific architecture, and likewise some processor architectures would dictate which OS had to be used. The servers themselves may have been freestanding, and as technology has advanced, servers got smaller and became rack mountable, enabling greater compression of the datacenter.

---

**UNDERSTANDING X86**

Often the term *x86* is used when talking about processor architecture, but its use has been generalized beyond just the original Intel processors that built on the 8086. *x86* does not refer to only Intel processors but is used more generally to refer to 32-bit operating systems running on any processor leveraging x86 instruction sets, including processors from AMD. *x64* represents a 64-bit instruction set extension processor (primarily from Intel and AMD), although you may also see amd64 to denote 64-bit. What can be confusing is that a 64-bit processor is still technically x86, and it has become more common today to simply use *x86* to identify anything based on x86 architecture, which could be 32-bit or 64-bit from other types of processor architecture. Therefore, if you see *x86* within this book or in other media, it does not mean 32-bit only.

---

Even with all this variation in types of server and operating systems, there was something in common. Each server ran a single OS, and that OS interacted directly with the hardware in the server and had to use hardware-specific drivers to utilize the capabilities available. In the rest of this book, I'm going to primarily focus on x86 Windows; however, many of the challenges and solutions apply to other OSs as well.

Every server comprises a number of resources, including processor, memory, network, and storage (although some modern servers do not have local storage such as blade systems and instead rely completely on external storage subsystems). The amount of each resource can vary drastically, as shown in the following sections.

## PROCESSOR

A server can have one or more processors, and it's common to see servers with two, four, or eight processors (although it is certainly possible to have servers with more). Modern processors use a core architecture that allows a single processor to have multiple cores. Each core consists of a discrete central processing unit (CPU) and L1 cache (very fast memory used for temporary storage of information related to computations) able to perform its own computations, and those multiple cores can then share a common L2 cache (bigger but not as fast as L1) and bus interface. This allows a single physical processor to perform multiple parallel computations and actually act like many separate processors. The first multicore processors had two cores (dual-core) and this continues to increase, with eight-core (octo-core) processors available and a new "many-core" generation on the horizon, which will have tens of processor cores. It is common to see a physical processor referred to as a socket and each processor core referred to as a logical processor. For example, a dual-socket system with quad-core processors would have eight logical processors (four on each physical processor, and there are two processors). In addition to the number of sockets and cores, there are variations in the speed of the processors and the exact instruction sets supported. (It is because of limitations in the continued increase of clock speed that moving to multicore became the best way to improve overall computational performance, especially as modern operating systems are multithreaded and can take advantage of parallel computation.) Some processors also support hyperthreading, which is a means to split certain parts of a processor core into two parallel computational streams to avoid wasted processing. Hyperthreading does not double computational capability but generally gives a 10 to 15 percent performance boost. Typically with hyperthreading, this would therefore double the number of logical processors in a system. However, for virtualization, I prefer to not do this doubling, but this does not mean I turn off hyperthreading. Hyperthreading may sometimes help, but it certainly won't hurt.

Previous versions of Windows actually supported different processor architectures, including MIPS, Alpha, and PowerPC in early versions of Windows and more recently Itanium. However, as of Windows Server 2012, the only supported processor architecture is x86 and specifically only 64-bit from Windows Server 2008 R2 and above (there are still 32-bit versions of the Windows 8/8.1 client operating system).

Prior to Windows Server 2008, there were separate versions of the hardware abstraction layer (HAL) depending on if you had a uniprocessor or multiprocessor system. However, given the negligible performance savings on modern, faster processors that was specific to the uniprocessor HAL on single-processor systems (synchronization code for multiple processors was not present in the uniprocessor HAL), this was removed, enabling a single unified HAL that eases some of the pain caused by moving from uni- to multiprocessor systems.

## MEMORY

The memory resource is generally far simpler and not really a huge variation. Some memory supports error-correcting code (ECC), which provides resiliency against the most common types of internal corruption, and memory has different speeds. However, for most environments, the memory considerations is simply how much there is! Generally, the more memory, the better, and with only 64-bit versions of Windows Server, there are no longer considerations around the maximum amount of memory that can be used by an operating system (a 4 GB limit exists for 32-bit operating systems).

## STORAGE

Storage will fall into one of two buckets. The storage is internal (direct-attached storage, or DAS), which means the disks are local to the server, and attached via a technology such as SCSI, SATA, or SAS (even if the storage is in an external storage enclosure but is connected via one of these means, it is still considered direct-attached). Alternatively, the storage is external, such as storage that is hosted on another server or on a storage area network (SAN) or on network-attached storage (NAS). Various protocols may be used for external storage access that offer either file-level or block-level access to the storage.

File-level access enables the requesting server to access files on the server, but this is offered over a protocol that hides the underlying file system and actual blocks of the file on disk. Examples of file-level protocols are Server Message Block (SMB) and Network File System (NFS), typically offered by NAS devices.

Block-level access enables the requesting server to see the blocks on the disk and effectively mount the disk, format the mounted disk with a file system, and then directly manipulate blocks on the disk. Block-level access is typically offered by SANs using protocols such as iSCSI (which leverages the TCP/IP network) and Fibre Channel (which requires dedicated hardware and cabling). Typically, block-level protocols have offered higher performance, and the SANs providing the block-level storage offer advanced features, which means SANs are typically preferred over NAS devices for enterprise storage. However, there is a big price difference between a SAN and potentially the dedicated storage hardware and cabling (referred to as storage fabric), and an NFS device that leverages the existing IP network connectivity.

The hardware for connectivity to storage can vary greatly for both internal storage such as SCSI controllers and external storage such as the host bus adapters (HBAs), which provide the connectivity from a server to a Fibre Channel switch (which then connects to the SAN). Very specific drivers are required for the exact model of storage adapter, and often the driver version must correlate to a firmware version of the storage adapter.

In all components of an environment, protection from a single point of failure is desirable. For internal storage, it is common to group multiple physical disks together into arrays that can provide protection from data loss due to a single disk failure, a Redundant Array of Independent Disks (RAID), although Windows Server also has other technologies that will be covered in later chapters, including Storage Spaces. For external storage, it is possible to group multiple network adapters together into a team for IP-based storage access. For example, SMB, NFS, and iSCSI can be used to provide resiliency from a single network adapter failure, and for non-IP-based storage connectivity, it is common for a host to have at least two storage adapters, which are in turn each connected to a different storage switch (removing single points of failure). Those storage adapters are effectively joined using Multi-Path I/O (MPIO), which provides protection from a single storage adapter or storage switch failure. Both the network and storage resiliency configurations are very specific and can be complex.

Finally, the actual disks themselves have different characteristics, such as size and also their speed. The higher availability of SSD storage and its increase in size and reduced cost is making it a realistic component of modern datacenter storage solutions. This is especially true in tiered solution, which allow a mix of fast and slower disks with the most used and important data moved to the faster disks. Disk speed is commonly measured in input/output operations per second, or IOPS (pronounced "eye-ops"). The higher the IOPS, the faster the storage.

The storage also contains the actual operating system (which can be local or on a remote SAN using boot-from-SAN capabilities).

## NETWORKING

Compute, memory, and storage enable a server to perform work, but in today's environments, that work often relies on work done by other servers. In addition, access to that work from clients and the communication between computers is enabled through the network. To participate in an IP network, each machine has to have at least one IP address, which can be statically assigned or automatically assigned. To enable this IP communication, a server has at least one network adapter, and that network adapter has one or more ports that connect to the network fabric, which is typically Ethernet. As is true when it is connecting to storage controllers, the operating system requires a driver specific to the network adapter to connect to it. In high-availability network configurations, multiple network adapters are teamed together, which can be done in many cases through the driver functionality or in Windows Server 2012 using the native Windows NIC Teaming feature. Typical networking speeds in datacenters are 1 gigabit per second (Gbps) and 10 Gbps, but faster speeds are available. Like IOPS with storage, the higher the network speed, the more data you can transfer and the better the network performs.

## How Virtualization Has Changed the Way Companies Work and Its Key Values

I spend quite a lot of time talking about the resources and how they can vary, and where specific drivers and configurations may be required. This is critical to understand because many of the benefits of virtualization derive directly from the complexity and variation in all the resources available to a server. Figure 1.1 shows the Device Manager output from a server. Notice all the very specific types of network and storage hardware.

**FIGURE 1.1**

The Device Manager view of a typical physical server with Task Manager showing some of its available resources

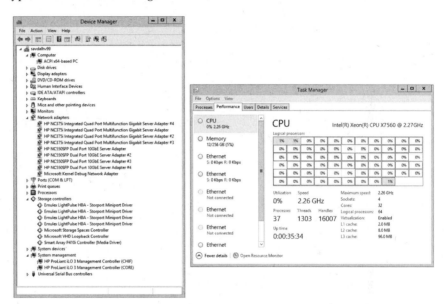

All these resources are very specific to the deployed operating system and are not easy to change in normal physical server deployments. If the boot disk from a server is placed in a different server with a different motherboard, network, or storage, there is a strong possibility the server will not boot, and it certainly will lose configuration settings and may not be able to use the hardware in the new server. The same applies to trying to restore a backup of a server to different hardware. This tight bonding between the operating system and the hardware can be a major pain point for organizations when they are considering resiliency from hardware failure but also for their disaster recovery planning. It's necessary to have near identical hardware in the disaster recovery location, and organizations start to find themselves locked in to specific hardware vendors.

Virtualization abstracts the physical hardware from that of the created virtual machines. At a very high level, virtualization allows virtual machines to be created. The virtual machines are assigned specific amounts of resources such as CPU and memory in addition to being given access to different networks via virtual switches; they are also assigned storage through virtual hard disks, which are just files on the local file system of the virtualization host or on remote storage. Figure 1.2 shows a high-level view of how a virtualized environment looks.

**FIGURE 1.2**

A high-level view
of a virtualization
host and resources
assigned to virtual
machines

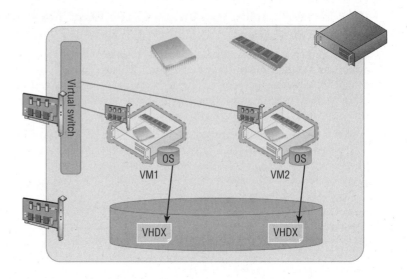

Within the virtual machine, an operating system is installed such as Windows Server 2012 R2, Windows Server 2008, Windows 8, or a Linux distribution. No special process is needed to install the operating system into a virtual machine, and it's not even necessary for the operating system to support virtualization. However, most modern operating systems are virtualization-aware today and are considered "enlightened" to be able to directly understand virtualized hardware. The operating system installed in the virtual machine, commonly referred to as the guest operating system, does not see the physical hardware of the server but rather a set of virtualized sets of hardware that is completely abstracted from the physical hardware. Figure 1.3 shows a virtual machine that is running on the physical server shown in Figure 1.1. Notice the huge difference in what is visible. All the same capabilities are available—the processor capability, memory (I only assigned the VM 212 GB of memory but up to 1 TB can be assigned), storage, and networks—but it is all through abstracted, virtual hardware that is completely independent of the physical server on which the virtual machine is running.

**FIGURE 1.3**

A virtual machine
running on a physi-
cal server

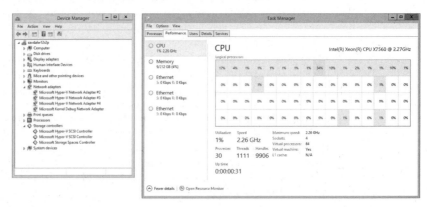

This means that with virtualization, all virtualized operating system environments and their workloads become highly mobile between servers. A virtual machine can be moved between any two servers, provide that those servers are running the same version of the hypervisor and that they have enough resource capacity. This enables organizations to be more flexible with their server hardware, especially in those disaster recovery environments that now allow any hardware to be used in the disaster recovery location as long as it runs the same hypervisor. When a backup needs to be performed, it can be performed at the hypervisor level and then at restoration provided the new server is running the same hypervisor version. As long as this is the case, the virtual machine backup can be restored and used without additional reconfiguration or manual repair.

The next major pain point with physical servers is sizing them—deciding how much memory they need, how many processors, how much storage (although the use of SANs has removed some of the challenge of calculating the amount of local storage required), how many network connections, and what levels of redundancy. I spent many years as a consultant, and when I was specifying hardware, it always had to be based on the busiest possible time for the server. It was also based on its expected load many years from the time of purchase because organizations wanted to ensure that a server would not need to be replaced in six months as its workload increased. This meant servers would be purchased that had far more resources than were actually required, especially the processor resources, where it was typical to see a server running at 5 percent processor utilization with maybe a peak of 15 percent at its busiest times. This was a huge waste of resources and not optimal resource utilization. However, because each OS instance ran on its own box and often server-class hardware only comes in certain configurations, even if it was known that the processor requirement would not be high, it was not possible procure lower-specification hardware. This same overprocurement of hardware applied to the other resources as well, such as memory, storage, and even network resources.

In most environments, different services need processor resources and memory at different times, so being able to somehow combine all the resources and share between operating system instances (and even modify the amounts allocated as needed) is key, and this is exactly what virtualization provides. In a virtual environment, the virtualization host has all of the resources, and these resources are then allocated to virtual machines. However, some resources such as processor and network resources can actually be shared between multiple virtual machines, allowing for a much greater utilization of the available resource and avoiding the utilization waste. A single server that previously ran a single OS instance with a 10 percent processor usage average could run 10 virtualized OS instances in virtual machines with most likely only additional memory being required in the server and higher IOPS storage. The details of resource sharing will be covered in future chapters, but resources such as those for processors and networks can actually be shared between virtual machines concurrently; resources like memory and storage can be segregated between virtual machines but cannot actually be shared because you cannot store different pieces of information in the same physical storage block.

The best analogy is to consider your Windows desktop that is running a single OS and likely has a single processor but is able to seemingly run many applications all at the same time. You may be using Internet Explorer to stream a movie, sending email with Outlook, and editing a document in Word. All of these applications seem to be running at the same time, but a processor core can perform only one computation at a time (ignoring multicores and hyperthreading). In reality, though, what is happening is that the OS is time-slicing turns on the processor and giving each application a few milliseconds of time each cycle, and with each application taking its turn on the processor very quickly, it appears as if all of the applications are actually running at the same time. A similar concept applies to network traffic, except this time there is a finite bandwidth size and the combined network usage has to stay within that limit. Many applications can send/receive data over a shared network connection up to the maximum speed of the network. Imagine a funnel. I could be pouring Coke, Pepsi, and Dr Pepper down the funnel and all would pour at the same time up to the size of the funnel. Those desktop applications are also assigned their own individual amounts of memory and disk storage. This is exactly the same for virtualization except instead of the OS dividing up resource allocation, it's the hypervisor allocating resources to each virtual machine that is running but uses the same mechanisms.

Building on the previous benefit of higher utilization is one of scalability and elasticity. A physical server has a fixed set of resources that are not easily changed, which is why physical deployments are traditionally overprovisioned and architected for the busiest possible time. With a virtual environment, virtual machine resources can be dynamically changed to meet the changing needs of the workload. This dynamic nature can be enabled in a number of ways. For resources such as processor and network, the OS will use only what it needs, which allows the virtual machine to be assigned a large amount of processor and network resources because those resources can be shared. So while one OS is not using the resource, others can. When it comes to resources that are divided up, such as memory and storage, it's possible to add them to and remove them from a running virtual machine as needed. This type of elasticity is not possible in traditional physical deployments, and with virtualization hosts generally architected to have far more resources than in a physical OS deployment, the scalability, or maximum resource that can be assigned to a virtualized OS, is much larger.

The consolidation of operating system instances onto a smaller number of more powerful servers exposes a number of additional virtualization benefits. With a reduced number of servers that are more powerful but more highly utilized, organizations see reduced datacenter space requirements, which leads to energy savings and also ultimately cost savings.

Many organizations have long struggled with a nontechnical aspect of their datacenters, and that is licensing. I'm going to cover licensing in detail later in this chapter, but when you have thousands of individual servers, each running a single operating system, it can be hard to track all the licenses and hard to know exactly what version you need based on the capabilities required, but most important, it just costs a lot of money. With virtualization, there are ways to license the virtualization hosts themselves and allow an unlimited number of virtual machines, making licensing of the OS and management software far more cost effective.

Another challenge with a single operating system per physical server is all the islands of resources you have to manage. Every server has its own local storage, and you have to somehow protect all that data. Utilizing centralized storage such as a SAN for every physical server is possible but typically cost prohibitive. It's not practical to purchase fibre-channel HBAs (cards that enable connectivity to fibre-channel switches), fibre-channel switches to accommodate all the servers, and all the cabling. Take those same servers and reduce the number of physical servers by even tenfold using virtualization and suddenly connecting everything to centralized storage is far more realistic and cost effective. The same applies to regular networking. Implementing 10 Gbps networking in a datacenter for 100 servers is far more possible than it is for one with 1,000 servers.

On the opposite side of the scale from consolidation and centralization is the challenge of isolating workloads. Consider a branch location that for cost purposes has only a single server to host services for the local workers. Because there is only a single server, all the various roles have to run on a single OS instance without virtualization, which can lead to many complications in configuration and supportability. With virtualization, that same server can host a number of virtual machines, with each workload running in its own virtual machine, such as a virtual machine running a domain controller and DNS, another running file services, and another running a line of business (LOB) service. This allows services to be deployed and isolated to standard best practices. Additionally, many remote offices will deploy two virtualization servers with some kind of external storage enclosure that can be connected to both servers. This enables virtual machines to actually be moved between the servers, allowing high availability, which brings us to the next benefit of virtualization.

Physically deployed services that require high availability must have some native high-availability technology. With virtualization, it's still preferred to leverage the service's native high-availability capabilities, but virtualization adds additional options and can provide solutions where no native capability exists in the virtualized service. Virtualization can enable virtual machines to move between physical hosts with no downtime using Live Migration and can even provide disaster recovery capabilities using technologies such as Hyper-V Replica. Virtualization also allows simpler backup and recovery processes by allowing backups to be taken of the entire virtual machine.

Consider the process of deploying a new service on a physical server. That server configuration has to be specified, ordered, delivered, and installed in the datacenter. Then the OS has to be installed and the actual service configured. That entire process may take a long time, which lengthens the time it takes to provision new services. Those delays may affect an organization's ability to respond to changes in the market and react to customer requirements. In a virtual environment, the provisioning of a new service consists of the creation of a new virtual machine for that service; with the right automation processes in place, that could take minutes from start to finish instead of weeks. Because resources are pooled together in a virtual infrastructure, it is common to always run with sufficient spare capacity available to allow for new services to be provisioned as needed, and as the amount of free resources drops below a certain threshold, new hardware is purchased and added to the virtual infrastructure ready for additional services. Additionally, because the deployment of a new virtual machine does not require any physical infrastructure changes, the whole process can be completely automated, which helps in the speed of provisioning. Additionally, by removing many manual steps, the chances of human error are removed, and with a high level of consistency between deployed environments comes a simplified supportability process.

Finally, I want to touch on using public cloud services such as Windows Azure Infrastructure as a Service (IaaS), which allows virtual machines to be hosted on servers accessed over the Internet. When using virtualization on premises in your datacenter, and in this case specifically Hyper-V, you have full compatibility between on and off premises, making it easy to move services.

There are other benefits that are specific to virtualization, such as simplified networking infrastructure using network virtualization, greater Quality of Service (QoS) controls, metering, and more. However, the benefits previously mentioned are generally considered the biggest wins of virtualization. To summarize, here are the key benefits of virtualization:

◆ Abstraction from the underlying hardware, allowing full mobility of virtual machines

◆ High utilization of resources

◆ Scalability and elasticity

◆ Energy, datacenter space, and cost reduction

- Simplification and cost reduction for licensing

- Consolidation and centralization of storage and other resources

- Isolation of services

- Additional high-availability options and simpler backup/recovery

- Speed of service provisioning and automation

- Compatibility with public cloud

Ultimately, what these benefits mean to the organization is either saving money or enabling money to be made faster.

## History of Hyper-V

So far in this chapter I have not really used the word *Hyper-V* very much. I have focused on the challenges of traditional datacenters and the benefits of virtualization. I now want to start looking at the changes to the various versions of Hyper-V at a high level since its introduction. This is important because not only will it enable you to understand the features you have available in your Hyper-V deployments if you are not yet running Windows Server 2012 R2 Hyper-V, it also shows the great advancements made with each new version. All of the features I talk about will be covered in great detail throughout this book, so don't worry if the following discussion isn't detailed enough. I will provide you with a very high-level explanation of what they are in this part of the chapter.

I'll start with the first version of Hyper-V, which was introduced as an add-on after the Windows Server 2008 release. Hyper-V was not an update to Microsoft Virtual Server, which was a virtualization solution Microsoft acquired as part of the Connectix acquisition. Microsoft Virtual Server was not well adopted in many organizations as a virtualization solution because it was a type 2 hypervisor, whereas Hyper-V is a type 1 hypervisor. There are numerous definitions, but I think of it quite simply as follows:

- Type 2 hypervisor runs on a host operating system. The host operating system manages the underlying hardware; the type 2 hypervisor makes requests to the host operating system for resource and to perform actions. Because a type 2 hypervisor runs on top of a host OS, access to all the processor rings of operating systems running in the virtual machine is limited, which generally means slower performance and less capability.

- Type 1 hypervisors run directly on the bare metal of the server and directly control and allocate resources to virtual machines. Many type 1 hypervisors take advantage of a Ring -1, which is present on processors that support hardware virtualization to run the hypervisor itself. This then allows virtual machines to still be able to directly access Ring 0 (kernel mode) of the processor for their computations, giving the best performance while still allowing the hypervisor management of the resource. All modern datacenter hypervisors are type 1 hypervisors.

It is very important at this stage to realize that Hyper-V is absolutely a type 1 hypervisor. Often people think Hyper-V is a type 2 hypervisor because of the sequence of actions for installation:

1. Install Windows Server on the physical host.

2. Enable the Hyper-V role.

3. Configure and manage virtual machines through the Windows Server instance installed on the physical host.

Someone might look at this sequence of actions and how Hyper-V is managed and come to the conclusion that the Hyper-V hypervisor is running on top of Windows Server; that is actually not the case at all. When the Hyper-V role is enabled on Windows Server, changes are made to the boot configuration database to configure the hypervisor to load first, and then the Windows Server operating systems runs on *top* of that hypervisor, effectively becoming a pseudo virtual machine itself. Run the command bcdedit /enum on a Hyper-V host and it shows that the hypervisor launchtype is set to automatically launch.

The Windows Server operating system becomes the management partition for the Hyper-V solution. The hypervisor itself is quite compact and needs to be as light as possible, so it's focused on interacting with compute and memory resources and controlling access for virtual machines to avoid introducing latencies in performance. The management partition works for the hypervisor and is tasked with a number of items, such as hosting worker processes to communicate with virtual machines, hosting drivers for storage and network adapter interactions, and more. However, all the virtual machines are running directly on the hypervisor and not on the host operating system that was installed. This is best shown by looking at the Hyper-V architecture in Figure 1.4, which clearly shows the hypervisor running in Ring -1 and both the management partition and all the virtual machines running side by side on the hypervisor. The management partition does have some additional privileges, capabilities, and hardware access beyond that of a regular virtual machine, but it is still running on the hypervisor.

**FIGURE 1.4**
Hyper-V
architecture

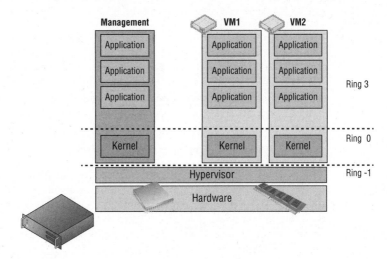

> ### WHAT IS A PARTITION?
>
> In the discussion of the history of Hyper-V, I referred to a management partition. The hypervisor runs directly on the hardware and assigns different amounts of resource to each virtual environment. These virtual environments can also be referred to as partitions because they are partitions of the underlying resource. Because the management partition is not a true virtual machine (because not all of its resources are virtualized) and it has privileged access, it is referred to as the management partition or the parent partition. Although it can be confusing, it's also common to see the management partition referred to as the host because it is the OS closest to the hardware and is directly installed on the server. Sometimes virtual machines are referred to as child partitions or guest partitions.

## Windows Server 2008 Hyper-V Features

The initial version of Hyper-V provided a solid foundation for virtualization and a fairly limited set of additional capabilities. As with all versions of Hyper-V, the processors must support hardware-assisted virtualization (AMD-V or Intel VT) and also Data Execution Prevention (DEP). Although Hyper-V is available only on 64-bit versions of Windows Server, it is possible to run both 32-bit and 64-bit operating systems. The initial version of Hyper-V included the following key capabilities:

- Up to 64 GB of memory per VM.

- Symmetric multiprocessing (SMP) VMs (up to four vCPUs each). However, the exact number differed depending on the guest operating system. For example, four vCPUs were supported on Windows Server 2008 SP2 guests but only two were on Windows Server 2003 SP2. The full list is available at

  http://technet.microsoft.com/en-us/library/cc794868(v=ws.10).aspx

- Virtual Hard Disk (VHD) format for virtualized storage up to 2 TB in size with multiple VHDs supported for each VM on either a virtual IDE controller or a virtual SCSI controller. VMs had to be booted from a VHD attached to a virtual IDE controller, but data VHDs could be connected to a virtual SCSI controller with higher performance through the virtual SCSI controller. Only 4 devices could be connected to the IDE controller (2 to each of the 2 IDE controllers), while each of the 4 virtual SCSI controllers supported up to 64 devices, each allowing up to 256 VHDs attached via the virtual SCSI.

- Leveraged Failover Clustering for high availability.

- Ability to move virtual machines between hosts in a cluster with minimal downtime using Quick Migration. Quick Migration worked by pausing the virtual machine and saving the device, processor, and memory content to a file on the cluster storage. It then moved that storage to another host in the cluster, reading the device, processor, and memory content into a newly staged virtual machine on the target and starting it. Depending on the amount of memory in the virtual machine, this may have meant minutes of downtime and the definite disconnect of any TCP connections. This was actually one of the biggest weaknesses of the Windows Server 2008 Hyper-V solution.

♦ Supported VSS live backup of virtual machines. This allowed a backup to be taken of a virtual machine from the host operating system. The VSS request for the backup was then communicated to the virtual machine's guest operating system through the Hyper-V integration services to ensure that the application data in the VM was in an application consistent state and suitable for a backup.

♦ The ability to create VM snapshots, which are point-in-time captures of a virtual machine's complete state (including memory and disk). This allowed a VM to be rolled back to any of these snapshots. The use of the term *snapshots* was confusing because the term is also used in the backup VSS nomenclature, but in this case it's referring to snapshots used in the backup process, which are different from VM snapshots. In Windows Server 2012 R2, VM snapshots are now called checkpoints to help remove this confusion.

♦ Pass-through disk access for VMs was possible even though not generally recommended. It was sometimes required if VMs needed access to single volumes greater than 2 TB in size (which was the VHD limit).

♦ Integration services available for supported guest operating systems, allowing capabilities such as heartbeat, mouse/keyboard interaction, backup services, time synchronization, and shutdown.

♦ Multiple virtual networks could be created with support for 10 Gbps and VLANs.

## Windows Server 2008 R2 Changes

While Windows Server 2008 Hyper-V offered a solid foundation and actually a very reliable solution for a v1, a number of limitations stopped Hyper-V from being seriously considered in many environments, among them the ability to move virtual machines between hosts in a cluster with no downtime. There were two challenges for Hyper-V to enable this:

♦ The VM had to be paused to enable the memory, processor, and device state to be saved to disk.

♦ NTFS is not a shared file system and can be mounted by only one OS at a time, which means when a virtual machine moves between hosts in a cluster the logical unit number, or LUN (which is a block of storage from a SAN), must be dismounted from the source host and mounted on the target host. This takes time.

Windows Server 2008 R2 solved both of these challenges. First, a new technology called Live Migration was introduced. Live Migration enabled the memory of a virtual machine and the virtual machine's state to be replicated to another host while the virtual machine was still running and then switched over to the new host with no downtime. I will cover this in detail in Chapter 7, "Failover Clustering and Migration Technologies," but the technology worked at a high level using the following steps:

1. A container VM was created on the target host using the existing VM's configuration.

2. The memory of the VM was copied from the source to the target VM.

3. Because the VM was still running while the memory was copied, some of the memory content changed. Those dirty pages were copied over again. This process repeated a number of iterations with the number of dirty pages shrinking by a magnitude each iteration, so the time to copy the dirty pages shrank greatly.

4. Once the number of dirty pages was very small, the VM was paused and the remaining memory pages were copied over along with the processor and device state.

5. The VM was resumed on the target Hyper-V host.

6. A reverse unsolicited ARP was sent over the network notifying routing devices that the VM's IP address was moved.

The whole process can be seen in Figure 1.5. One item I explained may have caused concern in the previous section, and that is that the VM is paused for a copy of the final few pages of dirty memory. This is common across all hypervisors and is necessary; however, only milliseconds of time are involved, so it's too small to notice and well below the TCP connection timeout, which means no connections to the server would be lost.

**FIGURE 1.5**

A high-level view of the Live Migration process

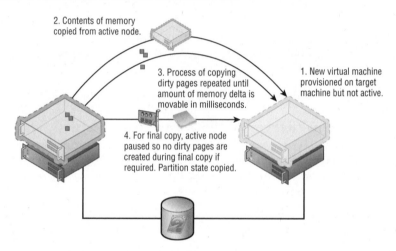

2. Contents of memory copied from active node.

3. Process of copying dirty pages repeated until amount of memory delta is movable in milliseconds.

1. New virtual machine provisioned on target machine but not active.

4. For final copy, active node paused so no dirty pages are created during final copy if required. Partition state copied.

Live Migration solved the problem of pausing the virtual machine to copy its memory between hosts It did not, however, solve the problem that NTFS couldn't be shared, so the LUN containing the VM had to be dismounted and mounted, which took time. A second new technology solved this problem: Cluster Shared Volumes, or CSV.

CSV allows an NTFS-formatted LUN to be simultaneously available to all hosts in the cluster. Every host can read and write to the CSV volume, which removes the need to dismount and mount the LUN as VMs move between hosts. This also solved the problem of having to have one LUN for every VM to enable each VM to be moved independently of other VMs. (The LUN had to move when the VM moved, which meant if other VMs were stored on the same LUN, those VMs would also have to move.) With CSV, many VMs could be stored on a single CSV volume, with VMs actually running throughout all the hosts in the cluster. Behind the scenes, CSV still leverages NTFS, but it controls the writing of metadata to the volume to a single host for each CSV volume to avoid any risk of NTFS corruption. This will also be explained in detail in Chapter 7.

With Live Migration and CSV technologies working in unison, the ability to move a virtual machine between hosts in a cluster with no downtime was now possible and removed a major obstacle to the adoption of Hyper-V. Windows Server 2008 R2 included other enhancements:

◆ A processor compatibility mode that allowed a virtual machine to be migrated between different versions of the same processor family. When a guest OS started within a virtual machine, it would commonly query the processor to find out all the instruction sets available, as would some applications, and those instruction sets would possibly be used. If a virtual machine was then moved to another host with a different processor version that did not support that instruction set, the application/OS would crash when it tried to use it. Download Coreinfo from

  `http://technet.microsoft.com/en-us/sysinternals/cc835722.aspx`

  and execute it with the `-f` switch. This will show which instruction sets are supported on your processor. When the processor compatibility feature was enabled for a virtual machine, the high-level instruction sets were masked from the VM so it did not use them, allowing the VM to be moved between different versions of the processor.

◆ Hot-add of storage to the SCSI bus. This enabled additional VHDs to be added to a virtual machine without shutting it down.

◆ Network performance improvements, including support for jumbo frames, VMQ, and allowing the use of NIC Teaming implemented by network drivers.

◆ If the processor supported it, Second Level Address Translation (SLAT), which allowed the processor to own the mapping of virtual memory to physical memory, therefore reducing overhead on the hypervisor. SLAT is used by Hyper-V when available.

## Windows Server 2008 R2 Service Pack 1

It's not common for a Service Pack to bring new features, but Windows Server 2008 R2 had one key feature missing, and this was the ability to dynamically change the amount of memory available to a virtual machine. SP1 for Windows Server 2008 R2 added the Dynamic Memory feature, which was very different from how other hypervisors handled memory optimization. Dynamic Memory worked by configuring a starting amount of memory and a maximum amount of memory. Hyper-V would then monitor the actual amount of memory being used within the virtual machine by processes via the integration services. If the amount of available memory dropped below a certain buffer threshold, additional memory was added to the virtual machine if it was physically available. If a virtual machine no longer needed all its memory, some was reclaimed for use with other virtual machines. This enabled Hyper-V to achieve great optimization of VM memory and maximize the number of virtual machines that could run on a host.

The other new technology in Service Pack 1 was RemoteFX, which was a technology based on those acquired through the Calista Technologies acquisition. The RemoteFX technology was focused on Virtual Desktop Infrastructure (VDI) deployments running on Hyper-V and making the VDI experience as rich as possible no matter what the capabilities of the client device. RemoteFX consisted of three technologies to offer this very rich capability:

◆ The first was the ability to virtualize a GPU in the Hyper-V server and then assign virtual GPUs to virtual machines. This works in a similar way to how CPUs are carved up between virtual machines. Once a virtual machine was assigned a vGPU, the OS within that VM could perform native DirectX processing using the GPU, allowing graphically rich applications to run, such as videoconferencing, Silverlight and Flash applications, and any DirectX application. As a demonstration, I installed Halo 2 in a RemoteFX-enabled virtual machine and played it over the network; you can see this at `http://youtu.be/CYiLGxfZRTA`. Without RemoteFX, some types of media playback would depend on the capability of the client machine, and certainly any application that required DirectX would not run. The key item is that all the graphical rendering is on the Hyper-V host's GPU and not on the local client.

◆ The second technology was related to the rich graphical capability and was an updated codec that was used to compress and uncompress the screen updates over the network.

◆ The final technology enabled USB device redirection at a port level. Typically with Remote Desktop Protocol (RDP), certain types of devices could be used in remote sessions, such as a keyboard, a mouse, a printer, and some devices with an inbox such as a scanner. However, many other types of devices and multifunction devices would not work. RemoteFX USB redirection enabled any USB device to be used in a remote session by redirecting at a USB port level all USB request blocks (URBs).

Note that the last two components of RemoteFX, the codec and USB redirection, are not Hyper-V features but rather updates to the RDP protocol. I still wanted to cover them because they are part of the RemoteFX feature family and really complete the remote client experience.

The combination of Dynamic Memory and RemoteFX made Hyper-V a powerful platform for VDI solutions, and Dynamic Memory on its own was useful for most server virtual machines as well.

## Windows Server 2012 Hyper-V Changes

Windows Server 2012 put Hyper-V to the top of the list of the true top hypervisors by closing nearly every gap it had with other hypervisors but also leapfrogging the competition in many areas. This entire book will focus on many of the changes in Windows Server 2012, but I want to call out some of the biggest improvements and new features.

One of the key reasons for the huge advancement of Hyper-V in Windows Server 2012 was not only the big focus on virtualization (to enable Hyper-V to compete and win against the competition) but also the success of Microsoft's public cloud service, Windows Azure. I'm going to briefly cover the types of cloud services later in this chapter and in far more detail later in the book, but for now, realize that Windows Azure is one of the largest public cloud services that exists. It powers many of Microsoft's cloud offerings and runs on Windows Server 2012 Hyper-V. All of the knowledge Microsoft gained operating Windows Azure and the enhancements it needed went into Windows Server 2012, and the engineering teams are now cloud first focused, creating and enhancing technologies that are then made available as part of new Windows Server versions. This is one of the reasons the release cadence of Windows Server has changed to an annual release cycle. Combining the development for the public and private cloud solutions makes Hyper-V a much stronger solution, which is good news for organizations using Hyper-V.

## SCALABILITY

The first grouping of changes relates to scalability, which was previously one of the weakest areas. Windows Server 2008 R2 did not change the scalability of virtual machines from Windows Server 2008 (although there were some modest improvements to the Hyper-V host limits). Windows Server 2012 made some big changes, as shown in Table 1.1.

**TABLE 1.1:**     Scalability changes from Windows Server 2008 R2 to Windows Server 2012

| ATTRIBUTE | WINDOWS 2008 R2 | WINDOWS 2012 | IMPROVEMENT |
| --- | --- | --- | --- |
| Logical processors on hardware | 64 | 320 (640 without Hyper-V role) | >5x |
| LP:VP ratio | 8:1 (12:1 for Windows 7 VDI) | No limit | |
| Physical memory | 1 TB | 4 TB | 4x |
| Virtual processors per host | 512 | 2,048 | 4x |
| Virtual processors per virtual machine | 4 | 64 (includes NUMA awareness) | 16x |
| Memory per virtual machine | 64 GB | 1 TB | 16x |
| Active virtual machines per host | 384 | 1,024 | 2.5x |
| Maximum cluster nodes | 16 | 64 | 4x |
| Maximum cluster virtual machines | 1,000 | 8,000 | 8x |
| Maximum VHD size | 2 TB | 64 TB (with VHDX) | 32x |

Some of the new scalability limits may almost seem ridiculously large: 64 TB virtual hard disks, 1 TB of memory in a single VM, and even 64 vCPUs in a single VM. But the point now is that almost any workload can be virtualized with Windows Server 2012 Hyper-V. Microsoft released an example of this ability to virtualize almost any workload with the statement that over 99 percent of the world's SQL Server deployments could now run on Windows Server 2012 Hyper-V. One aspect that is very important to the 64 TB VHDX scalability is that it removes most scenarios of having to use pass-through storage, which maps a virtual machine directly to some raw storage. The goal of virtualization is to abstract the virtual machine environment from the physical hardware, and directly mapping a virtual machine to physical storage breaks this abstraction and also stops some features of Hyper-V from being used, such as checkpoints, Live Migration, and Hyper-V Replica. In all my years of consulting, I have never seen an NTFS volume 64 TB in size. In fact, the biggest I have heard of is 14 TB, but a 64 TB limit means VHDX scalability would not limit the storage workloads that could be virtualized.

## WHY MOST NTFS VOLUMES ARE LESS THAN 2 TB

In most environments it's fairly uncommon to see NTFS volumes greater than 2 TB in size. One reason is that master boot record (MBR) partitioning had a limit of 2 TB. The newer GUID Partition Table (GPT) removed this limitation, but volumes still stayed at around the 2 TB size. Another reason concerns the unit of recoverability. Any set of data is typically restricted to the amount of data that can be restored in the required time frame. Legacy backup/restore solutions that were tape based could limit how large data sets would be, but modern backup/restore solutions that are primarily disk based remove this type of limit.

The number one reason for limits on volumes is if a corruption occurs on the NTFS volume. If a corruption occurs, the ChkDsk process must be run, which takes the volume offline while the entire disk is scanned and problems are repaired. Depending on the disk subsystem and its size, this process could take hours or even days. The larger the volume, the longer ChkDsk will take to run and the longer the volume would be offline. This meant companies would limit the size of volumes to minimize the potential time a volume would be offline if ChkDsk had to be run. In Windows Server 2012, ChkDsk has been rearchitected to no longer take the volume offline during the search for errors. Instead, it only has to take the disk offline to actually fix the problems discovered during an online scan. This means the maximum possible offline time for a volume is now 8 seconds, no matter how large the volume. With this change we can expect to see larger NTFS volumes as organizations adopt Windows Server 2012 and above.

Also important to note about scalability is that only very large virtual machines can be created with tens of virtual processors, but the non-uniform memory access (NUMA) topology is passed to the virtual machine, enabling the most optimal levels of performance. This scalability applies to both Windows guest operating systems and Linux, as Figure 1.6 shows with a 64 vCPU Linux virtual machine. Notice also in the figure the awareness of the NUMA nodes. This was another investment area in Windows Server 2012: making Linux a first-class guest operating system. Nearly every feature of Hyper-V worked equally for Windows guests and Linux guests.

**FIGURE 1.6**
Linux virtual machine running on Windows Server 2012 Hyper-V with 64 vCPUs

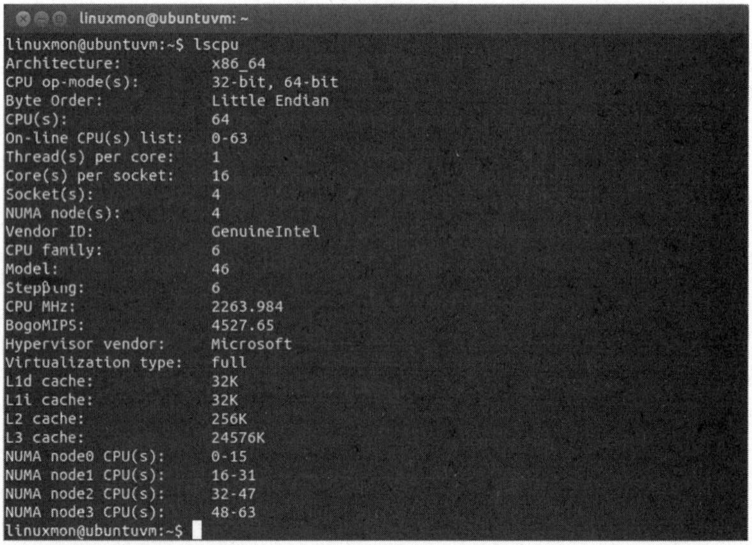

```
linuxmon@ubuntuvm: ~
linuxmon@ubuntuvm:~$ lscpu
Architecture:          x86_64
CPU op-mode(s):        32-bit, 64-bit
Byte Order:            Little Endian
CPU(s):                64
On-line CPU(s) list:   0-63
Thread(s) per core:    1
Core(s) per socket:    16
Socket(s):             4
NUMA node(s):          4
Vendor ID:             GenuineIntel
CPU family:            6
Model:                 46
Stepping:              6
CPU MHz:               2263.984
BogoMIPS:              4527.65
Hypervisor vendor:     Microsoft
Virtualization type:   full
L1d cache:             32K
L1i cache:             32K
L2 cache:              256K
L3 cache:              24576K
NUMA node0 CPU(s):     0-15
NUMA node1 CPU(s):     16-31
NUMA node2 CPU(s):     32-47
NUMA node3 CPU(s):     48-63
linuxmon@ubuntuvm:~$
```

## MOBILITY AND AVAILABILITY

As virtual machines became more scalable, the workloads that could be virtualized increased exponentially, which makes keeping the virtual machines available even more important. Windows Server 2012 made great advancements to the mobility and resiliency of virtual machines. Windows Server 2008 R2 had introduced Live Migration as a means to move virtual machines between nodes in a cluster that had shared storage. Windows Server 2012 took this to the next level by allowing multiple concurrent live migrations, which it would auto-scale based on available bandwidth and would queue until they could be performed based on network bandwidth availability.

A big shift for Hyper-V architecture options was support of SMB 3.0 for the storage of virtual machines, which allows Hyper-V virtual machines to be run from SMB 3.0 file shares, enabling a new file-based storage option. This change made it possible for Windows Server 2012 file share clusters to be used as the shared storage for Hyper-V environments in addition to any NAS or SAN solutions that support SMB 3.0. By using SMB 3.0 as the storage for virtual machines, an additional type of Live Migration was enabled, SMB Live Migration, which enabled virtual machines to be moved between *any* two Windows Server 2012 Hyper-V hosts, even if they were not part of a cluster. The Live Migration and SMB Live Migration processes remained similar except that the handles and locks to the files on the SMB share are transferred between hosts as part of the SMB Live Migration process.

Storage Live Migration was introduced with Windows Server 2012 Hyper-V. It allows all the storage-related items of a virtual machine to be moved between supported storage mediums with no downtime to the virtual machine. This included the virtual machine's configuration files, checkpoint data, smart paging files, and virtual hard disks. Any and all of these can be moved with no interruption to the virtual machine's availability. While this was an important feature to have because it was available in other virtualization solutions, its use must be accompanied with extreme caution. Consider the amount of IO that is required to move the storage of a virtual machine, both reading from the source and writing to the target. If a storage subsystem is currently having performance issues, which is a reason to want to move the virtual machine, then performing an actual storage migration would add substantial IO load and would likely worsen the situation in the short term. It is, however, an important feature to have and enables the true "Wow" mobility feature of Windows Server 2012, Shared Nothing Live Migration.

The ability to move a virtual machine without any constraints is the utopian goal of any virtualization solution: to be able to move a virtual machine between any hosts in the datacenter and between different storage subsystems without any downtime using only a 1 Gbps network connection. Windows Server 2012 delivers this in Windows Server 2012 with Shared Nothing Live Migration. Shared Nothing Live Migration allows a virtual machine to be moved between stand-alone hosts, from a cluster to a stand-alone, from a stand-alone to a cluster, or from cluster to cluster without any interruption to virtual machine communication. A Storage Live Migration is performed first if required to move the storage of the virtual machine to the destination. Then it is synchronized while the memory of the virtual machine is copied and synchronized again before the virtual machine is flipped and started on the destination. Being able to move virtual machines anywhere in the datacenter with no downtime is a useful capability, but the same cautions related to Storage Live Migrations apply: Understand the impacts of moving virtual machines.

Mobility is important for moving virtual machines in planned scenarios to enable hardware and software maintenance on hosts without affecting the availability of virtual workloads.

Beyond that, though, is making services available in unplanned events such as power outages, host crashes, and natural disasters. Windows Server 2012 greatly improved Failover Clustering, which is the backbone of Hyper-V high availability. However, what many customers asked for was a disaster recovery (DR) feature that would allow an asynchronous replication of virtual machines from one datacenter to another. Hyper-V Replica provides exactly this capability, allowing the virtualized storage of a virtual machine to be replicated to a DR location Hyper-V server every 5 minutes in addition to providing numerous failover options, including the ability to test failover without impacting production replication. I am going to cover high availability and disaster recovery in great detail later in the book, and I don't consider Hyper-V Replica the answer to all DR situations. Hyper-V Replica, which provides asynchronous replication between a primary VM and a replica VM, is one tool available that has specific scenarios in which it works very well.

---

#### WHY IS ASYNCHRONOUS REPLICATION A GOOD THING FOR DISASTER RECOVERY?

Typically, synchronous is best for any kind of replication. With synchronous replication, a change made to the primary store is not committed until it is also written to the secondary store. For the best assurance of the data integrity and to ensure no loss, this is a good thing. However, there is a substantial cost for synchronous replication. The connectivity required for synchronous replication needs to be resilient and fast enough with a low enough latency to ensure that the performance of the primary workload is not negatively affected. For the replication of a virtual machine across datacenters, only the highest levels of connectivity would enable the storage replication without affecting the primary workload, and while these solutions are possible, they are typically part of SAN solutions, which are usually costly. With asynchronous replication, the primary workload is not affected and the changes are replicated to the secondary store as quickly as possible or on a fixed interval. This achieves a good level of protection without requiring very fast, low-latency network connections, but it is not real-time replication. In the event of an unplanned failover to the DR site, a few minutes of data may be lost, but in a true disaster, a few minutes of state loss is typically accepted. Asynchronous brings disaster recovery to all workloads rather than just the tier 1 services that can utilize SAN-level synchronous replication.

---

### OTHER CAPABILITIES

Windows Server 2012 Hyper-V introduced a great number of other capabilities that greatly change virtual environments:

- Virtual fibre-channel support that allows virtual machines to directly communicate to fibre-channel-connected SANs, which is a necessity for guest clustering scenarios that need shared storage and cannot use iSCSI

- Network virtualizing that enables complete abstraction of the network viewed by virtual machines from the physical network fabric, enabling complete isolation between virtual environments and also enabling environments to span multiple datacenters without having to modify IP configuration

- SR-IOV and dynamic VMQ for the highest level of virtual machine network performance

- Improvements to Dynamic Memory

When I created presentations for Windows Server 2012 Hyper-V, I actually created a single slide that showcased the majority of the new Hyper-V features (Figure 1.7) and, as noted, all the new capabilities, none of which affected the ability to live migrate virtual machines. These technologies will all be covered throughout this book.

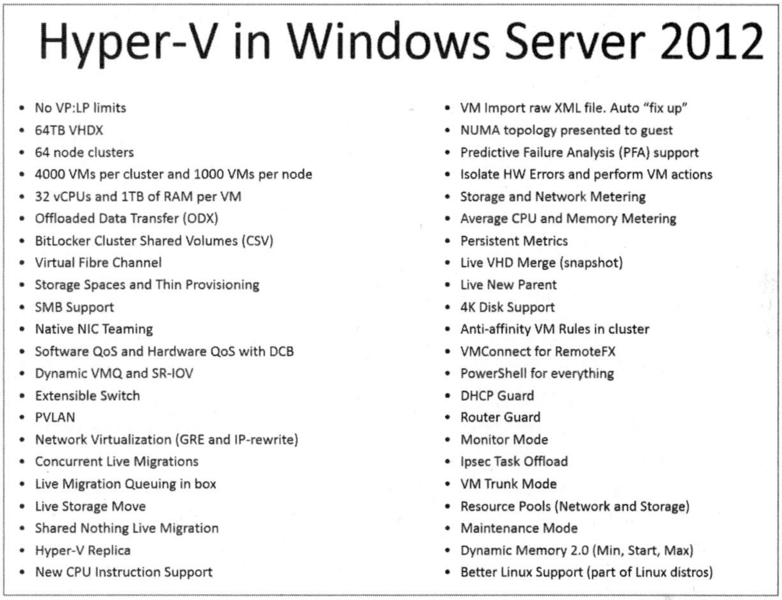

**FIGURE 1.7**

The major new features of Windows Server 2012 Hyper-V

# Hyper-V in Windows Server 2012

- No VP:LP limits
- 64TB VHDX
- 64 node clusters
- 4000 VMs per cluster and 1000 VMs per node
- 32 vCPUs and 1TB of RAM per VM
- Offloaded Data Transfer (ODX)
- BitLocker Cluster Shared Volumes (CSV)
- Virtual Fibre Channel
- Storage Spaces and Thin Provisioning
- SMB Support
- Native NIC Teaming
- Software QoS and Hardware QoS with DCB
- Dynamic VMQ and SR-IOV
- Extensible Switch
- PVLAN
- Network Virtualization (GRE and IP-rewrite)
- Concurrent Live Migrations
- Live Migration Queuing in box
- Live Storage Move
- Shared Nothing Live Migration
- Hyper-V Replica
- New CPU Instruction Support

- VM Import raw XML file. Auto "fix up"
- NUMA topology presented to guest
- Predictive Failure Analysis (PFA) support
- Isolate HW Errors and perform VM actions
- Storage and Network Metering
- Average CPU and Memory Metering
- Persistent Metrics
- Live VHD Merge (snapshot)
- Live New Parent
- 4K Disk Support
- Anti-affinity VM Rules in cluster
- VMConnect for RemoteFX
- PowerShell for everything
- DHCP Guard
- Router Guard
- Monitor Mode
- Ipsec Task Offload
- VM Trunk Mode
- Resource Pools (Network and Storage)
- Maintenance Mode
- Dynamic Memory 2.0 (Min, Start, Max)
- Better Linux Support (part of Linux distros)

I have focused on the changes to Hyper-V so far. However, there were a large number of other changes in Windows Server 2012 that enabled Windows Server 2012 to be an even better foundation for many Hyper-V services, such as changes to Failover Clustering, the new SMB 3.0 protocol, configuration levels that enable a server to be switched between server core and server with a GUI without having to reinstall, native NIC teaming, Server Manager, PowerShell v3, and much more. In addition, I will cover the non-Hyper-V features of Windows Server throughout this book where appropriate and where they bring value to a virtual experience.

## Windows Server 2012 R2

I look at Windows Server 2012 Hyper-V as a whole new generation of Hyper-V from the previous versions. It took Hyper-V to new levels of scalability and functionality and made it a true enterprise hypervisor, bringing in major new technologies such as Hyper-V Replica, Network Virtualization, SMB 3.0 usage, and Live Migration. I look at Windows Server 2012 R2 as the continued advancement of the Hyper-V technology, refining many of the capabilities based on the feedback of enterprises that deployed Windows Server 2012 Hyper-V. Many organizations will welcome the 2012 R2 enhancements.

There were no scalability changes in Windows Server 2012 R2. I think most people would agree that the scalability of Windows Server 2012 meets today's and tomorrow's requirements. The focus was on improving the utilization of environments and fully embracing the technologies that companies were utilizing.

### GENERATION 2 VIRTUAL MACHINE

The format of virtual machines has not really changed since the first version of Hyper-V. Looking at a virtual machine shows a lot of emulated hardware, which is required because operating systems don't natively understand virtualization. This was true 10 years ago but it's not true today. Nearly all modern operating systems understand virtualization and the synthetic types of resource available, making the emulated hardware previously required for compatibility not required. Windows Server 2012 R2 introduces a new type of virtual machine, a generation 2 virtual machine, which removes all the legacy emulated hardware previously present and shifts to a UEFI-based virtual machine exclusively using synthetic SCSI (allowing virtual machines to now boot from the synthetic SCSI) and network adapters (including PXE boot from a synthetic network adapter). Generation 1 virtual machines are still available, and there is no real performance improvement of a generation 1 vs. generation 2 virtual machine once the OS is installed and running, but a generation 2 virtual machine will install and boot faster.

### STORAGE ENHANCEMENTS

One feature that did not make Windows Server 2012 Hyper-V was the ability to dynamically resize a VHDX attached to a running machine, which was an issue for some organizations where just adding additional VHD/VHDX files to a running virtual machine was not sufficient. 2012 R2 Hyper-V supports the dynamic resizing of VHDX files attached to the virtual machine's SCSI controller. This dynamic resizing supports both increasing the size and reducing the size provided there is sufficient unpartitioned space within the VHDX file.

VHDX files can be shared among multiple virtual machines in 2012 R2 Hyper-V, and these shared VHDX files, which are hosted on Cluster Shared Volumes or a scale-out file server, are seen to the virtual machines as shared SAS storage and can be used as shared storage within the virtual machine for guest clustering scenarios. This removes the previous requirement to use iSCSI or virtual Fibre Channel to enable shared storage within virtual machines for guest clustering purposes.

Resource metering was introduced in 2012 Hyper-V for processor, memory, and network but not storage other than the amount of storage used. In Windows Server 2012 R2, the resource metering is expanded to give more detail on the IO profiles of storage, including average IOPS and data read and written. 2012 R2 also allows Quality of Service (QoS) to be used with storage to restrict the maximum IOPS of each individual virtual hard disk and also can alert administrators if the IOPS drops below a certain threshold.

### MOBILITY AND AVAILABILITY

Live Migration in Windows Server 2012 may seem to be the perfect solution, covering all scenarios, but in 2012 R2, it has been made more efficient. The Windows 2012 Live Migration method of copying memory over the networks specified for Live Migration is still available in 2012 R2. However, the default now utilizes compression, which reduces the amount of data sent over the network, thus reducing Live Migration durations potentially by a factor of five at the expense of some extra CPU cycles to both compress the memory at the source and decompress at the target. Another option is to utilize SMB Direct as the transport, which may not seem like a good option initially, but the goal is to use it if the network adapters support Remote Direct Memory Access (RDMA), which allows it to be used; SMB Direct will be faster than even compressed Live Migration, but it uses almost no CPU. Windows Server 2012 R2 also allows Live Migration from Windows Server 2012, which allows organizations to migrate from 2012 to 2012 R2 without downtime for virtual machines.

Hyper-V Replica is also enhanced to allow different choices for the frequency of the asynchronous replication of the storage changes. The 5-minute frequency from Windows 2012 Hyper-V is still available, but additional options of 30 seconds and 15 minutes are also now offered (see Figure 1-8). Extended Hyper-V Replica can be configured, allowing a replica to be created of a replica. Note that the extended replica is sourced from the existing replica and not from the original virtual machine. This is a useful capability for organizations using Hyper-V Replica within a datacenter that also want an additional replica in a separate datacenter for true DR.

**FIGURE 1.8**
Extended Hyper-V Replica allows different replication intervals between the different replicas

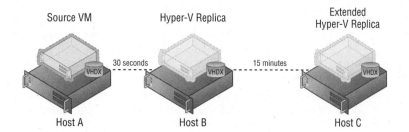

## OTHER CAPABILITIES

One major new feature in Windows Server 2012 R2 is the inclusion of a network virtualization gateway, which is critical to allow different virtual networks to communicate and also to be able to communicate with the physical network fabric. Prior to 2012 R2, a hardware gateway was required, and there really were not many of them.

In 2012 R2, it's possible to export virtual machines and virtual machine checkpoints while they are running, enabling a simple cloning process that can be very useful, especially in development and testing environments.

More capabilities were added for Linux virtual machines, including dynamic memory, live backup offering file consistency, and Hyper-V Replica IP reconfiguration during failover.

Activation can be a pain point in virtual environments. In Windows Server 2012 R2 Hyper-V, if the Hyper-V host is running Datacenter edition and is activated, then any Windows Server 2012 R2 virtual machine (Essentials, Standard, or Datacenter) on the server will automatically activate. No need for KMS or Active Directory Based Activation (ADBA). If the VM leaves the host, it will deactivate. The only required action is to use the Automatic Virtual Machine Activation key in the guest OS, which can be found at the following location:

```
http://technet.microsoft.com/en-us/library/dn303421.aspx
```

# Licensing of Hyper-V

The most painful aspect of most virtual environments is understanding the licensing of the hypervisor, the operating systems running in the virtual machines, and the management software. I don't want to go into great detail about licensing in this book because despite new licensing agreements, there are still special combinations of licensing through agreements with programs such as Server and Cloud Enrollment (SCM) and the legacy Enrollment in Core Infrastructure (ECI). For most organizations, the licensing is actually simple with Windows Server 2012 and above, as is picking which version of Windows Server you need to use.

## One Operating System (Well, Two, but Really One)

Prior to Windows Server 2012, there were numerous versions of Windows Server—Web, Standard, Enterprise, and Datacenter—and each version had different capabilities and different limits and were licensed differently. That all goes away in Windows Server 2012 and above, where for medium-size and large companies, there are only two versions of Windows Server: Windows Server 2012 R2 Standard and Windows Server 2012 R2 Datacenter. Both versions are *exactly* the same:

- ◆ They have the same limits, both supporting 64 processor sockets, 640 logical processors (320 with Hyper-V role enabled), and 4 TB of memory.

- ◆ Both have the same roles and features; for example, even Standard has Failover Clustering.

- ◆ They are essentially bit for bit the same operating system other than that each shows different versions in the About menu option and different background wallpaper.

- ◆ Both are licensed in two-socket increments, and all sockets in the server must be licensed. If a server has four sockets, then two licenses of either Standard or Datacenter must be purchased.

The difference between Standard and Datacenter is operating system environments (OSEs), or virtual instances for each license. This is the number of virtual machines running Windows Server that are included as part of your license: Standard allows two virtual instances per license, and Datacenter allows unlimited instances. From a virtualization environment perspective, this is a big difference. For each Standard license, I can run two virtual machines running Windows Server, while with Datacenter, I can run an unlimited number of virtual machines. This means Standard edition is now targeted at physically deployed operating system instances or very light virtualization, while Datacenter is targeted at virtualization hosts.

It is possible to stack licenses, and this means, for example, buying three Standard licenses for a server, which would allow me to run 6 virtual machines running Windows Server on that server (each Standard licenses essentially allows two "slots," with each "slot" supporting a Windows Server virtual machine), which would be cheaper than buying a Datacenter license. However, complications will occur if you want to move virtual machines between hosts.

Consider Figure 1.9, which shows two Hyper-V hosts in a remote office that needs only 6 virtual machines. The option shown in the example is using three copies of Windows Server Standard on one server and a single copy on the other server, and this is allowed. However, suppose you want to move the virtual machines to the other server, as shown in Figure 1.10, to perform maintenance on the first server. This can be done, but it requires actually moving two of the Windows Server Standard licenses between physical hosts. License mobility only allows the movement of licenses every 90 days, which means you could move the virtual machines and the licenses but you would not be able to move the virtual machines back for 90 days.

To allow free movement of the virtual machines, the high watermark of virtual machines ever present on the hosts would need to be used to calculate the required number of licenses, which would therefore be three copies of Standard on both servers, as shown in Figure 1.11.

Now consider having 8, 10, or 20 virtual machines and having clusters of 16 or even 64 hosts. The unlimited number of virtual machines that accompanies the Datacenter edition makes much more sense, as shown in Figure 1.12. Using Datacenter enables highly dense deployments of virtual machines without you needing to worry about the licensing of the virtual machines.

**FIGURE 1.9**
Using stacked Standard licenses for virtual machines

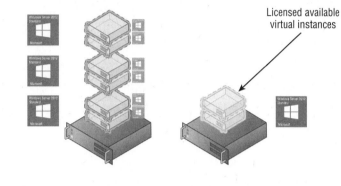

**FIGURE 1.10**
Moving Standard licenses to enable licensed virtual machine migrations

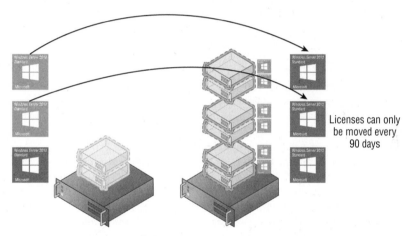

**FIGURE 1.11**
Required Standard licensing to enable virtual machine mobility

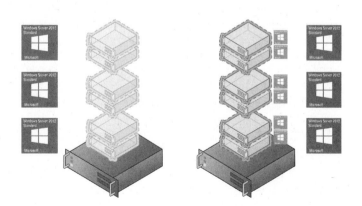

**FIGURE 1.12**
Using Datacenter
to enable an unlim-
ited number of
virtual machines
on the hosts for full
mobility

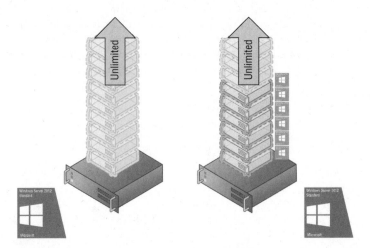

It's important to realize that the use of Standard or Datacenter is not actually related to Hyper-V specifically but rather the licensing of the operating systems running inside the virtual machines, and the same would apply to any hypervisor, such as XenServer or ESX.

This is an important point. Standard vs. Datacenter relates to the number of virtual instances running the Windows Server operating system. If you need to run something other than Windows Server, like Linux virtual machines or Windows Client virtual machines such as for a VDI environment, then these virtual instances do not apply and you need to license those operating systems to whatever licensing scheme is required. There is no limit to the number of virtual machines you can run on Windows Server Standard Hyper-V, and it would be possible to have hundreds of virtual machines running Linux or Windows Client without the need to use Datacenter or have multiple Standard licenses.

In fact, there is another option if a virtual environment needs to exclusively run Linux or Windows Client, and no virtual instance rights for Windows Server are required. Microsoft makes available Microsoft Hyper-V Server, which is a free download from Microsoft that is designed for environments that don't wish to run Windows Server virtual machines and don't need the virtual instance rights included with the Standard or Datacenter edition, making it perfect for Linux and VDI environments. Microsoft Hyper-V Server is updated with each version of Windows Server, making the version that's currently available Microsoft Hyper-V Server 2012 R2, and it has all the same capabilities of the version of Hyper-V that is available in Windows Server, but only the Hyper-V role is included. It cannot be a file server or a domain controller or be used for any other role, nor can the graphical interface or server management tools be installed; it runs in the Server Core configuration level.

## Choosing the Version of Hyper-V

Given the information in the previous section, determining which version of Hyper-V is required is actually a fairly simple decision. While it is technically possible to mix Standard and Datacenter in a single cluster, this makes tracking licensing complex. I use the following criteria to decide which version of Hyper-V I need in a virtual environment:

◆ If the virtual machines will all be running non–Windows Server operating systems, then use the free Microsoft Hyper-V Server.

◆ If the environment will be running only a few virtual machines with no plans to expand and with limited mobility required, then the Standard edition of Windows Server can be used.

◆ If there will be more than a few virtual machines with future growth possible and full mobility of virtual machines required, use the Datacenter edition of Windows Server.

## The Role of System Center with Hyper-V

The capabilities of the features for Hyper-V I described previously in this chapter are impressive, but it's important to realize that this is just for virtualization. Yes, Hyper-V is powerful and can enable almost any required scenario, but virtualization is the foundation and not the complete solution.

A production environment of any kind needs a number of management services, and virtualization adds additional requirements to those management capabilities. For Windows Server and Hyper-V, the management solution is System Center. While it is possible to deploy Hyper-V without System Center in a very small, limited capacity, it is required for any enterprise deployment. System Center actually comprises a number of separate components, each component separately deployed and offering its own discrete capabilities, and while deployment of the entire System Center product offers numerous benefits, some organizations will deploy only certain components. Chapter 9, "Implementing the Private Cloud and SCVMM," goes into detail on how System Center is leveraged, I want to briefly introduce all the components here because they will be discussed and used in the chapters before Chapter 9. Figure 1.13 shows the full System Center 2012 product.

**FIGURE 1.13**
Components of
System Center 2012

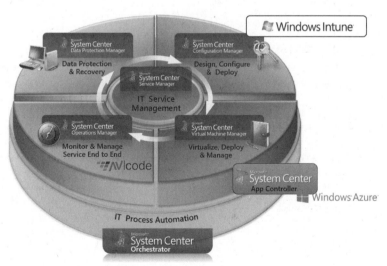

System Center is licensed exactly the same as Windows Server. It can be purchased in the Standard or Datacenter edition. The versions are identical except for the number of virtual instance rights: two for Standard, unlimited for Datacenter. It is licensed in two-socket increments, which makes it easy to know how many and of what type of System Center license you need for your Windows Server environment. Typically, it will match your Windows Server licenses, and there are combination licenses available, such as Enrollment for Core Infrastructure (ECI), where Windows Server and System Center are licensed together.

### System Center Configuration Manager

Moving through the products shown in Figure 1.13, I'll start with System Center Configuration Manager (SCCM). SCCM provides capabilities to deploy operating systems, applications, and OS/software updates to servers and desktops. Detailed hardware and software inventory and asset intelligence features are key aspects of SCCM, enabling great insight into an entire organization's IT infrastructure. SCCM 2012 introduces management of mobile devices such as iOS and Android through ActiveSync integration with Exchange and a user-focused management model. One key feature of SCCM for servers is settings management, which allows a configuration of desired settings to be defined (such as OS and application settings) and then applied to a group of servers (or desktops). This can be useful for compliance requirements.

### System Center Virtual Machine Manager and App Controller

Next in the circle of products in Figure 1.13, you see System Center Virtual Machine Manager (SCVMM). It will get a lot of focus in this book, but essentially it's the virtualization-specific management functionality across multiple hypervisors and gives insight and management into storage and network fabric resources. SCVMM allows the creation and deployment of virtual machine templates and even multitier services. It also lights up a number of Hyper-V features, such as network virtualization. App Controller provides a rich Silverlight web-based self-service interface for management of private and public cloud resources.

### System Center Operations Manager

System Center Operations Manager (SCOM) provides a rich monitoring solution for Microsoft and non-Microsoft operating systems and applications and also for hardware. Any monitoring solution can tell you when something is broken, and yes, SCOM does that, but its real power is in its proactive nature and best practice adherence functionality. SCOM Management Packs are units of knowledge about a specific application or component. For example, there is an Exchange management pack and a Domain Name System (DNS) for Windows Server management pack. The Microsoft mandate is that any Microsoft product should have a management pack that is written by the product team responsible for the application or operating system component. This means that all the knowledge of those developers, the people who create best practice documents, is incorporated into these management packs, which you can then just deploy to your environment. Operations Manager will raise alerts when potential problems are detected or when best practices are not being followed. There are often objections from customers that when first implemented, Operations Manager floods them with alerts. This could be for a number of reasons (perhaps there are a lot of problems in the environment that should be fixed), but often Operations Manager will be tuned to ignore configurations that perhaps are not best practice but are nevertheless accepted by the organization.

Many third parties provide management packs for their applications and hardware devices. When I think about "it's all about the application" as a key tenant of the private cloud, the Operations Manager's ability to monitor from the hardware, storage, and network all the way through the OS to the application is huge, but it actually goes even further in Operations Manager 2012.

System Center Operations Manager 2012 introduced a number of changes, but two huge ones were around network monitoring and custom application monitoring. First, Microsoft licensed technology from EMC called SMARTS, which enables a rich discovery and monitoring of network devices. With the network discovery and monitoring functionality, Operations Manager can identify the relationship between network devices and services to actually understand that port 3 on this switch connects to server A, so if there is a switch problem, Operations Manager will know the affected servers. CPU and memory information, among other types of information, is available for supported network devices.

The other big change was the acquisition by Microsoft of AVIcode, which is now Application Platform Monitoring (APM) in Operations Manager 2012. APM provides monitoring of custom applications without any changes needed by the application. APM currently supports .NET applications and Java Enterprise Edition (J2E).

## System Center Data Protection Manager

System Center Data Protection Manager (DPM) is Microsoft's best-of-breed backup, continuous data protection, and recovery solution for key Microsoft workloads, including SharePoint, SQL Server, Dynamics, Exchange, Hyper-V, file services, and desktops. DPM allows very granular recovery of information within the supported options for the product, including end-user self-recovery in certain scenarios. Where DPM can be useful in the private cloud is in the protection of the environment. DPM can back up and protect the Hyper-V servers, the SQL databases that are used by most of the System Center 2012 components, the management servers running the System Center infrastructure, and all the virtual machines running on Hyper-V that are created.

DPM supports backing up at the Hyper-V server level, and that backup request will be passed by Hyper-V to the virtual machines. That allows the virtual machines to ensure that information on disk is in a backup-ready state so when the virtual machine is backed up, the integrity and usability of that backup can be assured.

I do want to be very clear; just because you can back up at the Hyper-V level does not mean you should back up only at the Hyper-V level. If you want granular restoration capabilities of applications like SharePoint, SQL Server, and Exchange, you need to have the DPM agent installed within the virtual machine and actually be backing up from the VM directly to enable DPM to have the knowledge of the application configuration and data.

## System Center Service Manager

I'll spend more time on System Center Service Manager (SCSM) in a later chapter, but think of Service Manager as the configuration management database (CMDB) for the entire infrastructure, which is another ITIL key capability. Service Manager is shown in the center of the rest of the System Center components for a good reason. It has connectors into all the surrounding components, receiving feeds of information that it consolidates into a single view of everything related to an asset (such as a computer or person), giving a single point of truth for the entire organization.

Service Manager has capabilities commonly associated with a help desk solution, such as logging incidents, problems, and change requests, but it also handles change management and release management in addition to providing a powerful workflow engine to enable your organization's processes such as approvals to be replicated in Service Manager.

The key item that I will focus on later is the service catalog, which provides the organization with the ability to request services, including services for software and virtual infrastructures. Organizations often have a help desk solution already in place but realize Service Manager is far more than a ticketing system; it can be implemented and actually integrated with another ticketing solution, all the while leveraged for its other powerful capabilities and CMDB functionality.

### System Center Orchestrator

System Center Orchestrator is actually an acquisition of a product called Opalis that has been renamed System Center Orchestrator as part of System Center 2012. Orchestrator provides two key capabilities that, as with Service Manager, I want to dive into in more detail in a later chapter.

First, Opalis was acquired because it had connectivity to many of the major datacenter applications and systems that exist, which with the acquisition, now includes the Microsoft solutions. Integration packs exist for many systems and provide activities that are specific to the integration pack target, but Orchestrator can talk to targets that don't have integration packs, using many types of communication, including WMI, SSH, PowerShell, SNMP, and many more.

Second, Opalis had powerful runbook automation capabilities that leveraged all this connectivity. Runbooks that were typically manually actioned by IT administrators and business users can be migrated to Orchestrator using a great flowchart-type interface and can be completely automated. Orchestrator has a Silverlight console that gives access to not only launch the defined runbooks but also to see their progress.

It is because of these capabilities that Orchestrator is shown as the foundation of the System Center product; all of the other System Center 2012 components can leverage Orchestrator for actions requests made to other systems and complex processes, and Orchestrator can talk to the rest of System Center 2012, enabling automation of processes that use many components of System Center and other systems through a single runbook. As I will talk about later in this book, where Orchestrator becomes a key component of the private cloud is in its ability to communicate with systems like Service Manager, Operations Manager, and Virtual Machine Manager to actually orchestrate the creation of virtual machines and scaling actions.

## Clouds and Services

This book's primary focus is on Hyper-V, but the big technology investment area today is around various types of clouds and various types of capabilities offered "as a Service." I will focus on a number of these throughout the book, but I want to provide a high-level summary of the types of clouds and "as a Service" offerings commonly seen so they will make sense as I discuss their principles and use throughout this book.

There are two primary types of cloud: private cloud and public cloud. Virtualization focuses on services related to compute, such as actually creating, configuring, and running the virtual machines, but it does not focus on the storage or network fabrics that are major pieces of the datacenter. Virtualization does not help abstract the underlying resources from how they may be provisioned, and quotas to create resources are allocated to business units and users. Virtualization does not provide self-service capabilities and workflows to the clients. Cloud services enable this by providing rich management technologies that build on the virtualization foundation and enable intuitive, scalable, and controlled services that can be offered beyond just the IT team. With cloud services, different resources from the datacenter can be grouped together and offered to different groups of users with well-defined capabilities and capacity. There are many more benefits, and I will go into more detail on them throughout this book.

Cloud services that are offered using an organization's internal resources are known as private clouds. Cloud services that are offered external to the organization, such as from a hosting partner or even solutions such as Windows Azure, are called public clouds.

Within these clouds different types of services can be offered, and typically these are seen from public cloud providers. There is, however a movement of these types of services being offered in an organization's private cloud to its various business units, especially IaaS. There are three primary types of services: Infrastructure as a Service (IaaS), Platform as a Service (PaaS), and Software as a Service (SaaS). For each type, the responsibilities of the nine major layers of management vary between the vendor of the service and the client (you). Figure 1.14 shows the three types of service and also a complete on-premises solution.

**FIGURE 1.14**
The key types of management and how they are owned for the different types of cloud service

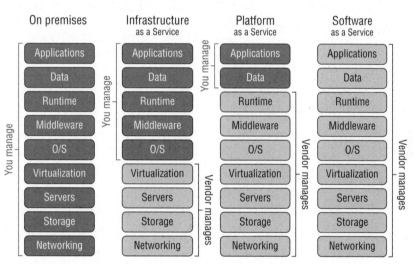

IaaS can be thought of as a virtual machine in the cloud. The provider has a virtual environment and you purchase virtual machine instances. You then manage the operating system, the patching, the data, and the applications within. Examples of IaaS are Amazon's Elastic Computing 2 (EC2) and Windows Azure IaaS, which give organizations the ability to run operating systems inside cloud-based virtual environments.

PaaS provides a framework in which custom applications can be run. Organizations only need to focus on writing the very best application within the guidelines of the platform capabilities and everything else is taken care of. There are no worries about patching operating systems, updating frameworks, backing up SQL databases, or configuring high availability. The organization just writes the application and pays for the resources used. Windows Azure is a classic example of a PaaS.

SaaS is the ultimate in low maintenance. The complete solution is provided by the vendor. There is nothing to write or maintain by the organization other than configuring who in the organization should be allowed to use the software. A commercial example of SaaS would be Hotmail, which is a messaging service on the Internet. The enterprise example could be Office 365, which provides cloud-hosted Exchange, SharePoint, and Lync services all accessed over the Internet with no application or operating system management for the organization.

Ideally, for the lowest management overhead, SaaS should be used, then PaaS if SaaS is not available, and then IaaS if PaaS is not an option. SaaS is gaining a great deal of traction with services such as Office 365, but PaaS adoption is fairly slow. The primary obstacle for PaaS is that applications have to be written within specific guidelines to be able to operate in PaaS environments. Many organizations have many custom applications that cannot be modified or don't have the budget to change the application, which is why IaaS is so popular. With IaaS, an existing virtual machine on-premises can fairly painlessly be moved to the IaaS solution. In the long term, I think PaaS will become the standard for custom applications, but it will take a long time, and I think IaaS can help serve as the ramp to adopting PaaS.

Consider a multitiered service that has a web tier, an application tier, and a SQL database tier. Initially, all these tiers would run as IaaS virtual machines. The organization may then be able to convert the web tier from IIS running in an IaaS VM and use the Windows Azure web role, which is part of PaaS. Next the organization may be able to move from SQL running in an IaaS VM to using SQL Azure. Finally, the organization could re-write the application tier to directly leverage Windows Azure PaaS. It's a gradual process, but the reduced overhead and increased functionality and resiliency at the end state is worth it.

## The Bottom Line

**Articulate the key value propositions of virtualization.**    Virtualization solves the numerous pain points and limitations of physical server deployments today. Primary benefits of virtualization include consolidation of resources, which increases resource utilization and provides OS abstraction from hardware, allowing OS mobility; financial savings through less server hardware, less datacenter space, and simpler licensing; faster provisioning of environments; and additional backup and recovery options.

**Master It**   How does virtualization help in service isolation in branch office situations?

**Understand the differences in functionality between the different versions of Hyper-V.**   Windows Server 2008 introduced the foundational Hyper-V capabilities, and the major new features in 2008 R2 were Live Migration and Cluster Shared Volumes (CSV). Windows 2008 R2 SP1 introduced Dynamic Memory and RemoteFX. Windows Server 2012 introduced new levels of scalability and mobility with features such as Shared Nothing Live Migration, Storage Live Migration, and Hyper-V Replica in addition to new networking and storage capabilities. Windows 2012 R2 Hyper-V enhances many of the 2012 features with generation 2 virtual machines, Live Migration compression and SMB support, new Hyper-V Replica replication granularity, and Hyper-V Replica Extended replication.

**Master It**   What is the largest virtual machine that can be created on Windows Server 2012 Hyper-V?

**Master It**   What features were enabled for Linux virtual machines in Windows Server 2012 R2 Hyper-V?

**Differentiate between the types of cloud service and when each type is best utilized.**   There are three primary types of cloud services. Software as a Service (SaaS), Platform as a Service (PaaS), and Infrastructure as a Service (IaaS). SaaS provides a complete software solution that is entirely managed by the providing vendor, such as a hosted mail solution. PaaS provides a platform on which custom-written applications can run and should be used for new custom applications when possible because it minimizes maintenance by the client. IaaS allows virtual machines to be run on a provided service, but the entire OS and application must be managed by the client. IaaS is suitable where PaaS or SaaS cannot be used and in development/test environments.

# Chapter 2

# Virtual Machine Resource Fundamentals

This chapter covers the primary building blocks of a virtual machine: the motherboard, processor, memory, and storage resources. We will look at the mechanics behind how these building blocks are virtualized on the physical host and explore the configuration options available for each of the virtualized resources when it's assigned to a virtual machine. We will also take a look at the advantages and limitations of the different options in the different common usage scenarios. By thoroughly understanding the fundamentals of virtual machine resources, you will be able to architect correctly the optimal virtual machine configuration based on the requirements available. You will also understand why the many other technologies are needed and how they should be utilized when they are explained later in this book.

In this chapter, you will learn to

- ◆ Describe how the resources of a virtual machine are virtualized by the hypervisor
- ◆ Use processor and memory advanced configuration options
- ◆ Explain the difference between VHD/VHDX and pass-through storage

## Understanding VMBus

Before we get into virtual machine resources, I want to cover the Hyper-V architecture in more detail than the high-level overview in Chapter 1, "Introduction to Virtualization and Microsoft Solutions." It is important to understand how the various resources for virtual machines are actually engineered and enabled. Figure 1.4 shows the hypervisor running directly on the hardware with all the virtual machine resource access serviced through the hypervisor. If you look carefully at the figure, I showed only the processor and memory resources being managed by the hypervisor, and this was deliberate. There are other resources that must be available for a full functioning environment, such as storage and networking. The mechanisms to communicate with the processor and memory in a system are quite standardized, removing the need for many different sets of code to handle the different types of processors and memory found in a system. This is not the case with storage controllers and network devices. Each vendor typically has it own specific implementation and must provide a driver to enable the operating system to correctly communicate with the hardware. There are literally thousands of these drivers for Windows, with most written by the independent hardware vendor (IHV). All these different types of storage and networks need to be usable by Hyper-V, and therefore the drivers need to be available. There are two different architectures for type 1 hypervisors: monolithic and micro-kernelized, as shown in Figure 2.1.

**FIGURE 2.1**
The monolithic and microkernelized hypervisors

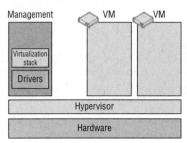

Monolithic hypervisor

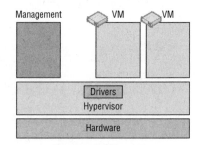

Microkernelized hypervisor

With a monolithic hypervisor, the drivers that are responsible for communication with the hardware sit in the actual hypervisor, which is a fairly complex kernel, basically a mini operating system. The virtual machines access the hardware via these specialized device drivers, which actually results in very good performance because the virtual machines can go directly to all hardware via these drivers in the hypervisor. However, there are issues. The first is that these shared drivers are specifically written for the hypervisor; that limits the hardware that is supported by a monolithic hypervisor, and virtualization solutions that use a monolithic hypervisor typically have a small hardware compatibility list. This shared driver base leads to the main concern, which is security and stability. With a shared driver for all the virtual machines, if a malware driver was placed in the hypervisor, all the partitions would be vulnerable to attack and snooping, plus if a driver is updated in the hypervisor that has an issue, it will cause problems for all the virtual machines.

Consider the Windows ecosystem with the huge number of hardware partners and the thousands of different storage controllers and network adapters that organizations may wish to use. Trying to create hypervisor drivers for all the different hardware would not be practical, and drastically reducing the supported hardware when using Hyper-V would also not be popular. So Microsoft choose the microkernelized hypervisor model, and this is why there is a Windows Server management/parent partition. With the microkernelized hypervisor model used by Hyper-V, all the Windows drivers created by vendors for their hardware can still be used and actually run in the management partition, removing the need for Hyper-V–specific drivers and not reducing the range of hardware usable with Hyper-V. This also keeps drivers out of the hypervisor, removing the security and stability concerns that relate to a monolithic hypervisor.

In actual fact, the hypervisor really just governs the allocation of CPU cycles and RAM and no other types of devices, such as storage and network. The parent partition hosts a virtualization stack that includes management components running in normal user mode. The Virtual Machine Management Service (VMMS) manages the state of virtual machines and launches the Virtual Machine Worker processes (VMWPs). There's one for each child partition running, and it controls the state changes of the child partition, enables certain types of emulated hardware, and enables management activities such as stopping and starting. Figure 2.2 shows Task Manager running on a Hyper-V server with a single vmms.exe instance but many vmwp.exe instances that correspond to each VM. In the background is a PowerShell command, which helps identify the worker process for a specific virtual machine. You need the parent partition along with the hypervisor to do anything useful such as creating child partitions. While you can install the hypervisor on its own, it won't really do much without a Windows Server 2012 R2 parent partition.

**FIGURE 2.2**
Task Manager showing a single vmms.exe instance and many vmwp .exe instances

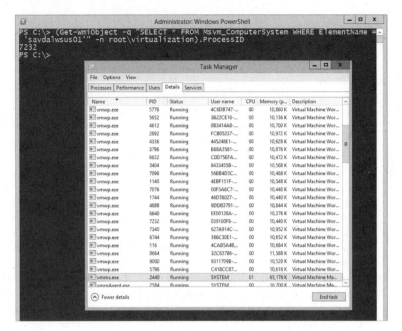

Components also run in kernel mode, such as the virtual machine bus (VMBus), which enables communication between a number of virtual service providers (VSPs) that enable support for non-CPU and memory hardware such as storage and networking. Each VSP corresponds to a number of virtual service clients (VSCs) running in the child partitions; for example, we have a virtual service provider and consumer for a network, a pair for storage, and so on. When a child partition wishes to access hardware resources that are not CPU or memory, its VSC makes a request to the VSP hosted in the VMBus on the parent partition, and the VSP performs the actual communication to the physical hardware. This is shown in Figure 2.3, which is an updated version of Figure 2.1 to show more clearly how the various types of hardware resource are actually serviced. The VMBus is not shared between all the child partitions, and there is one channel between each child and the parent so no communication or data can be seen by other child partitions running on the same server. This VMBus does not incur any significant performance penalty even though child partitions wanting to access hardware now essentially communicate via the VSC to a VSP on the VMBus hosted on the parent partition, which communicates to the hardware. This is because the VMBus is actually a pure memory bus running at a kernel level, so there is practically no latency introduced, and by using this model, Microsoft keeps the hypervisor small and secure while still allowing full hardware support for the breadth of the Microsoft hardware ecosystem.

**FIGURE 2.3**
Hyper-V VMBus
architecture

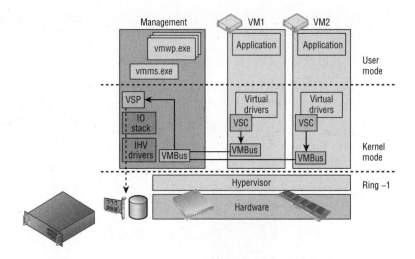

Essentially, the parent partition hosts all the VM support components that are not part of the hypervisor, and if the parent partition reboots or is unavailable, none of the child partitions are available either. There are components to the Hyper-V solution I did not show in Figure 2.3 to avoid confusion. There is a virtualization infrastructure driver (VID, vid.sys) that runs in the parent kernel mode and enables management services to the VMMS and VMWP that run in the user mode. The VID talks to the Windows Hypervisor Interface Library (WinHv) that communicates directly with the hypervisor via the hypercall interface, which communicates with the WinHv that runs in each VM (winhv.sys). There are a lot of moving parts, but for the most part you don't need to know about them. Things just work. It is, however, important to understand the VMBus and the role it plays in enabling very fast access to non-processor and non-memory resources via the parent partition.

## The Anatomy of a Virtual Machine

Consider the fundamental objectives of a virtualization environment. One objective is to enable multiple operating system instances to simultaneously execute on a single physical system, which enables the many benefits covered in Chapter 1. Another objective is to divide up and share the resources available on the physical host to many virtual machines, which act as their own, self-contained systems that are completely isolated from the other virtualized systems running on the host. Each virtual machine believes it is the sole user of the hardware it is running on. Within each virtual machine an operating system is installed, and into that operating system, applications are installed and configurations implemented to enable services to the organization.

Operating systems are written to run on hardware and expect certain components to be present that can be interacted with, such as the computer's BIOS, storage controller, input/output systems, and network device. Drivers are included in the operating system to see certain types of device like network and storage controllers to enable installation and startup of the operating system. It's also possible to add additional drivers for hardware that does not have drivers included as part of the operating system. This fundamental presence of hardware components does not apply to a virtual machine. The entire environment of a virtual machine is synthetic, with abstracted resources allotted to the virtual machine and many resources utilizing the VMBus as previously explained. However, the key aspects of a computer must be present for an operating system to install and function.

## Generation 1 Virtual Machine

All of the synthetic resources and devices that are exposed by Hyper-V provide the highest level of performance and functionality, but if an operating system cannot natively use them, then that operating system cannot be installed or started on that synthetic hardware. Even today with Hyper-V, there are large numbers of Windows 2000, Windows 2003, and Windows XP virtual machines running virtualized, and these operating systems are not virtualization aware. The use of the VMBus architecture within a guest operating system requires deep integration with other operating system components; it's not as simple as installing an additional storage or network driver during installation.

It is therefore often required to provide certain types of hardware as emulated, which means Hyper-V components provide to virtual machines what appear to be standard types of hardware such as an Intel 82371AB/EB IDE controller, an Intel 21140 Ethernet adapter, a PS/2 keyboard and mouse, and a complete virtual motherboard with BIOS. Behind the scenes, though, the Hyper-V solution is running code to pretend this hardware exists. Providing emulated hardware requires an additional workload in the hypervisor, predominantly provided by the worker process for the virtual machine, vmwp.exe.

Remember that the vmwp.exe runs in the user mode space of the parent partition, which means as emulated hardware is used, its performance will be poorer than the synthetic equivalents (which run purely in kernel mode and don't have the additional overhead of emulating physical pieces of hardware). The emulated hardware requires many context switches between user mode and kernel mode for the actual real hardware communications via the management partition's I/O stack, and the communication path is far more convoluted. Additionally, the interface to the emulated devices assumes things about a physical machine. For instance, setting up an IDE transfer involves seven I/O port writes, each of which is a separate round-trip to the emulator in the vmwp.exe and a huge performance penalty. This performance penalty is why synthetic hardware is always preferred over emulated hardware, but sometimes there isn't a choice, and for some types of hardware that is rarely used or primarily triggered by the user, the difference in performance is not noticeable (consider mouse or keyboard type hardware).

The term *generation 1 virtual machine* may be completely new to you. Prior to Windows Server 2012 R2 Hyper-V, it would have just been called a virtual machine. There is now a new type of virtual machine, which I will cover in the section, "Generation 2 Virtual Machine," and that is why there is now a name distinction. Consider the generation 1 virtual machine as the virtual machine you have known and loved since Windows Server 2008 Hyper-V but with a few improvements. Unless you are deploying all brand-new virtual machines on Windows Server 2012 R2 with the latest operating systems, you will continue to use generation 1 virtual machines for some time, and this is not a problem at all. Remember that generation 1 virtual machines fully support the VMBus and synthetic hardware but also provide support for emulated hardware when required.

## VIRTUAL MOTHERBOARD AND BIOS

At the core of a virtual machine is the virtual motherboard and the basic input/output system (BIOS). This provides the environment needed to initially start the virtual machine, choose the boot device, and hand over control to the operating system installed. Microsoft uses the American Megatrends Inc. BIOS for the virtual machines. However, you don't access the BIOS of a virtual machine the same way you access the BIOS of a physical machine (for example, by pressing the Esc or Delete key). Instead, the options related to BIOS startup and boot order are configured through the virtual machine properties using the BIOS area, as shown in Figure 2.4. Notice that the figure shows that the Num Lock state can be set as well as the types of boot devices supported in a generation 1 virtual machine (CD, IDE, legacy network Adapter, and floppy). The types of network adapters will be covered in the next chapter, but for now know that a legacy network adapter is an emulated network adapter instead of the synthetic network adapter which utilizes the VMBus. Typically, you *never* want to use the legacy network adapter except for a very specific use case, booting over the network.

**FIGURE 2.4**
The BIOS configurations possible for a generation 1 virtual machine. The boot order can be changed using the Move Up and Move Down buttons.

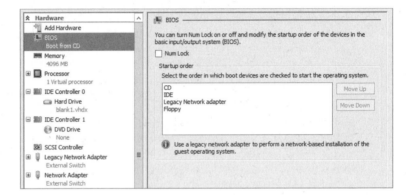

There are many other system devices enabled in the guest operating system through the virtual motherboard provided by Hyper-V. They can be seen in the System Devices section in Device Manager (devmgmt.msc), but typically they are not items you will interact with.

### WHAT ABOUT THE TIME?

A physical motherboard has a small battery and a real-time clock (RTC) to track time, but the way most operating systems work is to read the time from the RTC at startup and then use their own internal routines to calculate passed time. The problem for a virtual machine is that the routines used to calculate time do not work correctly due to the way virtual machine resources are actually delivered, which means time drifts in a virtual machine. To solve this problem, Hyper-V uses a time synchronization integration service that keeps the time correct within the virtual machine. There is a potential to see some time anomalies when a virtual machine is first booted or resumed from a saved state or checkpoint (point-in-time saved view of a virtual machine), but these should quickly be resolved once the time synchronization integration service loads, which will correct the issue. Even if the virtual machine is in a different time zone or is part of a domain that synchronizes time from domain controllers, you should leave the time synchronization integration service enabled. The time synchronization service will work well with other time sources. Run the w32tm /query /source command to check the time source for your operating system. A Hyper-V virtual machine should show the following:

```
C:\>w32tm /query /source
VM IC Time Synchronization Provider
```

The guidance for domain controllers has changed over the years. The recommendation was to disable time synchronization completely and then to disable only part of the service with the following command:

```
reg add HKLM\SYSTEM\CurrentControlSet\Services\W32Time\TimeProviders⏎
\VMICTimeProvider /v Enabled /t reg_dword /d 0
```

Once again, though, the recommendation is to just disable the time synchronization integration service completely, as documented in the time service section at the following location:

```
http://technet.microsoft.com/en-us/library/virtual_active_directory_
domain_controller_virtualization_hyperv(WS.10).aspx
```

My recommendation is to regularly check back, but fundamentally, Hyper-V has gotten better at controlling the drift, hence minimizing the time synchronizations needed for virtual machines that already synchronize from another source.

## IDE CONTROLLER

I'm going to cover processors and memory in great detail later in this chapter. The other "must have" component for a system is storage (technically, you don't need a network; a system is just not typically very useful without it). Generation 1 virtual machines must boot from storage connected to the IDE controller, which as previously explained emulates an Intel 82371AB/EB IDE controller. This enables almost any operating system to be installed in a Hyper-V virtual machine because the Intel 82371AB/EB IDE controller is common and the driver is built in to every major operating system.

There are two IDE controllers provided in a generation 1 virtual machine: IDE controller 0 and IDE controller 1. Each IDE controller can have up to two devices attached, which can be a hard drive or a DVD drive. Typically the only time a DVD drive is used is when there is an option to install the operating system into a new virtual machine by attaching an operating system installation ISO to the drive, although mapping to a physical DVD drive in the host is also possible. It's also possible to install or update the Hyper-V Integration Services, which are provided as an ISO.

Two IDE controllers with two devices each allows a maximum of four storage devices to be connected, which may seem limited. In most virtual machines you will use the IDE controller only for the boot hard disk and all data drives will be connected to the synthetic SCSI controller instead.

Something seemingly obvious may be occurring to you. In this chapter, I have been continually saying that emulated hardware is bad, that it is provided by a user mode process (vmwp.exe) in the parent partition (which gives poor performance), and wherever possible, to avoid using it. Now I'm saying every single Hyper-V virtual machine has to boot from a hard disk attached to the emulated IDE controller. Doesn't that mean every virtual machine will have terrible disk performance for the operating system disk? Yes, a little, but mostly no because the architects of Hyper-V did something very clever with the IDE controller.

The IDE controller had to emulate a common IDE controller to provide compatibility with all operating systems where the components needed to use synthetic, VMBus-enabled devices that would not natively be available. Once an operating system is installed in a Hyper-V virtual machine, one of the first steps is to install Hyper-V Integration Services, which enlightens the operating system to its virtualized state and allows it to leverage the synthetic devices available via the VMBus. It also enables tighter integration between Hyper-V and the operating system, such as time synchronization, data exchange, backup services, shutdown, and more. Once the integration services have been installed and loaded, the IDE controller switches under the covers from being an emulated IDE device to actually being a synthetic device that uses the VMBus and the VSC/VSP model via a component in the guest called the fast pass filter (storflt). It therefore matches the performance of the synthetic SCSI controllers that are also available. This means that providing Hyper-V Integration Services is installed, there is not a performance difference between using the IDE or SCSI controller in a virtual machine once the operating system has booted, but the SCSI controller does offer additional functionality, which is why its use is still preferred where possible for assets such as data disks.

### SCSI CONTROLLER

By default, a generation 1 virtual machine does not have a SCSI controller, but up to four SCSI controllers can be added to a virtual machine using the Add Hardware area of the virtual machine's property page as shown in Figure 2.5. Once a virtual machine has four SCSI controllers, the option to add additional SCSI controllers will be grayed out. The SCSI controller is a pure synthetic device fully leveraging the kernel, in-memory VMBus, which gives essentially the highest, bare-metal storage performance. The term *bare-metal* refers to a system that does not use virtualization. When something is compared to bare-metal, the comparison is to a nonvirtualized environment, and in this case, studies have shown there is no performance loss from using storage attached to the SCSI controller compared to the raw performance capabilities of the underlying storage.

**FIGURE 2.5**
Adding a SCSI controller to a generation 1 virtual machine

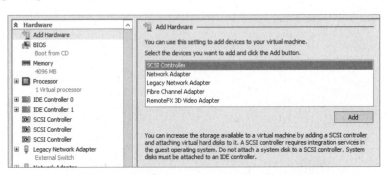

Each SCSI controller supports up to 64 hard drives attached, which equates to a maximum of 256 disks attached via the SCSI bus. Like the IDE controller, those hard disks can be virtual hard disks or mapped to physical hard disks on the host (pass-through storage). The SCSI controller also supports the hot-add/hot-plug of disks to a running virtual machine, which is a capability not available on the IDE controller. The SCSI controller offers even more functionality in Windows Server 2012 R2:

◆ Shared VHDX between multiple virtual machines

◆ Dynamic resizing of VHDX files

Always use SCSI-connected disks where possible in the virtual machine and restrict use of IDE-connected disks to the operating system and DVD drive.

## COM PORTS

Generation 1 virtual machines include two COM ports, COM 1 and COM 2, which can be connected to a named pipe either local to the Hyper-V host or on a remote computer. The use of COM ports is generally deprecated and is typically restricted to certain types of guest kernel debug scenarios.

## USB PORTS

If you are looking at a virtual machine settings dialog, you may wonder where USB devices are found. How do you map a USB device attached to the Hyper-V host directly through to a virtual machine? You won't find it, and the reality is you don't want to find it.

There are two scenarios for USB devices to be accessed in a virtual machine:

◆ As part of a user's session to a virtual machine

◆ Always available to the virtual machine, such as, for example, a USB dongle that must be available for a piece of software or service to function

Hyper-V does not allow the pass-through of a USB attached device on a host to a virtual machine. This would break the desired abstraction of the virtual machine from the hardware and therefore stop virtual machine mobility. This does not mean there are not solutions though.

For the first scenario, a USB device available as part of a user's session on a virtual machine, the solution is to use the Remote Desktop Protocol (RDP) capability to pass a locally attached USB device on the user's local device directly through to the remote virtual machine. With Windows Server 2012 and the RemoteFX technology, it is possible to redirect almost any USB device over RDP.

The second scenario, for a USB device to always be connected to a virtual machine even when a user is not logged on, requires the use of third-party solutions that enable USB over IP. The solutions work by having a physical server that has all the USB devices connected to it and runs a service that enables the USB devices to be accessed remotely over IP. The virtual machines then run a client piece of software that connects to the USB device over IP and looks to the VM like a local USB device. The benefit to these types of solutions is that the virtual machine can still be moved between hosts without losing connectivity to the USB device. There are many solutions available, but the two I have seen in customers' environments are described at the following locations:

```
http://www.silexamerica.com/products/usb_device_connectivity/sx-2000u2.html
http://www.digi.com/products/usb/anywhereusb#overview
```

## Generation 2 Virtual Machine

Earlier I made a statement, "Each virtual machine believes it is the sole user of the hardware it is running on," and the point was that the operating system was unaware it was running on a hypervisor, which is why there was so much emulated hardware in a generation 1 virtual machine. The various PS/2 keyboard and mouse devices, the IDE controller, the legacy network adapter for PXE boot, PCI controllers, and so on were required so operating systems could work in a virtual environment because they were inherently ignorant to virtualization, unable to natively use virtualized or synthetic devices. This was true when virtualization was first introduced and needed to support operating systems such as Windows NT 4 and Windows 2000, but the reality for modern operating systems such as Windows Server 2012 and even recent Linux distributions is that they natively understand virtualization and are fully virtualization enlightened. They can use virtual devices without additional drivers installed and don't require "physical hardware" elements to be present. Modern operating systems are designed to run in physical and virtual environments.

The generation 2 virtual machine was introduced in Windows Server 2012 R2 Hyper-V. It is focused on the new generation of operating systems that are natively enlightened to virtualization and don't require the emulated components such as IDE controllers, PS/2 IO devices, COM ports, legacy network adapters, floppy drives, and all the other emulated motherboard components (such as PCI-to-ISA bridge). A generation 2 virtual machine removes these emulated components to offer a simpler, streamlined virtual machine that also enables the latest operating system features by switching from BIOS to a Unified Extensible Firmware Interface (UEFI) such as Secure Boot (enabled by default). Secure Boot ensures a secure handoff from the UEFI to the operating system without any other party, such as malware, injecting itself between the hardware and the operating system.

Generation 2 virtual machines can boot from SCSI controller-connected hard disks and DVD drives and also from the synthetic network adapter to enable PXE boot scenarios. There is no IDE controller, floppy drive, or legacy network adapter option for a generation 2 virtual machine.

There are also no COM ports available via the Hyper-V Manager graphical interface. If a COM port is required in a generation 2 virtual machine for remote kernel debugging, then one can be added using the Set-VMComPort PowerShell cmdlet. There are, however, better options for virtual machines than using a serial port, such as using synthetic debugging. If the COM port has no named pipe associated at boot time, then the COM port will not be visible in the virtual machine. Remember also that kernel debugging is not compatible with Secure Boot, so if you need to perform kernel debugging (and many of us won't!), then turn of Secure Boot using Set-VMFirmware -EnableSecureBoot Off. In Figure 2.6, you see a generation 1 virtual machine next to a generation 2 virtual machine showing Device Manager and also the BIOS mode and version. Notice the large amount of hardware that is not present in a generation 2 virtual machine because this hardware is not required for an operating system that is natively virtualization enlightened.

**FIGURE 2.6**
Generation 1 compared to generation 2 hardware

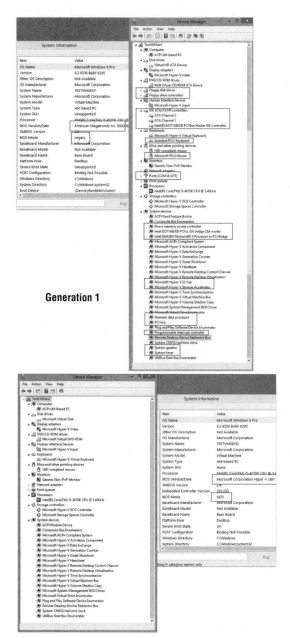

**Generation 1**

**Generation 2**

At time of this writing, the following operating systems can be installed in a generation 2 virtual machine:

◆   Windows Server 2012

◆   Windows Server 2012 R2

◆   Windows 8 64-bit

◆   Windows 8.1 64-bit

The biggest restriction is the need for the operating system to natively fully support UEFI, which is not available prior to Windows 8/Windows Server 2012, and only the 64-bit versions of Windows support UEFI. For a good overview of UEFI support with Windows, see

`http://msdn.microsoft.com/en-us/windows/hardware/gg463149.aspx`

The main benefits to using a generation 2 virtual machine are the ability to boot from the synthetic SCSI controller or network device and, by leveraging the UEFI Secure Boot capability, the minimized risks associated with boot-time malware. There is also a performance improvement in the time to install an operating system and the time to boot an operating system for a generation 2 virtual machine compared to a generation 1 virtual machine, but once the virtual machine has been booted, there is no performance difference. The choice of generation 1 vs. generation 2 is made when the virtual machine is created and cannot be changed. A single Hyper-V server can have a mix of generation 1 and generation 2 virtual machines.

When deciding to use generation 1 or generation 2, my advice would be to use generation 2 where possible, providing you do not need backward compatibility with Windows Server 2012 Hyper-V. Compatibility is not required with other public cloud services either, such as Windows Azure Infrastructure as a Service (IaaS), which at the time of writing does not support generation 2 virtual machines; this will change over time.

---

**CONVERTING A GENERATION 1 VIRTUAL MACHINE TO GENERATION 2**

The question of converting a generation 1 virtual machine to a generation 2 virtual machine comes up often, and the reality is that you really don't need to in most cases. Generation 1 virtual machines will continue to work and perform the same as a generation 2 virtual machine. But what if you really want to? You can't, or at least not without a huge amount of work.

A generation 1 virtual machine is BIOS based, which equates to a certain disk configuration such as an NTFS system partition. A generation 2 virtual machine is UEFI based and uses a FAT32 system partition. This alone prohibits moving virtual hard disks between generation 1 and generation 2 virtual machines. Also remember that generation 1 machines boot from the IDE controller and generation 2 machines boot from the SCSI controller.

The only way to move from generation 1 to generation 2 is to boot the virtual machine from Windows PE, capture the partitions to a WIM file, then redeploy to a generation 2 virtual machine, but this amount of effort is really not worth the benefit, and generation 2 is best saved for new virtual machines.

# Processor Resources

With the core fabric of a virtual machine understood, it's time to move on to the processor, which is one of the most interesting and used resources for a virtual machine. It's important to understand some of the terminology related to processor resources and how this relates to virtualization and Hyper-V.

There is a difference between the number of processors, cores, and logical processors and the amount of memory supported by Windows Server 2012 R2 and that supported by Hyper-V. With new processors having multiple processing cores and technologies such as hyperthreading, adding more complexity to understanding processors, a review of logical and virtual processors is important. Motherboards have one or more sockets, which can have processors installed. This is why the terms *socket* and *processor* are sometimes used interchangeably. Each processor has one or more processing cores. Early processors had only one core, but multicore processors became predominant starting with dual-core processors, then quad-core, and today there are 10-core processors available. Each core acts like a separate processor with the ability to perform its own execution of program instructions, though the cores share a common bus interface and certain types of processor cache, as explained in Chapter 1.

In many types of program instruction execution, not all of the core's execution resources are utilized, and so Intel introduced a hyperthreading technology that makes a single processor core look like two processor cores, known as logical processors, and allows two instruction threads to run on each processor core. This increases overall throughput by allowing the processor to switch between the two instruction threads to keep the cores busy because it's common for instruction threads to stall waiting on a resource. With hyperthreading, if one thread stalls, the other thread can be executed. There is still only a single execution resource on the core, so hyperthreading does not double performance; the actual improvement varies, but between a 10 to 15 percent performance improvement is an accepted value.

Figure 2.7 shows Task Manager on one of my Windows Server 2012 R2 boxes. It has four Intel Xeon processors, which are eight-core processors, and has hyperthreading enabled. Notice that the socket count is 4 and the core count is 32, while the logical processor count is 64 because the hyperthreading splits each core into two logical processors.

Prior to Windows Server 2012, there were different capabilities and scalability in the different SKUs (editions) of Windows Server. This changed with Windows Server 2012. Windows Server 2012 Standard and Datacenter have the same scalability and capabilities, supporting up to 320 logical processors addressable by the hypervisor and 4 TB of memory. Each virtual machine can be allocated up to 64 virtual processors. These scalability numbers did not change with Windows Server 2012 R2 Hyper-V because, in reality, they really didn't need to. With the Windows Server 2012 Hyper-V scalability capability of 64 vCPUs per virtual machine, Microsoft found that over 99 percent of the world's SQL Server instances could now be virtualized on Hyper-V.

Having multiple logical processors is very useful for virtualization. To take advantage of many logical processors on a normal system, the applications being used have to be written to take advantage of multiple threads of execution or many applications would be used at the same time, which the operating system would distribute over the available logical processors. With virtualization, each virtual machine is assigned a certain number of virtual processors (vCPUs), which then map to logical processors. A single logical processor can be used by multiple virtual processors because the logical processors' capacity is divided up among the utilizing virtual processors as computations are required. This works in a similar manner to the time slicing that occurs in between applications in an operating system sharing the processors. As virtual processors need to perform computations, they are scheduled on an available logical processor.

**FIGURE 2.7**
Task Manager in Logical Processor view showing the physical processors and logical processor details

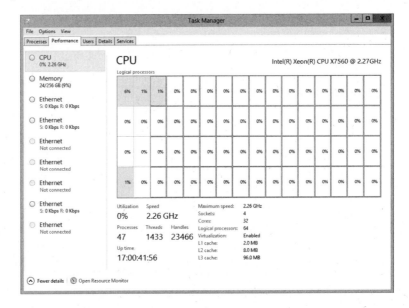

Prior to Windows Server 2012, there was a supported ratio of 8 virtual processors for every 1 logical processor (8:1) for all workloads except for Windows VDI environments, where a ratio of 12:1 was supported. This was stipulated to ensure that hosts were not overcommitted in terms of virtual processors assigned to virtual machines. For example, with a ratio of 8:1, if a system had a total of 8 logical processors, then up to 64 vCPUs could be assigned in total for all the virtual machines running on that host. Note that a single virtual machine can never be assigned more virtual processors than the number of logical processors present in the server. Taking the same 8 logical processors, this means a single virtual machine could not have more than 8 virtual processors assigned. However, I could have 8 virtual machines all with 8 virtual processors (or any other smaller combinations, providing the total does not exceed 64 virtual processors). The supportability ratio of virtual processors to logical processors was removed in Windows Server 2012. If you test the environment and it works, then it will be supported by Microsoft. You still cannot have more virtual processors in a virtual machine than logical processors that exist in the server. A Hyper-V host supports up to 2,048 virtual processors.

Even though the supported ratio has been removed, this does not mean careful planning is not required when architecting your Hyper-V environment. Virtualization cannot magically enable more processing resources than are physically available. For virtual machines with very low CPU utilization, such as around 10 percent, planning on 8 virtual processors to 1 logical processor would be fine and would yield an average utilization of around 80 percent on the physical core. If virtual machines have high processor utilization, a ratio of 8:1 would yield poor performance because virtual machines constantly wait for cycles on the physical cores.

Some applications, such as SQL Server and Exchange, have their own supported ratios of virtual processor to logical processor, which can be as low as 1:1. I will cover this in more detail later in this chapter. Because of the fairly low additional performance hyperthreading actually yields, though, I prefer to count processor cores only when thinking about my virtual to physical ratios. If I have a Hyper-V host with 4 processor cores, I would consider 32 my maximum number of virtual processors, even if hyperthreading was enabled. Figure 2.8 shows a high-level view of mapping of physical processors to cores to logical processors to virtual processors. Note that there is no concept of processor affinity in Hyper-V. You cannot force a certain virtual processor to always map to the same logical processor. That could lead to poor performance waiting for the processor to be available, and it also breaks the goal of abstracting the virtual resource from the physical resource.

**FIGURE 2.8**
A view of logical processor to virtual processor mapping

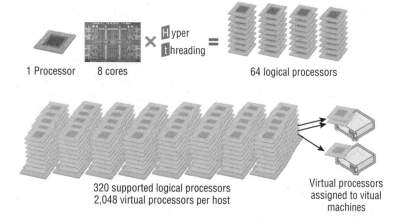

**SHOULD I TURN OFF HYPERTHREADING?**

Note that hyperthreading causes no harm and may help performance unless it pushes the number of logical processors above 320, which is the maximum number supported by Hyper-V. If hyperthreading means there are now more than 320, hyperthreading-provided logical processors will be used potentially instead of physical cores by the hypervisor. Therefore, if hyperthreading pushes the number of logical processors above 320, turn it off in the servers' BIOS/UEFI.

## Virtual Processor to Logical Processor Scheduling

How a virtual machine's virtual processors are assigned to logical processors for computations is actually very interesting. Consider the simplest possible scenario, a single virtual processor on a virtual machine. When the virtual processor needs to perform a computation, the hypervisor schedules the computation to an available logical processor, as shown in Figure 2.9.

**FIGURE 2.9**
A virtual processor from a single-processor VM assigned to a logical processor on the host

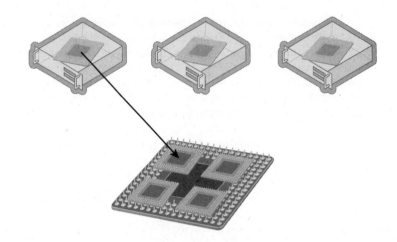

This gets more complicated for a virtual machine with multiple virtual processors, a symmetric multiprocessing (SMP) environment. The problem is that operating systems believe that all their processors are available to run at the same time because the operating system would exclusively own the hardware and can allow interdependencies between different computations on different processors. This is a problem in a virtual environment because many different virtual processors are using the same logical processors. This means the virtual processor scheduler in the hypervisor could have a problem. Consider Figure 2.10, where two of the virtual machines now have multiple processors. If the processor scheduler has to schedule all the virtual processors in a VM to logical processors at the same time, the virtual processor scheduler suddenly becomes inefficient. Even virtual processors not currently doing work would be scheduled on the logical processor as a set, and none of the virtual processors in a VM can be scheduled until there are an equal number of logical processors available to ensure that the computations for the VM can take place simultaneously. Consider a heavily used server and that virtual machines can have up to 64 virtual processors. Trying to group and schedule processors in this way is highly problematic. This type of scheduling is known as gang scheduling because when a multiprocessor virtual machine needs to schedule a processor, all of the virtual processors are "ganged" together and scheduled together against the available logical processors.

Here's a great analogy: Consider going out to dinner with a group of friends. You sit down, open the menu, and know exactly what you want to eat. You then have to proceed to sit there for 15 minutes until everyone else has decided what they will order because you have to all order at the same time. You are gang scheduled.

Nobody has been able to create a perfect gang scheduler that does not lead to delays and inefficiencies. It is because of this gang scheduling that with some hypervisors, you need to minimize the number of virtual processors per virtual machine as much as possible.

Hyper-V does not use gang scheduling and instead takes an alternate approach to handling multiprocessor virtual machines and the scheduling to logical processors. Remember, the problem is that operating systems believe that all their processors are available to run at the same time. Rather than trying to work around this problem, Microsoft actually fixed the operating system kernel itself so that the operating system no longer makes the assumption that all processors will be scheduled at the same time. This allows Hyper-V to be able to schedule virtual processors from a multiprocessor virtual machine independently of each other, which allows virtual processors to be scheduled only as they have workload, known as free processor scheduling. This fix was made in Windows Server 2008, which is why Windows Server 2000 supports only a single processor. A targeted change was made to the kernel in Windows Server 2003 Service Pack 2 and Windows XP Service Pack 3 that allows for two virtual processors to be configured. Because gang scheduling is not used with Hyper-V, there is no guidance to limit the number of virtual processors in a virtual machine where possible. There is still some overhead with having lots of idle processors, but it is fairly minimal and has nowhere near the impact as a hypervisor that uses gang scheduling. In my lab environment, nearly all my virtual machines have two processors and some have eight.

**FIGURE 2.10**
A virtual machine with multiple virtual processors being scheduled to the available logical processors

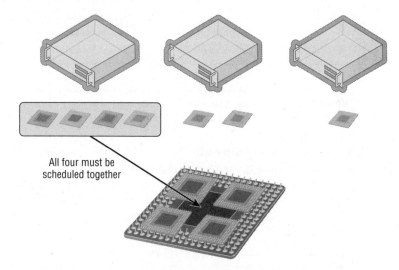

All four must be scheduled together

Using the same dinner analogy for Hyper-V would allow you to order dinner whenever you were ready and then get your food. This would be, however, poor dining etiquette on your part and would likely get you excluded from future dinner events and subject you to lots of future solo dining.

The exact number of virtual processors supported for each guest operating system for Hyper-V is documented and updated at

`http://technet.microsoft.com/en-us/library/hh831531.aspx`

but the primary numbers are shown in Table 2.1. Note that Windows Server 2000 is not listed on the Microsoft site because it is no longer a supported operating system; only one processor was supported.

**TABLE 2.1:**     Maximum number of virtual processors

| OPERATING SYSTEM | NUMBER OF VIRTUAL PROCESSORS |
| --- | --- |
| Windows Server 2008 R2 and above | 64 |
| Windows Server 2008 SP2 | 4 |

**TABLE 2.1:** Maximum number of virtual processors *(CONTINUED)*

| OPERATING SYSTEM | NUMBER OF VIRTUAL PROCESSORS |
| --- | --- |
| Windows Server 2003 [R2] SP2 | 2 |
| Modern supported Linux distributions (RHEL 5.9+, SUSE 11 SP2+, Ubuntu 12.04+) | 64 |
| Windows 8 and above | 32 |
| Windows 7 | 4 |
| Windows XP SP3/Windows Vista SP2 | 2 |

It's important to understand that gang scheduling is not bad; but rather there's just not an efficient algorithm to use it at this time. In the future, a perfect algorithm may be created, and then I would not be surprised to see Hyper-V implement some type of gang scheduling.

## Processor Assignment

When assigning processors to a virtual machine, between 1 and 64 (or the number of logical processors in the system) can be assigned. Additionally, it is possible to set three other values that help control the processor resource usage. These are Virtual Machine Reserve (Percentage), Virtual Machine Limit (Percentage), and Relative Weight, and they are described in the following list:

*Min*

**Virtual Machine Reserve (Percentage)** The amount of the processor that is reserved for this virtual machine and therefore always available. If a host has 4 logical processors and the virtual machine has 1 virtual processor and the reserve is set to 50 percent, then it means half of one of the logical processors is always available to this virtual machine. Note that it does not mean it's the same core or all from the same core, but the hypervisor will ensure that the virtual machine always has the equivalent of half of a logical processor of processing available to this virtual machine. If the virtual machine is not using the full reserve, other virtual machines may access the processor resource. However, as soon as the virtual machine with the reserve needs the CPU, it will take priority and be guaranteed its full allocation. The Percent Of Total System Resources value shows what percentage of the overall system resources the reserve that's assigned equates to. If a virtual machine has been assigned 8 virtual processors with a 25 percent reserve and the server has 16 logical processors in total, this means the percent of total system resources reserved is 12 percent (12.5 percent really).

*Max*

**Virtual Machine Limit (Percentage)** The maximum amount of processor that the virtual machine can use. The default is 100 percent, which means this virtual machine can use the entire resources of the allocated processors. Note that in times of resource contention, the virtual machine may not get a full 100 percent but will always get its reserve amount.

*Shares*

**Relative Weight** Used to determine the importance of a virtual machine getting shares of the CPU time in times of resource contention. For example, a virtual machine with a weight of 200 would get twice the number of CPU cycles that a virtual machine with a weight of 100 would.

Note that while the number of processors of a virtual machine cannot be changed once the virtual machine has been started, it is possible to modify the Virtual Machine Reserve (Percentage), Virtual Machine Limit (Percentage), and Relative Weight values while the virtual machine is running. This allows the ability to tweak the processor resources for a virtual machine dynamically. This would let you assign extra processors to a virtual machine than normally would be required but set the Virtual Machine Limit (Percentage) value to something like 50 percent so that only half the capacity could be used. If more processor is required while the virtual machine is running, that value can be increased. It should be noted that typically operating systems will not "waste" processor resources, so this type of limiting is typically not required unless you have a heavily overcommitted system or a virtual machine with rogue processes.

---

### SOLVING "HANGING" PROBLEMS FOR VERY LARGE HYPER-V VIRTUAL MACHINES

For a virtual machine with more than 32 virtual processors, I would sometimes see the virtual machine hang within 30 seconds of logging on (the same time Server Manager started and used processor resources). After investigation, I found that the problem was basically that a large number of the logical processors in the Hyper-V host had gone into a C3 sleep state, which is a deep sleep state to save power when the processor is idle. The problem seemed to be caused by all these logical processors trying to wake at the same time and getting into contention with each other. The solution for me was to simply disable the C3 sleep state on my processors on the Hyper-V host using the following command:

```
reg.exe add HKLM\System\CurrentControlSet\Control\Processor /v Capabilities /t
REG_DWORD /d 0x0007e066
```

Then I would reboot the server and my problem was solved.

---

Windows Server 2012 R2 Hyper-V has another processor-related setting that is set on a per-virtual-machine basis. This setting is "Migrate to a physical computer with a different processor version." It is not possible to migrate a virtual machine between Intel and AMD processors using migration technologies due to the completely different architecture and instruction sets of the processor. However, by default you also can't migrate between servers with different versions of the same processor family. This is because although both servers may have Intel processors, the different processors may have different capabilities and instructions, which is a problem because some applications perform tests when they start to check the capabilities of the processor. If an application checks the processor and decides it has a certain set of instructions and is then moved using migration technologies to a server with a different processor that does not support a particular instruction, when the application makes the call, the application may crash. To resolve this problem, Hyper-V adds the ability to hide many higher-level functions of processors in the guest operating systems. This means you can move guest operating systems between nodes in a cluster even if the processor versions are different because the virtual operating systems are exposed only to the generic instructions that are present in all versions of the processor family. Note that the functionality does not scan the processors and expose the lowest common set of functionality of all the processors in the cluster; it just limits to a generic basic set lower than all the processors in the cluster. This can also be set using PowerShell with the following command:

```
Set-VMProcessor -CompatibilityForMigrationEnabled $true
```

Prior to Windows Server 2012 Hyper-V, there was also a setting to enable running older operating systems such as NT 4, but this option has been removed from the Hyper-V manager graphical user interface. The problem for older operating systems is that modern processors return more information about the capabilities than can be handled by the operating system and it will blue screen (this was fixed in Windows NT 4.0 SP6). This option can still be set, but it must be configured using PowerShell:

```
Set-VMProcessor -CompatibilityForOlderOperatingSystemsEnabled $true
```

A great way to understand these two settings is by leveraging the Coreinfo utility from SysInternals, which can list all features for a processor. You'll find it at the following location:

```
http://technet.microsoft.com/en-us/sysinternals/cc835722.aspx
```

When running coreinfo on a processor without any compatibility enabled, I see all the features available for the operating system. An enabled feature shows an * instead of a -. When I run coreinfo on the same virtual machine but after setting CompatibilityForMigrationEnabled, all the items in bold changed from * to -, which meant they were now hidden, as shown in the following listing. In this example, it was SSSE3, SSE4.1, SSE4.2, and POPCNT that were hidden. Running with CompatibilityForOlderOperatingSystemsEnabled removed the entire Logical Processor to Cache Map section from the returned data, which means it was hidden from the operating system. It is important to use these features only when required because you are removing capability from the processor, which you don't want to do unless you absolutely have to.

```
S:\Tools>coreinfo

Coreinfo v3.2 - Dump information on system CPU and memory topology
Copyright (C) 2008-2012 Mark Russinovich
Sysinternals - www.sysinternals.com

Intel(R) Xeon(R) CPU           E5530  @ 2.40GHz
Intel64 Family 6 Model 26 Stepping 5, GenuineIntel
HTT             *       Hyperthreading enabled
HYPERVISOR      *       Hypervisor is present
VMX             -       Supports Intel hardware-assisted virtualization
SVM             -       Supports AMD hardware-assisted virtualization
EM64T           *       Supports 64-bit mode

SMX             -       Supports Intel trusted execution
SKINIT          -       Supports AMD SKINIT

NX              *       Supports no-execute page protection
SMEP            -       Supports Supervisor Mode Execution Prevention
SMAP            -       Supports Supervisor Mode Access Prevention
```

| | | |
|---|---|---|
| PAGE1GB | - | Supports 1 GB large pages |
| PAE | * | Supports > 32-bit physical addresses |
| PAT | * | Supports Page Attribute Table |
| PSE | * | Supports 4 MB pages |
| PSE36 | * | Supports > 32-bit address 4 MB pages |
| PGE | * | Supports global bit in page tables |
| SS | * | Supports bus snooping for cache operations |
| VME | * | Supports Virtual-8086 mode |
| RDWRFSGSBASE | - | Supports direct GS/FS base access |
| | | |
| FPU | * | Implements i387 floating point instructions |
| MMX | * | Supports MMX instruction set |
| MMXEXT | - | Implements AMD MMX extensions |
| 3DNOW | - | Supports 3DNow! instructions |
| 3DNOWEXT | - | Supports 3DNow! extension instructions |
| SSE | * | Supports Streaming SIMD Extensions |
| SSE2 | * | Supports Streaming SIMD Extensions 2 |
| SSE3 | * | Supports Streaming SIMD Extensions 3 |
| **SSSE3** | * | **Supports Supplemental SIMD Extensions 3** |
| **SSE4.1** | * | **Supports Streaming SIMD Extensions 4.1** |
| **SSE4.2** | * | **Supports Streaming SIMD Extensions 4.2** |
| | | |
| AES | - | Supports AES extensions |
| AVX | - | Supports AVX intruction extensions |
| FMA | - | Supports FMA extensions using YMM state |
| MSR | * | Implements RDMSR/WRMSR instructions |
| MTRR | * | Supports Memory Type Range Registers |
| XSAVE | - | Supports XSAVE/XRSTOR instructions |
| OSXSAVE | - | Supports XSETBV/XGETBV instructions |
| RDRAND | - | Supports RDRAND instruction |
| RDSEED | - | Supports RDSEED instruction |
| | | |
| CMOV | * | Supports CMOVcc instruction |
| CLFSH | * | Supports CLFLUSH instruction |
| CX8 | * | Supports compare and exchange 8-byte instructions |
| CX16 | * | Supports CMPXCHG16B instruction |
| BMI1 | - | Supports bit manipulation extensions 1 |
| BMI2 | - | Supports bit maniuplation extensions 2 |
| ADX | - | Supports ADCX/ADOX instructions |
| DCA | - | Supports prefetch from memory-mapped device |
| F16C | - | Supports half-precision instruction |
| FXSR | * | Supports FXSAVE/FXSTOR instructions |
| FFXSR | - | Supports optimized FXSAVE/FSRSTOR instruction |
| MONITOR | - | Supports MONITOR and MWAIT instructions |
| MOVBE | - | Supports MOVBE instruction |
| ERMSB | - | Supports Enhanced REP MOVSB/STOSB |
| PCLULDQ | - | Supports PCLMULDQ instruction |

| | | |
|---|---|---|
| **POPCNT** | **\*** | **Supports POPCNT instruction** |
| SEP | \* | Supports fast system call instructions |
| LAHF-SAHF | \* | Supports LAHF/SAHF instructions in 64-bit mode |
| HLE | - | Supports Hardware Lock Elision instructions |
| RTM | - | Supports Restricted Transactional Memory instructions |
| | | |
| DE | \* | Supports I/O breakpoints including CR4.DE |
| DTES64 | - | Can write history of 64-bit branch addresses |
| DS | - | Implements memory-resident debug buffer |
| DS-CPL | - | Supports Debug Store feature with CPL |
| PCID | - | Supports PCIDs and settable CR4.PCIDE |
| INVPCID | - | Supports INVPCID instruction |
| PDCM | - | Supports Performance Capabilities MSR |
| RDTSCP | - | Supports RDTSCP instruction |
| TSC | \* | Supports RDTSC instruction |
| TSC-DEADLINE | - | Local APIC supports one-shot deadline timer |
| TSC-INVARIANT | - | TSC runs at constant rate |
| xTPR | - | Supports disabling task priority messages |
| | | |
| EIST | - | Supports Enhanced Intel Speedstep |
| ACPI | - | Implements MSR for power management |
| TM | - | Implements thermal monitor circuitry |
| TM2 | - | Implements Thermal Monitor 2 control |
| APIC | \* | Implements software-accessible local APIC |
| x2APIC | - | Supports x2APIC |
| | | |
| CNXT-ID | - | L1 data cache mode adaptive or BIOS |
| | | |
| MCE | \* | Supports Machine Check, INT18 and CR4.MCE |
| MCA | \* | Implements Machine Check Architecture |
| PBE | - | Supports use of FERR#/PBE# pin |
| | | |
| PSN | - | Implements 96-bit processor serial number |
| | | |
| PREFETCHW | \* | Supports PREFETCHW instruction |

```
Logical to Physical Processor Map:
*-  Physical Processor 0
-*  Physical Processor 1

Logical Processor to Socket Map:
**  Socket 0

Logical Processor to NUMA Node Map:
**  NUMA Node 0
```

```
Logical Processor to Cache Map:
*-  Data Cache            0, Level 1,    32 KB, Assoc   8, LineSize  64
*-  Instruction Cache     0, Level 1,    32 KB, Assoc   4, LineSize  64
*-  Unified Cache         0, Level 2,   256 KB, Assoc   8, LineSize  64
*-  Unified Cache         1, Level 3,     8 MB, Assoc  16, LineSize  64
-*  Data Cache            1, Level 1,    32 KB, Assoc   8, LineSize  64
-*  Instruction Cache     1, Level 1,    32 KB, Assoc   4, LineSize  64
-*  Unified Cache         2, Level 2,   256 KB, Assoc   8, LineSize  64
-*  Unified Cache         3, Level 3,     8 MB, Assoc  16, LineSize  64

Logical Processor to Group Map:
**  Group 0
```

## NUMA Support

Consider the ability to now have virtual machines with 64 virtual processors and up to 1 TB of memory. I don't know of a physical processor with 64 logical processors on the market today, even with hyperthreading, which means a virtual machine with more virtual processors than can be provided by a single processor will receive resources from multiple physical processors. A multiprocessor motherboard has multiple sockets where processors can be installed and a corresponding number of memory slots directly linked to each of the sockets. A processor and the memory that is directly attached and managed by the processor is known as a non-uniform memory access (NUMA) node, and there is typically a 1:1 relationship between sockets and NUMA nodes, although some of the latest hardware does have more than one NUMA node per socket. A motherboard with four sockets would normally have banks of memory for each socket and would therefore have four NUMA nodes. A processor can access the local memory in its NUMA node faster than nonlocal memory, which means for best performance, processes running on a processor should use memory within that processor's NUMA node.

Windows Server 2012 introduced a new set of configurations for virtual machine processors, NUMA, but the reality is you should never touch these. Most likely bad things will happen and Hyper-V will make the right configurations for your environment without any manual intervention. However, I do want to cover what these settings are for and why NUMA is important. Note that Windows Server 2008 R2 Hyper-V host was NUMA aware and would always try to ensure that virtual processors and memory were assigned within the same NUMA nodes, but this NUMA topology was not made available to the virtual machine, which wasn't a problem considering virtual machines could only have four vCPUs and were therefore not likely to use more than one NUMA node.

Operating systems are aware of the NUMA nodes and the configuration, which enables the most optimal resource usage. With the large virtual machines possible in Hyper-V, the NUMA topology is also projected to the virtual machine, which is known as virtual NUMA or vNUMA. vNUMA uses the standard ACPI Static Resource Affinity Table (SRAT), which means the NUMA topology should be usable by any NUMA-aware operating system, including Linux.

This NUMA awareness is also a benefit for enterprise applications such as SQL, MySQL, and IIS that utilize resources based on NUMA configuration.

### VIRTUAL MACHINE NUMA CONFIGURATION

Figure 2.11 shows the NUMA configuration options available for the processor configuration of a virtual machine. These options are hidden away for good reason. In nearly all scenarios, you should not change these values. Hyper-V will do the best job of setting the right NUMA topology based on the physical Hyper-V host. There are, however, a few scenarios where you may need to change these values, which are related to the number of processors, memory, and number of nodes on a single socket.

**FIGURE 2.11**
Configuration
options for the
NUMA configuration of a virtual
machine

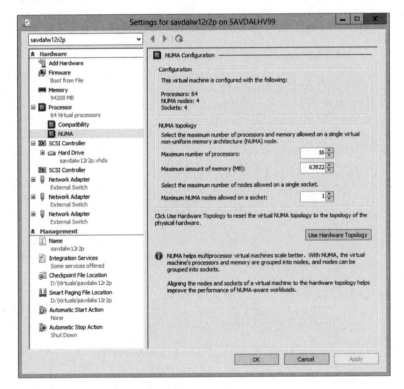

Consider a large Hyper-V environment with many different types of servers, with the physical servers having different NUMA topologies and where virtual machines may be live migrated between the servers. In this case, the NUMA configuration should be changed to match the smallest NUMA topology among all the servers to which the virtual machine may be migrated. For example, suppose I have two servers:

- Server 1 NUMA topology –Maximum number of processors is 16 and maximum amount of memory is 63822

- Server 2 NUMA topology – Maximum number of processors is 8 and maximum amount of memory is 22720

If a virtual machine was created on Server 1, that is the NUMA topology that would be configured for the virtual machine. If the virtual machine was then moved to Server 2, the VM would have incorrect NUMA configuration and will not have optimal resource assignments because what it believes is a single NUMA node would actually span multiple NUMA boundaries. It would therefore make sense to manually set the NUMA topology of the virtual machine to match that of Server 2. Hopefully, in the future the management solutions for Hyper-V will look at all the nodes in a cluster and automatically configure virtual machines with a NUMA topology that matches the smallest NUMA configuration in the cluster, but at time of this writing, this does not occur. Additionally, in most clusters the hosts all have the same NUMA topology, so in practice this is not a big issue. Another challenge with automated NUMA configuration is that with Shared Nothing Live Migration, virtual machines can be migrated outside of a cluster, which means any management solution would not be able to consider that. For most scenarios, virtual machines are created on the server they will run on, which means they will have the most optimal configuration and there are no manual actions necessary.

Notice there is the Use Hardware Topology button. If you change the settings and realize you don't know what the values were originally, you can click this button and the values will be reset back to the Hyper-V recommended values for that server.

Note that if a virtual machine uses Dynamic Memory, the vNUMA is disabled for the virtual machine.

## NUMA SPANNING

As previously discussed, the best performance comes from processes running on processor cores using local memory within the NUMA node rather than having to "span" NUMA nodes, which means the memory required is connected to another processor; it's known as foreign memory or remote memory and has a higher latency than local memory. There are two types of NUMA spanning configurations: configuration at a host level and configuration at a virtual machine level.

By default, Windows Server 2012 enables NUMA spanning at the host level, which provides the most flexibility because virtual machines can access and use memory in any NUMA node, but it may result in lower performance compared to forcing virtual machines to use memory on the same NUMA node as the processor cores. By disabling NUMA spanning at the host level, you disable it for all virtual machines on the host and you ensure that virtual machines' virtual NUMA nodes are backed by memory from one NUMA node giving the best performance. However, it could also mean there is a potential that virtual machines may not be able to start if the required amount of memory for the VM is not available on a single NUMA node. And it means you may not be able to live migrate virtual machines to other nodes if the target node cannot satisfy the NUMA requirements.

The NUMA spanning option should only be changed when, as an administrator, you feel comfortable with NUMA and the implications of disabling and also have an additional management suite that can help ensure best configuration. In reality, the best practice should be to leave NUMA spanning enabled, and that is what I recommend. To configure NUMA spanning, open the Hyper-V Settings page and deselect the NUMA spanning option, as shown in Figure 2.12, to disable NUMA spanning.

Note that System Center Virtual Machine Manager allows NUMA spanning to be configured on a per-virtual-machine basis, which behind the scenes is manually configuring virtual machine assignments to specific NUMA nodes, but this is not something you would ever want to try to perform manually. If you value having your workload always perform predictably, and you accept that your virtual machine may not start when memory is fragmented, turn off spanning for that guest. If you value having your workload start up predictably, with perhaps nonoptimal performance, leave spanning turned on. It's probably the right choice for most people to once again leave the NUMA spanning enabled for most virtual machines.

**FIGURE 2.12**
Changing the NUMA spanning option for a Hyper-V server

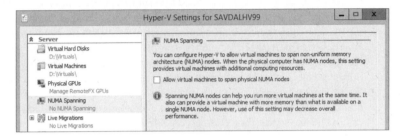

Note that whether NUMA spanning is enabled or disabled, the hypervisor will always make a best effort to be as efficient as possible and schedule the virtual processor on the appropriate physical NUMA node, backing the memory of the virtual machine. Hyper-V will also make an effort to not fragment memory among multiple NUMA nodes, if at all possible. NUMA spanning allows a way out only if there is no other option but to fragment. However, if no logical processor in the physical NUMA node is available, then the hypervisor may temporarily schedule the virtual processor to a remote logical processor in another NUMA node. Running a virtual processor on a remote NUMA node is still more efficient than not running it at all if no local NUMA node resource is available. Again, NUMA spanning does not change this behavior. The NUMA spanning configuration is primarily controlling if the memory for a virtual NUMA node can be sourced from multiple physical NUMA nodes if necessary (which is NUMA spanning enabled).

## Memory Resources

When you're looking at resources used in virtual environments, memory is the other major type of resource, along with processor, that typically dictates the number of virtual machines that can be supported on a host. While logical processors are shared by virtual processors by rapid context switching, the same technique does not work with memory. The context—the content of memory itself—cannot be swapped in and out fast enough to simulate simultaneous execution. For Windows 2008 and Windows Server 2008 R2 before Service Pack 1, the amount of memory that was assigned to a virtual machine could not be modified while the virtual machine was running. This means if a Hyper-V server had 16 GB of memory, and assuming 1 GB was kept for the Windows Server parent partition, then 15 GB could be assigned to virtual machines running on the server. That 15 GB could be consumed by 1 virtual machine with 15 GB of memory assigned or 30 virtual machines each using 512 MB of memory. In this model, each virtual machine must be assigned the most memory it will ever need. At any specific point in time, however, much of this memory may be unneeded. For example, half of the VMs on a host may require their full assignment, but the other half may be experiencing an idle period and not require anywhere near their full allotment of memory. This can lead to a lot of wasted memory during normal utilization, which reduces the number of virtual machines that can be hosted on each server.

Windows Server 2008 R2 Service Pack 1 introduced a new memory optimization feature, Dynamic Memory. This new technology allows the amount of memory allocated to a virtual machine to increase and decrease based on the amount of memory the processes running in the guest operating system actually need at any given moment in time. Dynamic Memory is different from memory overcommit used by other hypervisors. Memory overcommit strategies tell the VM it has a very large amount of memory in the hopes that not all VMs try to write to all the visible memory. If that were to happen, memory would have to be swapped with some other storage—say compressed memory, shared memory, or disk data—which can drastically impact VM performance.

Dynamic Memory uses three settings for each virtual machine: an initial, a maximum, and (in Windows Server 2012 and beyond) a minimum amount of memory. Hyper-V can intelligently add or remove memory to or from a virtual machine based on its real-time demand for memory and memory availability on the host. The virtual machine is initially allocated the amount of memory defined as the startup RAM, and then based on how the processes inside the virtual machine are using the memory, additional memory is allocated if available, possibly reallocated from other virtual machines with a lesser need or removed from the virtual machine. Figure 2.13 shows the actual dialog to configure memory in Windows Server 2012. Note that if the Enable Dynamic Memory check box is not selected, the virtual machine uses static memory and will use the amount defined in the Startup RAM setting. Checking Enable Dynamic Memory allows the Dynamic Memory setting to be changed. The value defined in Startup RAM is still used as the initial amount of memory, but Minimum RAM and Maximum RAM values are also available. Maximum RAM is the size to which the memory for the virtual machine can grow. The default Maximum RAM is 1,048,576 MB, the maximum Hyper-V allows. However, this can be configured to a more reasonable limit based on the expected and tolerated memory use to prevent depriving other virtual machines of memory if things go wrong and memory use grows unchecked. Minimum RAM was introduced in Windows Server 2012 and allows configuration of the virtual machine to shrink below its Startup RAM value. This is useful if you have an application that needs a certain amount of memory to initially launch but then no longer needs that amount.

Also in the figure are the option to set a percentage to use as an available memory buffer and a memory weight slider, which is the memory priority compared to other virtual machines running on the host. The memory buffer allows you to keep some extra memory assigned to the VM beyond its immediate need. This accomplishes two things. First, it's not desirable to let the operating system totally exhaust all memory before adding additional RAM, which may take a few seconds to be added and used. In those few seconds the performance of the virtual machine could be severely adversely affected, and it would have started to page out pages of memory to its pagefile. The pagefile is a file on disk that can be used by an OS's virtual memory manager to temporarily store pages from RAM when physical memory is low. This can deteriorate performance because disk is much slower than RAM to use. Second, it provides some extra memory to be used for cache and other memory consumers that use otherwise available memory behind the scenes.

To avoid this memory starvation and provide extra memory for caches, Dynamic Memory provides some memory beyond a virtual machine's instantaneous demand, up to the Maximum RAM setting (i.e., Hyper-V will never assign more than Maximum RAM). By default, this amount is 20 percent of demand. When the virtual machine has less than this available memory percentage, then more memory is added if physically available in the Hyper-V host to bring the virtual machine back to the desired percentage of available memory. The memory buffer can be changed to a desired amount based on the needs of the virtual machine and can be modified while the virtual machine is running.

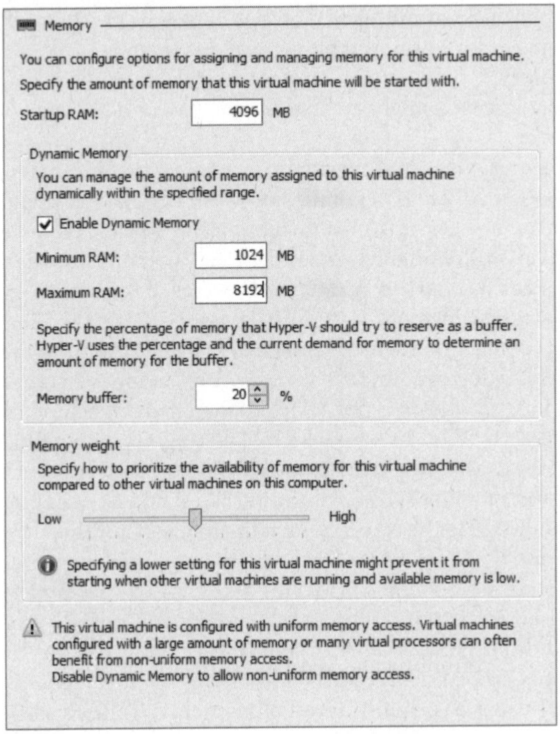

**FIGURE 2.13**
Configuring dynamic memory settings for a virtual machine

The other slider is used to set a priority of memory allocation in times when there is not enough physical RAM available to meet all the desired amounts for the VMs. Just as with CPU allocation, a VM with a higher memory priority will receive additional memory before VMs of a lower priority.

One aspect of Dynamic Memory that makes it special in terms of its memory optimization technique is how the decision to add or remove memory is made. I used the word *intelligently* earlier because Dynamic Memory does not just give more memory to a virtual machine if its free memory is low, but rather it's based on how much memory the workload needs. Figure 2.14 shows part of a Task Manager view of a Windows Server 2008 R2 server that has 8 GB of RAM. On first glance, this virtual machine only has 4 MB of free memory, so it would seem to need more memory. But this is not really the case.

Windows XP, Windows Server 2003, and earlier operating systems tried to use as little memory as possible, and so it was common to see systems with large amounts of free memory. Windows Vista, Windows Server 2008, and later operating systems use all the memory that they can use for cache purposes to help improve performance by preloading programs into memory. If memory is available, it makes sense to use it to try to improve performance. Leaving memory free does not benefit anyone, which is why it's rare to see a high Free Memory value on Windows Server 2008 and above. It is because nearly all memory is always used that memory overcommit technologies like allocate on first write (which assign memory as the virtual machine actually writes data) don't work well with modern operating systems and why Hyper-V does not use that memory optimization technique. The memory used for caching can be used by applications whenever needed, so the memory used for cache is largely still available, and therefore looking at free memory is fairly meaningless. We need to consider the available memory (which includes most of the memory being used for cache), which can be seen in Figure 2.14 as well.

**FIGURE 2.14**
An operating system with only 4 MB of free memory but still plenty of available memory

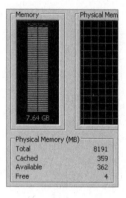

Dynamic Memory uses the commit value for memory to identify the amount of memory that is used, and therefore its memory demand, and is key to the intelligence it brings with memory allocation. Hyper-V Integration Services has a Dynamic Memory virtual service client (VSC) in the guest OS that communicates with its corresponding virtual service provider (VSP) in the parent partition to report its use of memory and specifically its amount of available memory. Based on the amount of available memory in the guest, the desired memory buffer configured for the virtual machine and the amount of physical RAM available in the host additional memory may be allocated to the guest. This type of intelligent memory allocation is only possible because of the guest OS insight provided by the Dynamic Memory VSC. It would not be possible if it was just the hypervisor looking at which memory is being used by a virtual machine externally because it would not be possible to tell if the memory was being used by an application or just for disposable purposes like precaching.

While adding memory to a virtual machine is fairly simple—more memory is simply presented to the guest OS for it to consume—the process to remove memory that is no longer needed is more complex. It is not possible to just take memory away from a guest operating system's memory manager and expect it to continue to function. The guest was probably using the memory (remember that little memory is actually free in a modern operating system) and, even it were truly free, expects it to be usable in the future. Moreover, even if memory could be taken from a virtual machine, it would be very difficult to know what memory is safest to take back! Hyper-V uses a process called ballooning to get around these problems and remove memory.

Ballooning is a clever way to get the guest operating system to decide which memory it no longer really needs and discontinue use of that memory. A "balloon" of memory is allocated by a kernel mode device driver under Hyper-V's control. When Hyper-V wants memory back from a Dynamic Memory VM, it requests the balloon driver to allocate memory inside that VM.

The driver, running inside the guest OS, allocates the memory and grows the "balloon" to a certain size. When a modern OS receives a memory allocation request, it uses insights into existing memory content and workload activity to decide where that memory can best come from. Free memory, cache memory, and unused or inactive application memory are all typical targets. If none of those are available, the guest OS may choose to page out memory content to the guest OS pagefile to generate free memory. The key is that the guest OS rather than some outside process that does not understand how memory is being used, gets to intelligently decide which pages should be given in the most unobtrusive way with the least hit to performance. Once the memory is allocated to the balloon driver, these addresses are communicated to the virtualization manager, which tells the hypervisor it can now effectively unmap those address ranges from physical RAM because the balloon driver will never actually touch them and no other part of the guest OS is allowed to. The memory has been reclaimed by Hyper-V and can be used with other virtual machines.

If the virtual machine needs additional memory in the future, then the VM management can "deflate" the balloon, either fully or by a certain amount. Physical RAM is provided by Hyper-V at its previous locations and then the balloon driver frees the previously allocated RAM back to the guest OS. This process is shown in Figure 2.15.

**FIGURE 2.15**
The inflation of the balloon driver to allow Hyper-V to reclaim memory from a virtual machine

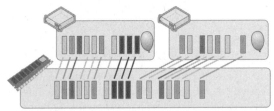

The balloon driver is deflated and not allocated any memory in the guest.

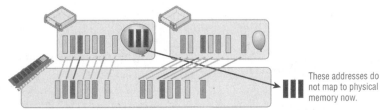

These addresses do not map to physical memory now.

Hyper-V under memory pressure sets a desired size for the balloon driver in the virtual machine. The balloon driver requests memory from the guest and reports the pages to Hyper-V, allocating the memory to be unwrapped from physical.

It is still critical to understand and plan placement of virtual machines based on expected memory usage and set realistic maximum values. Poor planning will result in the host running out of memory and virtual machines not getting enough RAM.

While Dynamic Memory is great for client operating systems in Virtual Desktop Infrastructure implementations, it also works well for many server workloads. I've seen many organizations use Dynamic Memory on all types of server workloads like file servers, domain controllers, System

Center servers, and more and get huge memory savings. Using Dynamic Memory can enable running many more virtual machines on a server thanks to the optimized use of memory.

There are also some types of services that need special considerations when using Dynamic Memory and those that should not use it. I've included some of the main ones in the following list. Ultimately check with the application vendors for their support of Dynamic Memory:

♦ Linux VMs were not able to utilize Dynamic Memory until the release of Windows Server 2012 R2, which provides updated Linux Integration Services. This allows recent distributions of Linux to leverage Dynamic Memory, but older releases without updated Integration Services may not be able to.

♦ The Exchange 2010 and above Mailbox server role actually checks the amount of memory when the mailbox server starts and then does not recheck, so it will not take advantage of additional memory if it's added to the virtual machine after the mailbox service has started.

♦ The Enterprise SKU of SQL Server supports the hot-add of memory into the operating system, which is how SQL Server treats Dynamic Memory. That means for SQL Server to leverage additional memory, you must be running the Enterprise SKU of SQL Server. With SQL Server Enterprise edition, the physical memory is checked every second, and if the memory has increased, the target memory size for SQL Server is recalculated, which is how the additions from Dynamic Memory will be seen. Because SQL Server has its own caching mechanisms regarding free memory, the buffer percentage should be set to 5 percent for a SQL Server virtual machine instead of the default 20 percent.

♦ Like SQL Server, Java also has its own caching mechanisms, which means the buffer percentage should be set to 5 percent for virtual machines running Java workloads instead of the default 20 percent.

It should be clear that Dynamic Memory is not a memory overcommit technology. Dynamic Memory gives a virtual machine an initial amount of memory and then, as the virtual machine uses the memory for processes, additional memory is added if available in the host. This assures the best use of memory while not running the risk of overcommitting the amount of memory available to virtual machines.

The maximum amount of memory that can be assigned to a virtual machine with Windows Server 2012 Hyper-V is 1 TB. There is one other memory-related setting for a virtual machine: the Smart Paging file location. Smart Paging files were necessary because of the change in Windows Server 2012 that introduced the Minimum RAM configuration memory option for a virtual machine. The new minimum RAM capability introduces a potential problem. Consider the following scenario on a host that is fully utilized from a memory perspective:

1. A virtual machine has been running for a period of time, and the amount of physical RAM allocated is set to its Minimum RAM value, 512 MB. The additional memory it was allocated when it started (startup RAM, which was 1 GB) has been taken by Hyper-V through the balloon driver process.

2. The virtual machine is restarted or the host is restarted.

**3.** To restart, the virtual machine needs 1 GB of memory, but it only has 512 MB available, and in this worst-case scenario, the Hyper-V host has no spare memory and no memory can be reclaimed from other virtual machines running on the host.

This one and only scenario is where the new Smart Paging feature is utilized:

◆ The virtual machine is being restarted (also caused by host restart).

◆ There is no available physical memory.

◆ No memory can be reclaimed from other virtual machines running on the host.

At this time, a Smart Paging file will be created for the virtual machine in the location specified in the configuration of the virtual machine and will be used by the virtual machine as memory to complete startup. As soon as possible, that memory mapped to the Smart Paging file will be ballooned out and the Smart Paging file will be no longer used and deleted. The target time to stop using the Smart Paging file is as soon as possible and no longer than 10 minutes. The Smart Paging feature is only used to provide reliable restart of virtual machines and is not used to
provide overcommit after boot.

---

### WHY PAGE SHARING TECHNOLOGIES ARE NOT USED WITH HYPER-V

When virtualization technologies are used, it's common to run many operating system instances (often similar versions) on one physical piece of hardware. On my main server I have 18 virtual machines all running Windows Server 2012 R2. The operating system version is the same, which means a large part of their memory content will have the same data as other virtual machines running the same guest operating system.

The idea of page sharing is storing only duplicate pages of memory from all the virtual machines once stored in physical RAM, basically Single Instance Storage for virtual machine memory. One way this can work is that a process in the hypervisor looks at every page of memory for every virtual, creates a hash value for each page of memory, and then compares the hash values. If a duplicate hash is found, a bit-by-bit comparison of the memory pages is performed to make sure the memory pages really are identical, and then the content is stored only once in memory and the duplicate virtual machine page addresses just point to the singly stored page. We are now sharing the page. This seems like a great idea, but unfortunately the reality is that with newer operating systems, Windows Server 2008 and later, it does not work well for many reasons.

First, page sharing works best on empty pages. However, as you saw in the previous section with Windows Vista and above, memory is rarely left empty and is used to cache as much as possible.

Second, memory pages are getting bigger, much bigger. In the past, memory pages were 4 KB in size, so the chances of finding 4 KB pages now with the same content across operating systems is quite possible and therefore physical memory space will be saved. Processors have supported large memory pages for a long time now, and a 2 MB memory page size is commonly recommended, which is what Windows Vista and Windows Server 2008 and above use by default (along with newer Linux operating systems). The chances of finding duplicate 2 MB memory pages is very slight, which is why as operating systems adopt large memory pages, memory sharing technologies lose their benefit.

Another factor is that Windows Vista and above use address space load randomization, which is a security technology that loads key components of the Windows kernel and user space into 1 of 256 possible locations. This makes it harder for malware to attack the kernel based on the components' location in memory because the locations will vary on different instances of the OS and at each reboot. This means duplicate instances of the same operating system will not have the same content in the same locations for this memory content, which will minimize the effectiveness of page sharing, but this is only for a small part of the operating system content.

# Virtual Storage

I previously covered the IDE controller and the SCSI controller, which support storage to be attached, and there are primarily two types of storage, virtual hard disks and pass-through storage. Before I even start discussing the technologies I want to be very clear: *always use virtual hard disks!* While pass-through storage was required in some scenarios in Windows Server 2008 R2 Hyper-V, it really should never be needed with the new VHDX format in Windows Server 2012 Hyper-V, so don't use it. I will, however, cover it briefly simply for completeness.

Processor and memory are very important resources to virtual machines, but storage is also critical. There are ways to enable a Windows Server 2008 R2 and above Hyper-V virtual machine to boot from a SAN by attaching to the LUN from the Hyper-V host and then mapping the disk directly to the VM using the pass-through disk capability of Hyper-V. In most cases, though, virtual machines will have some dedicated storage.

## VHD

The most common and recommended storage for a virtual machine is the use of a virtual hard disk, which prior to Windows Server 2012 was the VHD format. In Windows Server 2008 R2, the VHD format is a core part of the operating system and from a performance analysis there is only a negligible difference from using a pass-through disk. VHDs can be mounted using Windows Server 2008 R2 and above disk management tools, and physical computers can boot from VHDs using the Boot from VHD feature available in Server 2008 R2 and Enterprise and above versions of Windows 7.

A VHD can be up to 2 TB in size, and there are a number of different types of VHDs available:

♦ Dynamically expanding: This is the most popular format. Essentially the virtual hard disk is created using a minimal amount of disk space, and as the disk is used, the file expands on the file system to accommodate the data written to the disk up to the size specified as the size for the virtual hard disk. This option is the most efficient use of the disk space because space is not used on the physical hard drives unless needed. In Windows Server 2008, there was a performance penalty with dynamic disks, such as when a write was performed, the file had to grow. However, the VHD implementation was rewritten in Windows Server 2008 R2, and this performance penalty is negligible. A dynamically expanding disk does not shrink if data is deleted unless a compact operation is performed. This type of disk is also commonly referred to as thinly provisioned because it starts off thin and grows as data is written to it.

◆ Fixed size: In this case, the size specified for the virtual hard disk is allocated and used when the disk is created, and so if a 127 GB fixed size virtual hard disk is created, a 127 GB VHD file is created on the Hyper-V server. This is likely to lead to a less fragmented virtual hard disk.

◆ Differencing: A differencing hard disk is linked to a parent virtual hard disk and only stores the changes from the parent hard disk. As writes are made, the differencing (child) disk will have the writes committed, while read operations will be sourced from the parent VHD unless an update was made to the original data or its new data, in which case the data will be read from the differencing disk. Once a VHD becomes a parent disk, it becomes read-only. A differencing disk has a name of AVHD instead of VHD and will grow as data is written, behaving very similar to a dynamic disk.

Figure 2.16 gives an overview of the types of VHD and how they function.

**FIGURE 2.16**
The key types of
VHD disk

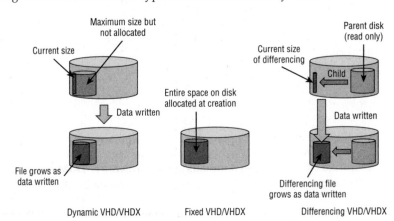

Although there is little performance difference between a dynamic and fixed VHD in Windows Server 2008 R2, the recommendation for production environments is to use a fixed VHD. The primary reason is that when dynamic VHDs are used, there is always the possibility that the underlying storage runs out of space, so as the dynamic VHD tries to grow, it will fail, causing unpredictable results. If systems have very well-defined processes to monitor disk space usage and alert as required, then the use of dynamic VHDs in production may be possible. VHD is a published standard by Microsoft and is used by other vendors, like Citrix. The specification can be found on the Microsoft Download Center website; just search for "VHD specification" at www. microsoft.com/download.

Virtual machines can have a number of VHDs attached to them, but a single VHD cannot be used by multiple virtual machines at the same time. Hyper-V supports both an IDE bus and a SCSI bus to connect VHDs to virtual machines. While the IDE bus must be used for DVD drives and the disk the virtual machine will boot from, for all other VHDs, the SCSI bus is recommended for best performance and maximum flexibility.

It is possible to perform conversions between dynamic and fixed VHDs using Hyper-V Manager and command-line tools. The conversion process actually creates a new VHD and copies over the content from the source VHD to the target.

## VHDX

The VHDX format was introduced in Windows Server 2012 to address some of the scalability and, to a lesser extent, performance challenges of the VHD implementation. VHD can still be used in Windows Server 2012 Hyper-V, but the recommendation is to always use VHDX unless backward compatibility is required with Windows Server 2008 R2 Hyper-V or, at the time of this writing, Windows Azure IaaS (which currently supports only VHD).

The same capabilities for VHD apply to VHDX, such as Boot from VHDX, the three types of VHDX (dynamic, fixed, and differencing), and native mounting and use within Windows Server 2012. VHDX essentially builds on VHD and provides new scalability and options.

VHDX supports a maximum virtual hard disk size of 64 TB, 32 times that of the VHD format. In all my years of consulting with the largest companies in the world, I have never seen an NTFS volume bigger than 14 TB. That means there is no workload that could not be contained within the new VHDX format, removing the few cases where pass-through storage was previously required because of size limitations with VHD. While it is true that the new ChkDsk features introduced in Windows Server 2012 will allow larger NTFS volumes because volumes can now have any corruption fixed with only seconds of downtime instead of hours or days, I still don't believe it will be common for any organization to require single volumes bigger than 64 TB.

VHDX also leverages an improved logging mechanism for updates to the VHDX metadata, which protects against corruption in the case of unplanned events such as power loss. In addition, VHDX features the ability to have custom metadata stored, which can be useful to store user notes about a virtual hard disk. The TRIM function is supported for VHDX files, which allows space to be reclaimed providing the hardware is TRIM-compatible.

VHDX files automatically align with the underlying physical structure of the disk, giving the most optimal performance, and also leverage larger block sizes for dynamic and differencing disk, giving better performance. When you're using dynamic VHDX files, the performance difference is even more negligible than with VHD, making dynamic the default choice when provisioning new VHDX files. However, the same guidance with VHD does apply if you don't have a good monitoring solution in place; to ensure that you don't run out of physical disk space, you would still use fixed VHDX format.

When VHDX is combined with the SCSI controller in Windows Server 2012 R2, the VHDX can be dynamically resized while being used by a running virtual machine, allowing the disk to be expanded and even shrunk provided there is sufficient unpartitioned space in the volume.

VHDX files can also be shared by multiple virtual machines in Windows Server 2012 R2 that are stored on a cluster shared volume or provided by a scale-out file server. I will cover this and dynamic resize in more detail in Chapter 4, "Storage Configurations."

If you have VHD disks, they can be converted to VHDX using Hyper-V Manager via the Edit Disk action and using the Edit Virtual Disk Wizard, which allows the Convert action.

An alternative is using PowerShell with the `Convert-VHD` cmdlet, as in the command `Convert-VHD .\test.vhd .\test.vhdx`.

## Creating a Virtual Hard Disk

Virtual hard disks can be created in a number of ways. Using Hyper-V Manager, you can create disks using the New – Hard Disk option, which I will walk you through in the following steps. Additionally, the same wizard is launched if you select to create a new virtual hard disk on a disk controller within a virtual machine settings dialog.

1. Select the New – Hard Disk option from Hyper-V Manager.

2. Click Next to open the New Virtual Hard Disk Wizard introduction screen.

3. Select the type of disk format: VHD or VHDX. Always use VHDX if possible. Click Next.

4. Select whether the disk is fixed size (the default if VHD is selected on the previous screen), dynamically expanding (the default if VHDX is selected on the previous screen) or differencing, and click Next.

5. Select a name for the new virtual hard disk and location, and then click Next.

6. If a fixed or dynamic disk is being created, you can use the Configure Disk screen to choose a size for the new disk or to copy the content from an existing physical or virtual hard disk, as shown in Figure 2.17. The default size is 127 GB, but you should change this to meet your needs. Click Next.

7. A summary of the choices will be shown. Click Finish to create the new virtual hard disk.

**FIGURE 2.17**
Selecting the size or source content for a new virtual hard disk

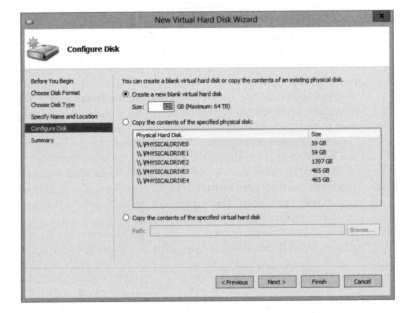

Also in Hyper-V Manager is the Edit Disk action, which when launched allows a virtual hard disk to be selected and then have actions such as the following performed on it:

◆ Compact: Reduces the size of the virtual hard disk. This is useful if large amounts of data within the virtual hard disk have been deleted and the dynamic disk should have physical space reclaimed.

◆ Convert: Allows conversion between virtual hard disk formats (VHD/VHDX) and between provisioning type (fixed/dynamic). The conversion works by creating a new virtual hard disk and copying the content so it will consume extra space on disk during the conversion process and may take a long time.

◆ Expand: Expands the capacity of a virtual hard disk.

The Inspect Disk action in Hyper-V Manager gives the basic information about a selected virtual hard disk, as shown in Figure 2.18. For a dynamic virtual hard disk, it shows its maximum size but also the amount of space currently used on disk.

**FIGURE 2.18**
The basic information about a virtual hard disk shown by the Inspect Disk option

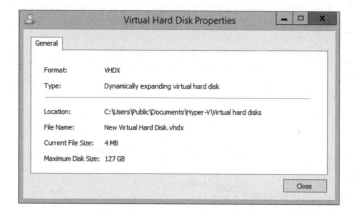

While graphical tools are highly intuitive for automation, a scripting language is typically leveraged, and PowerShell is the command-line interface and scripting language of choice for Microsoft.

Here are some of my favorite PowerShell commands related to virtual hard disks. Note that you do not have to specify if a disk is VHD or VHDX. Simply setting the file type to VHD or VHDX lets the commands know the type of virtual hard disk to create. I'll show later in the book how to create new virtual hard disks as part of a virtual machine creation.

Here's the command to create a fixed VHDX file:

```
New-VHD -Path D:\Virtuals\newfix.vhdx -Fixed -SizeBytes 10GB
```

To create a dynamic VHDX file, use this command:

```
New-VHD -Path D:\Virtuals\newdyn.vhdx -Dynamic -SizeBytes 1TB
```

The command to create a differencing VHDX file is as follows:

```
New-VHD -ParentPath D:\Virtuals\newfix.vhdx `
```

```
-Path D:\Virtuals\newdif.vhdx -Differencing `
-SizeBytes 1000000000
```

Here is the command to create a VHDX using very large block sizes:

```
New-VHD -Path D:\Virtuals\LargeBlockSize.vhdx –BlockSizeBytes 128MB `
-LogicalSectorSize 4KB –SizeBytes 1TB
```

A virtual hard disk can be added to a virtual machine using the `Add-VMHardDiskDrive` PowerShell cmdlet, as in this example:

```
Add-VMHardDiskDrive -VMName Demo1 -Path D:\Virtuals\newdyn.vhdx `
-ControllerType SCSI
```

## Pass-Through Storage

As I mentioned, one option is to use a pass-through disk, where a virtual machine has connectivity mapped directly to physical disks. However, this requires the physical disk to be used exclusively by a single virtual machine, and the benefits of abstracting the virtual machine from hardware is lost because the virtual machine is now directly linked to a physical piece of hardware. Other features, such as using checkpoints that provide a point-in-time saved state of a virtual machine, are not possible.

The Hyper-V host cannot access a disk that is passed-through to a VM. It becomes exclusively usable by the virtual machine. The disk must be offline on the Hyper-V host to be connected to a virtual machine. Pass-through disks may be used for very high I/O applications like SQL Server, but this is typically not actually required given the continued improvements in VHDX performance. Prior to VHDX, the use of pass-through storage was required if a volume larger than 2 TB was required because of the VHD size limit, but this is no longer a limiting factor because of VHDX.

# The Bottom Line

**Describe how the resources of a virtual machine are virtualized by the hypervisor.** The hypervisor directly manages the processor and memory resources with Hyper-V. Logical processors are scheduled to satisfy computer requirements of virtual processors assigned to virtual machines. Multiple virtual processors can share the same logical processor. Virtual machines are assigned memory by the hypervisor from the memory available in the physical host. Dynamic memory allows memory to be added and removed from a virtual machine based on resource need. Other types of resources, such as network and storage, are provided by the management partition through a kernel mode memory bus known as a VMBus. This allows existing Windows drivers to be used for the wide array of storage and network devices typically used.

**Master It** How is Dynamic Memory different from Memory Overcommit?

**Correctly use processor and memory advanced configuration options.** The compatibility configuration of a virtual machine processor should be used when a virtual machine may be moved between hosts with different versions of the same processor family. The processor compatibility option hides higher-level features from the guest operating system, enabling migrations without downtime to the virtual machine. Processor reserve and limit options ensure that a virtual machines coexists with other virtual machines without getting too many or too few resources. Dynamic Memory configurations allow the startup, minimum, and maximum amounts of memory for a virtual machine to be configured. It's important to note that the maximum amount of memory configured is available only if sufficient memory exists within the host.

**Master It**  When should the NUMA properties of a virtual machine be modified?

**Explain the difference between VHD/VHDX and pass-through storage.**  VHD and VHDX files are virtual hard disks that are files on a file system or share accessible to the Hyper-V host. They provide abstraction of the storage seen by the virtual machine and the underlying physical storage. Pass-through storage directly maps a virtual machine to a physical disk accessible from the host, which limits Hyper-V functionality and breaks one of the key principals of virtualization: the abstraction of the virtual machine from the physical fabric.

**Master It**  Why would VHD still be used with Windows Server 2012 Hyper-V?

# Chapter 3

# Virtual Networking

This chapter covers the networking elements that enable virtual machines to communicate with each other and also with the rest of your environment. Features that are specific to virtual machines will be covered, but also network technologies in the operating system that can bring additional benefit.

Windows 2012 introduced network virtualization, which closes the remaining gap between virtualization and the goal of complete abstraction of the virtual machine from the underlying fabric. Network virtualization allows virtual machines to be abstracted from the physical network fabric, allowing complete isolation between virtual networks and the ability to use IP schemes independently of the physical network fabric. This technology will be covered in detail along with all the various options available to you.

In this chapter, you will learn to

♦ Architect the right network design for your Hyper-V hosts and virtual machines using the options available

♦ Identify when to use the types of NVGRE Gateways

♦ Leverage SCVMM 2012 R2 for many networking tasks

## Virtual Switch Fundamentals

A typical server has one or more network adapters that are configured with an IPv4 and IPv6 address, either statically or dynamically, using services such as Dynamic Host Configuration Protocol (DHCP). The server may be part of a VLAN to provide isolation and control of broadcast traffic. It may require different network connections to connect to different networks, such as a separate, nonrouted network for cluster communications between servers in a failover cluster, a separate network for iSCSI traffic; a separate management network; and so on. With virtualization, the requirements for network connectivity is just as important as with a physical server. However, there are additional options available because essentially there are multiple server instances on a single physical asset, and in some cases they just need to communicate with each other and not externally to the virtualization host.

### Three Types of Virtual Switch

Virtual machines have a number of virtualized resources, and one type is the virtual network adapter (as discussed in the previous chapter, there are actually two types of network adapter for a generation 1 virtual machine, but their connectivity options are the same). One or more virtual network adapters are added to a virtual machine and then each virtual adapter is attached to a virtual switch that was created at the Hyper-V host level. A Hyper-V host can have many virtual switches created. There are three types of virtual switches available: external, internal, and private, as shown in Figure 3.1.

**FIGURE 3.1**
The three types of virtual switches available in Hyper-V

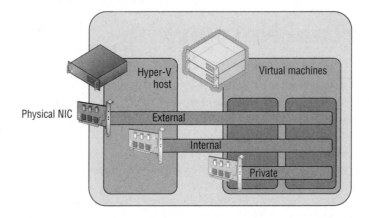

**External Virtual Networks**    These are bound to a physical network card in the host, and virtual machines have access to the physical network via the physical NIC, which is linked to the external switch the virtual network adapter is connected to. Virtual machines on the same virtual switch can also communicate with each other. If they are on different switches that can communicate through the physical network, through routing, then they can also communicate. The virtual machines each see a virtual network device, and the Hyper-V host still sees the network adapter—however, it will no longer use it. The network device on the Hyper-V host is the physical NIC, which is bound only to the Hyper-V extensible virtual switch, which means it is being used by a Hyper-V virtual switch.

It is also possible when creating a virtual switch to enable the Hyper-V host itself, the management OS, to continue using the network adapter even though it has been assigned to a virtual switch. Sharing the adapter works by actually creating a virtual network adapter in the management partition that is connected to the Hyper-V virtual switch so all communication still goes through the virtual switch, which exclusively owns the physical network adapter. In Windows Server 2012, it's actually possible to create multiple virtual network adapters in the management partition, which opens up some new configuration options and scenarios that I will cover later in this chapter. If you had only a single network adapter in the Hyper-V host, you should definitely select the option to share the network adapter with the management operating system. The option to share the network adapter can be enabled or disabled at any time after the external switch has been created.

**Internal Virtual Networks**    These are not bound to a physical NIC and so cannot access any machine outside the physical server. An internal network is visible to the Hyper-V host and the virtual machines, which means it can be used for communication between virtual machines and between virtual machines and the Hyper-V host. This can be useful if you are hosting services on the management partition, such as an iSCSI target, that you wish the virtual machines to be able to use. On both the Hyper-V host and virtual machines, a network device will be visible that represents the internal virtual network.

**Private Virtual Networks**   These are visible only on virtual machines and are used for virtual machines to communicate with each other. This type of network could be used for virtual machines that are part of a guest cluster, and the private network could be used for the cluster network, providing all hosts in the cluster are running on the same Hyper-V host.

In most cases an external switch will be used because most virtual machines will require communications beyond the local Hyper-V host with internal and private networks used in testing and niche scenarios, such as the guest cluster that is confined to a single host. However, most likely if you were creating a production guest cluster in virtual machines, you would want them distributed over multiple Hyper-V hosts to protect against a host failure—in which case an external switch would be required.

A single physical network adapter can only be bound to a single external switch, and in production environments it would be common to use NIC teaming on the Hyper-V host. This would allow multiple network adapters to be bound together and surfaced to the operating system as a single teamed network adapter, which provides resiliency from a network adapter failure but also potentially provides aggregated bandwidth, allowing higher speed communications (there are many caveats around this, which I will cover later in this chapter when I cover NIC teaming in detail). A teamed network adapter can also be used and bound for an external switch with Hyper-V, giving all the virtual network adapters connected to that switch additional resiliency.

If you have different network adapters in a host and they connect to different networks (which may, for example, use VLANs to isolate traffic), then if virtual machines need access to the different networks, you would create multiple external virtual switches, with each bound to the physical network adapter connected to one of the various networks. It may seem obvious, but virtual machines can communicate only with the other services that are available on that physical network or can be routed via that network. Effectively, you are just expanding the connectivity of the physical network adapter to virtual machines via the virtual switch.

Many virtual machines can be connected to the same virtual networks, and one nice feature is that if multiple virtual machines on the same Hyper-V host are connected to the same external network and communicate over that network, the traffic never actually goes to the physical network adapter. The Hyper-V networking stack is smart enough to know that the traffic is going to another VM connected to the same switch and directly passes the traffic to the VM without ever touching the physical network adapter or physical network.

When you start creating virtual switches, it's important to use a consistent naming scheme across all of your various hosts for the switches. This is important because when a virtual machine is moved between Hyper-V hosts, it will look for a virtual switch with the same name as its existing virtual switch connection on the target host. If there is not a matching virtual switch, the virtual network adapter will become disconnected and therefore the virtual machine will lose connectivity. This is critical in failover clusters where virtual machines can freely move between nodes in the cluster, but with the Windows Server 2012 capability of moving virtual machines between any host with no shared resources and no downtime, it's important to have consistent virtual switch naming between all Hyper-V hosts. Take some time now to think about a good naming strategy and stick to it.

It's also possible to create access control lists, called extended port access control lists, within the virtual switch to allow and block communication between different virtual machines connected to the switch based on IP address, protocol, and port. Additionally stateful rules can be created to allow communication only when certain conditions are met. Microsoft has a detailed walk-though on using the ACLs at the following location:

```
http://technet.microsoft.com/en-us/library/dn375962.aspx
```

## Creating a Virtual Switch

When the Hyper-V role is enabled on a server, an option is given to create an external switch by selecting a network adapter on the host. If this option is chosen, then a virtual switch will already be present on the host and it will be automatically configured to allow the management operating system to share the adapter, so an extra Hyper-V virtual Ethernet adapter will be present on the Hyper-V host. In general, I prefer not to create the virtual switches during Hyper-V role installation but to configure them postinstallation. Also, as you will read later, if your deployment is a production deployment and you're using System Center, then Virtual Machine Manager can do all of the switch configuration for you. I will, however, walk you through manually configuring virtual switches:

1. Launch Hyper-V Manager.

2. Select the Virtual Switch Manager action from the actions pane.

3. In the navigation pane, select New Virtual Network Switch, and in the details pane, select the type of virtual switch to create. In this case, select External and click the Create Virtual Switch button.

4. Replace the default New Virtual Switch name with a meaningful name that matches the naming standard for switches you have selected, such as, for example, External Switch. Optionally, notes can be entered.

5. If the switch type is external, the specific network adapter or the NIC team that will be bound to the virtual switch must be selected from the list of available network adapters on the system, as shown in Figure 3.2. Note that the type of switch can be changed in this screen by selecting another type of network, such as internal or private. Also note that network adapters/teams bound to other switches are still listed, but the creation will fail if they are selected.

   By default the "Allow management operating system to share this network adapter" option is enabled, which creates the virtual network adapter on the management partition, enabling the Hyper-V host to continue accessing the network through the new virtual switch that is bound to the network adapter. However, if you have a separate management network adapter or if you will create it manually later, then disable this option by unchecking the box. If you uncheck this box, you will receive a warning when the switch is being created that you will lose access to the host unless you have another network adapter used for management communication. The warning is shown to protect you from disabling anyway to communicate with the host.

6. If you plan to use SR/IOV, check the Enable Single-Root I/O Virtualization (SR-IOV) box. This cannot be changed once the switch is created. (SR-IOV will be covered later. It's a technology found in newer, advanced networking equipment and servers that allows virtual machines to directly communicate with the networking equipment for very high-performance scenarios.)

7. If the option to allow the management operating system to use the network adapter was selected, it is possible to set the VLAN ID used by that network adapter on the host operating system through the VLAN ID option by checking Enable Virtual LAN Identification

For Management Operating System and then entering the VLAN ID. Note that this does not set the VLAN ID for the switch but rather for the virtual network adapter created on the management partition.

8. Once all options are selected, click the OK button and the switch will be created (this is where the warning will be displayed if you unchecked the option to allow the management operating system to use the adapter).

**FIGURE 3.2**
Primary configuration page for a new virtual switch

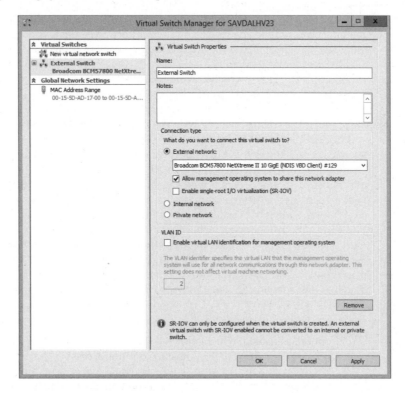

Creating switches is also possible using PowerShell, and the following commands will create an external (without sharing with the management operating system), internal, and private switch and then list switches that are of type External:

```
#Create new external (implicit external as adapter passed)
New-VMSwitch -Name "External Switch" -Notes "External Connectivity" ↵
-NetAdapterName "VM NIC" -AllowManagementOS $false
#Create new internal (visible on host) and private (vm only)
New-VMSwitch -Name "Internal Switch" -SwitchType Internal
New-VMSwitch -Name "Private Switch" -SwitchType Private
```

Once a switch is created, it can be viewed through the Virtual Switch Manager and modification of the properties is possible. A virtual switch's type can be changed at any time unless it is an external virtual switch with SR/IOV enabled. In that case, its type cannot be changed without deleting and re-creating it. Virtual network adapters can be connected to the switch through the properties of the virtual network adapter.

## Extensible Switch

The Hyper-V extensible switch provides a variety of capabilities that can be leveraged by the virtual network adapters that are connected to the virtual switch ports, including features such as port mirroring, protection from rogue DHCP servers and router advertisements, bandwidth management, support for VMQ, and more. However, there is still only a specific set of capabilities that cover the majority of scenarios and customer requirements; they might not cover every requirement that different clients may have. Those familiar with VMware may have heard of the Cisco Nexus 1000V, which is available for ESX and essentially replaces the VMware switching infrastructure completely. The Cisco Nexus 1000V is the only model VMware supports, and the challenge is that not many vendors have the resources available to write a complete virtual switching infrastructure. Microsoft went a different direction in Windows Server 2012.

Windows Server 2012 introduces the extensible switch for Hyper-V. With the extensible switch, it's possible for third parties to plug into the Hyper-V virtual switch at various points without having to completely replace it, thus making it far easier for organizations to bring additional value. It was common to have the ability to add functionality into the Hyper-V switch such as enhanced packet filtering capabilities, firewall and intrusion detection at the switch level, switch forwarding, and utilities to help sniff data on the network. Consider that Windows already has a rich capability around APIs and interfaces for third parties to integrate with the operating system, specifically Network Device Interface Specification (NDIS) filter drivers and Windows Filtering Platform (WFP) callout drivers. The Hyper-V extensible switch uses these exact same interfaces that partners are already utilizing, making it possible for vendors to easily adapt solutions to integrate directly into the Windows 2012 and above extensible switch. InMON's sFlow monitoring extension allows great trending analysis of traffic, NEC has OpenFlow extension, and 5Nine has a complete firewall extension for the Hyper-V extensible switch.

There are four specific types of extensions for the Hyper-V switch, which are listed in Table 3.1.

**TABLE 3.1:**     Types of extension for Hyper-V virtual switch

| EXTENSION | PURPOSE | POTENTIAL EXAMPLES | EXTENSIBILITY COMPONENT |
| --- | --- | --- | --- |
| Network packet inspection | Inspecting network packets, but not altering them | Network monitoring | NDIS filter driver |
| Network packet filter | Injecting, modifying, and dropping network packets | Security | NDIS filter driver |

**TABLE 3.1:**     Types of extension for Hyper-V virtual switch   *(CONTINUED)*

| EXTENSION | PURPOSE | POTENTIAL EXAMPLES | EXTENSIBILITY COMPONENT |
|---|---|---|---|
| Network forwarding | Third-party forwarding that bypasses default forwarding | Virtual Ethernet Port Aggregator (VEPA) and proprietary network fabrics | NDIS filter driver |
| Firewall/Intrusion detection | Filtering and modifying TCP/IP packets, monitoring or authorizing connections, filtering IPsec-protected traffic, and filtering RPCs | Virtual firewall and connection monitoring | WFP callout driver |

Multiple extensions can be enabled on a virtual switch, and the extensions are leveraged for both ingress (inbound) and egress (outbound) traffic. One big change from Windows Server 2012 is that in Windows Server 2012 R2, the Hyper-V Network Virtualization (HNV) module is moved into the virtual switch instead of being external to the virtual switch. This enables switch extensions to inspect both the provider and customer headers (more on this later, but for now the provider header is the packet that enables Network Virtualization to function across physical networks and the customer header is the IP traffic that virtual machines in a virtual network actually see) and therefore work with Network Virtualization. The move of the Network Virtualization module also enables third-party forwarding extensions like the Cisco Nexus 1000V to work with Network Virtualization, which wasn't the case in Windows Server 2012. And yes, Cisco has a Nexus 1000V for Hyper-V that works with the Hyper-V switch instead of completely replacing it. This is important because many organizations use Cisco networking solutions and the Nexus 1000V enables unified management of both the physical and virtual network environment through the Cisco network management toolset.

The Windows Server 2012 R2 extensible switch also supports hybrid forwarding, which allows packets to be forwarded to different forwarding agents based on the packet type. For example, suppose the Cisco Nexus 1000V extension (a forwarding agent) was installed. With hybrid forwarding, if network virtualization traffic is sent through the switch, it would first go through the HNV module and then to the forwarding agent, the Nexus 1000V. If the traffic was not network virtualization traffic, then the HNV module would be bypassed and the traffic sent straight to the Nexus 1000V.

Figure 3.3 best shows the extensible switch and how traffic flows through the extensions. Notice that the traffic flows completely through all layers of the switch twice, once "inbound" into the switch (which could be from a VM or from external sources) and once "outbound" from the switch (which could be to a VM or to an external source).

Extensions to the switch are provided by the third parties and installed onto the Hyper-V server and then enabled on a per-virtual-switch basis once installed. The process to enable an extension is simple. Open the Virtual Switch Manager and select the virtual switch for which you want to enable extensions. Then select the Extensions child node of the virtual switch. In the extensions area of the dialog, check the box for the extension(s) you wish to enable, as shown in Figure 3.4. That's it! The extensions are now enabled. In Figure 3.4, a number of different extensions types can be seen, and two are not part of standard Hyper-V: Microsoft VMM

DHCPv4 Server Switch Extension and sFlow Traffic Monitoring. When enabled, the sFlow Traffic Monitoring extension sends trending information and more to the sFlowTrend tool for graphical visualization and analysis. The Microsoft VMM DHCPv4 Server Switch Extension is a filter that, when it sees DHCP traffic, intercepts the requests and utilizes IP pools within Virtual Machine Manager to service DHCP requests over the virtual switch instead of using standard DHCP services, enabling VMM to manage all IP configuration.

**FIGURE 3.3**
How traffic flows through the extensible switch and registered extensions for the inbound path

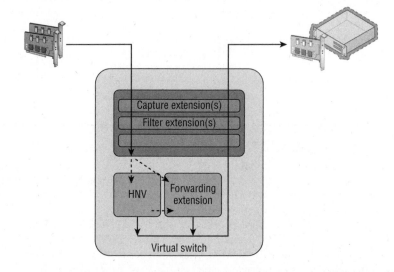

**FIGURE 3.4**
Enabling extensions for a virtual switch in Hyper-V

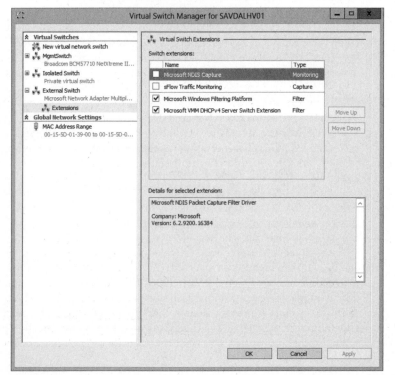

# VLANs and PVLANS

In most datacenters it is not uncommon to see widespread use of virtual LANs(VLANs), which allow for isolation of traffic without the need to use physical separation, such as using different switches and network adapters for the different types of isolated networks. While physical separation works, it is costly to maintain the additional physical infrastructure in terms of hardware, power, and even cooling in the datacenter. It can also be complex to manage large numbers of isolated physical network topologies.

## Understanding VLANs

A VLAN is a layer 2 technology that primarily adds the ability to create partitions in the network for broadcast traffic. Normally networks are separated using devices such as routers, which control the transmission of traffic between different segments (a local area network, or LAN) of the network. However, a VLAN allows a single physical network segment to be virtually partitioned so that different VLANs cannot communicate with each other and broadcast traffic such as ARP (to resolve IP addresses to MAC addresses) would not cross VLANs. A great example of explaining the broadcast boundary nature of a VLAN is to consider 10 machines plugged into a single switch and 1 of those machines is a DHCP server. Typically all 9 of the other machines plugged into that switch would be able to get an IP address from the DHCP server. If VLANs were configured and the DHCP server and a few of the machines were put in a specific VLAN, then only the machines in the same VLAN as the DHCP server would be able to get an IP address from the DHCP server. All the other machines not part of that VLAN would not be able to contact the DHCP server and would require another method for IP configuration.

Additionally, through network hardware configuration it is possible for a single VLAN to actually cross different physical network segments and even locations, allowing machines that are physically distributed to act and communicate as if they were on a single physical network segment. The VLAN is at a high level creating virtual LANs that are abstracted from the physical location. For VLANs to communicate with each, other layer 3 technologies (IP) would be used for IP-level routing.

The partitioning of communication and broadcast traffic enables VLANs to provide a number of key features to an environment that make VLANs an attractive technology to implement:

- **Separate broadcast domains**. This seems obvious, but it can be a huge benefit for larger networks where the amount of broadcast traffic may be causing network performance issues. This also enables a single network to be divided into separate networks as required.

- **Isolation between machines.** VLANs enable partitions between different groups of servers, which may be required in scenarios such as different departments, Internet-facing networks, hosting providers to separate clients, and more.

- **Administrative help.** With VLANs, it's possible to move servers between locations but maintain their VLAN membership, avoiding reconfiguration of the host.

- **A separation of physical networks from virtual networks.** This enables virtual LANs to span different physical network segments.

Typically a VLAN and IP subnet has a one-to-one mapping, although it is possible to have multiple subnets within a single VLAN. Remember, though, that a VLAN represents a broadcast boundary, which means a single subnet cannot cross VLANs because by definition, an IP subnet represents a group of machines with direct communication that rely on broadcasts for translating IP addresses to MAC addresses using ARP.

While VLANs seem like a useful technology, and they are, there are some drawbacks and complexity to their configuration. First, consider a typical datacenter network switch configuration with a number of racks of servers. There are typically two types of switches involved; servers within a rack connect to the top-of-rack (ToR) switch in each rack and then connect to aggregation switches. The configuration in Figure 3.5 shows three VLANs in use by Hyper-V servers for different virtual machines, which in this example are VLANs 10, 20, and 30. Notice that machines in VLAN 10 span different racks, which requires configuration of the VLAN in not just the ToR but also aggregation switches. For VLANs 20 and 30, all the VMs are in the same rack, so while the ports from the hosts in the rack to the ToR require access for VLAN 10, 20, and 30, the aggregation switches will see only VLAN 10 traffic passed to them, which is why only VLAN 10 has to be configured.

**FIGURE 3.5**

Three VLANs in a two-rack configuration. For redundancy, each ToR has a connection to two separate aggregation switches.

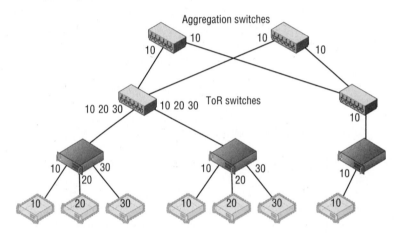

Notice in Figure 3.5 that single ports can be configured to allow traffic from different VLANs (ports between switches are known as trunk ports because they are configured for all the VLAN traffic that has to be passed between them). However, even normal ports to a host can be configured to allow multiple VLANs, which is especially necessary with virtualization where different virtual machines on a single host may be part of different VLANs. Realize that even in this very basic configuration with only two racks, the VLAN configuration can require changes on the network infrastructure at multiple points such as the ToRs and aggregation switches.

Consider now if a new virtual machine is required for VLAN 20 but there is no capacity in the first rack, which requires the virtual machine to be created in the second rack, as shown in Figure 3.6. This requires changes to the second rack ToR and both aggregation switches. Imagine there are hundreds of racks and hundreds of VLANs. This type of VLAN change can be very complex and take weeks to actually implement because all of the VLAN configuration is static and requires manual updating, which makes the actual network a bottleneck in provisioning new services. You've probably heard of some VLAN configuration problems, although you didn't know it was a VLAN configuration problem. Some of the major "outages" of Internet-facing services have been caused not by hardware failure but actually by changes to network configuration that "went wrong" and take time to fix, specifically VLANs! Suppose you wish to use Live Migration to easily move virtual machines between hosts and even racks; this adds even more complexity to the VLAN configurations to ensure that the virtual machines don't lose connectivity when migrated.

**FIGURE 3.6**
New VM in VLAN 20 added to the host in the second rack and the changes to the switch VLAN configuration required

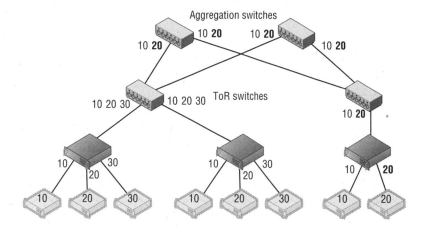

---

**TAGGED VS. UNTAGGED CONFIGURATION**

One thing regarding VLANs confused me when I first started with network equipment (well, lots of things confused me!), and that was whether to configure ports as tagged or untagged, which are both options when configuring a port on a switch.

When a port is configured as tagged, it means that port expects the traffic to already be tagged with a VLAN ID. This means the VLAN must be configured at the host connected to the port or at a VM level running on the host. Additionally, for a tagged port it is possible to configure inclusions and exclusions for the VLAN IDs accepted on that port. For example, a port configured as tagged may be configured to allow only VLAN ID 10 through. A trunk port would be configured with all the VLAN IDs that needed to be passed between switches.

When a port is configured as untagged, it means the port does not require traffic to be tagged with a VLAN ID and will instead automatically tag traffic with the default VLAN ID configured on the port for traffic received from the host and going out to other hosts or switches. For inbound traffic to the switch going to the host, the VLAN ID is stripped out and the packet is sent to the host. On many switches, by default all ports are configured as untagged with a default VLAN ID of 1.

To summarize:

Tagged = Port expects traffic to be tagged when receiving.

Untagged = Port expects traffic to not be tagged and will apply a default VLAN ID. Any traffic that has a VLAN tag will be dropped.

---

Another limitation with VLANs is the number of VLANs that can be supported in an environment, which is 4,095 because the VLAN ID in the header is 12 bits long and 1 VLAN ID is not usable. So 4,095 is the theoretical number, but most switches limit the number of usable VLANs to 1,000. This may still seem like a lot, but if an organization is a host with thousands of clients, then the 1,000 limitation, or even 4,095, would make it an unusable solution. Also remember the complexity issue. If you have a 1,000 VLANs over hundreds of servers, managing them would not be a pleasant experience!

## VLANs and Hyper-V

Even with the pain points of VLANs, the reality is you are probably using VLANs, will still use them for some time, and want to use them with your virtual machines. It is completely possible to have some virtual machines in one VLAN and other virtual machines in other VLANs. While there are different ways to perform configuration of VLANs, with Hyper-V there is really one supported and reliable way to use them and maintain manageability and troubleshooting ability:

◆ Configure the switch port that is connected to the Hyper-V host in tagged mode and configure it to have inclusions for all the VLAN IDs that will be used by VMs connected to that host. Another option is to run the port essentially in a trunk type mode and allow all VLAN IDs through the port to avoid potential configuration challenges when a new VLAN ID is used by a VM on the host. Definitely do not configure the port as untagged with any kind of default VLAN ID. I cannot stress this enough. If a switch port is configured as untagged and it receives traffic that is tagged, that traffic will be dropped even if the VLAN ID matches the VLAN the port has been configured to set via the untagged configuration.

◆ Do not set a VLAN ID on the physical NIC in the Hyper-V host that is used by the virtual switch that will be connected to the virtual machines.

◆ If you are using NIC Teaming, have only a single, default mode team interface configured on the team.

◆ Run all communications through the Hyper-V virtual switch and apply the VLAN ID configuration on the virtual switch ports that correspond to the virtual network adapters connected to the virtual switch.

This actually makes configuring a VLAN quite simple. The only VLAN configuration performed in the Hyper-V environment is within the properties of the virtual network adapter as shown in Figure 3.7, where I set the VLAN ID for this specific network adapter for the virtual machine. The `Set-VMNetworkAdapterVlan` PowerShell cmdlet can also be used to set the VLAN ID for a virtual network adapter, as in the following example:

```
Set-VMNetworkAdapterVlan -VMName test1 -Access -VlanId 173
```

If you refer back to Figure 3.2, there may be something that seems confusing and that is the option to configure a VLAN ID on the virtual switch itself. Does this setting then apply to every virtual machine connected to that virtual switch? No. As the explanation text in the dialog actually explains, the VLAN ID configured on the virtual switch is applied to any virtual network adapters created in the management OS for the virtual switch, which allows the management

OS to continue using a physical network adapter that has been assigned to a virtual switch. The VLAN ID configured on the switch has no effect on virtual machine VLAN configuration.

**FIGURE 3.7**
Setting the VLAN ID for a virtual machine's network adapter

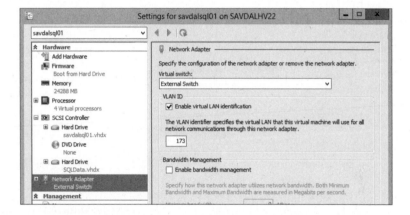

Note that if you do not require different VLAN IDs within the Hyper-V environment and all virtual machines effectively will use the same VLAN ID, then no VLAN configuration is required at the Hyper-V host or virtual machine level. Simply use untagged at the switch and configure whatever VLAN ID you wish all traffic to be tagged with as the default. The previous configuration is when you need different VLAN IDs for the various virtual machines and management OS.

## PVLANs

With all the scalability limitations of VLANs, you may wonder how large organizations and hosters specifically handle thousands of clients, which is where private VLANs (PVLANs) are a key feature. Through the use of only two VLAN IDs that are paired, PVLANs enable huge numbers of different environments to remain isolated from each other.

PVLANs enable three modes, as shown in Figure 3.8: isolated, community, and promiscuous. The primary mode that will be used with PVLANs is isolated; no direct communication is possible between hosts that are in isolated mode, but they can talk to their gateway and therefore out to the Internet and other promiscuous resources. This mode is useful if there are many different tenants that have only one host/VM each. Think about that large hosting company that hosts millions of VMs that don't need to communicate with each other or a hotel with 1,000 rooms. Also consider many workloads behind a load balancer that don't need to communicate with each other. Using PVLANs would stop the servers behind the load balancer from being able to communicate with each other, which would provide protection if one of them were compromised in some way, making it very useful for Internet-facing workloads. PVLANs are a great way to isolate every port from every other with only two VLANs required.

Community mode enables multiple hosts in the same community to communicate with each other. However, each community requires its own second VLAN ID to use with the shared primary VLAN ID. Finally, there are hosts in promiscuous mode that can communicate with hosts in isolated or community mode. Promiscuous PVLANs are useful for servers that are used by all hosts—perhaps they host a software share or updates that can be used by all.

**FIGURE 3.8**
PVLAN overview
and the three types

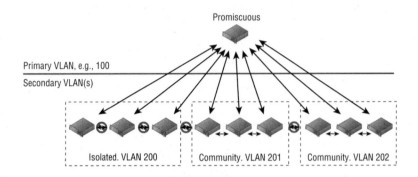

Hyper-V supports all three PVLAN modes, but this is not exposed through the graphical Hyper-V Manager and instead all configuration is done in PowerShell using the Set-VMNetworkAdapterVlan cmdlet. Remember that each VLAN can be used as the primary VLAN of only one isolated PVLAN, so ensure that different VLANs are used as primary for your isolated PVLANs. Note that the same secondary VLAN can be used in multiple isolated PVLANs without problem. The following configurations are some that you will perform for PVLAN using PowerShell.

To set a VM in isolated mode, use this command:

```
Set-VMNetworkAdapterVlan -VMName testvm -Isolated -PrimaryVlanId 100 `
 -SecondaryVlanId 200
```

Use this command to set a VM in community mode (note that the secondary VLAN ID sets the community the VM is part of):

```
Set-VMNetworkAdapterVlan -VMName testvm2 -Community -PrimaryVlanId 100 `
 -SecondaryVlanId 201
```

Use this command to set a VM in promiscuous mode (note that the secondary VLAN is now a list of all VLAN IDs used in community and for the isolated):

```
Set-VMNetworkAdapterVlan -VMName testvm3 -Promiscuous -PrimaryVlanId 100 `
 -SecondaryVlanIdList 200-400
```

To check the configuration of a virtual machine, use the Get-VMNetworkAdapterVlan cmdlet, as in this example:

```
Get-VMNetworkAdapterVlan -VMName testvm | fl *
```

The preceding commands assume that a virtual machine has a single network adapter, which essentially changes the configuration for the entire virtual machine. If a virtual machine has multiple network adapters and you wish to configure only one of the virtual network adapters, then pass the specific network adapter to the Set-VMNetworkAdapterVlan cmdlet. For example, the following command sets the VLAN for the virtual network adapter with the MAC address (remember, you can view the MAC addresses of all the virtual machines' NICs with the command Get-VMNetworkAdapter -VMName "VMName"). This command is working by listing all the adapters for the VM, then narrowing the list down by the one that matches the passed MAC address, and then passing that adapter to the Set-VMNetworkAdapterVlan cmdlet:

```
Get-VMNetworkAdapter -VMName "VMName" | where {$_.MACAddress -like
"00155DADB60A"} `
| Set-VMNetworkAdapterVlan -Isolated -PrimaryVlanID 100 -SecondaryVlanId 200
```

Some configuration of PVLANs is also possible using SCVMM, but only isolated mode is supported and not promiscuous or community. If you are using SCVMM and wish to have promiscuous and community mode virtual machines, you will need to continue using PowerShell for those virtual machines. To use SCVMM for isolated mode, it's actually a fairly simple configuration:

1. Open the Virtual Machine Manager interface, open the Fabric workspace, and select Networking ➤ Logical Networks.

2. Select the Create Logical Network action.

3. For VMM 2012 SP1 on the Name page of the Create Logical Network Wizard dialog check the "Network sites within this logical network are not connected" box and then check the "Network sites within this logical network contain private VLANs" box, as shown in Figure 3.9; then click Next. For VMM 2012 R2, there is actually a new option specifically for PVLAN. You would select the Private VLAN (PVLAN) networks option and click Next.

4. On the Network Site page of the wizard, add a site as usual. However, you will enter both a primary and secondary VLAN ID, as shown in Figure 3.10. Multiple rows can be added, each a separate isolated PVLAN if needed. When virtual networks are created later, each virtual network can be can be linked to a specific isolated PVLAN. Click Next.

5. Click Finish to create the new PVLAN isolated configuration.

**FIGURE 3.9**
Enabling a PVLAN using SCVMM on a new logical network

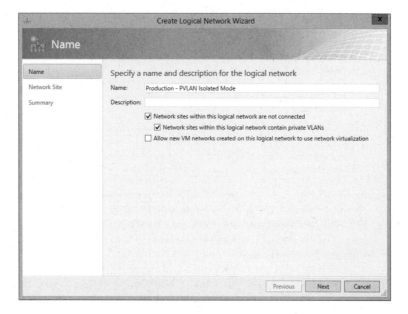

**FIGURE 3.10**
Using SCVMM to create multiple isolated PVLANs that use the same secondary VLAN ID

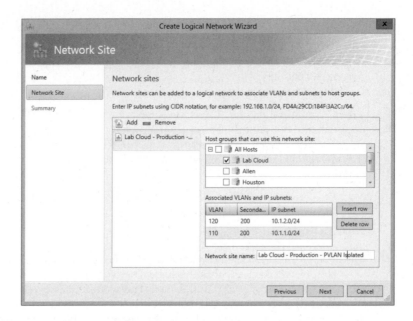

Here are the same PowerShell commands for SCVMM to create the isolated PVLAN configuration that matches the configuration previously performed using the SCVMM graphical interface:

```
$logicalNetwork = New-SCLogicalNetwork -Name "Production - PVLAN Isolated Mode" `
-LogicalNetworkDefinitionIsolation $true -EnableNetworkVirtualization $false `
-UseGRE $false -IsPVLAN $true

$allHostGroups = @()
$allHostGroups += Get-SCVMHostGroup -ID "<GUID>"
$allSubnetVlan = @()
$allSubnetVlan += New-SCSubnetVLan -Subnet "10.1.2.0/24" -VLanID 120 `
-SecondaryVLanID 200
$allSubnetVlan += New-SCSubnetVLan -Subnet "10.1.1.0/24" -VLanID 110 `
-SecondaryVLanID 200

New-SCLogicalNetworkDefinition -Name "Lab Cloud - Production - PVLAN Isolated" `
-LogicalNetwork $logicalNetwork -VMHostGroup $allHostGroups `
-SubnetVLan $allSubnetVlan -RunAsynchronously
```

It's very important with PVLAN that all the physical switch ports are configured correctly for the VLANs used as part of the PVLAN configuration or traffic will not flow between hosts correctly. While VLANs are used heavily in many environments, most organizations won't use PVLANs that are aimed at specific scenarios where there is a requirement to have large numbers of hosts/virtual machines that cannot talk to each other. The good news is they are all supported with Hyper-V.

# How SCVMM Simplifies Networking with Hyper-V

While SCVMM will be covered in detail later in the book, I've already mentioned its use a number of times in this chapter and I'm about to discuss it a lot more as it moves from being an optional management technology to being the *only* practical way to implement some technologies. I want to discuss some fundamental SCVMM logical components and how to quickly get up and running with them, including deploying some of the components we've already covered in this chapter the "SCVMM way."

When you consider what configuration was performed with Hyper-V, it really consisted of creating a virtual switch that was tied to a physical network adapter and how what we named the virtual switch could indicate what it would be used for. However, if that switch connected to an adapter that connected to a switch port that supported different VLANs for different networks, then there was no way to convey that and manage it effectively. Also, there was no concept of separating the network seen by the virtual machines from that defined on the Hyper-V server. Additionally, on each Hyper-V server the virtual switch configuration and any extensions were manually configured. Things get a lot more complicated when virtual switches are used for multiple virtual network adapters on the management operating system, as you'll see when we look at a more converged network infrastructure (and this will be covered in detail later this chapter).

SCVMM introduces quite a few new concepts and constructs that initially may seem a little overwhelming, but they are fundamentally designed to let you model your physical networks, your switch, and your network configurations on the Hyper-V hosts and then model a separate abstracted set of definitions for networks available to virtual machines. These constructs can broadly be divided into those that model connectivity and those that model capability.

I want to build these constructs out and then walk through a configuration for a new deployment. One key point is to ideally perform all your configuration through SCVMM for your Hyper-V host. Install the Hyper-V role with no virtual switches and do nothing else. Don't create virtual switches, don't create NIC teams, don't start creating virtual machines. The best experience is to define the configuration in SCVMM and let SCVMM perform all the configuration on the hosts.

One very important point for networking—whether for physical hosts, for virtualization with Hyper-V, or using SCVMM—is proper planning and design and understanding your physical network topology and your actual requirements and then translating this to your virtual network infrastructure. Why this gets emphasized with SCVMM is that SCVMM networking components will force you to do this planning because you need to model your network within SCVMM using its various networking architectural components to achieve desired results.

1. **Discovery.** Understand the network requirements of your datacenter and your virtual environments. This may require asking questions of the network teams and the business units to find out what types of isolation are required, what address spaces will be used, and what types of networks exist and need to be leveraged. Do certain types of traffic require guaranteed bandwidth, which would dictate the use of separate networks or use Quality of Service (QoS) technologies?

2. **Design.** Take the information you have discovered and translate it to SCVMM architectural components. Consider any changes to process as part of virtual environments.

This may be an iterative process because physical infrastructure such as hardware switches may limit some options and the design for the virtual network solution may need to be modified to match capabilities of physical infrastructure.

**3. Deployment.** Configure SCVMM with a networking design and deploy the configuration to hosts, virtual machines, and clouds.

## SCVMM Networking Architecture

The first architectural component for SCVMM is the logical network, which helps model your physical network infrastructure and connectivity in SCVMM. Consider your virtualization environment and the networks the hosts and the virtual machines will need to connect to. In most datacenters, at a minimum you would see something like Figure 3.11.

**FIGURE 3.11**
Common networks seen in a datacenter with virtualization

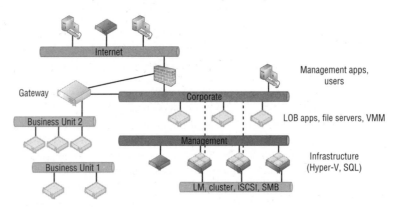

In this common datacenter, the different types of networks have different connectivity, different capabilities, and different routing available. The networks may require isolation from each other using various technologies, which is explained in more detail later. Remember, these are just examples. Some datacenters will have many more. Here are the different types of networks you could have:

**The Internet**   You may have customers or users that access the network via the Internet and connect to the Internet through various routes, so systems with Internet connectivity will likely need to be modeled as a separate network.

**Corporate**   This is usually the primary network in your company where users exist and will connect to the various services offered, such as line of business (LOB) applications, file servers, domain controllers, and more. Additionally, administrators may connect to certain management systems via systems available on the corporate network, such as your VMM server. The VMM environment will need to model the corporate environment so virtual machines can be given connectivity to the corporate environment to offer services.

**Management**   Infrastructure servers typically are connected on a separate management network that is not accessible to regular users and may not even be routable from the corporate network.

**Special Networks**   Certain types of servers require their own special types of communications, such as those required for cluster communications, live migrations, iSCSI, and SMB storage traffic. These networks are rarely routable and may even be separate, isolated switches to ensure desired connectivity and low latencies or they may use separate VLANs. Some organizations also leverage a separate network for backup purposes.

**Business Units/Tenants/Labs**    Separate networks may be required to isolate different workloads, such as different business units, different tenants (if you are a hoster), and lab/test environments. Isolation can be via various means, such as VLANs, PVLANs, or network virtualization. These networks may require connectivity out to the Internet, to other physical locations (common in hoster scenarios where a client runs some services on the hoster infrastructure but needs to communicate to the client's own datacenter), or even to the corporate network, which would be via some kind of gateway device. In Figure 3.11, Business Unit 2 requires connectivity out of its isolated network, while Business Unit 1 is completely isolated with no connectivity outside of its own network.

Each of these different types of networks would be modeled as logical networks in SCVMM. Additionally, an organization may have different physical locations/datacenters, and SCVMM allows you to define a logical network and include details of the sites where it exists along with the configuration required at each site, known as a network site. For example, suppose an organization has two locations, Dallas and Houston, and consider just the management network in this example. In Dallas, the management network uses the 10.1.1.0/24 subnet with VLAN 10, while in Houston, the management network uses the 10.1.2.0/24 subnet with VLAN 20. This information can be modeled in SCVMM using network sites, which are linked to a SCVMM host group and contained within a logical network. This enables SCVMM to assign not just the correct IP address to virtual machines based on location and network but also the correct VLAN/PVLAN. This is a key point. The logical network is modeling the physical network, so it's important that your objects match the physical topology, such as correct IP and VLAN configuration.

Note that a network Site in a logical network does not have to reflect an actual physical location but rather a specific set of network configurations. For example, suppose I had a management network that used two physical switches and each switch used a different VLAN and IP subnet. I would create a single logical network for my management network and then a separate site for each of the different network configurations, one for each VLAN and IP subnet pair.

A network site can be configured with just an IP subnet, just a VLAN, or an IP subnet/VLAN pair. You only need to configure IP subnets for a site if SCVMM will be statically assigning IP addresses to the site. If DHCP is present, then no IP subnet configuration is required. If VLANs are not being used, a VLAN does not need to be configured. If DHCP is used in the network and VLANs are not used, you do not have to create any network sites.

Once the sites are defined within a logical network, IP pools can then be added to the IP address subnet that's defined, which enables SCVMM to actually configure virtual machines with static IP addresses as the virtual machines are deployed. If DHCP is used in the network, there is no need to configure IP pools in SCVMM or even specify the IP subnet as part of the site configuration. DHCP would be leveraged for the IP assignment, but if you don't have DHCP, then creating the IP pool allows SCVMM to handle the IP assignment for you. The IP assignment is achieved by modifying the sysprep answer file with the IP address from the SCVMM IP pool as the virtual machine template is deployed. When the virtual machine is deleted, SCVMM reclaims the IP address into its pool. Even if DHCP is primarily used in the network, if you are using features such as load balancing as part of a service, then SCVMM has to be able to allocate and track that IP address, which will require the configuration of an IP pool. If no IP pool is created for a network site, SCVMM configures any virtual machines to use DHCP for address allocation. Both IPv4 and IPv6 are fully supported by SCVMM (and pretty much any Microsoft technology because a Common Engineering Criteria requirement for all Microsoft solutions is support for IPv6 at the same level as IPv4).

At a high level, this means the logical network models your physical network and allows the subnet and VLANs to be modeled into objects and then scoped to specific sites, which can also include static IP address pools for allocation to resources such as virtual machines and load balancer configurations. This is shown in Figure 3.12, with a management logical network that has two network sites, Dallas and Houston, along with the IP subnet and VLAN used at each location. For Dallas, an IP pool was also created for the network site to enable static IP configuration. Houston would use DHCP because no IP pool was created for the Houston network site within the logical network.

**FIGURE 3.12**
High-level view of logical networks

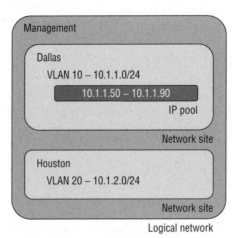

When planning your logical networks, try to stay as simple as possible. There should not be hundreds of logical networks. There should be fewer that contain different network sites that reflect the different network configurations within the type of network that is represented by the logical network. Microsoft has a good blog on designing logical networks at

http://blogs.technet.com/b/scvmm/archive/2013/04/29/logical-networks-part-ii-how-many-logical-networks-do-you-really-need.aspx

The information can really be summarized as follows:

1. Create logical networks to mirror the physical networks that exist.

2. Create logical networks to define the networks that have specific purposes.

3. Identify logical networks that need to be isolated and identify the isolation method.

4. Determine required network sites, VLANs, PVLANs, and IP pools required for each logical network and deploy them.

5. Associate logical networks to host computers.

## LOGICAL SWITCH

Earlier in this chapter, we created a virtual switch, and as part of that configuration there were options available and also the ability to enable certain extensions. While it is possible to perform a configuration on a server-by-server basis manually, this can lead to inconsistencies and inhibits automatic deployment of new Hyper-V hosts. SCVMM has the logical switch component, which acts as the container for all virtual switch settings and ensures a consistent deployment across all servers using the logical switch. The automatic configuration using the logical switch is not only useful at deployment, but SCVMM will continue to track the configuration of the host compared to the logical switch, and if the configuration deviates from that of the logical switch, this deviation will be flagged as noncompliant, and that can then be resolved. This may be important in terms of ensuring compliance enforcement in an environment. If the logical switch is updated (for example, a new extension is added), all the Hyper-V hosts using it will automatically be updated.

Logical switches use port profiles, which are another SCVMM architectural construct of which there are two types: virtual port profiles and uplink port profiles.

The virtual port profile enables settings to be configured that will be applied to actual virtual network adapters attached to virtual machines or created on the management host OS itself. This can include offload settings such as the settings for VMQ, IPsec task offloading, and SR-IOV and security settings such as those for DHCP Guard. It can also include configurations that may not be considered security related, such as guest teaming and QoS settings such as minimum and maximum bandwidth settings. A number of built-in virtual port profiles are provided in SCVMM for common network adapter uses, many of which are actually aimed at virtual network adapters used in the host OS. Figure 3.13 shows the inbox virtual port profiles in addition to the Security Settings page. Once a virtual port profile is used within a logical switch and the logical switch is deployed to a host, if the virtual port profile configuration is changed, the hosts will be flagged as noncompliant because their configuration no longer matches that of the virtual port profile. The administrator can easily remediate the servers to apply the updated configuration.

**FIGURE 3.13**
Viewing the security settings for the built-in Guest Dynamic IP virtual port profile

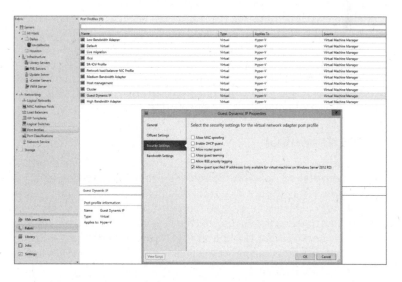

An uplink port profile defines the connectivity of the virtual switch to logical networks. You need separate uplink port profiles for each set of hosts that require the same physical connectivity (remember that logical networks define the physical network). Conversely, anytime you need to restrict logical networks to specific hosts in the same location or need custom connectivity, you will require different uplink port profiles. Logical networks can be selected that will be available as part of the uplink port profile and also NIC teaming configuration when used on hosts that will assign multiple network adapters. No inbox uplink port profiles are supplied because their primary purpose models the logical networks that can be connected to and by default there are no logical networks. If a change is made to the uplink port profile definition (for example, adding a new VLAN that is available), SCVMM will automatically update all the virtual switches on the Hyper-V hosts that use the uplink port profile via a logical switch with the new VLAN availability or any other settings within the uplink port profile.

When you put all these components together, it does require some additional upfront work, but the long-term deployment and manageability of the environment becomes much simpler and can help identify misconfigurations or where there are actual problems in network connectivity.

The logical switch is a Live Migration boundary for SCVMM's placement logic. Note that a logical switch can be deployed to many hosts, it can stretch clusters, and so on. However, SCVMM needs to ensure that the same capabilities and connectivity are available when virtual machines are moved between hosts, and so the SCVMM placement logic will not allow live migration to hosts using a different logical switch. If you had a scenario where you required different logical switches in the environment (for example, if you required different extension configurations), then a live migration would not be possible and may be a reason for those hosts to not use the logical switch and instead perform the switch configuration directly on the Hyper-V hosts; this type of switch is known as a standard switch. Standard switches are fully supported within SCVMM, and their deployment and configuration will be via Hyper-V Manager or with SCVMM. If you have an existing Hyper-V server with virtual switches defined that will be standard switches in SCVMM, there is no way to convert them to logical switches. The best option is to delete the standard switches and then re-create the switches as logical switches via SCVMM. To delete the standard switches, you would need to evacuate the host of virtual machines, which typically means you have a cluster. However, with Windows Server 2012, you can also move virtual machines with no downtime using Shared Nothing Live Migration between any Hyper-V hosts provided they have a 1 Gbps network connection.

## VM Networks

While the logical network provides the modeling of the networks available in the environment and the desired isolation, the goal for virtualization is to separate and abstract these logical networks from the actual virtual machines. This abstraction is achieved through the use of VM networks, which is another networking architectural component in SCVMM. Through the use of VM networks, the virtual machines have no idea of the underlying technology used by the logical networks, for example, if VLANs are used on the network fabric. Virtual machine virtual network adapters can only be connected to a VM network. When Network Virtualization is used, the Customer Address (CA) space is defined as part of the VM network, allowing specific VM subnets to be created as needed within the VM network.

There may be some scenarios where the isolation provided by VM networks is not actually required—for example, where direct access to the infrastructure is required, such as if your SCVMM server is actually running in a virtual machine, or where the network is used for cluster communications. It is actually possible to create a no isolation pass-through VM network that directly passes communication through to the logical network. The VM network is present only because a virtual machine network adapter needs to connect to a VM network. If a logical network has multiple sites defined, then when a virtual machine is deployed, it will automatically pick the correct IP subnet and VLAN configuration at deployment time based on the location to which it's being deployed. Users of self-service-type portals are exposed to VM networks but not the details of the underlying logical networks.

### PORT CLASSIFICATIONS

Port classifications are assigned to virtual machines that are containers for port profile settings. The benefit of the port classification is that it acts a layer of abstraction from the port profiles assigned to logical switches, which allows a port classification to be assigned to a virtual machine template. The actual port profile used depends on the logical switch the VM is using when deployed. Think of port classifications as being similar to storage classifications; you may create a gold storage classification that uses a top-of-the-line SAN and a bronze storage classification that uses a much lower tier of storage. I may create a port classification of High Bandwidth and one of Low Bandwidth. A number of port classifications are included in-box that correlate to the included virtual port profiles. Port classifications are linked to virtual port profiles as part of the logical switch creation process. Like VM networks, port classifications are exposed to users via self-service portals and not the underlying port profiles.

### MICROSOFT RESOURCE

Microsoft has a great poster available that details all the key networking constructs available. If possible, download this poster, get it printed, and put it up on your wall, or if you have a large monitor, set it as your background. The poster can be downloaded from

www.microsoft.com/en-us/download/details.aspx?id=37137

## Deploying Networking with SCVMM 2012 R2

For this part of the chapter, I will assume SCVMM 2012 R2 is up and running in your environment. I cover implementing SCVMM 2012 R2 in Chapter 6, "Maintaining Your Hyper-V Environment," so if you want to follow along, you may want to jump to Chapter 6 to get a basic deployment in place. The good news is that networking is one of the first components that needs to be configured with SCVMM, so once you have SCVMM deployed and you have created some host groups (which are collections of hosts), you will be ready to follow this next set of steps. Figure 3.14 gives a high-level view of the steps that will be performed.

**FIGURE 3.14**
The steps for
SCVMM network
configuration

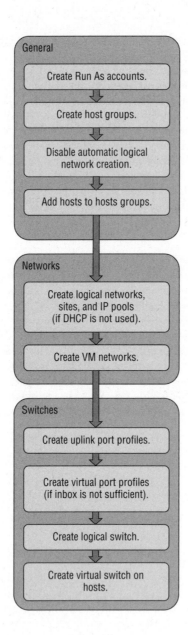

### DISABLE AUTOMATIC LOGICAL NETWORK CREATION

The very first action related to networking in SCVMM 2012 R2 is to disable the automatic creation of logical networks. This may seem strange that our first configuration is to disable functionality, but it will help ensure your SCVMM modeling consistency. With automatic logical network creation enabled, when a Hyper-V host that already has a virtual switch defined is added to SCVMM, a logical network will automatically be created in SCVMM if SCVMM does not find a match for an existing logical network based on the first DNS suffix label for the network adapter network (which is the default behavior). For example, if the DNS suffix for a network connection was lab.savilltech.net, then a logical network named lab would be used, and if not found, would automatically be created. This automatic creation of logical networks may be fine in a test environment, but in production, where you have done detailed planning for your logical networks and deployed accordingly, it is very unlikely that the automatic creation of logical networks based on DNS suffix labels would be desirable. Therefore, disable this automatic logical network creation as follows:

1. Open Virtual Machine Manager.

2. Open the Settings workspace.

3. Select the General navigation node.

4. Double-click Network Settings in the details pane.

5. In the Network Settings dialog, uncheck the Create Logical Networks Automatically option as shown in Figure 3.15 and click OK. Notice also in this dialog that it is possible to change the logical network matching behavior to a scheme that may better suit your naming conventions and design.

**FIGURE 3.15**
Disabling the automatic creation of logical networks in SCVMM 2012 R2

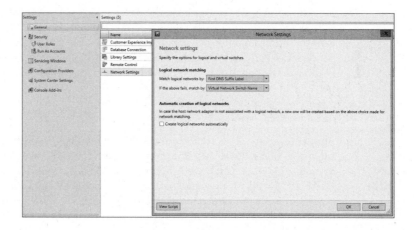

Those of you who used SCVMM 2012 SP1 will notice that the option to also automatically create virtual switches (VM networks) has been removed. The automatic creation of virtual switches, which virtual machines use to connect, actually caused a lot of confusion, so it was removed in R2. At this point you can safely add Hyper-V hosts to the SCVMM environment without them automatically creating logical networks you don't want in the environment.

## CREATING LOGICAL NETWORKS

In this environment I have three networks available that I will model as logical networks. However, they are all separate VLANs on the same physical network that will be controlled by setting the VLAN ID on the virtual network adapter. The physical ports on the switch have been configured to allow all the various VLANs that can be configured (similar to a trunk port):

◆ Corporate network. The main address space used by my organization, which on my switches uses VLAN 10 in all locations.

◆ Lab network. The network used for a number of separate lab environments that each have their own IP subnet and VLAN.

◆ Network virtualization network. Will be used in the future when network virtualization is explored

The steps to create a logical network are detailed here:

**1.** Open Virtual Machine Manager.

**2.** Open the Fabric workspace.

**3.** Select the Networking ➤ Logical Networks navigation node.

**4.** Click the Create Logical Network button, which launches the Create Logical Network Wizard.

**5.** As shown in Figure 3.16, a name and description for the logical network is entered along with the type of network. It can be a connected network that allows multiple sites that can communicate with each other and use network virtualization, a VLAN-based independent network, or a PVLAN-based network. Note that when you are creating a network with the One Connected Network option, the option to automatically create a VM network to map to the logical network is available, but in this example I will not use that, so we can manually create it. Because this is the corporate network, I do not intend to use network virtualization. Click Next.

**6.** The next screen allows configuration of the sites. For corporate, I only need a single site using VLAN 10 because the switch is configured to allow VLAN 10 through to the corporate network. Click the Add button to add a site and then click Insert Row to add VLAN/IP details for the site. The actual IP space is all configured by corporate DHCP servers in this example, so I will actually leave the IP subnet blank, which tells SCVMM to just configure the VM for DHCP.

If the network does not use VLANs, then set the VLAN ID to 0, which tells SCVMM that VLANs are not to be configured. By default, sites are given the name <Logical Network>_<number>, but you should rename this to something more useful. For example, as shown in Figure 3.17, I am renaming it Corp Trunk.

For each site, select the host group that contains hosts in that site. Because this can be used in all locations, I select the All Hosts group. Click Next.

**7.** The Summary screen will be displayed. It includes a View Script button that when clicked will show the PowerShell code that can be used to automate the creation. This can be useful when you are creating large numbers of logical networks, or more likely, large numbers of sites. Click Finish to create the logical network.

**FIGURE 3.16**
Creating a logical network that represents a connected collection of sites

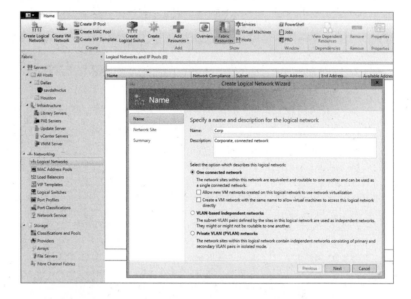

**FIGURE 3.17**
Adding a single site to a logical network

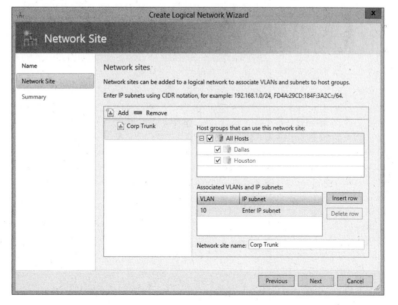

Here is the PowerShell code used to create my corporate logical network:

```
$logicalNetwork = New-SCLogicalNetwork -Name "Corp" `
-LogicalNetworkDefinitionIsolation $false -EnableNetworkVirtualization $false `
-UseGRE $false -IsPVLAN $false -Description "Corporate, connected network"

$allHostGroups = @()
$allHostGroups += Get-SCVMHostGroup -ID "0e3ba228-a059-46be-aa41-2f5cf0f4b96e"
$allSubnetVlan = @()
$allSubnetVlan += New-SCSubnetVLan -VLanID 10

New-SCLogicalNetworkDefinition -Name "Corp Trunk" `
-LogicalNetwork $logicalNetwork `
-VMHostGroup $allHostGroups -SubnetVLan $allSubnetVlan -RunAsynchronously
```

The next network I would create would be my set of lab networks. In this case I will select the VLAN-based independent networks type, and I will create a separate site for each of the VLAN/IP subnet pairs, which represent separate lab environments as shown in Figure 3.18. I'm creating only two of the VLANs in this example because performing this using the graphical tools is actually very slow. My lab environments are all based in Dallas, so only the Dallas host group is selected. Because the sites in this logical network have IP subnets defined, I would also create an IP pool for each site as in the next set of steps. You will notice most of these settings are similar to those configured for a DHCP scope because essentially SCVMM is performing a similar role; it just uses a different mechanism to assign the actual IP address. All of the details are those that will be configured on the virtual machines that get IP addresses from the IP pool.

**FIGURE 3.18**
Creating a VLAN-based logical network

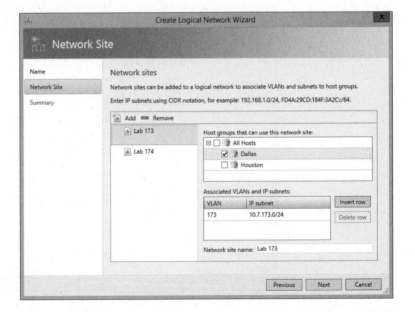

1. Click the Create IP Pool button or right-click on the logical network and select the Create IP Pool context menu action.

2. Enter a name and description and select the logical network the IP pool is for from the drop-down list.

3. The next screen, as shown in Figure 3.19, allows you to use an existing network site or create a new one. Choose to use an existing one and then click Next.

4. The IP Address Range page allows configuration of the IP address range that SCVMM will manage and allocate to resources such as virtual machines and load balancers. Within the range, specific addresses can be configured as reserved for other purposes or for use by load balancer virtual IPs (VIPs) that SCVMM can allocate. In Figure 3.20, you can see that I have reserved 5 IP addresses from the range for use by load balancer VIPs. Fill in the fields and click Next.

5. Click the Insert button and enter the gateway IP address. Then click Next.

6. Configure the DNS servers, DNS suffix, and additional DNS suffixes to append and then click Next.

7. Enter the WINS server details if used and click Next.

8. On the Summary screen, confirm the configuration, click the View Script button to see the PowerShell that will be used, and then click Finish to create the IP pool.

**FIGURE 3.19**
Choose the site for a new IP pool or create a new one.

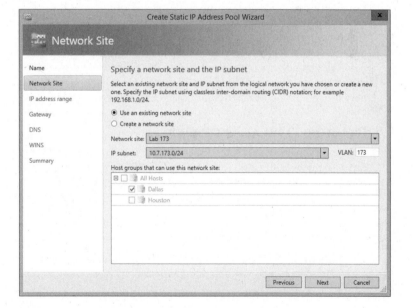

**FIGURE 3.20**
Configuring the IP
address range for
the IP pool

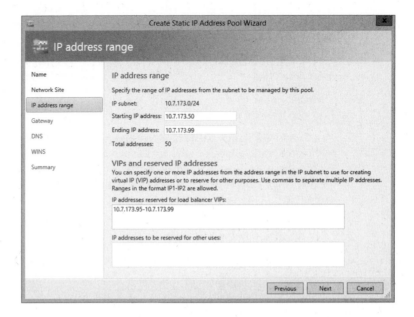

Finally, I will create my Hyper-V network virtualization logical network, which will support network virtualization and be configured with an IP pool that will be used for the provider space for the Hyper-V hosts. This will follow the same process as the other networks, except this time I will select the One Connected Network option and the option "Allow new VM networks created on this logical network to use network virtualization." A network site is created and a VLAN is configured if needed along with an IP subnet (this must be set), and this will purely be used so that the Hyper-V hosts that are hosting virtual machines that are participating in network virtualization can be allocated their provider address (PA). An IP pool must also be created for the site for the IP address allocation for the PA. No DNS servers are required for the PA network, but if you are using multiple subnets, then a gateway would need to be defined.

### CREATING VIRTUAL NETWORKS

With logical networks created, the next step is to create the VM networks that virtual machines can actually be connected to. In SCVMM 2012 R2, within the logical networks view, there is a convenient option to create the VM network using the Create VM Network button or by right-clicking on a logical network and selecting Create VM Network. For now we will use the "old-fashioned" way:

1. Open Virtual Machine Manager.

2. Open the VMs And Services workspace (not Fabric, because this is now a construct directly related to virtual machines).

3. Select the VM Networks navigation node.

4. Click the Create VM Network button.

5. Enter a name and description for the VM network, select the logical network, and click Next.

6. Depending on the logical network selected, this may be the end of the configuration. For example, a connected network without network virtualization requires no further configuration. A VLAN type network that is isolated will show an Isolation screen, which allows a specific VLAN (site) to be selected for this specific VM network, or you can select Automatic, which allows SCVMM to automatically select a site based on those available on the logical network. If a network that is enabled for network virtualization is selected, a number of additional configuration pages must be completed to define the configuration for the IP scheme in the virtual network space (CA). I will cover this in detail in the section "Network Virtualization."

Click Finish to complete the VM Network creation process.

My final configuration is shown in Figure 3.21 for my logical networks and VM networks.

**FIGURE 3.21**

The complete logical network and VM network configuration

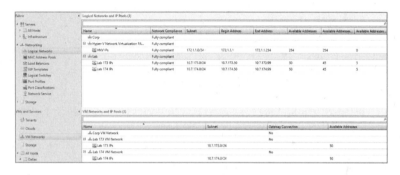

So far we have done a lot of configuration but have not modeled our network to SCVMM. Consider my lab environment. I configured 2 of the VLANs to separate the different lab environments, but suppose I have 40 or 80 or 200. This is where PowerShell is invaluable, and I created the script that follows to automate this configuration process.

This script creates a separate site for each VLAN with the appropriate IP subnet and also an IP pool (which in my case was just two addresses that were used for the first 2 machines that were domain controllers because the rest were assigned by DHCP). In my lab, the third octet matches the VLAN ID. This script automatically creates all 40 VLAN sites, which run from 150 to 190, and the appropriate IP pools. You can customize it to meet your own needs, including changing the name of the SCVMM server and also replacing with the logical network that all the sites should be added to (you have to create the logical network in advance, although this could also be added to this script if required). To find the GUID of your logical network, run the command Get-SCLogicalNetwork | ft Name, ID -Auto.

```
Import-Module virtualmachinemanager
Get-VMMServer -ComputerName scvmm
#Replace this with actual ID of the Logical Network.
#Get-SCLogicalNetwork | ft name, id
$logicalNetwork = Get-SCLogicalNetwork -ID "xxxxxxxx-xxxx-xxxx-xxxx-
xxxxxxxxxxxx"
```

```
$startNumber = 150
$endNumber = 190

$vlanID = $startNumber

do
{

    $allHostGroups = @()
    $allHostGroups += Get-SCVMHostGroup -ID "0e3ba228-a059-46be-aa41-
2f5cf0f4b96e"
    $allSubnetVlan = @()
    $allSubnetVlan += New-SCSubnetVLan -Subnet "10.1.$vlanID.0/24" -VLanID
$vlanID

    $logicalNetworkDefinition = New-SCLogicalNetworkDefinition -Name
"VLAN_$vlanID" `
-LogicalNetwork $logicalNetwork -VMHostGroup $allHostGroups `
-SubnetVLan $allSubnetVlan -RunAsynchronously

    # Gateways
    $allGateways = @()
    $allGateways += New-SCDefaultGateway -IPAddress "10.1.$vlanID.1" -Automatic

    # DNS servers
    $allDnsServer = @("10.1.$vlanID.10", "10.1.$vlanID.11")

    # DNS suffixes
    $allDnsSuffixes = @()

    # WINS servers
    $allWinsServers = @()

    $NewVLANName = "VLAN_" + $vlanID + "_IP_Pool"

    New-SCStaticIPAddressPool -Name $NewVLANName `
-LogicalNetworkDefinition $logicalNetworkDefinition -Subnet "10.1.$vlanID.0/24" `
-IPAddressRangeStart "10.1.$vlanID.10" -IPAddressRangeEnd "10.1.$vlanID.11" `
-DefaultGateway $allGateways -DNSServer $allDnsServer -DNSSuffix "" `
-DNSSearchSuffix $allDnsSuffixes -RunAsynchronously


    #Now create VM Network for each

    $vmNetwork = New-SCVMNetwork -Name "Customer_VLAN_$vlanID" `
-LogicalNetwork $logicalNetwork -IsolationType "VLANNetwork" `
```

```
-Description "VM Network for Customer VLAN $vlanID"
    $logicalNetworkDefinition = Get-SCLogicalNetworkDefinition -Name
"VLAN_$vlanID"
    $subnetVLAN = New-SCSubnetVLan -Subnet "10.7.$vlanID.0/24" -VLanID $vlanID
    $VMSubnetName = "Customer_VLAN_" + $vlanID + "_0"
    $vmSubnet = New-SCVMSubnet -Name $VMSubnetName `
-LogicalNetworkDefinition $logicalNetworkDefinition -SubnetVLan $subnetVLAN `
-VMNetwork $vmNetwork


    $vlanID += 1
}
until ($vlanID -gt $endNumber)
```

## CREATING THE PORT PROFILES AND LOGICAL SWITCH

Now that the logical networks and VM networks exists, I can create my logical switch, but remember, the logical switch uses the uplink port profiles to identify the connectivity available. I also use virtual port profiles and port classifications. I will use the built-in objects for those, but they are easy to create if required using the Fabric workspace and the Port Profiles and Port Classifications navigation areas. I recommend looking at the existing virtual port profiles and port classifications as the foundation of configuration should you need to create your own. Now is a good time to take a look at the inbox port profiles and port classifications, which you can choose to keep, delete, or even modify to exactly meet your own needs.

The first step is to create the uplink port profiles. Remember, the uplink port profile models the connectivity available for a specific connection from the host, that is, from the network adapter to the switch. If different network adapters have different connectivity to different switches, you will need multiple uplink port profiles. Here are the steps:

1. Open Virtual Machine Manager.

2. Open the Fabric workspace.

3. Select the Networking ➢ Port Profiles navigation node.

4. Click the Create button drop-down and select Hyper-V Port Profile.

5. Enter a name and description for the new port profile, as shown in Figure 3.22. Select the Uplink Port Profile radio button. You can additionally configure a teaming mode, which is used if the port profile is used on a host where NIC Teaming is required and the settings configured in the port profile will be applied. Because I am connecting all my Hyper-V boxes to ports configured on the switch with multiple VLANs allowed, I only need one uplink port profile that can connect any of the networks. Click Next.

6. Select the network sites (that are part of your logical networks) that can be connected to via this uplink port profile (Figure 3.23). Because all of my networks can, I will select them all and also check the box to enable Hyper-V Network Virtualization. On Windows 2012 Hyper-V hosts, this option enables Network Virtualization in the networking stack on the network adapter, but it does nothing on Windows Server 2012 R2 hosts, which

always have Network Virtualization enabled because it's part of the switch. Check the network sites that can be connected via this uplink port profile and click Next.

**7.** Click Finish to complete the creation of the uplink port profile.

**FIGURE 3.22**
Setting the options for a new uplink port profile and NIC Teaming options

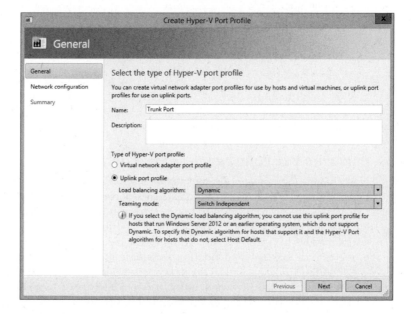

**FIGURE 3.23**
Selecting the network sites that can be connected to using the uplink port profile

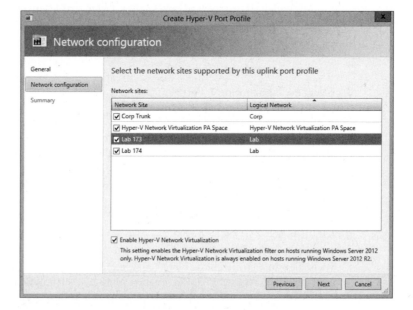

The final step of modeling is the creation of the actual logical switch, which will then be applied to the Hyper-V hosts. The logical switch will bring all the different components together. Follow these steps:

1. Open Virtual Machine Manager.

2. Open the Fabric workspace.

3. Select the Networking ➤ Logical Switches navigation node.

4. Click the Create Logical Switch button.

5. The Create Logical Switch Wizard will launch. Read all the text on the introduction page. It confirms all the tasks you should have already performed, such as creating the logical networks, installing extensions, and creating uplink port profiles (aka native port profiles). Click Next.

6. Enter a name and description for the new logical switch. If you wish to use SR-IOV, the Enable Single Root I/O Virtualization (SR-IOV) box must be checked, and this cannot be changed once the switch is created. Click Next.

7. The list of installed virtual switch extensions are displayed and can be selected for deployment as part of the logical switch usage. This can be changed in the future if required. Click Next.

8. The uplink port profiles must be selected. The first option is the uplink mode, which by default is No Uplink Team, but it can be changed to Team. Setting the value to Team tells SCVMM to create a NIC team (using the settings in the uplink port profile) if the logical switch is deployed to a host and multiple network adapters are selected. Click the Add button, select the uplink port profile to be added, and click OK. Multiple uplink port profiles can be added as required. Click Next.

9. The virtual port profiles should now be added to the logical switch. Click the Add button, and in the dialog that appears, click the Browse button to select the port classification (remember, this is the generic classification that is exposed to users of the environment). Then check "Include a virtual network adapter port profile in this virtual port" and select the virtual port profile that corresponds. For example, if I selected the high-bandwidth port classification, then most likely I would select the High Bandwidth Adapter virtual port profile object. Click OK. Repeat to add additional classifications. Select the classification you would like to be the default and click the Set Default button. Click Next.

10. Click Finish to create the logical switch.

### CONFIGURING A HYPER-V HOST WITH A LOGICAL SWITCH

The final step is to now configure Hyper-V hosts with the logical switch, which will trigger SCVMM to actually create virtual switches on the Hyper-V host that matches the configurations defined. It also sets up the environment for virtual machine and service deployments, and all the networking elements will be configured automatically.

In my lab, my Hyper-V hosts have three network adapters that I wish to have teamed to use for my Hyper-V virtual switch. I also have a separate network adapter for management actions such as RDP and file services and another network adapter for cluster and Live Migration operations. I don't use iSCSI or SMB in this environment because it uses Fibre Channel to connect to a SAN. I'm covering this so you understand why I will make the choices I make. However, if you need the virtual switch to use all your network adapters, including your management network adapter, SCVMM can take care of ensuring that you don't lose connectivity, which I will cover in the following walk-through.

1. Open Virtual Machine Manager.

2. Open the VMs And Services workspace.

3. Navigate to your Hyper-V hosts.

4. Right-click on a Hyper-V host and choose Properties.

5. Click the Hardware tab and scroll down to the Network Adapters section. Your network adapters will be shown, and right now they will all be disconnected from a logical network.

6. Click the Virtual Switches tab and click the New Virtual Switch button. The option to create a new logical switch or a new standard switch is displayed. Click the New Logical Switch option.

7. In this walk-through, only one logical switch was created, and that will be selected automatically along with one network adapter. This network adapter can be changed using the drop-down, as can the uplink port profile it uses. Additional network adapters can be added using the Add button if you wish to create a team.

   In most environments, the uplink port profile will need to be the same for all network adapters, and SCVMM will actually perform a check and gray out the option to change the uplink port profile for any additional network adapters, as shown in Figure 3.24. There are some third-party forwarder switch extensions that do allow different connectivity for different adapters in a team, which would be detected if configured for the logical switch by SCVMM and the option to set different virtual port profiles was enabled.

8. This step is needed only if virtual network adapters need to be created on the Hyper-V host, such as, for example, in the scenario in which I'm using the network adapter I use for management as part of the new virtual switch. Click the New Virtual Network Adapter button. Enter a name for the new network adapter. There is a check box enabled by default, "This virtual network adapter inherits settings from the physical management adapter," which tells SCVMM to copy the MAC address and IP configuration from the first adapter in the team into the new virtual network adapter it is creating, which will ensure continued connectivity for the host. Because the MAC address is copied, this would ensure that even if DHCP was used, the same IP address would be assigned. Click the Browse button in the Connectivity section to select the connectivity for the virtual network adapter and a port profile classification. Multiple virtual network adapters can be added as required.

9. Once all configuration is complete, click OK for the configuration to be applied. A warning that connectivity may temporarily be lost during configuration is displayed. Click OK. This would only happen if you are using your management network adapter in the new switch.

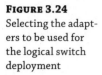

**FIGURE 3.24**
Selecting the adapters to be used for the logical switch deployment

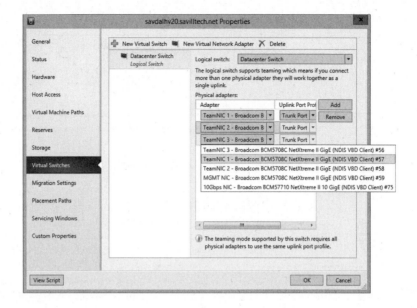

The progress of any action performed by SCVMM, known as a job, can be viewed via the Jobs workspace, and as Figure 3.25 shows, my switch deployment completed successfully. On the bottom of the figure, you can see each step that was actually performed. You will notice I actually configured the logical switch on two hosts, which are members of the same cluster, and it's important to have a consistent configuration across any clusters to ensure that no problems occur with connectivity and functionality as virtual machines are moved between hosts. Remember that SCVMM requires hosts to have the same logical switch to be available for placement during live migrations. The eagle-eyed reader may notice that the logical switch creation on savdalhv20.savilltech.net (second line down from the top of Figure 3.25) shows that it completed with information, which was not the case for the savdalhv21.savilltech.net, which I configured second (the top line). The information was as follows:

```
Information (26844)
Virtual switch (Datacenter Switch) is not highly available because the switch is not
available in host (savdalhv21.savilltech.net).
```

SCVMM was telling me that I had deployed a logical switch to a server that was part of a cluster and that because the same logical switch was not available in the other node of the cluster, it was not highly available. This is why I did not get an information message when adding the logical switch to the second node because then the logical switch was available on both nodes.

When connecting to the Hyper-V hosts where I deployed the logical switch, I now see that a new NIC team has been created and a new virtual switch in Hyper-V that matches the configurations of all those SCVMM networking constructs that I defined.

When a virtual machine is created, the VM networks that are available will be listed to choose from based on those available within the logical switch, which were set via the uplink port profile selections.

**FIGURE 3.25**

Viewing the status of logical switch deployment

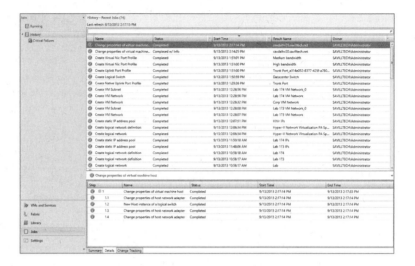

Looking at all the work that was done, it certainly seems like it was far more than just manually creating a switch in Hyper-V Manager, which can be automated with PowerShell. However, consider having hundreds of Hyper-V hosts, and also realize that now the environment has been fully modeled in SCVMM, allowing for very intricate deployments without the need for users to understand the underlying network fabric or for administrators to search for which IP address and VLAN to use. With the work done upfront, the ongoing management is far easier while also assuring compliance.

## Network Virtualization

Previously, I covered VLAN and PVLANs as technologies to provide some isolation between virtual machines and even abstract the connectivity from the physical network to a limited degree. However, the challenge was the scalability limits of VLANs, the narrow scenarios where PVLANs make sense, and the relative complexity and overhead of configuration required on the network equipment where VLANs are used and modified. Even with VLANs, there is not a true abstraction of the virtual network and the physical fabric.

Look at every aspect of the virtual environment. Memory, processor, and storage have all been virtualized very effectively for a virtual machine but not the network. Our goal when we talk about clouds is to pool all our resources together for greater scale and flexibility, but physical networks can impede this seamless pooling. When a virtual machine is attached to a virtual switch, it needs to match the IP scheme used on the underlying network fabric to be able to communicate. I spent a lot of time modeling the network in SCVMM, and once configured, it makes the management of the network much easier, but it also enables a far more powerful feature, network virtualization.

### Network Virtualization Overview

Network virtualization separates the address space seen by the virtual machines, the customer address (CA) space, from that used to actually send the packets over the network, the provider address (PA) space, providing abstraction of the network and complete isolation between different virtual networks. Because of this complete isolation of address space, it allows tenants to bring their own IP schemes and subnets to a virtual environment and also allows overlapping of IP subnets between different virtual networks. Additionally, because of this abstraction it's possible for virtual machines to actually move between locations without requiring changes to their IP configuration. This is very important in many scenarios. Hosting companies who want to host many tenants benefit greatly from network virtualization because each tenant is completely isolated from every other tenant with complete IP flexibility. Think about a company hosting Coke and Pepsi. It's important to be able to keep them completely isolated! Organizations who host different business units can also provide complete isolation and, again, flexible IP schemes. Even without the need for flexible IP schemes or complete isolation, a move to network virtualization and what is known as software-defined networking (SDN) removes the complexity of managing physical network infrastructure anytime a change is required that is commonly needed when using existing technologies such as VLANs. Network virtualization also removes the scalability challenges associated with VLANs.

This virtual network capability is enabled through the use of two IP addresses for each virtual machine and a virtual subnet identifier that indicates the virtual network to which a particular virtual machine belongs. The first IP address is the standard IP address that is configured within the virtual machine, the customer address (CA). The second IP address is the IP address the virtual machine actually communicates over the physical network with, known as the provider address (PA). The PA is actually invisible to the virtual machine; the Hyper-V host owns the PA.

This is best explored by an example. In this example, we have a single physical fabric, and running on that fabric are two separate organizations, the red and blue organizations. Each organization has its own IP scheme that can overlap, and the virtual networks can span multiple physical locations. This is shown in Figure 3.26. Each virtual machine that is part of the virtual red or blue networks would have its own customer address, and then a separate provider address would be used to send the actual IP traffic over the physical fabric. The important part is that like other aspects of virtualization, the virtual machines have no knowledge that the network is virtualized. The virtual machines in a virtual network believe they are operating on a physical network available only to them.

**FIGURE 3.26**
High-level overview of network virtualization

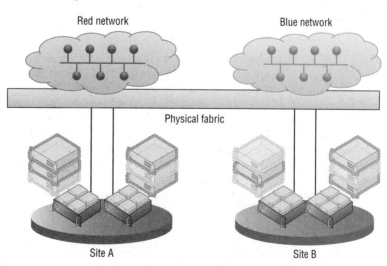

Network Virtualization Generic Routing Encapsulation (NVGRE) is used for the network virtualization implementation; it is an extension of GRE, an IETF standard. With NVGRE, the network virtualization works by wrapping the originating packet from the VM, which uses the CA addresses (which are all the virtual machine is aware of), inside a packet that can be routed on the physical network using the PA IP addresses. It also includes the actual virtual subnet, which represents a specific subnet within a virtual network. The virtual subnet is included in the wrapper packet, so each VM does not require its own PA address because the receiving host can identify the targeted VM based on the CA target IP address within the original packet and the virtual subnet ID in the wrapper packet. The virtual subnet ID is actually stored in the GRE key, which is a 24-bit key allowing over 16 million virtual subnets, very different scalability from the 4 thousand limit of VLANs. The only information the Hyper-V host on the originating VM needs to know is which Hyper-V host is running the target VM and can then send the packet over the network. This can be seen in Figure 3.27, where three virtual machines exist in a virtual network and are running across two separate Hyper-V servers. In the figure, CA1 is talking to CA2. However, note in the lookup table on the first Hyper-V server that the PA address for CA2 and CA3 are the same since they run on the same Hyper-V host. The PA address is for each Hyper-V host rather than each virtual machine.

**FIGURE 3.27**
High-level over-
view of network
virtualization using
NVGRE

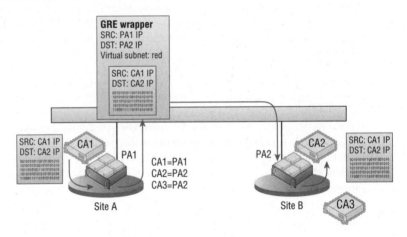

The use of a shared PA means that far fewer IP addresses from the provider IP pools are needed, which is good news for IP management and the network infrastructure. When thinking about the actual data going across the wire when using the NVGRE encapsulation, the packet structure would be composed as shown in the following list. As expected, the full Ethernet and IP header and payload from the virtual machine communication is wrapped in an Ethernet and IP header that can be used on the physical network fabric based on the Hyper-V host MAC addresses and PA IP addresses. The full specification for NVGRE can be found at

```
http://tools.ietf.org/html/draft-sridharan-virtualization-nvgre-01
```

Note that VLANs can still be used on the physical fabric for the PA and would just be part of the standard packet, completely invisible to the Network Virtualization traffic. The packet structure for NVGRE encapsulation is as follows:

- PA Ethernet MAC source and destination addresses

- PA IP source and destination addresses

♦ Virtual subnet ID (VSID)

♦ VM Ethernet MAC source and destination addresses

♦ CA IP source and destination addresses

♦ Original IP payload

There is a potential downside to using NVGRE that I at least want to make you aware of. Because the original packet is being wrapped inside the NVGRE packet, any kind of NIC offloading such as IPsec processing in the network adapter will break because the offloads won't understand the new packet format. The good news is that many of the major hardware manufacturers are looking to add support for NVGRE to all their network equipment, which will once again enable offloading even when NVGRE is used. Additionally, even without offloading, typically there is not a significant performance degradation until very high-bandwidth (over 5 Gbps) scenarios are reached.

---

### WHAT HAPPENED TO IP REWRITE?

If you looked at network virtualization for Windows Server 2012 early on, you would have seen two types of network virtualization technology: NVGRE and IP rewrite. IP rewrite was originally introduced at the same time NVGRE was introduced because there was a concern that the NVGRE encapsulation would introduce too much overhead. IP rewrite worked by rewriting the IP information of the packet as it was sent over the wire to use the PA space instead of the CA space, which meant a regular packet was being sent over the network instead of an encapsulated packet and therefore all existing offloads continue to function. When the packet reached the destination Hyper-V host, the IP address was rewritten again back to the CA space. This meant that there had to be a PA for every CA used, which was a lot of IP addresses from the PA space. The reality was that customers found the different technologies confusing. In addition, after testing, it was found that even without NVGRE optimized hardware, there was not the performance penalty expected by NVGRE until workloads started approaching 5 Gbps for a single VM, which would actually be a fairly isolated, extreme instance in most environments. Only at this time did NVGRE support in the networking equipment to enable offloads become a factor. For this reason, IP rewrite was actually deprecated in Windows Server 2012 and has been removed in SCVMM 2012 R2.

---

Virtualization policies are used between all the Hyper-V hosts that participate in a specific virtual network to enable the routing of the CA across the physical fabric and to track the CA-to-PA mapping. The virtualization policies can also define which virtual networks are allowed to communicate with other virtual networks. The configuration of the virtualization policies can be accomplished via PowerShell, which is the direction for all things Windows Server. However, trying to manually manage network virtualization using PowerShell is not practical. The challenge in using the native PowerShell commands is the synchronization and orchestration of the virtual network configuration across all Hyper-V hosts that participate in a specific virtual network. The supported solution, and really the only practical way, is to use the virtualization management solution to manage the virtual networks and not to do it manually using PowerShell, which means use System Center Virtual Machine Manager.

Referring back to the different planes required for network virtualization to work will help you understand the criticality of SCVMM. Whereas SCVMM can be considered "not essential" for some areas of Hyper-V where the end result could still be achieved, albeit with far more work and customization, this is really not the case for network virtualization that needs SCVMM. These planes are shown in Figure 3.28:

**FIGURE 3.28**
The three planes
that enable network
virtualization

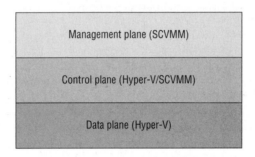

**Data Plane** Packets are actually encapsulated and decapsulated for communication over the wire on the data plane. This is implemented by Hyper-V and leverages NVGRE for the encapsulation.

**Control Plane** Controls how configuration is propagated to the networking equipment and the Hyper-V servers. This is handled very efficiently by Hyper-V and SCVMM by actually using SCVMM as a central policy store, which is then used by the Hyper-V servers, avoiding large amounts of network "chatter" related to control traffic. This provides a scalable solution, and as changes occur, such as to which host a virtual machine is hosted on, SCVMM, as that central policy store, can notify all Hyper-V hosts affected in real-time.

**Management Plane** The network is actually configured and managed on the management plane. This is SCVMM using its management tool and SCVMM PowerShell cmdlets.

So far when talking about network virtualization, I have focused on the virtual subnet ID (VSID). However, strictly speaking, the VSID is not actually the isolation boundary. The true boundary of a virtual network is the routing domain, which is the boundary of the routing policies that control the communication and therefore the isolation boundary. Think of the routing domain as the container that then contains virtual subnets, which can all communicate with each other. You may actually see three different names used, but they all mean a virtual network:

- ◆ Virtual network: The official nomenclature

- ◆ Routing domain: Name used when managing with PowerShell

- ◆ VM network: Name used within SCVMM

For efficiency of communications, you may still wish to define different virtual subnets for different locations or requirements within a virtual network (even though you don't have to). A virtual subnet, like a physical subnet, acts as a broadcast boundary. Later on I'll discuss using gateways to enable communication between different virtual networks and to the Internet or physical networks.

No separate gateway technology is required for different virtual subnets within a single virtual network to communicate. The Hyper-V Network Virtualization component within the Hyper-V switch takes care of routing between virtual subnets within a virtual network. The Hyper-V Network Virtualization filter that runs within the Hyper-V virtual switch always provides a default gateway for each virtual subnet, which is always the .1 address and is commonly referred to as the *.1 gateway*. For example, if the virtual subnet was 10.1.1.0/24, then the gateway address would be 10.1.1.1. The gateway will route traffic between the different virtual subnets within the same virtual network, so it's actually acting as a router.

Windows 2012 R2 uses a new intelligent unicast replication if there are CA broadcasts/multicasts on the network. What this means is that a VM sends a broadcast to its virtual subnet, then Hyper-V will actually only send this broadcast once to each Hyper-V host that hosts VMs on that virtual subnet. Then the target host sends the packet to each virtual machine. Only IP broadcast and multicast is supported, such as ARP, Duplicate Address Detection, and Neighbor Unreachability Detection.

Another benefit to network virtualization is that the networking visible to the virtual machines, which is now provided using software, can now be managed by the virtualization administrators and even the virtualization tenants instead of having to involve the networking team, who can focus on the physical network infrastructure.

## Implementing Network Virtualization

In many areas of this book I talk about natively performing configurations using Hyper-V capabilities and also how to perform them with SCVMM. For network virtualization, I will only show how by using SCVMM. Hopefully I've already made it clear that trying to implement network virtualization manually using PowerShell may work if you use complex PowerShell for a couple of hosts where you don't move virtual machines, but in any real world or even a lab environment, you have to use a management solution, which in this case is SCVMM. A key point is to make sure any virtual machine migrations are performed using SCVMM, which enables policies to be updated instantly. If a migration was performed using Hyper-V Manager or any non-SCVMM method, it will take time for SCVMM to notice that the virtual machine has moved and update policies accordingly, which will mean that routing of network virtualization traffic would be affected adversely until SCVMM detected the virtual machine move.

Virtual networks can be created only on logical networks that were enabled for network virtualization, and as long as you select a virtualization-enabled logical network, the process to create a virtual network with SCVMM is simple:

1. Open Virtual Machine Manager.

2. Open the VMs and Services workspace (not Fabric, because this is now a construct directly related to virtual machines).

3. Select the VM Networks navigation node.

4. Click the Create VM Network button.

5. Enter a name and a description for the VM network, select the logical network that was enabled for network virtualization, and click Next.

6. Select Isolate Using Hyper-V Network Virtualization and by default IPv4 will be used for the VM and logical networks. Click Next.

7. You will now create VM subnets, which are the IP addresses used within the virtual networks. Click the Add button and then enter a name and subnet in the CIDR syntax: <IP subnet>/<number of bits to use for subnet mask>, as shown in Figure 3.29. Click Next.

8. If gateways are configured in SCVMM, a gateway can be selected, but for now click Next because none are available.

9. Click Finish to create the new VM network and VM subnets.

Once the VM network is created, you must create IP pools for each of the VM subnets that were defined. Right-click the VM network and select Create IP Pool; then follow the same process you used to create IP pools for a logical network site, but select a VM subnet instead of a logical network site. Make sure an IP pool is created for every VM subnet because these IP pools are used for the IP address assignment for virtual machines connected to the virtual network.

**FIGURE 3.29**
Creating a VM subnet within a new VM network

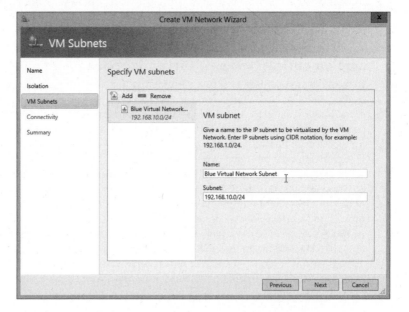

The next step is to actually connect virtual machines to a VM network, and this is done through the properties of a virtual machine, by selecting the Hardware Configuration tab. Select the network adapter to be connected, select the Connected To A VM Network button. Click the Browse button to select the specific VM network (for example, Blue Virtual Network), and then select the VM subnet, as shown in Figure 3.30. Click OK to make the change take effect.

At this point network virtualization is configured and being used. If the ping firewall exception is enabled within the virtual machines (the firewall exception is File And Printer Sharing [Echo Request - ICMPv4-IN]), then virtual machines within the same VM network will be able to ping each other and communicate using whatever protocols have been enabled. Different virtual networks will not be able to communicate, nor can the virtual networks communicate with anything outside of their own virtual network.

**FIGURE 3.30**
Connecting a virtual machine network adapter to a VM network

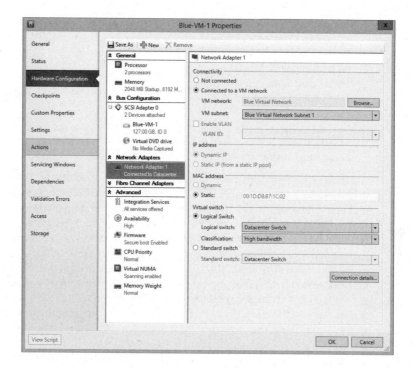

## Useful Network Virtualization Commands

If you're like me, you'll agree that it's great that SCVMM has really made network virtualization simple and it all just works, but when it comes to troubleshooting and just understanding technologies a little better, it's good to "peek behind the curtain" at what is actually happening on the Hyper-V hosts that are hosting virtual machines that are part of virtual networks, which is what I want to do in this part of the book.

Remember that as part of the logical network configuration for the network that is network virtualization enabled, an IP pool that would be used for the provider address space was created. When a Hyper-V host starts hosting virtual machines that are part of a virtualized network, it has an additional IP address in the provider space for each virtual network that is used by virtual machines that it hosts. You may expect to see these additional IP addresses when running ipconfig (or in PowerShell, Get-NetIPAdress). However, the PA IP addresses will not be shown. Instead, to see the IP addresses for a Hyper-V host from the PA, you must run the PowerShell command Get-NetVirtualizationProviderAddress. Here is the output shown on a host that is hosting virtual machines on two different virtual networks:

```
PS C:\Users\administrator.SAVILLTECH> Get-NetVirtualizationProviderAddress

ProviderAddress  : 172.1.1.6
InterfaceIndex   : 44
PrefixLength     : 0
VlanID           : 173
AddressState     : Preferred
```

```
MACAddress        : 001dd8b71c08
ManagedByCluster  : False

ProviderAddress   : 172.1.1.3
InterfaceIndex    : 44
PrefixLength      : 0
VlanID            : 173
AddressState      : Preferred
MACAddress        : 001dd8b71c03
ManagedByCluster  : False
```

I previously mentioned the lookup table, or routing table, that is used by the Hyper-V hosts to know which Hyper-V host should be communicated with when a virtual machine on a virtual network needs to talk to another virtual machine with a specific CA IP address on the same virtual network. This routing table is maintained by SCVMM and is populated to the Hyper-V hosts, and only the relevant records for a specific host are populated. For example, if two virtual networks exist, blue and red, and one host only hosts virtual machines connected to the blue virtual network, then none of the policies (routing records) related to the red virtual network would be populated on the host. To look at the lookup records for a host, use the Get-NetVirtualizationLookupRecord command, which will show the customer address (the IP address within the VM), the virtual subnet ID (the virtual subnet), and then the actual provider address (plus details such as the VM name). The following is the content of my environment that hosts four virtual machines that are connected to three different virtual subnets within two virtual networks. I've selected to show only certain fields in the output for readability:

```
PS C:\> Get-NetVirtualizationLookupRecord | Sort-Object VMName | Format-Table Customer
Address,VirtualSubnetID,ProviderAddress,VMName -AutoSize

CustomerAddress VirtualSubnetID ProviderAddress VMName
--------------- --------------- --------------- ------
192.168.10.4           6864375 172.1.1.3       Blue-VM-1
192.168.10.5           6864375 172.1.1.4       Blue-VM-2
192.168.11.2           6836310 172.1.1.3       Blue-VM-3
192.0.2.253           16200119 172.1.1.6       DHCPExt.sys
192.0.2.253            6864375 172.1.1.3       DHCPExt.sys
192.0.2.253            6836310 172.1.1.3       DHCPExt.sys
192.168.10.1          16200119 1.1.1.1         GW
192.168.11.1           6836310 1.1.1.1         GW
192.168.10.1           6864375 1.1.1.1         GW
192.168.10.2          16200119 172.1.1.6       Red-VM-1
```

As can be seen, there are the records you would expect for each of the virtual machines, and notice that the provider address is the same for Blue-VM-1 and Blue-VM-3, because both are running on the same Hyper-V host. Additionally, for each virtual subnet there is a GW (gateway) entry, which is facilitated by the Hyper-V virtual switch to send traffic between virtual subnets (that are part of the same virtual network) and also an entry for the SCVMM DHCP virtual switch extension. If I run the same command on my other Hyper-V host, which hosts only a single VM that is connected to the blue virtual network, I see a simpler lookup table, as shown in the following output. It does not see records for the red virtual network because it does not need to know. That's because it hosts no VMs connected to the red virtual network, and it has only a single GW and DHCP virtual switch extension because it only hosts a VM connected to a single virtual subnet.

```
PS C:\> Get-NetVirtualizationLookupRecord | Sort-Object VMName | `
Format-Table CustomerAddress,VirtualSubnetID,ProviderAddress,VMName -AutoSize

CustomerAddress VirtualSubnetID ProviderAddress VMName
--------------- --------------- --------------- ------
192.168.10.4            6864375 172.1.1.3       Blue-VM-1
192.168.10.5            6864375 172.1.1.4       Blue-VM-2
192.168.11.2            6836310 172.1.1.3       Blue-VM-3
192.0.2.253             6864375 172.1.1.4       DHCPExt.sys
192.168.10.1            6864375 1.1.1.1         GW
```

To make this easier to understand, I created a picture to show the actual virtual machines and hosts that are being examined with these commands, which can be seen in Figure 3.31. Hopefully this will help make the output from the above commands clearer.

**FIGURE 3.31**

Hyper-V configuration for my basic lab environment

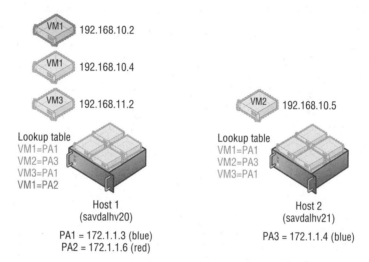

To view all the virtual subnets and the virtual network (routing domain) they are part of, a great command is Get-NetVirtualizationCustomerRoute, which shows the details. Note in the following output that we don't see *red* or *blue* in these names because they are names that SCVMM is managing. Hyper-V just sees GUIDs for the routing domains (the virtual networks) and the virtual subnet IDs.

```
PS C:\> Get-NetVirtualizationCustomerRoute


RoutingDomainID   : {3B10FAC6-5593-477B-A31E-632E0E8C3B5E}
VirtualSubnetID   : 16200119
DestinationPrefix : 192.168.10.0/24
NextHop           : 0.0.0.0
```

```
Metric              : 0

RoutingDomainID     : {0CF58B26-4E00-4007-9CD0-C7847D965BC9}
VirtualSubnetID     : 6836310
DestinationPrefix   : 192.168.11.0/24
NextHop             : 0.0.0.0
Metric              : 0

RoutingDomainID     : {0CF58B26-4E00-4007-9CD0-C7847D965BC9}
VirtualSubnetID     : 6864375
DestinationPrefix   : 192.168.10.0/24
NextHop             : 0.0.0.0
Metric              : 0
```

Notice that the two last virtual subnets have the same outing domain ID; this is because they are within the same virtual network (blue).

It's very common when troubleshooting to just want to test connectivity, and commonly the ping command is used. However, this won't actually work for provider addresses. The secret is to use the new -p switch, which tells ping to use the provider address instead of regular addresses:

```
C:\>ping -p 172.1.1.4

Pinging 172.1.1.4 with 32 bytes of data:
Reply from 172.1.1.4: bytes=32 time=1ms TTL=128
Reply from 172.1.1.4: bytes=32 time=1ms TTL=128
Reply from 172.1.1.4: bytes=32 time<1ms TTL=128
Reply from 172.1.1.4: bytes=32 time<1ms TTL=128

Ping statistics for 172.1.1.4:
    Packets: Sent = 4, Received = 4, Lost = 0 (0% loss),
Approximate round trip times in milli-seconds:
    Minimum = 0ms, Maximum = 1ms, Average = 0ms
```

It's also possible to use the new Test-VMNetworkAdapter cmdlet to actually ping CA addresses for a virtual machine from the Hyper-V host to ensure connectivity to the actual CA space. To use Test-VMNetworkAdapter, you need to know the MAC address of the next "hop" in communication between the source CA and destination CA address, which can be found using the Select-NetVirtualizationNextHop cmdlet as in the following example:

```
PS C:\> Select-NetVirtualizationNextHop -SourceCustomerAddress 192.168.10.4 `
-DestinationCustomerAddress 192.168.11.2 -SourceVirtualSubnetID 6864375


SourceCustomerAddress        : 192.168.10.4
DestinationCustomerAddress   : 192.168.11.2
SourceVirtualSubnetID        : 6864375
NextHopAddress               : 192.168.10.1
SourceMACAddress             : 001dd8b71c02
NextHopMACAddress            : 00508c125f46
```

Note that because these virtual machines are in different virtual subnets, the next hop is actually the gateway. If they were on the same virtual subnet, there would be no next-hop address and the next-hop MAC would be the target virtual machine network adapter, as shown in the following output.

```
PS C:\> Select-NetVirtualizationNextHop -SourceCustomerAddress 192.168.10.4 `
-DestinationCustomerAddress 192.168.10.5 -SourceVirtualSubnetID 6864375


SourceCustomerAddress       : 192.168.10.4
DestinationCustomerAddress  : 192.168.10.5
SourceVirtualSubnetID       : 6864375
NextHopAddress              : 0.0.0.0
SourceMACAddress            : 001dd8b71c02
NextHopMACAddress           : 001dd8b71c04
```

Once the MAC address of the next hop is known, the `Test-VMNetworkAdapter` cmdlet can be used to populate the required details, such as the source VM name and the MAC address for the next hop. Ensure that the virtual machine name specified is the source virtual machine name, and if the virtual machine had multiple network adapters, you need to pass the specific virtual network adapter to use. The way `Test-VMNetworkAdapter` works is to actually hook directly into the virtual switch, inject the ICMP packet to the destination, and then capture the return pack and return the result. The benefit of this command is that you can use it where you cannot just perform a ping from within the virtual machines, such as if you are an administrator at a service provider and the tenants using the virtual networks do not give you logon privileges. With the `Test-VMNetworkAdapter` cmdlet, you can test the communication between virtual machines in a virtual network without having to actually log on to them.

```
PS C:\> Test-VMNetworkAdapter -Sender -SenderIPAddress 192.168.10.4 `
-ReceiverIPAddress 192.168.11.2 -VMName "Blue-VM-1" `
-NextHopMacAddress "00508c125f46" -SequenceNumber 100
RoundTripTime : 2 milliseconds
```

Windows 2012 R2 introduces support for dynamic learning of IP addresses used in the CA space. This is useful if you're using DHCP within a CA space or running clusters within the CA space, which will have cluster IP addresses that will need to move between virtual machines. I do want to point out that SCVMM by default will intercept any DHCP requests via its DHCP virtual switch extension and allocate IP addresses from its IP pools. If this was disabled, though, it would then be possible to run DHCP servers within a CA space. I mention this here because if you wish to use this dynamic learning, then the configuration is performed using PowerShell. The following commands create a Layer 2 Only type lookup record, which means it's a dynamic learning record. Notice that I specify the MAC address of the virtual machine's network adapter. Now when the VM uses DHCP and gets an IP address, the routing table will be dynamically updated with this learned IP address.

```
$ProviderAddressHost="172.1.1.3"
$vsid = 6864375
$DHCPClientMAC = "020203030404"
New-NetVirtualizationLookupRecord -CustomerAddress 0.0.0.0 `
```

```
-VirtualSubnetID $vsid -MACAddress $DHCPClientMAC `
-ProviderAddress $ProviderAddressHost -Type L2Only `
-Rule TranslationMethodEncap
```

I've shown you the manual way of enabling a DHCP client using PowerShell on the Hyper-V host. Remember though, when using SCVMM, you need to not perform configurations directly on the Hyper-V hosts, especially configurations related to network virtualization, because the changes will not be known by SCVMM and therefore will get lost. To enable the guest learning IP address capability, you use the "Allow guest specified IP addresses (only available for virtual machines on Windows Server 2012 R2)" security setting for the virtual port profile used. This is configured by default in the Guest Dynamic IP inbox virtual port profile.

## Network Virtualization Gateway

While the isolation provided by virtual networks is a powerful feature and provides islands of communication, there will be times you want communication outside of a virtual network. To enable virtual machines in a virtual network to communicate outside of their network -virtualization-provided network, you must use a Network Virtualization Gateway, or NV Gateway. This is different from the gateway functionality that is provided by the Hyper-V network virtualization filter running in the Hyper-V switch, which routes traffic between virtual subnets in the same virtual network. The functionality I am referring to now is related to communication between different virtual networks and to other networks such as the Internet, a corporate network, or even another location. If you have a virtual network that wants to talk to the outside world, then it needs to use a NV Gateway. In the future, I think physical switches will start to support certain NV Gateway features such as switching and forwarding, but today a separate NV Gateway is required.

In Windows Server 2012 Hyper-V, this was a problem because no NV Gateway was provided and instead it was necessary to use a third-party NV Gateway solution. In Windows Server 2012 R2, you can still use a third-party NV Gateway, but one is also now provided in-box, the Hyper-V Network Virtualization Gateway, commonly known as HNV Gateway.

There are three types of gateway functionality provided by the HNV Gateway, and the one you will use depends on your requirements and configuration:

**Forwarding Gateway** This can be used if the IP scheme used in the virtual network is essentially an extension of your existing IP scheme and would be routable on the network. The gateway simply forwards packets between the physical network fabric and the virtual network. A HNV Gateway in forwarding mode only supports a single virtual network. This means if you need forwarding for 10 virtual networks, you need 10 separate HNV Gateways.

**NAT Gateway** If the IP schemes used in the virtual networks would not be routable on the physical fabric and/or have overlapping IP schemes between virtual networks, then Network Address Translation (NAT) must be used between the virtual network and the physical fabric. An HNV Gateway in NAT can support up to 50 virtual networks.

**Site-to-Site (S2S) Gateway** An S2S gateway provides a connection from a virtual network to another network using a VPN connection. In most enterprise environments, there is already IP connectivity between locations, so this would not be required. However, consider a hoster scenario where a tenant wants to talk to their on-premises network. The HNV Gateway S2S could be used to connect the tenant's virtual network to their physical network. A single gateway can support 200 VPN tunnels.

A single virtual network can have multiple S2S connections, providing redundancy of connectivity failure. If I wanted to connect an on-premises virtual network and a Windows Azure virtual network, I would also use the S2S Gateway option.

Also remember that SCVMM is key to the control and management plane. If different SCVMM instances are used for different locations, then you will require a gateway to connect the virtual networks together because they will not share policies and will have separate routing tables. S2S uses the RRAS functionality of Windows Server 2012 R2. The other types of gateways do not leverage RRAS.

### DEPLOYING A HNV GATEWAY

The HNV Gateway is a virtual machine (it cannot be a physical host) running on a Windows Server 2012 R2 Hyper-V host, but there is a caveat. The Hyper-V host running the HNV Gateway *cannot* host any virtual machines that are members of a virtual network. Essentially, you need a dedicated Hyper-V host that will not participate in network virtualization except for the purposes of the HNV Gateway virtual machines that will be deployed.

The virtual machines that act as HNV Gateways will have a number of virtual network adapters connected to different networks:

◆ Connection to the network that needs to be connected from the virtual networks (for example, connection to the corporate network or the Internet network)

◆ Connection to the virtual network(s)

◆ (Optional) Separate management network connection

◆ (Optional) Cluster networks if highly available

Note that when a HNV Gateway is enabling connectivity for multiple virtual networks such as with NAT or S2S, then each virtual network is implemented using a separate networking *TCP compartment*, which is a new Windows Server 2012 R2 concept and enables the different network connectivities to be isolated from other network connectivities.

The first step is to specify that the Hyper-V host that will host the HNV Gateway virtual machines should not be used for normal network virtualization.

1. In Virtual Machine Manager, select the Fabric workspace.

2. Under Servers, expand the All Hosts host group, right-click on the Hyper-V host that will host the gateways, and select Properties.

3. Select the Host Access tab.

4. Check the box labeled "This host is a dedicated network virtualization gateway, as a result it is not available for placement of virtual machines requiring network virtualization" and click OK, as shown in Figure 3.32.

**FIGURE 3.32**
Enabling a host for
HNV Gateway use only

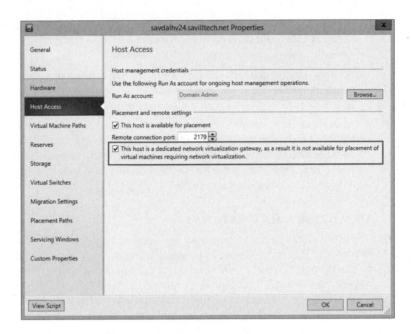

The next step is to actually deploy the gateway virtual machine. This will vary depending on the network being connected to; for example, high availability may be required, or you may need a separate management network. There is a great document available from

www.microsoft.com/en-us/download/details.aspx?id=39284

It covers every scenario, so I recommend downloading it and reading it. It walks you through setting up HNV Gateway for S2S, NAT, and Forwarding. It also covers creating a specific VM template and a service template to quickly deploy new gateways. This is important if you are hosting tenants and want to provide them with the ability to deploy their own gateways to connect their virtual networks to on-premises or even the Internet, they need a simple way which is provided by using service templates. Microsoft has a service template available for both standalone and highly available gateway deployments that simplifies the work. They are available from the Web Platform Installer (PI) feed in SCVMM. I highly recommend using the service templates because they automate all of the various configurations required.

For now, I will walk through a very basic setup with a gateway virtual machine with two network connections: one to the lab network to which I want to enable connectivity from the virtual networks and one that will eventually connect to the logical network that is used for network virtualization but initially must be configured as "Not connected."

1. Deploy a Windows 2012 R2 virtual machine and make sure it has two network adapters, one not connected to any network and the other connected to the network that is the target network for connectivity from the virtual networks configured with static IP from the

IP pool. Ensure that the VM is deployed to a Hyper-V host that has been configured to be used for network virtualization gateways.

2. Within the virtual machine you created, make sure the firewall is disabled for all profiles. This can be done through the Windows Firewall with Advanced Security application or with the following command:

```
Set-NetFirewallProfile -Profile Domain,Public,Private -Enabled False
```

3. The Routing and DirectAccess and VPN role services of Remote Access must be installed in the VM along with the Remote Access module for the Windows PowerShell feature. This can be done using Server Manager or using the following PowerShell command:

```
Install-WindowsFeature RSAT-RemoteAccess-PowerShell, DirectAccess-VPN, Routing
```

4. Once the virtual machine is deployed, open its properties page, select the Hardware Configuration tab, and navigate to the second network adapter that was not connected. Select the Connected To A VM Network option and click Browse. In the Select A VM Network window, click the Clear Selection button and then click OK. This allows the option to select a standard switch, which should be the switch that exists on the host. It is not connecting via a VM network, though, which is a key detail, as shown in Figure 3.33. Click OK. Once the change has taken effect, start the virtual machine.

**FIGURE 3.33**

Properties for the network adapter used to connect to the virtual networks

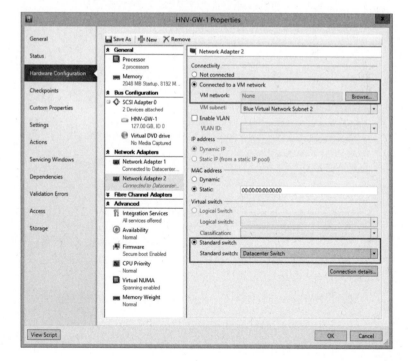

5. The next step is to configure the virtual machine as a gateway to SCVMM. Open the Fabric workspace and expand Networking ➢ Network Service. Right-click Network Service and select the Add Network Service action.

6. The Add Network Service Wizard will launch and ask for a name and description of the new service. I typically use the name of the gateway VM as the name for the service. Click Next.

7. Select Microsoft as the manufacturer and set the Model to Microsoft Windows Server Gateway. Click Next.

8. Select a Run As account that has local administrator privileges on the virtual machine and then click Next.

9. The connection string for the gateway needs to be configured. It is made up of the Hyper-V host hosting the virtual machine and the virtual machine's name; for example, in Figure 3.4 it is

   ```
   VMHost=savdalhv24.savilltech.net;GatewayVM=HNV-GW-1
   ```

   Click Next.

**FIGURE 3.34**
Configuring the connection string. Notice that a number of examples are shown on the dialog.

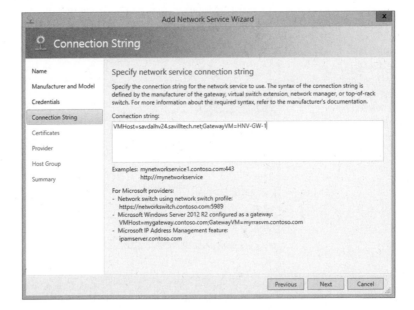

10. A certificates screen appears. It is not used for this configuration, so just click Next.

11. The connection to the virtual machine can be tested using the Test button. It's important that Test Open Connection, Test Capability Discovery, and Test System Info all show Passed. Click Next.

12. Next, specify the host group where the HNV gateway can be used. For example, I would specify my Dallas host group. Click Next.

**13.** Click Finish to go ahead and configure the gateway for virtualization.

**14.** Once the configuration is complete, right-click the new network service and select Properties. Then select the Connectivity tab.

**15.** You need to tell SCVMM which of the adapters in the VM is the backend connection (i.e., connects to the network virtualizations side and is the adapter we directly connected to the switch) and which is the front-end connection (i.e., connects to the target external network such as the Internet or corporate). It's very important that you get this right. In my gateway, I renamed the NICs to make it simpler, and the Microsoft service template actually does this for you automatically as well! You can see in Figure 3.35 that I made my selections.

Click OK and changes will be made to the gateway virtual machine. This may take a few minutes. Monitor the Jobs workspace to confirm when the gateway configuration has completed.

**FIGURE 3.35**
Configuring the new gateway network service

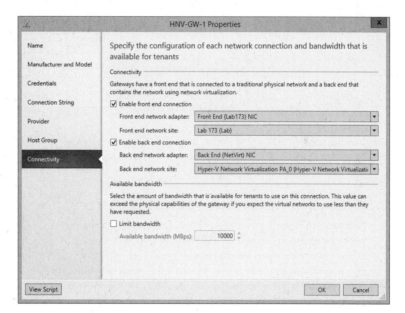

**16.** The final step is to configure a virtual network to use the new gateway service you created to enable connectivity beyond the virtual network. Open the virtual network via the VMs And Services workspace ➤ VM Networks. Select the Connectivity tab. It's now possible to select to enable additional types of connectivity using your new gateway for the various types of routing. As shown in Figure 3.36, I am using the gateway for NAT connectivity for this virtual network because its IP scheme is not routable on the network being connected to.

**FIGURE 3.36**
Configuring the
new gateway net-
work service

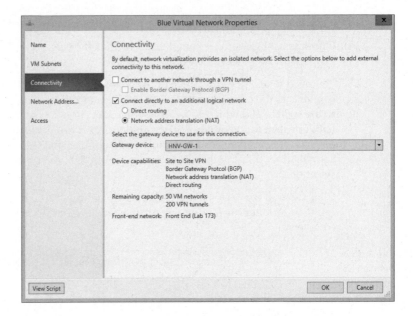

Within my virtual network I can now communicate with the external network. Providing I have DNS configured on the virtual machines in the virtual network, I can now access external resources.

That took quite a lot of steps. It would be simpler if you use the service templates provided by Microsoft, but it's good to know how to perform these steps manually, especially if you have to perform any troubleshooting.

## BEHIND THE CURTAIN OF THE HNV GATEWAY

Previously I talked about the TCP compartments that are used within the HNV Gateway to enable multiple tenants (virtual networks) to be serviced using a single HNV Gateway instance. During the whole process of creating the HNV Gateway, it was never required to perform any routing configurations on the actual virtual machine, but behind the scenes SCVMM was remotely configuring services and the TCP compartments required for the different types of gateways required. Figure 3.37 shows an example of the TCP compartments in my lab environment with the red and blue virtual networks for NAT gateway functionality. As can be seen, there is a default compartment for the operating system, which is also where NAT functionality is performed, and then there is a separate TCP compartment for each of the virtual networks that contains an interface for the virtual network to which it belongs.

**FIGURE 3.37**
Overview of TCP
compartments
used in the HNV
Gateway

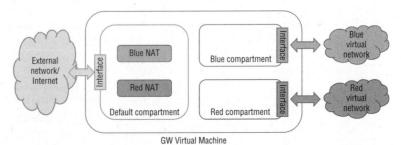

If you log on to the HNV Gateway virtual machine, you can use PowerShell commands to inspect the TCP compartments. To see all compartments, use the Get-NetCompartment command as shown here:

```
PS C:\> Get-NetCompartment


CompartmentId        : 1
CompartmentDescription : Default Compartment
CompartmentGuid      : {b1062982-2b18-4b4f-b3d5-a78ddb9cdd49}


CompartmentId        : 2
CompartmentDescription : Blue Virtual Network0cf58b26-4e00-4007-9cd0-c7847d965bc9
CompartmentGuid      : {0cf58b26-4e00-4007-9cd0-c7847d965bc9}


CompartmentId        : 3
CompartmentDescription : Red Virtual Network3b10fac6-5593-477b-a31e-632e0e8c3b5e
CompartmentGuid      : {3b10fac6-5593-477b-a31e-632e0e8c3b5e}
```

This shows my three compartments as previously mentioned. It is then possible to look at the actual interfaces configured in each compartment. The following output shows the interfaces for the blue compartment. Note that you should not have to ever look at this. SCVMM is doing all the work for you, but if you were not using SCVMM, you would need to manually create the compartments, perform the configuration, and so on.

```
PS C:\> Get-NetIPInterface -IncludeAllCompartments -CompartmentId 2


ifIndex InterfaceAlias            AddressFamily NlMtu(Bytes) InterfaceMetric
Dhcp      ConnectionState PolicyStore


------- --------------            ------------- ------------ ----------------
--------------- ---------
31      WNVAdap_6865744           IPv6          1458         5
Disabled Connected       Active...
30      Loopback Pseudo-Interface 2 IPv6        4294967295   50
Disabled Connected       Active...
31      WNVAdap_6865744           IPv4          1458         5
Disabled Connected       Active...
30      Loopback Pseudo-Interface 2 IPv4        4294967295   50
Disabled Connected       Active...
```

## Summary

There are some workloads that do not work with network virtualization today. PXE boot, which enables booting an operating system over the network, will not function. DHCP is supported in Windows Server 2012 R2 Hyper-V as previously mentioned, but SCVMM has its own switch extension to intercept DHCP to allocate from IP pools, so normal DHCP in a VM would not work when you're managing your network with SCVMM. The SCVMM load balancer configuration capability as part of a service deployment does not work when using network virtualization; the load balancer would have to be configured "out-of-band."

To summarize, you can use the following types of isolation methods in your Hyper-V environment:

**Physical**   Use separate physical network switches and adapters to provide isolation between networks. Not scalable and costly and complex.

**External**   Using virtual switch extensions, specifically the forwarding extension such as Cisco Nexus 1000V or NEC OpenFlow, can provide isolation in the switch using native technologies. This is, however, fairly opaque to SCVMM.

**VLAN**   Layer 2 technology provides isolation and broadcast boundary on a shared network, but the number of VLANs is limited and can become complex to manage. Does not allow IP address overlap between VLANs, nor does it allow flexibility for business units/tenants to bring their own IP scheme to the environment.

**PVLAN**   Utilizes a pair of VLANs to provide an isolated network in different modes, but most commonly allows many virtual machines to communicate with a common set of resources/Internet while being completely isolated from each other.

**Network Virtualization**   Abstraction of the virtual machine network from the physical network fabric provides maximum capability without the limitations and complexity of other technologies. Allows users of network virtualization to bring their own IP scheme and even IP overlap between different virtual networks. Network Virtualization gateways allow virtual networks to communicate with external networks.

Where possible, utilize network virtualization for its flexibility and relative ease of configuration. However, for some types of network, such as management networks, it will still be common to use more traditional isolation methods such as VLAN technologies.

# VMQ, RSS, and SR-IOV

So far we have covered a lot of technologies related to network connectivity. However, in the following sections, I want to cover a few technologies that can help with the performance of network communications. Although it can introduce some challenges when trying to maximize its utilization and gain the highest levels of performance and bandwidth, 10 Gbps and beyond is becoming more common in many datacenters.

SR-IOV and Dynamic Virtual Machine Queue (DVMQ) are two popular networking technologies that can help with network performance and also can minimize overhead for the hypervisor. These technologies are shown in Figure 3.38.

## SR-IOV

Single root I/O virtualization (SR-IOV) allows a single PCI Express network device to represent itself as multiple separate devices directly to virtual machines. In the case of SR-IOV and virtual machines, this means a physical NIC can actually present multiple virtual NICs, which in SR-IOV terms are called virtual functions (VFs). Each VF is of the same type as the physical card and is presented directly to specific virtual machines. The communication between the virtual machine and the VF is now completely bypassing the Hyper-V switch because the VM uses Direct Memory Access (DMA) to communicate with the VF. This makes for very fast and very low-latency communication between the VM and the VF because both the VMBus and the Hyper-V switch are no longer involved in the network flow from the physical NIC to the VM. Because the Hyper-V switch is bypassed when SR-IOV is used, SR-IOV is disallowed if any ACL checking, QoS, DHCP Guard, third-party extensions, Network Virtualization, or any other switch features are in use. SR-IOV use is permitted only when no switches' features are active.

**FIGURE 3.38**
Understanding the VMQ and SR-IOV network technologies compared to regular networking

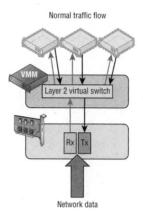

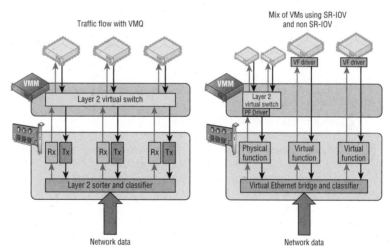

SR-IOV does not break Live Migration, a technology not covered yet, but allows virtual machines to move between hosts with no downtime, even when you're moving a virtual machine to a host that does not support SR-IOV. Behind the scenes when SR-IOV is used, the Network Virtualization Service Client (NetVSC) actually creates two paths for the virtual machine network adapter inside the VM. One path is via SR-IOV and one is using the traditional VMBus path, which uses the Hyper-V switch. When the VM is running on a host with SR-IOV, the SR-IOV path is used and the VMBus is used only for control traffic, but if the VM is moved to a host without SR-IOV, then the SR-IOV path is closed by NetVSC and the VMBus path is used for data and control traffic; this is all transparent to the virtual machine. It means you don't lose any mobility even when using SR-IOV. To use SR-IOV, both the network adapter and the motherboard must support it. To use SR-IOV with a virtual switch, the option to use SR-IOV must be selected at the time of the virtual switch creation as shown in Figure 3.39. If you're using the New-VMSwitch cmdlet to create the virtual switch, use the -EnableIov $True parameter to enable SR-IOV. On the Hardware Acceleration property tab of the virtual network adapter for a virtual machine that needs to use SR-IOV, ensure that the Enable SR-IOV check box is selected.

**FIGURE 3.39**
Enabling SR-IOV on a virtual switch at creation time

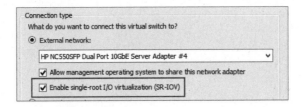

To check your server for SR-IOV support, there are a number of commands you can run. To start with, run PowerShell command Get-VMSwitch | Format-List *iov* as shown here. Note that this example shows that the network adapter supports SR-IOV, but it is not supported because of limitations on the server motherboard and BIOS.

```
PS C:\> Get-VMSwitch | Format-List *iov*


IovEnabled               : True
IovVirtualFunctionCount  : 0
IovVirtualFunctionsInUse : 0
IovQueuePairCount        : 0
IovQueuePairsInUse       : 0
IovSupport               : False
IovSupportReasons        : {To use SR-IOV on this system, the system BIOS
must be updated to allow Windows to control
PCI Express. Contact your system manufacturer for an update., This system has a
security
vulnerability in the system I/O remapping hardware. As a precaution, the ability
to use
SR-IOV has been disabled. You should contact your system manufacturer for an
updated BIOS
which enables Root Port Alternate Error Delivery mechanism. If all Virtual
Machines
intended to use SR-IOV run trusted workloads, SR-IOV may be enabled by adding a
registry
key of type DWORD with value 1 named IOVEnableOverride under
HKEY_LOCAL_MACHINE\SOFTWARE\Microsoft\Windows NT\CurrentVersion\Virtualization
and changing
state of the trusted virtual machines. If the system exhibits reduced performance
or
instability after SR-IOV devices are assigned to Virtual Machines, consider
disabling the
use of SR-IOV.}
```

The following output is from another system that has one adapter that does not support SR-IOV and additional adapters that do support it:

```
PS C:\> Get-VMSwitch | Format-List *iov*


IovEnabled                : False
IovVirtualFunctionCount   : 0
IovVirtualFunctionsInUse  : 0
IovQueuePairCount         : 0
IovQueuePairsInUse        : 0
IovSupport                : False
IovSupportReasons         : {This network adapter does not support SR-IOV.}

IovEnabled                : True
IovVirtualFunctionCount   : 62
IovVirtualFunctionsInUse  : 10
IovQueuePairCount         : 63
IovQueuePairsInUse        : 10
IovSupport                : True
IovSupportReasons         : {OK}

IovEnabled                : True
IovVirtualFunctionCount   : 6
IovVirtualFunctionsInUse  : 2
IovQueuePairCount         : 7
IovQueuePairsInUse        : 2
IovSupport                : True
IovSupportReasons         : {OK}
```

It's also possible to run the PowerShell command Get-NetAdapterSriov to get SR-IOV support adapter information on a system; it also shows the number of virtual functions (VFs) supported by the card. If a virtual machine is using SR-IOV successfully, then when you look at the Networking tab of the virtual machine in Hyper-V Manager, that status will show "OK (SR-IOV active)."

```
PS C:\> Get-NetAdapterSriov


Name                 : Ethernet 3
InterfaceDescription : Intel(R) Gigabit ET2 Quad Port Server Adapter #2
Enabled              : True
SriovSupport         : Supported
SwitchName           : DefaultSwitchName
NumVFs               : 6

Name                 : Ethernet 6
InterfaceDescription : Intel(R) Gigabit ET2 Quad Port Server Adapter #4
Enabled              : True
SriovSupport         : Supported
```

```
SwitchName            : DefaultSwitchName
NumVFs                : 6
```

The reality right now is that not many systems are SR-IOV capable and SR-IOV would be used in targeted scenarios because in most situations, the standard Hyper-V network capabilities via the virtual switch will suffice for even the most demanding workloads. SR-IOV is targeted at those very few highest networking throughput needs. The other common place where SR-IOV implementations can be found is in "cloud in a box" type solutions where a single vendor supplies the servers, the network, and the storage. The one I have seen commonly is the Cisco UCS solution that leverages SR-IOV heavily because many network capabilities are actually implemented using Cisco's own technology, VM-FEX. An amazing multipart blog is available from Microsoft on SR-IOV; it will tell you everything you could ever want to know.

```
http://blogs.technet.com/b/jhoward/archive/2012/03/12/everything-you-wanted-to-
know-about-sr-iov-in-hyper-v-part-1.aspx
```

## DVMQ

A technology that's similar to SR–IOV is Dynamic Virtual Machine Queue (DVMQ). VMQ, which was introduced in Windows Server 2008 R2, allows separate queues to exist on the network adapter, with each queue being mapped to a specific virtual machine. This removes some of the switching work on the Hyper-V switch because if the data is in this queue, the switch knows it is meant for a specific virtual machine. The bigger benefit is because there are now separate queues from the network adapter, that queue can be processed by a different processor core. Typically, all the traffic from a network adapter is processed by a single processor core to ensure that packets are not processed out of sequence. For a 1Gbps network adapter, this may be fine, but a single core could not keep up with a loaded 10 Gbps network connection caused by multiple virtual machines. With VMQ enabled, specific virtual machines allocate their own VMQ on the network adapter, which allows different processor cores in the Hyper-V host to process the traffic, leading to greater throughput. (However, each virtual machine would still be limited to a specific core, leading to a bandwidth cap of around 3 to 4 Gbps, but this is better than the combined traffic of all VMs being limited to 3 to 4 Gbps.)

The difference between VMQ and SR-IOV is that the traffic still passes through the Hyper-V switch with VMQ because all VMQ presents are different queues of traffic and not entire virtual devices. In Windows Server 2008 R2, the assignment of a VMQ to a virtual machine was static; typically first come, first served because each NIC supports a certain number of VMQs and each VMQ was assigned (affinitized) in a round-robin-type manner to the logical processors available to the host, and this would never change. The assignment of VMQs is still on a first come, first served basis in Windows Server 2012, but the allocation of processor cores is now dynamic and fluid. This allows the queues to be moved between logical processors based on load. By default, all queues start on the same logical processor, the home processor, but as the load builds on a queue, Hyper-V can move the individual queues to a different logical processor to more efficiently handle the load. As the load drops, the queues can be coalesced back to a smaller number of cores and potentially all back to the home processor.

Many modern network cards support VMQ, and this is easy to check using the PowerShell `Get-NetAdapterVmq` command. In the following example, I can see that VMQ is enabled on two of my network adapters because they are currently connected to a Hyper-V virtual switch. If network adapters are not connected to a virtual switch, their VMQ capabilities will not be shown.

```
PS C:\> Get-NetAdapterVmq |ft Name, InterfaceDescription,Enabled,NumberOfReceive
Queues -AutoSize

Name           InterfaceDescription                 Enabled NumberOfReceiveQueues
----           --------------------                 ------- ---------------------
J_ETH4         Broadcom BCM57800 NetXtreme    ) #132   False                     0
10Gbps NIC2    Broadcom BCM57800 NetXtreme IIt) #130    True                    14
MGMT NIC       Broadcom BCM57800 NetXtreme II) #131    False                     0
10Gbps NIC1    Broadcom BCM57800 NetXtreme Int) #129    True                    14
```

By default, if a virtual network adapter is configured to be VMQ enabled, there is no manual action required, and based on the availability of VMQs, a VMQ may be allocated and used by a virtual machine. Figure 3.40 shows the Hardware Acceleration setting for a virtual network adapter, and also notice in the main Hyper-V Manager window to the left, at the bottom of the screen, it shows that VMQ is actually being used because the Status column is set to OK (VMQ Active). Remember that just because a network adapter is configured to use VMQ does not mean it will be allocated a VMQ. It depends on if one is available on the network adapter when the VM is started.

**FIGURE 3.40**
Ensuring that VMQ is enabled for a virtual machine

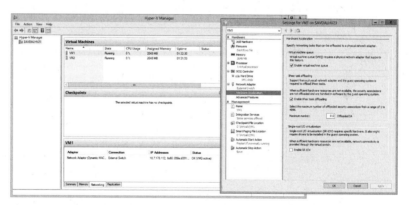

To check which virtual machines are actually using VMQs and also which processor core is currently being used by the queue, you can use the Get-NetAdapterVmqQueue PowerShell command. In the following example, you can see that VM1 and VM2 each have a queue but are running on the home processor, as is the default queue, which is used for traffic that is not handled by a separate VMQ. There is no way to force a virtual machine to always be allocated a VMQ. The only way would be to make sure those virtual machines that you want to have a VMQ are started first when the host is started.

```
PS C:\> Get-NetAdapterVmqQueue
```

```
Name              QueueID MacAddress         VlanID Processor VmFriendlyName
----              ------- ----------         ------ --------- --------------
10Gbps NIC2       0                                 0:0       SAVDALHV23
10Gbps NIC1       0                                 0:0       SAVDALHV23
10Gbps NIC1       1       00-15-5D-AD-17-00         0:0       VM1
10Gbps NIC1       2       00-15-5D-AD-17-01         0:0       VM2
```

You may wonder how VMQ works if you are using NIC Teaming, and the answer is that it actually varies depending on the mode of NIC Teaming. Consider that it's possible to mix network adapters with different capabilities in a NIC team. For example, one NIC supports 8 VMQs and another supports 16 VMQs in a two-NIC team. There are two different numbers that are important:

◆ Min Queues: The lower number of queues supported by an adapter in the team. In my example, 8 would be the Min Queue value.

◆ Sum of Queues: The total number of all queues across all the adapters in the team. In my example, this would be 24.

The deciding factor for how many VMQs are available to a NIC team depends on the teaming mode and the load balancing algorithm used for the team. If the teaming mode is set to switch dependent, then the Min Queues value is always used. If the teaming mode is switch independent and the algorithm is set to Hyper-V Port or Dynamic, then the Sum of Queues value is used; otherwise, Min Queues is used. Table 3.2 shows this in simple form.

**TABLE 3.2:** VMQ NIC Teaming options

|                         | **ADDRESS HASH** | **HYPER-V PORT** | **DYNAMIC**    |
| ----------------------- | ---------------- | ---------------- | -------------- |
| **SWITCH DEPENDENT**    | Min Queues       | Min Queues       | Min Queues     |
| **SWITCH INDEPENDENT**  | Min Queues       | Sum of Queues    | Sum of Queues  |

## RSS and vRSS

I previously talked about a 3 to 4 Gbps bandwidth limit, which was caused by the amount of traffic that could be processed by a single processor core, and even with VMQ, a virtual machine network adapter is still limited to traffic being processed by a single core. Physical servers have a solution to the single-core bottleneck for inbound traffic, Receive Side Scaling, or RSS. RSS must be supported by the physical network adapter, and the technology enables incoming traffic on a single network adapter to be processed by more than a single processor core. This is enabled using the following flow:

1. Incoming packets are run through a 4-tuple hash algorithm that uses the source and destination IP and ports to create a hash value.

2. The hash is passed through an indirection table that places all traffic with the same hash on a specific RSS queue on the network adapter. Note that there are only a small number

of RSS queues. Four is a common number, so a single RSS queue will contain packets from many different hash values, which is the purpose of the indirection table.

**3.** Each RSS queue on the network adapter is processed by a different processor core on the host operating system, distributing the incoming load over multiple cores.

Creating the hash value to control which RSS queue and therefore which processor core is important because problems occur if packets are processed out of order, which could happen if packets were just randomly sent to any core. Creating the hash value based on the source and destination IP addresses and port ensures that specific streams of communication are processed on the same processor core and therefore are processed in order. A common question is, What about hyper-threaded processor cores? RSS does not use hyperthreading and actually skips the "extra" logical processor for each core. This can be seen if the processor array and indirection table is examined for an RSS-capable network adapter, as shown in the following output. Notice that only even number cores are shown; 1, 3, and so on are skipped because this system has hyperthreading enabled and so the hyperthreaded cores are skipped.

```
PS C:\> Get-NetAdapterRss


Name                                      : MGMT NIC
InterfaceDescription                      : Broadcom BCM57800 NetXtreme II 1 GigE (NDIS
VBD Client) #131
Enabled                                   : True
NumberOfReceiveQueues                     : 4
Profile                                   : NUMAStatic
BaseProcessor: [Group:Number]             : 0:0
MaxProcessor: [Group:Number]              : 0:30
MaxProcessors                             : 16
RssProcessorArray: [Group:Number/NUMA Distance] :
0:0/0  0:2/0  0:4/0  0:6/0  0:8/0  0:10/0  0:12/0  0:14/0
0:16/0  0:18/0  0:20/0  0:22/0  0:24/0  0:26/0  0:28/0  0:30/0

IndirectionTable: [Group:Number] :
0:4    0:20    0:6    0:22    0:4    0:20    0:6    0:22
0:4    0:20    0:6    0:22    0:4    0:20    0:6    0:22
0:4    0:20    0:6    0:22    0:4    0:20    0:6    0:22
0:4    0:20    0:6    0:22    0:4    0:20    0:6    0:22
0:4    0:20    0:6    0:22    0:4    0:20    0:6    0:22
0:4    0:20    0:6    0:22    0:4    0:20    0:6    0:22
0:4    0:20    0:6    0:22    0:4    0:20    0:6    0:22
0:4    0:20    0:6    0:22    0:4    0:20    0:6    0:22
0:4    0:20    0:6    0:22    0:4    0:20    0:6    0:22
0:4    0:20    0:6    0:22    0:4    0:20    0:6    0:22
0:4    0:20    0:6    0:22    0:4    0:20    0:6    0:22
0:4    0:20    0:6    0:22    0:4    0:20    0:6    0:22
0:4    0:20    0:6    0:22    0:4    0:20    0:6    0:22
0:4    0:20    0:6    0:22    0:4    0:20    0:6    0:22
0:4    0:20    0:6    0:22    0:4    0:20    0:6    0:22
0:4    0:20    0:6    0:22    0:4    0:20    0:6    0:22
```

It's possible to configure the actual processor cores to be used for an RSS adapter by modifying the BaseProcessorNumber, MaxProcessorNumber, and MaxProcessors values using the Set-NetAdapterRss PowerShell cmdlet. This gives the administrator more granular control of the processor resources used to process network traffic. It's also possible to enable and disable RSS for specific network adapters using Enable-NetAdapterRss and Disable-NetAdapterRss.

RSS is a great technology, but it is disabled as soon as a network adapter is connected to a virtual switch. VMQ and RSS are mutually exclusive, which means I do not get the benefit of RSS for virtual network adapters connected to virtual machines, which is why if I have a virtual switch connected to a 10 Gbps NIC, the throughput to a virtual machine is only around 3 to 4 Gbps, the maximum amount a single processor core can process, and this is what was possible with Windows Server 2012. This changes with Windows Server 2012 R2 and the introduction of virtual RSS, or vRSS.

vRSS enables the RSS mechanism of splitting incoming packets between multiple virtual processors within the virtual machine. This means that a virtual machine could now leverage the full bandwidth available; for example, a virtual machine could now receive 10 Gbps over its virtual NIC because the processing is no longer bottlenecked to a single virtual processor core.

For vRSS, the network adapter must support VMQ. The actual RSS work is performed on the Hyper-V host, so using vRSS does introduce some additional CPU load on the host, which is why by default vRSS is disabled in the virtual machine. It must be enabled within the virtual machine the same way regular RSS would be enabled on a physical host:

◆ Use the Enable-NetAdapterRss PowerShell cmdlet.

◆ Within the properties of the virtual network adapter inside the virtual machine, select the Advanced tab and set the Receive Side Scaling property to Enabled.

With vRSS enabled, once the processor core processing the network traffic is utilized around 80 percent, the processing will start to be distributed among multiple vCPUs.

A great way to show and maximize the throughput of a network adapter is using Microsoft's ntttcp.exe test tool, which allows for multiple streams to be created as a sender and receiver, therefore maximizing the use of a network connection. The tool can be downloaded from the following location:

http://gallery.technet.microsoft.com/NTttcp-Version-528-Now-f8b12769

Once it's downloaded, copy ntttcp.exe into a virtual machine (with at least four vCPUs and with its firewall disabled) that is connected to a virtual switch that uses a 10 Gbps network adapter (this will receive the traffic) and also to a physical host with a 10 Gbps network adapter (that will send the traffic). Within the virtual machine, run the tool as follows:

```
Ntttcp.exe -r -m 16,*,<IP address of the VM> -a 16 -t 10
```

This command puts the virtual machine in a listening mode, waiting for the traffic to arrive. On the physical host, send the traffic using the following command:

```
Ntttcp.exe -s -m 16,*,<IP address of the VM> -a 16 -t 10
```

On the virtual machine, it will show that traffic is being received. Open Task Manager and view the CPU in the Performance tab. Ensure that the CPU graph is set to Logical Processors (right-click on the process graph and select Change Graph To ➤ Logical Processors). Initially, without vRSS, the bandwidth will likely be around 4 to 5 Gbps (depending on the speed of your processor cores, but most important, only a single vCPU will be utilized). Then turn on vRSS within the VM and run the test again. This time the bandwidth will be closer to 10 Gbps and many of the vCPUs will be utilized. This really shows the benefit of vRSS, and in Figure 3.41 and Figure 3.42, you can see my performance view without and with vRSS. Notice both the processor utilization and the network speed.

**FIGURE 3.41**
Network performance without vRSS enabled

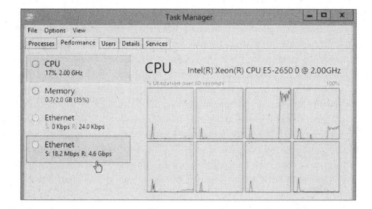

I do want to point out that there is no vRSS support in the host partition. This may not seem important because a host can normally just use RSS. It does become an issue, though, if you create multiple virtual network adapters within the host OS that is connected to a Hyper-V virtual switch. This is possible in Windows 2012 and above and is something I will be talking about later in this chapter. Realize that virtual network adapters in the host partition will be limited in bandwidth to what is possible through a single processor core for each virtual network adapter.

**FIGURE 3.42**
Network performance with vRSS enabled

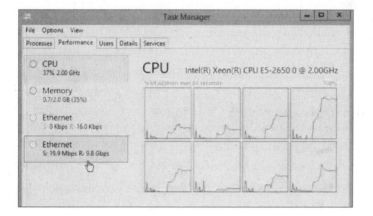

# NIC Teaming

As more resources are consolidated onto a smaller number of physical systems, it's critical that those consolidated systems are as reliable as possible. Previously in this chapter, we created virtual switches, some of which were external to connect to a physical network adapter. Many different virtual machines connect to a virtual switch for their network access, which means a network adapter failure in the host would break connectivity for a large number of virtual machines and the workloads running within them. It is therefore important to provide resiliency from network adapter failure and also potentially enable aggregation of bandwidth from multiple network adapters. For example, a solution would be to group four 1 Gbps network adapters together for total bandwidth of 4 Gbps.

The ability to group network adapters together, made possible by a feature known as NIC Teaming, has been a feature of many network drivers for a long time. However, because it was a feature of the network driver, the implementation differed by vendor. It was not possible to mix network adapters from different vendors, and strictly speaking, the technology was not "supported" by Microsoft because it was not Microsoft technology. Windows Server 2012 changed this by implementing NIC Teaming as part of the operating system itself. It allows up to 32 network adapters to be placed in a single NIC team, and the network adapters could be from many different vendors. It's important that all the NICs are the same speed because the Windows NIC Teaming algorithms do not consider NIC speed as part of their traffic balancing algorithms, so if you mixed 1 Gbps network adapters with 10 Gbps network adapters, the 1 Gbps network adapters would receive the same amount of traffic as the 10 Gbps network adapters, which would be far from optimal.

NIC Teaming is simple to configure using Server Manager or using PowerShell. For example, the following command would create a new NIC team using Switch Independent mode, the dynamic load balancing algorithm, and two network adapters:

```
New-NetLbfoTeam -Name "HostSwitchTeam" -TeamMembers NICTeam3,NICTeam4 `
-TeamingMode SwitchIndependent -LoadBalancingAlgorithm Dynamic `
-Confirm:$false
```

Additionally, as you saw earlier in the chapter, SCVMM can automatically create teams on hosts when deploying logical switches. There are two primary configurations for a NIC team (in addition to specifying which network adapters should be in the team), the teaming mode and the load balancing algorithm. There are three teaming modes:

◆ Static Teaming: Configuration is required on the switches and computer to identify links that make up the team.

◆ Switch Independent: Using different switches for each NIC in the team is not required but is possible, and no configuration is performed on the switch. This is the default option.

◆ LACP (dynamic teaming): The Link Aggregation Control Protocol (LACP) is used to dynamically identify links between the computer and specific switches.

For load balancing, there were two modes in Windows Server 2012 and three in Windows Server 2012 R2:

◆ Hyper-V Port: Each virtual machine NIC (vmNIC) has its own MAC address, which is used as the basis to distribute traffic between the various NICs in the team. If you have a large number of virtual machines with similar loads, then Hyper-V Port works well, but it can be nonoptimal with a small number of virtual machines or uneven loads. Because a specific vmNIC will always be serviced by the same NIC, it is limited to the bandwidth of a single NIC.

◆ Address Hash: Creates a hash value based on information such as the source and destination IP and port (although the exact mode can be changed to just use IP or just use MAC). The hash is then used to distribute traffic between the NICs, ensuring that packets with the same hash are sent to the same NIC to protect against out-of-sequence packet processing. This is not typically used with Hyper-V virtual machines.

◆ Dynamic: New in Windows Server 2012 R2 and really the best parts of Hyper-V Port and Address Hash combined. Outbound traffic is based on the address hash, while inbound traffic uses the Hyper-V Port methods. Additionally, the Dynamic mode uses something called flowlets as the unit of distribution between NICs for outbound traffic. Without flowlets, the entire stream of communication would always be sent via the same network adapter, which may lead to a very unbalanced utilization of network adapters. Consider a normal conversation: There are natural breaks between words spoken, and this is exactly the same for IP communications. When a break of sufficient length is detected, this is considered a flowlet and a new flowlet starts, which could be balanced to a different network adapter. You will pretty much always use the Dynamic mode in Windows Server 2012 R2.

Although it is possible to use the NIC Teaming feature within a virtual machine, only two vmNICs are supported (this is not a hard limit but a supportability limit), and a configuration change is required on the virtual network adapter properties of the virtual machine. This can be done in two ways:

◆ Within the properties page of the virtual machine, select Advanced Features for the network adapter and check the "Enable this network adapter to be part of a team in the guest operating system" option.

◆ Use PowerShell and run the following command:

```
Set-VMNetworkAdapter -VMName <VM Name> -AllowTeaming On
```

Typically, you will not need to use teaming within the virtual machine. The high availability would be enabled by using NIC teaming at the Hyper-V host level and then the created team would be bonded to the virtual switch. If, for example, you were leveraging SR-IOV, which bypasses the Hyper-V switch, you may wish to create a NIC team within the OS between two SR-IOV network adapters or one SR-IOV and one regular vmNIC.

The addition of NIC Teaming in Windows Server 2012 does not mean NIC Teaming capabilities will no longer be provided by network card vendors. Some vendors differentiate their cards based on teaming capabilities, but customers will have the choice to use teaming capabilities from the network adapter driver or use the Microsoft NIC Teaming functionality, which is fully supported by Microsoft. The decision should be made based on required functionality and supportability needs.

## Host Virtual Adapters and Types of Networks Needed in a Hyper-V Host

A Hyper-V host needs many different types of network connectivity, especially if it's part of a cluster. It's critical that each of these types of traffic get the required amount of bandwidth to ensure smooth operation. Additionally, resiliency is likely required for many types of connections to protect against a single network adapter failure. The following key types of network connectivity are required for a Hyper-V host:

◆ Management: Communication to the host for management such as remote desktop (RDP), WS-MAN for remote PowerShell and Server Manager, and basic file copy operations. Sometimes backup operations will be performed over the management network, or a separate backup network may be required.

◆ VM: Traffic related to virtual machines connected to a virtual switch.

◆ Live Migration: The data related to moving a virtual machine between hosts, such as the memory and even storage of a virtual machine.

◆ Cluster/CSV: Cluster communications and Cluster Shared Volume data.

◆ SMB 3: Windows 2012 makes SMB an option for accessing storage containing virtual machines, which would require its own dedicated connection.

◆ iSCSI: If iSCSI is used, a separate network connection would be used.

Traditionally, to ensure the required guaranteed bandwidth for each type of network communication, a separate network adapter was used for each type of traffic. Look at the preceding list again. That is a lot of network adapters, and that list is without resiliency, which may mean doubling that number, which is typically not practical. This is also outlined in the Microsoft networking guidelines at the following location:

```
http://technet.microsoft.com/en-us/library/ff428137(v=WS.10).aspx
```

Your connectivity may look like Figure 3.43. Not only does this require a lot of network adapters, but there is a huge amount of wasted bandwidth. For example, typically the Live Migration network would not be used unless a migration is occurring, and normally the Cluster network has only heartbeat and some minimal metadata redirection for CSV, but the high bandwidth is needed for when a Live Migration does occur or when a CSV goes into redirection mode. It would be better if the network bandwidth could be used by other types of communication when the bandwidth was available.

**FIGURE 3.43**
A nonconverged Hyper-V host configuration with separate 1 Gbps NIC teams for each type of traffic

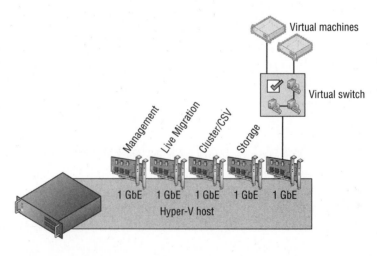

Having this many 1 Gbps network adapters may be possible, but as datacenters move to 10 Gbps, another solution is needed in keeping with the converged direction in which many datacenters are focused. Some unified solutions offer the ability to carve up a single connection from the server to the backplane into virtual devices such as network adapters, which is one solution to this problem. It's also possible, however, to solve this using the Hyper-V virtual switch, which traditionally was available only for virtual machines.

One of the properties of a virtual switch is the option to allow the management operating system to share the network adapter, which creates a virtual network adapter (vNIC) on the Hyper-V host itself that was connected to the virtual switch. This would allow the management traffic and the VM traffic to share the virtual switch. It's actually possible, though, to create additional vNICs on the management operating system connected to the virtual switch for other purposes using PowerShell. Quality of Service (QoS) can then be used to ensure that sufficient bandwidth is guaranteed for each of the different vNICs created so that one type of traffic would use up all the bandwidth and stop other types of communication. To add additional vNICs on the Hyper-V host connected to a virtual switch, use the following command (changing the switch name from External Switch to a valid virtual switch name in your environment):

```
Add-VMNetworkAdapter -ManagementOS -SwitchName "<External Switch>"
```

The ability to create vNICs in the management operating system connected to a virtual switch that can in turn be connected to a native NIC team that is made up of multiple network adapters makes it possible to create a converged networking approach for the Hyper-V host. Because separate vNICs are used for each type of traffic, QoS can be used to ensure that bandwidth is available when needed, as shown in Figure 3.44. In this example, four 1 Gbps NICs are used together and then used by the virtual switch, which now services virtual machines and the different vNICs in the management partition for various types of communication. However, it would also be common to now use two 10 Gbps NICs instead. I walk through the process in a video at www.youtube.com/watch?v=8mOuoIWzmdE, but here are some of the commands to create two vNICs in the host in a new NIC team and virtual switch. I assign a minimum bandwidth weight QoS policy. If required, each vNIC can be configured with a separate VLAN ID.

```
New-NetLbfoTeam -Name "HostSwitchTeam" -TeamMembers NICTeam3,NICTeam4 `
-TeamingMode Static -Confirm:$false
New-VMSwitch "MgmtSwitch" -MinimumBandwidthMode weight `
-NetAdapterName "HostSwitchTeam" -AllowManagement $false
Add-VMNetworkAdapter -ManagementOS -Name "LiveMigration" -SwitchName "MgmtSwitch"
Set-VMNetworkAdapter -ManagementOS -Name "LiveMigration" `
-MinimumBandwidthWeight 50
Add-VMNetworkAdapter -ManagementOS -Name "Cluster" -SwitchName "MgmtSwitch"
Set-VMNetworkAdapter -ManagementOS -Name "Cluster" -MinimumBandwidthWeight 50
```

I go into detail in an article at

```
http://windowsitpro.com/windows-server-2012/quality-of-service-windows-
server-2012
```

It is definitely worth reading if you want to understand the details of QoS and why minimum bandwidth is a better solution than the traditional maximum bandwidth type caps that always limited the available bandwidth to the cap value, even if there was more bandwidth available.

Using minimum bandwidth allows maximum utilization of all bandwidth until there is bandwidth contention between different workloads, at which time each workload is limited to its relative allocation. For example, suppose I have the following three workloads:

◆ Live Migration: MinumumBandwidthWeight 20

◆ Virtual Machines: MinumumBandwidthWeight 50

◆ Cluster: MinumumBandwidthWeight 30

**FIGURE 3.44**
A converged Hyper-V host configuration with a shared NIC team used

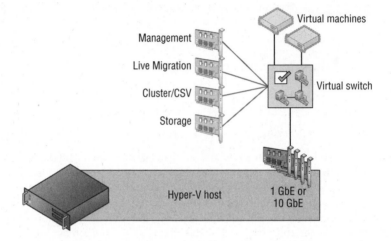

Under normal circumstances, the virtual machines could use all available bandwidth—for example, 10 Gbps if the total bandwidth available to the switch was 10 Gbps. However, if a live migration triggered and the virtual machines were using all the bandwidth, then the virtual machines would be throttled back to 80 percent and the Live Migration traffic would be guaranteed 20 percent, which would be 2 Gbps. Notice that my weights add up to 100, which is not required but is highly recommended for manageability.

Although using this new converged methodology is highly recommended, there is one caveat, and that is the new SMB 3.0 usage. SMB 3.0 has a feature named SMB Direct, which uses remote direct memory access (RDMA) for the highest possible network speeds and almost no overhead on the host. Additionally, SMB 3 has a feature called SMB Multichannel, which allows multiple network connections between the source and target of the SMB communication to be aggregated together, providing both protection from a single network connection failure and increased bandwidth, very similar to the benefits of NIC Teaming. (SMB Direct still works with NIC Teaming because when a NIC team is detected, SMB automatically creates four separate connections by default.) The problem is that RDMA does not work with NIC Teaming. This means if you wish to take advantage of SMB Direct (RDMA), which would be the case if you were using SMB to communicate to the storage of your virtual machines and/or if you are using SMB Direct for Live Migration (which is possible in Windows Server 2012 R2), you would not want to lose the RDMA capability if it's present in your network adapters. If you wish to leverage RDMA, your converged infrastructure will look slightly different, as shown in Figure 3.45, which features an additional two NICs that are not teamed but would instead be aggregated using SMB Multichannel. Notice that Live Migration, SMB, and Cluster (CSV uses SMB for its communications) all move to the RDMA adapters because all of those workloads benefit from

RMDA. While this does mean four network adapters are required to most efficiently support the different types of traffic, all those types of traffic are fault tolerant and have access to increased bandwidth.

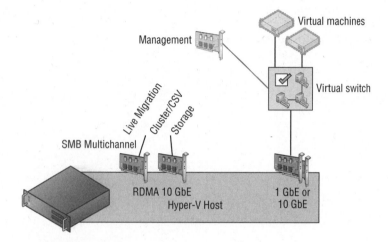

**FIGURE 3.45**
A converged Hyper-V host configuration with separate NICs for SMB (RDMA) traffic

Remember the bandwidth limitation when using vNICs in the host as I explained in the section "RSS and vRSS." vRSS cannot be used in the host partition for the vNICs, which means each vNIC will be limited to 3 to 4 Gbps. This likely will be enough bandwidth for each vNIC for most scenarios, but it's important to remember or you may be confused as to why your live migrations over a vNIC run at 3 Gbps instead of 10 Gbps.

## Types of Guest Network Adapters

There are two types of network adapters available to a generation 1 virtual machine: legacy (emulated Intel 21140-Based PCI Fast Ethernet) and synthetic. As was discussed in Chapter 2, "Virtual Machine Resource Fundamentals," emulated hardware is never desirable because of the decreased performance and higher overhead, which means the legacy network adapter is only really used for two purposes in a generation 1 virtual machine:

◆ Running an operating system that does not have Hyper-V integration services available and therefore cannot use the synthetic network adapter (this would mean the operating system is also unsupported on Hyper-V).

◆ Needing to boot the virtual machine over the network, known as PXE Boot. If this is the reason, then initially use a legacy network adapter, but once the operating system is installed, switch to the synthetic network adapter for the improved performance.

Additionally, QoS and hardware acceleration features are not available for legacy network adapters, making the standard network adapter your default choice. Each virtual machine can have up to eight network adapters (synthetic) and four legacy network adapters.

There are many options available for a network adapter that are configured through the virtual machine properties by selecting the network adapter (legacy network adapter or network adapter), and if there are multiple network adapters for a virtual machine, each adapter has its own set of configurations. These configurations are broken down into three areas: core configurations, hardware acceleration (not available for legacy network adapters), and advanced features, as shown in Figure 3.46. Figure 3.46 also shows Device Manager running in the virtual machine whose properties are being displayed, which shows the two network adapters. The Intel 21140-Based PCI Faster Ethernet Adapter (Emulate) is the legacy network adapter and the Microsoft Virtual Machine Bus Network Adapter is the network adapter.

**FIGURE 3.46**
Primary properties for a network adapter

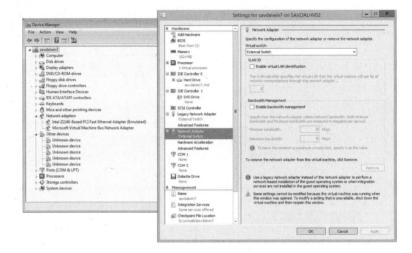

The core properties for a network adapter are as follows:

◆ Virtual Switch: The virtual switch the adapter should be connected to.

◆ Enable Virtual LAN Identification: If the switch port that the virtual switch is connected to is set to tagged and expects packets to be tagged with a VLAN ID, this option allows you to configure which VLAN ID packets from this network adapter will be tagged.

◆ Enable Bandwidth Management (not available for legacy network adapter): Enables limits to be specified in Mbps for the bandwidth available for the network adapter. The lowest value allowed for Minimum is 10 Mbps, while 0.1 is the lowest value that can be set for Maximum.

The Hardware Acceleration tab (not available to legacy network adapters) enables VMQ, IPsec, and SR-IOV by checking the appropriate box. Remember that even if these properties are set in a virtual machine, it does not guarantee their use. For example, if the physical network adapter does not support VMQ or has run out of VMQs, then VMQ will not be used for the vmNIC. Likewise, if SR-IOV is selected by the virtual switch, if the hardware does not support SR-IOV, or if the physical adapter has no more available virtual functions, then SR-IOV will not be used. Selecting the options simply enables the capabilities to be used if they are available without guaranteeing their actual use.

The Advanced Features tab enables a number of interesting options whose use will vary depending on the environment deploying the technology:

**MAC Address**  By default, a dynamic MAC address is used, which is configured when the VM is created and should not change. However, it's also possible to select Static and configure your own preferred MAC address. The option to enable MAC address spoofing can also be set, which enables the VM to change the MAC address on packets it sends to another MAC address. This would be necessary when using network load balancing, for example, within virtual machines.

**Enable DHCP Guard**  Network adapters configured with the DHCP Guard option will have any DHCP reply packets from the VM dropped by the Hyper-V switch. This means if the VM is pretending to be a DHCP server when it shouldn't be, although the server still sees the DHCP request from clients and responds, those responses never get to the network. Consider a multitenant environment. It's very important that one tenant not pretend it's a DHCP server and affect the others. The best practice is to enable this feature on all virtual machine network adapters and disable it only on the virtual machines that are known DHCP servers.

**Enable Router Advertisement Guard**  Very similar to DHCP Guard, but this will block router advertisements and redirection messages. Again, enable this by default unless a VM is acting as a router.

**Protected Network**  This feature specifies that if the network the virtual machine is connected to becomes disconnected, then failover clustering will move the virtual machine to another node in the cluster.

**Port Mirroring**  There are three settings; None, Destination, and Source. This allows network traffic from a vmNIC set as Source to be sent to vmNICs on other virtual machines that are set as Destination. Essentially, this allows network traffic from one virtual machine to be sent to another for analysis/monitoring.

**NIC Teaming**  This allows the network adapter to be used within a NIC team defined inside the virtual machine.

All of these various options can be set with the `Set-VMNetworkAdapter` PowerShell cmdlet in addition to being set through Hyper-V Manager.

A common question arises when the network adapters inside the virtual machine are inspected, which shows an actual speed for the virtual network adapter. This is always 10 Gbps for the network adapter (synthetic) and 100 Mbps for the legacy network adapter. People get very confused. They may say, "But my physical network card is only 1 Gbps; how can it be 10 Gbps?" The fact is, this number is meaningless. Some number has to be displayed, so Hyper-V tells the virtual machine a certain number, but the actual speed seen completely depends on a couple of factors:

◆ If the traffic is between two virtual machines on the same host, the traffic never touches a physical network adapter and will process between them as fast as the VMBus and processor can handle the traffic.

◆ If the traffic is external to the Hyper-V host, the speed is based on the speed of the network adapter (or adapters, if a team) and also the processor. For example, if you have a 10 Gbps network adapter, the speed will likely be determined by the processor that has to process the traffic, so you may not actually see 10 Gbps of speed. When receiving traffic, each virtual machine NIC may be assigned a VMQ from the NIC. The VMQ is processed by a single processor core (except in Windows Server 2012 R2, which supports virtual Receive Side Scaling, or vRSS), which likely will result in speeds between 3 and 4 Gbps.

To summarize, the speed shown in the virtual machine is irrelevant and does not guarantee or limit the actual network speed, which is based on the physical network adapter speed and the processor capabilities.

## Monitoring Virtual Traffic

Readers may be familiar with the Network Monitor (NetMon) tool that Microsoft has made available for many years as a method to monitor traffic. When it was installed on a machine, this tool could monitor the network in promiscuous mode to view all the traffic sent over the link. This is still an option. It can even be installed inside a virtual machine and the port mirroring feature of the network adapter could be used to send network traffic from one virtual machine to another for monitoring.

Microsoft has replaced NetMon with a new tool, Message Analyzer, which is available from the following location:

```
http://www.microsoft.com/en-us/download/details.aspx?id=40308
```

Going into detail about Message Analyzer is beyond the scope of this book. However, I want to focus on one new very powerful feature, and that is the ability to perform remote capture of a Windows Server 2012 R2 server or Windows 8.1 client, including specific virtual machines running on a Windows Server 2012 R2 Hyper-V host. The ability to perform remote capture is a key requirement when you consider many production servers now run Server Core, which has no ability to run graphical management tools such as the NetMon tool, and that would block performing network analysis.

Remote capture is made possible because the driver used by Message Analyzer, NDISCAP, is now built into the Windows 8.1 and Windows Server 2012 R2 operating systems. It was specifically written to enable remote capture, sending packets over the network to the box that is running the Message Analyzer tool. Message Analyzer can still be used on Windows 7 (with WMI 3 installed), Windows 8, Windows 2008 R2 (with WMI 3), and Windows Server 2012, and will install a capture driver, PEFNDIS, but it does not allow remote capturing of network data. When a remote capture is initially performed, a WMI call is made to the remote server to collect the information about what can be captured, and then RPC is used to send packets over the network to the Message Analyzer. Note that it's possible to configure only certain types of traffic to be sent to Message Analyzer, and by default, traffic is truncated to show only the first 128 bytes of each packet to minimize the amount of traffic sent over the network from the source to the analyzer machine.

Message Analyzer features a completely new interface, and I will walk through the basic steps to start a remote capture of a virtual machine on a remote Hyper-V host. Before running this process, add the remote host to the list of trusted WMI machines by running the following command below from an elevated command prompt:

```
WinRM set winrm/config/client @{TrustedHosts="RemoteHostName"}
```

Now you can continue with the remote capture:

1. Launch Message Analyzer.

2. Select the Capture/Trace tab.

3. In the Trace Scenario Configuration area, change the host from Localhost to the remote Hyper-V server by selecting Connect To Remote Host.

4. Enter the name of the host. Additionally, separate credentials for the remote host can be configured. Click OK.

5. The next step is to apply a template, and in this case I will apply the Remote Link Layer template by dragging it to the Trace Scenario Configuration area.

6. Next, click the Configure link next to the capture configuration as shown in Figure 3.47. This allows the configuration of the exact traffic to be captured. Note that it shows the actual virtual machines that are connected to the switch. In this case, I have selected to only capture data from my Blue-VM-1 virtual machine. Click OK.

7. Now click the Start With button to start the capture and view the packets.

8. Once the capture is finished, click the Stop button.

Figure 3.48 shows an example of my captured output from the virtual machine I selected. The ability to remotely monitor specific network adapters, specific virtual switches, and even specific virtual machines with no configuration on the source host is a huge benefit and really completes and emphasizes the capabilities available to us with Windows Server 2012 R2 networking.

**FIGURE 3.47**
Configuring the remote traffic to capture using Message Analyzer

**FIGURE 3.48**

Example view of
captured traffic

## The Bottom Line

**Architect the right network design for your Hyper-V hosts and virtual machines using the options available.** There are many different networking traffic types related to a Hyper-V host, including management, virtual machine, cluster, live migration, and storage. While traditionally separate, network adapters were used with each type of traffic; a preferred approach is to create multiple vNICs in the management partition that connect to a shared virtual switch. This minimizes the number of physical NICs required while providing resiliency from a NIC failure for all workloads connected to the switch.

**Master It** Why are separate network adapters required if SMB is leveraged and the network adapters support RDMA?

**Identify when to use the types of NVGRE Gateway.** There are three separate scenarios supported by NVGRE Gateway: S2S VPN, NAT, and Forwarder. S2S VPN should be used when a virtual network needs to communicate with another network such as a remote network. Forwarder is used when the IP scheme used in the virtual network is routable on the physical fabric, such as, for example, when the physical fabric network is expanded into the virtual network. NAT is required when the IP scheme in the virtual network is not routable on the physical network fabric and requires external connectivity, such as when tenants needed to access the Internet.

**Leverage SCVMM 2012 R2 for many networking tasks.** While Hyper-V Manager enables many networking functions to be performed, each of these configurations are limited to a single host and are hard to manage at scale. SCVMM is focused on enabling the network to be modeled at a physical level, and then the types of network required by virtual environments can be separately modeled with different classifications of connectivity defined. While the initial work may seem daunting, the long-term management and flexibility of a centralized networking environment is a huge benefit.

**Master It** Why is SCVMM required for network virtualization?

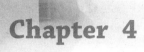

# Chapter 4

# Storage Configurations

In previous chapters, the compute and network resources of a virtual environment were examined, and this chapter deals with the final resource building block—storage. In Windows Server 2012 R2, there are many different storage options and topologies available, enabling organizations to implement different solutions to meet the many different requirements encountered.

Many organizations are familiar with using storage area networks (SANs) as the cornerstone for their storage requirements and leveraging connectivity such as Fibre Channel, and this is still a valid solution, and in certain scenarios, the right architecture. However, with Windows Server 2012, the focus was on choice and offering other storage solutions that can be more cost effective and more flexible, such as iSCSI, SMB 3, and Storage Spaces. Hyper-V fully leverages these technologies in addition to supporting a new virtual hard disk format that offers the highest scalability and performance.

In this chapter, you will learn to

◆ Explain the types of storage available to a virtual machine

◆ Identify when to use virtual Fibre Channel vs. Shared VHDX and the benefits of each

◆ Articulate how SMB 3 can be used

## Storage Fundamentals and VHDX

Chapter 2 covered the basics of virtual storage, and I want to quickly review those basics and the various limits and options provided. Nearly every virtual machine scenario will require some kind of "local" storage such as that used to host the boot and system partitions, which contain the operating system environment and locally installed applications and services. Additional storage may also be assigned to the virtual machine for data storage, although this could also be accessed using other network-based methods.

Storage that is assigned to the virtual machine from the host server (in most cases, but there are exceptions, which will be covered later in the book) must first be accessible to the Hyper-V host, such as direct-attached storage to the host or storage that the host can communicate with, such as on a SAN via iSCSI or fibre channel connectivity or even on a Windows file server or network-attached storage (NAS) device using SMB 3 with Windows Server 2012 and above, which introduced file-level access support. It is important that any storage used by the host to store virtual machines is resilient to failure. For direct-attached storage, use technologies to enable a disk to fail without losing data (such as RAID), and for remote-storage, ensure that there are multiple paths to the storage to avoid losing storage access if a single card, cable, or switch fails. The remote storage should also be fault tolerant. When Hyper-V hosts are clustered together, as they always should be to ensure availability of the virtual environment, it's important that storage used by virtual machines is available to all hosts in the cluster.

With storage available at the host level, it needs to be assigned to virtual machines. While it is possible to pass a disk directly from the Hyper-V host into a virtual machine known as a pass-through disk, this is not something that should ever be done, for the following reasons:

◆  The disk is solely usable by the virtual machine assigned the physical disk from the host so that not even the host can still use the disk.

◆  Virtual machine checkpoints that provide point-in-time captures of a virtual machine don't work.

◆  Migration technologies such as Live Migration do not work without an outage to availability.

◆  Replication technologies such as Hyper-V Replica do not work.

◆  Virtual machine backup at the host is not possible.

◆  Storage Quality of Service is not available.

With all of these problems, you may wonder why pass-through storage was even made available as an option, and the answer is that sometimes virtual machines needed access to volumes and storage that was larger or faster than what was possible with the VHD format, which had a 2 TB limit. Consider a large SQL database; a 2 TB limit was too restrictive, and also there was a performance hit when using VHD above the bare-metal storage, especially using dynamic VHD, which grows as data is written to it. In the scenarios in which very large volumes with the highest performance needs were required, the Windows Server 2008 VHD implementation would not suffice, and either pass-through storage had to be used or iSCSI within the VM. Windows 2008 R2 greatly improved the performance of VHD, but the 2 TB limit remained. This is why pass-through was required as an option.

In Windows Server 2012, you should *never* need pass-through storage. There is not a scenario in which it is required because of the new 64 TB VHDX virtual hard disk format, which also features greatly improved performance effectively matching the bare-metal storage performance. I've never seen a client with an NTFS volume that is 64 TB in size. The largest I have seen is 14 TB because most organizations will limit the size of a NTFS volume in case a volume becomes corrupt and CHKDSK has to be run, although this is no longer a problem with Windows Server 2012 and above.

With the need to use pass-through storage removed, all virtual storage assigned from the Hyper-V host for normal purposes will be through the use of VHDX files. VHD files should only be used if compatibility is required for pre–Windows Server 2012 Hyper-V or Windows Azure (at time of this writing, Windows Azure does not support VHDX but may by the time you read this).

VHDX has other advantages over VHD beyond just performance and scalability:

◆  Protection against corruption caused by unplanned power outages by logging updates to the VHDX metadata structures.

◆  Alignment with physical disk structures automatically and 4 KB sector support. Alignment was a big performance problem for early VHD, which was caused by the VHD file geometry, such as virtual sector size, being different from the underlying NTFS file system and disk. Even if the geometry was the same, there may have been an offset between where the VHD started and its header, causing a VHD block to not sit within a single NTFS cluster, which could result in spanning multiple NTFS clusters. This makes disk operations very inefficient because while the virtual OS may think it's fetching a single block, on the physical storage, many different clusters must be read. The good news is that the alignment issue is resolved in VHDX, which will always align correctly. Details can be found in the VHDX specification at the following location:

www.microsoft.com/en-us/download/details.aspx?id=34750

◆ Custom metadata, allowing management applications to store information such as the OS running inside the VHDX.

◆ Trim support, which enables the efficient reclaiming of blocks on SSD devices.

---

### WHAT IS THE CHKDSK PROBLEM?

ChkDsk is the utility that has to be run when a volume has problems. To fix the problems, the volume has to be taken offline, which means it's unavailable, while a thorough scan and fix is performed on it. The larger the number of files on a volume, the longer the scan for the problems will take and the longer the volume will be offline. For example, a 2 TB volume filled with many files could be offline for hours or days depending on the storage subsystem, which is a long time if the volume contains important data. Therefore, to avoid long outages, organizations would limit the size of NTFS volumes, which reduces the number of files. Think of this scenario as a highway that is closed while a crew walks along looking for potholes and fixing the few that it finds. This road may be closed for weeks or months while the crew is looking for the potholes.

Windows Server 2012 re-architected ChkDsk into a two-phase process. The long process of finding problems now occurs with the volume still online. Once the problems are found, the volume is taken offline and a spotfix of the problems is performed, but in the worst-case scenario, the volume is offline for only 8 seconds and commonly for only milliseconds, which is not noticeable at all. If Cluster Shared Volumes (CSV) is used, there is never downtime because CSV has its own layer of indirection, resulting in just a pause in I/O. Going back to the highway analogy, in Windows Server 2012, the road stays open as the crews hop between cars looking for the problems. Then once they have found all the potholes that are marked on a map, the road is closed for one night while all the found potholes are filled.

To perform the scan, use `chkdsk /scan <disk>:` or `Repair-Volume -Scan <disk>:` in PowerShell, and then once the search for problems is complete, perform the spotfix, which will take the volume offline for the maximum of 8 seconds to run the commands `chkdsk /spotfix <disk>:` or `Repair-Volume -SpotFix <disk>:`.

This means that NTFS volumes are no longer restricted to a certain size because of fears related to running ChkDsk.

---

An important point to remember about VHDX is that it is a core part of the operating system for both server and client. VHDX files can be mounted natively to the operating system, and physical machines can even boot from VHDX files, which allows great flexibility for moving an operating system instance from a virtual machine to a physical machine without any real changes being required. If you have a physical system that you would like to convert to a virtual machine, there are a number of technologies available for this physical-to-virtual (P2V) conversion. However, a nice free tool for a small number of conversions is disk2vhd from

```
http://technet.microsoft.com/en-us/sysinternals/ee656415.aspx
```

It will take the storage from physical machines and create equivalent VHD and VHDX (version 2) files that could then be used with Hyper-V virtual machines.

## Types of Controllers

In Chapter 2 I told you about two types of storage controllers available in a generation 1 virtual machine, IDE and SCSI, while a generation 2 virtual machine supports only the SCSI controller. In a generation 1 virtual machine, the operating system VHDX must be connected to the IDE controller because the SCSI controller does not support bootable devices. In a generation 2 virtual machine, though, the SCSI controller does support bootable devices, allowing the operating system VHDX file to be connected to the SCSI controller.

A generation 1 virtual machine has two IDE controllers, with each controller supporting up to two virtual devices, which could be VHD/VHDX files or virtual DVD drives. Both generation 1 and generation 2 virtual machines support up to four SCSI controllers, with each SCSI controller supporting up to 64 virtual hard disks. Even though the performance of the IDE controller and SCSI controller are equivalent, once the integration services are loaded, the fact that so many more disks are supported on the SCSI controller means that in most environments, the IDE controller is used solely for the operating system storage while all data disks connect to the SCSI controller.

There is one additional difference, or was, between the IDE and SCSI virtual controllers that is important to be aware of and that also makes the SCSI controller a better choice for any kind of database, and that is caching behavior, or more specifically, how write cache is reported. For any kind of database, you typically do not want any kind of write caching on the device. Write caching is a technology that enables storage to report a write has been committed to disk but actually is cached in the controller and will be written in the most optimal way at a later time. The danger with write caching is that if an unplanned outage occurs, the data in the volatile cache would never have been written to the disk and would be lost. This is bad for any kind of database, including Active Directory.

With Hyper-V, write caching cannot be disabled on virtual hard disks because there is no way to ensure that there is not an always-on write cache on the underlying storage or that the VHDX may one day be moved to a disk with an always-on write cache using storage or live migration technologies. Additionally, because many VHDX files can reside on a single physical disk, there is no way to be sure all VHDX files on the physical disk would want the write cache disabled and the configuration of write-cache is a physical disk setting. When the write cache is disabled on a disk that is using Device Manager and is connected to the virtual SCSI controller, an error is displayed, as shown in Figure 4.1. This is important because applications also try to disable write caching, and the error notifying that the write cache could not be disabled allows any application that needs to ensure data write integrity to use alternative methods, specifically Force Unit Access (FUA), to ensure that data is not cached.

**FIGURE 4.1**
An error occurred when the administrator was trying to disable write caching within a virtual machine. Applications would receive a similar error condition.

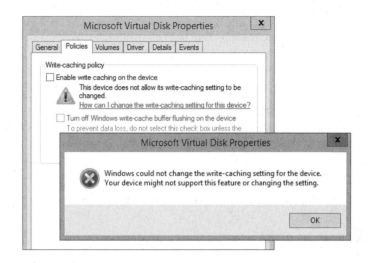

When applications try to disable write caching on a virtual disk connected to an IDE controller, no error is returned, which makes the application think that write caching has successfully been disabled, so no other actions to ensure data integrity are taken. In reality, though, write caching was not disabled. This can lead to data corruptions in the event of unplanned outages.

Windows Server 2012 R2 does not have this problem, and the good news for Windows Server 2012 and Windows Server 2008 R2 Hyper-V environments is that Microsoft released a fix, KB2853952. Once this fix is applied to the Hyper-V host, it will correctly return a failure error to the VM if write caching is disabled on the IDE controller, allowing the applications to then leverage FUA.

As you move forward with Windows Server 2012 R2 and generation 2 virtual machines, you don't have many choices to make; you will use a virtual SCSI controller and you will use VHDX files for the best set of features and scalability.

## Common VHDX Maintenance Actions

In Chapter 2 I covered basic commands to create VHDX files and also the basic Edit Disk actions that allow certain modifications and optimizations to be performed. I will go into some additional details in this section.

First, as mentioned, a VHDX file can be natively mounted in Windows Server by right-clicking it and selecting the Mount option or just double-clicking the file. To unmount, right-click the volume in Explorer and choose Eject. This can also be performed using the various disk management tools, but for automation, scripting the mount and unmounts can be very useful. PowerShell provides an easy way to mount and unmount a VHDX file:

```
Mount-VHD -Path D:\Virtuals\newdyn.vhdx
Dismount-VHD -Path D:\Virtuals\newdyn.vhdx
```

Throughout this chapter I talk about VHDX, but many environments will have VHD files from previous deployments and you might want to convert them to VHDX to gain the new capabilities. Using Hyper-V Manager, start the Edit Disk action and select the source VHD file.

Then under the action, select Convert and then select the VHDX format, which will convert the VHD to a VHDX file. This can also be done using PowerShell:

```
Convert-VHD -Path d:\temp\source.vhd -DestinationPath d:\temp\destination.vhdx
```

Note that any conversion process creates a new virtual hard disk file and copies the content across, which means you need sufficient free space to create the temporary new file until the old file is deleted. It is also possible to convert a VHDX to a VHD file using the same process providing the VHDX is less than 2,040 GB in size.

Dynamic VHDX files will grow as writes are performed, but they never shrink automatically, even if large amounts of data are deleted. This means that if you delete a large amount of data from a dynamic VHDX file and want to reclaim the space on the physical disk, you need to perform a compaction of the VHDX file, which can be performed by using the Hyper-V Manager Edit Disk action and selecting the Compact action. This can also be performed using PowerShell:

```
Optimize-VHD -Path d:\temp\data1.vhdx
```

There are optional parameters that can be used with Optimize-VHD that tune the type of optimization and are fully explained at

```
http://technet.microsoft.com/en-us/library/hh848458.aspx
```

However, in most cases the default optimization mode of Quick for a VHDX will yield the desired result.

When a VHDX file is created, it can be created as a fixed or dynamic VHDX file. This can be changed through the Edit Disk action or through PowerShell Convert-VHD, specifying the -VHDType parameter as Fixed or Dynamic.

The size of a VHDX file can also be changed using the same method, increasing the available space or even shrinking it, provided there is sufficient unallocated space on the disk inside the virtual machine. For example, if a VHDX file is 80 GB but the virtual machine inside has only allocated 60 GB of storage, it would leave 20 GB unallocated, as shown in Figure 4.2. This would allow the VHDX file to be shrunk by 20 GB. This can be confirmed when looking at the properties of a VHDX file and inspecting the MinimumSize attribute. Note that when working with dynamic disks, changing the size of the file changes only its maximum size; the actual amount of space used on disk is based entirely on the data written, which is shown in the FileSize attribute. If you wanted to reduce the size of a VHDX file more than the MinimumSize attribute, you should connect to the virtual machine and shrink the size of the volumes inside the virtual machine using Disk Management to increase the amount of unallocated space.

```
PS E:\Virtuals\win81nondomain\Virtual Hard Disks> Get-VHD .\win81nondomain.vhdx


ComputerName            : SAVDALHV01
Path                    : E:\Virtuals\win81nondomain\Virtual Hard Disks\
win81nondomain.vhdx
VhdFormat               : VHDX
VhdType                 : Dynamic
FileSize                : 11983126528
Size                    : 85899345920
```

```
MinimumSize            : 64423477760
LogicalSectorSize      : 512
PhysicalSectorSize     : 4096
BlockSize              : 33554432
ParentPath             :
DiskIdentifier         : ae420626-f01e-4dfa-a0a5-468ffdfe95ad
FragmentationPercentage : 6
Alignment              : 1
Attached               : True
DiskNumber             :
Key                    :
IsDeleted              : False
Number                 :
```

**FIGURE 4.2**
A virtual machine with 20 GB of space unallocated

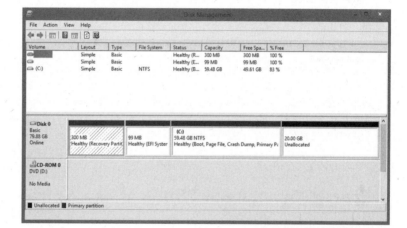

## Performing Dynamic VHDX Resize

Prior to Windows Server 2012 R2, any changes to the size of a VHDX file required the virtual machine using the VHDX file to be shut down. There was no way to dynamically resize a VHDX while the virtual machine was still running, which some organizations found to be a pain point. Windows Server 2012 R2 introduces dynamic resize for both increasing and decreasing the size of a file. The requirements for dynamic resize are as follows:

◆ Must be a VHDX file. Dynamic resize is not supported for VHD files.

◆ Must be connected to the SCSI controller. Dynamic resize is not supported for virtual hard disks connected to the IDE controller.

Performing a dynamic resize is exactly the same as performing an offline resize operation:

**1.** Within Hyper-V Manager, select the Edit Disk option.

**2.** Click Next on the Edit Virtual Hard Disk Wizard introduction page.

3. Select the VHDX file to modify (remember, the VM using it can still be running), and then click Next.

4. Select the Expand or Shrink option, depending on your desired action, and then click Next.

5. If you selected Shrink, the minimum possible size will be shown in brackets. If you selected Expand, the maximum possible size will be shown in brackets. Enter the new size and click Next.

6. Click Finish to perform the resize.

If you performed an expand of a virtual hard disk within the virtual machine, you need to use the newly available unallocated disk space. Either extend an existing volume or create a new volume in the unallocated space using the Disk Management MMC snap-in or PowerShell. If a shrink was performed, no actions are required; there will simply be less or no unallocated space on the disk.

To resize using PowerShell, utilize the `Resize-VHD` cmdlet, passing the new size using the `-SizeBytes` parameter (however, you do not have to type the size in bytes; you can type numbers such as 2 GB or 10 TB), which can be less or more than the current size, as long as it is a valid size (i.e., not smaller than the `MinimumSize` attribute and not larger than VHDX 64 TB limit or than is physically available if it is a fixed-size VHDX file). If you want to shrink the file as much as possible, instead of using `-SizeBytes`, use the `-ToMinimumSize` parameter, as in this example:

```
Resize-VHD .\win81nondomain.vhdx -ToMinimumSize
```

## Storage Spaces and Windows as a Storage Solution

While not strictly a Hyper-V topic, I want to briefly cover the big shift in storage introduced with Windows Server 2012 because it will most likely affect the way your Hyper-V environments are architected, especially in smaller organizations and branch offices.

In the introduction I talked about Fibre Channel– and iSCSI-connected storage area networks, which historically have been the preferred storage choice for organizations because they provide many benefits:

◆ Storage is centralized, allowing the highest utilization of the available space as opposed to many separate instances of storage with lots of wasted space.

◆ Centralized backup is possible.

◆ They offer the highest level of performance and scalability, which is possible because the storage is all centralized, allowing higher-specification storage solutions to be purchased.

◆ Storage is accessible to all servers throughout the datacenter, providing the server has the required connectivity, such as fibre channel or iSCSI.

◆ Centralized storage enables easy migration of virtual machines between physical hosts because the storage can be seen by multiple servers.

◆ They provide shared storage, which is required for many cluster scenarios.

The use of high-end, centralized storage is still a great option for many organizations and scenarios. However, there is also another model being adopted by many organizations and service providers, including Windows Azure, which is the move from centralized storage to the use of just a bunch of disks (JBOD) solutions that are either local to a server or in an external enclosure connected to a number of clustered hosts. This can provide great cost efficiencies because storage subsystems based on regular disks are much cheaper than SAN solutions. It is important, though, to build in resiliency and backup solutions for what is now local storage containing critical workloads, that is, your virtual machines.

Windows Server has long had the ability to create fault resilient storage using Redundant Array of Independent Disks (RAID) technology in one of two modes: RAID-1, which mirrored all data from one disk to another disk, and RAID-5, which used striping with parity. However, there were challenges with the software RAID implementation:

- It did not self-heal. If a disk was lost, another disk had to be manually configured to be the replacement.

- Only thick/fat provisioning was possible, which means a volume can be created only up to the physical space available. Thin provisioning, which allows volumes to be created beyond the physical space and allocated as data was written, was not possible.

- Management was quite painful, and RAID volumes could not be resized easily.

- Was not supported in a Failover Cluster.

Storage Spaces was introduced in Windows Server 2012 as a completely new way to think about managing and using direct attached storage. With Storage Spaces, the physical disks that are providing the underlying storage of data are completely abstracted from the process of requesting new volumes, now known as spaces, and any actions required to restore data redundancy in the event of a disk failure are performed automatically by the Storage Spaces technology as long as there are sufficient physical disks available.

The first step is to create a storage pool, which is a selection of one or more physical disks that are then pooled together and can be used by the Storage Spaces technology. Supported disk types in a storage pool are USB, SATA, and SAS connected disks. These disks are just standard disks, JBOD. With no hardware high availability such as RAID behind the scenes, Storage Spaces is going to take care of fault tolerance. The use of USB-connected drives is great on the desktop side, while servers will focus on SATA and SAS connected drives. Additionally, shared SAS is fully supported, which means a disk enclosure could be used that is then connected to a number of hosts in a cluster and the storage space created on those shared SAS drives would be available to all nodes in the cluster and can be used as part of Cluster Shared Volumes. This allows a cluster of Hyper-V hosts to use a clustered storage space as the storage for virtual machines. If an external disk enclosure is used, Storage Spaces supports the SES protocol, which enables failure indications on the external storage if available, such as a bad disk LED in the event Storage Spaces detects a problem with a physical disk. While there are many storage enclosures that work with clustered storage spaces, Microsoft does have a number certified enclosures for Windows Server 2012, which are documented at the Windows Server Catalog.

Other technologies, like BitLocker, can also be used with Storage Spaces. When a new storage pool is created, the disks that are added to the storage pool will disappear from the Disk Management tool because they are now virtualized and used exclusively by the Storage Spaces technology. The disks' state can be seen through the Storage Pools view within File and Storage Services in Server Manager. To create a storage pool, follow these steps:

1. From the Tasks menu, select New Storage Pool, which launches the New Storage Pool Wizard.

2. Enter a name for the new storage pool and an optional description and click Next.

3. On the next screen, select the physical disks that are available to be added to the new pool and their allocation. The default allocation for disks will be Data Store to be used as part of virtual disks created but can also be reserved for Hot Spare purposes. Click Next

4. Once the confirmation is displayed, click Create to create the storage pool.

A storage pool is now available, and the next step is to create virtual disks within the storage pool, which can then have volumes created on them to be used by the operating system. The nomenclature is unfortunate here. While the term *virtual disk* is used by Storage Spaces, it is not a virtual hard disk of any kind and does not leverage VHD or VHDX. A virtual disk is simply an object created within a storage pool that is seen as a disk by the operating system, which writes directly to blocks within the storage pool.

Storage Spaces introduces a feature that was previously only available using external storage solutions such as SANs and NAS devices, the ability to thin provision storage. During the creation of a virtual disk, the option is available to create the new virtual disk as fixed, which means all the space for the size of the virtual disk is allocated at creation time, or thin, which means space is taken from the pool only as needed. Using a thin provisioned disk would allow a virtual disk to be created far larger than the actual storage available. This allows you to create a large volume initially without having to preallocate physical storage.

Now, this does not mean you can store more data in the thinly provisioned disk than actually is allocated to the pool but that typically volumes fill up over time. I may create a 10 TB thin disk that initially only has 1 TB of physical storage associated with it, but as the amount data increases and approaches 1 TB, I would add another 1 TB of physical storage to the pool by just adding more disks. As it approaches 2 TB, I add another 1 TB of storage by adding more disks and so on. As long as I add physical disks before it fills, there is no issue. Alerts will be generated notifying me that a storage pool is reaching the threshold, giving me time to add the required storage. When a virtual disk is created, all that needs to be known is which storage pool to create the disk in. No knowledge of physical disks is required or even openly available. The point of storage spaces is this abstraction to just create virtual disks as needed to suit what is required. To create a virtual disk, perform the following steps:

1. Select a storage pool in which to create a new virtual disk, and in the Virtual Disks section, select the New Virtual Disk task.

2. Confirm the correct server and storage pool is selected in the Storage Pool selection page of the wizard and click Next.

3. Give a name and optional description for the new virtual disk and then click Next.

4. Select the storage layout. The options are Simple (no data redundancy and data striped over many disks), Mirrored (data duplicated to additional disks), and Parity (spreads data over multiple disk like Simple but adds parity data so in the event of a disk loss, no data is lost). Prior to Storage Spaces, these layouts would have been referred to as RAID-0, RAID-1, and RAID-5, respectively, but that nomenclature is not used with Storage Spaces layouts due to differences in implementation.

   Make the selection and click Next. This is shown in Figure 4.3. A three-way mirror is possible in Windows Server 2012 and beyond, but it must be configured using PowerShell instead of the graphical interface.

5. Choose a provisioning type of Thin or Fixed, and click Next.

6. Specify a size. Remember, if Thin was selected, a size larger than the physical free space available can be selected. Click Next.

7. A confirmation of options will be displayed. Confirm them and click Create.

**FIGURE 4.3**
Creating a new virtual disk within a storage space

Once the virtual disk is created, it will be available within Server Manager and the Disk Management MMC to create volumes and be formatted with a file system. The actual amount of space used from a pool can be seen in Server Manager or, if you're using a client, in the Storage Spaces Control Panel applet.

---

**PERFORMANCE AND STORAGE SPACES**

One concern I always had when using software RAID prior to Windows Server 2012 was performance because any parity calculation had to use the processor, which used up processor cycles and typically was just not optimal compared to a hardware RAID solution. This is still a concern with Storage Spaces.

Fundamentally, Storage Spaces is a software-implemented storage solution. This means that, when using any kind of parity virtual disk, it is the operating system, specifically the processor, that has to calculate the parity information. Using a parity resiliency will utilize additional processor resources. In my experience, parity utilizes only a single processor core and therefore can quickly become a bottleneck if you are performing large amounts of disk writes, making it unsuitable for some workloads. Therefore, my advice is as follows:

◆ Use mirroring for workloads requiring high performance.

◆ Use parity for archival and media streaming purposes where there are not performance-critical write operations.

---

Windows Server 2012 R2 Storage Spaces has a number of improvements, including the ability to have dual-parity spaces, which allows up to two copies of parity information instead of one. That provides additional resiliency (dual parity needs to be configured using PowerShell and is not exposed in Server Manager), support for parity spaces in cluster scenarios, and much faster rebuild in the event of a failure by rebuilding the missing information to many disks in the storage pool instead of rebuilding everything to a single disk, which limits the speed of resolution to the IOPS possible by a single disk.

There was a bigger change in Windows Server 2012 R2 Storage Spaces that can open up new levels of performance and that is the differentiation between traditional spinning hard disk drives (HDDs) and solid-state drives (SSDs). In a Windows Server 2012 R2 storage space, it is possible to create different tiers of storage, an HDD tier and a SSD tier, and the Storage Spaces technology will move the most-used blocks of a file from the HDD tier into the SSD tier, giving the highest levels of performance. Additionally, the SSD tier can be leveraged for a write-back cache. This means that as writes occur, they are written into the SSD tier initially, which is very fast, and then lazily written to the HDD tier for long-term storage. This new tiering model is shown in Figure 4.4. When you use tiering, you must have a sufficient number of disks from each tier to meet the data resiliency options. For example, if mirroring is selected for a virtual disk, at least two disks would need to be available with enough space in the HDD tier and in the SSD tier. The same applies for the write-back cache. Storage Spaces will not allow a drop in resiliency.

To utilize tiering and the write-back cache you can use PowerShell, which gives granular control (although by default a 1 GB write-back cache is created on all new virtual disks if sufficient SSD space and disks are available in the pool), or Server Manager for a simpler experience but with less granularity in the configuration. In the following PowerShell commands, I create a storage space from four physical disks, two HDDs and two SSDs, and then create a virtual disk and create a volume:

```
#List all disks that can be pooled and output in table format (format-table)
Get-PhysicalDisk -CanPool $True | `
ft FriendlyName,OperationalStatus,Size,MediaType
```

```
#Store all physical disks that can be pooled into a variable, $pd
$pd = (Get-PhysicalDisk -CanPool $True | Where MediaType -NE UnSpecified)
#Create a new Storage Pool using the disks in variable $pd
#with a name of My Storage Pool
New-StoragePool -PhysicalDisks $pd `
-StorageSubSystemFriendlyName "Storage Spaces*" `
-FriendlyName "My Storage Pool"
#View the disks in the Storage Pool just created
Get-StoragePool -FriendlyName "My Storage Pool" | `
Get-PhysicalDisk | Select FriendlyName, MediaType

#Create two tiers in the Storage Pool created.
#One for SSD disks and one for HDD disks
$ssd_Tier = New-StorageTier -StoragePoolFriendlyName "My Storage Pool" `
-FriendlyName SSD_Tier -MediaType SSD
$hdd_Tier = New-StorageTier -StoragePoolFriendlyName "My Storage Pool" `
-FriendlyName HDD_Tier -MediaType HDD

#Create a new virtual disk in the pool with a name of TieredSpace
#using the SSD (50GB) and HDD (300GB) tiers
$vd1 = New-VirtualDisk -StoragePoolFriendlyName "My Storage Pool" `
-FriendlyName TieredSpace -StorageTiers @($ssd_tier, $hdd_tier) `
-StorageTierSizes @(50GB, 300GB) -ResiliencySettingName Mirror `
-WriteCacheSize 1GB
#cannot also specify -size if using tiers and also
#cannot use provisioning type, e.g. Thin
```

**FIGURE 4.4**
Storage Spaces architecture showing a hot block moving from the HDD tier to the SSD tier

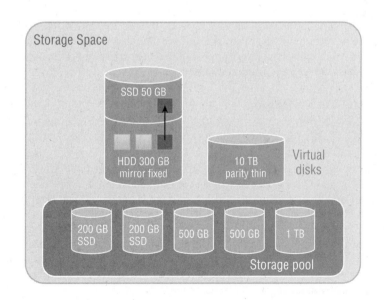

Normally the hot blocks are detected over time and moved into the SSD tier as part of a nightly optimization job at 1:00 a.m. However, certain files can be pinned to the SSD tier, which will keep them there permanently. To pin a file to the SSD tier and then force a tier optimization, use the following commands:

```
Set-FileStorageTier -FilePath M:\Important\test.vhd `
  -DesiredStorageTier ($vd1 | Get-StorageTier -MediaType SSD)
Optimize-Volume -DriveLetter M -TierOptimize
```

With Storage Spaces technology, you can create flexible and performant storage solutions using direct attached disks, which can be useful in a number of scenarios and architectures. I walk through Storage Spaces in a video at

www.youtube.com/watch?v=x8KlY-aP9oE&feature=share&list=UUpIn7ox7j7bH_OFj7tYouOQ

The use of tiering is a great feature for virtualization and will help you get the highest over-all performance without having to use high-end storage for the entire storage solution.

## Server Message Block (SMB) Usage

While SMB has been available in Windows for a very long time, its usage has been limited to basic file sharing scenarios such as users accessing their home drives or a file share containing some archived data. Hyper-V had long had the requirement of having block-level access to its storage; that is, the host mounted the volumes that contained the virtual machines, which could be direct attached or connected via mediums such as iSCSI or Fibre Channel. However, this was a challenge for many organization that were used to using file-level protocols with virtualiza-tion. Specifically, VMware supported NFS for virtual machine storage, which was available in many NAS solutions that typically are much cheaper than SAN solutions and are a good fit for many environments.

Windows Server 2012 invested greatly in SMB to make it an enterprise-ready solution suit-able for storing virtual machines and other enterprise workloads, such as SQL Server databases. SMB 3.0 introduced a large number of new features and performance improvements to make it a realistic choice for virtualization storage.

### SMB Technologies

I previously talked about SMB being used to store user documents, and now with SMB 3.0, it will be used to store mission-critical virtual machines. This requires a big shift in resiliency and failover technologies. When the user is editing their PowerPoint document from a SMB share, portions of the document are cached locally and occasionally the user clicks Save. If the SMB file server experiences a problem—for example, if it reboots or if it's clustered and the file share is moved to another node in the cluster—the user would lose their handle and lock to the file, but that really does not have any impact. The next time the user clicks Save, everything is rees-tablished and no harm is done. Now consider Hyper-V storing a virtual machine on a SMB file share that experiences a problem and the file share moves to another node in the cluster. First, the Hyper-V box will wait for the TCP time-out before realizing the original connection has gone, which can mean 30 seconds of pause to the VM, but also Hyper-V has now lost its handles and locks on the VHD, which is a major problem. Where user documents may be used for a few hours, enterprise services like a virtual machine or database expect handles on files to be available for months without interruption.

## SMB TRANSPARENT FAILOVER

Typically for a clustered file service, a single node of the cluster mounts the LUN containing the file system being shared and offers the share to SMB clients. If that node fails, another node in the cluster mounts the LUN and offers the file share but the SMB client would lose their handles and locks. SMB Transparent Failover provides protection from a node failure, enabling a share to move between nodes in a manner completely transparent to the SMB clients and maintaining any locks and handles that exist and also the state of the SMB connection.

The state of that a SMB connection is maintained over three entities: the SMB client, the SMB server, and the disk itself that holds the data. SMB Transparent Failover ensures that there is enough context to bring back the state of the SMB connection to an alternate node in the event of a node failure, which allows SMB activities to continue without the risk of error.

It's important to understand that even with SMB Transparent Failover there can still be a pause to IO because the LUN still has to be mounted on a new node in the cluster. However, the failover clustering team has done a huge amount of work around optimizing the dismount and mount of a LUN to ensure that it never takes more than 25 seconds, which sounds like a lot of time, but realize that is the absolute worst-case scenario with large numbers of LUNs and tens of thousands of handles. For most common scenarios, the time would be a couple of seconds, and enterprise services such as Hyper-V and SQL Server can handle an IO operation taking up to 25 seconds without error in that worst possible case.

There is another cause of a possible interruption to IO and that's the SMB client actually noticing that the SMB server is not available. In a typical planned scenario such as a node rebooting because it's being patched, it will notify any clients who can then take actions. If a node crashes, though, there is no notification to the client and so the client will sit and wait for TCP time-out before it takes action to reestablish connectivity, which is a waste of resources. Although a SMB client may have no idea that the node it's talking to in the cluster has crashed, the other nodes in the cluster know within a second thanks to the various IsAlive messages that are sent between the nodes. This knowledge is leveraged by a new witness service capability that is available in Windows Server 2012. The witness server essentially allows another node in the cluster to act as a witness for the SMB client, and if the node the client is talking to fails, the witness node notifies the SMB client straight away, allowing the client to connect to another node, which minimizes the interruption to service to a couple of seconds. When a SMB client communicates to a SMB server that is part of a cluster, the SMB server will notify the client that other servers are available in the cluster and the client will automatically ask one of the other servers in the cluster to act as the witness service for the connection.

There is no manual action required to take advantage of SMB Transparent Failover or the witness service. When you create a new share on a Windows Server 2012 or above failover cluster, SMB Transparent Failover is enabled automatically.

## SMB SCALE-OUT

In the previous section, I explained that there would be a pause in activity because the LUN had to be moved between nodes in the file server cluster, but this delay can be removed. This problem stems from the fact that NTFS is a shared-nothing file system and cannot be accessed by multiple operating system instances concurrently without the risk of corruption. This problem was solved with the introduction of Cluster Shared Volumes (CSV) in Windows Server 2008 R2. CSV allowed all nodes in a cluster to read and write to the same set of LUNs simultaneously using some very clever techniques, thus removing the need to dismount and mount LUNs between the nodes.

Windows Server 2012 extends the use of CSV to a specific type of file server, namely the Scale-Out File Server option, which is a new option available in Windows Server 2012 and targeted for use only when sharing out application data such as SQL Server databases and Hyper-V virtual machines. The traditional style of the general-use file server is still available for non-application data, as shown in Figure 4.5. When selecting the option to create a scale-out file server (SoFS), you must select a CSV as the storage when shares are subsequently created within the file server; the storage is therefore available to all nodes in the cluster. Because the storage for the share is available to all nodes in the cluster, the file share itself is also hosted by all the nodes in the cluster, which now means SMB client connections are distributed over all the nodes instead of just one. In addition, if a node fails, there is now no work involved in moving the LUNs, offering an even better experience and reducing any interruption in operations to almost zero, which is critical for the application server workloads to which this scale-out file server is targeted.

**FIGURE 4.5**
Enabling active-active through the selection of Scale-Out File Server For Application Data

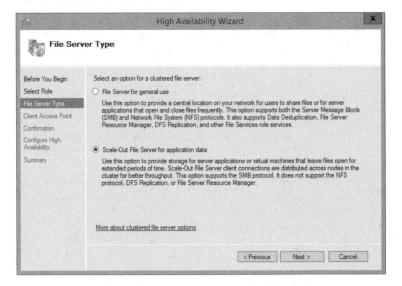

The use of scale-out file servers offers an additional benefit. Typically, when a general-use file server is created as part of the configuration, you have to give the new cluster file server a NetBIOS name and also its own unique IP address because that IP address has to be hosted by whichever node in the cluster is currently hosting the file server. With scale-out file servers, all nodes in the cluster offer the file service, which means no additional IP addresses are required. The IP addresses of the nodes in the cluster are utilized via the Distributed Network Name (DNN) that is configured.

All the nodes in the cluster are offering the same file service and therefore share with the scale-out file server, and there is a change in functionality between Windows Server 2012 and Windows Server 2012 R2. In Windows Server 2012, a single SMB client will only ever connect to one of the nodes in the cluster simultaneously even if establishing multiple connections. Essentially, when the SMB client initiates connections, it will initially get a list of all the IP addresses for the hosts in the cluster and pick one of them to initiate the SMB session with. It will then use only that node unless that node experiences a problem, in which case it will converse with an alternate node. The exception is that the SMB client does communicate with a second node when leveraging the witness service I previously discussed. Windows Server 2012 R2 introduces a rebalancing feature that will has two components:

◆ The CSV disk ownerships are distributed evenly between all nodes in the cluster, spreading the workload.

◆ SMB connections are rebalanced so clients are directed to the CSV owner, giving the most optimal connection when used with clustered Storage Spaces (this rebalancing is not required when using symmetrical storage such as a Fibre Channel connected SANs because every node has equivalent connectivity).

This means that a single SMB client could now be connected to multiple nodes in a cluster via SMB instead of a single node.

## SMB MULTICHANNEL

It is critical to avoid any single points of failure in any solution, and if SMB is being used to access the storage containing virtual machines, there must be resiliency to prevent a single network adapter, network cable, or network switch from failing. In storage fabrics, technologies such as Multi-Path I/O (MPIO) are used to provide multiple paths to storage, and this same idea is now possible with SMB using SMB Multichannel.

SMB Multichannel allows a SMB client to establish multiple connections for a single session, providing protection from a single connection failure and also adding additional performance. As with most of the SMB 3.0 features, there are no manual steps to utilize SMB Multichannel; it happens automatically. Once the initial SMB connection has been established, the SMB client looks for additional paths to the SMB server, and where multiple network connections are present, those additional paths are utilized. This would be apparent if you're monitoring a file copy operation as initially only a single connection's worth of bandwidth. However, the bandwidth would double as the second connection was established and the bandwidth aggregated, then the third connection, and so on. In the event a connection fails, there are still other connections to continue the SMB channel without interruption.

To see whether SMB Multichannel is being utilized from your server, use the `Get-SMBConnection` PowerShell cmdlet, which will show the SMB connections to a SMB share. In the following example, I see that I have only two connections to my server:

```
PS C:\> get-smbconnection

ServerName        ShareName  UserName       Credential      Dialect NumOpens
----------        ---------  --------       ----------      ------- --------
savdalsofs.sav... Virtuals   NT VIRTUAL ... SAVILLTECH.N... 3.02    4
savdalsofs.sav... Virtuals   SAVILLTECH\... SAVILLTECH.N... 3.02    2
```

If I run the `Get-SmbMultiChannelConnection` cmdlet from the client, it shows me all the possible paths that the server can accept connections over, as shown in the following output. Note that on the server side, networking uses a NIC team, which means only one IP address but can still leverage SMB Multichannel.

```
PS C:\> get-smbmultichannelconnection
```

| Server Name | Selected | Client IP | Server IP | Client | Server | Client |
|-------------|----------|-----------|-----------|--------|--------|--------|
| RSS | Client RDMA | | | | | |
| | | | | Interface | Interface | |
| Capable | Capable | | | | | |
| | | | | Index | Index | |
| ----------- | -------- | --------- | --------- | ------- | -------------- | ------- |
| ------- | -------------- | | | | | |
| savdalsofs.... | True | 10.7.173.101 | 10.7.173.20 | 14 | 15 | True |
| False | | | | | | |
| savdalsofs.... | True | 10.7.173.23 | 10.7.173.20 | 15 | 15 | True |
| False | | | | | | |

To confirm which path is actually being used between the client and the server, I can look at the TCP connections to the remote port 445, which is used for SMB. This confirms that I am using the two available paths with four connections for each path (which is the default number).

```
PS C:\> Get-NetTCPConnection -RemotePort 445
```

| LocalAddress | | LocalPort | RemoteAddress | |
|--------------|--|-----------|---------------|--|
| RemotePort State | AppliedSetting | | | |
| ------------ | | --------- | -------------- | --------- |
| - ----- | -------------- | | | |
| 10.7.173.23 | | 56368 | 10.7.173.20 | 445 |
| Established Datacenter | | | | |
| 10.7.173.23 | | 49826 | 10.7.173.20 | 445 |
| Established Datacenter | | | | |
| 10.7.173.23 | | 49825 | 10.7.173.20 | 445 |
| Established Datacenter | | | | |
| 10.7.173.23 | | 49824 | 10.7.173.20 | 445 |
| Established Datacenter | | | | |
| 10.7.173.101 | | 49823 | 10.7.173.20 | 445 |
| Established Datacenter | | | | |
| 10.7.173.101 | | 49822 | 10.7.173.20 | 445 |
| Established Datacenter | | | | |
| 10.7.173.101 | | 49821 | 10.7.173.20 | 445 |
| Established Datacenter | | | | |
| 10.7.173.101 | | 49820 | 10.7.173.20 | 445 |
| Established Datacenter | | | | |

## SMB DIRECT

While there are a number of other SMB technologies, such as encryption, Receive Side Scaling, VSS for SMB File Shares, and more, the last feature I want to mention is SMB Direct, which enables the use of RDMA-capable network adapters with SMB. I discussed remote direct memory access (RDMA) in the Chapter 3 as it relates to network adapters, and it's is equally important to SMB.

With SMB Direct leveraging the RDMA capability of the network adapter, there is almost no utilization of server processor resources. The network adapter is essentially pointed to a block of memory containing the data that needs to be sent to the target, and then the card takes care of sending it using the fastest possible speed with very low latencies. Behind the scenes, the RDMA network adapter may use iWARP, RDMA over Converged Ethernet (RoCE), or InfiniBand, but that does not matter to the SMB protocol, which just benefits from the RDMA capability.

There is no special requirement to leverage SMB Direct. Like everything else with SMB, if the capability exists, it just happens. Initially, a regular SMB connection is established between the client and server. A list of all possible connections is found, which enables the use of multi-channel, and then the capabilities of the network adapters are found. If it is found that both the sender and receiver support RDMA, then a RDMA connection is established and SMB operations switch from TCP to RDMA, completely transparently.

If you used SMB Direct in Windows Server 2012, you will see a 50 percent performance improvement using the SMB Direct v2 in Windows Server 2012 R2 for small IO workloads, specifically 8 KB IOPs, which are common in virtualization scenarios.

The performance improvement is important because SMB is leveraged for more than just file operations now. SMB is also used by Live Migration in some configurations, specifically to take advantage of RDMA-capable NICs. Remember, do *not* use NIC Teaming with RDMA-capable network adapters because NIC Teaming blocks the use of RDMA.

## How to Leverage SMB 3 in Your Environment

If right now your datacenter has every virtualization host connected to your top-of-the-line SAN using Fibre Channel, then most likely SMB 3 will not factor into that environment today. However, if not every server is connected to the SAN or you have new environments such as datacenters or remote locations that don't have a SAN or that will have a SAN but you want to try to minimize the fabric costs of Fibre Channel cards and switches, SMB 3 can help.

If you already have a SAN but do not currently have the infrastructure (for example, the HBAs) to connect every host to the SAN, then a great option is shown in Figure 4.6. A scale-out file server cluster is placed in front of the SAN, which provides access to the SAN storage via SMB 3. This allows the investment in the SAN and its capabilities to be leveraged by the entire datacenter without requiring all the hosts to be connected directly to the SAN. To ensure best performance, have at least as many CSV volumes as nodes in the cluster to allow the balancing to take place. Have double or triple the number of CSV volumes for even better tuning. For example, if I have four hosts in the SoFS cluster, then I would want at least eight CSV volumes.

Another option if you do not have a SAN or don't want to use it for certain workloads is to leverage Storage Spaces as the backend storage. While it would be possible to have a single server using Storage Spaces and hosting storage via SMB 3 to remote hosts, this would be a poor design because it introduces a single point of failure. If the SMB 3 server was unavailable, every workload hosted on the server would be unavailable as well. Always leverage a file server cluster and use a clustered storage space, which would have the disks stored in an external enclosure and be accessible to all the nodes in the cluster that are connected. Ensure that resiliency is enabled for the virtual disks created, most likely mirroring for best performance. This would look like Figure 4.7.

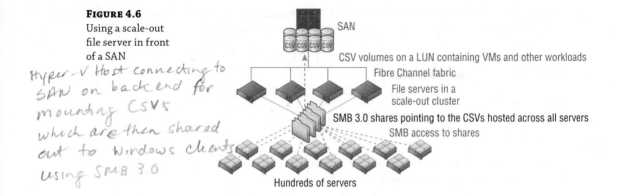

**FIGURE 4.6**
Using a scale-out file server in front of a SAN

*Hyper-V Host connecting to SAN on back end for mounting CSVs which are then shared out to Windows clients using SMB 3.0*

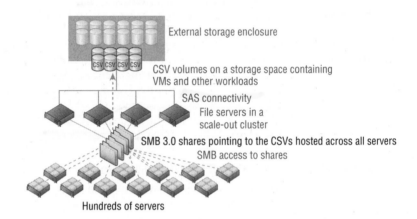

**FIGURE 4.7**
Using a scale-out file server and a clustered storage space

## Using SMB for Hyper-V Storage

Using SMB 3 with Hyper-V is easy. The Hyper-V host's computer account and the cluster account (if hosts are in a cluster) requires full control at the share and NTFS file system level. Additionally, the administrator creating or moving the virtual machines should have full control at the share and NTFS level. The easiest way to set the correct permissions is using PowerShell, which is simple in Windows Server 2012 R2. This could also be done through Failover Cluster Manager on shares created on scale-out file servers. The following command creates a folder and then gives the computer accounts for Hyper-V hosts HV01 and HV02 full control and the HVCLUS account for the failover cluster they are in full control as well. Note the $ after the computer account names, which must be typed. Additionally the administrator is given full control.

```
MD G:\VMStore
New-SmbShare -Name VMStore -Path G:\VMStore '
 -FullAccess domain\administrator, '
domain\HV01$, domain\HV02$, domain\HVCLUS$
Set-SmbPathAcl -Name VMStore
```

Note that in Windows Server 2012, the `Set-SmbPathAcl` cmdlet was not available and the NTFS permissions had to be set manually, as shown in the following command. Note this is *not* required in Windows Server 2012 R2 because the `Set-SmbPathAcl` cmdlet copied the share permissions to the NTFS file system.

```
ICACLS G:\VMStore /Inheritance:R
ICACLS G:\VMStore /Grant ' "domain\administrator:(CI)(OI)F"
ICACLS G:\VMStore /Grant domain\HV01$:(CI)(OI)F
ICACLS G:\VMStore /Grant domain\HV02$:(CI)(OI)F
ICACLS G:\VMStore /Grant domain\HVCLUS$:(CI)(OI)F
```

Once the permissions are correctly set, simply specify the SMB share as the location for VM creation or as the target of a storage migration. Figure 4.8 shows a virtual machine using the share `\\savdalsofs\Virtuals` for its storage. Note that not only is the disk stored on the share, but also the configuration files, checkpoint files, and smart paging files. It's actually possible to use different storage locations for the different assets of a virtual machine.

**FIGURE 4.8**
A virtual machine using SMB for its storage

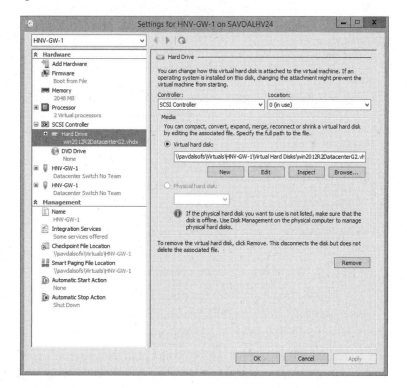

# iSCSI with Hyper-V

Previously I talked about assigning storage to the virtual machine in the form of a virtual hard disk, which required the Hyper-V host to connect to the storage and then create the VHDX files on it. There are, however, other ways to present storage to virtual machines.

iSCSI is a popular alternative to fibre channel connectivity that allows block-level connectivity to SAN storage using the existing network infrastructure instead of requiring a completely separate fabric (cards, cables, switches) just for storage. iSCSI works by carrying the traditional SCSI commands over IP networks. While it is possible to run iSCSI over the existing network infrastructure, if iSCSI is being used as the primary storage transport, it is common to have a dedicated network connection for iSCSI to ensure the required bandwidth or, ideally, to leverage larger network connections such as 10 Gbps and use QoS to ensure that iSCSI gets the required amount of bandwidth.

In addition to using iSCSI on the Hyper-V host to access storage, it can also be leveraged within virtual machines as a means to provide storage that is accessible to the virtual machine including providing storage that could be accessed by multiple virtual machines concurrently, known as shared storage, and is required in many cluster scenarios in which clusters are implemented within virtual machines, known as guest clustering. If you intend to leverage iSCSI within virtual machines, it is a good idea to have dedicated networking for iSCSI, which means creating a separate virtual switch on the Hyper-V hosts connected to the adapters allocated for iSCSI and then creating an additional network adapter in the virtual machines connected to the virtual switch. If the iSCSI communication is important to the business, you may want to implement redundant connectivity, which can be accomplished by creating multiple virtual switches connected to different network adapters, creating multiple virtual network adapters in the virtual machines (connected to the different virtual switches), and then using MPIO within the virtual machine. I will talk more about MPIO in the section "Understanding Virtual Fibre Channel." Do *not* use NIC Teaming with iSCSI because it's not supported, except in one scenario.

If you have a shared NIC scenario (as discussed in Chapter 3), which uses a number of separate network adapters that are teamed together using the Windows Server NIC Teaming solution (it *must* be the Windows in-box NIC Teaming solution) and the NIC team then has multiple virtual network adapters created at the host level for different purposes, one of which is for iSCSI, NIC Teaming *is* supported. But this is the only time it can be used with iSCSI. If you had dedicated network adapters for iSCSI, then use MPIO.

There are two parts to iSCSI: the iSCSI Initiator, which is the client software that allows connectivity to iSCSI storage, and the iSCSI target, which is the server software. The iSCSI Initiator has been a built-in component of Windows since Windows Server 2008/Windows Vista and is also available for Windows 2000 and above from

`www.microsoft.com/en-us/download/details.aspx?id=18986`

Windows also has a built-in iSCSI target from Windows Server 2012 and above and is available as a downloadable component for Windows Server 2008 R2 from

`www.microsoft.com/en-us/download/details.aspx?id=19867`

Additionally, most SAN solutions offer iSCSI as a means to connect and some NAS solutions. There are other components to iSCSI available, such as iSNS, which provides a centralized repository of iSCSI servers, making discovery simpler. A full deep dive into iSCSI is beyond the scope of this discussion. My focus will be on the mandatory requirements to enable an iSCSI connection.

## Using the Windows iSCSI Target

The Windows Server iSCSI target provides storage using the virtual hard disk format, which would be the equivalent of a LUN on a traditional SAN. The Windows Server 2012 iSCSI target used the VHD implementation for the storage, which limited iSCSI targets to 2 TB in size and to the fixed type that requires all storage to be allocated at target creation time. The Windows Server 2012 R2 iSCSI target leverages VHDX instead, which allows 64 TB iSCSI targets and also allows the option to use the dynamic type, removing the requirement for all storage to be allocated at creation and instead allocates as data is written.

The iSCSI target is not installed by default. It must be installed using Server Manager and is available at File And Storage Services ➤ File And iSCSI Services ➤ iSCSI Target Server. A VDS and VSS provider is also available (iSCSI Target Storage Provider [VDS and VSS hardware providers]). The target can also be installed using PowerShell:

```
Install-WindowsFeature FS-iSCSITarget-Server
```

Once the iSCSI target role service is installed, it is managed through Server Manager ➤ File And Storage Services ➤ iSCSI. Use the following basic steps to enable a new iSCSI target:

1. Navigate to File And Storage Services ➤ iSCSI in Server Manager on the iSCSI target server.

2. From the Tasks menu, select the New iSCSI Virtual Disk action.

3. Select the server to host the iSCSI target, and then select either a volume that will host the VHDX file (by default the VHDX will be created in a root folder named iSCSIVirtual-Disks on the selected volume) or a custom path. Click Next.

4. Enter a name and optional description for the VHDX file that will be created. Make the name descriptive so its use may be ascertained by looking at the VHDX filename only. Click Next.

5. Enter the size for the new VHDX file, which will be the size available for the iSCSI target. Note, as shown in Figure 4.9, that all the types of VHDX are available for the iSCSI target, including the option to zero out the content of the disk when creating a fixed-size VHDX to ensure that no old data would be exposed. Notice also that the option to create a differencing VHDX file is available, which is useful if you have a VHDX with existing content that you wish to make available as part of the new iSCSI target without copying all the content.

   While this is not iSCSI specific, it is vital that if you use any dynamic storage, such as dynamic or differencing, you have monitoring and processes in place to ensure that the underlying storage does not run out of space, which would cause problems for any services using the target. Click Next.

6. For the iSCSI target name, which is a unique name for each target, select New iSCSI Target (or an existing target could be selected) and click Next.

7. Enter a name for the new target. While the iSCSI target name syntax is complex, you only need to enter a unique name that represents how you wish to identify the new target (for example, ProjectOne). The wizard will take care of using the name you enter within the full iSCSI target name. Enter your unique portion of the new target name and an optional description and click Next.

8. The next step is to grant permission to the various iSCSI initiator names (the clients, known as the IQN) that should be allowed to connect to the new iSCSI target you are creating. Click the Add button to add each target. If you know the IQN of the iSCSI Initiator, select Enter A Value For The Selected Type and enter the value (the IQN for a client can be viewed via the Configuration tab of the iSCSI Initiator Control Panel applet on the client).

   An easier way is to select the Query Initiator Computer For ID option and enter the computer's name, which allows the wizard to scan the remote machine and find the correct IQN. That method works on Windows Server 2012 and later. Click OK. Once all the IQNs are added, click Next.

9. In the Enable Authentication section, leave all the options blank and click Next.

10. On the confirmation screen, verify all options and click Create. Once the target is created, click Close.

**FIGURE 4.9**
Selecting the options for the new iSCSI VHDX target

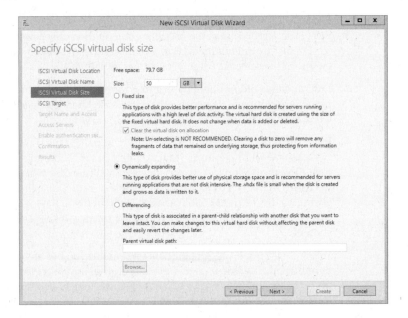

Note the whole creation can also be automated in PowerShell using the New-IscsiVirtualDisk and New-IscsiServerTarget cmdlets. At this stage, you have a Windows-hosted iSCSI target that has been configured so that specific IQNs can access it. If the Windows iSCSI target is used to host important data, then a cluster should be used to provide the iSCSI service, which is fully cluster supported.

## Using the Windows iSCSI Initiator

While the iSCSI target is built into Windows Server, by default the service, called Microsoft iSCSI Initiator, is not started, and its startup is set to manual. The first time you launch the iSCSI Initiator Control Panel applet you will be notified that the service is not running and asked if you wish the service to be modified so it starts automatically. Click Yes.

The iSCSI Initiator properties are accessed through a number of property tabs. The Configuration tab shows the IQN of the client (which can be modified) and also allows CHAP and IPsec configurations. Most of the actions you need to perform are through the Discovery and Targets tabs.

On the Discovery tab, click the Discovery Portal button, enter the DNS name or IP address of the iSCSI server, and click OK. This will perform a scan of all the targets on the specified server that the initiator has permission to access. To connect to one of the targets, select the Targets tab, select a discovered target, and click Connect. This will connect to the storage and add it as a favorite by default, which means it will automatically connect after reboots, as shown in Figure 4.10. Once connected in Disk Manager the new disk will be shown where it should be brought online, initialized and formatted.

**FIGURE 4.10**
Connecting to a new iSCSI target using the built-in iSCSI Initiator

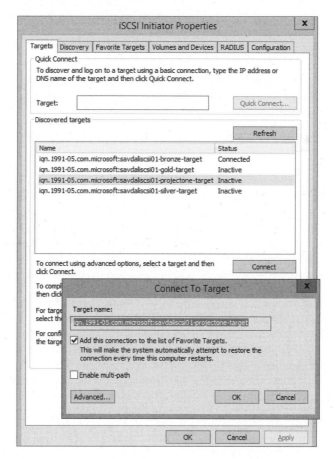

This connection could be made from a Hyper-V host to access storage or from within your virtual machine. The benefit of iSCSI is that multiple iSCSI Initiators can connect to the same iSCSI target, which would enable shared storage and numerous failover cluster scenarios within the virtual machines.

## Considerations for Using iSCSI

Using iSCSI to enable shared storage between virtual machines in Windows Server 2008 R2 was the only option and was also the only way to access volumes greater than 2 TB (when not connecting to a Windows iSCSI target, which still had a 2 TB limit because it used VHD as the storage) without using a pass-through disk. If iSCSI is the storage standard for your organization, then using it within virtual machines is still a workable solution. With Windows Server 2012 R2, though, there is a better option, which I will go into in section "Leveraging Shared VHDX." A benefit of iSCSI is that the Hyper-V host itself does not require any access to the storage. The virtual machine's guest OS IQN is what is given permission to the target and not the host.

There are also some challenges you should be aware of when using iSCSI:

- Hyper-V has no knowledge that the virtual machine is using iSCSI-connected storage.

- If a backup is taken of the virtual machine at the Hyper-V host, then none of the data stored in iSCSI targets would be backed up.

- While technologies like Live Migration and Hyper-V Replica (only if the VSS integration component is disabled for the VM) will still function, they protect and move only the VHDX/VHD content and not data stored on iSCSI targets.

- To use iSCSI, the guest operating system must know details of the iSCSI fabric, which may not be desirable, especially in hoster scenarios.

# Understanding Virtual Fibre Channel

While iSCSI provided a method to enable shared storage within virtual machines, many organizations did not use iSCSI and instead relied on fibre channel to access their SAN environments. These organizations wanted to enable virtual machines to be able to access the SAN directly using the host's fibre channel host bus adapter (HBA, basically similar to a network card but used to connect to storage fabric with technologies to enable very fast and efficient movement of data).

Windows Server 2012 introduced Virtual Fibre Channel to allow virtual machines to directly connect to storage on a fibre channel–connected SAN whose architecture is like that shown in Figure 4.11. The architecture is similar in structure to how networking works with Hyper-V.

Notice in Figure 4.11 that on the Hyper-V host one or more virtual SANs are created, and they connect to one or more HBAs on the Hyper-V host. The key is to not introduce a single point of failure, which means there are multiple virtual SANs connected to different HBAs that connect to different physical switches, and then within the virtual machines, there are multiple virtual adapters, each connecting to a different virtual SAN.

To use virtual fibre channel, the HBA must support and be enabled for N-Port ID Virtualization (NPIV), which allows virtual port IDs to share a single physical port. If your HBA does not support NPIV or NPIV is not enabled, this will be shown when you are trying to create a virtual SAN, as shown in Figure 4.12.

**FIGURE 4.11**
Using virtual fibre channel with Hyper-V

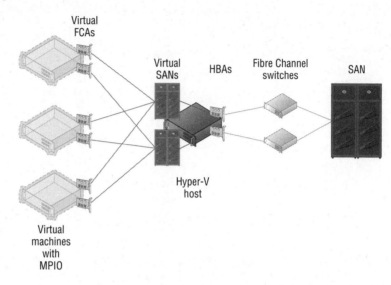

**FIGURE 4.12**
Problem with the ports that will block using in a virtual SAN

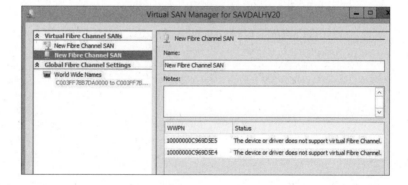

There are some key steps to take when trying to resolve supportability with NPIV:

1. Make sure the HBA supports NPIV. This seems obvious, but check the specifications of the HBA to ensure that it will work with NPIV.

2. Check if NPIV is enabled. Many HBAs ship with NPIV disabled by default. Use whatever management application is available to ensure that NPIV is enabled. As shown in Figure 4.13, I used the OneCommand Manager tool to see if NPIV is enabled on my Emulex card.

3. Update the firmware for the HBA and the driver on the Hyper-V host. Note that if you update the firmware, it may reset NPIV to disabled again, so you will need to reenable it. In my experience, a firmware and driver update is often required to fully enable NPIV.

**FIGURE 4.13**
Enabling NPIV using the OneCommand Manager tool

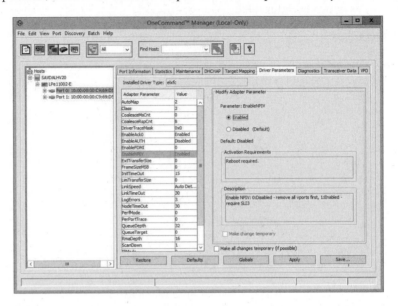

Assuming I have two HBA ports in my Hyper-V host, I will create two separate virtual SANs, each connected to one of the HBA ports. This assumes that each of the HBA ports is connected to a different fibre channel switch to remove single points of failure. If you have four HBA ports, each virtual SAN would be configured with two of the HBA ports. A single HBA port cannot be assigned to more than one virtual SAN. My configuration is shown in Figure 4.14 with two virtual SANs, each using one of the available ports.

**FIGURE 4.14**
A virtual SAN using one of the available HBA ports

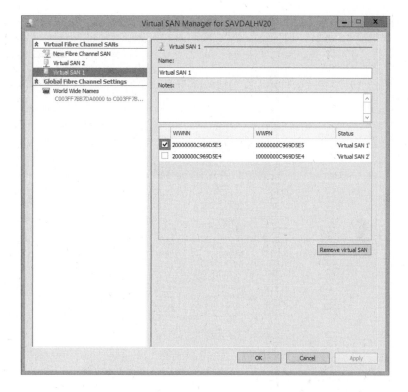

Once the virtual SANs are created, the next step is to add virtual fibre channel adapters (vFCAs) to the virtual machines that need to access the storage. Open the settings of the virtual machine, and in the Add Hardware section, select Fibre Channel Adapter and click Add. Each virtual machine should have two vFCAs, each connected to a different virtual SAN, providing the virtual machine with redundant connections and protection from a single point of failure as highlighted in Figure 4.11 previously. The only configuration for the vFCA is to select the virtual SAN it will connect to, and each vFCA is assigned two sets of World Wide Port Names (WWPNs), as shown in Figure 4.15, which are used to zone access to storage in the switches, effectively granting access to storage. I will cover why each vFCA gets two WWPNs later. Notice the Copy button that will take the WWPN and World Wide Node Name (WWNN) information for the vFCA and copy it to the Clipboard; it can then be used in your notes or in your switch configuration tool to zone storage.

**FIGURE 4.15**
A virtual fibre channel adapter for a virtual machine

With the WWPNs available, the next step would be in your switch to zone storage to the WWPNs (both of the WWPNs for each adapter) of the virtual machine and assign to LUNs on the SAN. When you start a virtual machine with vFCAs assigned but currently with no storage zoned to those vFCAs, you will notice that the virtual machine progress stays at 1% when starting for 90 seconds. This is because the vFCA picks a HBA from the virtual SAN it is connected to and calls the HBA driver to create a virtual port. The vFCA then looks for at least one LUN to be accessible before it continues. If there is no storage zoned to the vFCA, then this LUN check will not work and the 90-second time-out has to expire and an event log will be written:

```
Log Name:       Microsoft-Windows-Hyper-V-SynthFC-Admin
Source:         Microsoft-Windows-Hyper-V-SynthFcVdev
Date:           10/9/2013 2:13:08 PM
Event ID:       32213
Task Category: None
Level:          Warning
Keywords:
User:           NT VIRTUAL MACHINE\1F2AA062-7677-45C0-86F6-643C33796A9D
Computer:       savdalhv20.savilltech.net
Description:
'savdalfc01': No LUNs have appeared for Synthetic Fibre Channel HBA
Fibre Channel Adapter (BB50C162-40E7-412B-AB06-B34104CF6D17). The
VM has been started after the timeout period (90 seconds). Please
```

```
review the LUN mappings for the virtual port. (Virtual machine ID
1F2AA062-7677-45C0-86F6-643C33796A9D)
```

You may need to start this way initially so the WWPNs show on the fibre channel switch to allow them to be zoned. Then once available storage is zoned, the result will be another event log being written to show that storage is now available on the vFCA:

```
Log Name:      Microsoft-Windows-Hyper-V-SynthFC-Admin
Source:        Microsoft-Windows-Hyper-V-SynthFcVdev
Date:          10/9/2013 3:33:42 PM
Event ID:      32210
Task Category: None
Level:         Information
Keywords:
User:          NT VIRTUAL MACHINE\1F2AA062-7677-45C0-86F6-643C33796A9D
Computer:      savdalhv20.savilltech.net
Description:
'savdalfc01': A new LUN '\\?\SCSI#VMLUN&Ven_NETAPP&Prod_LUN#5&12d7e3f3&0&070000#{
6f416619-
9f29-42a5-b20b-37e219ca02b0}' has been added for the Synthetic Fibre
Channel HBA Fibre Channel Adapter (BB50C162-40E7-412B-AB06-B34104CF6D17).
(Virtual machine ID 1F2AA062-7677-45C0-86F6-643C33796A9D)
```

I want to step back now and cover why each vFCA has two WWPNs. One of the most used features of Hyper-V is Live Migration, which is the ability to move a virtual machine between hosts with no downtime to the virtual machine. It was important that virtual fibre channel did not break the ability to live migrate a virtual machine. However, if a vFCA had a single WWPN when a virtual machine was moved to another host as part of the migration, it would be necessary to temporarily disconnect the connection to the storage so the WWPN could be used on the target host, which would result in storage access interruption. Therefore, each vFCA has two WWPNs, which enables the second WWPN to be used on the target of the live migration, enabling both the source and targets to be connected to the storage during a live migration and avoiding any interruption. As live migrations are performed, the WWPN used will switch between the A and B set with each migration. This is important because when you are zoning the storage, you must zone both the A and B WWPN or if you live migrate the virtual machine, it will lose access. It may be necessary to perform a live migration of the virtual machines to activate the second set of WWPNs to allow them to be zoned on the switches if you cannot manually specify WWPNs that are not currently visible to the switch. This means the process may look like this:

1. Start the virtual machine.

2. Connect to the switch, and create an alias (or any other construct, depending on the switch) for the visible WWPNs.

3. Live migrate the virtual machine to another host, which will trigger the other set of WWPNs to activate.

4. On the switch, add the newly visible WWPNs to the alias.

5. Complete zoning to storage.

Figure 4.16 shows my switch with an alias created for each of the vFCAs for each virtual machine. Notice that each alias has two WWPNs, the A and the B set, but only one is active. Figure 4.17 shows the same view after I live migrate the two virtual machines to another host. Notice now the second set of WWPNs are active.

**FIGURE 4.16**

The A set of WWPNs being used

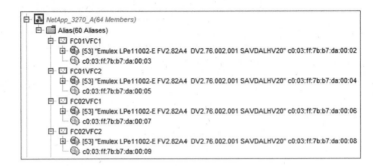

**FIGURE 4.17**

The B set of WWPNs being used

What is a great feature here is that the Hyper-V host itself has no access to the storage. Nowhere is the WWPN of the host zoned to storage; only the virtual machines have access to the storage, which is important from a security perspective and simplifies management because there is no need to ensure that every Hyper-V host is zoned to storage, only the virtual machines' vFCAs that actually need the access.

With storage now zoned to all the WWPNs for the vFCAs used, the virtual machines can be started and the storage can be accessed as shared storage, allowing guest clustering. While this is not a Hyper-V–specific step, it is important to realize in my architecture shown in Figure 4.11 that I have redundant paths to the storage through my two vFCAs and the two virtual SANs (which can both see the storage via redundant path), which means for each LUN zoned the storage will actually be seen four times, as shown in Figure 4.18. Basically, each virtual SAN sees each disk twice, once for each of its paths to the storage, and then the virtual machine has two connections to different virtual SANs, each telling it there are two disks! This would be the same experience if redundant path iSCSI was used.

**FIGURE 4.18**
A view of a single
disk without MPIO

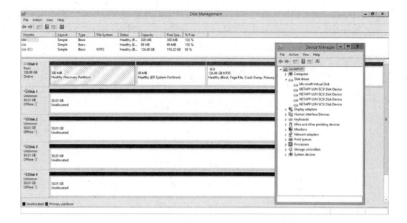

Windows has a feature called MPIO that solves this and adds the intelligence into Windows so it understands that it's actually seeing the same storage multiple times and it has redundant paths. Install the MPIO feature and then run the MPIO tool. On the Discover Multi-Paths tab, select the SAN device and click Add, and then you will be prompted to reboot. Once the machine reboots, there will be a single instance of each disk, as shown in Figure 4.19.

**FIGURE 4.19**
A view of a single
disk with MPIO

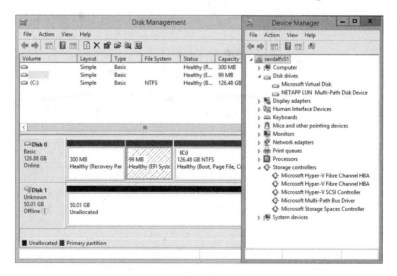

The addition of virtual Fibre Channel is a great feature for organizations that have a fibre channel–centric storage strategy, and Microsoft made great efforts to provide a flexible while secure implementation, enabling full Live Migration compatibility without giving the Hyper-V hosts themselves access. There are still considerations. As with iSCSI, a backup taken at the Hyper-V host will not back up any data stored on the SAN storage. To use Virtual Fibre Channel, you must have a guest operating system that is Windows Server 2008 or above and the latest version of Hyper-V Integration Services must be installed. At time of this writing, Virtual Fibre Channel does not work with Linux guest operating systems. Hyper-V Replica cannot be used with a virtual machine that has vFCAs. Also, as with iSCSI, to use Virtual Fibre Channel, the virtual machines need to have knowledge of the storage fabric, which is not desirable in many scenarios, especially those hoster scenarios.

## Leveraging Shared VHDX

Windows Server 2012 R2 provides a feature that for most environments will remove the need to use iSCSI inside the virtual machine or Virtual Fibre Channel and remove the need to expose the storage fabric details to the virtual machine. Shared VHDX allows a VHDX file to be connected to multiple virtual machines simultaneously, and the shared VHDX will be seen as shared storage (shared SAS) and therefore used as cluster storage within guest clusters. The requirements for shared VHDX are as follows:

◆ Must use Windows Server 2012 R2 Hyper-V.

◆ Guest operating systems must be Windows Server 2012 or above and must be running the Windows Server 2012 R2 Integration Services.

◆ The disk must be VHDX, not VHD, and must be connected to a SCSI controller, not IDE. It can be a generation 1 or generation 2 virtual machine.

◆ VHDX can be fixed or dynamic but not differencing.

◆ Can be used for data disks only. Cannot be used for operating system disks.

◆ The storage for the VHDX file being shared must either be a Cluster Shared Volume (CSV) or be hosted from a scale-out file server (SoFS) accessed using SMB 3 (the SoFS would be using CSV for its backend storage). The reason CSV must be used to store the VHDX is that the code to implement the VHDX sharing is part of CSV and not the regular NTFS code.

It is actually possible to force the process of loading and attaching the shared VHD filter driver to a non-CSV volume. However, this loading will survive only until the disk is offlined in some way, at which point you would have to load and attach again. Note that this is not supported or even tested by Microsoft and should be used only in basic test scenarios if a CSV is not available.

1. Install the Failover Clustering feature through Server Manager or through PowerShell:

```
Install-WindowsFeature Failover-Clustering
```

2. Run the following command, specifying the volume to attach the shared VHDX filter to:

```
FLTMC.EXE attach svhdxflt <volume>:
```

Providing a VHDX file is stored on a CSV volume or SoFS and it is connected via a SCSI controller, there is only one step to make it shared: Once it has been added to a virtual machine in the Advanced Features properties for the disk, check the Enable Virtual Hard Disk Sharing option, as shown in Figure 4.20. Repeat this for the same disk on all virtual machines that need to access the shared disk.

**FIGURE 4.20**

Setting a VHDX file
as shared

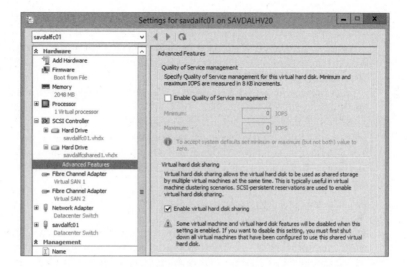

This process could also be accomplished using PowerShell. In the following example, I have two virtual machines, savdalfc01 and savdalfc02, to which I will add a shared VHDX file. Notice the use of the -ShareVirtualDisk switch when I add the VHDX file to the virtual machine.

```
New-VHD -Path C:\ClusterStorage\Volume1\SharedVHDX\Savdalfcshared1.vhdx '
-Fixed -SizeBytes 25GB
Add-VMHardDiskDrive -VMName savdalfc01 -Path '
C:\ClusterStorage\Volume1\SharedVHDX\Savdalfcshared1.vhdx -ShareVirtualDisk
Add-VMHardDiskDrive -VMName savdalfc02 -Path '
C:\ClusterStorage\Volume1\SharedVHDX\Savdalfcshared1.vhdx -ShareVirtualDisk
```

To check if a virtual disk is using a shared VHDX, the SupportPersistentReservations property can be examined. If it is set to True, then it is a shared VHDX. For example, notice that my shared VHDX file has a value of True:

```
PS C:\> Get-VMHardDiskDrive -VMName savdalfc01 | ft vmname, path, `
controllertype, SupportPersistentReservations -auto

VMName     Path                     ControllerType  SupportPersistentReservations
------     ----                     -------------   ----
-----
savdalfc01 C:\ClusterSto..\savdalfc01\savdalfc01.vhdx           SCSI      False
savdalfc01 C:\ClusterSto.. \Shared VHDX\savdalfcshared1.vhdx    SCSI      True
```

Within the virtual machine, the shared VHDX would be seen as a regular shared SAS disk and used like normal shared storage. The huge benefit with shared VHDX is that the virtual machine knows nothing about the underlying storage fabric and provides complete abstraction for the storage from the physical storage fabric.

Because the VHDX file is shared between multiple virtual machines, the ability to perform a backup at the Hyper-V host or even a checkpoint is not possible. Backups would need to be taken within the guest virtual machine. Storage migration is also not supported for shared

VHDX files. This also means Hyper-V Replica cannot be used for virtual machines that are connected to a shared VHDX file.

When using Shared VHDX on an SMB 3.0 share an entirely new protocol called Remote Shared Virtual Hard Disk Protocol is used. This protocol leverages SMB as a transport but is not actually part of the SMB protocol itself.

Hopefully, you can see that there is a large range of options for shared storage within virtual machines, including SMB 3, iSCSI, Virtual Fibre Channel, and shared VHDX. Each has its own benefits and considerations, and I don't think there is a right or wrong solution as long as you take time to fully understand each technology. I think where possible you should use shared VHDX first because it provides a true virtualized shared storage solution that removes the need for direct fabric knowledge and configuration from the virtual machines.

## Data Deduplication and Hyper-V

So far I hope I have covered some of the reasons Windows Server 2012 R2 is a great storage platform. Storage Spaces with its thin provisioning and auto-recovery, improved ChkDsk error correction, iSCSI and SMB 3.0 servers, and VHDX are amazing features. There are many other features, such as the new ReFS file system and industry-leading NFS implementation, but I want to touch on one more feature that in Windows Server 2012 I would not have covered but is now applicable to virtualization, and that is data deduplication.

Windows Server 2012 introduced the block-level data deduplication capability as an optional role available within the File and iSCSI Services collection of role services. In Windows Server 2012, data deduplication did not work on any file that had an exclusive lock open, which was the case for a virtual hard disk used by a virtual machine. This meant that the data deduplication feature was useful only for reducing space for archived virtual machine or libraries of content.

In Windows Server 2012 R2 the data deduplication functionality has been improved to work on exclusively locked files and can therefore deduplicate virtual hard disks used by Hyper-V virtual machines. For the Windows Server 2012 R2 release, though, deduplication is supported for only a single scenario, and that is for the deduplication of VDI deployment virtual machines, primarily personal desktop deployment that often results in a very large amount of duplicated content. When you leverage the data deduplication capability at the file system level, all the duplicated blocks within a virtual hard disk and between different virtual hard disks would be single-instanced, resulting in huge disk savings. Windows Server 2012 R2 also adds support for deduplication for Cluster Shared Volumes, which means deduplication can be used on shared cluster disks and on the storage of scale-out file servers.

The way the data deduplication works is that a periodic scan of the file system is performed and the blocks on disk have a hash value created. If blocks are found with the same value, it means the content is the same and the block is moved to a single instance store and the old locations now point to the single-instance store copy. The block size used is variable to achieve the greatest level of deduplication. It is not uncommon to see disk space savings of up to 95 percent in VDI environments because most of the content of each virtual hard disk is the same as the other virtual hard disk instances. Using deduplication actually speeds up the performance of VDI environments due to improvements in caching instead of having a negative performance impact, which may be expected.

It should be noted that while in Windows Server 2012 R2 the data deduplication is supported for VDI deployments, the actual data deduplication is a core part of the storage stack and so there is no block to stop data deduplication working with other virtual workloads. However, these workloads have not been tested. There are some types of workloads I would be very concerned about enabling data deduplication on, such as any kind of database. It is therefore important that when configuring data deduplication on a volume that has mixed workloads, you explicitly block folders containing virtual hard disks you do not want to be deduplicated.

VDI is actually one of the great scenarios for using differencing disks, which remember are child disks of a parent disk with only differences stored in them. If data that is being read is not in the differencing disk, it is read from the parent disk. Any write actions are performed into the differencing disk. Therefore, in a pooled VDI scenario, a master VHDX file would have the core Windows client image, the gold image, and then many VDM virtual machines created with their own differencing disks that are children of the master image. Each differencing disk would still be a couple of gigabytes due to changes made during the specialization phase, but using differencing disks is still a very efficient solution. The master image can be stored on a high tier of storage, such as the SSD tier if Storage Spaces is being used, and because the master would be read-only, it would also benefit from any caching. Figure 4.21 shows this architecture.

**FIGURE 4.21**
Using differencing disks in a VDI environment

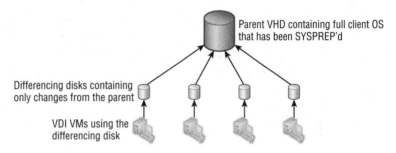

Parent VHD containing full client OS that has been SYSPREP'd

Differencing disks containing only changes from the parent

VDI VMs using the differencing disk

# Storage Quality of Service

Many organizations have long focused on ensuring that virtual machines correctly get the required amounts of memory and processor resources while network and storage controls historically have not been well implemented. Windows Server 2012 R2 introduces basic IOPS-based QoS on a per-virtual-hard-disk level. There are two settings:

- Minimum IOPS: If the virtual hard disk does not receive the configured minimum number of IOPS, an event log is generated.

- Maximum IOPS: The virtual hard disk will be hard limited to the number of IOPS specified.

You will notice that the minimum and maximum options are implemented very differently. There is no "guaranteed" minimum number of IOPS possible for a virtual machine because there is no way to ensure that the required number of IOPS is possible or even available. Therefore, the best solution at this time is for an event to be generated notifying that the virtual hard disk is not receiving the number of IOPS required which will be an Event ID 32930 under Applications and Services Logs\Microsoft\Windows\Hyper-V-VMMS\Admin and an Event ID 32931 when performance is back to the expected level. A WMI event is also triggered. It is simple to make sure a virtual hard disk does not exceed a certain number of IOPS, which is why the maximum value is a hard limit and simply limits the virtual hard disk to the configured number of IOPS. To configure the storage QoS, perform the following steps:

**1.** Open the settings of a virtual machine.

2. Navigate to the virtual hard disk and select Advanced Features.

3. Check the Enable Quality Of Service Management check box and set the Minimum and/or Maximum values as shown in Figure 4.22. A value of 0 means there is no configuration. Click OK.

**FIGURE 4.22**
Configuring QoS for a disk

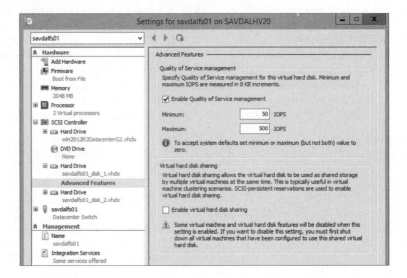

To configure storage QoS using PowerShell, use the `Set-VMHardDiskDrive` cmdlet and configure the `MaximumIOPS` and `MinimumIOPS` parameters.

In addition to enabling QoS on storage, storage details are also now reported as part of the resource metering introduced in Windows Server 2012. The storage-related data returned includes the average IOPS, average latency, and the data read and written in MB. An example of the information returned is shown in the following output:

```
PS E:\> Measure-VM -VMName savdalfs01 | fl


ComputerName                     : SAVDALHV01
VMId                             : 4c6db747-8591-4287-a8fc-ac55e37dba16
VMName                           : savdalfs01
HardDiskMetrics                  : {Microsoft.HyperV.PowerShell
.VirtualHardDiskMetrics, Microsoft.HyperV.PowerShell.VirtualHardDiskMetrics}
MeteringDuration                 :
AverageProcessorUsage            : 204
AverageMemoryUsage               : 3236
MaximumMemoryUsage               : 3236
MinimumMemoryUsage               : 3236
TotalDiskAllocation              : 260096
AggregatedAverageNormalizedIOPS  : 389
AggregatedAverageLatency         : 633
```

```
AggregatedDiskDataRead        : 103
AggregatedDiskDataWritten     : 367
NetworkMeteredTrafficReport   : {Microsoft.HyperV.PowerShell
.VMNetworkAdapterPortAclMeteringReport,
Microsoft.HyperV.PowerShell.VMNetworkAdapterPortAclMeteringReport,
Microsoft.HyperV.PowerShell.VMNetworkAdapterPortAclMeteringReport,
Microsoft.HyperV.PowerShell.VMNetworkAdapterPortAclMeteringReport}
AvgCPU                        : 204
AvgRAM                        : 3236
MinRAM                        : 3236
MaxRAM                        : 3236
TotalDisk                     : 260096
```

Another type of storage Quality of Service (QoS) is applicable with the adoption of SMB 3.0 for not just file traffic (default) but also for hosting virtual machines and even for Live Migration. The existing QoS technologies that could control SMB allocation is not granular enough to enable different bandwidth limits for the different types of SMB traffic. Windows Server 2012 R2 adds this new granularity for SMB bandwidth management: Default, LiveMigration, and VirtualMachine. This allows an amount of bandwidth to be specified for each of the types of SMB traffic. In most environments, this should not be required because SMB does a good job of fair-sharing the network, but if you need to better tune the bandwidth allocation, the new SMB bandwidth management will be useful.

To configure the SMB bandwidth management, perform the following steps:

1. Install the SMB Bandwidth Limit feature. This can be done through Server Manager (note that it is a feature and not a role) or using PowerShell.

   ```
   Install-WindowsFeature FS_SMBBW
   ```

2. Configure the limits for each type of traffic using the `Set-SMBBandwidthLimit` PowerShell cmdlet, as in this example:

   ```
   Set-SMBBandwidthLimit -Category LiveMigration - BytesPerSecond 2GB
   ```

3. To view the configured SMB QoS, use the `Get-SMBBandwidthLimit` cmdlet. Use the `Remove-SMBBandwidthLimit` cmdlet to remove it.

## SAN Storage and SCVMM

This chapter has shown a lot of great functionality that is enabled through the use of the Windows Server platform, but this does not mean that there are not investments related to leveraging SANs. One of the biggest features when utilizing SANs is offloaded data transfer, or ODX.

Typically, when any file move or copy operating occurs, the server becomes the bottleneck in the process and significant resources are used on the server as the following occurs:

1. The server reads a portion of the data from the SAN.

2. The server writes the portion of the data to the SAN.

3. Both steps are repeated until all data is read and written.

This is a highly inefficient process because the SAN is far more capable of natively moving or copying data. ODX allows the SAN to move or copy data itself through the use of a series of tokens, with each token representing a portion of the data at a point in time. The token, instead of the actual data, is passed by the host to the SAN, which then allows the SAN to natively move or copy the data.

To utilize ODX, the SAN must support it, and the good news is that by default, ODX will be utilized where possible automatically. Consider the action of deploying a virtual machine from a template. In the past, the Hyper-V host would copy the template to the new location, resulting in large amounts of processor utilization on the host and a copy operation that may take 10 minutes to perform. With ODX, the copy would use a negligible amount of processor resource and the copy operation would likely finish in about 30 seconds. File operations using Windows Explorer, the command prompt, PowerShell, and Hyper-V will all utilize ODX where possible.

System Center Virtual Machine Manager (SCVMM) 2012 R2 also now utilizes ODX when deploying a virtual machine from a template but not in any other scenario. If ODX cannot be used, SCVMM will use a regular file copy, and if that does not work, it will resort to BITS.

While native ODX allows very fast copies of data because the SAN can natively perform the copy/move directly, it also allows SAN vendors to improve the process. For example, there is no reason the SAN has to actually copy the data. SAN ODX implementations may use native capabilities such as just creating a pointer to the original data. The NetApp implementation uses its sub-LUN cloning technology, which creates two pointers to the same block of data, so the operation finishes almost instantly because no data is actually being moved or copied. A write-forward snapshot is then leveraged so changes to the new copy are written to a new area. Even without these additional optimizations, ODX provides a huge performance improvement during large move and copy operations.

Windows Server 2012 also introduced native support for Storage Management Initiative Specification (SMI-S), and in Windows Server 2012 R2, there is a built-in SMI-S provider for the inbox iSCSI solution, making it manageable from SMI-S–based management solutions without additional software required, which includes SCVMM 2012 R2.

I want to close by mentioning how SCVMM 2012 R2 can integrate with storage solutions to simplify management. The goal of SCVMM is to be the fabric management solution and not just for managing virtual machines. Storage providers can be loaded into SCVMM, which then displays the aggregates/volumes and the contained LUNs. Each aggregate/volume can be assigned a custom classification such as Gold, Silver, or Bronze. Figure 4.23 shows the Classifications And Pools view of the storage fabric. As you can see, I have three classifications of storage defined, and I have a number of different storage subsystems loaded, including a Windows Server 2012 R2 iSCSI server and two NetApp SANs. Using a common classification enables SCVMM to automatically create and allocate LUNs to hosts as required based on a storage classification in the virtual machine request.

SCVMM leverages industry standards to connect to the storage subsystems such as CIM- and WMI-based versions of SMI-S and also Windows storage APIs to manage Windows file servers, which can also be classified in SCVMM 2012 R2. I will cover SCVMM in more detail later in the book, but all of the storage features related to VHDX, SMB, and virtual fibre channel can be managed through SCVMM 2012 R2. In addition, SCVMM 2012 R2 can deploy complete file server clusters in addition to Hyper-V hosts.

**FIGURE 4.23**

A view of storage managed by SCVMM 2012 R2

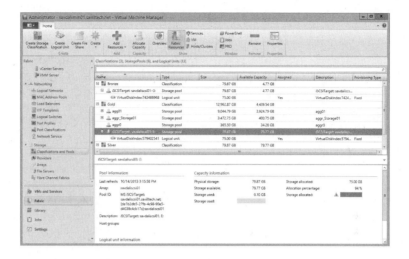

## The Bottom Line

**Explain the types of storage available to a virtual machine.** Windows Server 2012 R2 provides a number of different types of storage to a virtual machine. VHDX files provide a completely abstracted and self-contained virtual container for file systems available to virtual machines, and 2012 R2 allows a VHDX file connected to the SCSI bus to be shared between multiple virtual machines, providing shared storage. Additionally, storage can be exposed to virtual machines that are hosted in SAN environments through the use of iSCSI running inside the guest operating system or through the new virtual fibre channel capability.

**Master It** Why is MPIO required?

**Identify when to use Virtual Fiber Channel and when to use shared VHDX and the benefits of each.** Virtual Fibre Channel allows virtual machines to be directly connected to a fibre channel SAN without the host requiring zoning to the storage, but it requires knowledge of the storage fabric. Shared VHDX provides shared storage to the virtual machine without requiring that the users of the shared VHDX have knowledge of the storage fabric, which is useful in hosting the type of scenarios where all aspects of the physical fabric should be hidden from the users.

**Articulate how SMB 3.0 can be used.** SMB 3.0 went through a huge upgrade in Windows Server 2012, providing an enterprise-level file-based protocol that can now be used to store Hyper-V virtual machines. This includes additional storage options for Hyper-V environments, including fronting existing SANs with a Windows Server 2012 R2 scale-out file server cluster to extend the SAN's accessibility beyond hosts with direct SAN connectivity.

**Master It** Which two SMB technologies enable virtual machines to move between nodes in a SoFS without any interruption to processing?

# Chapter 5

# Managing Hyper-V

The previous chapters explained the key building blocks of virtualization, and this chapter shows how to begin bringing together those separate blocks through consolidated management. While basic management can be performed using Hyper-V Manager, for most enterprise deployments it will be necessary to use System Center Virtual Machine Manager (SCVMM) and also automation solutions such as PowerShell and System Center Orchestrator.

This chapter looks at installing and securing Hyper-V before looking at details around virtual machine deployments and converting physical servers into a virtual machine.

In this chapter, you will learn to

◆ Identify the different ways to deploy Hyper-V

◆ Explain why using Server Core is beneficial to deployments

◆ Create and use virtual machine templates

## Installing Hyper-V

Hyper-V is a role of Windows Server 2008 and above that is enabled after the installation of the Windows Server operating system, and it's simple to enable it. Remember from Chapter 1, "Introduction to Virtualization and Microsoft Solutions," that the Hyper-V role is available in both the Standard and Datacenter SKUs of Windows Server 2012 R2. It's also the only role available in the free Microsoft Hyper-V Server offering that is aimed at VDI and Linux workloads that don't need the Windows Server guest licenses that are part of Standard and Datacenter licenses. The capabilities and scalability are the same for all three versions, and the version you choose will depend on your exact requirements, but typically you'll choose the version based on the following:

◆ Windows Server Datacenter: Used when you have a large number of virtual machines running Windows Server operating systems, especially when clustering hosts to provide maximum mobility for virtual machines. Datacenter allows an unlimited number of licenses for Windows Server virtual machines (known as *virtual operating environments* in Microsoft parlance).

◆ Microsoft Hyper-V Server: Used when not running Windows Server guest operating systems, which means virtual instance rights that are provided with Standard and Datacenter are not needed. Primarily aimed at environments where VMs do not require Windows Server licenses, such as VDI environments that run Windows client operating systems in virtual machines and also Linux environments. Both scenarios require their own separate licensing of the operating systems in the virtual machines.

◆ Windows Server Standard: Not typically used in virtualization environments because Standard provides only two virtual OS instance rights running Windows Server that cannot be moved between servers. May be used in very lightly virtualized environments where clustering is typically not used.

Whether you use Standard or Datacenter, there is no difference in any operational activities; they are the same operating system. When you use the free Microsoft Hyper-V Server, the Hyper-V role is automatically enabled, removing the manual role additional action.

I should also note that Hyper-V is available as a feature in Windows 8 and Windows 8.1. It's the same Hyper-V code that is running in Windows Server; it is just missing some of the features that make no sense on a client operating system, such as Virtual Fibre Channel, SR-IOV, Live Migration, and Hyper-V Replica. It's the same hypervisor using the same virtual hard disk formats, which means you can take a virtual machine running on Windows 8.1 Hyper-V and run it on Windows Server 2012 R2 Hyper-V with no changes required. You can even move in the opposite direction.

On the server side, you should make sure servers are sized accordingly based on the desired usage and also that they have the required network and storage connectivity. Processors are required to support hardware-assisted virtualization (Intel VT or AMD-V) and data execution prevention in the form of Intel XD bit (execute disable bit) or AMD NX bit (no execute bit). The good news is that any server processor released within the last five years should definitely have these capabilities and likely even older processors.

It's nice to have Second Level Address Translation (SLAT) for improved performance. It allows the processor to handle mapping of physical memory to virtual machine memory, which otherwise has to be handled by the hypervisor, increasing resource usage of the hypervisor. Intel calls this technology Extended Page Tables (EPT) and AMD calls it Rapid Virtualization Indexing (RVI).

To check your server processors' capabilities, download `coreinfo.exe` from

`http://technet.microsoft.com/en-us/sysinternals/cc835722.aspx`

and execute with the `-v` switch, which shows virtualization-related processor features. A * means the feature is present, a - means it is missing.

```
PS C:\temp> .\Coreinfo.exe -v

Coreinfo v3.2 - Dump information on system CPU and memory topology
Copyright (C) 2008-2012 Mark Russinovich
Sysinternals - www.sysinternals.com

Intel(R) Xeon(R) CPU E5-2680 0 @ 2.70GHz
Intel64 Family 6 Model 45 Stepping 7, GenuineIntel
HYPERVISOR      -      Hypervisor is present
VMX             *      Supports Intel hardware-assisted virtualization
EPT             *      Supports Intel extended page tables (SLAT)
```

Providing you see a * for the hardware-assisted virtualization, your system is capable of running Hyper-V.

## Using Configuration Levels

Before discussing enabling the Hyper-V role, I want to cover configuration levels, which is a new concept in Windows Server 2012 that was built on Server Core and introduced in Windows Server 2008. Server Core was a minimal installation of the Windows Server operating system with no graphical shell, no management tools, no .NET, and no PowerShell and was designed to run certain Windows Server roles such as Active Directory Domain Controller, Hyper-V, and File Server. The goals behind Server Core were to have an operating system with fewer components that really were not required for many server roles and therefore to cut down on patches needed, reduce possible vulnerabilities, and reduce the number of reboots associated with patches. There was also a small resource overhead reduction. This goal was a good one, but the problem was that Server Core was hard to manage and could not be used with Server Manager remotely and people largely ignored it. Windows Server 2008 R2 improved on this with remote management via Server Manager and PowerShell support, but the hard choice at installation time made using Server Core scary and it's still avoided by most IT organizations.

Windows Server 2012 changed this inflexible choice at installation, making the graphic shell and management tools features that can be added and removed like any other feature, which made it easy to switch a server from being in Server Core mode to being a full server with a graphical interface. Additionally, more granularity was introduced to allow different configuration levels, which are shown in Figure 5.1. Notice that with configuration levels it is possible to remove the graphical shell but still have the management tools available locally to the server. The default installation option for Windows Server 2012 and above is now Server Core, which shows the shift to Server Core being "the norm" for a Windows server, with nearly every Windows role and feature supported on Server Core in Windows Server 2012 R2. In addition, for applications to receive Microsoft's Gold Certification, which is the highest level of application certification, the application must run without the graphical shell installed. The Windows Server 2012 R2 Server Core base footprint is actually about 1 GB smaller than Windows Server 2012 Server Core thanks to new optimizations and compression of optional features, which are not actually installed.

**FIGURE 5.1**
Configuration levels available in Windows Server 2012 R2

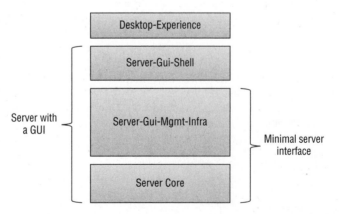

Consider a Hyper-V host. The host operating system is the management partition for the virtual machine, providing critical services and connectivity, which means if the host operating system must be restarted then every virtual machine also has to be restarted. For this reason it's critical that the maintenance and reboots required are as minimal as possible, and that means running all Hyper-V servers at the Server Core configuration level and managing them remotely. I should point out that in a production environment, the Hyper-V hosts should be clustered, which means a host can be patched and rebooted with no impact to virtual machine availability because virtual machines can be moved between hosts with no downtime. However, it is still desirable to minimize maintenance and reboots as much as possible.

> **SERVER CORE STILL SEEMS TO HAVE A LOT OF PATCHES IN WINDOWS SERVER 2012**
>
> In the Windows Server 2008 time frame, there were about 50 percent fewer patches that applied to Server Core compared to a full installation (Server with a GUI), enabling servers to go many months without a reboot. For Windows Server 2012, many organizations found that there were many patches required for Server Core, which meant similar reboots for Server Core and a Server with a GUI deployment.
>
> There are a number of binaries present on Server Core that are used, but vulnerabilities that may get patched in the binary do not always apply to Server Core. The problem is that Windows Update will see the binary present and patch it and therefore require a reboot, but if you read the security bulletin related to the patch, it will say whether it actually applies to Server Core or not. For example, in the past year there have been around 10 critical patches with bulletins, but you would find that fewer than half of these were actually needed on Server Core if you read the bulletin. If you just ran Windows Update, though, they would have all been applied.
>
> This means that if you want the most optimal Server Core patching with the least possible reboots, you cannot just run Windows Update and instead need to verify the security bulletins for critical updates to check if they actually apply to Server Core or not. On the plus side, this does show even without the patching that Server Core is inherently less susceptible to vulnerabilities.

While all management can be done remotely, if you ever experienced a problem where the management tools would aid the resolution or even the graphical shell, simply add the components using Server Manager or PowerShell. Once the problem is resolved, remove them again. Likewise, if you have not automated the deployment of servers and like to perform initial configuration using graphical tools, then you can install servers in the Server with a GUI mode, and then once the server is fully configured, the management tools and graphical shell can be removed to run in Server Core mode.

For example, to move from Server with a GUI to Server Core, I just need to remove `Server -Gui-Mgmt-Infra` (which also removes `Server-Gui-Shell` since `Server-Gui-Shell` is dependent on `Server-Gui-Mgmt-Infra`):

```
Uninstall-WindowsFeature Server-Gui-Mgmt-Infra –Restart
```

To take Server Core and make it a full server with a GUI, use this command:

```
Install-WindowsFeature Server-Gui-Mgmt-Infra,Server-Gui-Shell –Restart
```

## Enabling the Hyper-V Role

When the operating system has been installed on a server and has been patched, the next step is to enable the Hyper-V role. Because your server will be running in Server Core configuration level, there is no local way to graphically install the Hyper-V role; instead, PowerShell can be leveraged:

```
Install-WindowsFeature -Name Hyper-V -Restart
```

Notice that I am not including the `-IncludeManagementTools` switch because the management tools cannot install on Server Core and would require a change in the configuration level. The server will reboot and the Hyper-V hypervisor will be loaded on the bare-metal hardware and ready for use. The next step would be to start managing through SCVMM, creating virtual switches, virtual machines, and so on.

The Hyper-V role can also be enabled using Server Manager from a remote Windows 8.1 machine that has the Remote Server Administration Tools (RSAT) installed or from another Windows Server 2012 R2 server that has the management tools installed. The process to enable using Server Manager is as follows:

1. Launch Server Manager.

2. From the Manage menu, select Add Roles And Features.

3. Click Next on the wizard introduction screen.

4. For the installation type, select the Role-based Or Feature-based installation.

5. From the list, select the server that will have the Hyper-V role installed. If your target server is not shown, you must first add it as a managed server via the Manage ➤ Add Servers action in the main Server Manager interface.

6. In the Server Roles screen, select the Hyper-V role.

7. As shown in Figure 5.2, a dialog appears from which you can also install the management tools and PowerShell module. Uncheck the Include Management Tools check box and click Continue (the Add Features button changes to a Continue button). Click Next on the Server Roles screen.

8. Click Next on the Features screen.

9. There are a number of optional configurations that can be performed during the Hyper-V role installation from Server Manager, specifically creating a virtual switch, configuring migration options, and choosing the default locations for virtual machines. Click Next on the introduction screen for these options.

10. In the Create Virtual Switches page do not select any network adapters. It is better to create the virtual switches post deployment as discussed in Chapter 3, "Virtual Networking." Click Next.

11. On the Virtual Machine Manager screen, you can enable Live Migration and choose the authentication protocol to use. This can be changed at any time in the future, but for now, do not configure this. Just click Next again.

12. The Default Stores page allows you to specify the default location for virtual hard disks and virtual machine configuration files. These locations can be changed in the future and also will be overridden by SCVMM. Click Next.

13. On the Configuration page, check the Restart The Destination Server Automatically If Required check box (click Yes when you are prompted to verify that you are sure you

want the server to automatically reboot). Then click Install to complete the Hyper-V role installation. Once the reboot is complete, Hyper-V is installed.

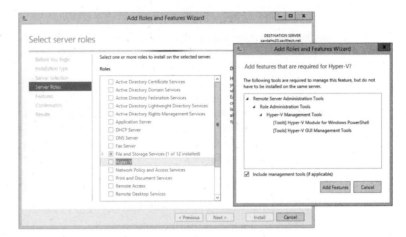

**FIGURE 5.2**
Local management tools are not wanted on a Hyper-V server that should be Server Core configuration level.

## Actions after Installation of Hyper-V

Once the Hyper-V role is enabled on a server, there are a number of important steps and processes that need to be in place. There are obvious actions, such as actually creating virtual machines, that are covered later in this section and throughout the book. There are some other items, though, that you need to ensure are implemented or at least considered:

◆ Add the server to SCVMM. This should be the first action before you create NIC teams, configure fibre channel, create virtual switches, join clusters, or anything else because all of these items can be configured and managed through SCVMM in a centralized fashion. Once the SCVMM agent is installed on the host and is being managed by SCVMM, you should add to clusters, deploy logical switches, and so on to make the server ready to host workloads.

◆ If you are not using SCVMM, you should create NIC teams and virtual switches according to the guidelines discussed in Chapter 3. Remember to use a consistent naming scheme for your switches to ensure that there is no network connectivity interruption when you're live migrating virtual machines between hosts.

◆ Add the server to a cluster or create a new cluster and add cluster disks to Cluster Shared Volumes to enable simultaneous access to the storage across the cluster.

◆ If you are running antivirus software on the Hyper-V hosts, ensure that you have the proper exclusions configured or problems can arise due to locking by the malware solution. The key exclusions for files and processes, documented at `http://support .microsoft.com/kb/961804/en-us`, are essentially blocking everywhere virtual machines are stored and the `vmms.exe` and `wmwp.exe` processes. Another option is to just not run malware protection, but most security departments would not be OK with this. If you consider that the Hyper-V server is running Server Core, with no one ever logging on to the box or running other applications, its vulnerability level would be very low. However, I don't advocate having no malware protection and instead I recommend running a supported malware solution with the exclusions just mentioned.

◆ Ensure that you have a patching strategy in place but also remember that a reboot will bring down all virtual machines unless they are live migrated to another server prior to reboot. Patching options range from using Microsoft Update to using Windows Server Update Services or System Center Configuration Manager, which both include a local patch repository of approved patches that can be deployed in a controlled manner, even adhering to configured maintenance windows. When you're using clusters of Hyper-V hosts, there are built-in capabilities (which will be discussed in the Chapter 7, "Failover Clustering and Migration Technologies") that allow an entire cluster to be patched with a single click without any virtual machine downtime. The important point is to have a patching strategy that will be adhered to and that ensures that patches are tested prior to implementation in production.

◆ As workloads are running in virtual machines on the Hyper-V host, it is important that they are backed up. This backup may be performed at the Hyper-V host level or potentially from within the virtual machine. The decision will depend on the workload being protected and the desired granularity of restoration. This decision will be discussed later in the book, but it's important that there is some backup solution running.

◆ Virtualization is moving many operating system instances on to a reduced number of physical hosts, which means it's critical that those physical boxes are healthy and available. Monitoring is a critical element to ensure that you have insight into the environment. Monitoring should be in place for all the various critical components, such as the physical server, operating system, networking, storage, and services within virtual machines. Additionally, a monitoring solution that proactively notifies you of problems and non-optimal configurations is preferred over a solution that just notifies you once something has failed. Users will notify you of failures for free.

---

### IMPORTANCE OF A PRODUCTION-EQUIVALENT TEST ENVIRONMENT

There are many moving parts to a Hyper-V solution, including the servers, operating system, additional management components, drivers for hardware (such as fibre-channel cards and network cards), firmware on servers and cards, and software versions on other components, such as storage area networks. It's important to test any changes you want to make to your production Hyper-V environment before you make them. That requires a testing/development environment that accurately reflects the production environment; otherwise, you will not have the required assurance that when you implement a change in production, it will be successful and not cause problems. This means you need to have servers with the same hardware, the same firmware versions, the same management, and so on in your testing environment. The closer it is to the production environment, the more confidence you'll have that a successful test process will result in success in production.

I heard of a company that tested an implementation in the test environment and then moved to production and within a few days, started suffering blue screens and huge service outages. It was caused by a mismatch of driver and firmware in production that was not present in the test environment. There are many similar stories, unfortunately.

This does not mean the testing environments needs to be on the same scale as the production environment. I may have 200 servers in production and 2 in development, and that's generally OK (unless you are performing scalability testing). What is important is that the components are the same.

This list is not definitive, and your organization may have other processes, such as adding to change control systems, but certainly these actions should be considered the minimum actions to take.

## Deploying Hyper-V Servers with SCVMM

You already have a method to deploy operating systems to your physical servers. This could be over the network from a solution like System Center Configuration Manager or Windows Deployments Services, installation locally from a USB device or CD, or even some other process. That process may be well understood and tested and should be maintained for your Hyper-V hosts as much as possible. Minimizing the number of different ways an action is performed reduces complexity and the chance of errors. If your process is not optimal, there is a solution to deploy Hyper-V hosts (and even file servers in the 2012 R2 release) included as part of SCVMM.

Rather than document the complete process to deploy a Hyper-V server with SCVMM, I will instead refer you to the Microsoft step-by-step detailed documentation available at the following location:

```
http://technet.microsoft.com/en-us/library/gg610634.aspx
```

I do, however, want to cover the high-level process and specifically what a Hyper-V host deployed using SCVMM will look like once deployed because SCVMM uses a feature, Boot from VHD, that allows a physical server (or desktop) to boot from a VHD file.

At a very high level, the following actions are performed:

1. Windows Deployment Services is deployed to the same subnet as the servers are being deployed to (or an IP helper-address is configured on the switch in the subnet with the servers and points to the WDS server) and is configured inside SCVMM as a PXE server (which allows SCVMM to configure and add required images to WDS).

2. You must have a sysprep'd VHDX file containing Windows Server 2012 R2. This could be the same VHDX file you use to deploy virtual machines, but it must match the type of system. For example, if the server is BIOS based, the VHDX should be from a generation 1 type VM.

3. A physical computer profile is created in SCVMM that SCVMM 2012 R2 allows you to configure if it will be used for a Hyper-V host or a Windows file server. In this profile, the VHDX file to be used is configured along with items such as domain membership, naming, product key, specific actions, and configurations. This profile will be used when deploying the physical host.

4. The physical server to be deployed is added to SCVMM via the Fabric workspace. The physical server must support one of the SCVMM-supported out-of-band management protocols such as IPMI or SMASH. You must have the address and credentials for the connection. Add the server to SCVMM (as shown in Figure 5.3), which will then deploy the new server by copying the VHDX file to the target server and configuring the host to boot from the VHDX file.

If you run into problems using the SCVMM host deployment, a great resource, which is a troubleshooting flow chart that can help identify problems, is available at the following location:

```
http://blogs.technet.com/b/scvmm/archive/2011/04/20/troubleshooting-os
-deployment-of-hyper-v-through-sc-vmm-2012.aspx
```

**FIGURE 5.3**
Selecting the protocol to be used for the new server to be provisioned

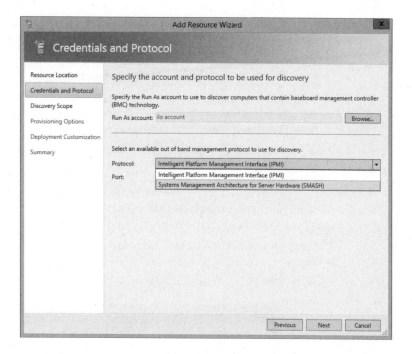

---

**MANUALLY CONFIGURING BOOT FROM VHD**

The option to use Boot from VHD simplifies the process used by SCVMM, but it can be used as part of a normal OS deployment with a few extra steps. I walk through the process at the following location (which also includes a video):

```
http://windowsitpro.com/virtualization/q-how-can
-i-install-windows-7-or-windows-server-2008-r2
-virtual-hard-disk-vhd-file
```

The process is the same for Windows Server 2012, as described in the article.

---

## Hyper-V Management Tools

Based on the assumption that your Hyper-V servers are all running Server Core, all graphical management tools will be run remotely, typically from a Windows 8.1 client operating system. There are three primary Hyper-V management environments. Additionally, remember that there are management functions that aren't specific to Hyper-V, such as management via Server Manager. Windows Server 2012 and above have remote management enabled by default, which means no configurations are required to be able to remotely manage a server instance.

The first management environment is the built-in Hyper-V Manager. Typically for a client operating system to manage server operating systems remotely, Remote Server Administration Tools must be installed. They are available from the following location:

```
www.microsoft.com/en-us/download/details.aspx?id=39296
```

This would include management tools such as Server Manager, but because Hyper-V is actually built into Windows 8.1, the Hyper-V graphical management tool and the PowerShell cmdlets are also built in and just need to be enabled as follows:

1. From the Desktop, open the charms (Windows key + C) menu, select Settings, and select Control Panel.

2. Launch the Programs And Features applet.

3. Click the Turn Windows Features On Or Off link.

4. Enable Hyper-V Management Tools, as shown in Figure 5.4. Do not select Hyper-V Platform because this will install the actual Hyper-V hypervisor on your Windows 8.1 machine.

5. Click OK. The Hyper-V tools will be available.

**FIGURE 5.4**

Enabling the Hyper-V management tools that are built into Windows 8.1

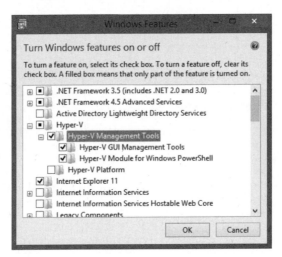

The second environment is PowerShell, which contains a large number of cmdlets that are specific to Hyper-V and are available by loading the Hyper-V PowerShell module:

```
Import-Module Hyper-V
```

The preceding command manually loads the Hyper-V module, which is always the best practice. However, PowerShell version 3 and above features a module auto-load capability that automatically loads modules as needed if cmdlets are used from modules not yet available.

The third environment is the SCVMM graphical tools (and strictly speaking, SCVMM also has its own PowerShell module, making it a forth environment). The SCVMM graphical tools will be covered in detail in the SCVMM chapter, but they can easily be installed on a Windows 8.1 client:

1. Launch the SCVMM setup routine.

2. Click Install.

3. On the Select Features To Install page, check the VMM Console option, as shown in Figure 5.5.

4. Complete all the other dialogs, which prompt you to accept the license agreement and configure update settings, and finally, click Install.

**FIGURE 5.5**
Selecting to install only the VMM console on a client operating system

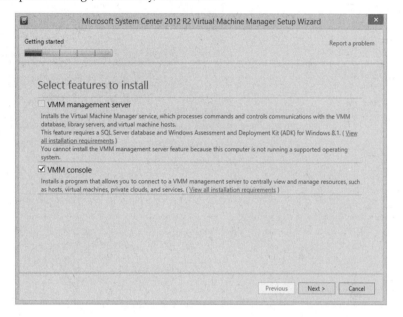

Figure 5.6 shows a Windows 8.1 client that has the Hyper-V Manager, Hyper-V PowerShell module, and SCVMM console running at the same time. The only requirement is that the user has the correct privileges on the Hyper-V hosts and SCVMM. The SCVMM 2012 R2 console is actually supported back to Windows 7 SP1, as documented at

http://technet.microsoft.com/en-us/library/gg610640.aspx

However, the Windows Server 2012 R2 Hyper-V Manager is only part of Windows 8.1, and the RSAT for Windows Server 2012 R2 will install only on Windows 8.1. If you really need to manage Windows 2012 R2 servers from an older client, there are some workarounds. I walk through a solution in a video at http://youtu.be/_dkxyr03Er4. The solution is to configure a Remote Desktop Session Host, which has the administration tools installed, and then publish them to other client operating systems. It's not ideal, but it does work.

## Using Hyper-V Manager

Many aspects of Hyper-V Manager are covered throughout this book. For example, virtual switches are covered in Chapter 3, virtual SANs are covered in Chapter 4, "Storage Configurations," and migration and replication settings will be covered in future chapters. In this section, I will cover the main components of Hyper-V Manager and some core configurations. If I don't cover a feature, it means it's covered elsewhere in the book in a section that's more specific to the topic.

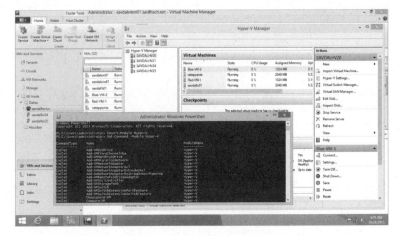

Figure 5.7 shows the Hyper-V Manager interface with the five main panes of information and capabilities exposed. Notice in the far-left server inventory pane that it is possible to add multiple Hyper-V servers to Hyper-V Manager. It is not possible to specify alternate credentials, which means only Hyper-V servers in trusting domains can be added where your current credentials have administrative rights. To add a new Hyper-V server to Hyper-V Manager, select the Connect To Server action available on the Hyper-V Manager navigation menu root in the navigation pane. You will need to perform this when managing from a Windows 8.1 client because by default, no Hyper-V servers will be shown. In previous versions of Windows there were various manual tasks to perform on the Hyper-V server to enable remote management, but this is no longer necessary; all configurations for remote management are enabled by default.

**FIGURE 5.7**

The Hyper-V
Manager interface

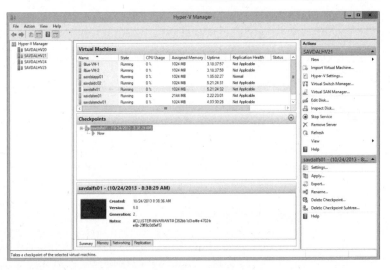

The Virtual Machines pane at the top center shows the virtual machines that are hosted by the currently selected Hyper-V server. Note that it is not possible to select multiple servers to see virtual machines from them. Only one server's virtual machine inventory can be shown. By default, a number of pieces of information are shown in the virtual machine's view, specifically its name, current state (such as Running, Paused, Saved, or Off), the CPU usage, assigned memory, uptime, and status. It's also possible to add a Replication Health column by right-clicking the column headings and selecting Add/Remove Columns, which also allows columns to be removed and the order rearranged. This view is useful to get a very high-level view of the virtual machines on a host. If a node is clustered, only the virtual machines running on the node will be shown and not all virtual machines in the cluster.

Note that the CPU Usage value shown is the percentage of resources used of the entire Hyper-V host and not the resource usage of the virtual processors within the virtual machine. For example, a virtual machine with a single vCPU may be running at 100 percent, but if a server has 24 logical processors in total, then 100 percent would only be around 4 percent of the total system resources, which is the number that would be visible in Hyper-V Manager. This is why on large systems it is common for virtual machines to show a value of 0 for CPU usage. Figure 5.8 shows an example of this with a virtual machine running a CPU stress test tool with its single processor running at 100 percent while Hyper-V Manager shows it using only 3 percent. SCVMM shows the actual CPU utilization of the virtual machine's allocated resources rather than the utilization as a percentage of the entire system, which means in my test it would have shown 100 percent processor utilization.

**FIGURE 5.8**

A virtual machine running at 100 percent processor utilization showing only 3 percent usage of a 24-core Hyper-V host

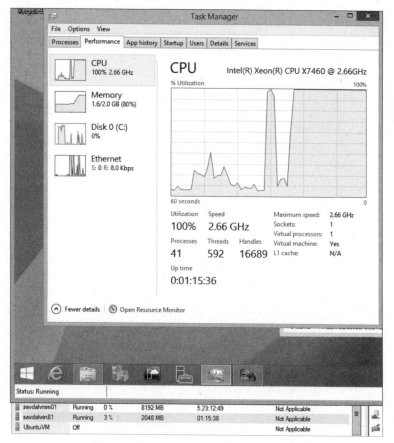

The next pane in Hyper-V Manager is Checkpoints, which is the new name for Snapshots. Checkpoints enable a point-in-time view of a virtual machine to be saved and used in the future. The view includes disk, memory, and device status. This will be covered in detail later in the book.

The bottom center pane shows some detailed information about the selected virtual machine, including a thumbnail of the console and basic information such as VM version, generation, notes, and a basic health status. There are also additional tabs related to memory, networking and Hyper-V Replica replication:

◆ Memory: For statically configured virtual machines, this tab offers no additional information beyond the assigned memory value shown already. For dynamically configured virtual machines, the minimum, startup, and maximum values are shown in addition to the currently assigned amount of memory, the actual memory demand of the VM, and the status of the memory, as shown in Figure 5.9. Remember that the Assigned Memory value is the actual memory currently allocated to the virtual machine from the physical memory of the host.

◆ Networking: Shows all adapters for a virtual machine, including IP address and status.

◆ Replication: Shows the status of replication when Hyper-V Replica is used.

**FIGURE 5.9**

Detail tabs for a virtual machine

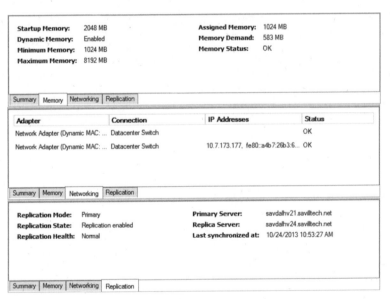

The Actions pane shows contextual actions depending on the currently selected item. Typically, a host and virtual machine are selected, which provides host-level configurations at the top of the pane and actions specific to virtual machines in the bottom half.

While there are numerous actions for the server, such as creating new virtual machines and disks, the key configuration for the Hyper-V host is via the Hyper-V Settings action, which opens up the key configurations for the server. The Server options, such as the default path for virtual hard disks, and configurations can be changed in addition to specifying which GPU can be used for RemoteFX, NUMA spanning, and other configurations (all covered throughout the book). In the User portion of the configurations, shown in Figure 5.10, I often like to change the Keyboard option to always send the special key combinations to the virtual machine, even when it's not running full screen.

**FIGURE 5.10**
Changing the keyboard behavior when the keyboard is connected to a virtual machine

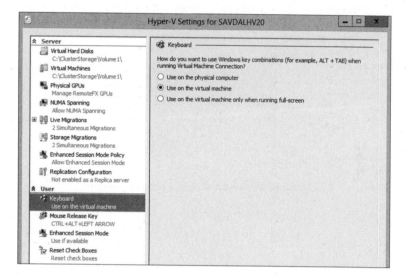

For virtual machines, the exact actions available will depend on the current state of the virtual machine. For example, the following actions are available for the Running state: Turn Off (doesn't gracefully shut down the guest operating system but is the same as just powering off a physical machine), Shut Down (sends a request to the guest operating system to perform a controlled shutdown, which is the same as selecting Shutdown within the guest operating system), Save (saves the current state, such as the memory and device state, to disk, allowing it to be resumed at a later time), Pause (suspends activity in the VM), and Reset (which is like powering off the VM and then starting it again). Options to connect to, move, export, checkpoint, rename, and enable replication are all available.

While Hyper-V Manager exposes many capabilities and configurations, it is suited only for a single host or a very small number of hosts because it does not allow configurations of multiple hosts in a single action. SCVMM provides the enterprise management solution, which is covered in Chapter 9, "Implementing the Private Cloud and SCVMM."

A common question related to Hyper-V Manager is whether it gives you the ability to control management of specific activities using role-based access control (RBAC). The original versions of Hyper-V enabled granular control of the actions available to different groups of users by utilizing the Windows Authorization Manager (AzMan) component. This authorization management approach was deprecated in Windows Server 2012 (although it still works) in favor of a new, simple authorization scheme that utilizes a new local group on each Hyper-V Server, Hyper-V Administrators. Any user who is in the Hyper-V Administrators group on a server has complete access and management rights for the Hyper-V server and the virtual machines. If you have a group of people who should be administrators for all Hyper-V servers, the best practice is to create a group in Active Directory, add the Hyper-V administrators into that group, and then add the Active Directory group into each server's local Hyper-V Administrators group. That way, as administrators change, only the single Active Directory group membership has to be updated. The true RBAC solution for Hyper-V is through SCVMM, which has full RBAC capabilities with very granular options for assigning different rights through the use of custom user roles that can be created and assigned the required configuration targeting specific resources. Figure 5.11 shows some of the actions that can be granularly assigned within SCVMM to user roles, which users are then made part of.

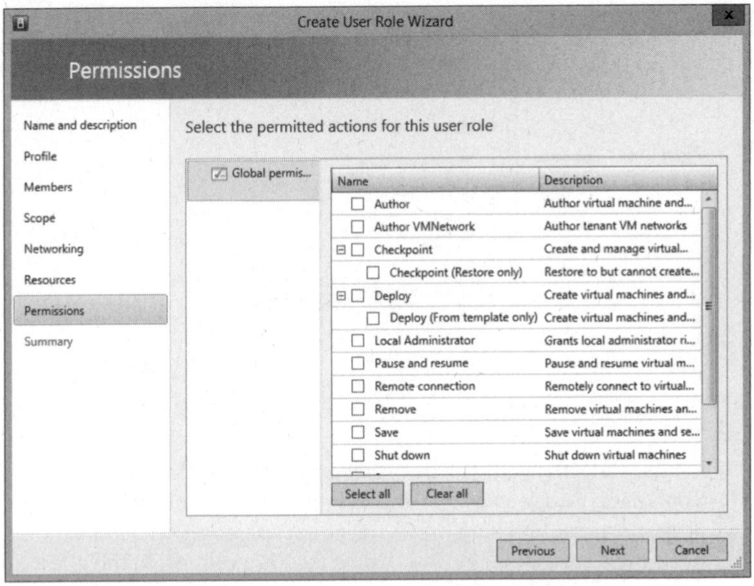

**FIGURE 5.11**
Configuring actions
for a specific new
user role

## Core Actions Using PowerShell

The Hyper-V PowerShell module enables complete management of Hyper-V. If an action is possible in the graphical shell, then it is possible using PowerShell. If the number of cmdlets in the Hyper-V module are counted, you see that there are 178 in Windows Server 2012 R2:

```
PS C:\> (Get-Command -Module Hyper-V).Count
178
```

If you are unfamiliar with PowerShell, I cannot stress enough how important PowerShell is to any Microsoft environment. At a high level, a PowerShell cmdlet (command) takes the form of <verb>-<noun>, where the verb is a specific type of action such as new, get, or start, while the noun is a particular type of object. They are many types of objects related to Hyper-V that can be acted upon:

```
PS C:\> Get-Command -Module Hyper-V | Select -Unique Noun | Sort Noun

Noun
----
VFD
```

```
VHD
VM
VMBios
VMComPort
VMConnectAccess
VMDvdDrive
VMEventing
VMFailover
VMFibreChannelHba
VMFile
VMFirmware
VMFloppyDiskDrive
VMHardDiskDrive
VMHost
VMHostNumaNode
VMHostNumaNodeStatus
VMIdeController
VMInitialReplication
VMIntegrationService
VMMemory
VMMigration
VMMigrationNetwork
VMNetworkAdapter
VMNetworkAdapterAcl
VMNetworkAdapterExtendedAcl
VMNetworkAdapterFailoverConfiguration
VmNetworkAdapterIsolation
VMNetworkAdapterRoutingDomainMapping
VmNetworkAdapterRoutingDomainMapping
VMNetworkAdapterVlan
VMProcessor
VMRemoteFx3dVideoAdapter
VMRemoteFXPhysicalVideoAdapter
VMReplication
VMReplicationAuthorizationEntry
VMReplicationConnection
VMReplicationServer
VMReplicationStatistics
VMResourceMetering
VMResourcePool
VMSan
VMSavedState
VMScsiController
VMSnapshot
VMStorage
VMStoragePath
VMSwitch
VMSwitchExtension
```

```
VMSwitchExtensionPortData
VMSwitchExtensionPortFeature
VMSwitchExtensionSwitchData
VMSwitchExtensionSwitchFeature
VMSystemSwitchExtension
VMSystemSwitchExtensionPortFeature
VMSystemSwitchExtensionSwitchFeature
```

Most of these various nouns are self-explanatory, and once you understand the noun you wish to act on, it is possible to see the verbs (actions) available. For example, to understand the actions available for a VM, I can use the following command:

```
PS C:\> Get-Command -Module Hyper-V -Noun VM

CommandType      Name                            ModuleName
-----------      ----                            ----------
Cmdlet           Checkpoint-VM                   Hyper-V
Cmdlet           Compare-VM                      Hyper-V
Cmdlet           Debug-VM                        Hyper-V
Cmdlet           Export-VM                       Hyper-V
Cmdlet           Get-VM                          Hyper-V
Cmdlet           Import-VM                       Hyper-V
Cmdlet           Measure-VM                      Hyper-V
Cmdlet           Move-VM                         Hyper-V
Cmdlet           New-VM                          Hyper-V
Cmdlet           Remove-VM                       Hyper-V
Cmdlet           Rename-VM                       Hyper-V
Cmdlet           Repair-VM                       Hyper-V
Cmdlet           Restart-VM                      Hyper-V
Cmdlet           Resume-VM                       Hyper-V
Cmdlet           Save-VM                         Hyper-V
Cmdlet           Set-VM                          Hyper-V
Cmdlet           Start-VM                        Hyper-V
Cmdlet           Stop-VM                         Hyper-V
Cmdlet           Suspend-VM                      Hyper-V
```

I cover many of these cmdlets throughout the book related to specific types of activity. Here I want to cover some commands that are useful to quickly get a view of your Hyper-V environment.

To view the basic information about a Hyper-V host, use `Get-VMHost -ComputerName server | Format-List`, and most attributes returned can be modified using the `Set-VMHost` cmdlet.

To view all virtual machines running on a Hyper-V host, use the `Get-VM` cmdlet. A key feature of PowerShell is the ability to pipe information from one cmdlet to another. This enables comprehensive feedback and also intelligent, automated sets of actions, which is why

PowerShell management is a much better option for performing actions across multiple servers with virtual machines. For example, I may want to export all virtual machines that are currently turned off. The first cmdlet gets all virtual machines, the second part identifies the VMs in the Off state, and then only those VMs are passed to the final cmdlet, which exports them.

```
Get-VM | where-object {$_.State -EQ "Off"} | Export-VM -Path D:\Backups
```

Likewise, I had a folder full of virtual machines I wanted to import into a Hyper-V server. This is very easy with PowerShell. The following code just looks for XML files (which is the format for virtual machine configurations) and then imports:

```
Get-ChildItem e:\virtuals\*.xml -recurse | Import-VM
```

In another case, I wanted to configure all virtual machines that were set to automatically start to not start if they were running when the Hyper-V server shut down. That's easy with PowerShell:

```
Get-VM | Where-Object {$_.AutomaticStartAction -eq "StartIfRunning"} | `
Set-VM -AutomaticStartAction Nothing -AutomaticStopAction ShutDown
```

SCVMM also has its own PowerShell module. Provided it's installed, it can be loaded using this command:

```
Import-Module virtualmachinemanager
```

The virtualmachinemanager module has 619 cmdlets! This is where using the same commands to view all the nouns available in the module is useful. There is, however, an even better way to learn how to use the SCVMM PowerShell cmdlets. Every action performed using the SCVMM graphical interface actually translates to PowerShell, and as each action is performed using SCVMM, there is an option to view the PowerShell, as shown in Figure 5.12, by clicking the View Script button. You can use the PowerShell that is displayed in your own scripts.

**FIGURE 5.12**
Viewing the PowerShell used by SCVMM

## Securing the Hyper-V Server

Your Hyper-V servers are running the majority of your server operating system instances and potentially your desktops if you're using VDI solutions. While an administrator on a Hyper-V server cannot bypass the regular logon to an operating system in a virtual machine, if you have access to the Hyper-V server, then you have access to the virtual machine storage. The storage could then be mounted and the content could be accessed.

The normal security best practices for servers should apply:

◆ Ensure that servers are physically secure.

◆ Ensure that the firewall is enabled.

◆ Patch servers.

◆ Run malware protection (with the required exclusions configured).

◆ Restrict who is an administrator (and by extension, domain administrators should be limited as well).

◆ Run Server Core on Hyper-V servers.

◆ Do not run other applications or browse the Web on Hyper-V servers. Running Server Core will help stop this.

◆ Use BitLocker to encrypt volumes containing virtual machines; it can also be used on Cluster Shared Volumes.

◆ Make sure administrators are well trained and understand their actions.

◆ Use Group Policy to ensure that policies are set as required.

◆ Have a monitoring solution in place, and also ensure that security logs are checked to detect any attack attempts.

The best Microsoft resource to help with security is the Microsoft Security Compliance Manager, which is available at the following location:

www.microsoft.com/en-us/download/details.aspx?id=16776

It is a large download at over 100 MB, but it provides not only documentation to help secure your entire environment but also tools and templates to ensure security.

## Creating and Managing a Virtual Machine

Ultimately you deploy Hyper-V to host virtual machines, and in this section I will walk through creating a basic virtual machine using Hyper-V Manager and PowerShell. Once the virtual machine is created, the next step is to actually deploy an operating system to it. That typically means attaching to the virtual machine an ISO containing an operating system installation or even booting the virtual machine over the network using a legacy network adapter for a generation 1 virtual machine or booting from the synthetic network adapter for a generation 2 virtual machine. This type of virtual machine creation is manually intensive and time consuming and is not taking advantage of the fact the virtual machine storage is essentially a file that could just be copied, which is why using templates is a much better option and is covered in the next section.

To create a virtual machine using Hyper-V Manager, perform the following steps:

1. Select the New ➤ Virtual Machine action.

2. Click Next on the introduction wizard screen.

3. Enter a name for the new virtual machine and optionally an alternate path for the virtual machine instead of the default location configured for the host. Click Next. There is a difference in behavior if the option to store the virtual machine in a different location is selected, even if the actual path is the same as the default. When Store Virtual Machine In A Different Location is selected, a folder is created under the specified location with the name of the new virtual machine, and that's where all its files and virtual hard disks are created. Without this setting enabled, the virtual machine configurations and disks are stored in the root of the default location in a standard structure.

4. Select the generation for the virtual machine. Remember, generation 2 virtual machines work only on Hyper-V 2012 R2, and only Windows Server 2012/Windows 8 64-bit and above is supported within the virtual machine. If you need compatibility with versions of Hyper-V prior to Windows Server 2012 or, at time of this writing, Windows Azure IaaS, you should use generation 1. You cannot change the generation of a virtual machine post creation. Click Next.

5. Select the amount of startup memory for the virtual machine. Note that the default value of 512 is insufficient for the latest generation of Windows client operating systems, which require 1 GB for 32-bit versions and 2 GB for 64-bit versions. Additionally, the option to use dynamic memory can be selected, and the values can be tweaked post creation. Click Next.

6. By default, virtual machines have a single network adapter, and the switch to connect it to should be selected. Click Next.

7. The virtual hard disk for the virtual machine is selected by default. This can be a new virtual hard disk, an existing virtual hard disk, or the option of choosing if a disk should be added later. Click Next.

8. If the option to create a new virtual hard disk was selected, the method to install the operating system is requested, as shown in Figure 5.13. You can choose to install the operating system later, install it from a bootable ISO, or install it from a network location. Note that if the virtual machine is generation 1 and you select to install from a network location, the network adapter created for the virtual machine will be a legacy network

adapter. Once the operating system is installed from the network, you will want to add a normal network adapter and remove the legacy network adapter to get the best performance. Click Next.

**9.** View the configurations in the Summary screen and click Finish to create the virtual machine.

**FIGURE 5.13**
Selecting the method to install the operating system into the virtual machine

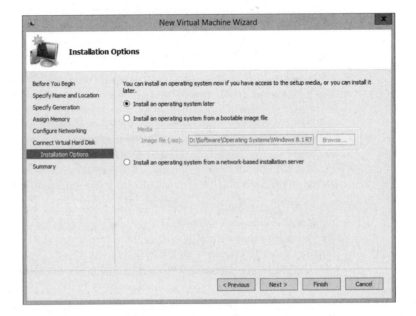

When the virtual machine is turned on, it will install the operating system from the ISO or over the network, and the standard operating system installation configurations will need to be performed within the guest operating system. If the operating system is not Windows Server 2012 R2, once the operating system is installed, the first action should be to install the 2012 R2 Hyper-V Integration Services, covered later in this chapter.

To actually connect to a virtual machine, use the Connect action for the virtual machine within Hyper-V Manager, which launches a connection that is connected to the virtual console of the virtual machine, allowing operating system installation. Make sure you click the mouse within the Virtual Machine Connection window when you first turn on the VM to be able to press a key to launch the boot from ISO or the network. The rest of the OS installation is the same as for a physical system. Note that if you are installing Windows 8/Windows Server 2012 into a generation 2 virtual machine, the physical keyboard will not work because the keyboard driver required is not part of the Windows 8 PE environment. Either use the onscreen keyboard during OS installation, or if you really want to fix the problem, follow my instructions at the following location:

```
http://windowsitpro.com/hyper-v/fix-vm-keyboard-problems-generation-2-virtual
-machine
```

---

### ACTIVATING THE GUEST OPERATING SYSTEM

There are numerous types of product keys available for operating systems, and your guest operating systems are still just operating systems that need to be activated. The product key specified during installation could be a Multiple Activation Key (MAK) key that enables multiple activations, or you may have a Key Management Server (KMS) in your organization, which provides the ability to locally activate operating systems. Windows Server 2012 introduces a new activation option, Active Directory Based Activation (ADBA), that automatically activates Windows Server 2012 and Windows 8 operating systems (physical or virtual) when they join the domain.

Windows Server 2012 R2 introduces a new option for Windows Server 2012 R2 virtual machines, Automatic Virtual Machine Activation (AVMA). With the AVMA technology, if the Hyper-V host is running Windows Server 2012 R2 Datacenter and is activated, then any virtual machine running Windows Server 2012 R2 (Essentials, Standard, or Datacenter) is automatically activated, provided the AVMA key is used during the guest OS installation. These keys are as follows:

Server Standard: DBGBW-NPF86-BJVTX-K3WKJ-MTB6V
Server Datacenter: Y4TGP-NPTV9-HTC2H-7MGQ3-DV4TW
Server Essentials: K2XGM-NMBT3-2R6Q8-WF2FK-P36R2

They are documented at the following location:

```
http://technet.microsoft.com/en-us/library/dn303421.aspx
```

The benefit of AVMA is that the virtual machine is activated only while running on an activated Windows Server 2012 R2 Hyper-V host. If the virtual machine was given to another organization or moved, it would be unactivated unless the target host was also Windows Server 2012 R2 Datacenter and activated. The Hyper-V host must be the Datacenter SKU because only Datacenter allows an unlimited number of guests VMs running Windows Server.

---

The actual virtual machine connection is enabled through the vmconnect.exe image, which is automatically launched through the Connect action with the target virtual machine specified for you. Vmconnect.exe can also be manually launched, which brings up the dialog shown in Figure 5.14, which allows a Hyper-V host to be selected and then a list of all the virtual machines on the selected Hyper-V host to be displayed.

**FIGURE 5.14**
Manually launching
vmconnect.exe
allows you to select
the host and virtual
machine

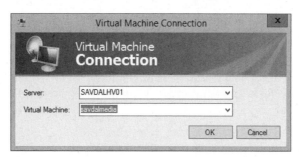

Windows Server 2012 R2 introduces a new set of capabilities related to the vmconnect; it's known as Enhanced Session Mode (ESM). Windows 8.1 and Windows Server 2012 R2, the only operating systems that work with Enhanced Session Mode, were enhanced so that the terminal services stack was tightly integrated with the Hyper-V VMBus.

This enables VM connections (via Hyper-V Manager or via `VMConnect.exe`) to leverage the following functionality traditionally associated with RDP connections:

◆ Rich display

◆ Audio

◆ Printers

◆ Clipboard

◆ USB devices

◆ Drives

◆ Plug and Play devices

◆ Smart cards

The requirements that need to be met are as follows:

◆ Guest OS in the VM supports Remote Desktop Services (e.g., Windows 8.1 Pro/Enterprise/Windows Server 2012 R2).

◆ The server policy in the Hyper-V Manager server settings for Enhanced Session Mode is enabled (the Server, Enhanced Session Mode Policy, Allow Enhanced Session Mode check box is selected). It's disabled by default.

◆ The user policy in the Hyper-V Manager server settings is enabled (User ➢ Enhanced Session Mode ➢ Use Enhanced Session Mode).

◆ The Remote Desktop Services service is running in the guest (but the Allow remote connections to this computer in System configuration doesn't need to be enabled).

◆ User logging on is as a member of local administrators or remote desktop users groups in the guest operating system.

◆ The Out Of Box Experience (OOBE) Wizard has been completed.

When you connect to a VM that supports ESM, an initial dialog allows the configuration of the display and local resources that are redirected in addition to letting you save the configuration, as shown in Figure 5.15. Any saved configurations are written to `%APPDATA%\Roaming\Microsoft\Windows\Hyper-V\Client\1.0` with a name format of `vmconnect.rdp.<GUID of VM>.config`.

**FIGURE 5.15**

The connection dialog when connecting using Enhanced Session Mode

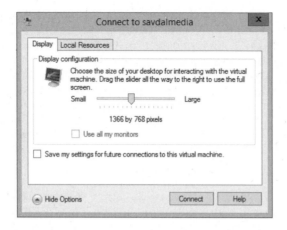

Finally, outside of the Hyper-V technologies is regular Remote Desktop Protocol (RDP). Windows natively supports RDP, and providing Remote Desktop is enabled (which it is not by default; only remote management is enabled by default) within the guest operating system, the guest operating system can be connected to via RDP, which would be the normal way for users of virtual machines to connect.

## Creating and Using Hyper-V Templates

In the previous section, a virtual machine was manually created, and all the attributes such as memory, CPU, network, and storage had to be configured. Then the operating system had to be manually installed. While PowerShell can help automate this process, a much better option is to use a template, which is a virtual machine configuration and virtual hard disk with a duplication-ready operating system installed that can be easily deployed just by copying the VHDX file and assigning it to a new virtual machine that is created from a template VM configuration.

The first step is to create the VHDX file containing the operating system that is suitable for duplication. Any readers who have ever deployed desktops will be used to the idea of building out one "gold" desktop and then preparing it for duplication so it could then be captured and deployed to many desktops very quickly. Windows has actually been using this method since Windows 2008, when the WIM format was introduced as the method of installing Windows. Inside the WIM file is an actual deployed operating system that has been prepared for duplication. All Windows installation actually does is deploy the content of the WIM file, which is why installation actually got faster between Windows 2003 and Windows 2008. When Windows is installed, there are a number of specializations performed, such as creating the Security ID, creating the Globally Unique ID, and other items. Many problems arise if different systems have the same SID, GUID, and other items. For this reason, sysprep is a utility built into the operating system that removes this unique information (the process is known as generalization), and once it is removed, the operating system can be duplicated and started on the target. When that happens, a specialization phase creates the required unique values and also runs certain critical processes to ready the copied operating system for usage. Once you have deployed the operating system to a virtual machine and tailored it, run the command at the end of this paragraph. This will generalize the operating system and shut it down. You can then copy the VHDX file to a template area and use that template for new virtual machines, essentially just copying the template to a new location for each new virtual machine that should run the same operating system. It's also possible to just launch sysprep.exe and a dialog will allow you to select the same options. However, when you are using the full command line, the /mode:VM parameter can be specified (covered in detail in Chapter 10, "Remote Desktop Services") but it enables sysprep to run in a mode that is optimized for virtualized hardware.

```
Sysprep.exe /generalize /oobe /shutdown /mode:VM
```

When a new virtual machine starts from a copy of your template, it will go through a very basic out-of-box-experience that will ask minimal questions regarding country, language, keyboard layout, accepting the EULA, and a new local administrator password. Those questions can be answered through the use of an unattended installation answer file, which is how SCVMM actually automates deployments.

Once you have the template VHDX file, there is a challenge to keep it updated, such as having the latest patches applied. You can only generalize an operating system so many times, so it is not an option to take a template, start it with a VM, patch it, then generalize it again with sysprep, and keep repeating this process. There are several options that I think are good and I have written instructions for the first two and even recorded a video for each:

1. Inject patches into the VHDX file directly using the Deployment Image Servicing and Management (DISM) tool. I created a script to do this, which is available at

   http://windowsitpro.com/windows/add-updates-offline-vhd-or-wim-file

   A video walk-through is available at

   http://www.youtube.com/watch?v=cOUlW2bJnK0

2. Use a virtual machine and utilize checkpoints to create a point-in-time capture of the VM before sysprep'ing, applying updates, and sysprep'ing again, and then export the updated image and revert back to the pre-sysprep'd checkpoint ready for the next set of updates. I detail this at

   http://windowsitpro.com/hyper-v/easily-maintain-hyper-v-template-image

   There is a video walkthrough at

   http://www.youtube.com/watch?v=1dddszeRHpM

3. In the past, Microsoft had the Virtual Machine Servicing Tool (VMST), which allowed the patching of Hyper-V virtual machines. However, the last supported version only worked up to SCVMM 2012. Microsoft has now released an updated solution based on Orchestrator SMA that can patch virtual machines stored in a SCVMM library from updates available in WSUS. The solution is available at

   http://blogs.technet.com/b/privatecloud/archive/2013/12/07/orchestrated-vm
   -patching.aspx

   The solution comes in the form of the SMA runbook and instructions on its actual usage.

One option with the template VHDX would be to write some basic PowerShell that creates a new folder for the new VM, copies the template VHDX into that folder, creates a new VM, and attaches the copied VHDX file to the new VM. It would even be possible to mount the VHDX file and inject a sysprep answer file into it to specify name, domain join instructions, and even network configuration so that when the virtual machine is turned on, it is fully configured (which is exactly what SCVMM does).

A better option is to leverage SCVMM, which has full template support and can even take an existing virtual machine and turn it into a template, including generalizing the guest operating system:

◆ The guest virtual machine must be a supported operating system, and the operating system in the guest must be known to SCVMM. When you are looking at the virtual machine in the VMs And Services workspace, it should show the operating system version. If it does not, right-click the VM and select Refresh while the virtual machine is running.

◆ The virtual machine must be shut down.

◆ The virtual machine must not have any checkpoints (to save the VM, create a clone of it first).

◆ The virtual machine administrator password does not need to be blank.

This allows you to create a virtual machine, customize as required, shut it down, and simply right-click it in SCVMM and select the Create VM Template option. Remember that this will generalize the operating system, and so if you wish to keep the state of the virtual machine, you should create a clone of it prior to using it as the source for a template creation. A warning is displayed that the template creation process will remove the state of the VM. When creating a VM template, the virtual hardware will copy the configuration of the source VM, but this can be changed in the Library post-template creation. The Operating System template properties can be modified, such as name, administrator password, time zone, and domain membership, and you can even install roles, features, and other software. A SCVMM library server must be selected as the target to store the new template, along with a location within the library. Once the template is created, the original virtual machine will be deleted. You can track the status of the template creation using the Jobs workspace in SCVMM, as shown in Figure 5.16. Note that the longest part of the process was copying the VHDX file to the library.

**FIGURE 5.16**

The full detail of a
template creation
using SCVMM

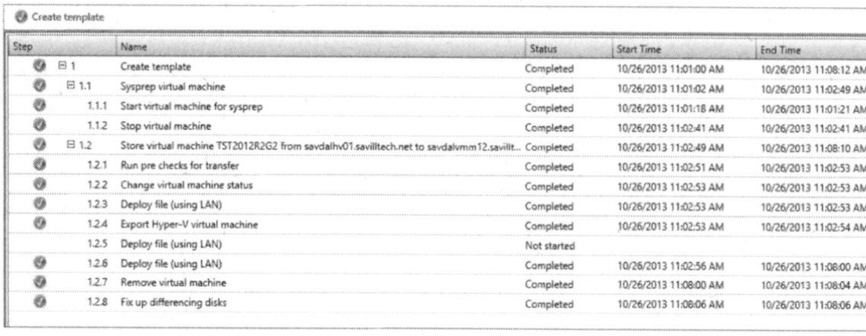

| Step | | | Name | Status | Start Time | End Time |
|---|---|---|---|---|---|---|
| ✅ | ⊟ 1 | | Create template | Completed | 10/26/2013 11:01:00 AM | 10/26/2013 11:08:12 AM |
| ✅ | ⊟ 1.1 | | Sysprep virtual machine | Completed | 10/26/2013 11:01:02 AM | 10/26/2013 11:02:49 AM |
| ✅ | | 1.1.1 | Start virtual machine for sysprep | Completed | 10/26/2013 11:01:18 AM | 10/26/2013 11:01:21 AM |
| ✅ | | 1.1.2 | Stop virtual machine | Completed | 10/26/2013 11:02:41 AM | 10/26/2013 11:02:41 AM |
| ✅ | ⊟ 1.2 | | Store virtual machine TST2012R2G2 from savdalhv01.savilltech.net to savdalvmm12.savilt... | Completed | 10/26/2013 11:02:49 AM | 10/26/2013 11:08:10 AM |
| ✅ | | 1.2.1 | Run pre checks for transfer | Completed | 10/26/2013 11:02:51 AM | 10/26/2013 11:02:53 AM |
| ✅ | | 1.2.2 | Change virtual machine status | Completed | 10/26/2013 11:02:53 AM | 10/26/2013 11:02:53 AM |
| ✅ | | 1.2.3 | Deploy file (using LAN) | Completed | 10/26/2013 11:02:53 AM | 10/26/2013 11:02:53 AM |
| ✅ | | 1.2.4 | Export Hyper-V virtual machine | Completed | 10/26/2013 11:02:53 AM | 10/26/2013 11:02:54 AM |
| | | 1.2.5 | Deploy file (using LAN) | Not started | | |
| ✅ | | 1.2.6 | Deploy file (using LAN) | Completed | 10/26/2013 11:02:56 AM | 10/26/2013 11:08:00 AM |
| ✅ | | 1.2.7 | Remove virtual machine | Completed | 10/26/2013 11:08:00 AM | 10/26/2013 11:08:04 AM |
| ✅ | | 1.2.8 | Fix up differencing disks | Completed | 10/26/2013 11:08:06 AM | 10/26/2013 11:08:06 AM |

SCVMM 2012 SP1 introduced the ability to also create Linux-based virtual machine templates that could then be deployed. There is an additional step because Linux does not have a built-in sysprep, which means a SCVMM agent must be installed into the Linux VM prior to using it for a template that allows SCVMM to customize the OS during deployment. The process for Linux is as follows:

1. Create a new virtual machine (VM) and install a SCVMM-supported Linux distribution into it (at the time of this writing, this includes Red Hat Enterprise Linux, [RHEL], CentOS, Ubuntu, and SUSE, with others coming in the future).

2. Install the latest version of Hyper-V Integration Services if needed (the Linux kernel 3.4 includes the Windows 2012 version of Hyper-V Integration Services).

3. Next, install the SCVMM Linux agent. This is found in the `C:\Program Files\ Microsoft System Center 2012 R2\Virtual Machine Manager\agents\Linux` folder on the SCVMM server. How you get the content of the folder to the Linux distribution will vary.

   One option, if the Linux distribution supports SMB, is to just connect to the C$ share on the SCVMM server. Or you could create an NFS share for Linux to connect to, although I found it easier to just create an ISO with the Linux agent in it and then map the ISO to the Linux VM, which will be available as the local CD. I found the easiest way to create the ISO is to use a software package such as MagicISO. Once the files are available, you must install the Linux agent by running the install script and pick the 32-bit or 64-bit version. To run the install script, you first need to set the install script to be executable: `chmod +x install`

   Then execute (I use sudo because I'm not logged on as administrator): `sudo ./install scvmmguestagent.1.0.2.1014.x64.tar`

   The agent is needed because it performs the customization of the Linux environment when a template is deployed. Once the Linux template is deployed, the SCVMM agent is automatically removed.

4. Shut down the Linux VM, and then save its VHDX file to the SCVMM library.

5. Now create a Linux template, and make sure you set the correct operating system, which will allow you to configure automatic naming (* is a complete random name, while ### specifies an automatically incrementing number) for the hostnames along with a password for the root account, the time zone, and any scripts you want to run. Save the Template.

6. You can now create new Linux VMs from the template. You will notice that when you deploy a Linux VM from the template, at one point an ISO is connected to the VM temporarily. This carries a customization file that contains the personalization data in the `linuxosconfiguration.xml` file in addition to the latest version of the SCVMM Linux agent (in case it's been updated).

Templates are visible through the Library workspace and shown in the Templates ➢ VM Templates area. Figure 5.17 shows the main configuration areas for a template. Notice that all the virtual hardware can be changed in addition to adding new hardware to the template hardware profile. If you will be creating many different types of templates rather than configuring the same hardware or operating system configurations each time, a good option is to navigate to Profiles within the Libraries workspace and create separate hardware profiles and guest OS profiles, which can then be used in templates you create, avoiding the need to perform the same configurations repeatedly. VM templates can also be exported and imported, allowing portability between SCVMM environments.

---

**USING APPLICATION, SQL, ROLE, AND FEATURE TEMPLATE CONFIGURATIONS**

You will notice that in the VM templates there are sections related to application configurations, SQL configuration, roles, and features. While it may seem that all of these configurations will be used when deploying the template, this is not the case. These components are used only when the VM template is deployed a part of a service template, which I will cover in Chapter 9. When you're deploying a template-based virtual machine, configurations related to application, SQL, roles, and features are ignored and not available. If you require this type of deployment, either use service templates or manage these configurations using PowerShell or System Center Orchestrator as an add-on to the VM deployment.

---

**FIGURE 5.17**
Modifying a template within SCVMM

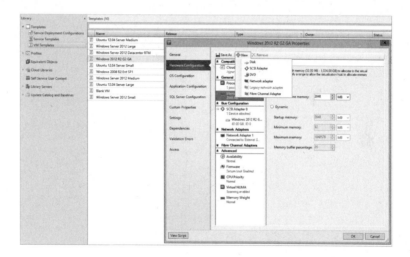

In most environments you will have a very few number of template VHDX files but many different templates that use the same VHDX and apply different configurations and applications. You do not want a large number of VHDX files with different configurations and applications installed. This is hard to maintain and patch. The goal is to have a plain, sometimes called vanilla, VHDX template with just the operating system and then deploy all other customizations using the template options.

A Linux OS configuration has far fewer options than a Windows OS configuration, and most customizations beyond root credentials and name will need to be performed using the RunOnce Commands option.

Deploying a virtual machine using a template is simple:

1. Within the VMs And Services workspace, select the Create Virtual Machine action, which has an option to create based on an existing virtual machine, VM template, or virtual hard disk in the library, as shown in Figure 5.18. Click Next.

**FIGURE 5.18**
Selecting a template as the source for a new virtual machine

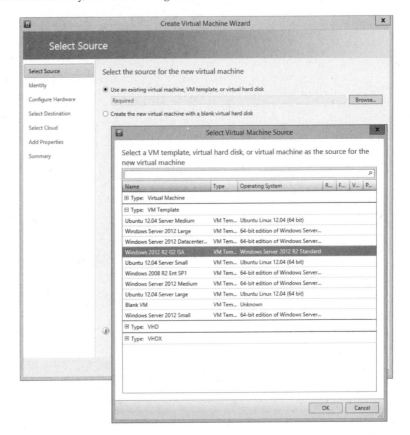

2. Enter a name and optional description and click Next.

3. The virtual hardware profile can be customized from the profile in the template or even a completely separate hardware profile can be loaded. If this virtual machine needs to be highly available, in the Advanced ➤ Availability section, ensure that the Make This Virtual Machine Highly Available box is checked, as shown in Figure 5.19. Click Next.

4. Customizations for the operating system can be performed, such as identity, answer file, and RunOnce commands. Notice that all the defaults from the template are populated automatically. Click Next.

5. Select the location for the deployment. This can be to a cloud or to a host group. When you have made your selection, click Next.

**FIGURE 5.19**
Setting a virtual
machine to be
highly available and
therefore requiring
deployment to a
cluster

6. An evaluation against all hosts is performed and each available host is given a rating, as shown in Figure 5.20, based on its suitability. The rating is explained in the Details section. The first two are good matches, but the third and fourth are not because the VM needs to be clustered and these nodes are not clustered, which is shown in the Rating Explanation section. Select a host and click Next.

7. The Configure Settings dialog allows changes to configurations such as the computer name and location. Make changes as required and click Next.

8. In the Select Networks dialog, select the VM network and click Next.

9. Set the automatic actions for startup and shutdown and choose whether the new VM should be excluded from placement optimizations. (This will be covered in Chapter 7, "Failover Clustering and Migration Technologies," but it's a technology that moves VMs between hosts if necessary for optimal resource utilization. This should be left enabled for most virtual machines.) Click Next.

10. A summary screen is displayed (along with the View Script button should you wish to capture the PowerShell). Click Create to create the virtual machine.

**FIGURE 5.20**

The ratings for possible hosts

Deploying a template is the single circumstance in which SCVMM 2012 R2 leverages ODX if possible, which needs to be a capability of the SAN, and the LUN containing the template VHDX file must be on the same volume as the LUN that is the target for the VM deployment for most SANs. If it's not possible to leverage ODX, SCVMM will try a regular Fast File Copy, and if that fails, it will resort to using BITS. Figure 5.21 shows the complete deployment of a VM from a template. Notice the various steps. First a virtual machine is created, and then the template VHDX file is copied to the target storage. Step 1.8.2 creates a temporary ISO that contains the answer file that performs all the configuration of the guest OS. This ISO is created in the root of the new virtual machine folder that has the name of the VM. For example, my test1 VM ISO would be called `C:\ClusterStorage\Volume1\test1\test1.iso`. This ISO is deleted once the VM is created, as are the additional virtual DVD drives that are added during deployment to attach the answer file ISO to as well as the VMM additions.

If you are quick enough, you can see the temporary ISO file created and could even copy it to another location. It contains a single file, `unattend.xml`, which contains all the guest OS customizations specified in the template and the selections during VM deployment. The following code is the content of my `unattend.xml` file that SCVMM created for the deployment shown in Figure 5.21. This is useful for your own education and understanding of how your OS customizations actually are implemented to the virtual machine.

**FIGURE 5.21**
A complete SCVMM VM deployment from a template

Create virtual machine

| Step | Name | Status | Start Time | End Time |
|---|---|---|---|---|
| 1 | Create virtual machine | Completed | 10/26/2013 2:18:01 PM | 10/26/2013 2:23:18 PM |
| 1.1 | Create virtual machine | Completed | 10/26/2013 2:18:05 PM | 10/26/2013 2:18:08 PM |
| 1.2 | Deploy file (using Fast File Copy) | Completed | 10/26/2013 2:18:08 PM | 10/26/2013 2:19:37 PM |
| 1.3 | Deploy file (using LAN) | Completed | 10/26/2013 2:19:38 PM | 10/26/2013 2:19:38 PM |
| 1.4 | Change properties of virtual machine | Completed | 10/26/2013 2:19:38 PM | 10/26/2013 2:19:52 PM |
| 1.5 | Fix up differencing disks | Completed | 10/26/2013 2:19:38 PM | 10/26/2013 2:19:38 PM |
| 1.6 | Change properties of network adapter | Completed | 10/26/2013 2:19:53 PM | 10/26/2013 2:19:56 PM |
| 1.7 | Install VM components | Completed | 10/26/2013 2:19:57 PM | 10/26/2013 2:20:08 PM |
| 1.7.1 | Start virtual machine to install VM components | Not started | | |
| 1.7.2 | Stop virtual machine | Not started | | |
| 1.8 | Customize virtual machine | Completed | 10/26/2013 2:20:08 PM | 10/26/2013 2:23:17 PM |
| 1.8.1 | Deploy file (using LAN) | Completed | 10/26/2013 2:20:08 PM | 10/26/2013 2:20:08 PM |
| 1.8.2 | Create an ISO file with the Unattend.xml file | Completed | 10/26/2013 2:20:08 PM | 10/26/2013 2:20:08 PM |
| 1.8.3 | Deploy file (using LAN) | Completed | 10/26/2013 2:20:08 PM | 10/26/2013 2:20:15 PM |
| 1.8.4 | Attach the ISO file in the virtual DVD drive to the virtual machine | Completed | 10/26/2013 2:20:15 PM | 10/26/2013 2:20:16 PM |
| 1.8.5 | Attach the ISO file in the virtual DVD drive to the virtual machine | Completed | 10/26/2013 2:20:16 PM | 10/26/2013 2:20:16 PM |
| 1.8.6 | Start virtual machine for customization | Completed | 10/26/2013 2:20:16 PM | 10/26/2013 2:20:20 PM |
| 1.8.7 | Shut down virtual machine | Completed | 10/26/2013 2:23:16 PM | 10/26/2013 2:23:16 PM |

```
<?xml version="1.0" encoding="utf-8"?>
<unattend xmlns="urn:schemas-microsoft-com:unattend">
    <settings pass="specialize">
        <component name="Microsoft-Windows-Shell-Setup"
processorArchitecture="amd64" publicKeyToken="31bf3856ad364e35"
language="neutral" versionScope="nonSxS" xmlns:wcm="http://schemas.microsoft.com/
WMIConfig/2002/State"
xmlns:xsi="http://www.w3.org/2001/XMLSchema-instance">
            <RegisteredOwner />
            <RegisteredOrganization />
            <ComputerName>test1</ComputerName>
            <ProductKey>Y4TGP-NPTV9-HTC2H-7MGQ3-DV4TW</ProductKey>
        </component>
        <component name="Microsoft-Windows-UnattendedJoin"
processorArchitecture="amd64" publicKeyToken="31bf3856ad364e35"
language="neutral" versionScope="nonSxS"
xmlns:wcm="http://schemas.microsoft.com/WMIConfig/2002/State"
xmlns:xsi="http://www.w3.org/2001/XMLSchema-instance">
            <Identification>
                <JoinDomain>savilltech</JoinDomain>
                <Credentials>
                    <Domain>savilltech</Domain>
                    <Username>administrator</Username>
                    <Password>passwordinplaintext</Password>
                </Credentials>
            </Identification>
        </component>
        <component name="Microsoft-Windows-Deployment"
processorArchitecture="amd64" publicKeyToken="31bf3856ad364e35"
language="neutral" versionScope="nonSxS"
```

```
xmlns:wcm="http://schemas.microsoft.com/WMIConfig/2002/State"
xmlns:xsi="http://www.w3.org/2001/XMLSchema-instance">
            <RunSynchronous>
                <RunSynchronousCommand wcm:action="add">
                    <Order>1</Order>
                    <Description>Install Guest agent</Description>
                    <Path>cmd.exe /c (for %1 in
(z y x w v u t s r q p o n m l k j i h g f e d c b a) do
@(if exist %1:\VMMGuestAgent.exe (sc create scvmmadditions binpath=%1:\
VMMGuestAgent.exe type=own start=auto &amp;
sc start scvmmadditions )))</Path>
                    <WillReboot>OnRequest</WillReboot>
                </RunSynchronousCommand>
            </RunSynchronous>
        </component>
    </settings>
    <settings pass="oobeSystem">
        <component name="Microsoft-Windows-Shell-Setup"
processorArchitecture="amd64" publicKeyToken="31bf3856ad364e35"
language="neutral" versionScope="nonSxS" xmlns:wcm="http://schemas.microsoft.com/
WMIConfig/2002/State"
xmlns:xsi="http://www.w3.org/2001/XMLSchema-instance">
            <UserAccounts>
                <AdministratorPassword>
                    <Value>localadminpasswordplaintext</Value>
                    <PlainText>true</PlainText>
                </AdministratorPassword>
            </UserAccounts>
            <TimeZone>Central Standard Time</TimeZone>
            <OOBE>
                <HideEULAPage>true</HideEULAPage>
                <SkipUserOOBE>true</SkipUserOOBE>
                <HideOEMRegistrationScreen>true</HideOEMRegistrationScreen>
                <HideOnlineAccountScreens>true</HideOnlineAccountScreens>
                <HideWirelessSetupInOOBE>true</HideWirelessSetupInOOBE>
                <NetworkLocation>Work</NetworkLocation>
                <ProtectYourPC>1</ProtectYourPC>
                <HideLocalAccountScreen>true</HideLocalAccountScreen>
            </OOBE>
        </component>
        <component name="Microsoft-Windows-International-Core"
processorArchitecture="amd64" publicKeyToken="31bf3856ad364e35"
language="neutral" versionScope="nonSxS" xmlns:wcm="http://schemas.microsoft.com/
WMIConfig/2002/State" xmlns:xsi="http://www.w3.org/2001/XMLSchema-instance">
```

```
        <UserLocale>en-US</UserLocale>
        <SystemLocale>en-US</SystemLocale>
        <InputLocale>0409:00000409</InputLocale>
        <UILanguage>en-US</UILanguage>
    </component>
  </settings>
  <cpi:offlineImage cpi:source="" xmlns:cpi="urn:schemas-microsoft-com:cpi" />
</unattend>
```

# Hyper-V Integration Services and Supported Operating Systems

When talking about the guest operating system running inside a virtual machine, I mentioned enlightened operating systems, which are guest operating systems that are aware they are running in a virtual environment and can leverage specific virtual features such as synthetic hardware via the VMBus through special drivers. Additionally, there are a number of services between the virtual machine and the Hyper-V host that are enabled when the guest has Hyper-V Integration Services installed. Hyper-V Integration Services is built into the Windows operating systems for the respective version of Hyper-V. For example, Windows Server 2012 R2 and Windows 8.1 have Hyper-V 2012 R2 Integration Services built in, and Windows Server 2012 and Windows 8 had the Hyper-V 2012 Integration Services built in. This means that if the guest operating system is running a version of an operating system older that the Hyper-V host, you will need to upgrade its version of Integration Services. This is the first action you should perform when deploying an operating system, and when creating a VM template, make sure you update Integration Services prior to capturing the VHDX for use with the template.

Each Hyper-V host has the latest version of Integration Services stored at C:\Windows \System32\vmguest.iso. When vmconnect is used to connect to a virtual machine, an action, Insert Integration Services Setup Disk, is available in the Action menu that attaches vmguest .iso to the virtual DVD for the virtual machine. The vmguest.iso file will then launch within the VM and update Integration Services, which will require a reboot for the guest operating system. While the version of Integration Services always increased between Windows Server versions, it may also increment as part of the updates. For example, an update related to backup operations was made to the Hyper-V Integration Services for Windows Server 2012 and Windows 8, which incremented Integration Services from 6.2.9200.16384 (the RTM) to 6.2.9200.16433. This was part of update rollup KB 2770917 (http://support.microsoft.com /kb/2770917). When the Hyper-V host reboots, it updates its vmguest.iso file with the latest integration services.

It is therefore important to track whether Hyper-V Integration Services is updated and whether you need to upgrade it inside virtual machines. Within the guest OS, Integration Services can be confirmed by looking at the VM's Registry at HKEY_LOCAL_MACHINE

\SOFTWARE\Microsoft\Virtual Machine\Auto\IntegrationServicesVersion for the IC version or from the host using the following command:

```
Get-VM | ft Name, IntegrationServicesVersion
```

Additionally, the Summary tab for a virtual machine will show whether an update is required in the Integration Services section, as shown in Figure 5.22.

**FIGURE 5.22**

A VM that requires an Integration Services upgrade

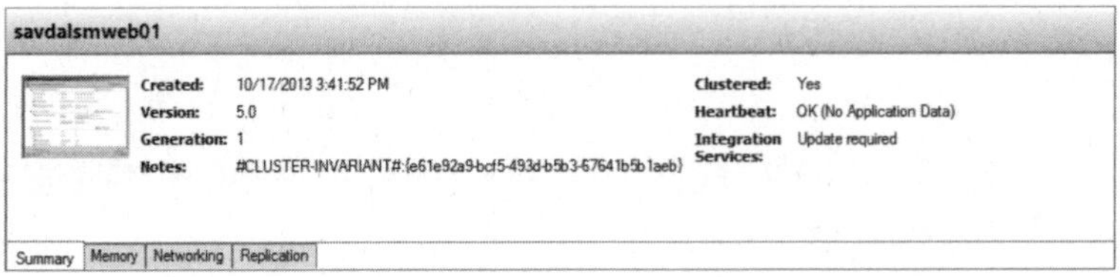

To update, the easiest way is to extract the contents of C:\Windows\System32\vmguest .iso from the Hyper-V host to a folder and then launch setup.exe from the relevant support\<architecture> folder on each VM, as in this example:

```
\\savdalhv01\HIS\support\amd64\setup.exe /quiet /norestart
```

Note that this will require a reboot of the VM at some point, but the /norestart suppresses the automatic reboot.

In addition to providing the drivers and components required for the most optimal utilization of resources between the guest and the hypervisor, there are a number of other integration services, which are described in the following list. Note that each service can be disabled if required through the settings of the virtual machine in the Management ➤ Integration Services section. Unless there is a specific reason not to, you should leave Integration Services enabled.

**Operating system shutdown**    Enables the guest operating system to be cleanly shut down from the Hyper-V manager or the management interfaces Hyper-V provides, such as PowerShell and Windows Management Instrumentation (WMI).

**Time synchronization**    Keeps the time of the guest OS synchronized with the host operating system.

**Data exchange**    Allows the exchange of specific Registry location values between a guest and the parent partition, known as key-value pairs. The Hyper-V host writes to location HKEY_LOCAL_MACHINE\SOFTWARE\Microsoft\Virtual Machine\Guest\Parameters within the VM, and the OS in the guest can then read from this location to gather information about the host. This information includes the Hyper-V host name (which is the cluster name if it's a cluster node), version information, its fully qualified name, and the actual VM's name and ID, as shown in Figure 5.23. This can easily be read using PowerShell. For example, within a virtual machine, to find which Hyper-V host it is on I use the following PowerShell command:

```
$regPath = "HKLM:\SOFTWARE\Microsoft\Virtual Machine\Guest\Parameters"
(Get-ItemProperty -Path $regPath).HostName
```

Conversely, the Hyper-V host reads information from HKEY_LOCAL_MACHINE\ SOFTWARE\Microsoft\Virtual Machine\Auto in the guest, which is populated by the guest OS, giving Hyper-V a lot of information about the OS, including version, naming, and IP configuration. This type of information exchange can be useful for many types of management operations, automation, and inventory. The complete list of values can be found at the following location, which documents the Msvm_KvpExchangeDataItem class:

http://msdn.microsoft.com/en-us/library/cc136850(v=vs.85).aspx

You can actually create your own custom values within the VM that can be read by the Hyper-V host by adding string values under HKEY_LOCAL_MACHINE\SOFTWARE \Microsoft\Virtual Machine\Guest. This would be useful to, for example, populate the type of server in the guest using a custom process, such as SQLServer or IISServer, which could then be read from the host to ascertain the type of server running in the VM. There is no PowerShell cmdlet available to read values set in the guest from the Hyper-V host. Instead, you use WMI. The following PowerShell script reads the fully qualified domain name from within the guest OS from the Hyper-V host for VM savdaldc02:

```
$vmName = "savdaldc02"

$vm = Get-WmiObject -Namespace root\virtualization\v2 `
    -Class Msvm_ComputerSystem `
    -Filter "ElementName='$vmName'"

$vm.GetRelated("Msvm_KvpExchangeComponent").GuestIntrinsicExchangeItems | % {
        $GuestExchangeItemXml = ([XML]$_).SelectSingleNode(`
  "/INSTANCE/PROPERTY[@NAME='Name']/VALUE[child::text()='FullyQualifiedDomainN
ame']")

        if ($GuestExchangeItemXml -ne $null)
        {
        $GuestExchangeItemXml.SelectSingleNode( `
        "/INSTANCE/PROPERTY[@NAME='Data']/VALUE/child::text()").Value
        }
    }
```

**Heartbeat**   Allows Hyper-V to check the responsiveness of the guest operating system by a heartbeat check.

**Backup (volume snapshot)**   A very powerful feature I will cover in Chapter 6, "Maintaining a Hyper-V Environment," this allows backup requests at the host level to be passed to the guest operating system, in turn allowing consistent file and application backups to be taken from the host.

**Guest services**   This is a new Integration Services component introduced in Windows Server 2012 R2 that is disabled by default. Guest services enables the copying of files to a virtual machine using WMI APIs or using the new Copy-VMFile PowerShell cmdlet.

**FIGURE 5.23**
Registry within a virtual machine showing information about the host

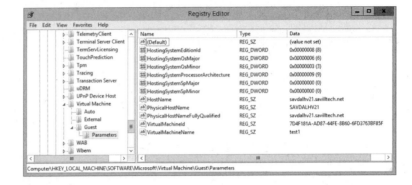

Microsoft provides Integration Services for the supported operating systems unless it is already part of the operating system; for example, many modern Linux distributions have the Hyper-V integration services built in (although Microsoft still releases updated Linux Integration Services, which are then integrated into newer distributions of Linux). The full list of the supported guest operating systems can be found at `http://technet.microsoft.com/library/hh831531`, but the primary supported operating systems for 2012 R2 Hyper-V are as follows:

- Windows Server 2012 R2

- Windows Server 2012

- Windows Server 2008 R2 SP1

- Windows Server 2008 SP2

- Windows Server 2003 [R2] SP2

- Windows 8.1

- Windows 8

- Windows 7

- Windows Vista SP2

- Windows XP SP3

- Windows XP x64 SP2

- CentOS 5.7-6.4

- Red Hat Enterprise Linux 5.7-6.4

- SUSE Linux Enterprise Server 11 SP2 and SP3

- Open SUSE 12.1

- Ubuntu 12.04, 12.10, 13.04 and 13.10

- Oracle Linux 6.4

Most of the Linux distributions have Integration Services built in. However, the previously mentioned article documents which ones need the Linux Integration Services downloaded and installed manually. At the time of this writing, the latest Linux Integration Services version is 3.4 and is available from the following location:

```
www.microsoft.com/en-us/download/details.aspx?id=34603
```

This is a large list that covers pretty much every operating system that is used in organizations today, but what if a company has another operating system? If it's not on this list of supported operating systems, will it not work? Remember that what Hyper-V provides in a generation 1 virtual machine is a virtual environment that does not require the guest operating system to be enlightened. To the guest it appears the virtual hardware being presented is a physical system that includes items such as the IDE controller and the emulated legacy network adapter. Even in the 2012 R2 version of Hyper-V, the processor compatibility for older operating systems (-CompatibilityForOlderOperatingSystemsEnabled), which was aimed at NT 4.0 systems, is still configurable using PowerShell. These nonenlightened systems that do not understand VMBus will have a higher overhead and see poorer performance because of the emulated nature of the storage and networking, but most likely they will work. There is a difference between what is supported and what will work. Microsoft supports only operating systems on Hyper-V that are themselves supported by the vendor. For example, Microsoft no longer supports Windows Server 2000, which means Hyper-V can no longer support it as a guest operating system, but it will run a single processor virtual machine. In a production environment you typically should be running only operating systems supported by the vendor to ensure that patches are received and that in the event of a problem you can get help from the vendor, but if you have a Windows Server 2000 application, it most likely would run on Hyper-V just fine.

## Migrating Physical Servers and Virtual Machines to Hyper-V Virtual Machines

For most organizations today, virtualization is a technology that is established in the environment and the number of operating systems deployed to bare-metal hardware (physical servers) is decreasing. It's more likely today that you have operating systems virtualized on another hypervisor, such as VMware ESX or Citrix XenServer. Moving from either a physical server or another hypervisor requires a migration known as physical to virtual (P2V) or virtual to virtual (V2V).

In the previous version of SCVMM, SCVMM 2012, the P2V feature was built into the product and allowed a physical server operating system to be captured and converted to a virtual machine. This worked in an online or offline mode depending on the operating system running on the server. Online P2V is used for operating systems that support the Microsoft Volume Shadow Copy Service (VSS) and works by deploying an agent to the physical computer operating system (although this could also be an operating system running inside a VM). A capture of the hardware configuration is performed and mapped to a virtual machine configuration, and then the content of the hard drives is captured using a VSS backup, which ensures the integrity of the backup, and is written to a VHD on the Hyper-V host. It is important that the application is stopped during this process because otherwise, once the backup is used with a virtual machine on Hyper-V, any subsequent changes on the physical host would be lost. This is not a problem if the application does not store application data or state locally. Because of the VSS requirement, the online P2V is available for Windows XP SP2 and Windows 2003 SP1 and above.

For those Windows 2000 SP4 machines that don't support VSS or for the other operating systems that perhaps you don't want to use online P2V because a VSS writer for the application is not available, an offline P2V is performed. With the offline P2V, a Windows PE OS is temporarily installed on the source server and the computer is rebooted into the Windows PE environment through a modification to the boot record. The VMM agent in the Windows PE environment captures the disk content and streams to the Hyper-V server, and once that's complete, the machine boots back into the regular operating system, the final P2V processes are completed, and the actual VM is created on the Hyper-V host.

This feature has been removed in SCVMM 2012 R2, which does leave a gap in the ability to perform P2V. The Microsoft recommended solution at this time is to deploy an instance of SCVMM 2012 as well and use that for the P2V migrations, as documented at the following location:

```
http://blogs.technet.com/b/scvmm/archive/2013/10/03/how-to-perform-a-p2v-in-a
-scvmm-2012-r2-environment.aspx
```

I believe, though, that they are working on a better solution, but the number of P2V migrations is decreasing because most organizations are virtualized and its mainly new workloads that are now being virtualized. There are third parties that offer P2V solutions, such as Double-Take, Quest, and PlateSpin. One manual approach is to use the SysInternals tool Disk2Vhd from the following location:

```
http://technet.microsoft.com/en-us/sysinternals/ee656415.aspx
```

It can be run on any system supporting VSS and creates a VHD of the system's content. The created VHD file could then be used when creating a new virtual machine.

The other migration type, V2V, is most commonly from VMware ESX to Hyper-V, and there are a number of different solutions. Many partners have V2V solutions, but Microsoft also provides a number of options for VMware migrations to Hyper-V.

SCVMM 2012 R2 still has built-in V2V supported from VMware and can convert either a VMware virtual machine running on an ESX host or a VMware virtual machine in the library. The major conversion task for VMware is converting the virtual hard disks because VMware uses the VMDK format, which needs to be converted to VHD. Additionally, VMware has its own version of Integration Services, called Integration Components, that is installed into guest operating systems. It must be removed from the operating system prior to starting on Hyper-V or the OS will most likely crash. Note that this does not happen with Hyper-V Integration Services if a Hyper-V VM is started on a different hypervisor. On startup, Hyper-V Integration Services is triggered via the BIOS in the virtual machine, which controls the starting of the VMBus. If the hypervisor is not Hyper-V, then the assertion to start VMBus will not occur and Integration Services is not started or used.

While SCVMM 2012 R2 does have V2V, Microsoft has, in my opinion, a better solution available, the Microsoft Virtual Machine Converter (MVMC) Solution Accelerator, which is available from the following location:

```
http://www.microsoft.com/en-us/download/details.aspx?id=34591
```

This solution seems to be where most of the engineering effort is—to provide the best VMware conversion experience. I would not be surprised if P2V was added to this in the future. In addition to the tool, the solution has complete documentation and even an add-on for the VMware vSphere client to expose the conversion functionality of MVMC. The MVMC converts the storage of the VM and removes VMware Integration Components. MVMC supports conversion of VMs on VMware vSphere 4.1 and 5.0.

While the MVMC converts virtual machines in an interactive fashion, it also provides scriptable command-line interfaces for providing automated conversions of large numbers of virtual machines. There are a number of solutions available that leverage MVMC. For example, there is a CodePlex solution to convert VMware to Windows Azure IaaS VMs at http:// vmware2windowsazure.codeplex.com/, and most useful is the Migration Automation Kit (MAT) available in the TechNet Gallery at

http://gallery.technet.microsoft.com/Automation-Toolkit-for-d0822a53

It provides a complete bulk migration solution from VMware that leverages MVMC for the conversion but provides a SQL database–backed solution that comprises three phases:

◆ Collection: Collects information about the VMware environment

◆ List Management: Select the VMs that you wish to be converted based on those found during the Collection phase

◆ Conversion: Automated conversion of all the virtual machines selected during the List Management phase

If you need to perform bulk migrations from VMware, I recommend using the MAT with MVMC. Another option is to leverage a partner who may have access to other tools to help with conversions. Microsoft Consulting Services (MCS) has its own migration solutions and offerings, including Datacenter Consolidation and Migration with some information available at the following location:

http://download.microsoft.com/download/9/4/1/9418922B-4E0D-4E8A-AAFE
-445A2B86E883/Datacenter%20Consolidation%20and%20Migration.pdf

When thinking about any migration, it's important to understand the workloads you currently have and the resources they are using. Microsoft provides a free tool, Microsoft Assessment and Planning Toolkit (MAP), which is available from http://technet.microsoft.com/en-us/ library/bb977556.aspx. MAP can be used for a very large number of scenarios, such as desktop migration, Office planning, and cloud migrations. However, one key capability is that it can inventory and scan the utilization of operating systems and then create reports on the findings to help identify good virtualization and consolidation targets. It is highly recommended to run MAP for a period of time before performing any migration project to ensure that you have a good knowledge of the current systems and their real resource utilization.

In Chapter 2 I talked about differences in how Hyper-V handles processor allocation compared to a hypervisor such as ESX. This can make a difference to how you allocate resources. When converting from ESX, you can match the hardware exactly or you can take the migration as a chance to optimize the resource allocation or increase it if required. With Hyper-V, there is not really a penalty to having additional virtual processors in a virtual machine and therefore you may choose to be more generous than with ESX. While it's important to be accurate in your planning for migrations to ensure that the right hardware is procured, there is quite a lot of flexibility available even for a running virtual machine:

◆ Processor: While processors cannot be hot-added to a virtual machine, the limits and weightings can be changed while the virtual machine is running. This is why potentially having additional virtual processors is a good idea, and the limits can be changed while the VM is running.

◆ Memory: With Dynamic Memory, a virtual machine can have additional memory added as required, and the settings for the memory can be changed while the VM is running, allowing the maximum to be increased.

◆ Network: If bandwidth management is used, the minimum and maximum bandwidth limits can be modified, and at the host level, it's possible to add additional network adapters to a team to increase available bandwidth.

◆ Storage: Additional virtual hard disks can be added to the SCSI controller, and with 2012 R2, a VHDX file attached to the SCSI controller can also be dynamically expanded.

## Upgrading and Migrating from Previous Versions

For an organization that is already using Hyper-V, the adoption of Windows Server 2012 R2 Hyper-V is actually a very simple process. For both stand-alone and clustered hosts Microsoft supports an n-2 upgrade support policy. This means upgrading from Windows Server 2008 R2 and Windows Server 2012 is supported.

It's important when upgrading your Hyper-V infrastructure that the upgrade is as transparent to the end users as possible, so minimizing downtime is very important. When thinking of your upgrade, make sure you consider the following:

◆ Can your hardware run the new version of Windows Server 2012 R2 (likely yes if you are running Windows Server 2008 R2), and even if it can, would this be a good time for a hardware refresh? I have seen big performance differences when running Hyper-V on newer processor generations.

◆ Is your management infrastructure compatible with Windows Server 2012 R2? Can it provide malware protection, monitoring, backup, and so on? It needs to!

◆ Have you upgraded System Center to the 2012 R2 version for full Windows Server 2012 R2 support?

◆ Are the administrators trained in Windows Server 2012 R2? Ensure that administrators can properly manager 2012 R2, especially if they are used to Windows 2008 R2.

◆ Are administrators using Windows 8.1? Only 8.1 can run the Windows Server 2012 R2 Remote Server Administration Tools to remotely manage Windows Server 2012 R2 servers.

◆ If you are migrating/upgrading from 2008 R2, you need to delete snapshots/checkpoints from the virtual machines and delete any Saved state. This is not required if you're upgrading from Windows Server 2012.

◆ Once you upgrade Hyper-V hosts, make sure you upgrade Integration Services on all the virtual machines with the Windows Server 2012 R2 version.

## Stand-Alone Hosts

For a stand-alone Hyper-V host, it is possible to perform an in-place upgrade. This means launching the Windows Server 2012 R2 setup process and selecting the option to perform an in-place upgrade. This will maintain all the server configurations but will mean a period of unavailability to the virtual machines because the virtual machines will all be shut down during the upgrade of the host operating system. Once the upgrade is complete, the virtual machines will start and then you can continue your management and post-upgrade actions.

Another option, if you have additional hardware available and are migrating from Windows Server 2012, is to create a new Windows Server 2012 R2 Hyper-V host and then perform a Shared Nothing Live Migration of the virtual machine from the Windows Server 2012 host to the Windows Server 2012 R2 host. For the first time it's possible to perform a cross-version live migration. This allows you to move the virtual machines to Windows Server 2012 R2 with no downtime to the virtual machine at all. Many companies use a type of rolling upgrade approach, providing they have one spare server available to use, and this is shown in Figure 5.24. In this process, a new box is stood up with Windows Server 2012 R2 (step 2) and the virtual machines from a host are migrated to this new box. The host that is now emptied is then reinstalled with Windows Server 2012 R2 (step 3), and the VMs from another host are then moved to this newly installed host (step 4) and the process continues (step 5). Note that while this process is targeted for Windows Server 2012 to Windows Server 2012 R2 with no downtime, you could use the same process from Windows Server 2008 R2, except there would be some downtime as part of the virtual machine migration and a storage migration or an export/import would be performed between hosts. If the stand-alone hosts were using SAN storage, it would be possible to just unmask the LUNs used by the source host to the target host and then import the virtual machines.

## Clusters

Most production Hyper-V environments will not be stand-alone hosts but rather have clusters of Hyper-V hosts, which means an in-place upgrade is not possible because it is not possible to have a cluster with a mix of operating system versions. This means a migration of virtual machines between clusters is required, with the exact approach differing depending on if you have new hardware for your Hyper-V 2012 R2 infrastructure.

Failover clustering provides the ability to migrate workloads between a source and target cluster, and Hyper-V virtual machines are a supported workload that can be migrated. The way the Cluster Migration Wizard works is that you tell the wizard that runs on the target Windows Serve 2012 R2 cluster that you wish to migrate roles and then point the wizard to the old Windows Server 2008 R2 or Windows Server 2012 cluster. The wizard will then show the roles running on specific storage volumes and will disconnect the storage from the old cluster, activate on the new cluster, migrate the roles (virtual machines) that are hosted on that storage. It's important to ensure that the switches have been zoned correctly so that the target cluster has rights to access the migrated LUNs and the old cluster has its access removed once the storage is migrated. This process is detailed by Microsoft at the following location and at a high level shown in Figure 5.25:

```
http://blogs.msdn.com/b/clustering/archive/2012/06/25/10323434.aspx
```

**FIGURE 5.24**
Rolling upgrade for
stand-alone hosts

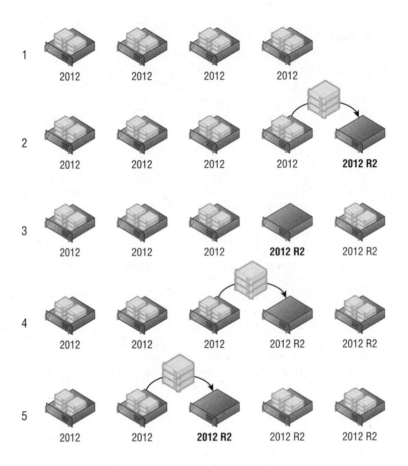

**FIGURE 5.25**
Using the cluster
migration wizard
between clusters

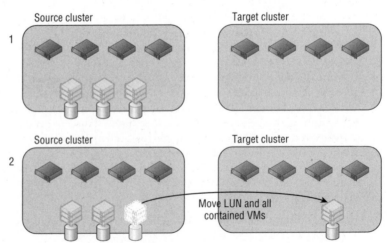

This is a great process but it requires a new cluster to migrate to. If you do not have spare hardware, then another approach is to evict nodes from your existing cluster, rebuild them with Windows Server 2012 R2, create a new cluster on those nodes (known as a seed cluster), and then move resources between clusters. As you move more resources, you evict more nodes from the source cluster. You rebuild a node and add it to the new cluster, move resources, then move another node until all nodes have been rebuilt and are part of the Windows Server 2012 R2 cluster. This approach does mean that there may be some reduction in resilience because the number of nodes in each cluster is reduced, but with careful planning it is still possible to maintain protection from a node failure. Just be sure you don't migrate more resources than can be hosted on the target if a node failed. Likewise, don't leave more resources on the source cluster than can be handled if a node failed on the source cluster. If you have a highly utilized cluster, this may be difficult and may require some additional hardware during the migration process. This approach is shown in Figure 5.26. Notice that I evict two nodes initially, so there is protection from a node failure. You never want fewer than two nodes in the source or target cluster.

I should note that you could take a different approach if you have sufficient spare storage that would perform a Shared Nothing Live Migration between a Windows Server 2012 cluster and a Windows Server 2012 R2 cluster. Using this method instead of using the cluster migration wizard, you would simply perform a Shared Nothing Live Migration of each virtual machine. The benefit over the cluster migration wizard is that the virtual machines do not have to be stopped during the migration and therefore there is no downtime. Once again, you could essentially move the VMs from one node at a time and then once each node is empty, remove it from the source cluster, rebuild it with Windows Server 2012 R2, and add to the new target cluster. If you are using a scale-out file server (SoFS) to host the virtual machines over SMB, then no extra storage would be required; you just need to ensure that the cluster and hosts have access to the file share and file system.

When you're moving from Windows Server 2012 to Windows Server 2012 R2, the key point is that whether the host is stand-alone or in a cluster, a migration with no downtime to the virtual machines is now possible.

**FIGURE 5.26**
Using a seed cluster
and node migration
approach

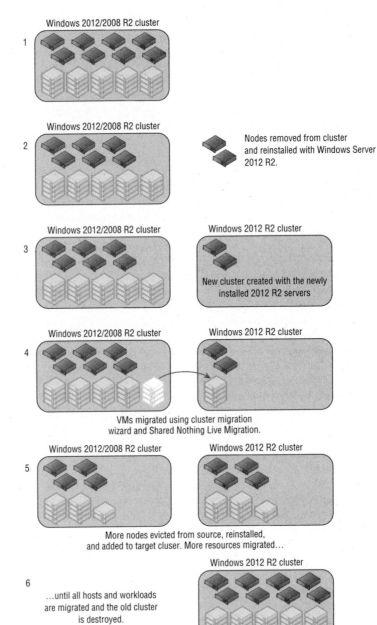

# The Bottom Line

**Identify the different ways to deploy Hyper-V.**   Windows Server 2012 R2 Hyper-V can be deployed using a number of methods. The traditional approach is to install a server from setup media, which could be a DVD, USB device, or even files obtained over the network. Enterprise systems management solutions such as System Center Configuration Manager and Windows Deployment Services can be used to customize deployments. System Center Virtual Machine Manager can also be deployed to deploy Hyper-V hosts using Boot to VHD technology, providing a single management solution for deployment of hosts and virtual machines.

**Master It**   What other types of server can SCVMM 2012 R2 deploy?

**Explain why using Server Core is beneficial to deployments.**   Windows Server and Windows client operating systems share a lot of common code, and a typical Windows Server deployment has a graphical interface, Internet browser, and many graphical tools. These components all take up space, require patching, and may have vulnerabilities. For many types of server roles, these graphical elements are not required. Server Core provides a minimal server footprint that is managed remotely, which means less patching and there-fore fewer reboots in addition to a smaller attack surface. Because a host reboot requires all virtual machines to also be rebooted, using Server Core is a big benefit for Hyper-V environ-ments to remove as many reboots as possible.

**Master It**   What was the big change to Server Core between Windows Server 2008 R2 and Windows Server 2012?

**Explain how to create and use virtual machine templates.**   While it is possible to manu-ally create the virtual machine environment and install the operating system for each new virtual machine, it's inefficient considering the virtual machine uses a file for its virtual storage. A far more efficient and expedient approach is to create a generalized operating sys-tem template VHDX file, which can then be deployed to new virtual machines very quickly. A virtual machine template allows the virtual hardware configuration of a virtual machine to be configured, including OS properties such as domain join instructions, local adminis-trator password, and more. The configuration is then linked to a template VHDX file. When the template is deployed, minimal interaction is required by the requesting user, typically just an optional name, and within minutes, the new virtual environment with a configured guest operating system is available.

# Chapter 6

# Maintaining a Hyper-V Environment

Once the Hyper-V environment is deployed and virtual machines are created, it is critical to ensure that your Hyper-V environment stays healthy, optimized, and available. In future chapters I will dive into details on technologies such as clustering to provide high availability, but this chapter will look at key processes and technologies that must be implemented to keep the environment running smoothly.

Every environment at some point will have performance challenges, and the final part of this chapter will dive into details of troubleshooting performance problems for the four key resources: computer, memory, network, and storage.

In this chapter, you will learn to

◆  Explain how backup works in a Hyper-V environment

◆  Identify where to use checkpoints and where not to use them

◆  Understand the benefits of service templates

## Patch Planning and Implementation

In the previous chapter I talked about some key processes and actions you must take on your Windows Server 2012 R2 Hyper-V servers. One of them was patching, and in this section, I want to dive into some additional detail, consider some options, and also cover some other factors that need to be considered in your patch solution planning.

In a virtual environment there are at least two workloads you have to consider patching:

◆  The Hyper-V host itself. The hypervisor itself would be updated via updates sent to the host.

◆  The virtual machines that are running on the Hyper-V hosts, including updates to Integration Services for Hyper-V (although this should not update frequently between versions of Hyper-V). The virtual machines may be running Windows operating systems but also Linux. I will focus on Windows updating, but you would also need processes to ensure that all workloads are updated. Virtual machines that are offline for long periods of time may also need to be patched, which can be accomplished using the same processes discussed in Chapter 5. "Managing Hyper-V," related to patching templates, such as using Deployment Image Servicing and Management (DISM).

I said at least two workloads because you most likely will need to ensure that items such as the management infrastructure (for instance, System Center) are patched and that firmware in hardware is kept up-to-date (for example, that updated drivers from vendors are downloaded and applied). These are not considerations specific to Hyper-V. They apply to any infrastructure, but it's especially important to ensure that your Hyper-V environment is patched and stable because it's not responsible for one operating system but instead is hosting possibly hundreds of operating systems.

If you already have a patching solution for your Windows-based servers, most likely that same solution can be leveraged to patch your Hyper-V servers. What is important is that patches are tested in a test environment prior to implementation in production, and also that care be taken when applying patches that require reboots. Remember, if the Hyper-V host reboots, then all virtual machines on the host will shut down for stand-alone hosts or be moved to other hosts in a clustered environment. It's therefore important to have the ability to define specific maintenance windows for your Hyper-V hosts, delaying reboots until that maintenance window is reached. In a cluster environment, you would make sure the maintenance windows are staggered to ensure that all hosts don't apply patches and reboot at the same time. There are better solutions for cluster environments, though, which I will touch on later in this chapter.

If you have stand-alone Hyper-V hosts in Windows Server 2012, it would be possible to perform a Shared Nothing Live Migration of virtual machines between hosts, or if SMB is used for the storage, then only the memory and state would need to be migrated. This would avoid any downtime to the virtual machines for planned outages; however, it would be an automated process you would need to create leveraging PowerShell or another automation solution. Additionally, if you have virtual machines that need to be protected from unavailability (e.g., unscheduled outages), then really the hosts should be clustered anyway. Generally if you have virtual machines on a stand-alone host, you should expect to have some periods of unavailability.

Microsoft maintains all updates on its Microsoft Update servers, and by default computers can connect to these servers, find the list of updated patches, download them, and apply them. This process works fine for a few machines, but if you have hundreds of servers, it's inefficient to have every machine downloading the updates over the Internet connection. This process will be slow and consume your Internet connection, which likely could be used more productively for other workloads. Additionally, if machines update directly from Microsoft Update using the built-in update component of Windows, the administrator of the organization has no ability to approve patches prior to their deployment.

## Leveraging WSUS

Windows Server Update Services (WSUS) is a role of Windows Server that acts as a local source for updates for machines within your organization. At a very high level, the process when leveraging WSUS is as follows:

1. Enable the WSUS role on a server and specify when synchronization with the Microsoft Update servers will occur.

2. Configure the WSUS server for the updates that should be downloaded, such as, for example, only critical and security updates and only for Windows Server 2012 R2.

3. Create computer groups in WSUS that will be the targets for patch deployment.

4. Specify whether any types of updates should be automatically approved. Any updates that are not automatically approved need to be manually approved by a WSUS administrator before they are deployed to specified computer groups.

5. Optionally, use Group Policy to automatically configure machines to use the WSUS server and to be part of a specific computer group. I document this at the following location:

   `http://windowsitpro.com/windows-8/group-policy-settings-wsus`

Machines will now utilize the WSUS server for available patches and also download them from the WSUS server instead of the Internet (although it is also possible to configure WSUS clients to pull updates from Microsoft Update if required). In very large organizations, it's actually possible to chain WSUS servers so a downstream WSUS server pulls approved updates from another WSUS server and then distributes them.

Configuring machines to pull down patches from Microsoft Update or a WSUS server via Group Policy is one option, but there are other enterprise solutions, such as System Center Configuration Manager, which actually leverages WSUS to ascertain that patches are available but then allows them to be packaged and targeted to different groups of servers at specific times with very granular tracking and reporting.

## Patching Hyper-V Clusters

The technologies I've been talking about are not specific to Hyper-V, which is logical since Hyper-V is a role within Windows Server and therefore its patch mechanisms are the same as for any other Windows Server machine. The good news is that the same patch deployment solution can be used for the Hyper-V hosts and for the virtual machines running Windows Server. There are, however, some solutions specific to Hyper-V patching and specific to patching clusters.

---

### IF YOU CARE ABOUT VM AVAILABILITY, DON'T USE STAND-ALONE HYPER-V HOSTS

As I have already mentioned, there are not really any special solutions to patch a stand-alone Hyper-V host. If you are deploying stand-alone Hyper-V hosts, then you don't really care about the availability of the virtual machines, so there are no special technologies in-box to patch stand-alone hosts and use Shared Nothing Live Migration to move VMs prior to the reboot and bring the VMs back. If you had that hardware available, you would have clustered them already, considering an SMB 3.0 file share can be used for the storage if a SAN is not available; you could even use a clustered external storage enclosure connected to both hosts and clustered storage spaces to provide shared access. The only time you should have an unclustered Hyper-V host is if you have a location with only one Hyper-V server.

---

Consider a clustered Hyper-V environment with shared storage and the ability to move virtual machines between hosts. In your Hyper-V environment, you are already using Server Core to minimize the number of patches that are applicable and therefore reducing the number of reboots. However, there will still be reboots required for patching and other purposes.

Utilizing the ability to move virtual machines between nodes with no downtime using Live Migration prior to reboots actually makes the actual impact of a Hyper-V node reboot in a cluster zero for the virtual machines. This means no loss of availability for the virtual machines, and only some minor administrative effort. This is why when you hear people hung up on having to patch Hyper-V, it's generally overblown as a real issue. Yes, you might need to patch, and there are times you need to reboot, but it has no impact on the availability of the virtual machines, which is what you care about in a virtual environment. The ideal process in a clustered environment is as follows:

1. The nodes in the cluster are scanned to ascertain which patches are required.

2. One node is placed in maintenance mode, drained of all virtual machines, which are Live Migrated to other hosts in the cluster.

3. The node has patches applied and rebooted.

4. The node is checked to ensure that no additional patches are needed, and if not, is brought out of maintenance mode.

5. Virtual machines are moved back to the node, and the process is repeated for the next node, and so on.

Most administrators who manage clusters are familiar with this process and perform it manually. SCVMM 2012 introduced the ability to patch an entire Hyper-V cluster using exactly the process just described. Each node is drained, patched, and rebooted for a complete cluster patch with no downtime to virtual machines with a click of a button. SCVMM leverages a WSUS server in the environment for the actual patch library, which does not have to be uniquely used by SCVMM. It could be a WSUS used for other purposes, such as, for example, by SCCM. Once the WSUS server is added to the SCVMM fabric, as shown in Figure 6.1, the SCVMM instance will be aware of all the updates known to the WSUS server. The next step is to create a baseline in the Library workspace ➤ Update Catalog and Baselines ➤ Update Baselines, which can then be assigned to specific host groups. Once a baseline is assigned, a scan can be performed on the host group via the Fabric workspace, which will show the compliance of each scanned node, and the details of the compliance can be viewed as shown in Figure 6.2. The administrator can click the Remediate button to patch the entire cluster. There's very little administrative work. It is important to note that SCVMM patches only Hyper-V hosts (even nonclustered) and *not* the actual virtual machines running on the hosts. You still require another patch strategy to patch the virtual machines.

**FIGURE 6.1**
Adding a WSUS
server to SCVMM

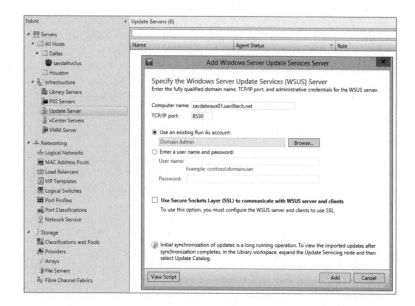

**FIGURE 6.2**
Viewing the compli-
ance details for a
noncompliant node

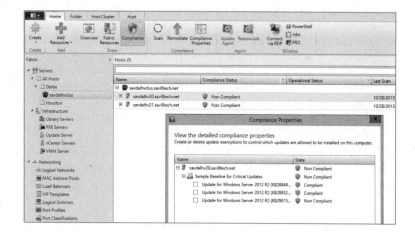

The SCVMM 2012 ability to patch an entire Hyper-V cluster with one click was a welcome feature and removed the need for many custom PowerShell and Orchestrator solutions, but Windows Server 2012 actually minimized the need to even use SCVMM. Windows Server 2012 introduced a native one-click patching of an entire cluster to the Failover Clustering feature. Once again, this Cluster-Aware Updating (CAU) leveraged WSUS and could patch not only Hyper-V clusters but any type of cluster with no downtime to the workloads running in the cluster. I will cover this in detail in Chapter 7, "Failover Clustering and Migration Technologies."

The key takeaway is that patching your Hyper-V cluster does not mean there is any downtime to your virtual machines.

Remember that all of the previous processes relate to the Windows operating system. You still need other processes to download drivers from the hardware vendor because even if there are drives built into Windows, for many types of hardware it's better to use drivers directly from the vendor.

## Malware Configurations

I briefly touched on antivirus recommendations in previous chapters, and there are two main schools of thought. One is that the Hyper-V server is running in Server Core configuration level, so it has no web browser, has limited vulnerabilities and a limited attack surface, is patched regularly, is never locally connected to because all management is remote, has a firewall enabled, and really does nothing but manage virtual machines. The chance of the server being infected is slight, so many people will say just don't run malware protection. Additionally, it's possible that malware protection could actually introduce problems because it runs at a very low level within the operating system. The Microsoft best practice are to run no additional applications on the Hyper-V host, and strictly speaking, this would include malware protection.

I personally lean a little more toward defense in depth. I prefer to have many layers of protection, which means malware support on the host. However, it's critical that any malware solution does not interfere with the Hyper-V processes or the resources of virtual machines. At the time of this writing, this means that exceptions should be configured in the malware solution to not scan the following:

◆ Default virtual machine configuration directory (`C:\ProgramData\Microsoft\Windows\Hyper-V`)

◆ Custom virtual machine configuration directories

◆ Default virtual hard disk drive directory (`C:\Users\Public\Documents\Hyper-V\Virtual Hard Disks`)

◆ Custom virtual hard disk drive directories

◆ Custom replication data directories, if you are using Hyper-V Replica

◆ Checkpoint directories

◆ `Vmms.exe` (Note that this file may have to be configured as a process exclusion within the antivirus software.)

◆ `Vmwp.exe` (Note that this file may have to be configured as a process exclusion within the antivirus software.)

Failure to correctly exclude Hyper-V resources will result in problems with virtual machines starting and functioning correctly, as documented at http://support.microsoft.com/kb/961804/en-us. There is a great malware exception article for more Microsoft solutions at

http://social.technet.microsoft.com/wiki/contents/articles/953.microsoft-anti-virus-exclusion-list.aspx

While the risk of infection is low, if an infection did hit your Hyper-V server, the impact would be large. There may also be audit problems for hosts with no malware protection. It's really an environment choice to be made after weighing the pros and cons. If you have great processes in place to patch your systems regularly, if they are running Server Core, and if people don't log on locally, you would probably be fine without malware. If you don't have a good patch strategy, if you are not running Server Core, and if administrators do log on to the servers and browse the Web, then malware protection is probably a good idea! If you do opt to use malware protection, ensure that you have processes in place to keep its signatures updated and that it is supported to run on Hyper-V. Microsoft provides enterprise malware protection with System Center Endpoint Protection.

What is important is that you still run malware protection within the virtual machines. You need malware protection running in the guest operating systems configured to whatever guidelines exist for the workload. Even if you run malware protection on the Hyper-V host, this does *not* protect the virtual machine guest operating system. There are special scenarios that need to be considered, such as, for example, VDI environments where there are many desktops that are created and deleted very quickly that have different malware protection requirements than regular, long-term servers. Investigate the different solutions available and tailor your solution based on the different services offered.

## Backup Planning

When virtualization is used in an environment, there is often a decision to be made as to whether backups will be taken from the virtualization host of the virtual machines or if backup agents should still run within the virtual machines and backups will be taken from inside the virtual machines. There is no "right" answer to which is the best approach, but what is running inside the virtual machines and where you take the backup can have a big impact on the granularity of any restore operations that are performed.

Windows Server has long standardized on the Volume Shadow Copy Service (VSS), which provides facilities that allow application vendors to write special VSS writers, which are application-specific modules used to ensure that application data is ready for backup and are registered with the operating system on which the application is installed. All VSS Writers registered on an operating system are called during a shadow copy backup initiated by a VSS-aware backup program. The VSS writers ensure that all data on disk for the application is in an application-consistent state and that other writers are quiesced (which means paused during the operation) while the backup is taken, maintaining the integrity of the on-disk data being backed up. An application-consistent backup means that the data is in a suitable state to be restored and used without corruption problems.

If a backup was taken at the Hyper-V host level of all the virtual machine assets, primarily the VHD files, then ordinarily the virtual machine would know nothing of the backup being taken at the host level, so the data backed up would likely not be in an application-consistent state. Hyper-V Integration Services includes a Backup (volume snapshot) service, and this allows the Hyper-V host to notify each virtual machine when a VSS backup is taken. The process then looks like the following and assures that backups of the virtual machines are in an application-consistent state.

1. The backup software (the VSS requestor) on the Hyper-V server makes a request for a VSS snapshot and enumerates the VSS writers (for example, the Hyper-V VSS writer) on the system to ascertain the data that can be backed up with VSS.

2. The Hyper-V VSS writer (in conjunction with the VSS coordination service) forwards the VSS snapshot request to each guest operating system via the Backup integration service.

3. Each guest operating system thinks it is receiving a native VSS request and proceeds to notify all VSS writers on the guest to prepare for a snapshot.

4. Each VSS writer in the guest operating systems writes any information to disk that relates to its service (for example, Exchange and SQL) and notifies the VSS coordinator that it is ready for a snapshot and tells it which data to back up (although this part is ignored because we'll be backing up the entire VHD from the Hyper-V host).

5. The Backup integration service for each VM tells the Hyper-V VSS writer that it is ready for a snapshot to be taken, and the Hyper-V VSS writer notifies the backup application via the VSS coordinator that it is ready for a snapshot.

6. The backup software takes a VSS snapshot of the file system containing the virtual configuration files and the virtual hard disks, and all data on the virtual hard disks is consistent thanks to the VSS request being passed into the virtual machines. Once the snapshot is taken, the VSS writer notifies the Hyper-V guests that the snapshot is complete and they continue their normal processing.

It should be noted that only VHD/VHDX content will be backed up using this method. If a virtual machine has pass-through storage, has iSCSI storage connected through the guest OS iSCSI Initiator, is connected to storage via fibre-channel, or is a shared VHDX, then that content would not be backed up via a backup at the Hyper-V server level through the Hyper-V VSS writer and would instead need to be backed up from within the guest virtual machine. The preceding scenario describes an online backup, also known as a Child VM Snapshot, where the guest operating system meets the following requirements:

♦ The integration services are installed with the Backup integration service enabled.

♦ The operating system supports VSS.

♦ NTFS file systems with basic disks (not dynamic) is used.

If you have guest operating systems that use dynamic disks, that use non-NTFS partitions, that don't have the integration services installed, or that don't have the Backup integration service enabled or it's just not supported (Windows 2000), then an offline backup will be taken of the virtual machine, also known as a Saved State backup. This is because virtual machines that can't support an online backup actually are placed into a saved state during the VSS snapshot, which actually means there is a period of downtime for the virtual machine during the backup. Operating systems that have to use saved state include Windows 2000, Windows XP, and Windows NT 4. Windows 2003, 2008, Vista, and above all support the online backup method with no virtual machine downtime.

Prior to Windows Server 2012 R2, a Linux system had to be backed up using an offline backup. Windows Server 2012 R2 introduces a number of new features for Linux virtual machines, one of which is live backup of Linux VMs. This is achieved through a new file-system snapshot driver that runs inside the Linux guest virtual machine. When a backup is performed on the Hyper-V host, the file-system snapshot driver is triggered in the guest, which enables a file-system-consistent snapshot to be taken of the VHDs that are attached to the Linux VM. It should be noted that this is a different experience from that available for Windows VMs, which provide file-system-consistent and application-consistent backups because applications have VSS writers that ensure that application data is consistent on the disk. This is because there is not a standardized VSS infrastructure in Linux, so there's no way to ask applications to make their data ready for a backup.

If you have guest operating systems that can't use the Hyper-V pass-through VSS capability, then perform backups within the virtual machine. There are also times when backing up within the virtual machine gives a better level of functionality, depending on the backup application. Suppose I want to use System Center Data Protection Manager (DPM), which is the Microsoft premium backup and recovery solution for Microsoft workloads. When you have the DPM agent on the virtual server in the main DPM administrator console, the level of granularity you have for what to protect would be at a virtual machine level. You can select which virtual machines to protect, but that's all you get. You can't go into detail about what to protect within the virtual machine. During a restore operation, you would be able to restore only the entire virtual machine or files from the VM, but nothing application aware such as restoring a SQL database or Exchange mailbox.

If you deploy the agent into the actual guest operating systems, you will have the full granularity of knowledge that comes with DPM. For example, if the virtual machine was running SQL Server, you would be able to select the actual databases to protect with the ability to capture the transaction logs and so on. The restore granularity would be the same, enabling the restore of just a specific database. Likewise, if I backed up a SharePoint server from within the SharePoint VM, I would be able to perform item-level recovery. Figure 6.3 shows an example where I have two virtual machines protected at the host level and two other virtual machines have the DPM agent installed locally, which allows me to protect application-aware workloads such as Exchange mailboxes and SQL databases.

**FIGURE 6.3**
Example view of protection using DPM

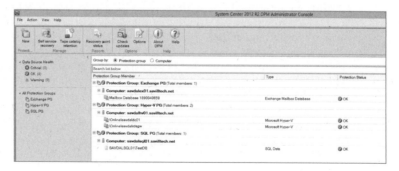

This means that for the best functionality, sometimes performing backups from within the guest OS give the best results, especially if your backup software has application-specific modules. Make sure you regularly test restoring the backups you take. Many times I have seen companies try to restore a backup when it's really needed and it fails or the right information was not actually being backed up.

No matter what other technologies are used, such as replication, multiple instances of applications, or even snapshots, none of these are replacements for backups. Backups should always be taken regularly for complete protection for all types of failure.

## Defragmentation with Hyper-V

On a physical system that uses hard disk drives (HDDs), it is common to defragment the file system. This is required because files can become fragmented, which means instead of a file being stored contiguously on the disk, it is broken up into many different pieces, or fragments, over the disk. This can affect performance because when data needs to be read, there are many seek operations (moving the disk head to the data location on disk). This will slow down operations compared to all the data being stored contiguously on disk, in which case the data can be read efficiently. Performing a disk defragmentation optimizes the disk by moving all the pieces of files so they are contiguous on the disk and therefore can be accessed efficiently. Files become fragmented for many reasons. Typically, when a file grows, if there is not empty space at the end of the file's current position, additional space must be allocated elsewhere on the disk. This would be very common with a dynamic VHDX/VHD that grows as data is written. Note that the problem with fragmentation is the seeking of the data. If you are using solid-state drives (SSDs), there is no seek time and therefore fragmentation does not incur a performance penalty. Moving data can actually decrease the life span of a SSD, so defragmentation is typically not performed or recommended. Windows 2012 and above automatically disables defragmentation on a SSD.

Consider local HDDs in a system. If you are using a fixed-size VHDX, it is likely not highly fragmented because it does not grow and therefore defragmentation should not be often required. If you use dynamic VHDX, the disk will most likely fragment over time and so performing a defragmentation will improve performance. The only caveat is to remember that a VHDX file contains a file system that itself contains files, so even if the VHDX file is not fragmented, when the VHDX file is used by a virtual machine, the content will be randomly accessed throughout the VHDX because the OS accesses various files, but defragmenting will still make it as contiguous as possible and certainly won't do harm.

If your storage is not local HDDs but a SAN, your virtual hard disks will be split over multiple disks anyway, there will be other optimizations in place on the SAN, and typically defragmenting is not recommended. Similarly, defragmenting a tiered volume that uses different types of storage is not recommended because this would touch different blocks of the disk and potentially interfere with the automatic tiering that optimizes performance.

The final type of defragmentation is performing a defragmentation within the actual virtual machine for its file system that is contained in the virtual hard disk. There is no definite answer here. My thinking on this is that fragmentation within the virtual hard disk is another level of fragmentation, but its effect will depend on the underlying storage. If the underlying storage is SSD or a SAN, I would not defragment. If the underlying storage is local HDD, a defragmentation within the VM would optimize the data within the virtual hard disk and therefore improve storage performance, which means I would defragment when necessary. Obviously, if you defragment within the virtual machine but not on the actual file system containing the virtual hard disk, you are likely not achieving any optimization because the actual virtual hard disk could still be fragmented on the actual physical drives.

Defragmentation can be performed using the Optimize Drives utility or using the defrag .exe utility. Very detailed information can be viewed about a volume using the /a and /v switches, as shown in this example:

```
PS C:\> defrag d: /A /V
Microsoft Drive Optimizer
Copyright (c) 2013 Microsoft Corp.

Invoking analysis on Data (D:)...



The operation completed successfully.

Post Defragmentation Report:


    Volume Information:
            Volume size                 = 1.81 TB
            Cluster size                = 4 KB
            Used space                  = 470.11 GB
            Free space                  = 1.35 TB


    Fragmentation:
            Total fragmented space      = 6%
            Average fragments per file  = 1.05

            Movable files and folders   = 100184
            Unmovable files and folders = 4


    Files:
            Fragmented files            = 742
            Total file fragments        = 3155


    Folders:
            Total folders               = 5552
            Fragmented folders          = 53
            Total folder fragments      = 248
```

```
Free space:
        Free space count          = 6505
        Average free space size   = 219.19 MB
        Largest free space size   = 604.87 GB


Master File Table (MFT):
        MFT size                  = 316.50 MB
        MFT record count          = 324095
        MFT usage                 = 100%
        Total MFT fragments       = 2

Note: File fragments larger than 64MB are not included in the fragmentation
statistics.


You do not need to defragment this volume.
```

Sysinternals has a tool, Contig, that shows the fragmentation of individual files and can even defragment individual files. It is available for download, along with documentation, at the following location:

```
http://technet.microsoft.com/en-us/sysinternals/bb897428
```

# Using Checkpoints

One fairly overlooked feature of Hyper-V is the checkpoint feature, which prior to Windows Server 2012 R2 was called snapshots. Checkpoints allow point-in-time views of a virtual machine to be saved. A checkpoint can be created when the virtual machine is turned off or when it's running. If a checkpoint is taken when a virtual machine is running, the current memory and device state is saved in addition to the virtual hard disk state, which is also taken when a snapshot is taken of a stopped virtual machine. When a checkpoint is taken, a number of files are created:

◆ XML file: Contains the information of the files and VM configuration associated with the checkpoint.

◆ VSV file: This contains the state of devices associated with the virtual machine. It is created only if a checkpoint is taken of a running virtual machine.

◆ BIN file: This contains the memory content of the virtual machine. It is created only if a checkpoint is taken of a running virtual machine.

◆ AVHDX file: To capture the state of the virtual hard disks, the differencing VHD capability is used. The current virtual hard disk state is frozen and marked read-only; this is what the checkpoint points to. A new differencing disk is created that uses the existing VHDX as the parent, and all future disk writes are written to the new differencing AVHDX file. Note that if the original file was a VHD, then a AVHD file is created.

Entire hierarchies of checkpoints can be created, and each checkpoint can be custom named, making it easy to understand what each checkpoint represents. Checkpoints can then be applied to a virtual machine. Applying a checkpoint reverts a virtual machine back to the state it was in when the checkpoint was created.

---

### Checkpoints with Fixed virtual Hard Disks

A fixed virtual hard disk preallocates all space at creation time, but if a checkpoint is created, a differencing virtual hard disk is created for future writes. This means a dynamic virtual hard disk is being used for writes and will therefore consume additional space that may not have been originally planned. There is also a small performance penalty as the dynamic differencing disk grows.

---

To create a checkpoint using Hyper-V Manager, select the virtual machine and select the Checkpoint action. This can be performed on a running virtual machine or on one that's shut down. For a running virtual machine, the creation may take a few seconds because the contents of the memory and configuration state must be saved. By default, the checkpoint will be named <VMname> - ( <date - time>), as shown in Figure 6.4, which shows a virtual machine with two checkpoints. They can be renamed simply by selecting and choosing the Rename action. Renaming the checkpoints is useful so you'll understand at a later time what the state of the virtual machine was at the point of checkpoint.

**FIGURE 6.4**
A VM with two checkpoints

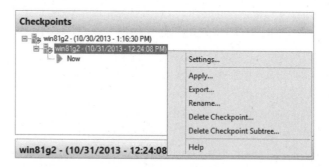

Checkpoints can be deleted via the Delete Checkpoint action and an entire subtree of multiple parent-child checkpoints can be deleted via the Delete Checkpoint Subtree action. What happens when you delete a checkpoint depends on where it is in the hierarchy of checkpoints and where the current Now state of the virtual machine is. If you delete a checkpoint that is on a different branch from the Now state and has no child checkpoints, its differencing virtual hard disk will just be deleted along with any state and configuration files. If you delete a checkpoint that is part of the Now branch or it has child checkpoints, when you delete the checkpoint, its state files will be deleted but the contents of its differencing virtual hard disk will be merged into its child object, which could be the Now state or another checkpoint. There is an exception. If you delete a checkpoint that has multiple child snapshots, the differencing virtual hard disk is kept; to remove it would require its content to be merged into each child virtual hard disk, which would actually mean additional space would be used up and that's likely not the experience administrators would expect. While the way in which a checkpoint deletion is handled differs, what is consistent is that the checkpoint is no longer usable.

You may wonder how you get different branches of checkpoints. The key is that you can apply a specific checkpoint and then create new checkpoints from that point. This would create different branches, as shown in Figure 6.5. If you perform a Revert action on a virtual machine, you will be prompted to create a new checkpoint of the current state of the virtual machine to avoid losing its state.

**FIGURE 6.5**

Example of checkpoint life cycle

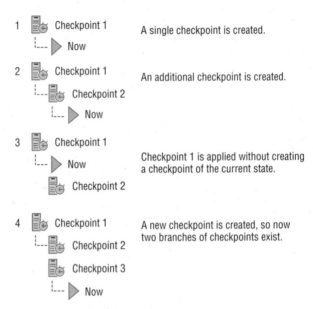

1. Checkpoint 1 / Now — A single checkpoint is created.

2. Checkpoint 1 / Checkpoint 2 / Now — An additional checkpoint is created.

3. Checkpoint 1 / Now / Checkpoint 2 — Checkpoint 1 is applied without creating a checkpoint of the current state.

4. Checkpoint 1 / Checkpoint 2 / Checkpoint 3 / Now — A new checkpoint is created, so now two branches of checkpoints exist.

Checkpoints can also be managed from PowerShell, but the naming is inconsistent. To create a checkpoint, use the `Checkpoint-VM` cmdlet as follows:

```
Checkpoint-VM -Name "TestVM10" -SnapshotName "Before change"
```

To list or apply a checkpoint, use the `Get-VMSnapshot` and `Restore-VMSnapshot` cmdlets. The following command finds the checkpoint for a VM and applies it:

```
Get-VM -Name "TestVM10" | Get-VMSnapshot | Restore-VMSnapshot
```

One great feature introduced in Windows Server 2012 was that the merging of differencing files that is required when a checkpoint is deleted was performed live while the virtual machine was still running. Prior to Windows Server 2012, the merging of differencing files related to a checkpoint deletion did not occur until the virtual machine was stopped.

Windows Server 2012 R2 introduced an even more powerful feature, or two, to be precise. First, checkpoints can be exported while the virtual machine is running, which previously was not possible. Additionally, an export of the Now state of a virtual machine (that is, the running state) is possible, which effectively creates a clone of the virtual machine. This is useful in debugging situations where a problem is occurring on a virtual machine, and instead of having to debug the virtual machine, it is possible to create an export/clone of its current state and then debug that clone state. The export of the live state includes a copy of the storage, the configuration, and the memory dump—all without any impact to the availability of the virtual machine.

How checkpoints should actually be used is something often discussed. They are not replacements for backups, but rather, checkpoints that are useful for development and testing environments. Imagine in a testing or development environment the ability to save the state of an operating system, make some changes, and then revert back to a state before the changes were ever made. For a developer, the ability to freeze a system at the point of a problem and be able to keep reverting back to that problem state again and again is invaluable.

The use of checkpoints in production environments is generally discouraged because their usage can cause problems, and as checkpoint hierarchies grow, there is some performance degradation. A virtual machine can have up to 50 checkpoints. Checkpoints are specifically hazardous and known to cause problems for some types of services, such as Active Directory domain controllers. Taking a checkpoint of a domain controller and then reverting the domain controller back to that checkpoint can result in replication problems, duplicate security identifiers, and therefore security vulnerabilities prior to Windows Server 2012.

Windows Server 2012 introduces "virtualization safe" Active Directory when it's running on Hyper-V 2012 or above. Prior to Active Directory running on Windows Sever2012 Hyper-V, there was a huge problem using snapshots with domain controllers. Directory services expect time to always go forward and need some way to track it, such as a logical clock, and Active Directory uses an update sequencer number (USN), which is incremented each time a new object is created along with other incremental values, such as the relative ID (RID). Look at Figure 6.6. Imagine you have a domain controller and at USN 2 a snapshot is created, and then the DC continues using USNs up to number 6 for created users. Then an administrator applies the snapshot that was created, which puts the domain controller back to USN number 2. The domain controller has no clue it has been put back in time, so it carries on back at USN number 2, creating objects with the same security IDs, which causes problems with security and the domain controller will no longer replicate correctly with the rest of the domain. We have divergence. This is a terrible problem for organizations and one of the biggest causes of Active Directory issues for Microsoft customers. Even though it's stated in many articles to never use snapshots with domain controllers, it still happens.

**FIGURE 6.6**
Update sequence number problems when applying a snapshot to a domain controller

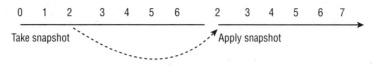

Windows Server 2012 fixes this through the use of a VM-generationID, which is provided by the Windows Server 2012 Hyper-V hypervisor. This VM-generationID is changed anytime something happens to a virtual machine that affects its point in time, such as applying a snapshot or duplicating the virtual machine. Active Directory stores the VM-generationID in the

AD database, and every time an operation is performed, such as creating or changing an object, the VM-generationID stored in the AD database is compared against the VM-generationID provided by the hypervisor. If the VM-generationIDs do not match, it means something has happened to the VM in logical time, and at this point the Active Directory service stops AD actions to protect Active Directory and performs the following:

- Discards the RID pool.

- Resets the invocation ID, which is a database identifier and is reset to ensure no replication problems with other domain controllers. When the invocation ID is reset, there is no USN reuse problem because USNs are paired with the invocation ID.

- Reassert the INITSYNC requirement for flexible single-master operation (FSMO) roles, which forces the domain controller to replicate with another domain controller that holds a copy of the partition in which the FSMO role is maintained.

These actions allow the domain controller to continue functioning without any risk to ongoing replication or security ID duplication. Even with this technology, there is still impact to the domain controller because it has to take corrective actions, so do not start using checkpoints with domain controllers but rather feel more secure that if they are used accidentally, it will not cause problems.

## Using Service Templates

In previous chapters I talked about the idea of virtual machine templates, which enable single virtual machines to be deployed. They are useful in typical deployment scenarios for individual workloads that are not dependent on other services, but few server applications work in isolation. Server applications talk to other server applications, and often multiple instances of server applications are required for availability and load balancing needs.

Multitiered services can be deployed manually using templates by creating eight virtual machines, four for the web front-end tier, two for the middle tier, and two for the backend storage/database tier, for example. When it comes time to update a service, each virtual machine would need to be manually updated because once a normal virtual machine is deployed, there is no ongoing relationship between the virtual machine and the template. This means a virtual machine is not refreshed if the virtual machine template from which it was created is updated.

Service templates provide a new capability, introduced in SCVMM 2012, that allows complete services to be defined in SCVMM. The capability and service template introduced in 2012 can be one-, two-, or three-tiered applications by default, as shown in Figure 6.7, but addition tiers can be added if required. The virtual machine template for each tier can be specified in addition to which applications should be deployed, such as an IIS site using Web Deploy for the front end, a regular application for the middle tier, and a database application using SQL DAC for the backend tier. SCVMM 2012 introduced the concept of Server App-V, which allowed server applications to be virtualized, allowing abstraction from the underlying operating system and simple deployment and migration. This feature has been deprecated in SCVMM 2012 R2 because it was not widely adopted and there are currently other initiatives to provide a better type of functionality, which means it's not a technology to invest in.

**FIGURE 6.7**
The default tiering options for a new service template. You'll see that a three-tier application is also available if you scroll down.

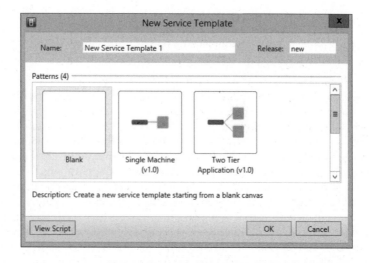

Web applications (Web Deploy) and database applications (SQL DAC) are considered first class in service templates because service templates understand the metadata of these types of application and can enable parameters to perform the configuration when the application is deployed, such as by the end user. Other types of application install are fully supported through the service template Generic Command Execution (GCE) feature because many organizations are not using SQL DAC, Server App-V, or maybe even Web Deploy yet. By using GCE, you can run both pre- and post-scripts for any type of application installation. The customization of non-first-class applications would need to be through the application's native unattended configuration capabilities or scripting and would not integrate with the service deployment interface in the same way first-class applications do. Standard Windows Server roles and features can also be added through standard virtual machine guest OS definitions.

A minimum, maximum, and initial number of instances of each tier are specified, which allows for easy scale out and scale in, depending on utilization. Service instances created from a service template maintain a link back to the template and that template becomes read-only, so it becomes the source of truth for how the service looked, and if an update is required, a new version of the service template is created and that updated service template is applied to deployed instances. The deployment of the new service template version will update the services while maintaining application state through the Server App-V state backup and restore feature.

The use of services enables fewer OS images to be managed by the IT department because of the abstraction of the actual services, roles, features, and applications needed on the operating system, which traditionally may have been part of the OS image. Services also enable the related VMs to be treated as a single unit. Another very nice bonus feature is that if SCVMM is integrated with Operations Manager, then Operations Manager will understand the service definition and show the VMs as part of a service.

A four-stage life cycle is the focus for service templates, as I've already alluded to:

◆ Create the service template.

◆ Customize the deployment at the deployment time of the service template.

◆ Deploy the service to environments.

◆ Update the service template to a new version and apply it to running instances of the service.

When an update to an existing instance of a service is made, there are three update types. First is a settings-only update mode, which only changes application settings but does not replace the OS image. The second update type is new, an in-place update, where updates to the template settings are applied but the actual OS images are not replaced. This would be used to update applications and modify configuration of the virtual machines in the service. Last is the image-based update, which replaces the actual deployed instance operating system images with the new OS image and performs a reinstallation of applications but maintains the application state. If you have modified a virtual machine configuration that is part of a service, for example, and you changed the memory from 1 GB to 4 GB and then applied an update to the service from a new version of the service template, then any customizations you made to the configuration would be lost. Remember, with services, the service template is always the source of truth. This can be useful, for example, if your service instance has lost some VMs and you want to bring it back within the parameters of the service template. Instances can be refreshed from the service template, which will look for any missing elements of tiers that have less than the minimum number of instances and fix them by deploying additional required VMs.

In addition to allowing the definitions of virtual machine templates to use, applications to install, and various other settings, it is within a service template that you can also utilize load balancers and logical networks. By using the other fabric elements, service templates can enable rich capabilities in a completely automated fashion.

Service templates are created and maintained in the Service Designer, which is shown in Figure 6.8 and consists of the familiar ribbon, a designer canvas (which is the majority of the interface) and a small properties area at the bottom that shows the properties of the currently selected object. Once configurations are made, you run the Save And Validate action, which checks for any problems in the service template definition.

Once a service is deployed within the VMs And Services workspace in SCVMM, it is viewed as a single unit in addition to viewing the individual virtual machines that make up the service. Within the VMs And Services workspace view, you can view the application settings configured for the service, which helps to identify individual instances of deployed services.

One of the great features of using a service template is the easy ability to scale out and scale in as required. Selecting the service within the VMs And Services workspace will expose a Scale Out action that launches a wizard. You can use the wizard to select the tier to be scaled out and then specify the degree of the scale out. Additional VMs will be created based on the scale properties. To scale in, instances of the VM in the tier are deleted.

The best way to really understand the service templates is to just fire up the Service Designer and start playing with the settings and looking at the options available. Even for basic services, the use of a service template is likely to make the management far easier, especially when you want to make the service available for end-user deployment with some deployment time configuration options.

**FIGURE 6.8**
The Service
Designer

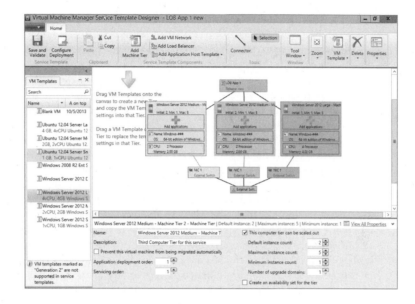

**FIGURE 6.8**
The Service
Designer

# Performance Tuning and Monitoring with Hyper-V

When an operating system is deployed to a physical machine, it is the only operating system using that hardware. If there are performance problems, it's fairly simple to ascertain the cause by using Task Manager and also Performance Monitor. When virtualization is introduced, looking at performance problems becomes more complex because now there is the host operating system (management partition) and all the various virtual machines. Each virtual machine has its own virtual resources, which are actually allocated from the shared resources of the host.

It's important to be proactive and try to avoid performance problems. You can do that by being diligent in the discovery of your environment, understanding the true resource needs of the various workloads running in virtual machines, and allocating reasonable resources. Don't give every virtual machine 64 virtual processors, don't set every virtual machine's dynamic memory maximum to 1 TB, and do consider using bandwidth management and storage QoS on virtual machine resources. Resource leaks can occur, bad code is written, or a user of a virtual machine may perform "tests." Any number of problems may cause guest operating systems to consume all of the available resources, so only give virtual machines access to resources they reasonably need based on your discovery and analysis. In most cases, additional resources can be added painlessly if they are truly required fairly.

Even with all the planning in the world, there will still be performance problems that you need to troubleshoot. One of the first questions ever asked about using virtualization is about the "penalty"—that is, what performance drop will I see running workloads virtualized compared to running them directly on bare metal? There is no exact number. Clearly, the hypervisor and management partition consumes some resource, such as memory, processor, storage, and limited network traffic, but there is also a performance cost in certain areas caused by virtualization, such as additional storage and network latency, which although very small, does exist (although if this small additional latency is a problem for the highest-performing workloads, there are solutions such as SR-IOV to remove network latency and various options for storage).

Some people will say that for planning purposes, you should consider the worst-case scenario, and I've seen the number 10 percent used commonly, not for Hyper-V specifically, but for any virtualization solution. When planning out the available resources, remove 10 percent of the bare-metal server capability and the 90 percent that's left is what you can expect for virtualized workloads. In reality, I've never seen anything close to this. I commonly see workloads running virtualized on Hyper-V that are on par with a nonvirtualized workload or even exceed what performance you see on the physical hardware, which at first glance seems impossible. How can virtualization improve performance above running directly on bare metal? The reason is that some workloads use only a certain amount of resources efficiently. Once you go beyond a certain number of processors and memory, the additional resources bring diminishing returns. If I have a large server with 256 GB of RAM and 128 processor cores and I install an OS directly on that box and then run an instance of a server application, it may only be able to use 64 GB of memory and 32 cores efficiently. If I use virtualization on that same server and create four virtual machines with an instance of the server application in each, I'll efficiently use all of the processor cores and memory in the server, giving much better overall performance. It's the difference between scaling up (adding more resources to an instance) and scaling out (adding more instances). Remember that even if there is some small performance penalty or, more realistically, some small amount of resource lost that is used by the management partition, the benefits of virtualization outweigh this with greater utilization, faster provisioning, easier management, and so on.

I want to recap the limits of Hyper-V in terms of what the Hyper-V host can leverage and then the limits for each virtual machine. Each Hyper-V host can address the following:

◆ 320 physical logical processors. (If you have more than this and are using hyperthreading, turn off hyperthreading so Hyper-V can access more of the real cores on the system.)

◆ 4 TB of physical RAM.

◆ There are no real limits you will hit for networking or storage.

◆ Each host can be allocated up to 2,048 virtual processors and can run up to 1,024 virtual machines.

Each virtual machine can be allocated the following:

◆ 64 virtual processors (assuming the physical host has 64 logical processors, otherwise the limit per VM will be the number of logical processors in the host).

◆ 1 TB of RAM.

◆ Up to 256 VHDX files connected via the four possible SCSI controllers, and each VHDX can be up to 64 TB in size. In terms of storage performance, Microsoft has demonstrated IOPS in excess of one million to a VHDX file. Obviously you need a powerful backend storage solution to get one million IOPS, but the point is that even when using virtual hard disks, you can really get any level of performance that is needed without needing direct access via virtual fibre channel, iSCSI, etc.

◆ Eight network adapters. (An additional four legacy network adapters can be added, but this should not be used due to poor performance and increased overhead.)

It's because of the huge scalability of Hyper-V with Windows Server 2012 and above that there is almost no workload that cannot be virtualized on Hyper-V. Over 99 percent of the world's SQL Server instances could now be virtualized on Hyper-V.

The key tool you will use to troubleshoot performance problems or even just to see the utilization of a Hyper-V host is Performance Monitor. Task Manager is of limited use. It will not show processor utilization by virtual machines because the host OS is just another operating system running on top of the hypervisor. This is also why the management OS can use only 64 processors on a system with more than 64; even the management OS is still accessing processor resources via the hypervisor, but as Figure 6.9 shows, Task Manager does at least show the total number of processors in the Logical Processors field even though the host logical processors are limited to 64. This is not a problem because the host OS does very little processing, while the actual hypervisor can access up to 320. Task Manager will also not show resources by virtual machine, so it's really not a useful tool for troubleshooting the performance of a Hyper-V environment.

**FIGURE 6.9**

Only 64 are processors visible on the Hyper-V host of an 80-processor system

| Sockets: | 4 |
| Cores: | 40 |
| Logical processors: | 80 |
| Host logical processors: | 64 |
| Virtualization: | Enabled |

Performance Monitor running on a Hyper-V host has access to very detailed information on not just performance of the management OS but also the resources used for each virtual machine. It shows information for all the different types of resources, including processor, memory, networking, and storage. I will cover the performance counters to use for each of these key types of resources. Remember that while most resource utilization should be consumed by virtual machines, it's always important to view the resource utilization of the host OS as well because the host performs certain functions for the guests that can consume resources and processes may be running on the host that are misbehaving and need to be corrected. When I refer to performance counters, I will refer to the group of the counters first and then the actual counter. For example, Hyper-V Hypervisor Logical Processor is the counter group and % Total Run Time is a counter within that group.

For the processor resource, we can examine the total busy time of each logical processor in the host (used by the host or virtual machines), the processor usage by the actual host OS, and the individual virtual machines.

◆ Hyper-V Hypervisor Logical Processor – % Total Run Time: The utilization of the actual logical processors as managed by the hypervisor, which is usage by the host OS and all the virtual machines.

◆ Hyper-V Hypervisor Root Virtual Processor – % Total Run Time: The amount used by just the Hyper-V host OS.

◆ Hyper-V Hypervisor Virtual Processor – % Total Run Time: The amount of processor used by each virtual processor for each virtual machine. There is a value for each virtual processor, which means if a virtual machine has eight virtual processors, it will have eight values.

If you see overall that the logical processors are consistently over 90 percent busy, then this would show overall that the host is too overloaded. You can look at what is using the processor by looking at the Root Virtual Processor (if it's the Hyper-V host using it) and Virtual Processor counters for each virtual machine (if it's a specific virtual machines). If the Virtual Processor counter for each virtual processor for each virtual machine will also show if it's simply a specific virtual machine that is overloaded, that means it's likely the virtual machine needs additional virtual processors added as opposed to the host being overcommitted in terms of resources.

For the memory resource there are two pieces. First, has the virtual machine been allocated enough memory? That can easily be seen by Hyper-V Manager, which shows the memory status (also visible through the Hyper-V Dynamic Memory VM – Current Pressure performance counter), and if the memory is too low, additional memory can be added through means such as Dynamic Memory, but this assumes that the host has enough memory to even allocate. Looking at Memory – Available MBytes shows the available memory on the host, but to check the amount of memory that can be allocated to virtual machines, look at Hyper-V Dynamic Memory Balancer – Available Memory, which shows memory available over the complete system or for each NUMA node (if NUMA spanning is disabled).

By default, Hyper-V enables NUMA spanning, which allows a virtual machine to be allocated memory across the boundary of the NUMA node of the processor cores being used. While allowing more virtual machines to run, NUMA spanning may also lead to an overall decrease in performance because using memory outside of the NUMA node of the processor is more "expensive" in performance terms. If you disable NUMA spanning (in the Hyper-V settings, select NUMA Spanning and uncheck Allow Virtual Machines To Span Physical NUMA Nodes), then a virtual machine *cannot* be allocated memory from remote NUMA nodes and would be limited to using memory on its local NUMA node.

If you disable NUMA spanning, then if you look at the performance counter Hyper-V Dynamic Memory Balancer – Available Memory, you will see multiple values, one for each NUMA node. If you have NUMA spanning turned on, you see only a single counter, System Balancer.

Potentially, more memory may be needed in the host if the available memory is low and you are seeing high memory demand from virtual machines.

The overall number of network bytes for each network adapter can be seen by looking at Network Adapter – Bytes Total/sec, and to see how much each virtual network adapter for each virtual machine is using, look at Hyper-V Virtual Network Adapter – Bytes/sec.

Finally, for storage we typically care about the latency of reads and writes, which we can see for each physical disk (or if SMB/iSCSI, etc. the equivalent counter) by looking at PhysicalDisk – Avg. Disk sec/Read and Avg. Disk sec/Write, and this should generally be less than 50 ms. Knowing the queue length can also be useful. You can see the number of IOs waiting to be actioned via the Physical Disk – Avg. Disk Read Queue Length and Avg. Disk Write Queue Length counters; you'll know you have a problem if you see sustained queues.

By looking at all these performance counters together, it should be possible to ascertain the cause of any degraded performance on your system. I actually create a custom MMC console, add all performance MMC snap-ins, and then add my counters and save the customized console so all my counters are easily available, as shown in Figure 6.10.

**FIGURE 6.10**

A nice view of the key resources for my Hyper-V host using the report graph type

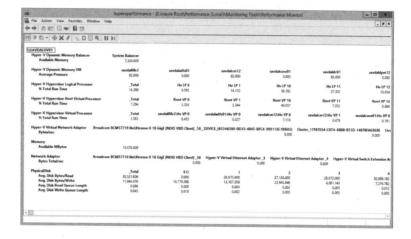

One important point is to benchmark your system. When you first deploy the server, run the counters to see how the machine runs "new" and store the results. Performance Monitor is not just for viewing live data, it can also log the data to a file so you can save the state of a monitoring session, which is a great feature. Then once a server has been running for a while, you can run the same counters again to see how it's performing and look for any signs of performance degradation.

In Chapter 7, I will talk about optimization technologies that will use Live Migration to move virtual machines between nodes in a cluster automatically if the current node cannot adequately handle the requirements of its virtual machines. This provides some breathing room regarding exactly estimating the resource needs of every virtual machine, but it's still important to ensure that the overall cluster has sufficient resources and that it has sufficient resources even if a certain number of nodes fail within the cluster.

## Resource Metering

Performance monitoring is useful to troubleshoot performance problems and even see details of virtual machines, but it's a fairly involved process. You will end up with a lot of data if you leave performance monitoring running for a long duration, and it's server specific, which means if a virtual machine was moved between servers using Live Migration or any other migration technology, you would have to start monitoring the virtual machine on the new server and add all the counters together across multiple nodes.

Windows Server 2012 introduced a better option if you want to track the resource utilization of one or more virtual machines, typically for the purpose of billing based on the resource utilization of the virtual machine. Instead of detailed metrics of the resource usage every 5 seconds, the resource metering functionality simply tracks the total and average resource utilizations of a virtual machine, which can then be viewed at any time. The great thing about the resource metering featuring is not just its simplicity but that the metering data persists even if the virtual machine is moved between Hyper-V nodes using any of the migration technologies.

The resource metering metrics that are gathered can be accessed via PowerShell cmdlets or using WMI.

To enable resource metering for a virtual machine, use this command:

```
Enable-VMResourceMetering -VMName <VM name>
```

To view the current measurements for a virtual machine in a detailed list format, use the following command:

```
Measure-VM -VMName <VM name> | fl
```

The metrics for a virtual machine never resets unless you either disable metering or perform a manual reset. Use this command to perform a manual reset:

```
Reset-VMResourceMetering -VMName <VM name>
```

Finally, to disable the metering, use this command:

```
Disable-VMResourceMetering -VMName <VM name>
```

To check which virtual machines have metering enabled, run the following command:

```
Get-VM | Format-Table Name, ResourceMeteringEnable
```

Here is an example of the output of metering from a Hyper-V 2012 R2 virtual machine. If you used metering in Hyper-V 2012, you will notice new metrics, specifically around storage performance.

```
PS C:\> Measure-VM -VMName savdalfs01 | fl


ComputerName                  : SAVDALHV01
VMId                          : 4c6db747-8591-4287-a8fc-ac55e37dba16
VMName                        : savdalfs01
HardDiskMetrics               : {Microsoft.HyperV.PowerShell
.VirtualHardDiskMetrics,Microsoft.HyperV.PowerShell.VirtualHardDiskMetrics}
MeteringDuration              :
AverageProcessorUsage         : 115
AverageMemoryUsage            : 2352
MaximumMemoryUsage            : 2352
MinimumMemoryUsage            : 2352
TotalDiskAllocation           : 261128
AggregatedAverageNormalizedIOPS : 5
AggregatedAverageLatency      : 316
AggregatedDiskDataRead        : 49666
AggregatedDiskDataWritten     : 87172
NetworkMeteredTrafficReport   : {Microsoft.HyperV.PowerShell
.VMNetworkAdapterPortAclMeteringReport,
 Microsoft.HyperV.PowerShell.VMNetworkAdapterPortAclMeteringReport,
```

```
                              Microsoft.HyperV.PowerShell
.VMNetworkAdapterPortAclMeteringReport,
 Microsoft.HyperV.PowerShell.VMNetworkAdapterPortAclMeteringReport}
AvgCPU                        : 115
AvgRAM                        : 2352
MinRAM                        : 2352
MaxRAM                        : 2352
TotalDisk                     : 261128
```

Most of the values shown are fairly self-explanatory. Information is given about the average, minimum, and maximum memory usage in addition to the average processor usage, which is measured in megahertz. You may wonder why the processor is shown in megahertz instead of CPU%. The reason is that virtual machines can move between servers, so a percentage of a CPU depends entirely on the server the virtual machine is running on, whereas megahertz is a fairly consistent value no matter which servers the virtual machine is moved between.

You will notice that there seem to be duplicate values related to processor, memory, and total disk allocation. AverageProcessorUsage is the same as AvgCPU, AverageMemoryUsage is the same as AvgRAM, and so on. These are in fact the same values. The reason for two different names is the output from Measure-VM by default will be in a table format and the regular titles such as AverageProcessorUsage would use up a lot of screen space and limit the data that's visible. Therefore, the short names are there to ensure that as much information as possible is shown when viewing in table mode, as in this example:

```
PS C:\ > Measure-VM -VMName savdalfs01


VMName      AvgCPU(MHz) AvgRAM(M) MaxRAM(M) MinRAM(M) TotalDisk(M) NetworkIn- NetworkOut-
                                                                  bound(M)   bound(M)
--------    ----------- --------- --------- --------- ------------ ---------- ----------
savdalfs01 113          2352      2352      2352      261128       2206       3478
```

Also shown is disk information related to IOPS, latency, and read and write information, but there are also cryptic values related to HardDiskMetrics and NetworkMeteredTrafficReport, which don't actually give any useful information. Each of those entries are actually separate reports that have to be viewed as specific report entities. You do this by saving the metering to a variable and then inspecting the separate report elements. Here is an example.

```
PS C:\> $report =  Measure-VM -VMName savdalfs01

PS C:\> $report.NetworkMeteredTrafficReport

LocalAddress RemoteAddress Direction TotalTraffic(M)
------------ ------------- --------- ---------------
             0.0.0.0/0     Inbound   2121
             0.0.0.0/0     Outbound  3479
```

```
                    ::/0           Inbound   88
                    ::/0           Outbound  2

PS C:\> $report.HardDiskMetrics


VirtualHardDisk         : Microsoft.HyperV.PowerShell.HardDiskDrive
AverageNormalizedIOPS : 2
AverageLatency          : 0
DataRead                : 38465
DataWritten             : 72908

VirtualHardDisk         : Microsoft.HyperV.PowerShell.HardDiskDrive
AverageNormalizedIOPS : 0
AverageLatency          : 0
DataRead                : 11213
DataWritten             : 14302
```

The resource metering functionality gives a great view into the metrics of a single virtual machine, but if there are 10 virtual machines in a certain group—for example, all the virtual machines for a certain client or all the SQL servers—then to get the total resource for all of the groups' virtual machines, you would have to manually add all the metrics together or write something. This is where the concept of resource pools can be useful. CPUs, memory, storage (VHD, ISO, fibre channel, and virtual floppy disk), and network adapters can be added to a resource pool from a number of virtual machines. Once the resources are added to the resource pool, metering can be enabled for the resource pool and subsequently measured. The one drawback with resource pools is that they are host specific, so if virtual machines are moved between hosts, you would need to ensure that the same resource pools are available on every node, which is why resource pools are typically not widely used.

By default, a number of resource pools, known as Primordial, exist on the system which can be viewed as follows:

```
PS C:\> Get-VMResourcePool


Name        ResourcePoolType        ParentName ResourceMeteringEnabled
----        ----------------        ---------- -----------------------
Primordial  FibreChannelConnection             False
Primordial  VHD                                True
Primordial  FibreChannelPort                   False
Primordial  VFD                                False
Primordial  ISO                                False
Primordial  Ethernet                           True
Primordial  Memory                             True
Primordial  Processor                          True
```

A new resource pool is created for each of the types of resource, but the same resource pool name is specified, which makes it a single, reportable pool. For example, in the following code snippet, I create a resource pool for a group of virtual machines, GroupA, for the four types of resources and then add virtual machine CPU and memory to each created pool in addition to virtual hard disks and the virtual switch the virtual machines use. In the following example, I actually add new hard disks and network adapters to a VM, but you can also use Set-<resource> -ResourcePoolName to set the pool. Notice that when the VHD resource pool is created, you must specify the path where the VHDs will be stored.

```
New-VMResourcePool -Name GroupA -ResourcePoolType Processor
New-VMResourcePool -Name GroupA -ResourcePoolType Memory
New-VMResourcePool -Name GroupA -ResourcePoolType Ethernet
New-VMResourcePool -Name GroupA -ResourcePoolType VHD `
-Paths @("\\savdalfs01\HVShare")
Add-VMSwitch -ResourcePoolName GroupA -Name "External Switch"
Set-VMProcessor -VMName savdal08R2 -ResourcePoolName GroupA
Set-VMMemory -VMName savdal08R2 - ResourcePoolName Group A
Add-VMHardDiskDrive -VMName savdal08R2 -ControllerType SCSI `
-ResourcePoolName GroupA `
 -Path "\\savdalfs01\HVShare\savdal08R2\data1.vhdx"
Add-VMNetworkAdapter -VMName savdal08R2 -ResourcePoolName GroupA
```

Additionally, once you create a resource pool for networking and storage, the resource pools will become visible in the Hyper-V Manager GUI (but not for processor and memory), as shown in Figure 6.11.

**FIGURE 6.11**
Viewing resource pools in Hyper-V Manager

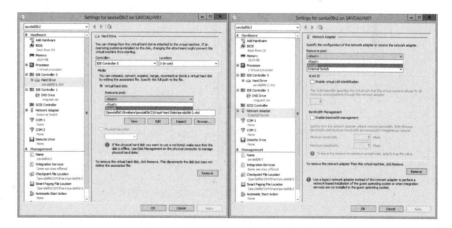

Once the resource pool is created, it can be enabled for metering using the normal cmdlets, except instead of a virtual machine name (VMName), specify the name of the resource pool (ResourcePoolName), as in this example:

```
Enable-VMResourceMetering -ResourcePoolName GroupA
```

If you create a resource pool, run the `Get-VMResourcePool` cmdlet again. You will see a lot of new entries. Remember, if you use resource pools, by default you would not be able to move a virtual machine configured in a resource pool if the target host does not have the same resource pool defined. I think resource pools are an interesting concept, but they really need to be easily managed across multiple hosts to be a useful feature.

While resource pools are primarily aimed at metering, they can also be used for actual resource allocation. Notice in the `Add-VMNetworkAdapter` command earlier, I don't specify a switch but rather just a resource pool that has switches added to it. This allows me to easily provision virtual machines on different hosts (providing the resource pool is defined on multiple hosts) and not worry about the actual switch name. I really don't expect many people to use resource pools in this manner. Using SCVMM to manage resource allocation is a much better and more enterprise-ready approach.

## Monitoring

I want to close on the concept of monitoring your environment. When you virtualize, as I've said previously, you are putting all your eggs into a much smaller number of baskets, and it's critical that those baskets are healthy and being proactively monitored so not only are you alerted when something breaks, you are notified when something is not performing as expected, when best practices aren't used on something, and when there are signs of impending failure.

When thinking about monitoring, you have to consider not just the Hyper-V host but all the other resources that are required for the host to run and be accessible and for the virtual machines to be able to function. At a minimum, you need to monitor the following:

◆   The Hyper-V host operating system (including the Hyper-V role-specific intelligence)

◆   Server hardware

◆   Storage subsystems (such as SANs)

◆   Networking equipment

◆   Active Directory

◆   SCVMM and its SQL database

It's also a good idea to monitor the OS within the virtual machines to get the best insight.

There are many monitoring solutions available. System Center 2012 R2 includes System Center Operations Manager, which is a powerful monitoring solution for not just Microsoft environments but also for the entire infrastructure. Operations Manager has management packs, which are imported and give insight into each element of the environment. Figure 6.12 is an example view from Operations Manager 2012 R2 of the heath status of a virtual machine. Operations Manager also has a great dashboard view of actual clouds that you define within SCVMM.

**FIGURE 6.12**

Operations Manager view of virtual machines

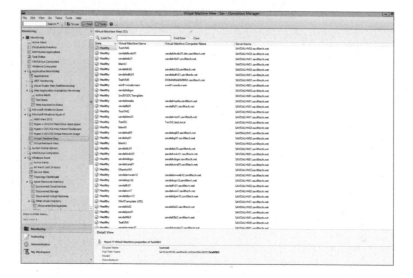

## The Bottom Line

**Explain how backup works in a Hyper-V environment.** Windows features the VSS component that enables application-consistent backups to be taken of an operating system by calling VSS writers created by application vendors. When a backup is taken of a virtual machine at the Hyper-V host level, the VSS request is passed to the guest operating system via the backup guest service, which allows the guest OS to ensure that the disk is in a backup-ready state, allowing the virtual hard disk to be backed up at the host and be application consistent.

**Master It** Is shared VHDX backed up when you perform a VM backup at the host level?

**Understand how to best use checkpoints and where not to use them.** Checkpoints, previously known as snapshots, allow a point-in-time view of a virtual machine to be captured and then applied at a later time to revert the virtual machine back to the state it was in at the time the snapshot was taken. This is useful in testing scenarios but should not be used in production because the effect of moving a virtual machine back in time can cause problems for many services. It can even cause domain membership problems if the computer's AD account password changes after the checkpoint creation.

**Understand the benefits of service templates.** Typically a virtual machine is created from a virtual machine template, which allows a single virtual machine to be deployed. A service template allows a complete, multitiered service to be designed and then deployed through a single action. Additionally, each tier can be configured to scale up and down as workloads vary, which enables additional instances of the virtual machine for a tier to be created and deleted as necessary. Deployed instances of a service template retain their relationship to the original service template, which means if the original service template is updated, the deployed instances can be refreshed and updated with the service template changes without losing application state.

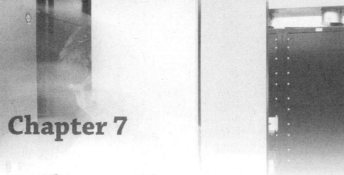

# Chapter 7

# Failover Clustering and Migration Technologies

As previously discussed, when implementing virtualization, you consolidate your operating systems onto fewer pieces of hardware, effectively putting your eggs in a smaller number of baskets. It's therefore important that those baskets are as secure as possible and, in the event a basket breaks, there is another basket underneath to catch the eggs that fall.

Failover clustering provides resiliency for Windows services such as SQL, Exchange, file, and print, and now Hyper-V. By leveraging the failover cluster feature, Hyper-V servers can share storage resources such as LUNs on a SAN. But more important, clustering provides high availability from a node failure by moving virtual machines to another node, plus it enables highly efficient migrations of virtual machines between nodes in planned scenarios such as hardware maintenance. Clustering also ensures that if a break occurs between nodes in a cluster, only one part of that cluster will offer services to avoid any chances of corruption. Windows Server 2012 introduced new types of mobility, both within a cluster and outside of a cluster, providing even more flexibility for Hyper-V environments.

In this chapter, you will learn to

◆ Understand the quorum model used in Windows Server 2012 R12

◆ Identify the types of mobility available with Hyper-V

◆ Understand the best way to patch a cluster with minimal impact to workloads

## Failover Clustering Basics

Failover clustering was first introduced in Windows NT 4.0, known then as Microsoft Cluster Services, and was developed under the very cool codename of Wolfpack. Prior to Windows Server 2012, the clustering feature was available only in the Enterprise and above SKUs of Windows Server, but with the standardization of features and scalability between the Standard and Datacenter SKUs with Windows Server 2012, the failover clustering feature is now available in the Standard SKU in addition to Datacenter.

Failover clustering is a feature and not a role in Windows Server because clustering just helps make another role more available. The difference between roles and features is that a role, such as Hyper-V or File Services, designates the primary purpose of a server. A feature, such as backup, BitLocker, and clustering, helps a server perform its primary purpose.

Failover clustering can be installed through Server Manager or through PowerShell as follows:

```
Install-WindowsFeature Failover-Clustering
```

A cluster consists of two or more nodes that offer services to the network, as shown in Figure 7.1. While the cluster itself has a name, IP address, configuration, and optionally, storage available to all nodes in the cluster, the actual services offered by the cluster have their own resources, such as an IP address, network name, and disks from those available to the cluster. The types of service offered by a cluster include file servers, print servers, DHCP servers, Hyper-V virtual machines, or any other application that has been written to be cluster aware, such as, for example, Exchange and SQL Server.

---

### A ONE-NODE CLUSTER?

I stated that a cluster consists of two or more nodes, but strictly speaking, that is not accurate. A cluster can consist of a single node, and many times you may start with a one-node cluster. Remember, the point of a cluster is to provide high availability of services by enabling services to move between servers if a server fails. With a single-node cluster, if the node fails, there is nowhere for the services to move to. Therefore, you always want at least two nodes in a cluster to provide high availability services.

This does not mean you won't ever see a single-node cluster. There are some features of failover clustering that apply even to single-node environments, such as the ability to monitor services that run inside virtual machines and restart the virtual machine if a service fails three times.

---

**FIGURE 7.1**
The components of a failover cluster

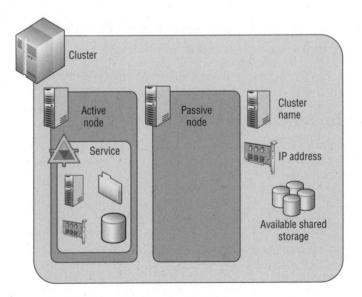

Figure 7.1 shows an active node and a passive node. In the example there is a single service configured in the cluster. The node the service is running on is the active node. The node not running the service is the passive node, but it would become the active node if the service moved to it as part of a planned move or if the existing active node failed.

While we will talk about active and passive nodes, in reality we can configure multiple services and applications within a cluster that can be hosted on different nodes in the cluster, and so at any time every node may be running a specific server or application. You just need to ensure that the resources in the cluster nodes is sufficient to run the services and applications from other nodes in the cluster in the event of planned failover of services or server failure or if applications are stopped for maintenance purposes.

The cluster consists of a number of nodes that can be active or passive. An active node is simply a node that currently owns a service or application. Windows Server 2012 allows up to 64 nodes in a cluster, up from the 16 nodes in previous versions of Windows Server.

A cluster can contain multiple services and applications, and these can be spread among all the nodes in the cluster. A service or application consists of a number of resources that enable the service or application to function, such as, for example, a disk resource, a share, a name, and an IP address. Different types of services and applications use different resources.

Any resource that is cluster aware and hosted in a cluster can move between nodes in the cluster to increase its availability. In an unplanned failure, such as a node failing, there may be a small period of service interruption because the node failure must be detected and then the service's resources moved to another node and restarted. In most planned scenarios, such as moving resources from one node to another to enable maintenance on the source node, any outage can be avoided, such as using Live Migration when a Hyper-V virtual machine moves between nodes in a cluster.

If you used clustering prior to Windows Server 2008, then you will have experienced an extremely long and painful cluster creation process that required pages of configuration information, was hard to troubleshoot, and required special hardware from a cluster-specific hardware compatibility list. This completely changed with Windows Server 2008. Windows Server 2008 introduced a greatly simplified cluster creation process that required you to specify only the nodes to be added to the cluster and to provide a name for the cluster and an IP address if DHCP was not used. All the other details are automatically configured by the cluster setup wizard. Additionally, the separate cluster hardware compatibility list was removed, replaced with a new cluster validation process that is run on the desired nodes prior to cluster creation. If the cluster validation passes, the cluster will be supported by Microsoft.

## Understanding Quorum and Why It's Important

With a cluster, there are multiple nodes that share a common cluster database in which services are defined that can run on any node in the cluster. The goal of the cluster is to provide high availability so if something bad happens on a node, the services move to another node. What is important is that there are scenarios where it may be a network problem that stops different parts of a cluster from being able to communicate rather than actual node problems. In the case of a communication problem between different parts (partitions) of the cluster, only one part of the cluster should run services to avoid the same service starting on different parts of the cluster, which could then cause corruption.

The detection of "something bad" happening within a cluster is facilitated by cluster heartbeat communications. The nodes in the cluster communicate constantly via a heartbeat to ensure that they are available. In the event of a change of cluster status, such as a node becoming unavailable or network problems stopping the cluster nodes from communicating, the cluster goes into arbitration, which is where the remaining nodes basically fight out to decide who should be hosting which services and applications to avoid split-brain. *Split-brain* describes a situation in which multiple nodes in a cluster try to bring online the same service or application, which causes the nodes to try to bring online the same resources.

## Quorum Basics

*Quorum* is the mechanism used to ensure that in the event of a break in communication between parts of the cluster or the loss of parts of the cluster, we always have to have a majority of cluster resources for the cluster to function. Quorum is the reason it is common to have a shared disk or file share that can be used in arbitration when there is an even number of nodes in different parts of the cluster.

Imagine that we had a cluster of four nodes without any shared disk or file share used for quorum and arbitration. If a split occurred and for some reason each node could contact only the node next to it, each half of the cluster would have two nodes, which would be a disaster because both halves may think they should own all the services and applications. That is why the quorum model is based on a majority, that is, *more* than half is needed for the cluster to function. In our example of two nodes on each side, neither side would have majority (half is not majority), so no cluster resources would be serviced. This is far better than multiple nodes trying to service the same resources. In actual fact, the behavior in the scenario I just outlined, with exactly half the nodes in each partition of the cluster, has changed in Windows Server 2012 R2, so services would be offered by one of the partitions. Each node can be seen as having a vote. By adding an extra vote with a file share or disk, you can ensure that one part of the cluster can always get more than 50 percent by claiming the file share or disk vote.

Let's look in detail at quorum. Prior to Windows Server 2012 there were a number of different quorum models, and even with Windows Server 2012 there was specific guidance about when to use a file share witness or disk witness. In Windows Server 2012 R2, this has all changed.

Prior to Windows Server 2012, there were various different cluster models, but in Windows Server 2012, this has been simplified to a single model. Within a cluster, by default each node has a vote. These votes are used in times of arbitration to decide which partition of a cluster can make quorum, that is, has more than half the number of votes. When creating a cluster, you also define either a disk witness or a file share witness, which also has a vote. Prior to Windows Server 2012 R2, a file share witness or disk witness was configured only if you had an even number of nodes. That meant an even number of votes, and therefore, in the event of partitioning of the cluster, neither partition would have more votes than the other side because there is an even number of nodes. When you configure the file share witness or disk witness, the extra vote assured that one partition of the cluster could claim that vote and therefore have more than 50 percent of the votes and make quorum. Only when the witness is required to make quorum is it locked by one partition of the cluster. For a file share witness, the lock is performed by locking the witness.log file on the share by one of the cluster partitions. To lock a disk witness, the disk has a SCSI persistent reservation made by one of the partitions. Both types of locks stop another partition of the cluster from being able to take ownership of the witness and try to use its vote to make quorum. This is shown in Figure 7.2 along with an odd number of vote scenarios showing why the witness is not required.

**FIGURE 7.2**

Quorum in a
failover cluster

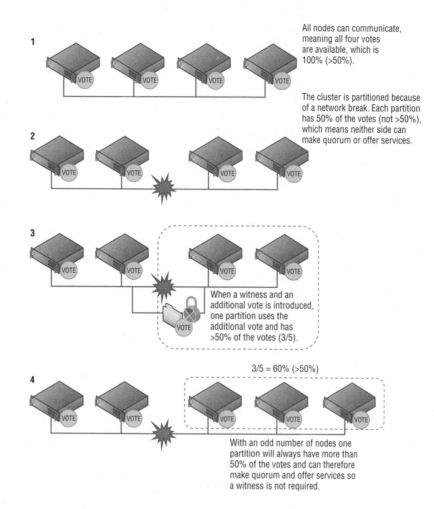

1

All nodes can communicate, meaning all four votes are available, which is 100% (>50%).

The cluster is partitioned because of a network break. Each partition has 50% of the votes (not >50%), which means neither side can make quorum or offer services.

2

3

When a witness and an additional vote is introduced, one partition uses the additional vote and has >50% of the votes (3/5).

3/5 = 60% (>50%)

4

With an odd number of nodes one partition will always have more than 50% of the votes and can therefore make quorum and offer services so a witness is not required.

Windows Server 2012 R2 changed the recommendation to always configure the disk witness or file share witness. It enhances the dynamic quorum feature introduced in Windows Server 2012 to extend to the additional witness to give it a vote only *if* there are an even number of nodes. If there are an odd number of nodes, then the witness does not get a vote and is not used.

A file share witness is simply a share on an SMB file server that is running Windows Server 2003 or above and is on a node that is in the same forest as the cluster. The file share should not be hosted on the actual cluster. If you have a multisite cluster, host the file share witness on a server in a third site to avoid any dependence on one of the two sites used by the cluster. A single file server can host file shares for different clusters. The cluster object in Active Directory (Cluster Name Object, or CNO) must have full control on both the file share and the folder that the file share is sharing. A good naming convention to use to avoid confusion for the share is FSW_<Cluster Name>. It's actually possible to have the file share witness for a cluster hosted on a different cluster to provide additional resiliency to the file share. Note that the clustered file share can be hosted on a traditional file server or a scale-out file server. Both will work well.

A disk witness can be any cluster disk, which means it's accessible from all nodes in a cluster that is NTFS or Resilient File System (ReFS) formatted and is at least 512 MB in size. You may wonder why the cluster disk needs to be 512 MB in size. The cluster disk stores a copy of the cluster database, hence the size requirement. By default, when you're creating a cluster, the smallest cluster disk that is over 512 MB is automatically made the disk witness, although this can be changed. The disk witness is exclusively used for witness purposes and does not require a drive letter.

To modify the witness configuration for a cluster, perform the following steps:

1. In Failover Cluster Manager, select the main cluster object in the navigation pane.

2. From More Actions, select Configuration Cluster Quorum Settings.

3. Click Next on the introduction page of the wizard.

4. Select the Select The Quorum Witness option and click Next. Note also the option Use Default Quorum Configuration, which allows the cluster to automatically configure witness configuration as it would during the initial cluster creation process.

5. Select the option to use a disk witness, file share witness, or no witness (never recommended) and click Next.

6. Depending on the option selected, you now must select the disk witness or file share. Then click Next.

7. Click Next on the remaining pages to complete the quorum configuration.

This can also be configured using PowerShell with one of the following commands depending on your desired quorum configuration:

- `Set-ClusterQuorum -NoWitness` (Don't do this.)

- `Set-ClusterQuorum -DiskWitness "<disk resource name>"`

- `Set-ClusterQuorum -FileShareWitness "<file share name>"`

- `Set-ClusterQuorum -DiskOnly "<disk resource name>"` (Don't do this either.)

---

**FILE SHARE WITNESS AND A DISK WITNESS? WHICH ONE?**

You never want two additional votes. The entire point of the witness vote is to provide an additional vote where there are an even number of votes caused by an even number of nodes.

You can make a decision as to whether is it better to have a disk witness or a file share witness. If you have a multisite cluster, then most likely you will have to use a file share witness because there would not be shared storage between the two sites. Additionally, the file share witness should be placed in a third site to provide protection from a site failure.

In a cluster where shared storage is available, always use a disk witness over a file share cluster, and there is a very good reason for this.

When you use a file share witness, a folder is created on the file share named with the GUID of the cluster, and within that folder a file is created that is used in times of arbitration so only one partition of a cluster can lock the file. Also, the file shows a time stamp of the last time a change was made to the main cluster database, although the file share does not actually have a copy of the cluster database. Every time a change is made to the cluster database, the time stamp on the file share witness is updated but the actual data is not stored on the file share witness, making the amount of actual network traffic very light.

Consider a scenario of a two-node cluster, node A and node B. If node A goes down, node B keeps running and makes updates to the cluster database, such as adding new resources, and also updates the time stamp of the witness.log on the file share witness. Then node B goes down and node A tries to start. Node A would see that the time stamp on the file share witness is in advance of its own database and realize its cluster database is stale and so will not start the cluster service. This prevents partition-in-time from occurring because node A is out-of-date (which is a good thing because you don't want the cluster to start out-of-date) and you would have different cluster states on different nodes, but you can't start the cluster without node B coming back or forcing quorum on node A.

Now consider a disk witness that actually stores a complete copy of the cluster database. Every time a change is made to the cluster database, that change is also made to the copy of the cluster database on the disk witness.

Now in the same two-node cluster scenario, when node A tries to start and sees that its database is out-of-date, it can just copy the cluster database from the disk witness, which is kept up-to-date, so while a file share witness prevents partition-in-time from occurring, a disk witness *solves* partition-in-time.

For this reason, always use a disk witness over a file share witness if possible.

As can be seen, the number of votes is key for cluster quorum, specifically having more than 50 percent of the total number of votes, but the total number of votes can be a problem. Traditionally, the number of votes is set when the cluster is created, when the quorum mode is changed, or when nodes are added or removed from the cluster. For any cluster, the total number of votes is a hard number that can be changed only through one of the actions previously mentioned. Problems can occur though. Consider a five-node cluster with no witness configured, which means there are five possible votes and three votes must be available for the cluster to make quorum. Consider the following sequence of actions:

◆ An administrator performs patching on a node, which requires reboots. The node would be unavailable for a period of time and therefore its vote is not available. This leaves four out of the five possible votes available, which is greater than 50 percent, so the cluster keeps quorum.

◆ The administrator starts to perform maintenance on another node, which again requires reboots, losing the vote of the additional node and leaving three out of the five possible votes available. That is still greater than 50 percent, which keeps quorum and the node stays functional.

♦ A failure in a node occurs or the administrator is an overachiever and performs maintenance on another node, losing its vote. Now there are only two votes out of the five possible votes, which is less than 50 percent, so the cluster loses quorum, the cluster services stop on the remaining two nodes, and all services in the cluster are no longer offered.

In this scenario, even though planned maintenance was going on and even though there were still two healthy nodes available, the cluster could no longer make quorum because there were less than 50 percent of the votes available. The goal of clustering is to increase availability of services, but in this case it actually caused services to become unavailable.

Windows Server 2012 changed how the vote allocation works and cures the scenario just described with a feature called dynamic quorum. With dynamic quorum, the total number of votes available in the cluster changes as node states change; for example, if a node is taken down as part of maintenance, then the node removes its vote from the cluster, reducing the total number of votes in the cluster. When the node comes out of maintenance, it adds its vote back, restoring the total number of possible votes to the original value. This means the cluster has greater resiliency when it comes to problems caused by a lack of votes. Consider the preceding scenario in Windows Server 2012 with dynamic quorum:

♦ An administrator performs patching on a node, which requires reboots, so the node would be unavailable for a period of time. As the node goes in to maintenance mode, it removes its vote from the cluster, reducing the total number of votes from five to four.

♦ The administrator starts to perform maintenance on another node, which again requires reboots. The node removes its vote, reducing the total number of votes in the cluster to three.

♦ A failure in a node occurs or the administrator is an overachiever and performs maintenance on another node, losing its vote. Now there are only two votes left out of the three total votes, which is greater than 50 percent, so the cluster stays running! In actual fact, that node that is now unavailable will have its vote removed from the cluster by the remaining nodes.

The dynamic quorum feature may seem to possibly introduce a problem to clustering, considering the whole point of the votes and quorum is to protect the cluster from becoming split-brain, with multiple partitions offering services at the same time. With dynamic quorum in place and votes being removed from the cluster when nodes go into maintenance or fail, you may think, "Couldn't the cluster split and both parts make quorum?" The answer is no. There are still rules for how dynamic quorum can remove votes and keep quorum.

To be able to deterministically remove the vote of a cluster node, the remaining nodes must have quorum majority. For example, if I had a three-node cluster and one of the nodes fails, the remaining two nodes have quorum majority, two out of three votes, and therefore are able to remove the vote of the failed node, which means the cluster now has two votes. Let's go back to our five-node cluster, which experiences a network failure. One partition has three nodes and the other partition has two nodes. The partition with three nodes has quorum majority, which means it keeps offering services and can therefore remove the votes of the other two nodes. The partition with two nodes does not have quorum majority, so the cluster service will shut down. The partition with three nodes now has a total vote count of three, which means that partition can now survive one of the three nodes failing, whereas without dynamic quorum, another node failure would have caused the cluster to shut down. This is shown in Figure 7.3.

**FIGURE 7.3**
Dynamic quorum in
action

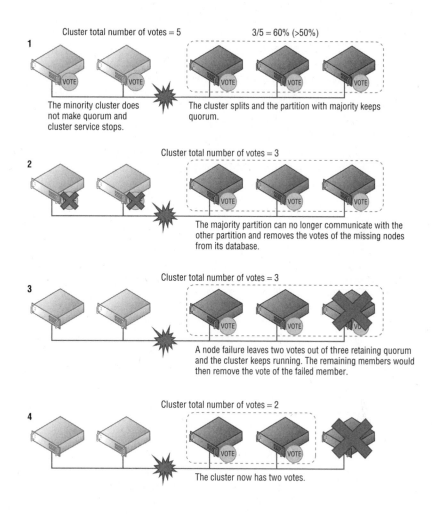

Cluster total number of votes = 5    3/5 = 60% (>50%)

**1**

The minority cluster does
not make quorum and
cluster service stops.

The cluster splits and the partition with majority keeps
quorum.

Cluster total number of votes = 3

**2**

The majority partition can no longer communicate with the
other partition and removes the votes of the missing nodes
from its database.

Cluster total number of votes = 3

**3**

A node failure leaves two votes out of three retaining quorum
and the cluster keeps running. The remaining members would
then remove the vote of the failed member.

Cluster total number of votes = 2

**4**

The cluster now has two votes.

With the ability to remove votes from the cluster as nodes fail or are shut down in a planned
manner, it is now possible to go from a 64-node cluster all the way down to a single node,
known as last man standing, providing the node shutdowns are sequential and a majority quorum is maintained with simultaneous node removals. It is important to note that if you remove
a large number of nodes from a cluster, it is unlikely the remaining nodes would be able to run
all the services present in the cluster unless you had a highly underutilized cluster. Dynamic
quorum is enabled by default, and the recommendation is to leave it enabled. Dynamic quorum
is a cluster property, and if you wanted to disable it, this is done through PowerShell by setting
the cluster DynamicQuorum property to 0 instead of the default 1, as in (Get-Cluster)
.DynamicQuorum = 0. Note that as nodes are resumed/fixed and communication is restored,
the nodes votes are restored to the cluster. To summarize the dynamic quorum scenarios:

◆   When a node shuts down in a planned manner (an administrator shutdown or automated
    shutdown such as cluster-aware updating), the node removes its own vote.

◆   When a node crashes, the remaining active nodes remove the vote of the downed node.

◆   When a node joins the cluster, it gets its vote back.

There is a feature called Node Vote Weights that actually enables certain nodes to be specified as not participating in quorum calculations by removing the vote of the node. The node still fully participates in the cluster, it still has a copy of the cluster database, and it still runs cluster services and can host applications, it simply no longer affects quorum calculations. There is really only one scenario where you would want to make this type of change, and that is for multisite clusters where failover must be manually performed, such as with a SQL Always On High Availability configuration using asynchronous replication that requires manual interaction to failover. In this scenario, the nodes in the remote site would have their votes removed so they cannot affect quorum in the primary site.

### Modifying Cluster Vote Configuration

Modification of votes can be performed using the Failover Cluster Manager graphical interface and PowerShell. To modify votes using the graphical tools, perform the following steps (note that the same process can be used to revert the cluster back to the default configuration of all nodes having votes):

1. In Failover Cluster Manager, select the main cluster object in the navigation pane.

2. From More Actions, select Configuration Cluster Quorum Settings.

3. Click Next on the introduction screen of the wizard.

4. Select the Advanced Quorum Configuration option and click Next.

5. On the Select Voting Configuration page, choose the Select Nodes option and then uncheck the nodes that should not have a vote and click Next (Figure 7.4). Note that on this screen, the default is All Nodes, meaning all nodes should have a vote, but also there is an option that no nodes have a vote, which means that only the disk witness has a vote. This is the original cluster quorum model and frankly, it should never be used today because it introduces a single point of failure. It is there for historical reasons only.

6. Click Next to all remaining screens. The witness configuration will be changed and the modification will then be made to the cluster.

To make the change using PowerShell, set the vote of the node to 0 (instead of the default value of 1), as in this example:

```
(Get-ClusterNode <name>).NodeWeight=0
```

To view the current voting state of nodes in a cluster, use the Nodes view within Failover Cluster Manager as shown in Figure 7.5. Note that two values are shown. The administrator-configured node weight is shown in the Assigned Vote column, while the cluster-assigned dynamic vote weight as controlled by dynamic quorum is shown in the Current Vote column. If you run a cluster validation, the generated report also shows the vote status of the nodes in the cluster. Remember, only use the node vote weighting in the very specific geo-cluster scenarios where manual failover is required. In most scenarios, you should not manually change the node weights.

**FIGURE 7.4**
Changing the
votes for nodes in a
cluster

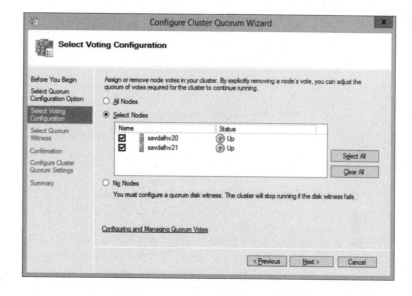

**FIGURE 7.5**
Viewing the current
voting state of a
cluster

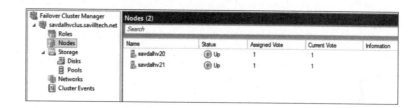

Earlier in this chapter I explained that in Windows Server 2012 R2, the guidance is to always configure a witness for the cluster. This is because the dynamic quorum technology has been extended to the witness in Windows Server 2012 R2; this technology is known as dynamic witness. Failover clustering is now smart enough to decide if the witness should have a vote or not:

◆ If there are an even number of nodes that have a vote (dynamic weight = 1), the witness dynamic vote = 1.

◆ If there are an odd number of nodes that have a vote (dynamic weight = 1), the witness dynamic vote = 0.

This is very logical because the witness is only needed when there is an even number of nodes, which ordinarily would not be able to make quorum in the event of a split. If the witness goes offline or fails, its witness dynamic vote value will be set to 0 in the same manner a failed nodes vote is removed. To check if the witness currently has a vote, run the following PowerShell command:

```
(Get-Cluster).WitnessDynamicWeight
```

A return value of 1 means the witness has a vote; a return value of 0 means the witness does not have a vote. If you look at the nodes in the cluster, the witness vote weight should correlate to the dynamic votes of the cluster nodes. To check the dynamic votes of the cluster nodes from PowerShell, use the following:

```
PS C:\> Get-ClusterNode | ft Name, DynamicWeight -AutoSize

Name         DynamicWeight
----         -------------
savdalhv20               1
savdalhv21               1
```

## Advanced Quorum Options and Forcing Quorums

In all of the quorum explanations so far, the critical factor is that there must be a majority of votes available for the cluster to keep running, greater than 50 percent. There will be times when there are an even number of votes in the cluster due to other failures (although dynamic witness should help avoid ever having an even number of votes unless it's the witness that has failed) or misconfiguration. Windows Server 2012 R2 provides tie-breaker code so that the cluster can now survive a simultaneous loss of 50 percent of the votes while ensuring that only one partition keeps running and the other partition shuts down. In the event of the loss of 50 percent of the votes, clustering will automatically select one of the partitions to "win" using a specific algorithm. The way the winning partition is selected is as follows: If there are an even number of node votes in the cluster, the clustering service will randomly select a node and remove its vote. That will change the number of votes in the cluster to odd again, giving one of the sites a majority vote and therefore making it capable of surviving a break in communication. If you want to control which of the sites should win if there is a break of communication, a cluster attribute, LowerQuorumPriorityNodeId, can be set to the ID of the node that should lose its vote when there are an even number of nodes and no witness available. Remember, providing you have configured a witness, this functionality should not be required.

Even in single-site configurations, the same last man standing code will be implemented. If I have a single site with only two nodes left in the cluster and no witness, one of the nodes would lose its vote. I want to look in more detail at this "last two vote standing" scenario as shown in Figure 7.6, which continues with the scenario we looked at in Figure 7.3. Note that in this example, there is no witness, which would not be best practice.

**FIGURE 7.6**
Two remaining nodes in a cluster

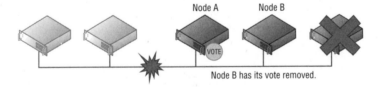

◆ If node B now has a failure, the cluster continues running on node A because node A has the last remaining vote and has quorum majority (it has the single vote, so it has 100 percent of the vote and therefore >50 percent).

♦ If node A has a failure and shuts down, then node B's cluster service will stop because node A had the only vote and therefore node B has no vote and cannot make quorum.

♦ If a communication failure happens between node A and node B, then node A will keep running with quorum majority while node B's cluster service will stop.

♦ If node A shuts down cleanly, then before it shuts down it will transfer its vote to node B, which means the cluster will continue running on node B.

With all these new technologies, it's actually very hard for the cluster to lose quorum. To lose quorum, the cluster would have to simultaneously lose more than half the number of votes, in which case you should shut down the cluster to protect the integrity of the services.

This brings us to forcing quorum. Consider a remote site that has a minority number of votes but in a disaster the cluster service must be started. Even in normal circumstances there may be times when nodes are lost and the cluster service must be started even without quorum majority. This is known as Forced Quorum, and it allows the cluster to start without a majority of votes. When a cluster is started in Forced Quorum mode, it stays in that mode until a majority of nodes is available as they come online again, at which point the cluster automatically switches from Forced Quorum mode to the normal mode. To start the cluster in Forced Quorum mode, perform one of the following on *one* node that will be part of the Forced Quorum partition:

♦ Run the command `Start-ClusterNode -ForceQuorum`.

♦ Run the command `Net start clussvc /ForceQuorum`.

♦ Perform a force start in Failover Cluster Manager.

All other nodes that will be part of the Forced Quorum should be started in Prevent Quorum mode, which tells the nodes it must join an existing cluster, preventing different nodes from creating their own partitions using one of the following methods:

♦ Run the command `Start-ClusterNode -PreventQuorum`.

♦ Run the command `Net start clussvc /PQ`.

♦ If you used the Failover Cluster Manager to perform a force start, then no action is required on other nodes. When you Force Quorum through the management tool, one node is picked to start with Force Quorum and then all other nodes that can be communicated with will be started with Prevent Quorum.

Windows Server 2012 R2 introduces Force Quorum resiliency, which is important when Force Quorum is used. Consider Figure 7.7, which shows how the cluster works when Forced Quorum is used. Step 1 shows that the partition with two nodes is started with Force Quorum. In step 2, the other partition starts and makes quorum because it has three out of five votes, so it has majority but no communication to the partition that started with Force Quorum. In step 3, the communication is restored and the partition with three nodes detects a partition that was started with Force Quorum. At this point, the three-node partition restarts the cluster service in Prevent Quorum mode on all nodes, which forces them to join the Force Quorum partition. In step 4, the merged cluster now has quorum majority and exits Force Quorum mode.

Care should be taken when using Forced Quorum because it would potentially be possible to start the cluster service on multiple cluster partitions, which could cause big problems.

Make sure you understand what is happening within the cluster that has caused the cluster to lose quorum and be 100 percent positive that the cluster is not running in another location before performing Forced Quorum.

**FIGURE 7.7**

Force quorum resiliency in action

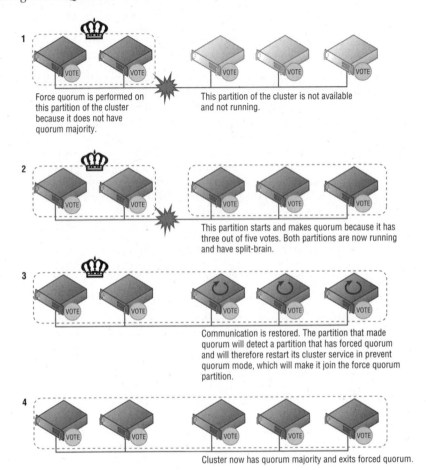

1. Force quorum is performed on this partition of the cluster because it does not have quorum majority.

   This partition of the cluster is not available and not running.

2. This partition starts and makes quorum because it has three out of five votes. Both partitions are now running and have split-brain.

3. Communication is restored. The partition that made quorum will detect a partition that has forced quorum and will therefore restart its cluster service in prevent quorum mode, which will make it join the force quorum partition.

4. Cluster now has quorum majority and exits forced quorum.

## Geographically Distributed Clusters

With enhancements to networking, storage, and particularly failover clustering in Windows Server, it is much easier to have multisite clusters and many of the quorum features discussed previously can be very useful. The first decision that must be made when dealing with a multisite environment is how the switch of services between sites should be performed.

If the failover between sites is automatic, then the sites can be considered equal. In that case, it's important to use a file share witness in a third location to ensure that if one site fails, the other site can use the witness vote and make quorum and offer services. If you have a synchronous storage replication solution that supports arbitration of storage, a disk witness could be used, but this is rare, which is why in most cases a file share witness would be used. It is important that both sites have an equal number of nodes. You would need to leverage a technology to replicate the storage used by Hyper-V virtual machines to the other location. If this type of SAN replication of storage is not available, the Hyper-V Replica technology can be leveraged. However, this would actually require separate clusters between locations and would not be an automated failover.

---

### CAN I HOST MY FILE SHARE WITNESS IN WINDOWS AZURE IAAS?

Windows Azure IaaS enables virtual machines to run in the Windows Azure cloud service, which can include a file server offering a file share that can be domain joined, making it seem a plausible option to host the witness for a cluster.

Technically the answer is that the file share for a cluster could be hosted in a Windows Azure IaaS VM and the Windows Azure virtual network can be connected to your on-premises infrastructure using its site-to-site gateway functionality. In most cases it would not be practical because most likely the desire to use Windows Azure is because you have two datacenters hosting nodes and wish to use Windows Azure as the "third site." The problem is, at the time of this writing, a Windows Azure virtual network supports only a single instance of the site-to-site gateway, which means it could be connected to only one of the datacenters. If the datacenter that the virtual network was connected to failed, the other datacenter would have no access to Windows Azure and therefore would not be able to see the file share witness, use its vote, and make quorum, making it fairly useless. Once Windows Azure supports multiple site-to-site gateways, then using it for the file share witness would become a more practical solution.

---

The other options is a manual failover where services are manually activated on the disaster recovery site. In this scenario, it would be common to remove votes from the disaster recovery site so it does not affect quorum on the primary location. In the event of a failover to the disaster recovery location, the disaster recovery site would be started in a Force Quorum mode.

In reality, it is not that common to see stretched clusters for Hyper-V virtual machines because of the difficulty and high expense of replicating the storage. Additionally, if virtual machines moved between locations, most likely their IP configuration would require reconfiguration unless network virtualization was being used or VLANs were stretched between locations, which again is rare and can be very expensive. In the next chapter, I will cover Hyper-V Replica as a solution for disaster recovery, which solves the problems of moving virtual machines between sites. Multisite clusters are commonly used for application workloads such as SQL and Exchange instead of for Hyper-V virtual machines.

## Why Use Clustering with Hyper-V?

In the previous sections I went into a lot of detail about quorum and how clusters work. The key point is this: clusters help keep the workloads available with a minimal amount of downtime, even in unplanned outages. For Hyper-V servers that are running many virtual machines, keeping the virtual machines as available as possible is critical.

When looking at high availability, there are two types of outage: planned and unplanned. A planned outage is a known and controlled outage, such as, for example, when you are rebooting a host to apply patches or performing hardware maintenance or even powering down a complete datacenter. In a planned outage scenario, it is possible to avoid any downtime to the virtual machines by performing a Live Migration of the virtual machines on one node to another node. When Live Migration is used, the virtual machine is always available to clients.

An unplanned outage is not foreseen or planned, such as, for example, a server crash or hardware failure. In an unplanned outage, there is no opportunity to perform Live Migration of virtual machines between nodes, which means there will be a period of unavailability for the virtual machines. In an unplanned outage scenario, the cluster will detect that a node has failed and the resources that were running on the failed node will be redistributed among the remaining nodes in the cluster and then started. Because the virtual machines were effectively just powered off without a clean shutdown of the guest OS inside the virtual machines, the guest OS will start in what is known as a "crash consistent state," which means when the guest OS starts and applications in the guest OS start, there may be some consistency and repair actions required.

In Windows Server 2008 R2, the Live Migration feature for moving virtual machines with no downtime between servers was available only between nodes in a cluster because the storage had to be available to both the source and target node. In Windows Server 2012, the ability to live migrate between any two Hyper-V 2012 hosts was introduced. It's known as Shared Nothing Live Migration, and it migrates the storage in addition to the memory and state of the virtual machine.

One traditional feature of clustering was the ability to smoothly move storage between nodes in a cluster. It was enhanced greatly with Windows Server 2008 R2 to actually allow storage to be shared between the nodes in a cluster simultaneously; it's known as Cluster Shared Volumes (CSV). With CSV, an NTFS volume can be accessed by all the nodes at the same time, allowing virtual machines to be stored on a single NTFS-formatted LUN and run on different nodes in the cluster. The sharing of storage is a huge feature of clusters and makes the migration of virtual machines between nodes a much more efficient process because only the memory and state of the virtual machine needs to be migrated and not the actual storage. Of course, in Windows Server 2012, nodes not in a cluster can share storage by accessing a common SMB 3 file share, but many environments do not have the infrastructure to utilize SMB 3 at a datacenter level or already have large SAN investments.

As can be seen, some of the features of clustering for Hyper-V are now available outside of a cluster at some level, but not with the same level of efficiency and typically only in planned scenarios. Additionally, a cluster provides a boundary of host membership, which can be used for other purposes, such as virtual machine rebalancing, placement optimization, and even automation processes such as cluster patching. I will be covering migration, CSV, and the other technologies briefly mentioned in detail later in this chapter.

Clustering brings high availability solutions to unplanned scenarios, but it also brings some other features to virtual machine workloads. It is because of some of these features that occasionally you will see a single-node cluster of virtual machines. Hyper-V has a number of great availability features, but they are no substitute for clustering to maintain availability during unplanned outages and to simplify maintenance options, so don't overlook clustering.

## Service Monitoring

Failover clustering provides high availability to the virtual machine in the event of a host failure, but it does not provide protection or assistance if a service within the virtual machine fails. Clustering is strictly making sure the virtual machine is running; it offers no assistance to the operating system running within the virtual machine.

Windows Server 2012 clustering changed this by introducing a new clustering feature, service monitoring, which allows clustering to communicate to the guest OS running within the virtual machine and check for service failures. If you examine the properties of a service within Windows, there are actions available if the service fails, as shown in Figure 7.8. Note that in the Recovery tab, Windows allows actions to be taken on the first failure, the second failure, and then subsequent failures. These actions are as follows:

◆ Take No Action

◆ Restart The Service

◆ Run A Program

◆ Restart The Computer

**FIGURE 7.8**
Service retry actions

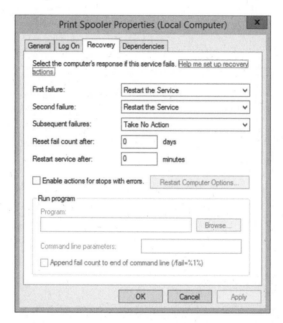

Consider if a service fails three times consecutively; it's unlikely restarting it a third time would result in a different outcome. Clustering can be configured to perform the action that is known to fix any problem, reboot the virtual machine on the existing host. If the virtual machine is rebooted by clustering and the service fails a subsequent time inside the virtual machine, then clustering will move the virtual machine to another host in the cluster and reboot it.

For this feature to work, the following must be configured:

◆ Both the Hyper-V servers must be Windows Server 2012 and the guest OS running in the VM must be Windows Server 2012.

◆ The host and guest OSs are in the same or at least trusting domains.

◆ The failover cluster administrator must be a member of the local administrator's group inside the VM.

◆ Ensure that the service being monitored is set to Take No Action (see Figure 7.8) within the guest VM for subsequent failures (which is used after the first and second failures) and is set via the Recovery tab of the service properties within the Services application (services.msc).

◆ Within the guest VM, ensure that the Virtual Machine Monitoring firewall exception is enabled for the Domain network by using the Windows Firewall with Advanced Security application or by using the following Windows PowerShell command:

```
Set-NetFirewallRule -DisplayGroup "Virtual Machine Monitoring" -Enabled True
```

After everything in the preceding list is configured, enabling the monitoring is a simple process:

1. Launch the Failover Cluster Manager tool.

2. Navigate to the cluster and select Roles.

3. Right-click the virtual machine role you wish to enable monitoring for, and under More Actions, select Configure Monitoring.

4. The services running inside the VM will be gathered by the cluster service communicating to the guest OS inside the virtual machine. Check the box for the services that should be monitored, as shown in Figure 7.9, and click OK.

**FIGURE 7.9**
Enabling monitoring of a service

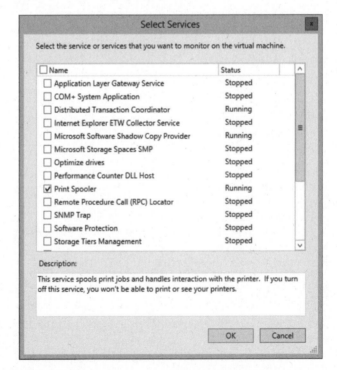

Monitoring can also be enabled using the `Add-ClusterVMMonitoredItem` cmdlet and `-VirtualMachine`, with the `-Service` parameters, as in this example:

```
PS C:\ > Add-ClusterVMMonitoredItem -VirtualMachine savdaltst01 -Service spooler
```

After two service failures, an event ID 1250 is logged in the system log. At this point, the VM will be restarted, initially on the same host, but on subsequent failures it will restart on another node in the cluster. This process can be seen in a video at `http://youtu.be/H1EghdniZ1I`.

This is a very rudimentary capability, but it may help in some scenarios. As mentioned in the previous chapter, for a complete monitoring solution, leverage System Center Operations Manager, which can run monitoring with deep OS and application knowledge that can be used to generate alerts. Those alerts can be used to trigger automated actions for remediation or simply to generate incidents in a ticketing system.

## Protected Network

While the operating system and applications within virtual machines perform certain tasks, the usefulness of those tasks is generally being able to communicate with services via the network. If the network is unavailable on the Hyper-V host that the virtual machine uses, traditionally clustering would take no action, which has been a huge weakness. As far as clustering is aware, the virtual machine is still fine; it's running with no problems. Windows Server 2012 R2 introduces the concept of a protected network to solve this final gap in high availability of virtual machines and their connectivity.

The Protected Network setting allows specific virtual network adapters to be configured as protected, as shown in Figure 7.10, via the Settings option of a virtual machine and the Advanced Features options of the specific network adapter. In the event the Hyper-V host loses network connectivity that the virtual machine network adapters configured as a protected network are using, the virtual machines will be live migrated to another host in the cluster that does have network connectivity for that network. This does require that the Hyper-V host still have network connectivity between the Hyper-V hosts to allow Live Migration, but typically clusters will use different networks for virtual machine connectivity than those used for Live Migration purposes, which means Live Migration should still be possible.

It is important to try to provide as much resiliency as possible for network communications, which means using NIC teaming on the hosts as described Chapter 3, "Virtual Networking," but the protected network features provides an additional layer of resiliency to network failures.

## Cluster-Aware Updating

Windows Server 2012 placed a huge focus on running the Server Core configuration level, which reduced the amount of patching and therefore reboots required for a system. There will still be patches that need to be installed and therefore reboots, but the key point is to reduce (or ideally, eliminate) any impact to the virtual machines when hosts have to be rebooted.

In a typical cluster, any impact to virtual machines is removed by Live Migrating virtual machines off of a node, patching and rebooting that node, moving the virtual machines back, and repeating for the other nodes in the cluster. This sounds simple, but for a 64-node cluster, this is a lot of work.

SCVMM 2012 introduced the ability to automate the entire cluster patching process with a single click, and this capability was made a core part of failover clustering in Windows Server 2012. It's called Cluster-Aware Updating. With Cluster-Aware Updating, updates are obtained from Microsoft Update or an on-premises Windows Server Update Services (WSUS) implementation and the entire cluster is patched with no impact to availability of virtual machines.

I walk through the entire Cluster-Aware Updating configuration and usage at the following location:

```
http://windowsitpro.com/windows-server-2012/cluster-aware-updating-windows-
server-2012
```

**FIGURE 7.10**
Configuring a protected network on a virtual machine network adapter

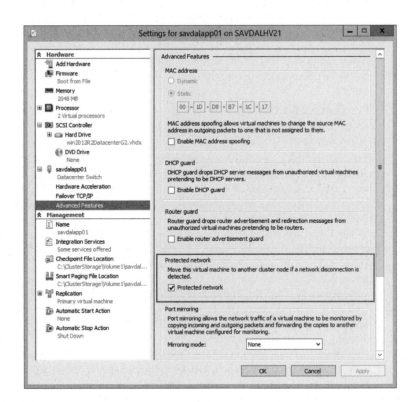

## Where to Implement High Availability

With the great features available with Hyper-V clustering, it can be easy to think that clustering the Hyper-V hosts and therefore providing high availability for all the virtual machines is the only solution you need. Clustering the Hyper-V hosts definitely provides great mobility, storage sharing, and high availability services for virtual machines, but that doesn't mean it's always the best solution.

Consider an application such as SQL Server or Exchange. If clustering is performed only at the Hyper-V host level, then if the Hyper-V host fails, the virtual machine resource is moved to another host and then started in a crash consistent state, which means the service would be unavailable for a period of time and likely an amount of consistency checking and repair would be required. Additionally, the host-level clustering will not protect from a crash within the virtual machine where the actual service is no longer running but the guest OS is still functioning, and therefore no action is needed at the host level. If instead guest clustering was leveraged, which means a cluster is created within the guest operating systems running in the virtual machines, the full cluster-aware application capabilities will be available, such as detecting if the application service is not responding on one guest OS, allowing another instance of the application to take over. Guest clustering is fully supported in Hyper-V virtual machines, and as covered Chapter 4, "Storage Configurations," there are numerous options to provide shared storage to guest clusters, such as iSCSI, Virtual Fibre Channel, and shared VHDX.

The guidance I give is as follows:

♦ If the application running inside the virtual machine is cluster aware, then create multiple virtual machines, each with the application installed, and create a guest cluster between them. This will likely mean enabling some kind of shared storage for those virtual machines.

♦ If the application is not cluster aware but works with technologies such as Network Load Balancing (NLB), for example IIS, then deploy multiple virtual machines, each running the service, and then use NLB to load balance between the instances.

♦ If the application running inside the virtual machine is not cluster aware or NLB supported but multiple instances of the application are supported and the application has its own methods of distributing load and HA (for example, Active Directory Domain Services), then deploy multiple instances over multiple virtual machines.

♦ Finally, if there is no application-native high availability option, rely on the Hyper-V cluster, which is better than nothing.

It is important to check whether applications support not only running inside a virtual machine (nearly all applications do today) but also running on a Hyper-V cluster, and extending that, whether they support being live migrated between hosts. Some applications initially did not support being live migrated for technical reasons, or they were licensed by physical processors, which meant it was expensive if you wanted to move the virtual machine between hosts because all processors on all possible hosts would have to be licensed. Most applications have now moved beyond restrictions of physical processor instance licensing, but still check!

There is another configuration you should perform on your Hyper-V cluster for virtual machines that contain multiple instances of an application (for example, multiple SQL Server VMs, multiple IIS VMs, multiple domain controllers, and so on). The goal of using multiple instances of applications is to provide protection from the VM failing or the host that is running the virtual machines failing. Having multiple instances of an application across multiple virtual machines is not useful if all the virtual machines are running on the same host. Fortunately, failover clustering has an anti-affinity capability, which ensures where possible that virtual machines in the same anti-affinity group are not placed on the same Hyper-V host. To set the anti-affinity group for a virtual machine, use `cluster.exe` or PowerShell:

♦ `(Get-ClusterGroup "<VM>").AntiAffinityClassNames = "<AntiAffinityGroupName>"`

♦ `cluster.exe group "<VM>" /prop AntiAffinityClassNames="<AntiAffinityGroup Name>"`

The cluster affinity can be set graphically by using SCVMM, as shown in Figure 7.11. SCVMM uses *availability set* as the nomenclature instead of *anti-affinity group*. Open the properties of the virtual machine in SCVMM, navigate to the Hardware Configuration tab, and select Availability under the Advanced section. Use the Manage Availability Sets button to create new sets and then add them to the virtual machine. A single virtual machine can be a member of multiple availability sets.

**FIGURE 7.11**
Setting affinity
using SCVMM

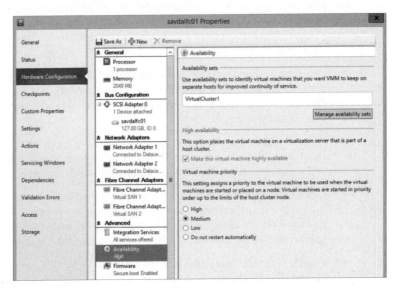

By default, this anti-affinity solution is a soft enforcement, which means clustering will do its best to keep virtual machines in the same anti-affinity group on separate hosts, but if it has no choice, it will place instances on the same host. This enforcement can be set to hard by setting the cluster ClusterEnforcedAntiAffinity attribute to 1, but this may mean virtual machines may not be able to be started.

For virtual machines that are clustered, it is possible to set the preferred owners for each virtual machine and set the order of their preference. However, it's important to realize that just because a host is not set as a preferred owner for a resource (virtual machine), that doesn't mean the host can't still run that resource if none of the preferred owners are available. To set the preferred owners, right-click on a VM resource and select Properties, and in the General tab, set the preferred owners and the order as required.

If you want to ensure that a resource never runs on specific hosts, you can set the possible owners, and when a resource is restricted to possible owners, it cannot run on hosts that are not possible owners. This should be used with care because if no possible owners are available that are configured, the resource cannot start, which may be worse than it just not running on a nonoptimal host. To set the possible owners, you need to modify the cluster group of the virtual machine, which is in the bottom pane of Failover Cluster Manager. Right-click the virtual machine resource group and select Properties. Under the Advanced Policies tab, the possible owners are shown. If you unselect servers, then that specific virtual machine cannot run on the unselected servers.

The same PowerShell cmdlet is used, Set-ClusterOwnerNode, to set both the preferred and possible owners. If the cmdlet is used against a cluster resource (that is, a virtual machine), it sets the preferred owners. If it is used against a cluster group, it sets the possible owners.

It's common where possible to cluster the Hyper-V hosts to provide mobility and high availability for the virtual machines and create guest clusters where applications running within the virtual machines are cluster aware. This can be seen in Figure 7.12.

**FIGURE 7.12**
Guest cluster running within a Hyper-V host cluster

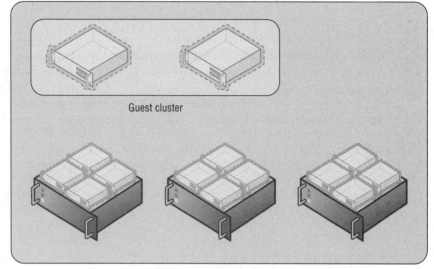

Guest cluster

Hyper-V host cluster

## Configuring a Hyper-V Cluster

Creating a Hyper-V cluster is essentially the same process as creating any cluster running on Windows Server 2012 R2. You need to follow some general guidelines:

◆ Ensure that the nodes in the cluster are running the same hardware, especially for the processor. If different generations of processor are used, it may be required to configure the processor compatibility attribute on virtual machines to enable migration between hosts without downtime.

◆ Ensure access to shared storage to enable virtual machines to be stored on Cluster Shared Volumes.

◆ Network connectivity is required, such as for virtual machines and management but also for cluster communications and Live Migration. I went over the network requirements in detail in Chapter 3, but I'll review them in the next section. It is important that all nodes in the cluster have connectivity to the same networks to avoid loss of connectivity if VMs move between different servers.

◆ Each node must be running the same version of Windows and also should be at the same patch/service pack level.

The good news that is the process to create a cluster actually checks your potential environment through a validation process and then only if everything passes validation do you proceed and actually create the cluster. The validation process gives a lot of information and performs very in-depth checks and should be used anytime you wish to make a change to the cluster, such as, for example, adding another node. It's also possible to run the validation without any changes because it can be a great troubleshooting tool. If you experience problems or errors, run the cluster validation, which may give you some ideas of the problems. The validation process also has some checks specific to Hyper-V.

## Cluster Network Requirements and Configurations

Before I go into detail on validating and creating a cluster, I want to touch on the networking requirements for a Hyper-V cluster and specifically requirements related to the cluster network.

The cluster network is critical to enable hosts in a cluster to communicate with each other. This is important for health monitoring to ensure that hosts are still running and responsive. If a server becomes unresponsive, the cluster takes remedial actions. This is done via a heartbeat that is sent by default every second over port 3343 (both UDP and TCP). This heartbeat is not a basic "ping" but rather a Request-Reply type process for the highest level of reliability and security that is actually implemented as part of the cluster NetFT kernel driver, which I will talk more about in the next section "Cluster Virtual Network Adapter." By default, if a node does not respond to five consecutive heartbeats, it is considered down and the recovery actions are performed.

If the cluster network fails, clustering will use another network that has been configured to allow cluster communications if needed. It is important to always have at least two networks configured to allow cluster communications.

The requirements of the cluster network have changed since early versions of clustering because the cluster network is not just used for heartbeat communications but is also used for Cluster Shared Volumes communications, which now leverage SMB. The use of SMB means that the cluster network adapter must have both the Client for Microsoft Networks and File and Printer Sharing for Microsoft Networks bound, as shown in Figure 7.13. Note that you can disable the Link-Layer services because they are not required for the cluster communications.

**FIGURE 7.13**
Binding for network adapters used for cluster communications

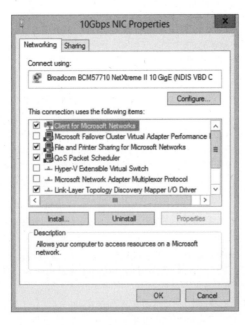

It's also important the Server and Workstation Services are running on the hosts and NTLM is used for authentication, so they must be enabled. Both IPv4 and IPv6 are supported for cluster communications, and although Microsoft performs most testing with IPv6 enabled, if it's disabled, clustering will still work fine. However, where possible leave IPv6 enabled. If both IPv4 and IPv6 are enabled, clustering will use IPv6. Disabling NetBIOS, as shown in Figure 7.14, has been shown to increase performance, and while enabling jumbo frames will not hurt, it has not been found to make any significant performance difference.

**FIGURE 7.14**
Disabling NetBIOS for the IPv4 protocol

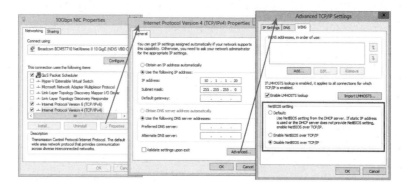

The binding order for the network adapters in a multinetwork adapter system is very important. It tells Windows which network adapter to use for different types of communication. For example, you would not want normal management traffic trying to use the Live Migration or the cluster network. You can change the binding order for network adapters using the following steps:

1. Open the Network And Sharing Center Control Panel applet.

2. Select the Change Adapter Settings action.

3. In Network Connections, press the Alt key to see the menu and select Advanced ➢ Advanced Settings.

4. The binding order is displayed. Make sure your management network/public network is at the top of the binding order. Your cluster networks should be at the bottom as shown in Figure 7.15.

5. Click OK to close the dialog.

A Network Topology Generator is used to build the various cluster networks that are available to clustering. If multiple network adapters exist that are on the same IP subnet, they will automatically be grouped into the same cluster network. This is important to understand from a resiliency perspective. Imagine you place two NICs in a node, both on the same subnet, that you wish clustering to use for high availability. What will actually happen is that both NICs would be placed in the same cluster network and only one of them will be used, removing any redundancy. The correct way to achieve redundancy in this situation is to actually use NIC Teaming to join the two NICs. When you have NICs on different subnets, they will be seen as different cluster networks and then clustering can utilize them for high availability across the different network routes. If you were looking to leverage SMB multichannel, you would need to place each NIC on a different subnet, which is a cluster-specific requirement because normally SMB multichannel will work with NICs on the same subnet.

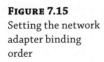

**FIGURE 7.15**
Setting the network
adapter binding
order

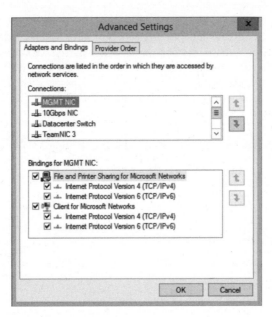

By default, during the cluster creation process, the cluster creation will use the Network Topology Generator and the most appropriate network to be used for clustering will be automatically selected based on connectivity. However, this can be changed after the cluster is created. Automatic metrics are used to determine the network used for clustering and other services based on the automatic configurations made by the cluster wizard and your customizations post creation. Figure 7.16 shows the properties available for each network available to Failover Clustering. Note that the network adapters used by Hyper-V virtual switches are not shown because they effectively offer no services to the Hyper-V host itself.

**FIGURE 7.16**
Cluster network
properties

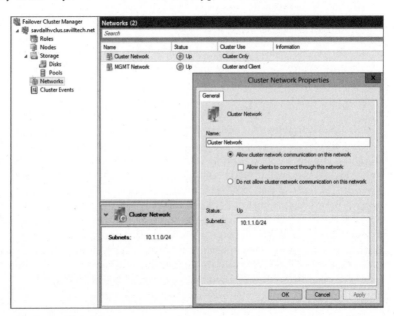

Notice that for each network, the following options are available, which are initially config-ured during clustering setup based on the IP configuration of the network adapter and whether a gateway was configured. These configure the role of the networks in relation to cluster activi-ties, and they also have a numeric value, shown in square brackets.

◆ Allow Cluster Network Communication On This Network [1]. This is set automatically for any IP-enabled network adapter and allows the cluster to use this network if necessary unless the iSCSI Software Initiator is bound to the IP address, in which case this is not configured.

◆ Allow Clients To Connect Through This Network [3]. This is set automatically if the IP configuration for the network adapter has a gateway defined, which suggests external communication and therefore client communication.

◆ Do Not Allow Cluster Network Communication On This Network [0]. The cluster cannot use this network. This would be configured on something like an iSCSI network, which is automatically set if the iSCSI Software Initiator is bound to the IP address.

These roles can also be configured using PowerShell using this command:

```
(Get-ClusterNetwork "<network name>").Role=<new role number>
```

These three settings are used by clustering to create an automatic metric for each network adapter, which sets the priority for the preferred network to be used for cluster communications for all those available for cluster communications. The metrics can be seen using the following PowerShell:

```
PS C:\> Get-ClusterNetwork | ft Name, Role, AutoMetric, Metric -AutoSize

Name             Role AutoMetric Metric
----             ---- ---------- ------
Cluster Network   1       True   30240
MGMT Network      3       True   70384
```

The lower the metric value, the cheaper it is considered to be and therefore a greater prefer-ence to be used for cluster communications. The way these values are calculated is primarily on the role of the cluster, which sets a starting value for the metric:

◆ Role of 1 - Starting metric 40000

◆ Role of 3 - Starting metric of 80000

Then the metric is reduced for each NIC based on its link speed and if it's RDMA capable and has RSS capabilities. The higher the performance and feature set of the NIC, the greater the metric reduction, making it cheaper and therefore more appealing to be used for cluster com-munications. It is possible to change these metric values by disabling AutoMetric on the cluster network and then manually setting a Metric value, but generally this should not be performed. Note that this prioritization of networks for cluster communications does not apply to SMB-based communications; SMB uses its own selection mechanism. If you did need to modify the metric, use the following:

```
(Get-ClusterNetwork "<cluster network>".AutoMetric = $false
(Get-ClusterNetwork "<cluster network>".Metric = 42
```

When considering network capacity planning for the network traffic, it's important to realize that in addition to the network health monitoring (heartbeats) traffic, the cluster network is used for intra-cluster communications such as cluster database updates and also CSV I/O redirection.

The heartbeat communications are very lightweight, 134 bytes to be exact in Windows Server 2012 R2, and are sent by default once a second. This means you don't require a big network pipe (that is, bandwidth), but the heartbeats are sensitive to latency (the lag between a request and response) because if too many heartbeats are not acknowledged in a period of time, the host is considered unavailable.

Intra-cluster communications type of traffic related to cluster database changes and state changes is light but does vary slightly depending on the type of workload. Our focus is Hyper-V, which has light intra-cluster communications, but a SQL or Exchange cluster tends to have a higher amount of traffic. Once again, though, the size of the pipe is not as important as the latency. This is because in the event of a cluster state change, such as a node being removed from the cluster, the state change is synchronous among all nodes in the cluster. This means before the state change completes, it must have been synchronously applied to every node in the cluster, potentially 64 nodes. A high-latency network would slow down state changes in the cluster and therefore affect how fast services could be moved in the event of a failure.

The final type of communication over the cluster network is the CSV I/O redirection, and there are really two types of CSV communications, which I'll cover in detail later in this chapter, but both actually use SMB for communication. There are metadata updates such as file extend operations and file open/close operations that are lightweight and fairly infrequent, but they are sensitive to latency because latency will slow down I/O performance. Then there is asymmetric storage access, where all I/O is performed over the network instead of just the metadata. This asymmetric access, or redirected mode, is not the normal storage mode for the cluster and typically happens in certain failure scenarios such as a node losing direct access to the storage and requiring its storage access to be fulfilled by another node. If asymmetric access is used, the bandwidth of the network is important to handle the I/O.

The takeaway from the preceding explanation is that typically the bandwidth is not important; the latency is the critical factor, which is why traditionally the cluster had a dedicated network. As described in Chapter 3, it is now possible to use a converged network, but you should leverage Quality of Service (QoS) to ensure that the cluster network does get the required bandwidth and, more important, priority for its traffic because a high priority will ensure as low a latency level as possible. In Chapter 3 I focused on the bandwidth aspect of QoS because for most workloads that is most critical. However, you can also use QoS to prioritize certain types of traffic, which we want to do for cluster traffic when using converged fabric. The code that follows is PowerShell for Windows Server 2012 R2 that sets prioritization of the types of traffic. Note that the priority values range from 0 to 6, with 6 being the highest priority.

Once created, the policies can be applied using the `Set-NetQoSPolicy` cmdlet:

```
New-NetQoSPolicy "Cluster" -Cluster -Priority 6
New-NetQoSPolicy "Live Migration" -LiveMigration -Priority 4
```

You can find details on `New-NetQoSPolicy` and the different types of built-in filters available here:

```
http://technet.microsoft.com/en-us/library/hh967468.aspx
```

With QoS correctly configured, you no longer have to use a dedicated network just for clustering and can take advantage of converged environments without sacrificing performance.

I've mentioned a number of times about the heartbeat frequency of once a second and that if five consecutive heartbeats are missed, then a node is considered unavailable and removed from the cluster and any resources it owns are moved to other nodes in the cluster. Remember that the goal of clustering is to make services as available as possible, which means a failed node needs to be detected as quickly as possible so its resources and therefore workloads are restarted on another node as quickly as possible. The challenge here, though, is if the networking is not as well architected as would be liked, there may be times that 5 seconds was just a network hiccup and not actually a failure of a host (which with today's server hardware is far less common as most components are redundant in a server and motherboards don't catch fire frequently). The outage caused by taking virtual machines and moving them to other nodes and then booting them (because remember, the cluster considered the unresponsive node gone and so could not live migrate them) is far bigger than the few seconds of network hiccup. This is seen commonly in Hyper-V environments where networking is not always given the consideration it deserves, which makes 5 seconds very aggressive.

The frequency of the heartbeat and the threshold for missed heartbeats is actually configurable:

- `SameSubnetDelay`: Frequency of heartbeats, 1 second by default and maximum of 2

- `SameSubnetThreshold`: Number of heartbeats that can be missed consecutively, 5 by default with maximum of 120

You should be careful when modifying the values. Generally, don't change the delay of the heartbeat. Only the threshold value should be modified, but realize that the greater the threshold, the greater the tolerance to network hiccups but the longer it will take to react to an actual problem. A good compromise threshold value is 10, which actually happens automatically for a Hyper-V cluster. As soon as a virtual machine role is created on a cluster in Windows Server 2012 R2, the cluster goes into a relaxed threshold mode (instead of the normal Fast Failover), where a node is considered unavailable after 10 missed heartbeats instead of 5. The value can be viewed using PowerShell:

```
(Get-Cluster).SameSubnetThreshold
 10
```

This means without any configuration, the Hyper-V cluster in Windows Server 2012 R2 will automatically use the relaxed threshold mode, allowing greater tolerance to network hiccups. If you have cluster nodes in different locations, and therefore different subnets, there is a separate value for the heartbeat delay, `CrossSubnetDelay` (new maximum is 4), and the threshold, `CrossSubnetThreshold` (same maximum of 120). Once again, for Hyper-V the `CrossSubnetThreshold` value is automatically tuned to 20 instead of the default 5. Note that the automatic relaxed threshold is only for Hyper-V clusters and not for any other type of workload.

## CLUSTER VIRTUAL NETWORK ADAPTER

When talking about the cluster network, it's interesting to actually look at how the cluster network functions. Behind the scenes there is actually a Failover Cluster Virtual Adapter implemented by a `NetFT.sys` driver, which is why it's common to see the cluster virtual adapter referred to as NetFT. The role of the NetFT is to build fault-tolerant TCP connections across all available interfaces between nodes in the cluster, almost like a mini NIC Teaming implementation. This enables seamless transitions between physical adapters in the event of a network adapter or network failure.

The NetFT virtual adapter is actually a visible virtual device. In Device Manager, it can be seen if you enable viewing of hidden devices and also with the `ipconfig /all` command as shown here:

```
Tunnel adapter Local Area Connection* 11:

    Connection-specific DNS Suffix  . :
    Description . . . . . . . . . . . : Microsoft Failover Cluster Virtual Adapter
    Physical Address. . . . . . . . . : 02-77-1B-62-73-A9
    DHCP Enabled. . . . . . . . . . . : No
    Autoconfiguration Enabled . . . . : Yes
    Link-local IPv6 Address . . . . . : fe80::80fc:e6ea:e9a4:a940%21(Preferred)
    IPv4 Address. . . . . . . . . . . : 169.254.2.5(Preferred)
    Subnet Mask . . . . . . . . . . . : 255.255.0.0
    Default Gateway . . . . . . . . . :
    DHCPv6 IAID . . . . . . . . . . . : 688049663
    DHCPv6 Client DUID. . . . . . . . : 00-01-00-01-19-B8-19-EC-00-26-B9-43-DA-12
    NetBIOS over Tcpip. . . . . . . . : Enabled
```

Remember, this is not a real network adapter but rather a virtual device that is using whatever network has the lowest cluster metric but can move between different physical networks as required. The MAC address of the NetFT adapter is generated by a hash function based on the MAC address of the local network interface. A nice change in Windows Server 2012 is that it is now supported to sysprep a cluster member because during the specialize phase a new NetFT MAC address will be generated based on the new environment's local network adapters. Previously, the NetFT MAC was set at cluster membership and could not be changed or regenerated.

The user of the NetFT adapter is the cluster service. It communicates using TCP 3343 to the NetFT, which then tunnels over the physical network adapters with the fault-tolerant routes using UDP 3343. Figure 7.17 shows this. Notice that there are two physical network adapter paths because two network adapters in this example are enabled for cluster communications and the NetFT has built the fault-tolerant path.

What is interesting here is that the cluster service traffic essentially flows through the networking stack twice, once through the NetFT bound stack and then through the stack bound to the network adapter being used. In Windows Server 2012, a new component was introduced, the NetFT Virtual Adapter Performance Filter that was automatically bound to physical network adapters. When it sees any cluster traffic on the physical network adapter, it sends it to the NetFT adapter directly, bypassing the redirection through the physical network stack. This sounds good, but if you also have a guest cluster running on virtual machines within the

Hyper-V host cluster and guest VMs are running on different nodes in the cluster, the performance filter would grab not only the host cluster communications but also the guest cluster communications, which means the communication would never reach the virtual machines and therefore break clustering. To resolve this problem, the Microsoft Failover Cluster Virtual Adapter Performance Filter would need to be disabled in Windows Server 2012, which is why it's disabled by default in Windows Server 2012 R2.

**FIGURE 7.17**
Cluster network
properties

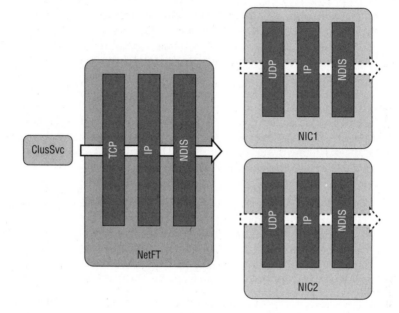

There are no manual firewall configurations required when using clustering. When the Failover Clustering feature is installed, a number of built-in inbound and outbound rules are automatically enabled for the inbox Windows Firewall. If you are using a third-party firewall solution, however, it's important that you enable the required firewall exceptions. The best way to do this is look at all the Failover Cluster firewall exceptions and emulate them in whatever firewall product you are using.

## Performing Cluster Validation

Now that you understand the importance of the cluster network and communications, it's time to actually get a cluster up and running, which is a simple process. The cluster validation process performs detailed tests of all the major areas related to the cluster configuration, such as network, storage, and OS tests and tests specific to Hyper-V to ensure that the cluster will be workable and supported by Microsoft.

As previously mentioned, the cluster validation should be performed prior to creating a cluster and anytime you make a major change to the cluster, such as adding a new node to the

cluster, adding a new network or adding new types of storage. Additionally, the cluster validation tool is a useful tool to run if you are experiencing problems with the cluster; it allows specific groups of tests to be run instead of all tests.

Provided the failover clustering feature is installed on the cluster nodes to perform a validation, follow these steps:

1. Start Failover Cluster Manager.

2. The root Failover Cluster Manager navigation node will be selected, which in the
   Management section has a Validate Configuration action, as shown in Figure 7.18, that
   you should click. If you wish to validate an existing cluster, select the cluster in Failover
   Cluster Manager and then click its Validate Cluster action.

3. Click Next on the introduction screen of the Validate a Configuration Wizard.

4. If this is a validation for what will be a new cluster, you must add all the servers that
   will become members of the new cluster by entering their names or clicking Browse and
   selecting them. Remember that all members of a cluster must be part of the same domain.
   As each name is entered, a check will be performed on the node. Once all machines are
   added to the server list, click Next.

5. The tests to be performed can be selected. For a new cluster, you should always leave the
   default of Run All Tests selected. Even for a validation of an existing cluster, it's a good
   idea to run all tests. However, you can select the Run Only Tests I Select option to expose
   an additional configuration page that allows you to select the specific tests you wish to
   run (shown in Figure 7.19, which I've edited to show all the Hyper-V options in detail). If
   the Hyper-V role is not installed, then the Hyper-V tests are not run. Notice the level of
   depth the cluster tests perform on Hyper-V. Click Next.

6. If you selected to perform storage checks on an existing cluster, you can select which storage will be validated. Storage validation involves testing arbitration and moving tested
   storage units, which would shut down any roles using the storage, so do not test any storage running roles such as virtual machines. I like to have a small LUN that I don't use
   that I keep for storage validations. If this is a validation for what will be a new cluster,
   then you are not prompted for which storage to validate. Click Next.

7. A confirmation is shown of the tests that will be performed. Click Next to start the
   validation.

8. The validation can take some time, especially if there is a large amount of storage
   attached, but the progress of the test and its success/failure is shown (Figure 7.20).

9. Once the validation is complete, a summary is displayed. The success/failure of each test
   is shown and a View Report button can be clicked to see the report results in the web
   browser with the details of each test. If the validation is for servers not yet in a cluster, a
   check box is automatically selected, Create The Cluster Now Using The Validated Nodes,
   which means when Finish is clicked, the Create Cluster Wizard will launch with the
   servers automatically populated. Click Finish to exit the validation wizard.

**FIGURE 7.18**
The empty Failover
Cluster Manager
interface

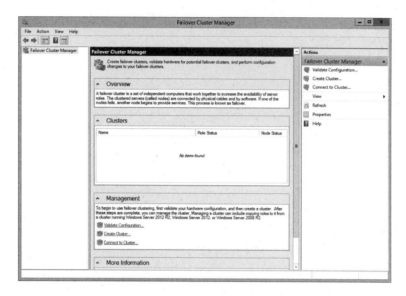

**FIGURE 7.19**
Cluster tests
available

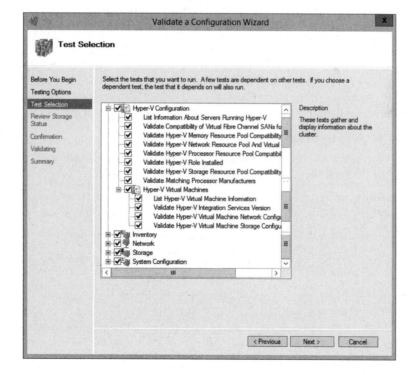

**FIGURE 7.20**
Cluster validation
in progress

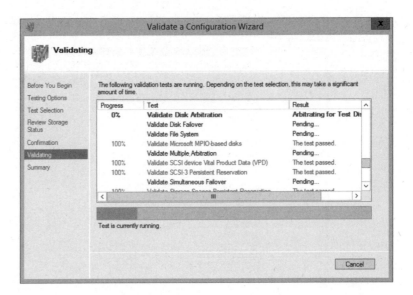

The validation reports are also saved to the folder C:\Windows\Cluster\Reports, which can be viewed at any time. The report name contains the date and time of execution. Open up a report and look; there is a huge amount of detail. These reports can be useful to keep as a record of the server configuration.

Validation can also be performed using PowerShell with the Test-Cluster cmdlet. This can be used to validate an existing cluster by passing a cluster name (or no cluster name and it will be performed on the local cluster) or used to validate nodes that will join a cluster by passing the server names of the future cluster members, as shown in these examples:

◆ Use Test-Cluster to validate the local cluster.

◆ Use Test-Cluster -Node node1,node2 to validate nodes node1 and node2 for a potential new cluster.

For more examples of Test-Cluster, view the Microsoft documentation at the following location:

http://technet.microsoft.com/en-us/library/ee461026.aspx

One useful tip is to select a specific disk for the purpose of storage testing. The disk can be passed using the -Disk parameter. For example, this just runs the storage test on a specific disk:

```
Test-Cluster -Cluster <cluster> -Disk "<disk, for example Cluster Disk 5>" `
-Include Storage
```

## Creating a Cluster

Once the validation process has been run, the next step is to create the cluster, which is actually very simple. At the end of the validation there was a check box option, Create The Cluster

Now Using The Validated Nodes. Keep that selected, and when you click Finish it will launch the Create Cluster Wizard. If you did not select the Create Cluster option, simply run the Create Cluster action and the only additional step you will need to perform is to specify the servers that will be joining the cluster. The only information you need to create the cluster is a name for the cluster and an IP address if you don't wish to use DHCP. Perform the following steps to complete the cluster process:

1. Click Next on the introduction page of the Create Cluster Wizard.

2. Enter the NetBIOS name that will be used to manage/access the cluster. If DHCP is used for the network adapters in the cluster servers, DHCP will automatically be used. If DHCP is not used, an IP address should be configured. Click Next.

3. The confirmation screen will be displayed. Leave the Add All Eligible Storage To The Cluster box checked because this will automatically add all storage that is accessible to all nodes in the cluster and that supports being clustered. Click Next.

4. The cluster will be created and a summary displayed. When the report is visible, review it and click Finish.

A computer object would have been created in Active Directory automatically and named the same as the cluster name specified during cluster creation. By default it will be created in the Computers container.

Note that by default the create cluster process selected the smallest cluster disk that was 512 MB or greater and initialized and formatted for the disk witness, whether there was an even or odd number of nodes. If you wish to change the witness use the More Actions ➤ Configure Cluster Quorum Settings and change it as previously described in this chapter.

## Creating Clusters with SCVMM

SCVMM can also help with clustering your Hyper-V hosts (and with 2012 R2, your Scale-Out File Server clusters). SCVMM can be used to initially deploy Hyper-V hosts as part of a cluster or take existing Hyper-V hosts and join them to a cluster. To use SCVMM to create and manage the cluster, it's important that SCVMM also fully manages the storage it uses. There are other requirements for using SCVMM to create and manage clusters:

◆ The cluster should meet the normal cluster requirements (part of Active Directory domain, same OS, and configuration level) and pass validation.

◆ The domain of the Hyper-V hosts must be trusted by the domain of the SCVMM management server.

◆ The Hyper-V hosts must be in the same host group in SCVMM.

◆ Hyper-V hosts must be on the same IP subnet.

Microsoft has detailed documentation on the requirements at

http://technet.microsoft.com/en-us/library/gg610630.aspx

The actual cluster creation is a wizard-driven process that validates the requirements of the cluster, enables the failover cluster feature on the hosts if it's not already installed, ensures that all storage is correctly unmasked to the hosts (remember, SCVMM must be managing the storage that is presented to the cluster), and makes each disk a Cluster Shared Volume. Follow these steps to create a cluster:

1. Open the SCVMM console and open the Fabric workspace.

2. Select Servers in the navigation pane.

3. From the Home tab, select Create ➤ Hyper-V Cluster.

4. Enter a name for the new cluster and select the Run As account to use to actually perform the configurations on each host. Click Next.

5. On the Nodes page, add the nodes that will be part of the cluster by selecting the servers and clicking the Add button. Then click Next.

6. If any of the nodes are using static IP configuration, you will be prompted for the IP configuration, which can be either an IP pool or a specific IP address to use. Enter the IP configuration and click Next.

7. Storage that can be clustered (that is, storage that is available to all the nodes) will be displayed. Select the storage to be used for the cluster, and then select the classification, partition style, file system, format instructions, and whether to make the disk a CSV. By default, a format is performed, so all data would be lost, although you can select Do Not Format in the File System area. Click Next.

8. Configure the virtual networks that will be available for all cluster nodes. Click Next.

9. On the Summary page, click Finish and the cluster will be created. Once the creation process is complete, the cluster will be shown in the Servers view of SCVMM.

Once the cluster is created, it can be fully managed with SCVMM, and there are some attributes you may want to customize. Right-click the cluster and selecting Properties. On the General page of the properties is a cluster reserve value that by default is set to 1. This defines the number of nodes in this cluster you want to be tolerant of failure. For example, a value of 1 means you want the cluster to be able to tolerate the failure of 1 node. This is used when deploying resources because SCVMM will ensure that the cluster is not overutilized so that it would not be able to run all deployed virtual machines in the event of a node failure. If you had a 4-node cluster and had the reserve set to 1, SCVMM would allow the deployment of only virtual machines that could be run on 3 nodes. If this was a lab environment where you just wanted to fill every node, then you could set the cluster reserve to 0. Alternatively, in a larger cluster, such as a 64-node cluster, you may want to increase the reserve value to 2 or 4 to support more nodes being unavailable. This value is important not just for node failures but also for maintenance where a node is drained of all virtual machines so it can be patched and rebooted. This means it's important in a production environment to always have the reserve set to at least 1 so that maintenance can be performed without having to shut down virtual machines.

The other tabs of the cluster properties show information about the status, storage, and networks. Figure 7.21 shows the view of the current shared volumes, giving easy insight into the utilization.

**FIGURE 7.21**
Shared volumes

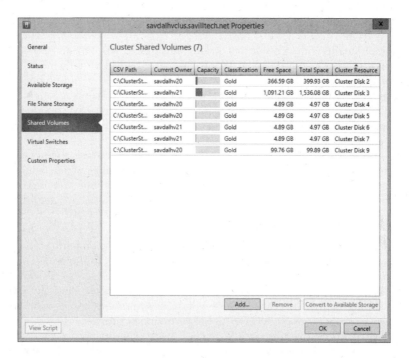

Another nice feature for the cluster is the ability to view the networking details via the View Networking action, as shown in Figure 7.22. This shows the cluster, the nodes in the cluster, and the networks that are connected to from each node.

**FIGURE 7.22**
Viewing the net-
working available
for a cluster

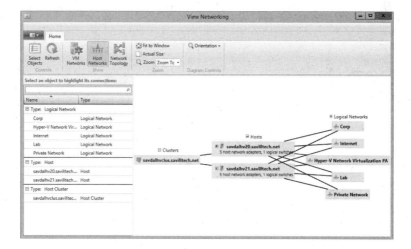

As with networking guidance, the best practice when using SCVMM to manage Hyper-V is to perform all actions from SCVMM, including creating clusters. If you do create clusters outside of SCVMM, then SCVMM will still detect them and allow them to be configured.

## Using Cluster Shared Volumes

Traditionally, with a cluster that has shared storage (which means the storage is accessible to all nodes in the cluster), only one node in the cluster would actually mount a specific LUN that is NTFS formatted. The basic problem is that NTFS is a shared nothing file system. It does not support multiple operating system instances connecting concurrently to it, which is the limitation. More specifically metadata updates such as file open/close of extension operations cannot be performed by multiple operating system instances; the actual SAN holding the LUNs supports multiple concurrent connections with no problem.

One solution would have been to create a new cluster-aware file system that could be mounted on multiple nodes in the cluster at the same time, which would remove the LUN failover requirement. However, this would have been a huge undertaking both from a development perspective and from a testing perspective when you consider how many services, applications, and tools are based around features of NTFS.

With this in mind, Microsoft looked at ways to make NTFS-formatted LUNs available to multiple nodes in a cluster concurrently, enabling all the nodes to read and write at the same time, and came up with Cluster Shared Volumes (CSV). In Windows Server 2012, when you're viewing a CSV in Disk Manager, the file system type shows as CSVFS instead of NTFS. Under the covers, CSVFS is still NTFS, but the CSVFS adds its own mini file system, which is leveraged to enable many of the capabilities I will discuss in this section. For the most part, though, it just acts as a pass-through to NTFS (or ReFS in Windows Server 2012 R2).

Prior to Windows Server 2012, to use Cluster Shared Volumes, the feature had to be manually enabled. CSV is now available by default, and to make a cluster disk a CSV, you select the disk in the Storage ➤ Disks view of Failover Cluster Manager and use the Add To Cluster Shared Volumes action, shown in Figure 7.23. This can also be performed using the Add-ClusterSharedVolume cmdlet and passing the clustered disk name, as in the following example:

```
Add-ClusterSharedVolume -Name "Cluster Disk 1"
```

**FIGURE 7.23**

Making a cluster disk a CSV

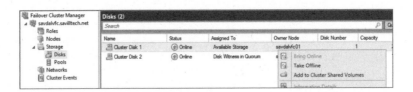

When a disk is enabled for CSV, any previous mounts or drive letters are removed and the disk is made available as a child folder of the %systemroot%\ClusterStorage folder as Volume<n>—for example, C:\ClusterStorage\Volume1 for the first volume, C:\ClusterStorage\Volume2 for the next, and so on. The content of the disk will be visible as content within that disk's Volume folder. Place each virtual machine in its own folder as a best practice, as shown in Figure 7.24.

The ClusterStorage structure is shared, providing a single consistent filename space to all nodes in the cluster so every node has the same view. Once a disk is added to Cluster Shared Volumes, it is accessible to all nodes at the same time. All nodes can read and write concurrently to storage that is part of ClusterStorage.

**FIGURE 7.24**

Viewing cluster shared volumes in Explorer

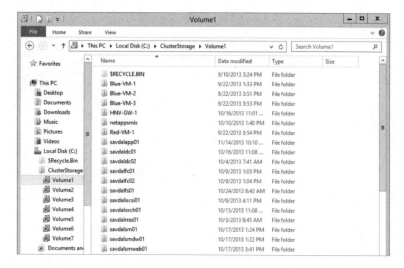

Remember that the problem with NTFS being used concurrently by multiple operating system instances is related to metadata changes and the chance of corruptions if multiple operating systems make metadata changes at the same time. Cluster Shared Volumes fixes this by having one node assigned to act as the coordinator node for each specific CSV. This is the node that has the disk online locally and has complete access to the disk as a locally mounted device. All of the other nodes do not have the disk mounted but instead receive a raw sector map of the files of interest to them on each LUN that is part of CSV, which enables the non-coordinator nodes to perform read and write operations directly to the disk without actually mounting the NTFS volume. This is known as Direct IO.

The mechanism that allowed this Direct IO in Windows Server 2008 R2 was the CSV filter (CsvFlt) that was injected into the file system stack in all nodes in the cluster that received the sector map from the coordinator node of each CSV disk and then used that information to capture operations to the ClusterStorage namespace and perform the Direct IO as required. In Windows Server 2012, this changed to the CSVFS mini file system. The CSV technology allows the non-coordinator nodes to directly perform IO to the disk, which is the most common activity when dealing with virtual hard disks. However, no namespace/metadata changes can be made by non-coordinator nodes, such as, for example, creating, deleting, resizing, and opening files. These operations require management of the NTFS file system structure, which is carefully controlled by the coordinator node to avoid corruption. Fortunately these types of actions are relatively rare, and when a non-coordinator node needs to perform such an action, it forwards the action via SMB to the coordinator node that then makes the namespace changes on its behalf since the coordinator has the NTFS locally mounted and thus has full metadata access. This is shown in action in Figure 7.25, where a single node is acting coordinator for both disks.

The CSV technology actually provides another very useful feature. In the event a non-coordinator node loses direct access to the LUN—for example, its iSCSI network connection fails—all of its IO can be performed over SMB via the coordinator node using the cluster network. This is known as redirected IO and is shown in Figure 7.26.

**FIGURE 7.25**
Cluster Shared
Volume normal
operation

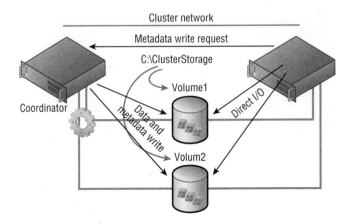

**FIGURE 7.26**
Cluster Shared
Volume in redi-
rected mode

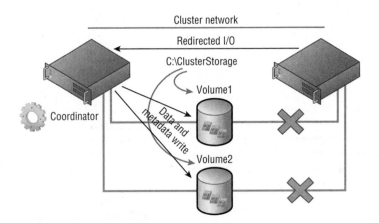

The actual coordinator node can be changed with minimal impact. There is a slight pause in IO if you move the coordinator to another node because the IO is queued at each node, but the pause is unlikely to be noticed, which is critical given how important the coordinator node is to CSV. Windows Server 2012 R2 introduces an automatic rebalancing of coordinator roles for CSV volumes, which is why typically you will see each node in the cluster having an equal number of disks it is coordinator for.

There are some considerations when you have multiple nodes directly writing to blocks on the disk in some operations, such as disk maintenance like defragmentation or performing a backup. In Windows Server 2008 R2, manual actions were required before performing these maintenance-type actions in addition to ensuring that actions were taking on the coordinator node for the disk. Windows Server 2012 really optimized this process to automatically place the CSV in maintenance mode when required, and it also moves the coordinator of the CSV between nodes as required. In Windows Server 2012, the backup applications are all CSV aware to ensure proper actions, plus in Windows Server 2012 R2, VSS actually got more intelligent; it understands when the VSS snapshot is performed even when running on a non-coordinator node. The ChkDsk process was completely rewritten in Windows Server 2012 to reduce the amount of volume offline time for potentially hours to at most 8 seconds, and on CSV there is actually no offline time at all because of the additional redirection introduced by CSV. Behind the scenes, if ChkDsk needs to run against a CSV volume, the handles between the physical disk and CSV are released, but CSV maintains the handles applications have to CSV. This means once ChkDsk has completed, within a few seconds the handles are restored between the disk and CSV. CSV can then map the restored handles back to the original and persisted handles of the applications to CSV, which means no break in access, only a slight pause in I/O.

Cluster Shared Volumes in Windows Server 2008 R2 supported only Hyper-V virtual machine workloads. In Windows Server 2012, CSV was also supported for a special type of cluster file share, a scale-out file server, which leveraged CSV as the storage for a file share that could be shared by multiple nodes in the cluster simultaneously. This was targeted to provide SMB 3 services for enterprise workloads such as Hyper-V virtual machines running over SMB 3, but it also allowed SQL Server databases to run over SMB 3. Windows Server 2012 R2 further adds to CSV-supported workloads, including SQL Server databases, without connecting to storage via SMB 3.

With CSV, all nodes in the cluster can access the same storage at the same time. This makes moving virtual machines between nodes simple because no dismount/mount is required of LUNs, but it also means you can reduce the number of LUNs actually required in the environment since virtual machines can now run across different servers, even when stored on the same LUN.

Windows Server 2012 introduced some additional features to CSV, specifically around performance with CSV Cache. CSV uses unbuffered IO for read and write operations, which means no caching is ever used. Windows Server 2012 introduced the ability to use a portion of the system memory as a read cache for CSV on each node in the cluster, which improves read performance. There are two steps to enable CSV Cache in Windows Server 2012 and only one step to enable it in Windows Server 2012 R2.

First, the amount of memory that can be used by the host for CSV Cache must be configured. In the following examples, I set a value of 4 GB.

Windows Server 2012:

```
(Get-Cluster).SharedVolumeBlockCacheSizeInMB = 4096
```

Windows Server 2012 R2:

```
(Get-Cluster).BlockCacheSize = 4096
```

For Windows Server 2012, the CSV Cache must be enabled on a per-disk basis. For Windows Server 2012 R2, the CSV Cache is enabled by default. To enable a disk for CSV Cache with Windows Server 2012, use the following command:

```
Get-ClusterSharedVolume "Cluster Disk 1" | `
Set-ClusterParameter CsvEnableBlockCache 1
```

The property is renamed EnableBlockCache in Windows Server 2012 R2 if you ever want to disable CSV Cache for a specific disk. No reboot is required when changing the CSV cache configuration.

In Windows Server 2012, the CSV Cache could be set to up to 20 percent of the system memory only. In Windows Server 2012 R2, it can be set to up to 80 percent of the system memory. The ability to set such a large cache is aimed at scale-out file servers, where committing more memory to cache will result in great performance gains. For Hyper-V clusters, typically it's better to have memory available to virtual machines, while some CSV cache will help overall performance.

Windows Server 2012 R2 adds support for ReFS with CSV. However, Hyper-V virtual machines are not supported on ReFS, which means you will still use NTFS to store your active virtual machines. Windows Server 2012 R2 also adds extended clustered storage space support, including support for storage spaces that use tiering, write-back cache, and parity. Data deduplication is also supported with CSV in Windows Server 2012 R2.

A nice addition in Windows Server 2012 R2 is increased diagnosibility for CSV. You can see the actual reason a CSV is in redirected mode, which previously was very hard to ascertain. Using the Get-ClusterSharedVolumeState PowerShell cmdlet will show the CSV state and the reason for the state. In the following example, all my CSVs are not redirected, but you can see where the reason for redirection would be displayed:

```
PS C:\> Get-ClusterSharedVolumeState


Name                         : Cluster Disk 2
VolumeName                   : \\?\Volume{2574685f-9cc6-4763-8d4b-b13af940d478}\
Node                         : savdalhv21
StateInfo                    : Direct
VolumeFriendlyName           : Volume2
FileSystemRedirectedIOReason : NotFileSystemRedirected
BlockRedirectedIOReason      : NotBlockRedirected

Name                         : Cluster Disk 2
VolumeName                   : \\?\Volume{2574685f-9cc6-4763-8d4b-b13af940d478}\
Node                         : savdalhv20
StateInfo                    : Direct
VolumeFriendlyName           : Volume2
FileSystemRedirectedIOReason : NotFileSystemRedirected
BlockRedirectedIOReason      : NotBlockRedirected
```

In a Hyper-V environment, I would recommend making every cluster disk used for storing virtual machines a CSV. There is no downside, and it enables the very efficient mobility of virtual machines and limits the number of LUNs required.

## Making a Virtual Machine a Clustered Virtual Machine

To create a new clustered virtual machine using Failover Cluster Manager, select the Virtual Machines ➤ New Virtual Machine action from the Roles navigation node, as shown in Figure 7.27. This will prompt for the node on which to initially create the virtual machine, and then the normal New Virtual Machine Wizard as seen in Hyper-V Manager will launch and allow all the attributes of the virtual machine to be specified.

**FIGURE 7.27**
Creating a new clustered virtual machine using Failover Cluster Manager

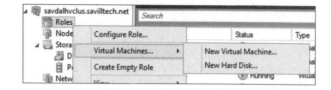

If you have existing virtual machines that are hosted on cluster nodes but are not actually cluster resources, it is easy to make a virtual machine a clustered resource:

1. Within Failover Cluster Manager, select the Configure Role action from the Roles navigation node.

2. Click Next on the wizard introduction screen.

3. From the list of available role types, scroll down and select Virtual Machine and then click Next.

4. You'll see a list of all virtual machines that are running on the cluster hosts but are not clustered. Check the boxes for the virtual machines you wish to cluster, as shown in Figure 7.28, and click Next.

5. Click Next on the configuration screen.

6. Once complete, click Finish.

**FIGURE 7.28**
Selecting the virtual machines to be made clustered resources

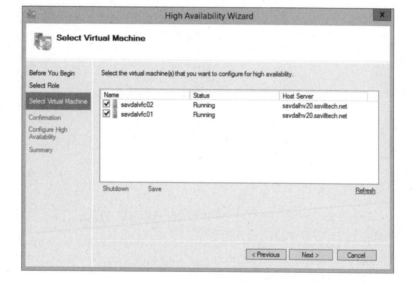

If you have virtual machines that are cluster resources but you wish to make them nonclustered, select the resource in Failover Cluster Manager and select the Remove action. This has no impact on the availability of the virtual machine and does not require the virtual machine to be stopped.

To create a clustered virtual machine in SCVMM, the process is exactly the same as creating a regular virtual machine. There is only one change to the virtual machine configuration. On the Configure Hardware page of the Create Virtual Machine Wizard, look at the Advanced options and select the Availability section. Check the Make This Virtual Machine Highly Available box, as shown in Figure 7.29. This will tell SCVMM to deploy this virtual machine to a cluster and make the virtual machine highly available.

**FIGURE 7.29**
Setting the high availability option for a virtual machine

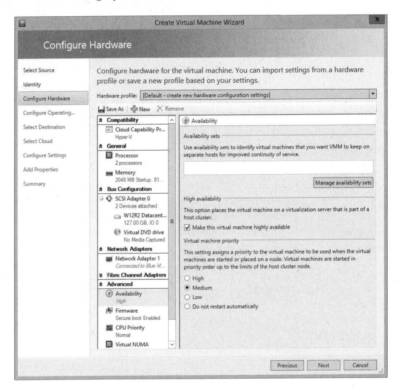

Once a virtual machine is clustered, a priority for the virtual machine can be configured via the virtual machine's properties within Failover Cluster Manager. The property can be set to Low, Medium, or High and is used when virtual machines need to be started, ensuring that the high-priority virtual machines start first and so on. This is also used where there are not enough resources to start all virtual machines and lower-priority virtual machines can be stopped to allow higher-priority virtual machines to start.

## Live Migration

Live Migration is the Hyper-V technology that enables a virtual machine to be moved between Hyper-V hosts. In Windows Server 2008 R2, Live Migration provided the functionality to migrate the memory and state of a virtual machine between hosts in a cluster while the virtual machine was still running. The storage of the virtual machine was available to both hosts in the cluster simultaneously through the use of Cluster Shared Volumes.

There are really six key stages to the original Live Migration process in Windows Server 2008 R2, and they remain today when using shared storage:

♦ A Live Migration connection is made between the source and target Hyper-V hosts.

♦ The virtual machine configuration and device information is transferred and a container virtual machine is created on the target Hyper-V host.

♦ The memory of the virtual machine is transferred.

♦ The source virtual machine is suspended and the state and remaining memory pages are transferred.

♦ The virtual machine is resumed on the target Hyper-V host.

♦ A reverse ARP is sent over the network to enable network traffic to find the virtual machine on the new host.

The transfer of the memory is the most interesting aspect of Live Migration. It's not possible to just copy the memory of a virtual machine to another node because as the memory is being copied, the VM is still running, which means parts of the memory being copied are changing, and although the copy is from memory to memory over very fast networks, it still takes a finite amount of time, and pausing the VM while the memory is copied would be an outage. The solution is to take an iterative approach that does not result in a perceived period of unavailability by any clients of the virtual machine and ensures that any TCP/IP connections do not timeout.

An initial transfer of the VM memory is performed, which involves the bulk of the information and the bulk of the time taken during a Live Migration. Remember that the virtual machine is still running and so we need a way to track pages of memory that change while we are copying. To this end, the worker process on the current node creates a "dirty bitmap" of memory pages used by the virtual machine and registers for modify notifications on the pages of memory used by the VM. When a memory page is modified, the bitmap of memory is updated to show that a page has been modified. Once the first pass of the memory copy is complete, all the pages of memory that have been marked dirty in the memory map are recopied to the target. This time only the changed pages are copied, which means there will be far fewer pages to copy and the operation should be much faster. Once again, though, while we are copying these pages, other memory pages may change and so this memory copy process repeats itself.

In an ideal world, with each iteration of memory copy, the amount of data to copy will shrink as the time to copy decreases and we reach a point where all the memory has been copied and we can perform a switch. However, this may not always be the case, which is why there is a limit to the number of memory copy passes that are performed; otherwise, the memory copy may just repeat forever.

Once the memory pages have all been copied or we have reached our maximum number of copy passes (five with Windows Server 2012 R2), it comes time to switch the virtual machine to execute on the target node. To make this switch, the virtual machine is suspended on the source node, and any final memory pages that could not be copied as part of the memory transfer phase are transferred along with the state of the VM to the target; this state of the VM that is transferred includes items such as device and processor state. The virtual machine is then resumed on the target node and an unsolicited ARP reply is sent, notifying that the IP address used by the VM has moved to a new location, which enables routing devices to update their tables. It is at this moment that clients connect to the target node. Yes, there is a slight suspend of the VM, which is required to copy the state information, but this suspend is milliseconds and below the TCP connection time-out threshold, which is the goal because clients will not disconnect during the Live Migration process and users are unlikely to notice anything. Once the migration to the new target is complete, a message is sent to the previous host notifying it that it can clean up the VM environment. This whole process is shown in Figure 7.30 to help clarify the sequence of steps.

**FIGURE 7.30**

The complete Live Migration process

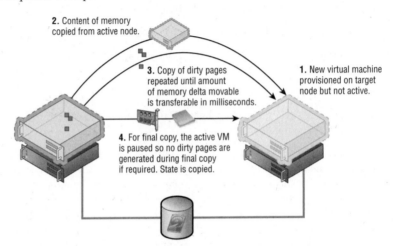

A Live Migration operation uses a large amount of network bandwidth, which meant in the 2008 R2 time frame a dedicated 1 Gbps network was advised for Live Migration. That then changed in the 2012 time frame to leverage converged networking and to use QoS to ensure that Live Migration received sufficient bandwidth.

When I talked about cluster networks, I mentioned that there was a metric used for the cluster networks to determine the prioritization of the networks to be used for cluster communications and the cluster network would use the lowest-cost network. The same prioritization is used for Live Migration, but to avoid conflicting with cluster traffic, Live Migration will automatically select the second-least-cost network. If you have a wish to use the same network for Live Migration as for cluster communications, you can override this using the graphical interface and using PowerShell.

In Windows Server 2008 R2, the network used for Live Migration was set on the virtual machine group properties via the Network For Live Migration tab. I have a write-up on the 2008 R2 method at the following location:

http://windowsitpro.com/windows/q-which-network-does-live-migration-traffic-use

This was changed in Windows Server 2012 to be a property of the cluster networks for the cluster. This can be set as follows:

1. Launch Failover Cluster Manager.

2. Right-click Networks and select Live Migration Settings.

**3.** A list of all cluster networks will be displayed. Check the networks that should be used for Live Migration and move them up and down to set their priority. As shown in Figure 7.31, I used the cluster network, which is a 10 Gbps network, and I leveraged QoS to ensure that Live Migration gets sufficient bandwidth. Click OK.

**FIGURE 7.31**
Setting the Live Migration network for a cluster

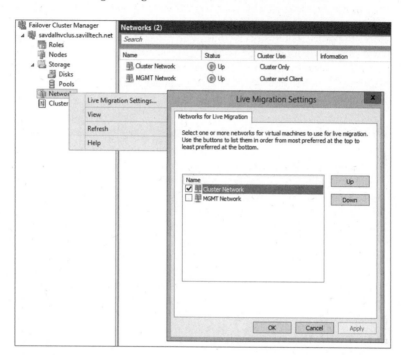

The Live Migration network can be changed using PowerShell, but it's the configuration to actually specify the name of the networks that should *not* be used for Live Migration. Therefore, if you have a specific network to be used for Live Migration, it should be placed in the following PowerShell command (in the example, my Live Migration network is named Migration Network):

```
Get-ClusterResourceType -Name "Virtual Machine" | Set-ClusterParameter `
 -Name MigrationExcludeNetworks -Value ([String]::Join(";",(Get-ClusterNetwork `
 | Where-Object {$_.Name -ne "Migration Network"}).ID))
```

In Windows Server 2008 R2, only one concurrent Live Migration could be performed between any two nodes in a cluster. For example, a Live Migration could be performed between node A and node B and a separate Live Migration could be performed between node C and node D, but it would not be possible to have two Live Migrations between A and B, nor would it be possible to have a Live Migration between node A and node B and between node A and node C. Failover Cluster Manager would also not allow the queuing of Live Migrations (although SCVMM did). The logic was that a single Live Migration would saturate a 1 Gbps network link and most datacenters were 1 Gbps. This has changed in Windows Server 2012 to allow multiple concurrent Live Migrations between hosts up to the limit you specify as part of the Live Migration configuration, which I will cover later in this chapter. Windows Server 2012 Failover Cluster Manager also introduces the concept of queuing Live Migrations that can not be actioned immediately.

In Windows Server 2012 and Windows Server 2012 R2 failover clusters, the Live Migration process remains the same. Virtual machines are always created on shared storage. However, instead of the virtual machines having to be stored on cluster storage, they can be stored on an SMB 3 file share that has been configured so each node in the cluster and the cluster account have full permissions. Note that if you are storing virtual machines in a cluster on a SMB 3 file share, it's important that the file share is not a single point of failure; it should be a scale-out file server, which itself is actually using Cluster Shared Volumes for the share storage. This also allows the use of Shared VHDX.

## Windows Server 2012 Live Migration Enhancements

One of the key reasons that Live Migration was restricted to within a cluster in Windows Server 2008 R2 was that the storage between the source and the target must be available, which meant Cluster Shared Volumes had to be used. Windows Server 2012 introduces the ability to use a SMB file share to store virtual machines, enabling hosts outside of a cluster to view the same storage provided they had the right permissions. This enabled a new type of Live Migration in Windows Server 2012, where SMB is leveraged to store the virtual machine and then the Live Migration technology is leveraged to move the virtual machine state and memory before the handle of the virtual machine's resources on the SMB share switches to the target node.

In a cluster environment, the network used for Live Migration is configured as part of the cluster network configuration. For nonclustered hosts, Live Migration must be configured and enabled if it was not enabled when you enabled the Hyper-V role on the server. The configuration for Live Migration is part of the Hyper-V host's core configuration, which is as follows:

1. Launch Hyper-V Manager (this can also be configured using SCVMM in the Migration Settings area of the server's properties).

2. Select the Hyper-V host, and select the Hyper-V Settings action.

3. Select the Live Migrations area.

4. Check the Enable Incoming And Outgoing Live Migrations check box, as shown in Figure 7.32.

5. Note that the number of simultaneous Live Migrations allowed can be configured, and this number is the maximum allowed and not necessarily the number of simultaneous Live Migrations that will always be performed. The migration module examines the amount of available bandwidth and dynamically ascertains if an additional Live Migration could be supported by the amount of bandwidth available on the migration network. If not, the migration is queued.

6. The configuration allows any network that is available to be used for Live Migration. Or you can select a specific network or networks by checking Use These IP Addresses For Live Migration and then adding and ordering IP networks that should be used in CIDR notation—for example, $xxx.xxx.xxx.xxx/n$, where the $n$ is the number of bits to use for the subnet mask, so 10.1.2.0/24 is the same as 10.1.2.0 with a subnet mask of 255.255.255.0. This would allow any IP address in the 10.1.2.0 network to be used for Live Migration.

To set this using PowerShell use the `Add-VMMigrationNetwork` and `Set-VMMigrationNetwork` cmdlets. Note that this setting is for the networks that can be used to receive incoming Live Migration. When a host is the source of a Live Migration, it will use whatever network it has available that can communicate with the Live Migration network configured to receive on the Live Migration target.

**7.** Click OK.

**FIGURE 7.32**
Enabling Live Migration for a stand-alone Hyper-V host

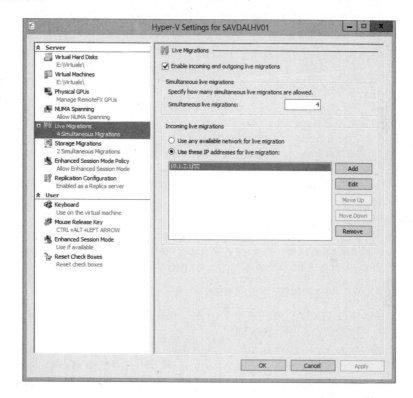

By default, CredSSP is used for the security between the source and target Hyper-V host, but there is another configuration option, known as constrained delegation, which I will cover later.

## Live Storage Move

Windows Server 2012 introduced the ability to move the storage of a virtual machine without having to shut down the virtual machine first, sometimes call Live Storage Move or Storage Migration.

Windows Server 2012 supports three main types of storage for virtual machines: direct attached; SAN based, such as storage connected via Fibre Channel or iSCSI; and new to Windows Server 2012 is support for SMB 3.0 file shares such as those hosted on a Windows Server 2012 file server or any NAS/SAN that has SMB 3.0 support. Windows Server 2012 Storage Migration allows the storage used by a virtual machine, which includes its configuration and virtual hard disks, to be moved between any supported storage with zero downtime to the virtual machine. This could be migration just to a different folder on the same disk, between LUNs on the same SAN, from direct attached to a SAN, from a SAN to a SMB file share—it doesn't matter. If the storage is supported by Hyper-V, then virtual machines can be moved with no downtime. It should be noted that storage migration cannot move nonvirtualized storage, which means if a virtual machine is using pass-through storage, that cannot be moved. The good news is with the new VHDX format that allows 64 TB virtual disks, there really is no reason to use pass-through storage anymore from a size or performance perspective. It is also not possible to perform a storage migration for a Shared VHDX.

The ability to move the storage of a virtual machine at any time without impacting the availability of the virtual machine is vital in two key scenarios:

◆ The organization acquires some new storage, such as a new SAN, or is migrating to a new SMB 3.0–based appliance and needs to move virtual machines with no downtime as part of a planned migration effort.

◆ The storage in the environment was not planned out as well as hoped and now either it's run out of space or it can't keep up with the IOPS requirements and virtual machines need to be moved as a matter of urgency. In my experience, this is the most common scenario, but it is important to realize that performing a storage migration puts a large additional load on the storage because every block has to be read and written to. Therefore, if you are having a storage performance problem, the problem will be worse during a storage migration.

The mechanics behind the Windows Server 2012 storage migration are actually quite simple, but they provide the most optimal migration process. Remember that the virtual machine is not moving between hosts; it's only the storage moving from a source location to a target location. Storage migration uses a one-pass copy of virtual hard drives that works as follows:

1. The storage migration is initiated from the GUI or PowerShell.

2. The copy of the source virtual hard disks, smart paging file, snapshots, and configuration files to the target location is initiated.

3. At the same time as the copy initiates, all writes are performed on the source and target virtual hard disks through a mirroring process in the virtual storage stack.

4. Once the copy of the virtual hard disks is complete, the virtual machine is switched to use the virtual hard disks on the target location (the target is up-to-date because all writes have been mirrored to it while the copy was in progress).

5. The virtual hard disks and configuration files are deleted from the source.

The storage migration process is managed by the VMMS process in the parent partition, but the heavy lifting of the actual storage migration is performed by the virtual machine's worker process and the storage virtualization service provider (VSP) in the parent partition. The mechanism for the copy of the storage is just a regular, unbuffered copy operation plus the additional IO on the target for the mirroring of writes occurring during the copy. However, in reality the additional IO for the ongoing writes is negligible compared to the main unbuffered file copy. The path used is whatever path exists to the target, which means if it's SAN, it will use iSCSI/ Fibre Channel, and if it's SMB, it will use whichever network adapter or network adapters have a path to the share. Any underlying storage technologies that optimize performance are fully utilized. This means if you are copying over SMB (from or to) and you are using NIC Teaming,

SMB direct, or SMB Multichannel, then those technologies will be used. If you are using a SAN and that SAN supports offloaded data transfer (ODX) and a virtual machine is being moved within a single LUN or between LUNs, ODX will be utilized, which will mean the move uses almost no load on the host and will complete very quickly.

The SAN ODX scenario is the best case, and for all the other cases, it is important to realize exactly what an unbuffered copy means to your system. The unbuffered copy is used because during the storage migration it would not be desirable on a virtualization host to use a large amount of system memory for caching of data. When a copy is performed, it can cause a significant amount of IO load on your system for both the reading of the source and writing to the target. To get an idea, try a manual unbuffered copy on your system using the xcopy command with the /J switch (which sets the copy to unbuffered). That is similar to the load a storage migration would inflict on your system (once again considering the ongoing mirrored writes as fairly negligible). Consider, therefore, moving a virtual machine between folders on a local disk, likely a worst-case scenario. The data would be read from and written to the same disk, causing a huge amount of disk thrashing. It would likely take a long time and would adversely affect any other virtual machines that use that disk. That is a worst-case scenario though. If the source and target were different storage devices, the additional load would not be as severe as a local move but would still need to be considered.

There is nothing Hyper-V specific about the disk IO caused by moving a VM. It would be the same for any data migration technology (except that other technologies may not have capabilities like ODX if a SAN is involved); ultimately the data has to be read and has to be written. This does not mean you should not use storage migration, but it does mean you should plan carefully when you use it. It's not something you would likely want to perform during normal working hours because of the possible adverse effect to other loads, and I suspect that's why at this time there is no automated storage migration process as part of the Dynamic Optimization in System Center Virtual Machine Manager that rebalances virtual machines within a cluster. If you detected a large IO load on a storage subsystem in the middle of the day, the last thing you would want to do is add a huge extra load on it by trying to move things around. The best option is to track IO over time and then at a quiet time move the virtual machines' storage, which would be easy to script with PowerShell or automate with technologies like System Center Orchestrator.

There is no specific configuration to enable storage migration. As previously stated, storage migration uses whatever path exists to communicate with the source and target storage and is enabled by default (in fact, you can't disable it). The only actual configuration is setting how many simultaneous storage migrations are allowed, and this is configured via the Hyper-V Settings action in the Storage Migrations area.

This can also be configured using PowerShell:

```
Set-VMHost -MaximumStorageMigrations <number to allow>
```

There is only one scenario where some extra configuration is required and that is if you are using SMB storage for the target of a storage migration and are initiating the migration remotely, either through Hyper-V Manager or PowerShell; that is, you are not running the tools on the actual Hyper-V host, which is the preferred management approach for Windows Server 2012 because all management should be done remotely using PowerShell or from a Windows 8/8/1 machine. When you configure SMB storage for use with Hyper-V, there are a number of specific permissions you set, including giving the administrators full control as the person creating a

VM on SMB or moving to SMB as part of a storage migration as their credential are used. To enable the credential to be used on a remote SMB file server, constrained delegation must be used, which I mentioned earlier related to Live Migrations in nonclustered environments. I will cover constrained delegation in detail later.

Storage migrations can be triggered through Hyper-V Manager or through PowerShell, and there are two different options when performing a storage migration. Move everything to a single location or select different locations for each item stored as part of a virtual machine, that is, one location for the configuration file, one for the snapshots, one for smart paging, one for virtual hard disk 1, one for virtual hard disk 2, and so on, as shown in Figure 7.33.

**FIGURE 7.33**
The different storage objects for a virtual machine

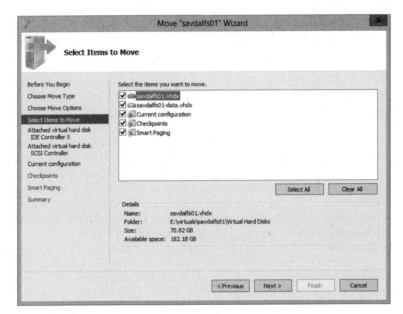

Start with performing the move using Hyper-V Manager, which will help you understand the options that are possible:

1. Launch Hyper-V Manager.

2. Select the virtual machine whose storage needs to be moved and select the Move action.

3. Click Next on the Before You Begin page of the wizard.

4. Since we are moving only the storage, select the Move The Virtual Machine's Storage option.

5. You can now choose to move all the virtual machine's data to a single location, which is the default, or you can select to move the virtual machine's data to a different location or move only the virtual hard disks for the virtual machine but none of its other data. Make your selection and click Next.

6. If you selected the default to move everything to a single location, you will be prompted for the new storage location. Just click next. If you selected either of the other two options,

you will have a separate page to select the target location for each element of the virtual machine's data, so set the location for each item and click Next.

**7.** Review your options and click Finish to initiate the storage migration.

To perform the storage migration from PowerShell, the `Move-VMStorage` cmdlet is used. If you're moving everything to a single location, it's very easy; you just pass the virtual machine name and the new target location with the `DestinationStoragePath` parameter (note that a subfolder with the VM name is not created automatically, so if you want the VM in its own sub-folder, you need to specify that as part of the target path), as in this example:

```
Move-VMStorage -DestinationStoragePath <target path> -VMName <vmname>
```

If, however, you want to move the parts to different locations, it's more complicated. Instead of `DestinationStoragePath`, the `SmartPagingFilePath`, `SnapshotFilePath`, and `VirtualMachinePath` parameters are used to pass the location for the smart paging file, snap-shots, and virtual machine configuration, respectively, but this still leaves the virtual hard disks. For the VHDs, the `Vhds` parameter is used. You could have more than one VHD for a single virtual machine (in fact you could have hundreds), and PowerShell does not really like an arbitrary number of parameters, so to pass the virtual hard disk's new location, you actually have to create a hash value for the `SourceFilePath` and `DestinationFilePath` for each virtual hard disk and then place those into an array that is passed to the –Vhds parameter. Pleasant!

In the following example, a virtual machine is being moved with three hard disks and its smart paging file, configuration, and snapshots. You don't have to move all elements of a virtual machine; you only need to specify the pieces you wish to move. Other elements not specified would just stay in their current location. Note that in the following command, squiggly brackets {} are used for the hash values (value pairs) while regular brackets () are used for the array.

```
Move-VMStorage -VMName <vmname> -SmartPagingFilePath d<smart paging file path> `
 -SnapshotFilePath <snapshot path> -VirtualMachinePath <vm configuration path> `
 -Vhds @(@{ "SourceFilePath " = "C:\vm\vhd1.vhdx "; `
 "DestinationFilePath " = "D:\VHDs\vhd1.vhdx "}, `
 @{ "SourceFilePath " = "C:\vm\vhd2.vhdx ";`
 "DestinationFilePath " = "E:\VHDs\vhd2..vhdx "}, `
 @{ "SourceFilePath " = "C:\vm\vhd3.vhdx ";`
 "DestinationFilePath " = "F:\VHDs\vhd3.vhdx "})
```

Once the storage migration is initiated, it will run until its finished; it will never give up no matter how long it may take. As the administrator, you can cancel the storage migration manu-ally through the Cancel move Storage action, or if you rebooted the Hyper-V host, this would also cause all storage migrations to be cancelled. The progress of storage migrations can be seen in the Hyper-V Manager tool or they can be queried through WMI, as shown here:

```
PS C:\ > Get-WmiObject -Namespace root\virtualization\v2 -Class Msvm_MigrationJob `
|`
 ft Name, JobStatus, PercentComplete, VirtualSystemName

Name            JobStatus       PercentComplete VirtualSystemName
----            ---------       --------------- -----------------
Moving Storage  Job is running               14 6A7C0DEF-9805-...
```

## Shared Nothing Live Migration

With the existing Live Migration technology and the new ability to move the storage of a virtual machine with no downtime, Windows Server 2012 introduced Shared Nothing Live Migration, which allows you to move virtual machines between any two Windows Server 2012 Hyper-V hosts with no downtime and no shared resource. This means no shared storage, no shared cluster membership; all that is needed is a gigabit network connection between the Windows Server 2012 Hyper-V hosts. With this network connection, a virtual machine can be moved between Hyper-V hosts, which includes moving the virtual machine's virtual hard disks, the virtual machine's memory content, and then the processor and device state with no downtime to the virtual machine. Do not think that the Shared Nothing Live Migration capability means Failover Clustering is no longer needed. Failover Clustering provides a high availability solution, while Shared Nothing Live Migration is a mobility solution but does give new flexibility in the planned movement of virtual machines between all Hyper-V hosts in your environment without downtime. It can supplement Failover Cluster usage. Think of now being able to move virtual machines into a cluster, out of a cluster, and between clusters with no downtime to the virtual machine in addition to moving them between stand-alone hosts. Any storage dependencies are removed with Shared Nothing Live Migration.

There is some assurance that the hosts in a failover cluster have a similar configuration, providing a confident migration of virtual machines between hosts without the fear of misconfigurations and therefore problems with virtual machines functioning if migrated. When Shared Nothing Live Migration is used to migrate virtual machines between unclustered Hyper-V hosts, there is no guarantee of common configuration, and therefore you need to ensure that the requirements for Shared Nothing Live Migration are met:

- At a minimum, there must be two Windows Server 2012 installations with the Hyper-V role enabled or the free Microsoft Hyper-V Server 2012 OS.

- Each server must have access to its own location to store virtual machines, which could be local storage, SAN attached, or an SMB share.

- Servers must have the same type of processor or at least the same family of processor (i.e., Intel or AMD) if the Processor Compatibility feature of the virtual machine is used.

- Servers must be part of the same Active Directory domain.

- Hosts must be connected by at least a 1 Gbps connection (although a separate private network for the Live Migration traffic is recommended but not necessary), which the two servers can communicate over. The network adapter used must have both the Client for Microsoft Networks and File and Printer Sharing for Microsoft Networks enabled because these services are used for any storage migrations.

- Each Hyper-V server should have the same virtual switches defined with the same name to avoid errors and manual steps when performing the migration. If a virtual switch has the same name as that used by a virtual machine being migrated, an error will be displayed and the administrator performing the migration will need to select which switch on the target Hyper-V server the VM's network adapter should connect to.

- Virtual machines being migrated must not use pass-through storage or shared VHDX (with Windows Server 2012 R2).

Earlier, in the section "Windows Server 2012 Live Migration Enhancements," I described how to enable and configure Live Migration in the scenario of using Live Migration when using SMB as the storage. It is the same for Shared Nothing Live Migration; there is no additional configuration required.

To perform a Shared Nothing Live Migration, select the Move action for a virtual machine, and for the move type, select the Move The Virtual Machine option, type the name of the destination Hyper-V server, and finally choose. how the virtual machine should be moved. For a Shared Nothing Live Migration, you need to select one of the first two options available: move the virtual machine's data to a single location or move the virtual machine's data by selecting where to move the items. The first option allows you to specify a single location where you want to store the virtual machine's configuration, hard disks, and snapshots on the target. The second option allows you to select a specific location for each of the virtual machine's items in addition to selecting which items should be moved. Make your choice and select the folder on the destination server. The move operation will start and will take a varying amount of time based on the size of the virtual hard disks and memory to move and also the rate of change. The move will be completed without any downtime or loss of connectivity to the virtual machine. This can be seen in a video at the following location:

www.savilltech.com/videos/sharednothinglivemigration/sharednothinglivemigration.wmv

The move can also be initiated using the `Move-VM` PowerShell cmdlet.

In my experience, the Shared Nothing Live Migration can be one of the most troublesome migrations to get working, so here are my top troubleshooting tips:

- First, make sure you have adhered to the requirements I listed previously.

- Check the Event Viewer for detailed messages. The location to check is `Applications and Services Logs > Microsoft > Windows > Hyper-V-VMMW > Admin`.

- Make sure the IP configuration is correct between the source and target. The servers must be able to communicate. Try pinging the target Live Migration IP address from the source server.

- Run the following PowerShell command in an elevated session to show the IP addresses being used for a server and the order in which they will be used:

  ```
  gwmi -n root\virtualization\v2 Msvm_VirtualSystemMigrationService |`
   select MigrationServiceListenerIPAddressList
  ```

- Make sure the Hyper-V (MIG-TCP-In) firewall exception is enabled on the target.

- The target server must be resolvable by DNS. Try an nslookup of the target server. On the target server, run the command `ipconfig /registerdns` and then run `ipconfig / flushdns` on the source server.

- On the source server, flush the Address Resolution Protocol (ARP) cache with the command `arp -d *`.

- To test connectivity, try a remote WMI command to the target (the Windows Management Instrumentation (WMI-In) firewall exception must be enabled on the target), such as the following:

  ```
  gwmi -computer <DestinationComputerName> -n root\virtualization\v2 Msvm_
  VirtualSystemMigrationService
  ```

- Try changing the IP address used for Live Migration; for example, if you're currently using 10.1.2.0/24, try changing to the specific IP address (e.g., 10.1.2.1/32). Also check any IPsec configurations or firewalls between the sources and target. Check for multiple NICs on the same subnet that could be causing problems, and if you find any, try disabling one of them.

◆ Try setting authentication to CredSSP and initiate locally from a Hyper-V server. If this works, the problem is the Kerberos delegation.

The most common problems I have seen are a misconfiguration of Kerberos and the IP configuration, but failing to resolve the target server via DNS will also cause problems.

## Configuring Constrained Delegation

Performing a Live Migration within a cluster removed the need for any special security considerations when moving virtual machines because the cluster account was used throughout migration operations. However, with Shared Nothing Live Migration, Live Migration using SMB, and the ability to move storage to SMB shares introduce some additional security, specifically credential considerations.

Outside of a cluster, each Hyper-V host has its own computer account without a shared credential, and when operations are performed, the user account of the user performing the action is normally used. With a Live Migration, actions are being taken on the source and target Hyper-V servers (and also file servers if the VM is stored on an SMB share, but more on that later), which both require that the actions be authenticated. If the administrator performing the Live Migration is logged onto the source or the target Hyper-V server and initiates Shared Nothing Live Migration using the local Hyper-V Manager, then the administrator's credentials can be used both locally and to run commands on the other Hyper-V server. In this scenario, CredSSP works fine and allows the user's credentials to be used on the remote server from the client, basically a single authentication hop from the local machine of the user performing the action (which happens to be one of the Hyper-V servers) to a remote server.

Remember, however, the whole goal for Windows Server 2012 and management in general: remote management and automation. Having to actually log on to the source or target Hyper-V server every time a Live Migration outside of a cluster is required is a huge inconvenience for remote management. If a user was logged on to their local computer running Hyper-V Manager and tried to initiate a Live Migration between Hyper-V host A and B, it would fail. The user's credential would be used on Hyper-V host A (which is one hop from the client machine to Hyper-V host A) but Hyper-V host A would not be able to use that credential on Host B to complete the Live Migration because CredSSP does not allow a credential to be passed on to another system (more than one hop).

This is where the option to use Kerberos enables full remote management. Kerberos supports constrained delegation of authentication, which means when a user on their local machine performs an action on a remote server, that remote server can use that user's credentials for authentication on another remote server. This initially seems to be a troubling concept, that a server I remotely connect to can just take my credentials and use them on another server, potentially without my knowing. The constrained part of constrained delegation comes into play and requires some setup before Kerberos can be used as the authentication protocol for Live Migration. To avoid exactly the problem I just described, where a server could use a remote user's credentials on another server, delegation has to be configured for each computer account that is allowed to perform actions on another server on behalf of another user. This delegation is configured using the Active Directory Users and Computer management tool and the computer account properties of the server that will be allowed to delegate. Additionally, when leveraging SMB file shares for Shared Nothing Live Migration or part of a storage migration, constrained delegation must be configured for the cifs service to each SMB file server. Follow these steps:

1. Launch Active Directory Users and Computers.

2. Navigate to your Hyper-V servers, right-click on one, and select Properties.

3. Select the Delegation tab.

4. Make sure Trust This Computer For Delegation To Specified Services Only is selected and that Use Kerberos Only is selected.

5. Click Add.

6. Click Users or Computers and select your other Hyper-V servers or SMB file servers. Click OK.

7. In the list of available services, select Microsoft Virtual System Migration Service or cifs for each server, depending on if it's a Hyper-V host (Microsoft Virtual System Migration Service) or SMB file server (cifs). Click OK.

8. Repeat the steps for all the Hyper-V hosts or SMB file shares it will communicate with that need constrained delegation as shown in Figure 7.34.

9. Repeat the whole process for each other Hyper-V so every Hyper-V host has constrained delegation configured to the other Hyper-V hosts and SMB file shares.

**FIGURE 7.34**
The different storage objects for a virtual machine

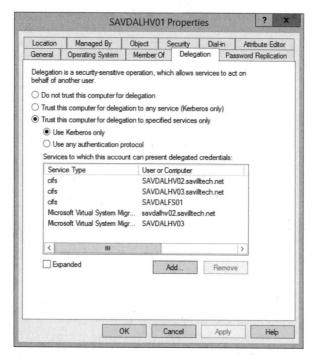

You *must* set authentication to Use Kerberos Only. It will not work if you select Use Any Authentication Protocol. It also won't work if you use the Trust This Computer For Delegation To Any Service (Kerberos Only) option. In my example configuration, I have a number of Hyper-V hosts, and in Figure 7.34, the configuration for savdalhv01 is shown. It has been configured for constrained delegation to the Hyper-V hosts savdalhv02 and savldalhv03 for cifs and migration in addition to the file server savdalfs01 for cifs only. I would repeat this configuration on savdalhv02 and savdalhv03 computer accounts, allowing delegation to the other hosts. The reason I have cifs enabled in addition to Microsoft Virtual System Migration Service for each Hyper-V host is in case virtual machines are using SMB storage that is being migrated, in which case cifs is required.

Once the Kerberos delegation is configured, the Live Migration will be able to be initiated from any remote Hyper-V Manager instance between trusted hosts. Remember also that all hosts that are participating in the Live Migration must have the same authentication configuration. While there is more work involved in the use of Kerberos authentication, the additional flexibility makes the additional work worthwhile and definitely recommended. To configure the authentication type to use from PowerShell, use the Set-VMHost cmdlet and set VirtualMachineMigrationAuthenticationType to either CredSSP or Kerberos.

### Initiating Simultaneous Migrations Using PowerShell

The Move-VM PowerShell cmdlet can be used to trigger Live Migrations, and to trigger multiple Live Migrations, the following can be used:

```
Get-VM blank1,blank2,blank3 | Move-VM -DestinationHost savdalhv02
```

The problem is this would live migrate blank1, and once that is finished, it would live migrate blank2, then blank3, and so on. It is not performing a simultaneous Live Migration, which is possible in Windows Server 2012.

One solution is to use the -parallel option available in PowerShell v3 workflows to trigger the Live Migrations to occur in parallel, as in this example:

```
Workflow Invoke-ParallelLiveMigrate
{
    $VMLIST = get-vm blank1,blank2,blank3
    ForEach -Parallel ($VM in $VMLIST)
    {
        Move-VM -Name $VM.Name -DestinationHost savdalhv02
    }
}

Invoke-ParallelLiveMigrate
```

The Live Migrations will now occur in parallel. Make sure your Hyper-V hosts are configured with the needed setting for the number of concurrent Live Migrations you wish to perform on both the source and destination Hyper-V hosts.

### Windows Server 2012 R2 Live Migration Enhancements

Windows Server 2012 R2 introduced performance improvements to Live Migration by allowing the memory transferred between hosts to be compressed or sent using SMB. The option to use compression means less network bandwidth and therefore faster Live Migrations, but additional processor resources are used to compress and decompress the memory. The option to use SMB is targeted to environments that have network adapters that support Remote Direct Memory Access (RDMA), which gives the fastest possible transfer of data with almost no server resource usage (compression is not used; it's not needed). By selecting SMB when network adapters support RDMA, you leverage the SMB Direct capability, which gives the best possible performance. Do *not* select SMB if your network adapters do not support RDMA.

By default, the compression option is selected for Live Migration, but it can be changed as follows:

1. Launch Hyper-V Manager (this can also be configured using SCVMM using the Migration Settings area of the server's properties).

2. Select the Hyper-V host and select the Hyper-V Settings action.

3. Select the Live Migrations area.

4. Click the plus sign next to Live Migrations to enable access to the Advanced Features configuration area.

5. Select the desired Performance Options setting, as shown in Figure 7.35. Notice also that the authentication protocol (CredSSP or Kerberos) is also selected in this area.

6. Click OK.

**FIGURE 7.35**
Setting the advanced configurations for Live Migration

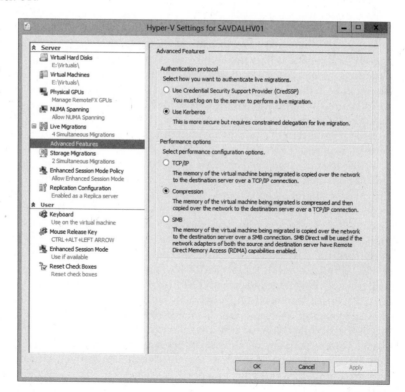

Windows Server 2012 R2 also enables cross-version Live Migration. This allows a Live Migration from Windows Server 2012 to Windows Server 2012 R2 (but not the other way). This Live Migration enables an upgrade from Windows Server 2012 to Windows Server 2012 R2 Hyper-V hosts without requiring any downtime of the virtual machines.

## Dynamic Optimization and Resource Balancing

When a virtual machine is created with SCVMM to a cluster, each node is given a star rating based upon its suitability to host the new virtual machine, and one of the criteria is the host's current utilization. Over time as new virtual machines are created, your cluster may become uneven with some hosts running many more virtual machines than others.

Dynamic Optimization (DO) is a new feature in SCVMM 2012 that is designed to ensure that the hosts within a cluster (Hyper-V, ESX, or XenServer) are spreading the virtual machine load as evenly as possible, avoiding certain hosts being heavily loaded (potentially affecting the performance of virtual machines) while other hosts are fairly lightly loaded. Dynamic Optimization is one of the most used features in almost all virtualized environments because of the dynamic balancing of virtual machines and because it removes a lot of the manual activities required of administrators around the placement of virtual machines. It is important to note that no amount of dynamic balancing can compensate for a poorly architected or over-loaded environment, and it's still critical to perform accurate discovery and design of virtual environments.

DO is not considered a replacement for Performance Resource Optimization (PRO), which was present in SCVMM 2008 and leveraged System Center Operations Manager for detail on utilization of the environment. Instead, DO is considered a complementary technology that does not rely on Operations Manager and is seen very much as a reactive technology. DO works by periodically looking at the resource utilization of each host in a cluster, and if the utilization drops below defined levels, a rebalancing is performed of the virtual machines to better equalize host utilization throughout the cluster. As Figure 7.36 shows, thresholds for CPU, memory, disk, and network can be defined in addition to how aggressive the rebalancing will be. The more aggressive it is, the quicker DO will be to move virtual machines for even a small gain in performance, which means more Live Migrations.

While any host group can have the DO configurations set, the optimizations will be applied only to hosts that are in a cluster, plus that cluster must support zero downtime VM migrations such as Live Migration on Hyper-V, XenMotion, and vMotion on ESX. A manual DO can be initiated at any time by selecting a host cluster and running the Optimize Hosts action, which will display a list of recommended migrations. The great part is that this manual DO can be used even if DO is not configured on the actual host group, allowing one-off optimizations to be performed.

PRO is still present in SCVMM 2012. It leverages Operations Manager and is used as a more long-term placement technology, and it's also the only extensible placement technology. Third-party PRO packs can be installed to extend the placement logic.

Also in Figure 7.36 is an option to enable Power Optimization (PO, but I'm not going to refer to it as that). While Dynamic Optimization tries to spread load across all the hosts in a cluster evenly, Power Optimization aims to condense the number of hosts that need to be running in a cluster to run the virtual machine workload without negatively affecting the performance of the virtual machines and powering down those not required. Consider a typical IT infrastructure that during the workday is busy servicing employees and customers but during non-work hours is fairly idle. Power Optimization allows thresholds to be set to ensure that VMs can be consolidated and evacuated hosts can be powered down, provided the remaining running hosts don't have any CPU, memory, disk, or network resource drop below the configured thresholds.

**FIGURE 7.36**
Dynamic
Optimization
options for a host
group

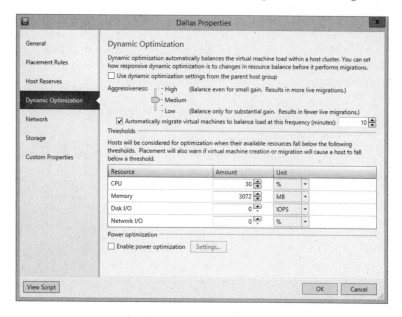

This is similar to the configuration options we set for DO, but this time it's controlling how much consolidation can occur. Your Power Optimization thresholds should be set higher than those for Dynamic Optimization because the goal of Power Optimization is to consolidate in quiet times and if the Power Optimization thresholds were lower than the Dynamic Optimization thresholds, then hosts would be powered off and lots of Live Migrations would occur. VMs would be moved around and the hosts that were just powered off would be powered on again. The Power Optimization thresholds also need to be generous, leaving plenty of spare resource because resource utilization fluctuates even in quiet times and eventually it will pick up again during busy times. It will take time to power on and boot the servers that were powered down during Power Optimization times, so plenty of buffer capability is required to ensure no resource shortage.

Additionally, as Figure 7.37 shows, you can set the times Power Optimization can occur. In this example, I don't want Power Optimization to occur during business hours except for a few exceptions, however there is no reason to stop Power Optimization during working hours providing you set well-defined thresholds to ensure that hosts have sufficient spare resources and won't suddenly be overtaxed during the time it takes to power back on servers that were powered down.

Waking servers is actually important because we don't want to power down servers that are not needed at a certain time and then be unable to start them up when they are needed again. A powered-down host is started using the host's Baseboard Management Controller (BMC), which needs to be configured on a per-host basis, and if the BMC is not present in a host or not configured, the host will not be able to be powered off as part of the Power Optimization process.

In partnership with the SCVMM placement logic and the Dynamic Optimization is the ability to create placement rules that can guide where virtual machines are placed. SCVMM contains 10 custom properties named Custom1 through Custom10. You can also create additional custom properties for the various types of SCVMM objects, such as a virtual machine (VM), a virtual machine template, hosts, host groups, clouds, and more.

You might create a custom property to store information, such as a VM's cost center, primary application function, desired physical location, or a contact email address—anything you can think of. These properties can then be used for administrators and business users to more easily understand information about assets in SCVMM and for reporting. The real power is realized when your custom properties are combined with custom placement rules that can utilize the custom properties to help control where VMs are placed.

**FIGURE 7.37**

Power Optimization options for a host group

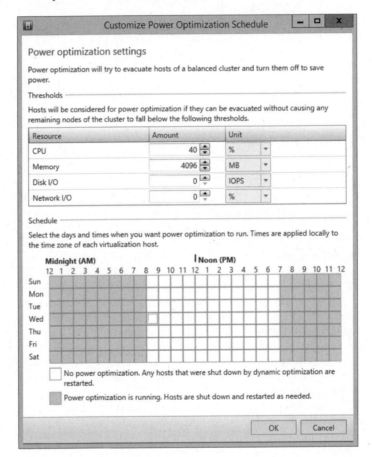

For example, consider the scenario in which each business unit group has its own set of hosts. You could create a cost center property for VMs and hosts and then create a custom placement rule that says the cost center of the VM must match that of the host for placement.

These rules are used both for initial placement and as part of Dynamic Optimization. It's important to note when you create your custom placement rules that you have options if the rule *should*, *must*, or *not* match. *Should* means the placement will try to match but doesn't have to and if placement violates the rule, a warning is generated. If *must* is used, then placement isn't possible if the rule is violated. To create a custom property, use the following procedure:

1. Start the Virtual Machine Manager console.

2. Navigate to the VMs And Services workspace, select the VM you want to set a custom property for, and open its properties.

3. Select the Custom Properties area, and click the Manage Custom Properties button.

4. In the Manage Custom Properties dialog, click the Create button.

5. Enter a name and description for the custom property and click OK.

6. The new custom property will be available in the list of available properties. Select it and click the Add button so it becomes an assigned property, then click OK. Note that the View Script button is available to show Windows PowerShell script to perform the action you just performed in the GUI, such as, for example:

```
New-SCCustomProperty -Name "Cost Center" `
-Description "Cost Center of the object" -AddMember @("VM")
```

7. You can now set a value for the custom property, and again the View Script button will show you the PowerShell script to perform the action.

8. Now select the properties of a host group, select the Custom Properties area, and click Manage Custom Properties. The custom property you already created is available. Add it to the assigned properties and enter a value.

9. In the same host group properties dialog is the Placement Rules page, which allows you to select custom properties. It also shows you how the custom property must/should relate to the host, as shown in Figure 7.38.

10. Click OK to all dialogs.

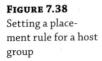

**FIGURE 7.38**
Setting a place-
ment rule for a host
group

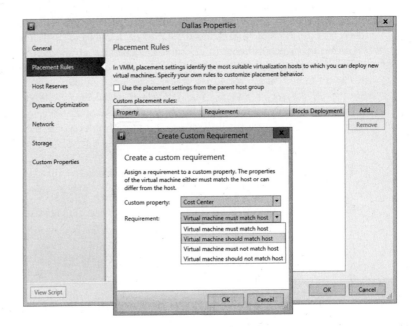

# The Bottom Line

**Understand the quorum model used in Windows Server 2012 R12.**   Windows Server 2012 R2 removes all the previous different models that were based on how votes were allo-cated and the type of quorum resource. In Windows Server 2012 R2, each node has a vote and a witness is always configured, but it's only used when required. Windows Server 2012 intro-duced dynamic quorum, which helps ensure that clusters stay running for as long as pos-sible as nodes' votes are removed from quorum because the nodes are unavailable. Windows Server 2012 R2 added dynamic witness to change the vote of the witness resource based on if there are an odd or even number of nodes in the cluster.

**Identify the types of mobility available with Hyper-V.**   Mobility focuses on the ability to move virtual machines between Hyper-V hosts. Virtual machines within a cluster can be live migrated between any node very efficiently since all nodes have access to the same storage, allowing only the memory and state to be copied between the nodes. Windows Server 2012 introduced the ability to move the storage of a virtual machine with no downtime, which when combined with Live Migration enables a Shared Nothing Live Migration capability that means a virtual machine can be moved between any two Hyper-V hosts without the need for shared storage or a cluster, with no downtime to the virtual machine.

Shared Nothing Live Migration does not remove the need for failover clustering but provides the maximum flexibility possible, enabling virtual machines to be moved between stand-alone hosts, between clusters, and between stand-alone hosts and clusters.

**Master It**   Why is constrained delegation needed when using Shared Nothing Live Migration with remote management?

**Understand the best way to patch a cluster with minimal impact to workloads.** All virtual machines in a cluster can run on any of the member nodes. That means before you patch and reboot a node, all virtual machines should be moved to other nodes using Live Migration, which removes any impact on the availability of the virtual machines. While the migration of virtual machines between nodes can be performed manually, Windows Server 2012 failover clustering provides Cluster Aware Updating, giving you a single-click ability to patch the entire cluster without any impact to virtual machines' availability. For pre–Windows Server 2012 clusters, SCVMM 2012 also provides an automated patching capability.

# Chapter 8

# Hyper-V Replica and Cloud Orchestration

High availability is essential for providing the most resilient infrastructure possible for a Hyper-V environment in order to ensure the availability of virtual machines; however, the ability to provide disaster recovery services to protect against the loss of an entire site is becoming a higher priority for many organizations. Windows Server 2012 introduced a new capability to Hyper-V that provides replication from one Hyper-V server to another, independent of any cluster or storage replication capabilities.

This chapter covers the options for providing disaster recovery for services in an organization and explains how Hyper-V Replica fits into a complete disaster recovery solution. The chapter also presents the options for providing orchestration of disaster recovery failover.

In this chapter, you will learn to

- Identify the best options for providing disaster recovery for the different services in your organization

- Describe the types of failover for Hyper-V Replica

- Explain the automated options for Hyper-V Replica failover

## The Need for Disaster Recovery and DR Basics

Modern organizations have various applications that are used internally by partners and by customers. These applications range from ones that are "nice to have" but not essential to doing business to those that would shut down the company if not available. Even the briefest outage of these business-critical applications can cause organizations harm in multiple ways, including the following:

- Financial loss through not being able to perform normal business functions

- Damage to reputation through publically visible outages that erode confidence in the organization for external parties

- Potential compliance gaps to regulatory requirements

It is therefore important to ensure that business-critical applications are always available, both within the primary datacenter through high availability technologies and also in alternate locations through disaster recovery technologies (although often a single technology can be leveraged for both high availability and disaster recovery). To provide disaster recovery, the data related to an application must be available in the alternate location, which means data replication. There must be means to run the application and connect to it, which means compute and network resources are required.

It is important to understand which applications are critical to the organization, and that can be ascertained only with the involvement of the business groups. Once the business-critical applications are identified, you must understand the dependent applications and services of those applications because protecting the business-critical applications without their dependencies would result in a nonfunctional solution in the event of a system outage or disaster scenario.

As an example, consider a typical line-of-business application that may run on one or more application servers. That application may leverage a SQL database that runs on a separate infrastructure, it may publish services through a corporate reverse proxy that is Internet facing, and it may require Active Directory for authentication. For the line-of-business application to be functional, all those dependent services must be available. In fact, when planning for high availability and disaster recovery, it's necessary to protect the applications and services that the target application depends on at the same or higher protection level.

There are many ways to provide resiliency and availability to services locally within a location and between locations, and there is no single "best" technology; rather, it is important to utilize the best availability technology for specific applications and services. Many availability solutions leverage the failover clustering feature that was covered in the previous chapter. A cluster-enabled application is protected from the failure of a node and will either seamlessly transition to another node or restart on another node without any administrator intervention.

Traditionally, a physical location was the boundary for a cluster for the following reasons:

◆ Cluster applications historically required access to shared storage that was facilitated via SAN storage and connected using technologies such as iSCSI and Fibre Channel. Making shared storage available to a remote SAN was typically not possible because of the latencies introduced with remotely accessing storage, and having a remote site dependent on storage in another remote site defeated the point of having a multisite cluster, which was to protect from a site failure. The solution was to have SAN-level replication, which historically was not available or was prohibitively expensive.

◆ Nodes in a cluster required a high-quality connection between nodes that was not tolerant to latency. This network was used for heartbeats between nodes to ensure all nodes were healthy and available. Cluster resources required an IP address that could not be changed between locations. Most multisite environments use different IP networks at the different locations, which meant that using clustering in a multisite environment, complex VLAN configurations, and geonetworks were required.

◆ Clusters used a special quorum disk that provided the foundation for partitioning protection. This quorum disk had to always be available, which typically meant it was located in one physical location.

Windows Server 2008 and a new shift in many datacenter applications removed these barriers for enabling multisite clusters. Key datacenter applications such as SQL Server and Exchange introduced options that did not require shared storage and instead leveraged their own data replication technologies. Failover clustering introduced changes that enabled multiple IP addresses to be allocated to a resource, and whichever IP address was required for the site that the resource was active in was used. Failover clustering also enabled more flexible heartbeat configurations, which tolerated higher latency networks; in addition, the reliance on a quorum disk was removed, offering additional quorum models based on the number of nodes and even a file share located at a third site. Being able to run clusters over multiple locations without shared storage enables certain disaster recovery options that will be discussed.

When designing a disaster recovery solution, there are typically many options available that offer different levels of recoverability. The *recovery point objective* (RPO) is the point you want to recover to in the event of a disaster. For example, only 30 minutes of data should be lost. The *recovery time objective* (RTO) is how quickly you need to be up and running in the event of a disaster. For example, the systems should be available within 4 hours in the event of a disaster. It's important to understand the RPO and RTO requirements for your systems when designing your disaster recovery solution. Also, different systems will likely have different requirements.

It is important to be realistic about the capabilities of your organization. An alternative to implementing new disaster recovery solutions for services may be to host the service in a public cloud infrastructure that provides site resiliency as part of the service. Using the public cloud as the disaster recovery location can also be an option.

Create very detailed processes that will be used in the event of a disaster to facilitate the failover. These processes should be updated any time a system changes or a new system is added. Disaster recovery tests should be performed at least every six months. Ensure the disaster recovery plans do not assume any amount of knowledge because the regular IT personal may not be available in the event of a disaster.

## Asynchronous vs. Synchronous Replication

As discussed, disaster recovery requires having the application data available in the disaster recovery location. This either requires the data to be stored somewhere that is available to both locations such as in the public cloud or, more commonly, requires the data to be stored in both locations and replication technologies to be used to keep the replica copy of the data synchronized with the primary (live) copy of the data.

The mode of the replication can be either asynchronous or synchronous.

**Asynchronous Mode**    This mode allows transactions to be committed on the primary source before the transaction has been sent to the replicas or has been acknowledged. The exact mechanism for asynchronous replication differs, but the key point is the primary source can continue working independently of the replica receiving and acknowledging the data. This gives the best performance on the primary replica (although there is always a slight risk of data loss in a failure situation because data is committed on the primary before it's committed or potentially even sent to the replica).

**Synchronous Mode**    This mode ensures no transactions are committed on the primary source until they are acknowledged on the replica. This ensures there is no risk of data loss, but this will incur some performance impact because of the additional delay while waiting for the acknowledgments from the replica. The higher the latency between the primary and the replica, the greater the performance impact.

Nearly every type of cross-site replication leverages asynchronous as the replication type because of the typical high latency between different locations and the performance impact that synchronous replication across high latency links imposes. Synchronous replication is typically reserved within a datacenter for highly critical data that cannot risk any kind of data loss.

SQL Server is a good example of a workload that leverages both asynchronous and synchronous replication with its AlwaysOn technology. AlwaysOn provides the replication of

SQL databases between a primary replica and one or more secondary replicas. Within a data-center, synchronous AlwaysOn replication may be used; between locations, the asynchronous AlwaysOn replication is typically used. SQL AlwaysOn actually allows switching between replication types, which opens up some interesting failover solutions such as running in asynchronous normally but switching to synchronous prior to failover to ensure no data loss.

Many storage solutions such as SANs offer replication at a storage level from one SAN to another, and very high-end SANs can actually offer a synchronous replication capability. This is typically expensive and is specific to the type of SAN used. The benefit of using SAN-level replication where available is that a cluster can then use the SAN storage in multiple locations as a single logical storage device, enabling clusters to span multiple locations with "shared" storage. Some large organizations leverage this type of SAN replication for their tier 1 workloads.

## Introduction to Hyper-V Replica

The news over the past few years has been filled with natural disasters such as Hurricane Sandy that have caused a loss of life and huge impacts to the infrastructure of entire cities. Even if the possibility of this type of disaster is known about weeks in advance, many organizations lack the technologies to enable disaster recovery to alternate locations. In the previous section, I talked about SAN-level replication, which is expensive and has high requirements that are not available to many organizations. Some applications such as SQL, Exchange, and Active Directory have their own replication technologies to enable disaster recovery protection, but many other applications do not have any kind of replication capability. As more and more of the datacenter is using virtualization, organizations are looking for a solution at the virtualization layer to help in disaster recovery planning.

Windows Server 2012 was an enormous release, particularly with regard to virtualization and enabling cloud services. One of the biggest new features was the introduction of Hyper-V Replica. Hyper-V Replica introduces the ability to replicate a virtual machine asynchronously to a second Hyper-V host. The target Hyper-V server, the *replica*, does not have to be part of a cluster with the primary Hyper-V host (in fact, the replica cannot be in the same cluster as the primary), does not need any shared storage, and does not even require dedicated network infrastructure for the replication. The goal of Hyper-V Replica is to enable disaster recovery capabilities for any Hyper-V environment without steep requirements, and this is achieved through its use of asynchronous replication.

Hyper-V Replica uses asynchronous replication efficiently and at a high level works as follows:

1. When a virtual machine is enabled for replication, a new virtual machine is created on the Hyper-V replica host that matches the configuration of the primary virtual machine, and the replica virtual machine is turned off.

2. The storage of the primary virtual machine is replicated to the replica virtual machine, and a log is started on the primary virtual machine for the VHDs being replicated that stores the writes to the VHDs. The log file is stored in the same location as the source VHD.

3. Once the initial replication of the storage is complete, the log file is closed. A new log file is started to track ongoing changes, and the closed log file is sent to the replica Hyper-V host and merged with the VHDs for the replica VM. The replica VM remains turned off.

4. At a defined time interval, the log file is closed, a new one is created, and the closed log file is sent to the replica and merged.

Note that the only replication is of the virtual hard disks of the virtual machine, not the ongoing configuration of the virtual machine and not the memory. This is why you cannot enable Hyper-V Replica for virtual machines that leverage virtual Fibre Channel, iSCSI, or pass-through storage. The virtual machine must use virtual hard disks for all storage because it is through the VHD implementation that replication is enabled. If you use virtual Fibre Channel or iSCSI, the assumption would be that the SAN is performing some level of replication between the primary and replica locations, which means it would make more sense for that SAN replication to replicate the VHDs of the virtual machine as well as the LUNs attached to the VM using virtual Fibre Channel/iSCSI. You would not want two different replication technologies used that would be out of sync with each other.

Because Hyper-V Replica uses asynchronous replication, there is a period where the replica is missing some of the data from the primary source. Potentially, in an unplanned failure, a certain amount of data may be lost. The exact amount of loss depends on how frequently the replica is updated. In Windows Server 2012, this was every 5 minutes, but in Windows Server 2012 R2, it can be every 30 seconds, every 5 minutes, or every 15 minutes. This possible data loss needs to be compared against the RPO of the application. If the application has an RPO of 5 minutes, then you can replicate at a 5-minute or 30-second interval. If the RPO is 1 minute, then you must replicate at the 30-second interval and also ensure there is sufficient bandwidth to handle the transmission of logs from the source to the replica. The good news is that because the replication is asynchronous, the introduction of the replica does not introduce any performance degradation on the source virtual machine and does not require very fast, low-latency network connections between the source host and the replica host.

The use of asynchronous replication by Hyper-V Replica opens up the use of replication for disaster recovery scenarios to many more scenarios and types of companies. These are some key ones that are often considered:

◆ Datacenter-to-datacenter replication for tier 1 applications for organizations without SAN-level replication such as small and medium-sized organizations

◆ Datacenter-to-datacenter replication for tier 2 applications for organizations with SAN-level replication but that don't want to use the SAN-level replication for applications that are not tier 1

◆ Branch office–to–head office replication to protect applications hosted at the branch location

◆ Hoster location 1–to–hoster location 2 replication for hosting companies

Small organizations that do not have a second datacenter can replicate to a hoster as the secondary datacenter for DR needs or even to a consulting organizations datacenter for their clients.

There are many more scenarios, including anything that is enabled through the asynchronous replication of a virtual machine. The key point is that with Hyper-V Replica, the ability to replicate virtual machines is now an option for any organization with two locations. As I will cover later in the chapter, it's an option even if an organization has only one location. It is also important to note that Hyper-V Replica is completely agnostic of the underlying storage technology used.

## Enabling Hyper-V Replica

Hyper-V Replica is simple to configure, and the easiest way to really understand how Hyper-V Replica works is to walk through its setup options and enable replication for a virtual machine. The first step in using Hyper-V Replica is to configure the replica Hyper-V server to accept requests for it to host a replica. This is performed using Hyper-V Manager. Select Hyper-V Settings from the server's list of actions, and in Hyper-V Settings, select the Replication Configuration list of configurations, as shown in Figure 8.1. Check the Enable This Computer As A Replica Server. Then you have a couple of choices to make.

**FIGURE 8.1**
Enabling inbound replication for a Hyper-V server

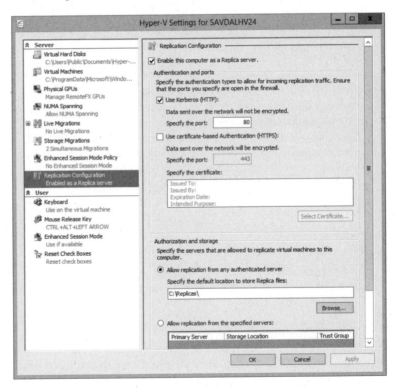

The first choice is to enable the use of Kerberos, which uses HTTP, or certificate-based authentication, which uses HTTPS. Kerberos is the simpler option to configure but requires that the primary and replica Hyper-V servers use Kerberos authentication and therefore are part of the same Active Directory forest or trusted domain. When using Kerberos, the replication of data between the primary and replica is not encrypted and is sent over the standard HTTP port 80. If encryption is required, then the Windows IPsec implementation could be used. The other option is to use certificate-based authentication, which enables the primary and replica to *not* be part of the same Active Directory forest or even organization and requires a certificate to be specified for use with an added benefit of using HTTPS, meaning all data transferred is now encrypted. Both Kerberos and certificate-based authentication can be enabled; in that case, when a new replication relationship is established, the administrator configuring the replication will be given a choice to use either Kerberos or certificate-based authentication. The option to use certificate-based authentication would be useful if you wanted to replicate to a Hyper-V server that's not part of your organization, such as a host offered by a hosting company as part of an external disaster recovery solution.

The only other configuration choice is to specify which servers the replica server will accept replication requests from and where those replicas will be stored. One option is to allow replication from any authenticated server, in which case a single location is selected where all replicas will be stored. The other option is to specify specific servers that can replicate to the server; in this case, each server can have a different storage location. When specifying specific servers, it is possible to use the wildcard character within the server name (but only one wildcard is supported in the server name); this allows the enablement of a group of servers such as `*.savilltech.net` for all servers whose fully qualified domain name ends in `savilltech.net`. The Trust Group setting is simply a tag to allow VMs to move between Hyper-V hosts with same trust group and continue replicating without issue. With Shared Nothing Live Migration, virtual machines can be moved between Hyper-V hosts that are not clustered with no downtime. With this new mobility capability you need to ensure groups of servers have the same trust group tag to enable replication to be unaffected if virtual machines are moved between servers within a trust group.

You can also perform this configuration using PowerShell via the `Set-VMReplicationServer` cmdlet. For example, to enable replication with the default settings (allow replication from any server and use Kerberos), I use the following:

```
Set-VMReplicationServer -ReplicationEnabled 1 -ComputerName savdalhv24
```

Further configuration can be performed using `Set-VMReplicationServer`. The easiest way to see the options is to view the output of `Get-VMReplicationServer`, as shown here:

```
PS C:\> get-vmreplicationserver -computername savdalhv24 | fl


ComputerName                          : savdalhv24
ReplicationEnabled                    : True
ReplicationAllowedFromAnyServer       : True
AllowedAuthenticationType             : Kerberos
CertificateThumbprint                 :
KerberosAuthenticationPort            : 80
CertificateAuthenticationPort         : 443
KerberosAuthenticationPortMapping     :
CertificateAuthenticationPortMapping  :
MonitoringInterval                    : 12:00:00
MonitoringStartTime                   : 15:00:00
```

```
DefaultStorageLocation              : C:\Replicas\
OperationalStatus                   : {Ok}
StatusDescriptions                  : {The Replication Service is fully
operational.}
AuthorizationEntries                : {*}
Key                                 :
IsDeleted                           : False
RepEnabled                          : True
KerbAuthPort                        : 80
CertAuthPort                        : 443
AllowAnyServer                      : True
AuthType                            : Kerb
```

Additionally, replication entries from specific hosts can be added using the New-VMReplicationAuthorizationEntry cmdlet. Here's an example:

```
New-VMReplicationAuthorizationEntry -AllowedPrimaryServer <primary server>
 -ReplicaStorageLocation <location> -TrustGroup <tag if needed>
```

The final step to complete a server to accept replication is to enable the required firewall exception for the port used: 80 for HTTP and 443 for HTTPS. The firewall exceptions are built into Windows Server but are not enabled even after replication configuration is complete. So, you will need to start the Windows Firewall with Advanced Security administrative tool, select Inbound Rules, and enable either (depending on your authentication methods) Hyper-V Replica HTTP Listener (TCP-In) or Hyper-V Replica HTTPS Listener (TCP-In), or both.

Once the replica server has been enabled for replication, it is important to also enable the primary Hyper-V server as a replica. This allows the reversal of replication in the event the virtual machine is activated on the replica server and now needs to start replicating to the server that was previously the primary but would now be considered the replica.

One item you do not need to configure as part of the replication configuration is the network to use for the replication traffic. The assumption is this technology is used between datacenters and there would be only one valid path between them; therefore, Hyper-V Replica will automatically choose the correct network to use for the replication traffic.

If you have existing Windows Server 2012 Hyper-V Replica environments to upgrade to Windows Server 2012 R2, you must upgrade the replica Hyper-V server first.

## Configuring Hyper-V Replica

Once the Hyper-V hosts are configured to enable the Hyper-V Replica capability, the next step is enabling virtual machines to be replicated. To show how to enable replication, I will initially use Hyper-V Manager, although PowerShell can also be used and would be used in any kind of automated bulk configuration. You select the virtual machine you want to enable replication on and select the Enable Replication action. The Replication Configuration Wizard will launch. Then follow these steps:

1. Specify the replica server that will host the replica and be sure the authentication type to use is selected. A check is performed against the replica server to check the types of authentication that are supported. If both Kerberos and certificate-based authentication are supported on the target replica server and are usable, you will need to select the

authentication method to use, typically Kerberos. Additionally, you can select whether the data sent over the network should be compressed, which will save network bandwidth but will use additional CPU cycles both on the primary and replica Hyper-V servers. The option to use compression is enabled by default.

2. Select the actual virtual hard disks that should be replicated. If a virtual machine has multiple virtual hard disks, then the hard disks to be replicated can be selected to ensure only the required virtual hard disks are replicated. For example, you could do this in order to not replicate VHDs containing just a pagefile, although this does cause more management overhead and, given the churn of pagefiles, is typically quite light; so, this is not a mandatory step. Be aware that only VHDs can be replicated; if a virtual machine uses pass-through disks, they cannot be replicated with Hyper-V Replica (another reason to avoid pass-through disks).

3. Identify the frequency of replication, which can be 30 seconds, 5 minutes, or 15 minutes. This step was not present in Windows Server 2012, which supported a 5-minute replication frequency only.

4. Configure the recovery history. By default the replica will have a single recovery point: the latest replication state. An extended recovery history is optional additional hourly recovery points, as shown in Figure 8.2. The additional recovery points are manifested as snapshots on the virtual machine that is created on the replica server; you can choose a specific recovery point by selecting the desired snapshot. Windows Server 2012 R2 increased the number of hourly recovery points from 16 to 24, which provides the ability to have a full day of incremental protection. Windows Server 2012 R2 also improves the mechanics of how the replica works, which now behaves more like a copy-on-write backup because writes written to the replica VHD have the replaced blocks now written to undo logs. This provides performance improvements.

**FIGURE 8.2**
Recovery point configuration

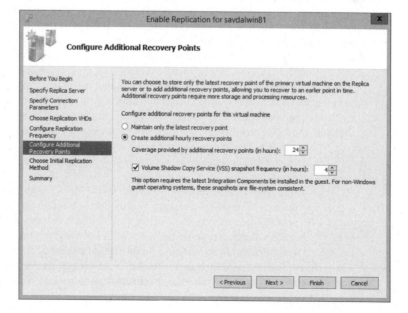

An additional option to create an incremental VSS copy at a configurable number of hours is also available. This gives an additional level of assurance in the integrity of the replica at that point in time. The normal log files sent at the replication interval provide the latest storage content, but at that point the disk may have been in an inconsistent state on the source virtual machine. Therefore, when the replica was started, the replica VHD might not have been in a consistent state. The incremental VSS option, when enabled, triggers a VSS snapshot on the source prior to that cycle's replication, which forces the source virtual machine to ensure the disk content is in an application-consistent state (in the same manner as if a backup were taken, the log file was closed and sent to the replica, and then that state was saved as the application-consistent recovery point on the target). If the virtual machine contains an application that has VSS writers, I suggest using the option to create an application-consistent recovery point. The default of 4 hours is a good balance between integrity and the additional work caused by creating a VSS recovery point on the source virtual machine.

Once the recovery point configuration is complete, you need to choose the method to initially replicate the storage. It can be accomplished by any of the following:

◆ Sending the VHD content over the network.

◆ Sending the VHD content via external media and specifying a location for the content to be exported to.

◆ Using an existing virtual machine on the replica server as the initial copy. This can be used if you already restored the virtual machine to the target Hyper-V server or perhaps if you previously had replication enabled and broke the replica but now want to enable again. An efficient bit-by-bit comparison will be performed between the primary and replica to ensure consistency.

The initial replication can be configured to begin immediately or at a later time, such as outside of normal business hours when contention on the network resources would be less. Depending on the choices made, the virtual machine would be created on the replica Hyper-V server in the off state, and the initial replication would begin. Once complete, at the replica time interval the Hyper-V Replica log (HRL) file is closed, sent to the replica, and merged into the replica VHD. The entire time the replica virtual machine is turned off. No memory, processor, or device state is replicated to the replica virtual machine; only disk content is. In the event the replica is activated, it will be turned on and booted similar to a crash-consistent state as if it previously just had been powered down without a clean shutdown. This is one of the reasons performing the periodic VSS snapshot recovery point is useful to ensure disk integrity.

To view the exact replication configuration of a virtual machine once the configuration has been performed, view the settings of the virtual machine. The Replication tab shows all the details of the Hyper-V Replica configuration, including the replica interval and authentication and recovery point configuration.

You can also enable replication using PowerShell with the Enable-VMReplication cmdlet. The only parameters to enable replication are to specify VMName for the virtual machine to be replicated, to specify the replica server using ReplicaServerName and ReplicaServerPort, and to specify the authentication type using AuthenticationType. Once replication is enabled, you need to start the initial replication using Start-VMInitialReplication.

Once the replica virtual machine is created, it is now a separate virtual machine from the primary virtual machine. Any changes in configuration to the primary virtual machine are not reflected in the replica virtual machine. This allows changes to be made on either side, and the replication of the VHD content will continue. Still, if there are changes made to the primary source such as increasing resources like memory or processor, you will need to manually reflect that change on the replica.

The fact the virtual machine on the primary and on the replica are actually separate virtual machines in terms of configuration enables some nice functionality. In most environments, the primary and secondary datacenters will use different IP networks, which means when a virtual machine is started in the disaster recovery site, it needs a new IP address. As part of the Hyper-V Replica functionality, an additional configuration is available on the virtual machine once replication has been enabled, namely, a failover TCP/IP configuration (found under the Network Adapter configuration of the virtual machine). This allows an alternate IPv4 and IPv6 configuration to be specified on each virtual network adapter for the replica virtual machine, which is injected into the virtual machine in the event of a failover, as shown in Figure 8.3. It is important to understand that this process works by Hyper-V updating the virtual machine through the Windows Server Hyper-V integration services running on the virtual machine. This works only on synthetic network adapters, not legacy network adapters, and it requires Windows XP SP2/Windows Server 2003 SP2 and newer to be running on the virtual machine to work. This also works with Linux virtual machines that are running the latest Linux distributions. A good practice is to complete the failover TCP/IP configuration on the primary virtual machine with its normal IP configuration. That way, if the replica is ever activated, replication is reversed, and the virtual machine is then failed back to what was the primary, and the correct IP address for the primary location can automatically be put back.

**FIGURE 8.3**
Configuring alternate IP configuration to be used during failover

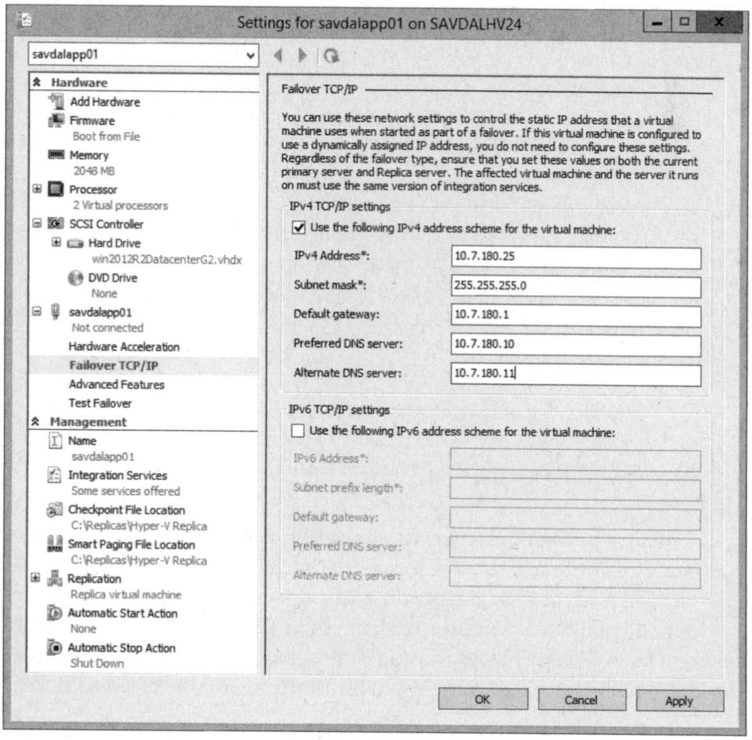

**INJECT IP CONFIGURATION OUTSIDE OF HYPER-V REPLICA USING POWERSHELL**

Hyper-V Replica offers the ability to inject an IP address into a virtual machine; you can also use this functionality outside of Hyper-V Replica.

To perform the injection using PowerShell, use the following code, which leverages the `Msvm_GuestNetworkAdapterConfiguration` class (http://msdn.microsoft.com/en-us/library/hh850156(v=vs.85).aspx). Replace the name of the VM and the IP configuration as needed.

```
$vmName = "win81g2"

$Msvm_VirtualSystemManagementService = Get-WmiObject `
    -Namespace root\virtualization\v2 `
    -Class Msvm_VirtualSystemManagementService

$Msvm_ComputerSystem = Get-WmiObject -Namespace root\virtualization\v2 `
    -Class Msvm_ComputerSystem -Filter "ElementName='$vmName'"

$Msvm_VirtualSystemSettingData = ($Msvm_ComputerSystem.GetRelated(«Msvm_
VirtualSystemSettingData», `
    "Msvm_SettingsDefineState", $null, $null, "SettingData", `
    «ManagedElement», $false, $null) | % {$_})

$Msvm_SyntheticEthernetPortSettingData = $Msvm_VirtualSystemSettingData
.GetRelated(«Msvm_SyntheticEthernetPortSettingData»)

$Msvm_GuestNetworkAdapterConfiguration = ($Msvm_SyntheticEthernetPortSettingData
.GetRelated( `
    "Msvm_GuestNetworkAdapterConfiguration", "Msvm_SettingDataComponent", `
    $null, $null, "PartComponent", "GroupComponent", $false, $null) | % {$_})

$Msvm_GuestNetworkAdapterConfiguration.DHCPEnabled = $false
$Msvm_GuestNetworkAdapterConfiguration.IPAddresses = @("192.168.1.207")
$Msvm_GuestNetworkAdapterConfiguration.Subnets = @("255.255.255.0")
$Msvm_GuestNetworkAdapterConfiguration.DefaultGateways = @("192.168.1.1")
$Msvm_GuestNetworkAdapterConfiguration.DNSServers = @("192.168.1.10",
«192.168.1.11»)

$Msvm_VirtualSystemManagementService.SetGuestNetworkAdapterConfiguration( `
    $Msvm_ComputerSystem.Path, $Msvm_GuestNetworkAdapterConfiguration.GetText(1))
```

There is a disadvantage to separating the virtual machine between the primary and the replica. If additional virtual hard disks are added to the primary virtual machine, the additional virtual hard disks will not automatically start replicating to the replica. The only way to add the new virtual hard disks for the virtual machine to those being replicated is to break the replication between the primary and the replica and then reestablish replication by selecting the new virtual hard disks as part of the replication set. When reestablishing replication, you can specify to use the existing virtual machine for the initial data, which will optimize the amount of data required to seed the replica.

One key point of Hyper-V Replica is that a virtual machine can have only one replica; this means a single virtual machine cannot have more than one replica. Additionally, in Windows Server 2012 you cannot create a replica of a replica VM, known as *extended replication*. This is not a problem if you consider the original goal of Hyper-V Replica, which is having a replica of a virtual machine in a disaster recovery location. This is also why the fixed interval of 5 minutes was a good default value. A number of organizations actually used Hyper-V Replica differently. They used Hyper-V Replica within a single datacenter where they could not use clustering or did not want to use it. This is also the reason the 5-minute replication frequency was too restrictive and organizations wanted to replicate more frequently. These same organizations still wanted to be able to have a replica to an alternate site, which required extending replication. As mentioned, the ability to add a replica to the existing replica virtual machine was added in Windows Server 2012 R2. Note you still cannot have more than one replica for a single VM; so, with Windows Server 2012 R2, the primary virtual machine can still have only one replica, but that replica can now have its own replica, as shown in Figure 8.4.

**FIGURE 8.4**
Windows Server 2012 R2 Hyper-V extended replication

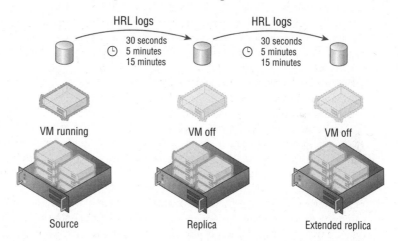

Note that an extended replica can be used in any situation, not just if you have the main replication within a datacenter. If you have two DR locations, Hyper-V extended replica can be beneficial. I've also seen it when in the primary datacenter the standard Hyper-V Replica feature is used to replicate a virtual machine from one cluster to another cluster and then extended replica is used to replicate to the DR datacenter. The extended replica has its own replication interval that is independent of the primary replica, but its interval cannot be less than that of the primary replica. For example, if the primary replica replicates every 5 minutes, then the extended replica can replicate every 5 minutes or 15 minutes but not at the 30-second interval.

To enable the extended replication, perform the following steps:

1. Open Hyper-V Manager and select the Hyper-V host that hosts the replica virtual machine (note the replica and not the source virtual machine).

2. Right-click the replica virtual machine and select the Extend Replication action from the Replication menu.

3. Click Next on the introduction screen of the Extend Replication Wizard.

4. Select the server that will host the extended replica and click Next.

5. The rest of the configuration is the same as enabling a normal replica: Select the authentication type, the frequency of replication, the additional recovery points, and the initial method of replication.

There is no separate PowerShell cmdlet to enable extended replication. The same `Enable-VMReplication` cmdlet is used for extended replication by specifying the replica VM. For `ReplicaServerName`, specify the extended replica Hyper-V server.

Replication can be removed for a virtual machine using the Replication – Remove Replication action or using the `Remove-VMReplication` PowerShell cmdlet.

## Using Hyper-V Replica Broker

If you use failover clustering, there is an additional requirement since a failover cluster consists of multiple Hyper-V hosts. If a failover cluster is the target for Hyper-V Replica, it's important the whole cluster can host the replicated virtual machine and not just a single host. This means the storage of the replica must be on a SMB share or cluster-shared volume. Hyper-V Replica support in a failover cluster is enabled by adding the Hyper-V Replica Broker role to the failover cluster. This will require a name and IP address for the Hyper-V Replica Broker role, which serves as the client access point (CAP) for Hyper-V Replica and will be the name used when selecting the cluster as a target for a replica.

When enabling replication within a cluster, once the Hyper-V Replica Broker role is added, the replication configuration is performed within the Failover Cluster Manager tool. Once the configurations for replication are completed (which are the same as for a stand-alone Hyper-V host), all hosts in the cluster will automatically be configured, unless certificate-based authentication was selected, in which case each host needs its own certificate configured.

You must configure the Hyper-V Replica Broker role in the cluster even if the cluster is not a replica target (although this is highly unlikely since in the event of a failover replication is typically reversed). This means you always need the Hyper-V Replica Broker role for a cluster that is participating in Hyper-V Replica in any way. If the cluster is the replica target, then the broker redirects the replication traffic because the VM may move between hosts in the cluster. If the cluster is the source of the replica, then the broker enables authorization of the primary hosts at a cluster level, and of course the replica is needed if the replication is reversed.

Once the Hyper-V Replica Broker role is created, you should modify its configuration by selecting the Replication Settings action for the broker. Then select to enable the cluster as a replica server and choose the various configurations, which are the same as for a normal replica server, as shown in Figure 8.5. Once replication is enabled, you will need to manually enable the required firewall exceptions on each host because this is not performed by the broker configuration; an example is the Hyper-V Replica HTTP Listener (TCP-In) firewall exception.

**FIGURE 8.5**
Enabling inbound
replication for the
Hyper-V Replica
Broker role

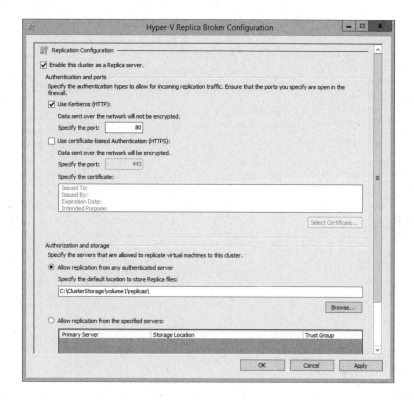

## Performing Hyper-V Replica Failover

Once replication is configured, the next step is to perform failovers. But before failing over, it's important to ensure the ongoing health of the replication. In Hyper-V Manager, each virtual machine has a Replication tab as part of its high-level status. This tab shows the mode of replication, the health of the replication, and the time of last synchronization. This same information is available in Failover Cluster Manager for the virtual machine, and you can view more detailed health of the replication state using the Replication – View Replication Health action, as shown in Figure 8.6. The replication health view shows the same basic overview information but also details of the average and maximum size of the transferred data, the average latency, any errors, and the number of replication cycles. It also shows pending replication data. It may be confusing because there is a Replication State entry and a Replication Health entry, but Replication State shows the current state of replication, and Replication Health factors in events over a period of time, which helps identify whether there has been a problem at some point in that evaluation time period. You can find a full list of possible values for Replication State and Replication Health at http://blogs.technet.com/b/virtualization/archive/2012/06/15/ interpreting-replication-health-part-1.aspx.

**FIGURE 8.6**
Viewing the health of replication

You can also see this health information with PowerShell using Measure_VMReplication. As shown here, the output contains the same basic information as in the replication health graphical interface. If you need a detailed level of monitoring for Hyper-V Replica, one option is to use System Center Operations Manager and the Hyper-V Management Pack, which monitors the health of Hyper-V Replica and many other Hyper-V aspects.

```
PS C:\> Measure-VMReplication -ComputerName savdalhv21 -VMName savdalapp01 | fl


VMName                     : savdalapp01
ReplicationState           : Replicating
ReplicationHealth          : Normal
LastReplicationTime        : 12/10


/2013 9:30:17 AM
PendingReplicationSize     : 4096
AverageReplicationLatency  : 00:00:00
SuccessfulReplicationCount : 223
MissedReplicationCount     : 0
```

If a virtual machine is the replica virtual machine and also has its own extended replica, `Measure-VMReplication` will return information about its relationship with the primary and extended replica. If you want to view information about only one of the relationships, add `-ReplicationRelationshipType` and specify either `Simple` (to view the primary relationship) or `Extended` (to see the extended relationship).

You can see the actual HRL files used by Hyper-V Replica if you look at the folder containing the VHD files being replicated. It is possible to pause and resume replication, but be careful to not pause replication for too long because this will cause the log files to build up. You can also pause and resume the replication using the `Suspend-VMReplication` and `Resume-VMReplication` cmdlets. Once again, you can specify `ReplicationRelationshipType` for a virtual machine that is the replica of the primary and the source for the extended replica, in other words, the one in the middle.

This can also happen if there is a network break between the primary and replica that stops transmission of the log files. If the size of the log files is greater than 50 percent of the size of the actual VHD file, a resynchronization is required. Resynchronization performs a block-by-block comparison of the source of the replica, with only different blocks being sent over the network. This is deemed more efficient than sending over the accumulated log files, although there is a performance impact during a resynchronization. Other scenarios can force a resynchronization, but they are rare. See `http://blogs.technet.com/b/virtualization/archive/2013/05/10/resynchronization-of-virtual-machines-in-hyper-v-replica.aspx`, which is a great blog post and worth reading for more information on the exact resynchronization process.

Now that you understand how to view the ongoing health of your Hyper-V Replica environment, you can look at the types of failover you want to perform with Hyper-V Replica. There are three types of failover used with Hyper-V Replica, as detailed here. Depending on the type of failover, the actual failover is triggered from either the primary or replica Hyper-V host by selecting one of the failover actions from the Replication action menu.

**Test Failover**    This is triggered on the replica virtual machine, which allows the replica VM to be started on the replica Hyper-V host by creating a temporary virtual machine based on the recovery point selected. Testing is performed to ensure replication is working as planned and as part of a larger site failover test process. During the test failover, the primary VM continues to send log updates to the replica VM, which are merged into the replica VHDs, ensuring replication continues. Once testing is complete, the temporary virtual machine is deleted. When triggering the test failover, you have the option to select the point in time to use for the failover if the virtual machine was enabled to store multiple points in time when replication was enabled, as shown in Figure 8.7. The test failover virtual machine is not connected to the regular network to avoid interfering with normal network communications.

**FIGURE 8.7**
Selecting the point in time for the test failover

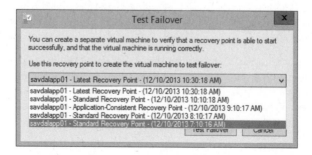

**Planned Failover**   This is triggered on the primary virtual machine and is the preferred failover type. This process shuts down the primary VM, replicates any pending changes to ensure no data loss, fails over to the replica VM, reverses the replication (if the option is selected) so changes flow in the reverse direction, and then starts the replica VM, which becomes the primary (while the old primary becomes the replica). Figure 8.8 shows the options for the planned failover that include whether replication should be reversed and whether the virtual machine should be started on the replica side. You should enable the reversal of replication unless there is a specific reason not to, such as if you are using extended replication (this will be discussed later in this section). Note that even though this is a planned failover, the virtual machine is still shut down during the failover, which is different from a Live Migration operation.

**FIGURE 8.8**

Performing a
planned failover

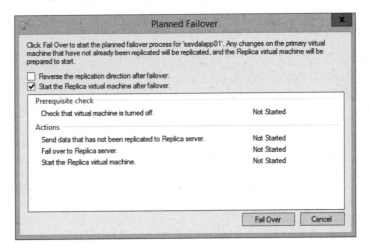

**Unplanned Failover (Failover)**   This is triggered on the replica virtual machine because the assumption is the failover was not planned and the primary is not available because a disaster has occurred. When this is performed, a replication of pending changes is not possible, and reverse replication has to be manually enabled with a resynchronization required because there is no way to know where the primary and the replica stopped replicating. When starting the reverse replication, choose Do Not Copy The Initial Replication on the Initial Replication page. The VM on the original primary VM can be used, and a block-by-block comparison will be performed to synchronize between the replica VM and the original primary VM. Only the delta content needs to be sent over the network. When performing an unplanned failover, an option to select the point in time is available in the same way as for the test failover.

In Windows Server 2012 if the option to maintain periodic snapshots of the primary virtual machine was enabled with Hyper-V Replica, then the replica virtual machine would show those point-in-time snapshots in the Snapshots view. This is no longer the case in Windows Server 2012 R2 Hyper-V, which may initially lead you to believe the snapshots are not being maintained for the replica, which is not the case. The various points in time are available and listed when performing a failover with Hyper-V Replica, as previously discussed. You can also see this using PowerShell, as shown here:

```
PS C:\> Get-VMSnapshot savdalapp01

VMName       Name        SnapshotType                                    CreationTime
------       ----        ------------                                    ------------
savdalapp01 savdalapp01 - Standard Replica - (12/2/2013 - 7:08:59 AM) Replica
12/2/2013 7...
savdalapp01 savdalapp01 - Standard Replica - (12/2/2013 - 8:09:00 AM) Replica
12/2/2013 8...
savdalapp01 savdalapp01 - Application-consistent Replica - (12/2/2013 - 9:09:00
AM) AppConsistentReplica 12/2/2013 9...
savdalapp01 savdalapp01 - Standard Replica - (12/2/2013 - 10:09:01 AM) Replica
12/2/2013 1...
```

To perform a failover using PowerShell, you use the `Start-VMFailover` cmdlet with different switches depending on the type of failover.

For a test failover, typically you need to list all the snapshots and save to an array, so a specific snapshot can be selected to be used for the test. Next, one of the snapshots in the array is used as part of the test failover. Zero would be the first item in the array, so take care to look at the snapshots to ensure the correct one is selected. This is performed on the replica virtual machine.

```
$VMSnapshots = Get-VMSnapshot -VMName <vm> -SnapshotType Replica
Start-VMFailover -Confirm:$false -VMRecoverySnapshot $VMSnapshots[0] -AsTest
```

A planned failover is a bit more involved and involves running commands against the primary VM to prepare it for failover and then activating on the replica VM. On the primary VM, the following commands are run:

```
Stop-VM <VM>
Start-VMFailover -VMName <VM> -prepare
```

Next, on the replica VM, the following commands are run to actually perform the failover, reverse the replication, and then start the replica VM.

```
Start-VMFailover -VMName <VM>
Set-VMReplication -reverse -VMName <VM>
Start-VM <VM>
```

An unplanned failover is used when the primary has been lost and you need to force the replica to start. If multiple points in times are available, then one of those times can be selected in a similar fashion to the test failover, with the major difference that the `-AsTest` switch is not used. Remember to select the right snapshot or don't use a snapshot at all, and use `-VMName` instead of the `-VMRecoverySnapshot` parameter.

```
$VMSnapshots = Get-VMSnapshot -VMName <vm> -SnapshotType Replica
Start-VMFailover -Confirm:$false -VMRecoverySnapshot $VMSnapshots[0]
```

At this point, you would check that the virtual machine is in the desired state and then complete the failover using this command:

```
Complete-VMFailover -VMName <VM> -Confirm:$false
```

The actual failover is invisible to the virtual machine guest operating system. The operating system is aware only of a reboot and likely its IP address change, which is performed by Hyper-V if alternate IP configuration was configured as part of the network adapter configuration. If you performed a planned failover, then the replication is reversed, providing you selected that option. To fail back so the virtual machine is running in the main datacenter, you perform another failover, which will move the virtual machine back to the main datacenter and then reverse the replication to resume the normal operation. This is why even on the primary virtual machine you typically configure its IP configuration in the failover IP section so that when you use Hyper-V Replica to fail back, the correct IP configuration will be injected back into the virtual machine.

There is a complication for the failback scenario if you are using extended replication where you have a replica of the replica. The reason for the complication is that if you have the configuration where A is replicating to B and then the replication is extended from B to C (where A, B, and C are Hyper-V hosts), you cannot reverse replication if you failover from A to B; therefore, B is now replicating to A. This is because B is already replicating to C and a single virtual machine cannot have more than one replica. When performing the initial failover from A to B, you should not select the option to reverse replication. Once you have performed the failover from A to B, you do have a choice on server B. You can choose to continue the replication from B to C or you can select to replicate from B to A, which will halt the replication to C. In many instances, you will select the option to continue replication to C since A is likely not available. To perform the continued replication, select the Resume Extended Replication action. You can also use `Resume-VMReplication -VMName <name> -Continue` to continue using PowerShell. If you do want to replicate to A, you select the option Reverse Replication, which will break the Hyper-V Replica extended relationship. The virtual machine on C has now become orphaned. With PowerShell, you first need to remove the extended replica and then reverse the replication.

```
Remove-VMReplication -VMName <name> -ReplicationRelationshipType Extended
Set-VMReplication -VMName <name> -Reverse
```

Assuming the option to continue replication from B to C was selected, this makes the failover of the virtual machine to run on server A a more complex operation because the virtual machine on server A is no longer receiving updates. The process involves manually performing the following steps:

1. Break the replication relationship between B and C.

2. Set up replication from B to A, which can use the existing virtual machine on server A, and the resynchronization process will be used to minimize data sent over the network.

3. Perform a failover from B to A and reverse the replication, which means A is now replicating to B.

**4.** Reestablish the extended replica from B to C, and once again the existing virtual machine on server C can be used as the base, and resynchronization is used to minimize data sent over the network.

# Sizing a Hyper-V Replica Solution

After understanding the capability of Hyper-V Replica, the first question from my clients is "What is the impact on my storage and network, and what are the requirements?" This is a valid question and is fairly complex. The answer ultimately boils down to the rate of change on the storage of the virtual machines that need to be replicated because Hyper-V Replica works by replicating the changes. The higher the rate of change to the storage of the virtual machine, the greater the size of the Hyper-V Replica log (HRL) files and the more data that needs to be sent over the network from the primary to the replica.

There is also the consideration of the impact on the storage, both on the primary storage hosting the primary VM VHDs, which also store the HRL files, and on the replica storage hosting the replica VM that receives the update files and then has to merge them into the replica VHDs and also maintain snapshots if configured. It is not possible to configure the HRL files to be written to different storage than the actual VHD files, which means the storage containing the VHD will incur whatever storage IO is associated with the log files.

There is a negligible impact for processor and memory, but it is generally not considered as part of your Hyper-V Replica planning, which is focused on the network and storage. The network is fairly simple, and the amount of network bandwidth relates directly to the rate of change of the virtual machine. While compression does decrease the amount of network traffic (and incur some processor overhead) by compressing all the zeros in the data, there is not really any additional consideration. The amount of network traffic relates directly to the rate of change. If you need a higher rate of network compression, then one option is to leverage WAN optimizers such as those from Riverbed, which will provide greater network bandwidth savings.

If you need to throttle the amount of bandwidth used for Hyper-V Replica, you should use network Quality of Service (QoS). QoS could be based on the target subnet (assuming the only traffic to the target subnet is Hyper-V Replica traffic), or you can throttle based on the destination port, which is possible because Hyper-V Replica uses port 8080 for the actual transmission of the log data. For example, here I limit the replica traffic to 200 Kb:

```
New-NetQoSPolicy "Replication Traffic to 8080" -DestinationPort 8080
 -ThrottleRateActionBitsPerSecond 200000
```

The storage consideration is more complex, specifically on the replica side where the changes have to be merged into the replica VHDs. On the primary side, the additional storage required to host the log files is equal to the rate of change, and the additional IO impact is less than 1.5 times that of the IOPS of the actual workload, so less than 50 percent additional IO. This is achieved by the use of a 32 MB memory buffer to track writes to optimize the actual writes to the log files.

On the replica side, there has been a major change between Windows Server 2012 and Windows Server 2012 R2 related to both the amount of storage and the IOPS. In Windows Server 2012, the IOPS requirement on the replica storage was between one and five times that of the workload, a big range. Windows Server 2012 R2 changes this to between one and two times that of the workload, which is a huge improvement and enabled by the new mechanism to manage changes to the storage. The change in applying the changes also reduces the storage required if recovery points are used. In Windows Server 2012, each recovery point would be around 10 percent of the size of the base VHD, which could be very large. In Windows Server 2012 R2, each recovery point is equal to the actual change between the recovery points, which is a huge improvement.

Actually ascertaining the rate of change for each virtual machine is the key factor for all of these estimates. To help with this, Microsoft has created a capacity planner available at www .microsoft.com/en-us/download/details.aspx?id=39057. Once the capacity planner is downloaded and installed, the application should be executed. The tool asks for the primary Hyper-V server or the broker if it's a cluster and the replica Hyper-V server or the broker of the replica cluster. It will also ask for the estimated WAN bandwidth and a duration to collect data for. Next the tool will display a list of virtual machines running on supported storage such as local and CSV and allow you to select the specific VHDs that you want to gather information for on the change, as shown in Figure 8.9. The tool will then monitor those VHDs for the period of time you specify. Once collection is complete, it will know the rate of change of the VHD and ascertain the actual processor, memory, network, and storage impact for using Hyper-V Replica with those VHDs. A full report is generated that shows the before and after impact to help you plan for the Hyper-V Replica implementation; I definitely recommend using it. Figure 8.10 shows an example of the process in action.

**FIGURE 8.9**

Selecting the VHDs to use for the planner

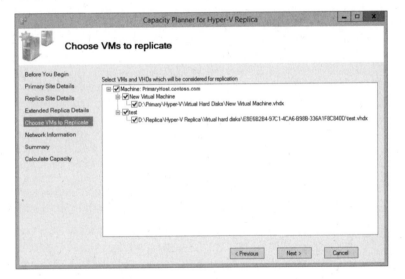

Microsoft also has a performance optimization document at http://support .microsoft.com/kb/2767928 that discusses some registry changes you can apply. One key setting is MaximumActiveTransfers, which may be of interest if you are replicating a large number of virtual machines. The default number of active transfers in Windows Server 2012 R2 is six (up from three in Windows Server 2012); however, you may need to increase this per the article instructions if you have a large number of replicated virtual machines.

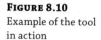

**FIGURE 8.10**
Example of the tool
in action

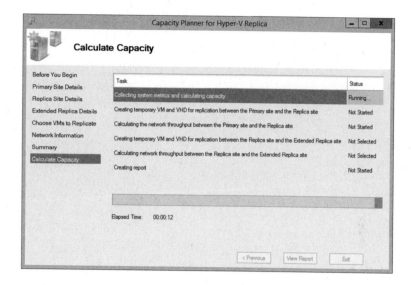

# Using Hyper-V Replica Cloud Orchestration for Automated Failover

Hyper-V Replica is a great technology, but as you have seen, it's very manual. You trigger the failover for each virtual machine. There is no automated or bulk failover capability. Most organizations don't want an automated DR failover because there are too many false positives that could trigger a DR failover. What organizations do want is the ability to perform an orchestrated disaster recovery failover, allowing scripts to be run, VMs to be failed over in a specific order, and all of this performed from a single interface using predefined failover plans.

Like all of Windows Server 2012, PowerShell can be used for every aspect of Hyper-V Replica. You can use it to craft your own solution to perform your Hyper-V Replica DR failover, but that would be a lot of work, and each time you added new virtual machines, you would have to update your process.

Microsoft actually released some Hyper-V Replica runbooks that leverage System Center Orchestrator to enable an orchestrated failover process. They are available from http://blogs .technet.com/b/privatecloud/archive/2013/02/11/automation-orchestrating-hyper-v-replica-with-system-center-for-planned-failover.aspx. While a nice solution, System Center Orchestrator is really focused on Windows Server 2012 and has not been updated for Windows Server 2012 R2; still, it's still a great starting point.

A better solution is provided by the Microsoft Hyper-V Recovery Manager (HRM) solution. You can find details at www.windowsazure.com/en-us/manage/services/recovery-services /configure-a-hyper-v-recovery-vault/. In the following section, I will walk through its main capabilities, its integration with Hyper-V Replica, and SCVMM, as well as how to get started.

## Overview of Hyper-V Recovery Manager

Figure 8.11 shows the main architectural view of an HRM-based solution. First notice that HRM is a service provided by Windows Azure and acts as a cloud-based broker and orchestration engine for Hyper-V Replica activities and failovers. The actual replication of the virtual machines is still from the Hyper-V servers in datacenter 1 to the Hyper-V servers in datacenter 2. No virtual machine storage replication happens to Windows Azure, and instead only metadata of the Hyper-V configuration is sent to Windows Azure to enable management.

**FIGURE 8.11**
HRM architectural
overview

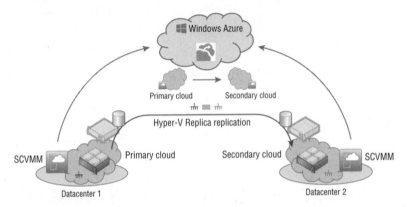

The actual communication to HRM is via an SCVMM instance at each datacenter; you enable this by downloading an HRM provider that installs into SCVMM and enables SCVMM to communicate to HRM using HTTPS. A certificate is used for the secure communications that you configure in HRM and in the SCVMM HRM provider, which gives a mutually trusted certificate. A proxy can be configured for the communication from SCVMM to HRM, and the only configuration is outbound HTTPS. HRM never contacts SCVMM; all communication is initiated from SCVMM outbound to HRM.

HRM works at a cloud level. Specifically, in SCVMM at each datacenter you need to create one or more clouds that contain the Hyper-V host groups that will be participating in Hyper-V Replica replication. The clouds within SCVMM are then enabled to send information to HRM by checking the Send Configuration Data About This Cloud To The Windows Azure Hyper-V Recovery Manager option on the General tab of the cloud properties.

Once the clouds are known to HRM, a relationship is created between two clouds. This is a *pairing*, which tells the primary cloud it has a replication relationship to a target cloud. As part of the pairing of clouds, HRM will trigger workflows on SCVMM that automatically configure the Hyper-V hosts for Hyper-V Replica replication using certificate-based authentication. There is no manual configuration for Hyper-V Replica required on the hosts. Once the cloud relationship is established, a relationship between networks on the primary and replica cloud are configured in HRM. This enables virtual machines to be updated with the correct connectivity when established on the replica Hyper-V server, and a new IP address is injected into the virtual machine from the IP pool of the new network, ensuring continued connectivity.

A recovery plan is then created in HRM that defines groups of virtual machines to be failed over, defines the ordering of failover, and even defines optional scripts to be executed that need to be present on the SCVMM servers. The final step is to enable virtual machines for protection using HRM via SCVMM, which behind the scenes configures the virtual machine to use Hyper-V Replica and makes the replication known to HRM. The option to use HRM can also be made part of a virtual machine template in SCVMM. This makes it easy to let the user deploy virtual machines that will be protected with Hyper-V Replica.

In the event a failover is required, one of the defined recovery plans can be initiated that triggers workflows on the SCVMM servers to perform the orchestrator Hyper-V Replica failovers and reverse replication as required.

As this high-level overview shows, no virtual machine or data ever goes to Windows Azure. All replication is directly between Hyper-V hosts in the organization's datacenters. The HRM service in Windows Azure is simply communicating with the SCVMM instances at each location to help orchestrate the initial configuration of Hyper-V Replica between the hosts, enabling replication for virtual machines and then actually triggering workflows to perform failovers, all from a separate cloud-based location.

## Getting Started with HRM

Microsoft has great documentation for Windows Azure that details the steps to implementing HRM. This section walks you through some of the key points involved in using HRM.

At the time of this writing, the HRM is currently in preview, but by the time you read this, it should be a released feature. If not, you will need to request access to the preview, which is linked from the location when trying to actually create a new Hyper-V Recovery Manager vault. Log on to the Windows Azure portal (https://manage.windowsazure.com) and then create a new Hyper-V Recovery Manager vault, as shown in Figure 8.12, via the New action at the bottom of the screen and by selecting Data Services ➤ Recovery Services ➤ Hyper-V Recovery Manager Vault – Quick Create. You will need to enter a name for the new vault and select a region that will host it from the drop-down.

**FIGURE 8.12**
Creating a new
Hyper-V Recovery
Manager vault

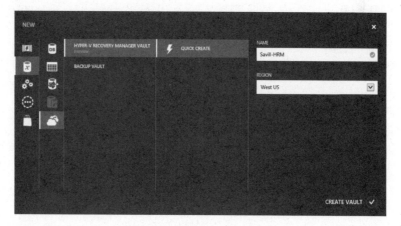

Once the HRM vault is created, the next step is to download the provider for SCVMM from the Dashboard page of the vault. The HRM vault is available within the Recovery Services navigation node. Once the provider is downloaded, store this in a location available to your SCVMM servers.

A certificate must be uploaded into the HRM vault that will also be used with the HRM SCVMM provider. This certificate can be an SSL certificate from an external CA or can be self-signed. Microsoft describes in detail the certificate requirements at `http://msdn.microsoft.com/en-us/library/dn169036.aspx`, including how to create your own self-signed certificate. You upload the certificate through the Dashboard page of the HRM vault by clicking the Manage Certificate action.

Once the certificate is uploaded to the HRM vault in Windows Azure, the next step is to install the partner certificate that contains the private key onto each SCVMM server. A `.pfx` file that contains the private key of the certificate can be created by exporting the certificate from the machine that originally created the certificate.

The downloaded HRM provider must be installed on your SCVMM servers, and during the installation of the provider, you will need to specify the same certificate that was uploaded to Windows Azure. The System Center Virtual Machine Manager service on the SCVMM host should be stopped during the installation of the HRM provider; you can stop it by using the `Services.msc` snap-in. During the provider installation, a proxy can be configured for the connectivity to the Internet and the certificate selected that you imported. Once the certificate is selected, the provider will automatically connect to Windows Azure and show all vaults that are using the equivalent public key certificate, as shown in Figure 8.13. Select the vault; the next step is to enter a friendly name for the SCVMM server, and by default the option to synchronize information about clouds to HRM is selected, which enables all existing clouds to send data to HRM. The SCVMM server will then be registered with the HRM vault, and data will start to be populated into HRM. The installation will prompt to restart the VMM service by default. Remember that all steps performed on the primary SCVMM environment must be repeated on the replica side of the SCVMM environment.

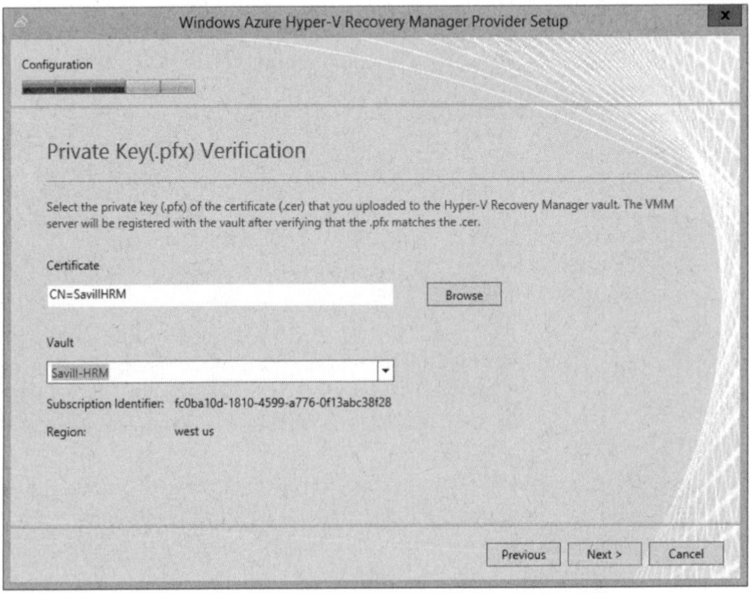

**FIGURE 8.13**
Selecting the vault as part of the HRM SCVMM provider installation

All of the clouds for the registered SCVMM servers will be displayed in the Protected Items view, but at this point none of them is actually being protected nor has actually been configured, and the status will show as (Not Configured). If you did not select the option during the provider installation to synchronize information about clouds to HRM for each cloud you want to be managed by HRM, you should open the properties of the cloud and on the General tab check the option Send Configuration Data About This Cloud To The Windows Azure Hyper-V Recovery Manager (available only once the HRM provider is installed). Note that because clouds are the unit of configuration for HRM that includes specific host groups, the host group is the level of granularity for the configuration of the Hyper-V Replica configuration via HRM. You may need to divide your servers into specific host groups to match your goals for configuration.

The next step is to create pairings of clouds, in other words, between the primary and the replica. Within the Protected Items view, click the primary cloud to launch a new screen where you should click the Configure Protection Settings action. This will launch the pairing process. You will need to select the target location, which is named based on the friendly name of the registered SCVMM server. Select the cloud hosted by the target SCVMM instance and then configure values for the copy frequency (which can be only 30 seconds or 15 minutes rather than the default 5 minutes if the servers are running Windows Server 2012 R2), additional recovery point settings, compression, and initial replication settings. These values will be used when enabling virtual machines for replication via SCVMM. Figure 8.14 shows the pairing wizard. When you click Save, a number of workflows will be triggered on the SCVMM instances to configure the Hyper-V hosts within the affected host groups that are part of the selected clouds to enable Hyper-V replication. These workflows include configuring certificate-based authentication and enabling the servers to receive Hyper-V Replica replicas from the required servers.

The next step, under the Resources navigation area, is to create relationships between the networks on the source SCVMM server and the target SCVMM server. This will allow the virtual machine to be reconfigured with the correct network mapping and a new IP address from the IP pool on the target network (if applicable and available) if a failover occurs.

With the cloud and network relationships defined in HRM and those configurations propagated to the SCVMM instances, it will be possible to enable virtual machines to be protected using HRM through the SCVMM management console. You do this through the properties of the virtual machine; under Hardware Configuration – Hyper-V Recovery Manager, check the option Enable Hyper-V Recovery Manager Protection For This Virtual Machine and select the replication frequency (which needs to match those configurations defined in the cloud protection relationships). The replication can also be enabled using the Set-SCVirtualMachine cmdlet with the parameters -DRProtectionRequired $true -RecoveryPointObjective <time in seconds, e.g. 900 for 15 minutes>. You can enable the same option in a virtual machine template, as shown in Figure 8.15.

The final step is to create recovery plans that contain specific virtual machines placed into groups, along with the order to failover those groups and any scripts that should be executed. Once the recovery plan is created, it can be used in a similar way to a standard Hyper-V Replica failover of a single virtual machine, a test failover, a planned failover, or an unplanned failover. Be careful because these plans will failover every virtual machine that is part of the recovery plan, so they could impact the availability of virtual machines. It's important to also have good processes in place to control access to being able to perform the various types of failover as well as checks that should be performed prior to performing failovers.

A great resource for details on all these steps is available at www.windowsazure.com/en-us/manage/services/recovery-services/configure-a-hyper-v-recovery-vault/. While HRM is not a requirement to use Hyper-V Replica, the reality is that Hyper-V Replica is a fabric feature that replicates virtual machines, and the actual enterprise management and failover orchestration is achieved through HRM and SCVMM. At the time of this writing, HRM does not support the Windows Server 2012 R2 extended replication scenarios that provide a third replica or tertiary replication.

**FIGURE 8.14**
Enabling relationship between the two clouds

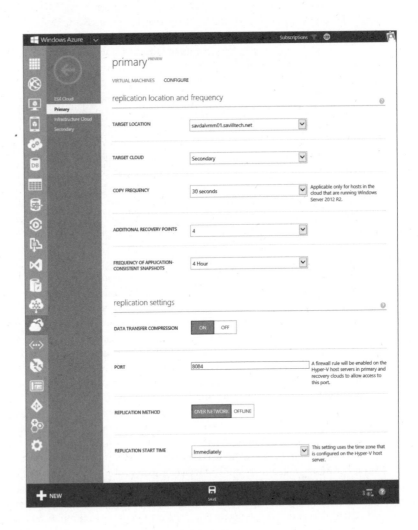

**FIGURE 8.15**
Enabling HRM
protection for
an SCVMM VM
template

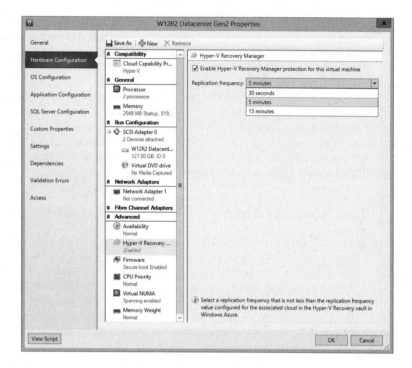

# Architecting the Right Disaster Recovery Solution

After reading this chapter, you may think you will just use Hyper-V Replica for all your disaster recovery needs. The reality is that should not be the case. It's a good technology, but there may be better options for specific workloads and applications.

Your first preference should be to use an application's replication and disaster recovery capabilities if it has them because it's always better for the application to be aware of a failover and manage its own data if possible. For example, SQL has its AlwaysOn replication and failover technology, which means if I had data in SQL Server, I would always use AlwaysOn first. Likewise, Exchange has database availability groups and replicates mailboxes. In that case, I would use that technology. Active Directory has multimaster replication, which means I would simply have domain controllers running in my DR location that would replicate from my primary location for normal operation.

If the application is not stateful, such as a website, then I could have instances of the application running in the primary and DR locations and use network load balancing to spread the load. Another option is to update DNS to point to DR instead of primary. Although there are some considerations around caching of DNS records, there are solutions for this.

My next preference would be if the storage had some kind of synchronous replication capability that could be used as if it were a single logical piece of storage that would allow a cluster to be used, treating the replicated SAN as shared storage and enabling any cluster-aware application to leverage the SAN. This could also include virtual machines running on the replicated SAN.

If none of those other options were available, then I would use Hyper-V Replica. That is not to say it's not a great solution, but a hypervisor-level asynchronous replication solution that is not application aware is simply not as rich in its functionality as one that is part of an application. In most organizations, there are a lot of applications that don't have their own replication technology and can't run on a replication SAN, so there is a huge number of virtual workloads that can benefit greatly from Hyper-V Replica.

## The Bottom Line

**Identify the best options to provide disaster recovery for the different services in your organization.** When planning disaster recovery, an application-aware disaster recovery should be used first where possible, such as SQL AlwaysOn, Exchange DAG, Active Directory multimaster replication, and so on. If no application-aware replication and DR capability is available, another option is to look at the replication capabilities of the SAN such as synchronous replication. Additionally, replicating at the virtual machine disk level such as Hyper-V Replica provides a replication solution that has no requirements on the guest operating system or the application.

**Master It** Why is Hyper-V Recovery Manager useful?

**Describe the types of failover for Hyper-V Replica.** There are three types of Hyper-V Replica failover. A test failover is performed on the replica server and creates a clone of the replica virtual machine that is disconnected from the network and allows testing of the failover process without any impact to the ongoing protection of the primary workload as replication continues. A planned failover is triggered on the primary Hyper-V host and stops the virtual machine, ensures any pending changes are replicated, starts the replica virtual machine, and reverses the replication. An unplanned failover is triggered on the replica Hyper-V host and is used when an unforeseen disaster occurs and the primary datacenter is lost. This means there may be some loss of state from the primary virtual machine. When possible, a planned failover should always be used.

**Master It** In an unplanned failover how much data could be lost?

**Explain the automated options for Hyper-V Replica failover.** Hyper-V Replica has no automated failover capability. To automate the failover steps, PowerShell could be used, System Center Orchestrator could be used, or for a complete solution Hyper-V Recovery Manager could be used. The key point is the actual decision to failover should not be automatic because there could be many conditions such as a break in network connectivity that could trigger a false failover. The automation required should be the orchestration of the failover once a manual action is taken to decide a failover should occur.

# Chapter 9

# Implementing the Private Cloud and SCVMM

So far this book has covered aspects of Hyper-V, such as types of resources, high availability, and management. This chapter takes the capabilities enabled through Hyper-V and shows how to build on them by using the System Center management stack and by leveraging the virtual infrastructure.

In this chapter, you will learn to

♦ Explain the difference between virtualization and the private cloud

♦ Describe the must-have components to create a Microsoft private cloud

## The Benefits of the Private Cloud

What is the private cloud? Understanding this is actually the hardest part of implementing the private cloud. One of my customers once said the following, and it's 100 percent accurate:

*If you ask five people for a definition of the private cloud, you will get seven different answers.*
*Very smart customer in 2011*

I like to think of the private cloud as having the following attributes:

♦ Scalable and elastic, meaning it can grow and shrink as the load on the application changes

♦ Better utilization of resources

♦ Agnostic of the underlying fabric

♦ Accountable, which can also mean chargeable

♦ Self-service capable

♦ All about the application

Let me explain this list in more detail. First, the all about the application attribute. In a physical setup, each server has a single operating system instance, which, as I've explored, means lots of wasted resources and money. The shift to virtualization takes these operating system instances and consolidates them to a smaller number of physical servers by running each operating system instance in a virtual machine. Virtualization saves hardware and money but doesn't actually change the way IT is managed. Administrators still log on to the operating system instances at the console and still manage the same number of operating system instances. In fact, now administrators also have to manage the virtualization solution. While you may not log on to the actual console of a server, you are still remoting directly into the operating system to do management, and this is basically managing at the console level. The private cloud shifts the focus on the actual service being delivered and the applications used in that service offering. The private cloud infrastructure is responsible for creating the virtual machines and operating system instances that are required to deploy a service, removing that burden from the administrator.

Think back to the service templates covered in Chapter 6. Service templates in System Center Virtual Machine Manager allow the design of multitiered services, with each tier having the ability to use different virtual machine templates and different applications and configurations. Service templates allow administrators (and users, as I will explore later) to easily deploy complete instances of services without any concern for the actual virtual machine configuration or placement. Those service templates also integrate with network hardware such as load balancers, enabling automatic configuration of the network hardware when services are deployed that require hardware load balancing.

Initial deployment is fine, but what about maintenance, patching, and scaling? I'll cover other components of System Center 2012, such as Configuration Manager, which can simplify automated patching of both server and desktop operating systems, but you can still use service templates. Unlike a normal virtual machine template, which loses any relationship with a virtual machine deployed from the template, any instances of a service deployed from a service template maintain the relationship to the template.

Think about being scalable and elastic. Those same service templates allow a minimum, maximum, and initial instance count of each tier of service. Let's look at the web tier as an example. I could configure the tier to have a minimum instance count of 2, a maximum of 20, and an initial of 4. This means when load increases, the user can just access the tool and scale out the tier to a higher number, such as 10, and the back-end infrastructure automatically takes care of creating the new virtual machines, setting up any configuration, and adding the new instances to the load balancer and any other associated actions. When the load dies down, the user can scale in that service, and once again the back-end infrastructure will automatically delete some virtual machines that make up that tier to the new target number and update the hardware load balancer. I'm focusing on the user performing the scale-out and scale-in, but that same private cloud could have monitoring in place, such as with System Center Operations Manager; when load hits a certain point, it runs some automated process using System Center Orchestrator that actually talks to System Center Virtual Machine Manager to perform the scaling. That's why when I talk about the private cloud and focus on the application, it's not just about System Center Virtual Machine Manager; the entire System Center product plays a part in the complete private cloud solution. This scalability and elasticity—meaning having access to resources when needed but not using them and allowing other services to leverage them when not needed—are key traits of the private cloud. Many organizations will charge business units for the amount of computer resources that are used by their applications, which is why the ability to scale is important. By running many different services on a single infrastructure, you will see high utilization of available resources, getting more bang for the infrastructure buck.

**Agnostic of the Underlying Fabric**   This can be confusing. For example, say I want to offer services to my customers, which could be my IT department, business units in the organization, or individual users. To those customers I want to provide a menu of offerings, known as a *service catalog* in ITIL terms. When those customers deploy a virtual machine or service, they should not need to know what IP address should be given to the virtual machine or virtual machines if deploying a single or multitiered service. The customer should not have to say which storage area network to use and which LUN should be used. Imagine I have multiple datacenters and multiple types of network and multiple hypervisors. If I want to allow non-IT people to deploy virtual machines and services, I need to abstract all that underlying fabric infrastructure from them. The user needs to be able to say (or request through a self-service interface), "I want an instance of this service in Datacenter A and B, and it should connect to the development and backup networks on a silver tier of storage." Behind the scenes, the private cloud infrastructure works out that for the development network in Datacenter A, the network adapter needs an IP address in a certain subnet connected to a specific VLAN and some other subnet and VLAN in Datacenter B. The infrastructure works out that silver-tier storage in Datacenter A means using the NetApp SAN and only certain LUNs, while in Datacenter B the EMC SAN is used with other specific LUNs. The user gets the service and connectivity they need with zero knowledge of the actual infrastructure, which is exactly as it should be.

Self-service by the user for the provisioning of these services is a great way to think of the difference between virtualization and the private cloud. Let me walk through the most basic case: creating a new virtual machine for a user. Provisioning virtual machines in a virtual world goes like this (Figure 9.1):

1. The user makes a request to the IT department. This could be a phone call, an email, or some help-desk request.

2. The IT department gets the request and may do some validation such as checking with their manager if it's approved.

3. IT will then launch their virtualization management tool and create a virtual machine from a template.

4. IT will then contact the user giving them the IP address of the VM.

This sounds fast, but in reality this process ranges from a few days to six weeks in some companies I've worked with. It's a manual process, IT teams are busy, they just don't like the particular business user, or there could be "solar activity disrupting electronics" (which is the same as not liking the user). Whatever the case, because it's a manual process, it takes time and is often fairly low on the priority list.

It can also be fairly hard to track the allocation of virtual machines, which means often there is no ability to charge business units for the requested virtual machines. This can lead to virtual machine sprawl because to the business the virtual machines are free.

In the private cloud, this changes to the process shown in Figure 9.2. The resources used are the same, but the order of the steps and method has changed.

1. The IT team use their management tool to carve out clouds of resources, which include compute, storage, and network resources, and assign clouds to users or groups of users with certain quotas. This is all done before any users request resources and is the only time the IT team has to do any work, freeing them up to spend their time on more forward-looking endeavors.

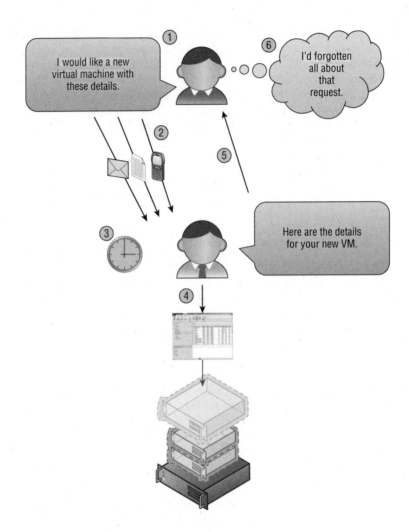

**FIGURE 9.1**
Traditional process for requesting virtual machines that is hands-on for the administrator

2. The user accesses a self-service portal and fills out a basic request letting them select the type of VM or application and the cloud they want to create it in based on their allocations and quotas.

3. The private cloud infrastructure takes the request and automatically provisions the VM, which could include workflows to request authorization from management if required. The user would see the details of their new VM in the self-service portal and could even get an automated email giving them details.

4. The user is happy, and if they had a red button that said "That was easy," they would be pressing it.

**FIGURE 9.2**

Provisioning process when using private cloud

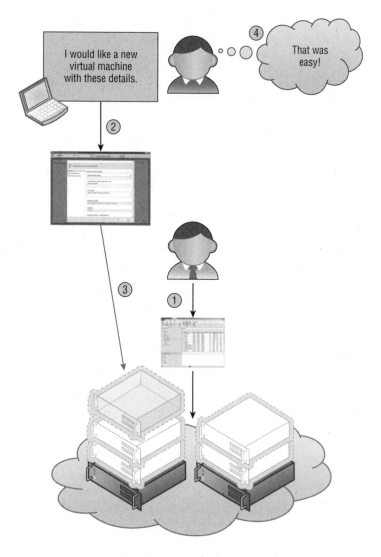

The number-one fear of many IT departments I talk to about the private cloud is that the ability for users and business units to self-serve themselves to virtual machines will result in millions of virtual machines being created for no good reason, plunging the IT infrastructure into a dark age of VM sprawl beyond any previously envisioned nightmare scenario. But that is simply not the case.

Remember what you are doing. First, you are creating clouds of resources. You are defining what these clouds can access in terms of which virtualization hosts and, on those virtualization hosts, how much memory, virtual CPU, and disk IOPS can be consumed. You are setting which tiers of storage that cloud can access and how much space. You are setting which networks that cloud can connect to. You are setting which VM templates can be used by the users to create the virtual machines. For each user or group of users, you set the quotas of how many virtual machines they can create or how much memory and virtual CPUs they can use in each cloud. You can even set what the virtual machines can look like in terms of CPU and memory allocations. With a private cloud solution, you can set charge-back and show-back capabilities, so if a business unit creates a large amount of virtual resource, they get charged accordingly, so the solution is fully accountable. You can set expiry of virtual machines so they are automatically deleted after a period of time. Users can create only on the resources you have defined and within the limits you have configured. If they have a limit of five virtual machines and want to create a sixth, they would have to either delete a virtual machine, export a virtual machine to a library that you have granted them, or request an extension of their quota and go through an approval process.

I think you will find this is more controlled and enforceable than any manual process you may have today. Users request a VM today, and you give it to them; it just takes you weeks, which may discourage business units from asking for virtual resources unless they really need them. That's a terrible way to control resources—by making it painful. Business users will just go elsewhere for their services such as setting up their own infrastructures or using public cloud services, which I've seen happen at a lot of organizations. It's far better to get good processes in place and enable the business so they can function in the most optimal way and use internal services where it makes sense. Remember with the private cloud, you can configure costs for virtual resources and charge the business, so if more virtual resources are required because the business units can now provision resources more easily, the IT department has the ability to gain the funding to procure more IT infrastructure as needed.

You can start slow. Maybe you use the private cloud for development and test environments first, get used to the idea, and get the users used to working within quotas. The private cloud infrastructure can be used in production, but perhaps it's the IT department using the private cloud and maybe even the self-service portal initially and then over time you turn it over to actual end users.

## Private Cloud Components

The difference between virtualization and the private cloud is simply the management infrastructure. The same compute, network, and storage resources used for a virtualization infrastructure can be used for a private cloud. To turn virtualization into a private cloud solution, you need the right management stack. For a Microsoft private cloud, this is System Center 2012 R2 added to the virtualization foundation provided by Hyper-V 2012 R2. I provided a brief overview of System Center in Chapter 1; however, here I will cover the components that are critical for a private cloud and why they are critical.

Many of the benefits of virtualization are related to the abstraction of resources, scalability, and controlled self-service. All of these benefits primarily come through SCVMM, so I will cover some of these.

Consider a typical virtualization administrator who has full administrative rights over the virtualization hosts and the compute resource but no insight into the storage and network. This leads to many problems and challenges for the virtualization administrators:

- "I have no visibility into what is going on at a storage level. I would like to have insight into the storage area networks that store my virtual machines from SCVMM."

- "Deploying server applications requires following a 100+ page procedure, which has human error possibilities and differences in implementation between development, test, and production. I want to be able to install the server application once and then just move it between environments modifying only changes in configuration."

- "My organization has many datacenters with different network details, but I don't want to have to change the way I deploy virtual machines based on where they are being deployed. The management tool should understand my different networks, such as production, backup, and DMZ, and set the correct IP details and use the right NICs in the hosts as needed."

- "I need to save power, so in quiet times I want to consolidate my virtual machines on a smaller number of hosts and power down unnecessary servers."

While the name System Center Virtual Machine Manager might make it seem like it's focused on the virtual machine management, some of its most powerful features relate not to virtualization but to the storage and network fabric, as discussed in this book. SCVMM integrates with the storage in your environment using SMI-S to give insight into the storage but also classifies and assigns storage to hosts as required. SCVMM allows the network to be designed in SCVMM, providing easy network assignment for the virtual workloads, including providing network virtualization with connectivity to nonvirtualized networks with 2012 R2. All of this insight into the compute, storage, and network resources is completely abstracted for the end user, enabling simple provisioning. Because all the resources are exposed and managed centrally, this leads to a greater utilization of resources, which is a key goal of the private cloud.

Once all the types of resources are centrally managed and abstracted, a key piece to the private cloud is actually creating clouds that can be consumed by different groups within an organization, which could be business units, teams of developers, or different parts of IT, or they could even be used by the same group of administrators for provisioning. But using separate clouds for different uses/groups provides a simpler tracking of resources. A cloud typically consists of a number of key resources and configurations that include the following:

- The capacity of the cloud, such as how much memory, processor, and storage resources can be used by the cloud and which hosts are used

- The classifications of storage exposed to the cloud

- Which networks can be used by the cloud

- The capabilities exposed to the cloud such as maximum number of vCPUs per VM

- Library assets available to the cloud such as templates

- Writable libraries for the purposing of storing virtual machines by cloud users

Notice that the cloud has specific capacity assigned rather than exposing the full capacity of the underlying resources. This means there could be a single set of hosts and storage that could be used by many different clouds. Once clouds are created, the cloud is assigned to different groups of users, or *tenants*, and those specific tenants have their own quotas within the capacity of the cloud. Individual users in the tenant group have their own subset of quota if required, giving very high levels of granularity and control over the consumption of resources in the cloud. Like clouds and underlying resources, many different tenants can be created for a single cloud. Clouds and tenants are defined and enabled through SCVMM. SCVMM also enables visibility into the usage of current cloud capacity and features role-based access control, which means end users could be given the SCVMM console to use for the creation of virtual machines because they would only see options related to their assigned actions; however, this is not really a good interface for end users to consume.

To provide the self-service capability commonly associated with the private cloud, you use the System Center App Controller component. App Controller provides a web-based front end to expose the clouds defined in SCVMM to the user and also to integrate with Windows Azure–based clouds and even hosting partners that leverage the Service Provider Framework (SPF). App Controller provides the ability to create virtual machines and also basic management such as snapshot creation and stop and start actions, plus a way to connect to the virtual machine consoles. App Controller also provides a bridge between on-premises private clouds and Windows Azure by allowing virtual machines to be migrated from on-premises to Azure.

While App Controller surfaces the clouds defined in SCVMM to the end user and allows self-service within the quotas defined as part of the cloud capacity and the tenant quotas, there is no concept of a provisioning workflow nor approval of requests. SCVMM and App Controller also lack detailed reporting on resource usage and the ability to charge business units based on resource consumption. You can use the Orchestrator and Service Manager components to leverage these features, as I will explain later in this chapter.

What does all this mean? For the key features of the private cloud such as scalability, utilization of resources, abstraction of the fabric, and self-service, the key components required for a Microsoft solution are Hyper-V, SCVMM, and App Controller. Other components such as Orchestrator and Service Manager bring additional functionality such as workflow, approval, and chargeback but are not required for a core private cloud solution. In this chapter, I will focus on SCVMM and App Controller as the foundation for the private cloud before briefly covering the additional features from the rest of System Center. Note that SCVMM no longer has its own self-service portal in the 2012 R2 version; App Controller replaces it.

## SCVMM Fundamentals

There are many sayings in the world; two that apply to Hyper-V and SCVMM especially are "A poor workman blames his tools" and "Behind every great man is a great woman" (or maybe that's a song lyric). With virtualization and Hyper-V, the tools that are used to manage and interact with Hyper-V are critical to a successful virtualization endeavor. I would not blame an administrator for blaming an inefficiently run Hyper-V implementation on his tools if all the administrator had access to was the Hyper-V management tool that is supplied in the box, "A poor Hyper-V admin blames Hyper-V manager, and so he should." For effective and comprehensive management of a Hyper-V environment and a heterogeneous virtualization environment including ESX and XenServer, System Center Virtual Machine Manager is a necessity. "Behind every great Hyper-V implementation is a great SCVMM."

## Installation

SCVMM 2012 R2, like the rest of the System Center 2012 R2 components, supports installation only on Windows Server 2012 or Windows Server 2012 R2, which requires a 64-bit server. The other software requirements are fairly minimal, and the only requirement you will have to manually install is the Windows Assessment and Deployment Kit (WADK), which includes components to create and manage operating system images that are required for SCVMM's bare-metal deployment features. You can download the correct WADK version from www.microsoft.com/en-eg/download/details.aspx?id=39982. The other requirements are actually part of the Windows Server 2012 R2 operating system such as Microsoft .NET Framework 4.5 and are automatically installed by the SCVMM installation process. SCVMM must be installed on a server that is part of an Active Directory domain but does not have any strict requirements such as a Windows Server 2008 domain or forest-level mode.

SQL Server 2008 R2 or SQL Server 2012 is required for SCVMM 2012 R2 to store its configuration and data, but this does not need to be installed on the SCVMM server. I recommend having a separate SQL server used for SCVMM and leveraging an existing SQL server farm in your organization that is highly available and maintained by SQL administrators. If you are testing SCVMM in a lab with a small number of hosts, then installing SQL on the SCVMM server is fine, but, where possible, you should leverage an external, dedicated SQL environment.

If you are running an older version of SCVMM 2012, there are specific operating system and SQL server requirements that are documented at the following locations:

- Operating system requirements: http://technet.microsoft.com/en-us/library/gg610562.aspx

- SQL Server requirements: http://technet.microsoft.com/en-us/library/gg610574.aspx

The actual hardware specifications required will vary based on the number of virtualization hosts being managed by SCVMM. A single SCVMM 2012 R2 server can manage up to 1,000 hosts containing up to 25,000 virtual machines. The Microsoft recommendations actually state that when you have fewer than 150 hosts per SCVMM, you can run the SQL Server on the SCVMM instance. I still prefer to limit the number of SQL instances in my environment, and it's better to invest in that well-architected and maintained highly available SQL farm rather than a local SQL install. Also, if you are planning on implementing a highly available SCVMM installation, then you need SQL Server separate from your SCVMM server. Virtualizing SCVMM 2012 is fully supported and indeed recommended. In my experience, all of the clients I work with virtualize SCVMM.

As with any virtualized service, it is important that you make sure the necessary resources are available to meet your virtualized loads and you don't overcommit resources beyond acceptable performance. Because SCVMM is so important to the management of your virtual environment, I actually like to set the reserve on the vCPUs for my SCVMM to 50 percent to ensure it always can get CPU resources in times of contention. Of course, as you will see, SCVMM should be doing a great job of constantly tweaking your virtual environment to ensure the most optimal performance and ensuring all the virtual machines get the resources they need, moving the virtual machines between hosts if necessary. If you have severely over-committed your environment by putting too many virtual machines on the available resources, performance will suffer, which is why proper discovery and planning are vital to a successful virtual environment.

Dynamic memory is fully supported by SCVMM. My recommendation for the dynamic memory setting for production environments is to set the startup memory to 2,048 and the maximum to 4,096 (the Microsoft minimum and recommended values) for environments managing fewer than 150 hosts. Set startup to 4,096 and maximum to 8,192 for SCVMM instances managing more than 150 hosts. This way, your environment is being efficient in the amount of memory it's using, but it stays within limits supported by Microsoft. You can certainly exceed these maximums if you find memory is low (but that should be unlikely), but I don't recommend you go below the minimum supported for the startup unless perhaps it's in a small lab environment with only a couple of hosts and you are short on memory.

Note that during the installation of SCVMM, the install process performs a check for the minimum amount of memory. If the OS has less than 2000 MB of RAM, the install process will error and refuse to continue. If you are using dynamic memory and set the startup to less than 2048, you will likely hit this problem, so turn off the VM, set the startup memory to 2048, start the VM, and restart the installation. You will get a warning that the memory does not meet the recommended amount of 4000 MB, but this is just a warning and won't stop the installation process. Once the SCVMM install is complete, you can power down the VM, modify the startup value to less than 2048, and continue using SCVMM. It does not check for minimum memory anytime other than install, but remember that using less than 2048 really is not recommended and definitely should not be done in any production environment.

You must specify an account during the installation of SCVMM, which is used to run the actual SCVMM service. During installation you are given the option to either specify a domain account or use Local System. Don't use Local System; while it may seem like the easy option, it limits a number of capabilities of SCVMM such as using shared ISO images with Hyper-V virtual machines, and it can make troubleshooting difficult because all the logs will just show Local System instead of an account dedicated to SCVMM. On the flip side, don't use your domain Administrator account, which has too much power and would have the same problem troubleshooting because you would just see Administrator everywhere. Create a dedicated domain user account just for SCVMM that meets your organization's naming convention, such as svcSCVMM or VMMService. Make that account a local administrator on the SCVMM server by adding the account to the local Administrators group. You can do this with the following command, or you can use the Server Manager tool to navigate to Configuration ➤ Local Users And Groups ➤ Groups and add the account to the Administrators group.

```
C:\ >net localgroup Administrators /add savilltech\svcSCVMM
The command completed successfully.
```

Do not use a generic domain service account for different applications. This can cause unexpected results and once again makes troubleshooting hard. Use a separate account for each of your services, that is, one for SCVMM, one for System Center Operations Manager (in fact, you need more than one for Operations Manager), another for System Center Configuration Manager, and so on. What do I mean by unexpected results? When SCVMM manages a host, it adds its management account to the local Administrators group of that host, in my case svc-SCVMM. If that host is removed from SCVMM management, that account is removed from the local Administrators group of that host. Now imagine you used a shared service account between SCVMM and another application that also needed its service account to be part of the local Administrators group. When you removed the host from SCVMM management, that shared service account would be removed from the local Administrators group on that host, and you just broke that other application.

If you have multiple SCVMM servers in a high availability configuration, the same domain account would be used on all servers, and it's actually a requirement to use a domain account in a SCVMM high availability scenario or if you have a disjointed namespace in your domain. For information on disjointed namespaces, see `http://support.microsoft.com/kb/909264`. Ideally, this is not something you have in your environment because it can be a huge pain for many applications.

During the installation of SCVMM, there is an option to specify the storage of the distributed keys that are used for the encryption of data in the SCVMM database. Normally these keys are stored on the local SCVMM computer, but if you are implementing a highly available SCVMM installation, then the keys need to be stored centrally. For SCVMM this means storing in Active Directory. For details on creating the necessary container in Active Directory for the distributed key management, refer to `http://technet.microsoft.com/en-us/library/gg697604.aspx`.

The actual installation process for SCVMM 2012 is a simple, wizard-driven affair that will guide you through all the required configuration steps, so I won't go into the details here. Just remember to specify your domain account for the service.

SCVMM 2012 supports being installed on a failover cluster now, which means the SCVMM service becomes highly available and can be moved in planned and unplanned scenarios using failover clustering technologies. An external SQL Server should be used to host the SCVMM database, and the installation of SCVMM to a highly available configuration is very simple. Start the SCVMM 2012 installation to an operating system instance that is part of a failover cluster, and the SCVMM install process will detect the presence of the failover clustering feature and prompt if the SCVMM installation should be made highly available. If you answer yes, then you will be prompted for an additional IP address and a name that will be used for the cluster SCVMM service, and that is really the only change in the installation process. A domain account will need to be specified for the VMM service to run as, and Active Directory will be used for storing the encryption keys. You would need to also install SCVMM on all the other nodes in the failover cluster so the SCVMM service can run on all nodes.

## SCVMM Management Console

The SCVMM management console looks different from consoles you may be used to because System Center has moved away from the Microsoft Management Console (MMC) standard in favor of a new workspace-based layout. This does not have an official name, but I like System Center Console Framework. Figure 9.3 shows the new console for SCVMM and is broken down into five main elements (also known as *panes*):

◆ Ribbon: The ribbon has become a standard in most Microsoft applications, and you will quickly come to appreciate the dynamically changing ribbon showing the actions available for the selected object that highlights the actions that are most popular based on a lot of research by the SCVMM team.

◆ Workspaces: The entire console is workspace based, and in the workspace area you select the workspace you want to work in, which is reflected in all other areas of the console. The workspace area shows the five available standard workspaces: VMs And Services, Fabric, Library, Jobs, and Settings. You will also hear workspaces unofficially referred to as *wunderbars*. After the initial configuration of SCVMM, you will not use Settings much, but the other workspaces will be used as you enhance your environment.

◆ Navigation: This shows the areas of management available in the current workspace.

◆ Results: Based on the current navigation node selected, this area will show all the results for that area. Note the Results pane will also be affected by elements selected in the ribbon, which can control what is shown in the Results pane based on the current workspace and Navigation area.

◆ Details: The Details pane is not always shown but, when available, will show detailed information on the currently selected object in the Results pane.

**FIGURE 9.3**
All elements of the SCVMM console change based on the current work-space and selected element of the workspace.

Navigation                                                    Ribbon

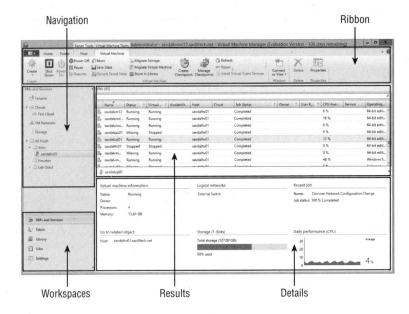

Workspaces                    Results                    Details

The best way to learn the SCVMM console is to fire it up and just look around. Explore all the workspaces, select the different nodes in the Navigation pane, and pay attention to the ribbon, which will change and show some interesting options that you will want to play with.

The MMC was great for its original concept of a standardized interface that could actually allow different snap-ins to be placed and organized in a single console, but there were restrictions, particularly around role-based access control (RBAC), which is a key tenant of System Center 2012 and newer. I'm talking about System Center here instead of SCVMM because the focus on RBAC is common for all of System Center and not just SCVMM. As System Center is used more broadly across an organization, it's likely different groups of users will be given access to only certain functionality areas of System Center 2012 components and within those functionality areas only be able to perform actions on a subset of all the objects. In the past, while delegating different permissions was possible, the people delegating rights would still see all the elements of the administrative console and would get "Access Denied" messages. With the new System Center model and RBAC, delegated users see only the areas of the console they have rights to and only the objects they are allowed to work with. A great example in SCVMM would be granting delegated rights to a group of users for only a specific collection of virtual-ization hosts. As Figure 9.4 shows, full administrators see the entire host hierarchy and all the available clouds on the left side, while application administrators (a self-service user) for the Lab Cloud servers cannot see any of the clouds nor do they have any knowledge of other host groups except for Lab Cloud, which they have been assigned to. By showing application administrators only console elements and objects that they have rights to, it makes the console easier to use, makes it more intuitive, avoids the "why don't I have access to x, y, and z?" questions, and makes the administrative tool usable by normal users such as self-service users. Notice the delegated user also has no view of the fabric workspace at all, and the other workspaces have information limited to their specific cloud.

In SCVMM user roles are created and assigned in the Settings workspace in the Security ➤ User Roles navigation area. By default, user roles exist for administrators and self-service users, but additional roles can be defined. Other profiles beyond application administrators include fabric administrators (delegated administrators), who have administrative rights on objects within their assigned scope; read-only administrators, which is great for users like the help desk who need to see everything but should not be able to change anything and can be scoped to specific host groups and clouds; and additional self-service roles, which can be scoped to different clouds and can have different actions available to them and different quotas such as Tenant Administrator. The adoption of the new interface also enables the ribbon, which really does help interact with System Center.

**FIGURE 9.4**
The view on the left shows a normal SCVMM administrator, while on the right you see the view for a Lab Cloud host group delegated administrator.

The SCVMM 2012 R2 console can be installed on any Windows 7 SP1 x86 or x64 Professional or newer operating system in addition to Windows Server 2008 R2 SP1 servers. By installing the SCVMM 2012 console on machines, you can remotely manage SCVMM and avoid having to log on to the SCVMM 2012 server. I like to install all the various management consoles from Windows and System Center on a remote desktop session host and then publish the administrator tools using the RDP protocol. I can then get to the admin tools from any device and operating system. I walk through the process in the video at http://youtu.be/_dkxyr03Er4.

Once you start using SCVMM for managing your Hyper-V environments, you should not use Hyper-V Manager or the Failover Cluster Management tool for normal virtualization resource management. If you do make changes using Hyper-V Manager directly, then SCVMM may not be aware of the change, and it can take some time for SCVMM to detect it, giving inconsistent views between Hyper-V Manager and SCVMM. For best results, once SCVMM is implemented and managing virtualization resources, don't use other management tools to manage the same resources.

---

**UNLOCKING ALL POSSIBILITIES WITH POWERSHELL**

When you look at any resource on System Center 2012 and newer or on Windows Server 2012 or newer, one common theme will be the prevalence of PowerShell. Everything that is done in the System Center consoles is actually performed by an underlying PowerShell cmdlet. As you make a selection in a console and click an action behind the scenes, the console composes the correct PowerShell command and executes it behind the scenes. There are actually many actions you can take only with PowerShell, and as you become more acquainted with System Center, you will start to use PowerShell more and more. I'm not talking about manually running actions, but when you consider you can perform every management action for the entire System Center 2012 product using PowerShell, the automation possibilities can truly be realized, and you will start to automate more and more processes.

A great way to get started with PowerShell is to use the graphical interface to perform an action, such as creating a new virtual machine, and in the Summary stage of the wizard you will see a View Script button at the bottom-right corner. Click the View Script button, and you will be shown all the PowerShell commands the console is going to run to perform the actions selected. You can now take all these commands and add them into your own scripts or automation processes.

---

## Libraries

Throughout this book I talk about many aspects of SCVMM, but I wanted to spend some time on the concept of libraries in SCVMM because they are critical when thinking about many activities. While it would be possible to store all these resources in various locations, the best way is to utilize the SCVMM library feature, which allows one or more file shares to be used by SCVMM as a central repository for assets that can be used in the virtualization management. Typical assets placed in the library include the following:

- Virtual machine templates, which include the virtual machine hardware configuration, OS configuration information such as domain membership, the product key, and other configuration options for enabling the fast creation of new virtual machines.

- Virtual hard disks, which will primarily be VHD for Hyper-V virtual machines (and XenServer) but can also store VMDK for ESX. VHD files can also be used to deploy physical Hyper-V servers.

- Virtual machines that are not in use. This allows saving disk space on the virtualization hosts or shared storage for unused machines and storing in the SCVMM library. You can then deploy them again if needed. For end users, this saves their VM quota!

- ISO files, which are images of CDs and DVDs that can be attached to virtual machines to install operating systems or applications.

- Drivers.

- Service templates, which describe multitiered services.

- Various types of profiles such as hardware profiles and guest OS profiles that are used as building blocks for creating templates. Host profiles (for physical deployments of Hyper-V servers), capability profiles that describe the capabilities of different hypervisors or environments, SQL Server profiles when installing SQL Server, and application profiles for application deployment. Think of profiles as building blocks for use in other activities within SCVMM.

- Updated baselines and catalogs.

- Scripts and commands used for management, which can be grouped together into packages called custom resources (which as previously mentioned are just folders with a `.cr` extension).

I should be clear that while libraries do have a physical manifestation by storing content on the file shares you specify when you add new library servers, not everything in the library is saved as a file. You will not find virtual machine templates or profiles as files on the file system; instead, templates and profiles are stored as metadata in the SCVMM SQL database.

The file system that corresponds to a location in the library can be accessed by right-clicking a library branch and selecting Explore or by selecting Explore from the ribbon. To add non-virtual-machine-type content such as drivers and ISO files, you would just use the Explore feature and then copy content onto the file system using Windows Explorer. When the library content is refreshed, the new content would be displayed, which can be forced to occur by selecting the library server and selecting the Refresh action on the Library Server ribbon tab. By default library content is automatically refreshed once an hour, but you can change this in the Settings workspace and in the General navigation area select the Library Settings and change the refresh interval per your organization's requirements.

I previously covered the creation of templates, so I'm going to move on to using other types of resources. Templates are one of the primary reasons to use SCVMM. While a single SCVMM library server is added during the installation of SCVMM, additional library servers can be added. It's common to add multiple library servers, particularly so you have a library server in each datacenter where you have virtualization hosts to ensure content that may need to be accessed by the hosts is locally available, and so you do not have to traverse a WAN connection. When you add a library server when the share is selected, check the Add Default Resources box for all the SCVMM default library content to be copied to the share. It is fully supported to host the file share that stores the library content on a highly available file server, which means it's part of a failover cluster and helps ensure the content is available even if a node fails.

To ensure hosts use a library server that is closest to them, library servers can be assigned to host groups by selecting the properties of the library server and setting up the host group, as shown in Figure 9.5. The recommendation is that virtualization hosts should be connected by at least a 100 Mbps link to the library server they use, but ideally 1 Gbps.

**FIGURE 9.5**
Specifying the
library server for a
specific host group

---

**REPLICATING LIBRARY CONTENT BETWEEN MULTIPLE LIBRARY SERVERS**

SCVMM has no capability to replicate the content of the library servers. If your organization has 20 SCVMM library servers, that means there are 20 file shares all with their own content that you need to keep maintained. If you add a VHD to one library, you need to add it to the other 19 manually.

There are a number of solutions to keep the content replicated, but all involve initially having a single "master" library, which is the library you add new content to and update/remove existing content from. A technology is then used to synchronize this master copy to all the other library servers. One way to replicate the content is to use the Microsoft Robust File Copy tool (Robocopy), which will copy the content from the master to all the other libraries in the organization. Once the copy is complete, a manual refresh of the library would be performed in SCVMM to load in the new content, which can be performed in PowerShell using the Read-SCLibraryShare cmdlet. Another option is to use Distribute File System Replication (DFSR), which allows master-slave relationships to be created and will automatically replicate changes from the master to the slave library shares, but the new content would not show until a library refresh was performed. You *cannot* use Distributed File System Namespaces (DFSN) as a location for libraries, only the DFSR replication component.

If you have other replication technologies in your organization, that is fine. The two technologies mentioned here are free, Microsoft-provided technologies.

If you have multiple libraries, you will end up with the same content on many different library servers, and your templates will refer to the content on a specific library server such as \\londonlib\SCVMM\VHDs\2008R2.vhd. But you are actually deploying to a server in New York, and there is a library server in New York, \\newyorklib\SCVMM, that has exactly the same file, which you would rather use than copying the content over the North Atlantic. SCVMM allows equivalencies to be created in the library, which as the name suggests allows you to specify that various content from all the different libraries are actually the same object. This means that even though a template may say to deploy \\londonlib\SCVMM\VHDs\2012R2.vhd, because you created an equivalency between the \\londonlib\SCVMM\VHDs\2012R2.vhd and \\newyorklib\SCVMM\VHDs\2012R2.vhd files, if you deployed the template in New York, it would use the VHD from the New York share. This also provides redundancy because if the New York library was not available, then the London library could be used.

To create an equivalency, you select the root Library Servers node in the Navigation pane in the Library workspace. You can then add a filter in the Results pane to show the objects of interest. Select the objects that are the same and then select the Mark Equivalent action; a dialog will open that will ask for a family for the objects and then a release. Both of these values are just text values but are used to help find other objects that match the family and release, so be consistent in your naming. As you type in the values, autocomplete will show existing values, or you can select from the drop-down.

One of the interesting ways library content is used is the use of ISO files, which are files that contain the content of a CD or DVD. To inject a CD/DVD into a virtual machine, you access the properties of a virtual machine by selecting the VM in the Results pane of the VMs And Services workspace and selecting the Properties action. Within the properties of the virtual machine, you select the Hardware Configuration tab, and under Bus Configuration you will find a Virtual DVD Drive. Select Virtual DVD Drive, and notice there is an option for No Media, which means the drive is empty. Physical CD or DVD Drive links it to the physical optical drive in the virtualization host, and Existing ISO Image File allows you to select an ISO file from the library.

Notice an interesting option in Figure 9.6: Share File Instead Of Copying It. A CD/DVD image is normally used to install some software onto an operating system. If the VM accessed the ISO file over the network and that connectivity was lost, it may cause unexpected results because it would appear the media was suddenly ripped out. To avoid this happening by default, when an ISO is attached to a VM drive, the ISO is first copied using BITS over the HTTPS protocol to the Hyper-V host in the virtual machine's folder, and then the VM attaches to the local copied ISO file. This means any network interruption would not stop the access to the ISO. When the ISO is ejected from the VM, the copied ISO file is deleted from the local host. While this does use disk space while the ISO is being used, it gives the safest approach. This same copy approach is used for ESX and XenServer but uses a different file copy technology specific to the virtualization platform. For Hyper-V, only SCVMM gives the option of not copying the ISO to the virtualization host and actually attaches the virtual drive to the ISO on the SCVMM library file share, which is the Share File Instead Of Copying It option. There are some specific configurations required to enable sharing; see http://technet.microsoft.com/en-us/library/ee340124.aspx.

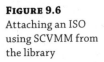

**FIGURE 9.6**
Attaching an ISO
using SCVMM from
the library

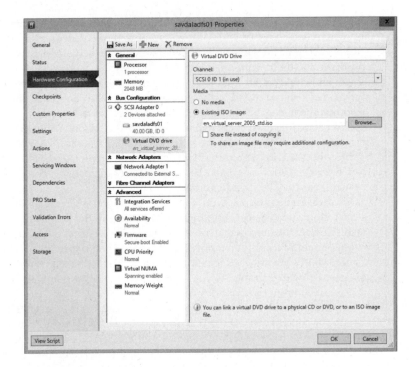

The library is one of the key capabilities of SCVMM. All types of resources can be stored in the library, even entire virtual machines, so it's important to architect the right number of library servers, ensuring proximity of a library server to your hosts in all your datacenters.

## Creating a Private Cloud Using System Center Virtual Machine Manager

I'm going to assume System Center Virtual Machine Manager is fully configured with all your hypervisor compute resources, such as all the Hyper-V servers that have been placed into failover clusters that have been dynamic- and power-optimized to get the most performant and highly available solution, which minimizes power wastage by turning off hosts when not needed. SCVMM has been connected to your hardware load balancers, all the storage area networks have their SMI-S providers in SCVMM, and the storage has been classified such as gold, silver, and bronze for all locations. Logical networks and sites have been defined. Virtual machine templates for all common configurations have been created, and common services have been modeled as a service template. System Center Operations Manager is performing monitoring of the environment, System Center Data Protection Manager is backing up and protecting the environment, and System Center Configuration Manager is providing patching, desired configuration, and inventory information. Everything is well configured and healthy, so you are ready to create a cloud.

To really understand what goes into creating a cloud in System Center Virtual Machine Manager and all the options, I will walk you through creating a cloud and granting users access to it. This will show all the capabilities and the delegation options for different groups of users.

You use the Virtual Machine Manager Console to create a new cloud, which is achieved through the VMs And Services workspace by selecting the Create Cloud action from the ribbon. The first step is to specify a name and description for the cloud. A good example may be Development for the name and then Cloud for development purposes, with access to the development network only and silver tier storage. Make it something useful.

The next step sets the actual resources that will be included in the cloud, as shown in Figure 9.7. The host groups will govern the computer resources (virtualization hosts) that will be included in the created cloud in addition to the various storage and networks that are available in those host groups. Remember that just because a host group is specified, it does not mean the entire capability or connectivity of that host group is exposed to the cloud. You can specify exactly what you want to give access to later in the wizard. The same host groups can be included in multiple clouds. Also note in the dialog that a VMware resource pool can be selected directly.

**FIGURE 9.7**
Selecting the host group that is available for utilization by the cloud

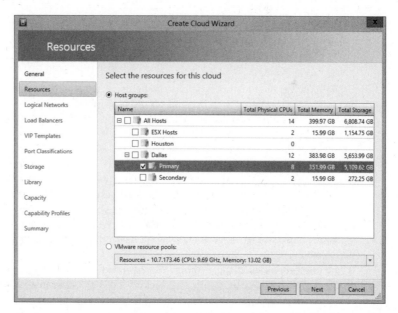

The next stage of the wizard allows the selection of which logical networks are available to the cloud. The logical networks displayed will vary depending on the connectivity available to the hosts in the host groups specified in the previous screen. Select the logical networks this cloud should have access to, as shown in Figure 9.8, and click Next to continue with the wizard.

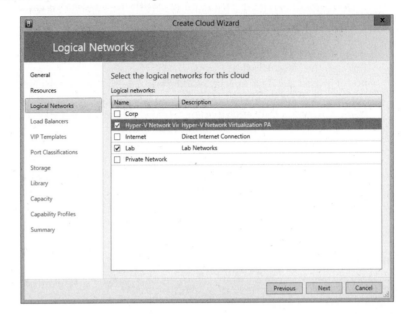

The hardware load balancers that can be used can be selected on this screen. The hardware load balancers displayed will depend on the host groups selected and the logical networks selected since a hardware load balancer is tied to host groups and logical networks. Once again, click Next to continue, which will allow you to select which virtual IP profiles to make available to the cloud; these are tied to the load balancers selected on the previous screen (do you see the pattern now?). Make the selections and click Next. The various types of port classifications for the cloud are displayed; you should select the ones desired for the cloud and click Next.

The Storage stage of the wizard displays all tiers of storage that are available within the selected host groups. Select the tiers of storage that should be available to the cloud, as shown in Figure 9.9. For a development cloud, as an example, I would select lower tiers of storage such as bronze. Only storage tiers that are available to the selected host groups will be displayed. Click Next.

The next step is selecting a library configuration. There are two parts to this. The first is the selection of the read-only library shares, and these are standard SCVMM libraries in the environment you want to grant this cloud access to and the contained resources that can be used to create virtual machines and services. You could create libraries with a subset of ISO images to limit what can be created in the clouds. The read-only library needs to be unique and not used as part of a normal library. A stored VM path is also specified, which is an area in which the users of the cloud can actually store content. Why do you want to give the cloud users a writable library area? Consider that users of the cloud will have a certain quota that limits the number of virtual machines they can create. It is possible they may run out of quota and need to create another VM or simply don't need a VM right now but don't want to lose its configuration. When you give the users a place where they can store VMs, the users can save a VM to storage, which removes it from the virtualization host and thus frees up their quota. In the future, the VM could be deployed from the library back to a virtualization host and once again count against their quota. Note that the path specified for the storage of VMs cannot be part of a library location specified as a read-only library. An easy solution is to create a new share on a file server, add it to SCVMM as a library, and then use it as the writable area for a cloud. Once everything has been configured, click Next.

**FIGURE 9.9**
Selecting the storage classifications available to the cloud

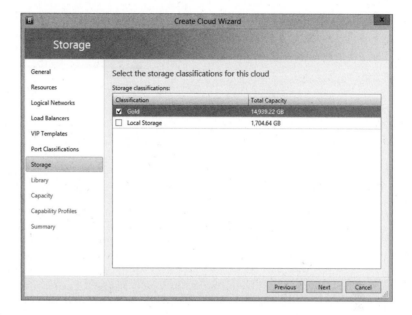

The next stage is configuring the capacity for the cloud (Figure 9.10), and this gets very interesting because there are different approaches an organization can take to managing capacity for the cloud. By default the capacity is unlimited, but I can change any of the dimensions of capacity, such as virtual CPUs, memory, storage, custom quota (which is carried over for compatibility with SCVMM 2008 R2), and virtual machines. I can set the values to use the maximum, a smaller amount, or a higher amount as I did with memory in Figure 9.11. Remember, this is the capacity available to this cloud, so I don't have to expose the full capabilities of the underlying host groups; I may have 10 different clouds on a single set of host groups and want to divide the resources between clouds. But wait a minute; I just set the memory to *higher* than I have available in the underlying hosts in the selected host groups. How does this work? It's quite acceptable to set the capacity of a cloud to exceed that of the current underlying resources of the cloud. It is just important that the proper resource utilization mechanisms and processes are in place so that as a cloud starts to approach the capacity of the underlying resources, additional resources are added to the host groups. This is where System Center Operations Manager is great for monitoring the usage of resources and can then work with System Center Virtual Machine Manager and System Center Orchestrator to add new Hyper-V hosts and place them into host groups. The same could be done for storage by adding new LUNs to the required storage tiers. Scalability is a key attribute of the private cloud. Set the capacity for the cloud and click Next.

**FIGURE 9.10**
Configuring the
capacity for the
cloud

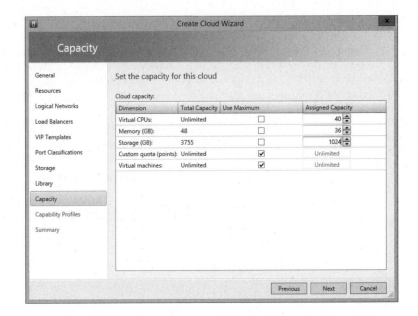

The next stage, capability profiles, is an interesting concept. This is different from capacity. Capacity is the limit of what can be stored in the cloud, while capability defines what the virtual machines created in the cloud are, well, capable of. For example, what is the maximum number of virtual CPUs that can be assigned to a virtual machine, and what is the maximum amount of memory for a VM? By default three capability profiles exist—one for Hyper-V, one for ESX, and one for XenServer—which profile the maximum capabilities for each hypervisor platform. For example, the Hyper-V capability profile sets the processor range from 1 to 64 and sets the memory from 8 MB to 1 TB, which are the limits for Hyper-V 2012. The ESX capability profile sets the processor range from 1 to 8 and the memory from 4 MB to 255 GB, which are the ESX 4.1 limits. By default you can select any combination of the three built-in, locked capability profiles for your cloud based on the hypervisors used in the cloud, but you don't have to.

Imagine you are creating a development cloud today. Windows Server 2012 and 2012 R2 Hyper-V are available with their support for virtual machines with 64 virtual CPUs and 1 TB of RAM. I may give a user a quota of 20 virtual CPUs and 24 GB of memory, so do I want that user consuming their whole quota with a single VM? Not likely. Instead, I could create a custom capability profile in the Library workspace and under Profiles ➤ Capability Profiles create a new profile to meet the capabilities I want in a specific cloud. In Figure 9.11, I have created a custom capability profile that has a limit of virtual CPUs and a memory range from 512 MB to 4 GB, and I could also mandate the use of dynamic memory. Note that I can also set the number of DVD drives allowed; if shared images are used, I could set the number of hard disks allowed and their type and size, number of network adapters, and even whether high availability is available or required.

There is a potential pitfall of creating customer capability profiles if you don't plan well. Many resources such as virtual machine templates have a configuration that sets the required capability profile. If you don't update the resources with your custom capability profile, you won't be able to assign any resources to your new cloud. This is configured through the

Hardware Configuration area of the VM template; select the Compatibility option and ensure the new capability profile is selected.

**FIGURE 9.11**
Custom capability profile

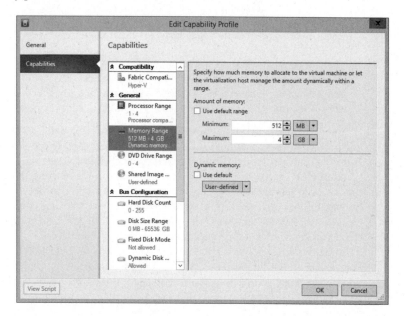

Once you've created your custom capability profiles, you can elect to use them for your cloud. The custom capability profiles created can be used in addition to, or instead of, the built-in capability profiles. Click Next.

A summary of all my choices are displayed in a confirmation screen along with the magic View Script button that would show the PowerShell code to create a complete new cloud. This is a basic example without hardware load balancers or virtual IP templates but gives an idea of what is going on. Now that you have the PowerShell code, you could use this in other components like System Center Orchestrator to automate the creation of clouds based on requests from Service Manager.

```
Set-SCCloudCapacity -JobGroup "XXXXXX" -UseCustomQuotaCountMaximum $true
-UseMemoryMBMaximum $false -UseCPUCountMaximum $false -UseStorageGBMaximum $false
-UseVMCountMaximum $true -MemoryMB 36864 -CPUCount 40 -StorageGB 1024

$resources = @()
$resources += Get-SCLogicalNetwork -Name "Hyper-V Network Virtualization PA" -ID
"c75b66eb-c844-49a2-8bbd-83198fc8ccc0"
$resources += Get-SCLogicalNetwork -Name "Lab" -ID " XXXXXX "


$resources += Get-SCStorageClassification -Name "Gold" -ID " XXXXXX "
```

```
$addCapabilityProfiles = @()
$addCapabilityProfiles += Get-SCCapabilityProfile -Name "Hyper-V"

Set-SCCloud -JobGroup " XXXXXX" -RunAsynchronously -AddCloudResource $resources
-AddCapabilityProfile $addCapabilityProfiles

$hostGroups = @()
$hostGroups += Get-SCVMHostGroup -ID " XXXXXX "
New-SCCloud -JobGroup " XXXXXX " -VMHostGroup $hostGroups -Name "Test Cloud"
-Description "" -RunAsynchronously -DisasterRecoverySupported $false
```

You now have a cloud that no one can use, so the next step is to assign the cloud to users and groups. To assign access to clouds, you use user roles. These can be either a Delegated Administrator who can do anything to the objects within their scope, a Read-Only Administrator who can view information about everything but can see nothing that is useful for auditors and interns, or a Self-Service user. Each user role has a scope that defines the clouds it applies to and the capabilities and the users/groups within that user role. It is common therefore that you will create a new Self-Service user role and possibly a Delegated Administrator user role for every cloud you create to enable granularity in assigning cloud access.

Open the Settings workspace, navigate to Security ➤ User Roles, and select the Create User Role action on the ribbon. The Create User Role Wizard will open, and a name and description for the object being created are requested. If the user role is cloud specific, then include the name of the cloud in the name. Click Next and the type of user role is requested; select Self-Service User and click Next.

The next stage prompts for the users and groups that are part of this role. Normally my recommendation would be always use Active Directory groups and add users to the AD group that need access to the user role so it's not necessary to keep modifying the user role. When a user is added to the AD group, the user automatically gets the cloud rights that the AD group has. This works great if you are creating a cloud for a certain business unit and that business unit already has an AD group. Just grant that business unit's AD group access to the cloud-specific Self-Service user role, then as users join the business unit they just get access to the cloud. Even if the cloud is not business-unit specific, but you have good processes in place to add users to groups, you could use an AD group. For example, developers could have access to a development cloud. Where my guidance changes is when there are not good processes in place to add users to groups and it's beyond the control of the team implementing the private cloud to fix it or effect change. In those cases, I may lean to adding users directly into user roles within SCVMM, which can be automated through PowerShell and cut out potentially large delays associated with adding the user to an AD group. Add the users and/or groups and click Next.

On the next page, you select the clouds the user roles apply to. Note there are no host groups shown, only clouds. System Center Virtual Machine Manager is the cloud or nothing. Select the clouds and click Next.

Next you set the quotas for the user role. Remember, when creating the actual cloud, you set the capacity. Now you are setting the quotas for this specific user role in the cloud as well as the quotas of each user within the user role. Note that you may have multiple Self-Service user roles for a single cloud with different quotas and different actions available. In Figure 9.12 I have set an unlimited quota for the role, giving it full access to the cloud, but each user has far smaller limits. Make your configurations and click Next.

**FIGURE 9.12**

Setting the quotas
for a specific tenant

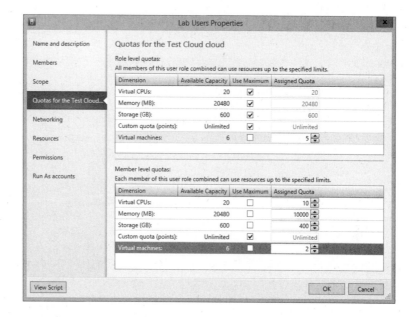

The next step is adding the resources that should be available to the role such as virtual machine templates, hardware profiles, service templates, and so on. These resources are what will be available when the users of this role create virtual machines, so ensure the right templates are available for them. Additionally, you can specify a location for user role data that is shared between all members of the role. Click Next to continue.

You can now configure permitted actions for the user role, which are fairly granular and fully documented at `http://technet.microsoft.com/en-us/library/gg610613.aspx`. Once the actions have been configured, the next step allows any specific Run As accounts to be made available to the user role. Take caution in what Run As accounts are made available because you don't want to give basic users access to highly privileged Run As accounts. Click Next, and a summary will be shown; then the role will be created. Once again, you can export the PowerShell code used.

## Granting Users Access to the Private Cloud with App Controller

I've talked about installing the SCVMM management console for end-user access, but this is really not practical. Instead, the preferred interface for users is via a web browser, which is primarily achieved using System Center App Controller.

System Center App Controller is a thin installation. It can be installed on the System Center Virtual Machine Management server, but for busy environments, you will gain better performance by running App Controller on its own server. App Controller uses a SQL database for its configuration storage, but the rest of its requirements are light. The install media is around 23 MB at time of writing. What System Center App Controller delivers is a web-based Silverlight experience, which means it's a rich, interactive interface that provides access to both private clouds provided by System Center Virtual Machine Manager and public cloud services such as Windows Azure, as shown in Figure 9.13.

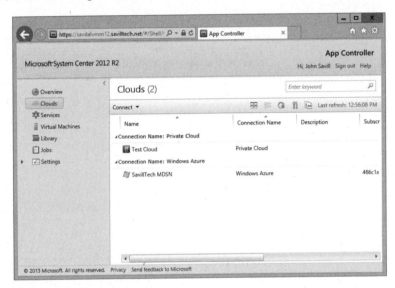

Virtual machines can be managed within SC App Controller, but SC App Controller can do so much more. It can deploy entire services that are based on the service templates that you created in SCVMM; these templates could have many tiers with different applications at each tier level. If you have a Windows Azure application, it can be deployed to your Windows Azure subscription from within App Controller and it can be fully managed and fully scaled instead of having to use the Windows Azure website. Services can be moved between your on- and off-premise clouds, giving you power, flexibility, and portability. App Controller can also hook into hosting partners that leverage the Service Provider Foundation (http://technet.microsoft .com/en-us/library/jj642895.aspx).

App Controller is supported on Windows Server 2008 R2 SP1 and newer, but if you are installing App Controller on the same server as Virtual Machine Manager 2012 R2, you have to use Windows Server 2012 or Windows Server 2012 R2 because VMM 2012 R2 does not support Windows Server 2008 R2. App Controller leverages its own database to store its configuration information, which can be SQL Server 2008 R2 or SQL Server 2012. It is common to deploy App Controller on the same server as Virtual Machine Manager because they work so closely together; however, in large environments that require greater scalability, App Controller can be deployed on its own operating system instance. App Controller can be made highly available and/or load balanced using a number of mechanisms. Make sure the SQL database is part of a highly available SQL cluster, and then for the App Controller server either make the App Controller virtual machine highly available or deploy multiple App Controller instances that use the same SQL database and share a common encryption key.

## Installation and Initial Configuration

The installation of App Controller is simple because most of its actual configuration comes from Virtual Machine Manager in terms of users and resources that are available. This means before deploying App Controller, it's important you have deployed Virtual Machine Manager 2012 R2 and have created clouds of resources and defined tenants (which are groups of users who have various rights and quotas for those clouds). This is the fundamental building block to enable App Controller to integrate with on-premises virtual environments. It's also necessary to have created virtual machine templates and optionally service templates because these are how users will deploy environments through App Controller. This also means your App Controller administrators must also be virtual machine manager administrators. The account you will use to install App Controller must be a member of the local Administrators group on the server and will become the first App Controller administrator.

The actual installation of App Controller is documented at `http://technet.microsoft` `.com/en-us/library/gg696046.aspx` and is intuitive because there are so few installation options. Provided you have the SQL Server deployment available to be used by App Controller and your server meets the requirements, the only change you may want to make to the standard installation is using a trusted SSL certification instead of a self-signed certificate generated by the install process. This means your users won't get warnings that the certificate is not trusted. I definitely recommend against using the self-signed certificate unless App Controller is being used only in a limited test environment.

The only configuration you must perform is to connect App Controller to the Virtual Machine Manager instance, which is performed by logging on to the App Controller website, `https://<App Controller Server>`, and then selecting the Settings navigation node and the Connections child navigation option. Select the Connect ➤ SCVMM action, as shown in Figure 9.14, which will launch the Add A New VMM Connection screen. Enter a name for the new VMM connection, a description, and then the actual VMM server name (remember, you should be logged on as an account that is both an App Controller and a VMM administrator). You will notice a Windows Azure connection exists by default and is what allows the addition of Azure subscriptions to App Controller. Also notice the option to add a service provider, which could be a company you use that offers virtual machine hosting and has implemented the Microsoft Service Provider Framework, which allows it to be managed via App Controller. Think of the SPF as exposing the hoster's own VMM deployment to your on-premises App Controller. It's necessary for the hoster to give you the URI for your tenant ID in their environment to complete the connection from App Controller.

**FIGURE 9.14**
Adding a VMM connection to App Controller

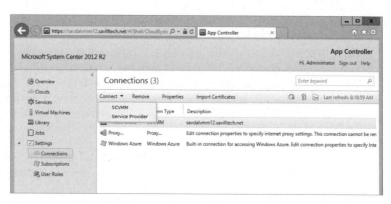

If your organization leverages Windows Azure, then those subscriptions should be added to App Controller via the Clouds navigation view and the Connect ➤ Windows Azure Subscription action (or Settings ➤ Connections ➤ Add). To link to Azure, it is necessary to have created a management certificate and imported it into the Azure subscription so it is available for importing into App Controller as part of the process to connect App Controller to Azure. I detail the whole process including how to create the certificate and use it at `http://windowsitpro.com/system-center/q-how-do-i-create-certificate-enable-system-center-app-controller-manage-windows-azure`.

Under the Settings navigation node is the User Roles node, where you can configure additional App Controller administrators by adding members to the Administrators built-in user role. If you added Windows Azure subscriptions or connections to SPF hosters, then additional user roles can also be created to control App Controller user access to Azure subscriptions and SPF services since these can't be controlled through your on-premise VMM instance, which manages only the on-premise, private cloud infrastructure.

Consider what you now have with App Controller. You have access to your on-premises private clouds defined and managed in Virtual Machine Manager, access to your Windows Azure subscriptions, and access to your services at hosting partners that leverage SPF. Initially, most organizations will just use App Controller for their on-premises private cloud management, but the ability to grow its reach will really help organizations embrace a hybrid cloud approach.

Some customization of App Controller is possible. It's easy to change the graphics for App Controller. The logos are just two image files in the `%PROGRAMFILES%\Microsoft System Center 2012 R2\App Controller\wwwroot` folder, called `SC2012_WebHeaderLeft_AC.png` and `SC2012_WebHeaderRight_AC.png`. Just back up and replace these images; your replacements must be the same dimensions as the originals, 213×38 and 108×16, respectively, or they won't work.

All App Controller configuration is performed through the website; there is no separate management tool. Because the App Controller web interface is based on Silverlight, the browser used must be a 32-bit browser that supports Silverlight version 5. This means you will need to use Internet Explorer 8 or newer. Other browsers will not work at this time. If you are embracing PowerShell, there is a PowerShell module for App Controller that enables all of the key configurations related to App Controller. Run the following PowerShell command to see all the available cmdlets:

```
Get-Command -Module AppController
```

## User Interaction with App Controller

App Controller is ready to be used and is functional straightaway once it's been connected to your cloud services. Users navigate to `https://<App Controller Server>` and log on using their domain credentials in a forms-based interface. If desired, it is possible to enable single sign-on, which will remove the forms-based authentication completely. Once the user is authenticated, they will see whatever clouds have been defined in VMM that they have access to in addition to their Azure and SPF-based services on the Overview screen. If a user is not a tenant (which means they are not part of any role that has rights) of a cloud defined in VMM, then they will not see any private clouds in App Controller. Think of App Controller just as an interface into the VMM configurations for private cloud. The actual granting of rights is all performed through VMM.

The actual App Controller interface is highly intuitive, and users can typically pick up its use easily. Figure 9.15 shows a default view for users when they log in and navigate to the Clouds view. In the example, you can see the user has access to a single on-premises cloud and no Azure subscriptions. For the on-premises cloud, it shows the users' current resource usage and their remaining quota. Any time a user deploys a new VM or service, App Controller shows the quota impact and ensures users cannot exceed quota. Notice that for standard users the Settings navigation node is not shown.

**FIGURE 9.15**

A cloud view for a cloud tenant

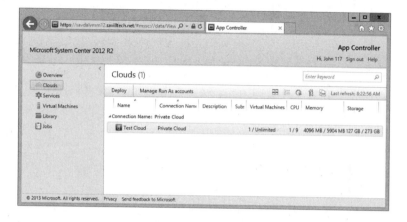

The deployment experience is one of the highlights of App Controller. Once the deploy has been initiated via the Deploy action, the New Deployment screen opens, which by default will have selected the cloud that was selected when the Deploy button was clicked. Initially, the only configuration possible is to select a template, which is a composite view of all the initial options depending on the cloud selected. The templates available will depend on which cloud you are deploying and what templates your user has been given access to. If you deploy to Azure, you get the standard Azure list of templates and any custom ones you may have added. If you deploy to your on-premises private cloud, you see the templates and services available for your user role. Once a virtual machine is selected, configuration is then possible, such as naming the virtual machine and perhaps some customization depending on the template selected. If you have defined service templates (which are scalable, multitiered complete services designed within VMM) and made them available to the tenant, then selecting a service results in a rich view in App Controller, as shown in Figure 9.16. This allows all the VMs for the *initial* service deployment to be configured and then deployed, but no configuration is actually necessary. Default virtual machine and computer names are autogenerated for all the virtual machines that are deployed as part of the service. I say the initial deployment because the whole point of service templates is that each tier can have a variable number of virtual machines depending on load, so App Controller just deploys the initial number of VMs defined for each tier, but as the service runs, that number may grow and shrink. App Controller actually allows the addition of virtual machines for a deployed service via the Scale Out action when using the diagram view of a deployed service. To scale in a tier of a service, you just manually delete virtual machines; there is no specific "Scale In" action.

Once all customization is complete, click the Deploy button to create a deployment job. If the deployment is to a private cloud, then the job is created in VMM. If to Azure, then the job is created in Azure, and if to an SPF-hosted cloud, then the job is created on the SPF infrastructure. No matter where the target is, the users' deployment experience is the same, and the deployment progress can be seen in their Jobs view, which is available via the navigation node. The actual time of deployment depends entirely on the size and number of virtual machines that make up the deployment and the service being deployed to, but the progress can be tracked in detail using the Jobs view.

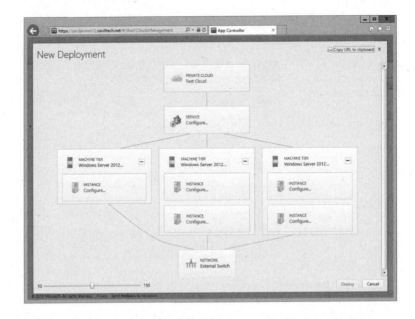

Once the services/virtual machines are deployed, they can be viewed using either the Services or Virtual Machines view. For now I will focus on the Virtual Machines view because this will be the primary way App Controller is used by most companies in the near term (although I strongly encourage you to look at service templates in VMM because they provide some amazing capabilities in terms of scalability and manageability). The Virtual Machines view will show all the provisioned virtual machines, the virtual machines stored in the library that the current user owns, and those they have been given access to. Default actions for virtual machines include Startup, Shutdown, Pause, Turn Off, Save, Store, Mount Image, Remote Desktop, and Connect To The Console. The exact options available will depend on the current state of the virtual machine, as shown in Figure 9.17. If the Properties option is select, additional options are available such as configuring access for other users and creating and applying snapshots. Remember that the actions available will depend on those granted to the users. Take some time to look around the App Controller interface, both as an administrator and as a regular user, including looking at the information and options for the Library and Jobs views.

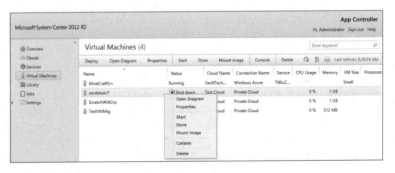

While App Controller provides huge benefit from a single view for all virtualization services used by an organization, App Controller also opens up some great hybrid capabilities. It is possible to deploy virtual machine templates stored on premises in VMM to Windows Azure. It is possible to take a virtual machine that is stored in the VMM library and deploy it to Windows Azure, and this is how you migrate a VM from on-premises Hyper-V to Azure using App Controller. There is no live migration type of functionality possible. You stop the VM running on premises and save it in the library using the Store action before it can be deployed to Azure using its Copy action. Bringing a virtual machine back from Azure to App Controller requires copying the VHDs from Azure into your VMM library and then redeploying. Another option for VM migration between on premises and Azure is to leverage System Center Orchestrator, which gives a lot more flexibility and power to the migrations.

## Enabling Workflows and Advanced Private Cloud Concepts Using Service Manager and Orchestrator

System Center Orchestrator provides two primary great capabilities: the ability to communicate with many different systems and the ability to automate defined series of activities that could span many different systems through runbooks. These two abilities can be highly beneficial to your private cloud implementation.

At the most basic level, Orchestrator can be leveraged to actually create virtual machines, deploy service templates, and even create entire clouds through runbooks. In Figure 9.18, I show a really basic runbook that receives some initialization data, makes a call to SCVMM to create a VM, and then runs some PowerShell to configure ownership of the VM.

**FIGURE 9.18**
This shows a basic Orchestrator runbook.

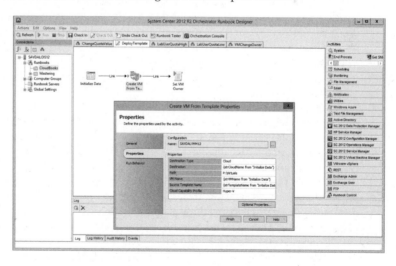

This is really just the tip of the iceberg. Running PowerShell scripts to perform actions through Orchestrator is great, and error checking and updating of other applications like Service Manager are benefits. But you can run PowerShell without Orchestrator. If you look again at Figure 9.18, you will see on the right side a list of activity groups, known as *integration packs,*

including System Center Virtual Machine Manager, System Center Configuration Manager, and VMWare vSphere. Each integration pack contains activities specific to the target. For vSphere there are activities for virtual machine creation and management; the same type of activities are available for SCVMM and for Configuration Manager activities including deploying software. Using integration packs for systems, the built-in Orchestrator activities, and PowerShell, it is possible to automate any action related to the private cloud (and anything else) and to customize exactly how your organization functions. Once you create the runbooks, they can then be called by the rest of System Center or triggered automatically. Here are some great scenarios where Orchestrator can be used:

◆ Creating a new cloud based on an IT request though a service catalog that calls a created Orchestrator runbook

◆ Deploying a new virtual machine or service instance

◆ Offering a runbook that automatically patches and reboots all virtual machines for a particular user or business group

◆ Automatic scaling up and down of deployed services by triggering runbooks that perform scaling based on performance alerts from Operations Manager

◆ Deprovisioning virtual machines or services that have passed a given length of time or date in development purposes

Remember that the point of the private cloud is its automation, and you can't automate by using graphic consoles. Therefore, as you learn System Center and Virtual Machine Manager in particular, look at the series of actions you perform, look at PowerShell, look at the activities in integration packs, and start creating runbooks in Orchestrator that can be used. Once the runbooks are created, they can be manually triggered using the Silverlight web-based Orchestrator interface or triggered from other systems such as an item in Service Manager's service catalog. With Orchestrator being able to connect to almost any system, with a little bit of work any manual process you perform should be able to be automated and more importantly orchestrated with System Center Orchestrator.

I talked about System Center Service Manager a number of times in this chapter and quite a few times in the previous section. Service Manager is the Configuration Management Database (CMDB) of your organization. It has feeds and connections to all the other System Center components and can offer various services such as basic ticketing activities such as incidents (things not doing what they should), problems (something is broken), and change requests (I want something). When there are problems in the environment because Service Manager connects to all the different systems, when you look at a computer in Service Manager, information from all the different systems is visible and gives you a single point of truth about the asset and aiding solutions. In Service Manager you can see all of the hardware, software, and patch status gathered from Configuration Manager. You can see AD information that was pulled from AD. You can see any alerts that were generated by Operations Manager plus any more complex service dependencies such as all the systems that are responsible, from providing messaging services to the organization.

Because of all these connections to systems, Service Manager can provide a great service for your private cloud. So far I've talked about creating clouds, virtual machines, and services with the SCVMM console, App Controller, PowerShell, and Orchestrator. There are problems, though, when you think of end users for all these approaches. Users don't really want a separate interface just for requesting a virtual machine typically. Users are not going to run PowerShell scripts you give them, and giving them a list of runbooks they can run through a web interface is likely to baffle them.

So, Service Manager 2012 introduced a new feature called a *service catalog*. The service catalog is a single source that can contain all the different types of services offered by the organization. This could include creating a new user, requesting the installation of a software package through SCCM, asking for a new keyboard, or really anything that Service Manager has some ability to enable through its connections to other systems. The service catalog is primarily available to end users through a SharePoint site that uses Service Manager Silverlight web parts. Users can browse the service catalog as a single go-to place for all their needs, which makes it a perfect place to offer virtual services on the private cloud. How do you offer the private cloud services in the service catalog? You just add the runbooks from Orchestrator, and then when a user makes a request from the service catalog, the normal Service Manager workflows can be used such as request authorization. Then the workflow will call the runbook in Orchestrator to actually perform the actions. Service Manager and Orchestrator have great bidirectional communications in System Center, allowing the status of the runbook execution to actually be visible within Service Manager, as shown in Figure 9.19. Once the process is complete, the service request would be marked as completed, and the user could even be sent an email. I walk through creating this type of service using Service Manager in a video at http://youtu.be/T1jTX9xE66A.

**FIGURE 9.19**
Service catalog view in Service Manager of request offerings that call Orchestrator runbooks

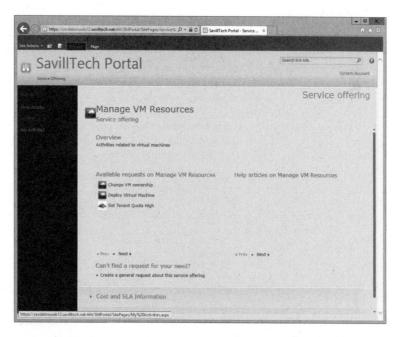

Service Manager also has the ability to create charge-back price sheets that allow prices to be assigned to different aspects of the virtual environment such as price per day for the VM, price per core, memory, and storage per day and then additional items such as a price for a highly available VM or static IP address. These price sheets can then be used within Service Manager to allow charge-back to business units based on their utilization.

## How the Rest of System Center Fits into Your Private Cloud Architecture

In this chapter I've touched on a number of components of System Center 2012 R2, such as Virtual Machine Manager, App Controller, Orchestrator, and Service Manager. There are others that, while not a key private cloud building block, are still important to a complete infrastructure. I will touch on them briefly here and finish with a new solution from Microsoft that builds on System Center 2012 R2 to bring a Windows Azure–like experience to your on-premises private clouds.

Fabric management and deployment of services are critical, however, to ensuring the ongoing health of the fabric, the Hyper-V hypervisor, the virtual machines, and the applications running inside the virtual machines monitoring is necessary to ensure the long-term availability and health of the environment.

System Center Operations Manager (SCOM) provides a rich monitoring solution for Microsoft and non-Microsoft operating systems, applications, and hardware. Any monitoring solution can tell you when something is broken. SCOM does that, but its real power is in its proactive nature and best-practice adherence functionality. SCOM management packs are units of knowledge about a specific application or component. For example, there is an Exchange Management Pack, and there is a Domain Name System (DNS) for Windows Server management pack. The Microsoft mandate is that any Microsoft product should have a management pack that is written by the product team responsible for the application or operating system component. This means all the knowledge of those developers, the people who create best-practice documents, are creating these management packs that you can then just deploy to your environment. Operations Manager will then raise alerts of potential problems or when best practices are not being followed. There are often objections raised from customers that when first implemented Operations Manager floods them with alerts. Well, this could be for a number of reasons; perhaps there are a lot of problems in the environment that should be fixed, but often Operations Manager will be tuned to ignore configurations that while perhaps not best practice are accepted by the organization.

Many third parties provide management packs for their applications and hardware devices. When I think about "all about the application" as a key tenant of the private cloud, the ability for Operations Manager to monitor from the hardware, storage, network, and everything all the way through the OS to the application is huge, but it actually goes even further in Operations Manager 2012.

System Center Operations Manager 2012 introduced a number of changes, but two huge ones were around network monitoring and custom application monitoring. First, Microsoft licensed technology from EMC called SMARTS that enables a rich discovery and monitoring of network devices. With the network discovery and monitoring functionality, Operations Manager can identify the relationship between network devices and services to actually understand that port 3 on this switch connects to server A, so that if there is a switch problem, Operations Manager will know the affected servers. Information such as CPU and memory information among other information is available for supported network devices.

The other big change was the acquisition of AVIcode by Microsoft, which is now Application Platform Monitoring (APM) in Operations Manager 2012. APM provides monitoring of custom applications without any changes needed by the application. APM currently supports .NET applications and Java Enterprise Edition (J2E), and a great example to understand this is to look at a custom web application in your environment today without APM when performance problems occur.

> User phones IT: "Application X is running slow and sucks."
> IT phones the app developer: "Users say Application X is running really slow and really sucks."
> App developer to self: "I suck and have no clue how to start troubleshooting this. I will leave the industry in disgrace."

With System Center Operations Manager's Application Platform Monitoring configured to monitor this custom application, it changes.

> User phones IT: "Application X is running slow and sucks."
> IT phones the app developer: "Users say Application X is running really slow. I see in Operations Manager the APM shows that in function X of module Y this SQL query 'select blah from blah blah' to SQL database Z is taking 3.5 seconds."
> App developer to self: "It must be an indexing problem on the SQL server and the index needs to be rebuilt on database Z. I'll give the SQL DBA the details to fix."
> App developer to SQL DBA: "Your SQL database sucks."

Operations Manager can be used in many aspects of the private cloud. While it's great that it monitors the entire infrastructure to keep it healthy, the Operations Manager ability to monitor resource usage and trending helps plan growth and can trigger automatic scaling of services if resources hit certain defined thresholds. Figure 9.20 shows an example view through Operations Manager of a complete distributed service that is comprised of many different elements. To prove the flexibility of Operations Manager in this example, I'm actually monitoring an ESX host through information gained through SCVMM and also my NetApp SAN, some processes running on Linux, and a SQL database. All of those different elements make up my complete application to show an overall health rollup, but I can drill down into the details as needed.

**FIGURE 9.20**
A view of a distributed service and its various services visible through Operations Manager

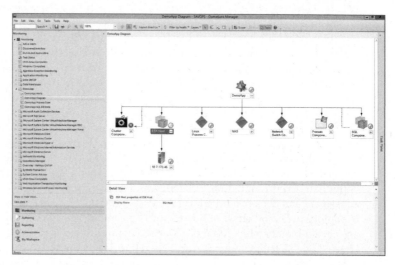

Operations Manager 2012 R2 also understands clouds and has a cloud view capability. Once the SCVMM MP has been imported into Operations Manager and the SCVMM connector to Operations Manager has been configured, you will be able to navigate to Microsoft System Center Virtual Machine Manager ➤ Cloud Health Dashboard ➤ Cloud Health within the Monitoring workspace. This will list all the clouds. Select a cloud and in the Tasks pane select the Fabric Health Dashboard, which, as shown in Figure 9.21, gives some insight into all the fabric elements that relate to the cloud.

**FIGURE 9.21**
The Fabric Health Dashboard for a SCVMM cloud

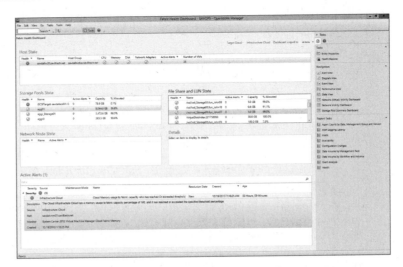

With the environment being monitored, a key aspect is the backup that I talked about in Chapter 6, namely, Data Protection Manager. As discussed previously, DPM is a powerful solution for the backup and restore of not just Hyper-V but also key Microsoft applications such as Exchange, SQL, and SharePoint. Although it has limited Linux VM backup on Windows Server 2012 R2 Hyper-V, DPM is still very much a Microsoft-focused protection solution.

The final component of System Center is Configuration Manager. SCCM provides capabilities to deploy operating systems, applications, and OS/software updates to servers and desktops. Detailed hardware and software inventory and asset intelligence features are key aspects of SCCM, enabling great insight into the entire organization's IT infrastructure. SCCM 2012 introduced management of mobile devices such as iOS and Android through ActiveSync integration with Exchange and a user-focused management model. One key feature of SCCM for servers is settings management, which allows a configuration of desired configuration to be defined such as OS and application settings and then applied to a group of servers (or desktops). This can be useful for compliance requirements. The challenge I face in recommended SCCM for servers today is that its focus seems to be shifting for SCCM to be mainly desktop. The benefits SCCM can bring to servers such as patching, host deployment, and desired configuration are actually better handled through other mechanisms. For patch management both SCVMM and Failover Clustering one-click patching leverage WSUS and not SCCM. For host deployment, SCVMM has the ability to deploy physical servers for Hyper-V and for file servers and automatically manage cluster membership and more. Desired configuration is possible through PowerShell v4's Desired State Configuration feature. Therefore, if you are already using SCCM, you can take advantage of some of those capabilities in your environment. I would not implement SCCM for the sole purpose of server management; there are better options in my opinion in the other components and base operating systems.

So far, I have talked about many different components and how they can be brought together to provide a private cloud solution. However, a fair amount of work is involved in producing a full private cloud offering. For System Center 2012 Microsoft has a solution accelerator, the System Center Cloud Service Process Pack (http://technet.microsoft.com/en-us/library/hh562067.aspx), that has guidance and add-ons for System Center 2012 to create a fully functioning private cloud. This is no longer provided for System Center 2012 R2. Instead, for System Center 2012 R2, Microsoft introduces the Windows Azure Pack (WAP), which builds on System Center 2012 R2, SPF, and a new component in System Center 2012 R2, Orchestrator Service Management Automation (SMA), to bring a Windows Azure–like experience to your on-premises private cloud.

You can find information on the Windows Azure Pack at www.microsoft.com/en-us/server-cloud/products/windows-azure-pack/ along with detailed deployment guidance. At the time of this writing, WAP brings a number of Windows Azure experiences to your on-premises private cloud such as IAAS, Web PAAS, and database as a service, but there are also other services that can be made available through custom services. Microsoft has already published some WAP gallery items for Exchange, Lync, and SharePoint services at http://blogs.technet.com/b/privatecloud/archive/2013/12/11/building-clouds-blog-windows-azure-pack-vmrole-gallery-items.aspx. Right now I think of WAP as focused on hosters and organizations that offer a hoster-type experience to their business units/users. In other words, they are very mature in their private cloud adoption and are focused on providing services. I think longer term the Microsoft direction for the end-user interaction will be via WAP because Microsoft will want to consolidate the number of different end-user experiences from having the separate App Controller, Service Manager, and WAP options.

# The Bottom Line

**Explain the difference between virtualization and the private cloud.**   Virtualization enables multiple operating system instances to run on a single physical piece of hardware by creating multiple virtual machines that can share the resources of the physical server. This enables greater utilization of a server's resource, reduction in server hardware, and potential improvements to provisioning processes. The private cloud is fundamentally a management solution that builds on virtualization but brings additional capabilities by interfacing with the entire fabric including network and storage to provide a complete abstraction and therefore management of the entire infrastructure. This allows a greater utilization of all available resources, which leads to greater scalability. Because of the abstraction of the actual fabric, it is possible to enable user self-service based on their assignment to various clouds.

**Master It**   Do you need to change your fabric to implement the private cloud?

**Describe the must-have components to create a Microsoft private cloud.**   The foundation of a Microsoft private cloud solution would be virtualization hosts using Hyper-V and then SCVMM and App Controller to provide the core fabric management, abstraction, cloud creation, and end-user self-service functionality. Orchestrator and Service Manager can be utilized to build on this core set of private cloud functionality to bring more advanced workflows, authorization of requests, and charge-back functionality.

# Chapter 10

# Remote Desktop Services

Up to this point in the book I have focused on the core technologies of virtualization, and for examples I primarily have used server operating system workloads. Historically this has been the principal usage for machine virtualization. You can, however, use virtualization with a client operating system to offer virtualized desktops.

This chapter looks at the Windows Server Remote Desktop Services (RDS) that enable remote access to operating systems, both server and desktop, with the primary goal of providing users with a desktop experience. As I will explain, there are a number of ways to achieve this, and I will focus on where Hyper-V is critical.

In this chapter, you will learn to

◆ Explain the types of desktop virtualization provided by RDS

◆ Describe the benefits of RemoteFX and its requirements

◆ Articulate the other technologies required for a complete virtualized desktop solution

## Remote Desktop Services and Bring Your Own Device

Remote Desktop Services is a core role of Windows Server; it was called Terminal Services before Windows Server 2008 R2 but was renamed to better reflect the range of its functionality. If you are familiar with Terminal Services, you know Terminal Services was focused on providing a complete desktop to remote users that was hosted on a server operating system. Each connected user had their own Windows session on the server operating system, which provided them with a level of isolation from other users connected to the same server operating system. The remote connection was enabled through the Remote Desktop Protocol (RDP). RDP is a core part of all Windows operating systems and is also what enables Remote Desktop to a desktop operating system remotely. Terminal Services, or Remote Desktop Session Host (RDSH) as it is now known, provides a desktop to the remote user including the Start menu, desktop icons, Internet Explorer, and the various applications installed on the server operating system, which could include Microsoft Office and line-of-business (LOB) applications. To the end user, there is really no difference in experience from a desktop operating system; however, actions that affect all users such as reboots and application installations are blocked in a session virtualization environment. Figure 10.1 shows a typical session virtualization solution with Remote Desktop Session Host. In this example, the session host is running as a virtual machine on a Hyper-V server, but it could also be running on a physical host directly. As you can see, many different users connect for their own desktop. As I cover later in this chapter, while RDSH provides a desktop environment, other technologies are required to give the users a full experience such as profile, applications, and their data.

**FIGURE 10.1**
Session virtualiza-
tion using Remote
Desktop Session Host

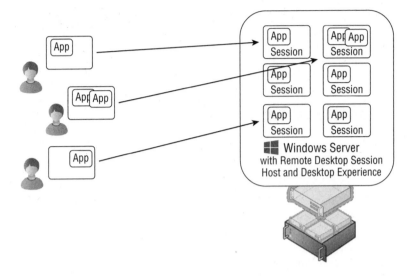

---

**ENABLING A RICH DESKTOP EXPERIENCE USING RDSH**

I've talked about configuration levels for the operating system, which could be Server Core for most server uses. For a session host that is providing an environment for a user, the full graphical experience is required. At a minimum this requires the Server Graphical Shell configuration level, which provides the graphical shell, Windows Explorer, Internet Explorer, and more. For the complete desktop experience of a client operating system, you will also want to enable the Desktop Experience configuration level, as shown in Figure 10.2. This adds features such as themes, Windows Media Player, and photo tools.

This is really the only time you should enable the Desktop Experience configuration level because it consumes more resources on the server operating system. However, there are some applications that require Desktop Experience, specifically for the graphical codecs it includes.

---

While Remote Desktop Services provides a complete desktop with the Start menu (or Start screen for Windows Server 2012/Windows 8 and newer), sometimes end users don't want a complete desktop. Instead, they want a specific application displayed on their device, such as a line-of-business application or an office application. This is especially true when using a smaller device such as a phone or tablet. Imagine trying to interact with the complete Windows desktop on a 4-inch iPhone compared to just launching a specific Windows application. Another example is where a user is already running a Windows desktop but has to run a specific application remotely. In these cases, the users just want the application's window to be displayed on their existing desktop or device without a completely separate desktop in order to launch applications from a website or some kind of local application catalog. Windows Server 2008 introduced the ability to publish applications in addition to a full desktop, which allowed just the application window to be sent to the user's local device.

**FIGURE 10.2**
Enabling the
Desktop Experience
configuration level

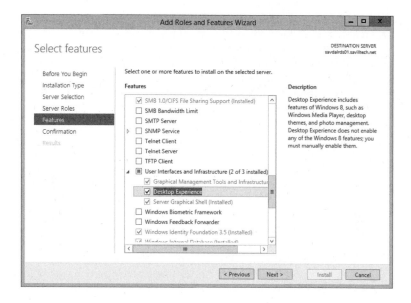

For a long time, this type of session virtualization was the most popular way to provide a virtualized desktop. Recently, Virtual Desktop Infrastructure (VDI) has been getting a lot of attention and is being touted as the best solution by many vendors. A VDI solution differs from session virtualization because each end user connects to a separate client operating system running in a virtual machine, as shown in Figure 10.3. This gives a greater level of isolation for each user since the users are now running in their own isolated operating system; therefore, it is a good fit for power users and developers who need to customize the operating system or reboot it. The downside is that a VDI solution uses up far more resources because each VDI desktop is a complete desktop environment with the memory, processor, and desk utilization that accompany that.

**FIGURE 10.3**
VDI solution in
action

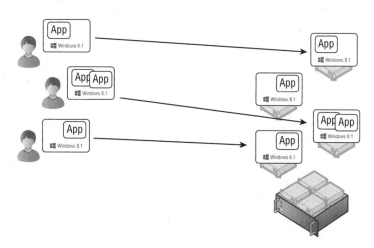

There are two modes for a VDI deployment: pooled and personal desktops. Most VDI deployments will leverage a pooled deployment for the majority of VDI users. Pooled VDI is a configuration where a number of virtual machines running the client OS are grouped together into a pool. As a user connects, the user is automatically assigned one of the VMs not currently in use. Once the user has logged off, the VM is placed back into the pool. Because a user potentially (and probably) gets a different VM each time they connect, it is essential you have solutions to maintain the user's profile and data between logons. After a user logs out, the VM in the pool is reset to a clean state in case anything was changed by the previous user.

Pooled desktops should be the default for all users, but there may be certain users who need the same client OS instance every time they connect. Maybe they are modifying the OS in some way, or perhaps they have an application that needs to be installed because it can't be virtualized. Whatever the reason, you have the capability to statically assign a VM to a particular user so they always get the same client OS. This is known as a *personal desktop*. A pooled desktop environment allows a gold image to be used as the template for all the VMs in the pool, and because no user state is stored in the VMs in the pool, there is no need to patch or maintain the VMs in the pool. The only maintenance required is to patch and manage the gold image, which will then refresh all the VMs in the pool. This is not possible for a personal desktop because the VM is maintained for the specific user between logons and therefore must be patched just like a regular desktop. It also may lay dormant if not used by the user but will still consume resources. It is therefore far more preferable to use pooled VMs over personal VMs where you use VDI.

It won't come as any surprise to you to learn that vendors that push VDI as the best solution for every scenario are those virtualization vendors that don't have a session virtualization solution, so that is their only way to expand into the desktop market. Vendors that have both VDI and session virtualization such as Microsoft and Citrix take a more balanced approach. I will give more guidance later in this chapter on when to use each type of desktop virtualization because certainly most organizations will need some of each.

Whether session virtualization or VDI is used, the end result is virtualization of the desktop, or simply virtual desktops. So, why do people even want these virtual desktop solutions? The following are some of the most common reasons:

- Disaster recovery situations where the normal work office for the users is not available because of some disaster or for some other reason. Consider a huge blizzard where workers cannot leave their homes. With a virtual desktop environment available, users can connect to the virtual desktop, and their complete desktop environment is available.

- Contract users with their own computers who need a corporate desktop environment. Rather than rebuild their computers, just give them access to a desktop in the corporate virtual desktop environment.

- Users who need to use many different devices and require a consistent desktop experience. This could include users who use shared devices such as in hospital environments.

- High-security situations where data cannot leave the datacenter, which requires the user's desktop to also be housed in the datacenter. It's not practical to sit users in the actual datacenter, so remotely accessing the desktop that is co-located in the datacenter is the best of both worlds.

- Certain applications that access huge amounts of data that is stored in the datacenter. Sending the data over the network may be impractical or give poor performance, so hosting the desktop in the datacenter with the application effectively running on the same local network gives great performance.

◆ Critical desktops that need high resilience. Consider that with virtual desktops the desktop operating system is actually running on server hardware, which means server-class performance and server-class high availability and redundancy including RAID-based storage.

◆ Remote developers who need to be able to customize their operating system environment and reboot.

◆ CEOs who need to bring in their iPad and access Windows applications.

◆ Bring Your Own Device (BYOD), where organizations allow users to bring their own computers into the office (and may even give them money each year to buy a device). Installing the corporate image on these devices does not make sense, so a virtual desktop can give the users a desktop.

BYOD has become the driving force behind the huge interest in desktop virtualization because many organizations are looking at ways to enable their users to work from any device and from anywhere. Microsoft has made huge strides in its Remote Desktop Services solution that minimize the need to leverage third-party solutions such as those from Citrix and Quest, although they still have a place in certain scenarios.

In the rest of this chapter, I will look at the key components of Microsoft Remote Desktop Services and how it's used to deliver a virtual desktop solution.

## Microsoft Desktop and Session Virtualization Technologies

To offer a virtual desktop solution, whether session virtualization or VDI, there are a number of components required to complete the solution and enable connectivity from the end users:

◆ Machine virtualization to host the virtual machines, for example, Hyper-V

◆ Virtualization management to enable the creation of virtual machines and stopping/starting them as needed in addition to passing information back to the VDI components

◆ Client platform to actually run inside the virtual machines, meaning Windows 8 or Windows 8.1

◆ Access protocol to actually communicate with the virtual desktop OS, which is Remote Desktop Protocol for native Windows

◆ Connection Broker to decide which virtual desktop a user should be connected to, which could be via session virtualization or VDI, and to remember which desktop a disconnected user was last using for reconnections

◆ Gateway capability for users connecting from outside of the corporate network and avoiding the need for VPN connections or technologies like DirectAccess

◆ Licensing

I will step you through the typical process of connecting to a hosted desktop in a Microsoft VDI implementation and demonstrate the actual Microsoft role services used and how they interact. In Figure 10.4, I walk through the major steps required for VDI functionality, from the initial user contact all the way to a usable VDI session with an empty Windows 8 operating system. If using session virtualization, the flow is similar except that the endpoint for the virtual desktop is a session host instead of a virtual machine; in addition, step 6 in the flow is not performed.

**FIGURE 10.4**
The full VDI implementation has many components to give a rich capability set while being invisible to the end user.

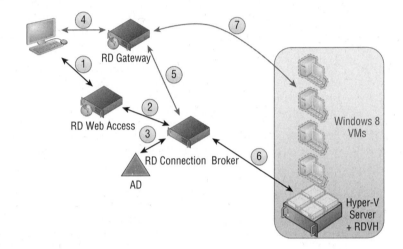

1. Users need to find the remote desktops they can connect to, which can be desktop virtualization sessions (Remote Desktop Session Host), published applications, and the VDI sessions. While a RDP file can be created and deployed to users using various methods, a more dynamic approach is to use the Remote Desktop Web Access role service, which presents a browser-based list of available connections that the user can choose from.

2. To create the list of published applications and connections that are presented to the user, the Remote Desktop Web Access server communicates with the Remote Desktop Connection Broker, which has knowledge of the VDI pools, personal desktops, and other published connections and applications through its own communications with configured RemoteApp sources.

3. To ascertain the exact access a user has, the Connection Broker communicates with Active Directory, which also provides any personal desktop configurations.

4. No matter what the exact method, be it Remote Desktop Web Access, RemoteApp, and Desktop Connections, or a deployed RDP file, the users now have an RDP file that can be used to initiate the connection. If the user is outside the corporate network, a direct RDP connection would be blocked by most organizations' firewalls. So, traditionally, the user would need to initiate a virtual private network (VPN) secure connection or use DirectAccess. But you have an alternate solution that does not require any end-user

action or additional client-side software. Windows Server 2008 introduced TS Gateway, which allows the RDP traffic to be encapsulated in HTTPS (port 443) packets, which is the RD Gateway component.

5. The user needs an initial RDP connection point since their VDI client VM destination will not be known yet unless the user has a personal desktop configured. The RD Connection Broker acts as the connection point for the user's RDP connection and then redirects the client to the true endpoint, the VDI session. The RD Connection Broker knows what the RDP target should be for the requesting client.

6. The RD Connection Broker communicates with the Remote Desktop Virtualization Host role service that is enabled on the Hyper-V boxes to check the state of the VMs, start the VM if required, and gather any needed information such as IP address of the client VM OS. This information is then passed back to the RD Connection Broker, to the RD Session Host in redirection mode, and then back to the client.

7. The client now makes an RDP connection to the destination client VM via the RD Gateway (if connecting from outside the corporate network), and the connection is complete. The logon process for the user would now be complete.

One part I haven't mentioned is the role of System Center Virtual Machine Manager, which while not a requirement definitely helps in the management of the virtual machines and helps automate the bulk creation and updating of virtual machines. I will spend a little time looking at each component in a bit more detail. It should go without saying, but all of the roles can be virtualized on Hyper-V, and it is common practice to do so.

## RD Web Access

The RD Web Access role provides the initial entry point for users; it provides a web-based interface to select the desired VDI or published desktop/application target. While not absolutely required, this helps give a simple-to-use portal that supports form-based authentication, provides single sign-on, and differentiates between public and private computers for credential caching. The Web Access portal utilizes HTTPS to protect the credentials that are passed and could be made available to the Internet through publishing enabled by gateway services such as Microsoft User Access Gateway.

Although not directly part of RD Web Access, Windows 7 introduced RemoteApp and Desktop Connections, which allows a feed from RD Web Access to populate the same content shown in the website directly into the Start menu, avoiding the need to use the website. The standard URL is `https://<RD Web Access server>/RDWeb/Feed/webfeed.aspx`.

This was continued in Windows 8 and extended with the new modern Remote Desktop application. The Remote Desktop application enables easy access to the feeds provided by RD Web Access. The Manage RemoteApp and Desktop Connections setting in the application enable a new connection to be added, as shown in Figure 10.5. The web feed URL or the user's email address can be specified. Behind the scenes, when an email address is entered, the domain part of the email address is extracted and then used to perform a DNS lookup for `_msradc.<domain from email>`. The record in DNS is a TXT type record that must be created by administrators, and the value of the DNS record is the URL of the RD Web Access feed.

**FIGURE 10.5**
Adding a new
connection

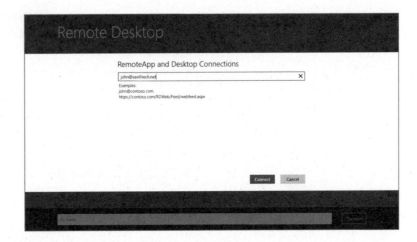

**FIGURE 10.5**
Adding a new
connection

## RD Connection Broker

The updated Connection Broker in Windows Server 2008 R2 was one of the major components that allows an all-Microsoft VDI solution and gives Remote Desktop Services the ability to balance and track connections to nonsession hosts, specifically the ability to manage connections to client operating systems. It's important to note that the Connection Broker still helps balance connections to session hosts as well. Additionally, Windows 2008 R2 introduced the ability for the Connection Broker to balance RemoteApps and support servers with different published applications, allowing a sum view of all the different applications gathered from all servers in the farm to be displayed to the user. This removes the need for all servers to have the same applications. The Connection Broker is the brains of the virtual desktop environment and communicates and controls the other components; it works particularly closely with the RD Session Host in redirection mode, which is why they are frequently placed on the same OS instance. However, when you start having more than 250 simultaneous connections, you may need to consider breaking the roles onto separate servers.

Windows Server 2012 also enabled the Connection Broker to act as the initial entry point for the incoming RDP connection, which previously required a dedicated RD Session host in redirection mode. This has removed the need to ever have an RD Session Host in a redirection part. Prior to Windows Server 2012, the RD Session Host in redirection mode was required because when you have a large session host server farm, to avoid users having to connect to different session hosts, the initial entry point is always a designated session host that does nothing more than talk to the broker and then redirect the RDP connection to the right RDP endpoint. This is the same concept in a VDI environment; you still need an initial RDP connection point for the RDP clients, which is exactly what the RDSH in redirection mode provides. It then redirects the RDP client to the right client OS VM that will be providing their desktop OS. By moving the functionality into the Connection Broker, it is one less component to have to deploy.

The Connection Broker is also in charge of cleaning up the VDI instance once the user logs off. This is achieved by the actual creation of a checkpoint, RDV_Rollback, when the VM instance is created from the template, which is in a clean state before a user logs on. Once a user logs off, the RDV_Rollback checkpoint is applied to the VM instance, reverting the VM to the pre-user logon state and making it ready for the next logon. In Windows Server 2008 R2, the RDV_Rollback checkpoint had to be manually created, but this is done automatically in Windows Server 2012 and newer.

## RD Virtualization Host

The RD Virtualization Host role service is installed on any Hyper-V host that will be participating in a VDI pool. It enables the Connection Broker to communicate with the Hyper-V hosts, start/stop VMs, and gather information from within to enable client connections. The RD Virtualization Host role also enables the use of RemoteFX.

## RD Gateway

The RD Gateway allows RDP traffic to be encapsulated in HTTPS packets, allowing secure RDP connection through corporate firewalls without having to open up firewall ports or use additional VPN solutions. Figure 10.6 shows a high-level overview.

**FIGURE 10.6**
How RD Gateway
works

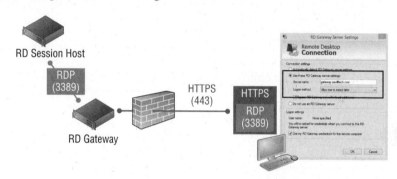

The RD Gateway is placed in the DMZ (or, more securely, behind some kind of firewall/proxy), and the clients connect to the RDP destination via the RD Gateway, which is accomplished by adding the RD Gateway server as part of the RDP file configuration that is given to the client. The client encapsulates the RDP traffic in HTTPS and sends it to the RD Gateway, which extracts the RDP and forwards it to the RDP destination. When traffic comes back from the RDP destination bound for the client, the RD Gateway encapsulates it in HTTPS and sends it to the client. With this technology, users outside the corporate network can still access all RDP resources without additional steps or software. Users who are on the corporate network would bypass the RD Gateway and communicate directly with the RDP destination.

Using RD Gateway, you can configure who can connect through the RD Gateway service, what they can connect to, the supported RDP settings such as device redirection, and so on. This allows access from outside the organization without the use of a separate VPN-type technology while still maintaining control of the levels of access. RD Gateway can be used with any RDP connection, which means it can be used with session virtualization, VDI, and application publishing.

# Requirements for a Complete Desktop Virtualization Solution

Everything I have talked about so far is about providing an operating system environment for the end users, but what the users actually care about is accessing applications and the related data in a familiar environment. This requires much more than just an operating system. Additionally, you must provide the following:

◆ Access to a user's data

◆ A consistent set of user customizations, that is, their profile

◆ Access to a user's applications

Many organizations already have solutions to protect and provide access to user data. The most important data actually resides in collaboration solutions such as SharePoint, and with features like SkyDrive Pro, it's possible to have a local cache on a user's machine that is a local copy of the data stored in the user's SharePoint area. For unstructured data such as that stored on a user's home drive, it is possible to use work folders (introduced in Windows Server 2012 R2) and the more traditional offline files with folder redirection.

Folder redirection allows well-known folders such as Documents to be redirected to a corporate file server but also cached locally using offline files/client-side caching to make the data available even when the machine is not connected to the corporate network. These technologies are mature and should be used at a minimum for the Documents and Desktop user folders. By redirecting these locations to a central file server, the user's data is always available, no matter which device a user is connected to. Granular controls are available to manage which data is redirected to a corporate file server and which data stays local to a machine and therefore will not roam with the user.

While providing access to data is a no-brainer for most organizations, providing a consistent user experience by making the user's profile move between different machines, known as roaming profiles, is a different story. While roaming profiles have existed in Windows for many versions, they have a history of problems. Roaming profiles in Windows 7 and newer are a fairly solid solution, but they have numerous limitations. For instance, you cannot use a single roaming profile between Windows XP and Windows 7 machines. You won't use a single profile between client and server operating systems. In addition, application settings don't work well between locally installed applications and those that are virtualized with solutions such as App-V. The root problem is that roaming profiles work by synchronizing predominantly a single file, ntuser.dat, which contains the registry of the user, and this synchronization occurs at logon and logoff with some limited synchronization periodically. This means for many settings to synchronize, the user must log off, which is a problem if the user is utilizing many devices simultaneously or needs to use different types of devices or connections that differ for certain parts of the profile.

Microsoft provides an alternate solution for roaming the user's settings, called User Experience Virtualization (UE-V), which is available as part of the Microsoft Desktop Optimization Pack (MDOP). UE-V is enabled on a per-application basis in addition to basic desktop settings. The locations in the registry and the file system for the user settings for each application are defined and therefore should be captured and virtualized by UE-V. This allows granularity in which application settings should be roamed between user environments, and each application has its own setting store, enabling much more flexible synchronization of settings. Let's imagine a user has two logon sessions, their local Windows 8 PC and a Windows 2012 R2 Remote Desktop Services session, and walk through the experience of using roaming profiles. I should point out that sharing a profile between a Windows 8 desktop and a 2012 R2 RDS server is not recommended, but it helps you see the problem.

1. In the Windows 8 session, the user launches PowerPoint, customizes the environment, and then closes PowerPoint.

2. In the 2012 R2 session, the user launches PowerPoint and none of the customizations made on the Windows 8 session are available. The user sets different customizations and then logs out of 2012 R2 session, at which point roaming profiles replicate the new profile.

3. The user logs out of the Windows 8 session, and the profile overwrites that of the 2012 R2 session.

With UE-V, which has been configured to virtualize settings for Microsoft Office, this is what happens:

1. In the Windows 8 session, the user launches PowerPoint. As the application launches, the UE-V service hooks into the application, pausing the start, and checks for any updates to the settings package for PowerPoint from the UE-V remote repository, which is just a file share. If there is an updated settings package, it synchronizes it using offline files to a local cache, and the application starts using the settings in the settings package exposed by the UE-V service. The UE-V service provides the technology to inject the user's application settings that are stored in the registry and file system onto their current OS as the application starts and then saves them back to the UE-V settings package when the application closes. This allows the abstraction of the application settings from the OS without any changes being needed by the application. The user now customizes the environment and then closes PowerPoint. As the application is closed, UE-V saves the updated settings to the settings package for the application and writes to the remote repository.

2. In the 2012 R2 session the user launches PowerPoint, and once again UE-V hooks into the application and pulls down and presents the user's customizations. Now the user sees the changes made in the Windows 8 session for PowerPoint and can get on with their work. If they make changes to the application settings, then on application close, those changes would be saved to the remote repository.

This demonstrates how UE-V really changes the user experience. Roaming profiles replicate changes only at logon and logoff. UE-V replicates application settings when the application launches and is closed. For desktop settings such as the theme (desktop background, sounds, and so on) and accessibility configurations, the changes are replicated at logon, logoff, lock, unlock, connect, and disconnect. Internet Explorer 9 (and newer) is supported and is treated like any other application; settings are replicated as the application is opened and closed. UE-V also works seamlessly with a mix of locally installed applications and virtualized applications with App-V, giving a single configuration for an application, no matter how it is implemented for user. For power users, there is a PowerShell cmdlet that enables an individual application settings to be rolled back to the default configuration. This is useful if a user has completely corrupted their settings for an application. The default configuration is created the first time an application is launched for a user and stored away in case a settings rollback is required.

From a platform perspective, UE-V 2.0 is supported on Windows 7, Windows 8, Windows 8.1, Windows Server 2008 R2, Windows Server 2012, and Windows Server 2012 R2, which means a single application configuration for any session on any supported platform. As long as the UE-V agent is installed and has the template registered for the applications and desktop, then the user will have a consistent experience.

There is no server infrastructure for UE-V other than a file share to store the settings packages for each user (who would have their own subfolder), or the user's settings packages could be part of their standard Active Directory–specified home drive. The templates that detail what applications should have settings virtualized and that document the various registry and file system locations that make up those settings and need to be intercepted can be registered at the time of the UE-V agent installation or can be stored on a file share where the UE-V agent can be configured to check for updates every 24 hours. This makes UE-V easy to deploy because most of the work will be just deploying the agent, which can be done manually, through an Enterprise Software Deployment (ESD) solution such as System Center Configuration Manager or even through Group Policy.

The final component is to provide the actual applications. One option is to install the applications into the actual operating system such as the RD Session Host or client OS in the VM for VDI; however, this is a lot of overhead and hard to maintain. Another option is to separately run applications on specific farms of session hosts that publish just the applications to the virtual desktop. Another option is to leverage App-V, which like UE-V is part of MDOP and is a great solution not just for virtual desktops but for physical desktops as well.

App-V virtualizes the application separately from the operating system, with each application running in its own virtual environment, or bubble. This bubble contains a virtual file system, registry, and many other system resources that sit on top of the operating system resource. These virtual layers contain the resources specific to the application. This allows the application to run on the operating system without having any footprint on the local resource such as writing to the file system or changing the registry. There is a single cache on each machine that holds the virtualized streams for each App-V application along with application icons and file type associates. The experience to the end user is completely seamless. App-V also streams applications to machines on first use where required; however, for session virtualization and VDI, that is typically not used, and instead a central cache can be shared that is prepopulated with all the virtualized applications.

Figure 10.7 shows a Microsoft technology-complete solution with session virtualization or VDI providing the operating system and other technologies providing the data, profile, and applications. This is not the only possible solution; rather, it's an example of how different technologies work together to create the complete end-user experience. The key point is these technologies can all be used on physical desktops and also enable a single set of technologies to provide a consistent and manageable experience for all the types of desktop in your organization.

There is another RDS-specific solution for the user profile and parts of the data, called *user profile disks*. The option to use a user profile disk is available when creating the VDI or session-based pools, also known as *collections*, and is a VHDX file for each user that uses the pooled virtual desktops. The first time a user connects to the pool, a new VHDX file is created and attached to the virtual machine (if VDI) or the RD Session Host that is hosting the user's session (if session-based). The entire user's profile is stored on the attached user profile disk by default. This means all the user's data and settings are stored on the user profile disk since Documents is part of the user profile area. On subsequent logons by the user, the user profile disk VHDX is attached to the required VM image or RD Session Host, providing the same user profile area and therefore the same user experience and data access. Within the virtual desktop that is using the user profile disk, the VHDX is seen as mounted for the location of the user's profile using the MOUNTVOL command.

**FIGURE 10.7**
Providing the complete user experience

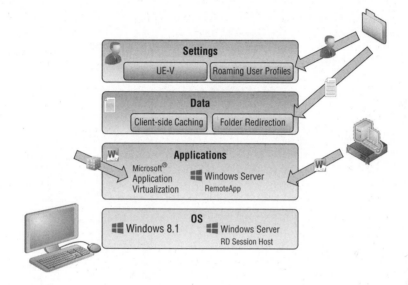

User profile disks can be enabled when creating a VDI or session-based pool or after the creation of the pool. Granular control of the data stored on the user profile disk is possible as shown in Figure 10.8; a maximum size for the data stored on the VHDX is also shown.

Using user profile disks has some advantages and disadvantages. The big advantage is that they are easy to use and provide users with a consistent profile and data experience without having to use roaming profiles, UE-V, folder redirection, or any other technology. The disadvantage is the user profile disks are specific only to the RDS environment, and the profile/data will not be available to other environments such as a physical desktop. In fact, it's more restrictive than that. When VDI or session-based deployments are created with RDS, specific servers are selected to be part of the deployment, which makes up a specific collection. An environment may have many different collections, which could be VDI or session based for different types of users. The user profile disks are specific to a specific collection defined in RDS, which means they cannot be shared between different RDS collections. Therefore, if users leverage virtual desktops from different collections, they would have a different user profile disk and therefore a different profile for each collection, which would not be a good end-user experience.

I think of user profile disks as a great solution for pilot environments where integration with a normal desktop environment is not required or for production environments where you have a set of users who will leverage only a specific RDS collection or do not need access to their normal profile or data. Outside of that, I think it is better to leverage user state virtualization technologies that are usable across all desktop environments such as the aforementioned roaming profiles, UE-V, and folder redirection.

**FIGURE 10.8**
User profile disk
configuration
options

## Creating the VDI Template

One of the most important decisions when using VDI is which operating system you will use in the image. Where possible, a consistent operating system between your physical desktops and the virtual desktops is advantageous because it will avoid additional application testing and different OS configuration and validation exercises. This may not be practical, however. One reason VDI may be attractive is because the physical desktops are all running Windows XP and you need a more modern operating system for some users or applications.

There are three client operating system options for a Windows Server 2012 R2 VDI deployment:

◆ Windows 7 Enterprise (with the RDP 8.0/8.1 update)

◆ Windows 8/8.1 Pro

◆ Windows 8/8.1 Enterprise

Where possible, Windows 8/8.1 Enterprise is the best option because it gives the richest client experience and highest set of functionality. Compared to Windows 8/8.1 Pro, the Enterprise edition has the following additional capabilities:

◆ RemoteApp: This offers application publishing and enables specific applications running on the operating system to be published and used by users instead of a complete desktop, bringing a far more seamless experience in addition to being more accessible and usable on smaller form-factor devices where a full desktop is not optimal. The Pro edition does not enable RemoteApp.

◆ RemoteFX Device Redirection: RemoteFX has a number of technologies, one of which enables the redirection of almost any USB device at a port level. Only Enterprise has this feature.

◆ RemoteFX vGPU: The feature of RemoteFX most people think of is the virtual GPU capability, which enables a physical GPU in a server to be virtualized and made available to virtual machines. Even if a server does not have a GPU or a certain level of graphical capability, it can still be exposed to the virtual machine through a software rastorizer. This enables the virtual machine to see a vGPU and perform local graphics rendering such as with DirectX enabling advanced graphics applications to be executed in the VDI environment. This is enabled only on the Enterprise edition.

◆ User profile disk: This enables a VHD to be attached to the virtual machine and used for profile and data storage so that a user's experience is consistent even when connecting to different VDI VM instances. This is available only on the Enterprise edition.

Windows 7 Enterprise edition with the RDP 8/8.1 update also has the features listed here. A feature that Windows 8/8.1 (Pro and Enterprise) has that Windows 7 Enterprise does not is support for RemoteFX Multi-Touch, which is far more than just enabling multiple contact points. It enables a "touch frame" that contains rich metadata about the complete set of touch contacts, on-screen location of contacts, bounding rectangles for each contact, and timing information relative to the previous frame. RemoteFX Multi-Touch supports up to 256 active contacts, which for most people will be plenty. Practically speaking, the reason for so many contacts is in multitouch-monitor scenarios, where up to 16 monitors are supported for RDP. Windows 7 and Windows 8 have a very different Start experience, plus Windows 8 and 8.1 support the new fully immersive modern applications. This means for the most complete user experience you should use Windows 8.1 Enterprise edition for your VDI environment where possible.

For the 32-bit vs. 64-bit decision, I generally recommend using whatever version you use on your physical desktops in the organization to avoid a large amount of additional software testing. Obviously, if you have 64-bit desktop applications and if you need more than 4 GB of memory, you will need to use the 64-bit version of Windows. The one downside of 64-bit Windows is it uses around 2 GB of additional disk space per virtual machine, but that is really the only difference in overhead. Memory and processor are about equal.

Once you decide on the version of operating system, there are many steps to optimize the image that will be the gold image and template for all the VM instances that will be created for the VDI collection. You will likely be running hundreds of instances of this VM template, so you want to optimize it as much as possible. Microsoft has a number of great resources to help with this. I recommend the following:

◆ `http://download.microsoft.com/download/6/0/1/601D7797-A063-4FA7-A2E5-74519B57C2B4/Windows_8_VDI_Image_Client_Tuning_Guide.pdf`: This is a great tuning guide that talks about OS considerations and customizations, services to disable, and software such as malware usage. This is a mandatory read.

◆ `http://blogs.technet.com/b/jeff_stokes/archive/2013/04/09/hot-off-the-presses-get-it-now-the-windows-8-vdi-optimization-script-courtesy-of-pfe.aspx`: This is a great script to automate most of what is discussed in the previous reference. It also has some guidance at the start of the script for actions to be performed on the image. Although it is for Windows 8, it works for Windows 8.1 as well.

You may also choose to install certain applications into the image. Generally I recommend keeping the image as light as possible, meaning don't install many applications into the image because each application update will require an update to the image. Instead, use technologies such as App-V and RemoteApp to deliver the applications. There may still be times you have to install applications into the image, but try to keep these to a minimum. You must not install modern applications into the reference image because you have to run Sysprep at the end of the image creation process and modern applications are currently not understood by Sysprep, which means the applications will have to reinstall anyway during the template's deployment in the VDI collection.

On this same theme, don't use a Microsoft account when creating the reference image. Use a local account because you also don't want to join the reference image to the domain, which would be removed during the Syspres process and can confuse things.

Once the image is how you want it, the next step is to prepare it to be used by an RDS collection. This involves generalizing it, which is achieved by running Sysprep. The command to be used in the OS is as follows:

```
Sysprep /generalize /oobe /shutdown /mode:vm
```

Windows 8 introduced the /mode:vm switch, which should be used when preparing a Windows 8 virtual machine (VM) that is being used as part of a VDI deployment. When Sysprep runs, it performs several actions, including removing unique information such as the SID and GUID; but it also resets the hardware information. In a VDI environment where all the duplicates are running on the same hypervisor as the source VM, there's no need to reset the hardware information. Not resetting the hardware is what the /mode:vm switch enables. This speeds up the startup of the duplicates on first boot.

I recommend an extra step before running Sysprep. Over time you will want to update the template, including adding patches. There are ways to patch the virtual machine without starting it, and I walked through some options in Chapter 5. Still, it's useful to be able to start the virtual machine, but remember it is not possible to continually run Sysprep on an operating system. Instead, I recommend doing the following:

1. Complete the customization of your reference image and shut down the virtual machine.

2. Create a checkpoint and label it Reference Pre-Sysprep.

3. Start the virtual machine and run Sysprep, which will then shut down the virtual machine and is ready for duplication.

If at any point in the future you need to boot the image to modify it, you apply the pre-Sysprep checkpoint, make the changes needed, shut down the VM, delete the original checkpoint, and create a new pre-Sysprep checkpoint (you want to save this state because it has the updates applied but is pre-Sysprep allowing this to be used for future changes), boot the virtual machine, and then run Sysprep again. The important part is that the checkpoint is updated with the updates but is always before the Sysprep action. Don't worry about having the checkpoint; when a virtual machine is used by the VDI collection creation, the virtual machine is exported to the target collection, the latest state is used, and the checkpoints are ignored. What is important is that the virtual machine should have no checkpoints that were taken while the virtual machine was running because this causes problems for the collection creation because the detection will show the virtual machine as running, even though it isn't.

You will now have a virtual machine template that will be referenced when creating a VDI collection. Don't forget to use dynamic memory for the virtual machine because this will give the most efficient use of memory and the greatest density of virtual machines on the server. Make sure the virtual machines have at least 1024 MB of memory.

One great feature in Windows Server 2012 R2 Hyper-V and the file services is that data deduplication is supported for virtual machines that are used in a VDI scenario. Remember that the free Microsoft Hyper-V Server is a great solution in VDI scenarios because the included Windows Server guest OS licenses with Windows Server Standard and Datacenter are not required, so using the free Microsoft Hyper-V Server makes great sense.

Even though the VDI collection automatically uses differencing disks for each VM instance in the collection to save space, the use of data deduplication will further save disk space and some guidelines will say to not use differencing disks at all and instead rely entirely on data deduplication. Note that while data duplication is supported for VDI environments only, it is not blocked for other purposes. You should be careful if you decide to use data deduplication for other workloads because some workloads may not behave as expected if deduplicated.

## Deploying a New VDI Collection Using Scenario-Based Deployment

I will focus on a pooled scenario in this walk-through because it's by far the most common VDI deployment. The process is intuitive with minimal changes required. If you do need some personal VDI images, the personal VDI assignment is configured through the Active Directory Users and Computers MMC snap-in via the Personal Virtual Desktop tab. A user can be assigned only one personal desktop, and a VM can be assigned to one user as a personal desktop. A personal desktop must not be in a VDI pool. Make sure the personal desktop name exactly matches the name of the VM. The name needs to be the FQDN, which means you need to give the VMs the name of the FQDN of the client OS. When using personal virtual desktops, you need to ensure the name of the virtual machine in Hyper-V matches the fully qualified domain name of the OS within the virtual machine.

If I had walked through deploying VDI in Windows Server 2008 R2, this would be a very different section. I would direct you to the 50-page Microsoft "quick-start" guides that require huge amounts of complicated configuration. Windows Server 2012 completely changed this with the new scenario-based deployments available in Server Manager. Remote Desktop Services deployment is now performed through Server Manager where all the different servers that will participate in the scenario are deployed through the single wizard to a best-practices configuration. While it is still possible to manually deploy each server role and configure them manually, it's strongly discouraged and offers no advantage. The management of Remote Desktop Services is also through Server Manager for nearly all actions (except for licensing management and troubleshooting).

Server Manager supports deployment for all the major scenarios, including session virtualization with application publishing, VDI with pooled desktops, and VDI with personal desktops. The scenario deployment also features two types of deployment. The quick-start installs all the required components on a single server and is designed to be used in a test or pilot-type scenario or small environment. The standard deployment option allows multiple servers to be selected for a more production-ready deployment. The easiest way to understand the scenario-based deployment is to walk through a deployment. For a session virtualization deployment, the entire process can be performed through Server Manager, but for VDI there are some extra steps because of the additional configurations required. The basic process to use RDS scenario deployments is as follows:

1. Launch Server Manager.

2. From the Manage menu select the Add Roles And Features action.

3. Click Next on the introduction page of the Add Roles And Features Wizard.

4. The installation type must be selected. Select the Remote Desktop Services installation option, which performs the scenario-based deployment instead of the standard role or feature-based installation. Click Next.

5. The type of deployment must be selected: Standard deployment or Quick Start. I will use a Standard deployment so multiple servers can be selected. Click Next.

6. The next step is to select the type of deployment. In this case I will select a virtual machine–based desktop deployment.

7. Complete the remaining configurations by selecting the servers to be used for the required RDS roles, which are RD Connection Broker, the RD Web Access, and RD Virtualization Host. You can find the full walk-through at http://technet.microsoft .com/en-us/library/hh831541.aspx.

Once RDS is deployed on the various required servers, to complete the environment, the next step is to deploy the actual VDI collection. This is all performed through Server Manager.

1. In Server Manager navigate to Remote Desktop Services ➤ Collections.

2. From the Tasks menu select Create Virtual Desktop Collection, which will launch the Create Collection Wizard.

3. Click Next on the introduction screen.

4. Enter a name for the collection and an optional description and click Next.

5. Select the Pooled Virtual Desktop Collection option and leave the Automatically Create And Manage Virtual Desktops option selected. Click Next.

6. Select the virtual machine that will act as the gold image for the VDI collection. Remember, this virtual machine must be shut down and has been sysprep'd, as shown in Figure 10.9.

7. When the virtual machine template is deployed to the many VM instances in the collection, the VM instances are customized. You can specify an unattended answer file that exists or complete settings through the wizard by leaving the default Provide Unattended Installation Settings option selected. Click Next.

8. Select the time zone, domain, and organizational unit the VMs in the VDI collection should use and click Next.

9. The next screen, as shown in Figure 10.10, specifies the users who can use the collection, the number of virtual desktops to be created in the collection, and a prefix and suffix for the VM instances. Configure the options you require and click Next.

10. The next step allows the Hyper-V hosts to be selected that will host the VDI VM instances and click Next.

11. The storage location to be used for the VM instances can be selected, which can be a local location on the Hyper-V hosts, a SMB file share, or a cluster shared volume. Note that even if you have an alternate storage location configured for virtual machines on the Hyper-V host, this location is not used unless you specify a location explicitly in this wizard. By default the VDI collection VMs will be created in the location `C:\ProgramData\Microsoft\Windows\RDVirtualizationHost\<collection name>`. By default the option to automatically roll back the virtual desktop when the user logs off will be selected, which creates the RDV_Rollback checkpoint that is applied when users log off; this checkpoint reverts the VM to a clean state. Click Next.

12. Select the option to use user profile disks and specify the share (making sure the computer accounts of the servers in the collection have full control for the share).

13. A summary of the configurations selected are shown. Click Create.

14. The progress will be displayed, which includes creating the virtual desktop template image, importing on the target, and then creating the new virtual machines that are part of the VDI collection. The exact duration will depend on the size of the image and your storage subsystem.

**FIGURE 10.9**
Selecting the
virtual machine
to be the reference
image for the VDI
collection

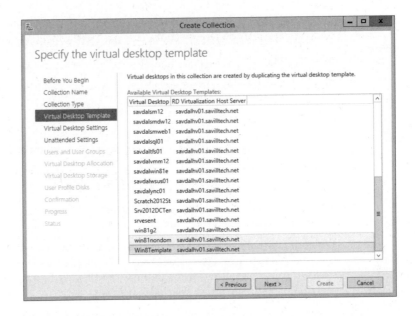

**FIGURE 10.10**
Configuring the
options for the VDI
VM instances

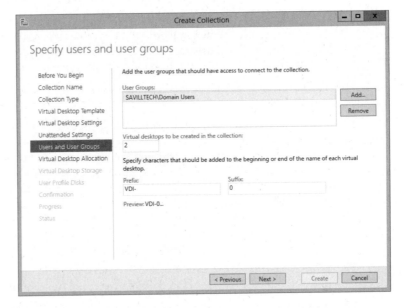

Once the deployment is complete, the collection will show in Server Manager, and the virtual machines will display in Hyper-V Manager, as shown in Figure 10.11. Note that for the VDI virtual machines the RDV_Rollback checkpoint was automatically created. What is more interesting is to look at the file system on the Hyper-V host to understand exactly what happened.

**FIGURE 10.11**
The deployed
VDI collection

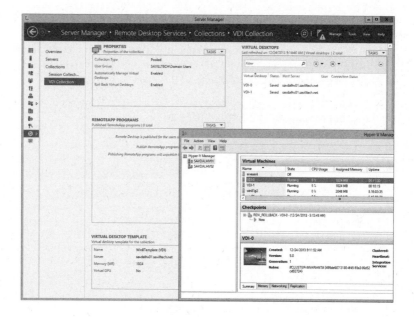

Figure 10.12 shows the file system objects related to my collection. You can see the copy of the actual reference virtual machine and its storage and then folders for each of the virtual machines. Notice the size of the VHDX files. The VHDX file in the IMGS subfolder is the original VHDX file that was exported from the reference virtual machine, so it has the same original size, 13 GB. For each of the virtual machines, VDI-0 and VDI-1, there are two virtual hard disk files. The first is the `VDI-n.VHDX` file, which is the original virtual machine checkpoint state, RDV_Rollback, and then there is an AVHDX file, which is the current state of the virtual machine that has the differences from the checkpoint state (this is normal).

**FIGURE 10.12**
The deployed VDI
collection file sys-
tem content for the
virtual hard disks

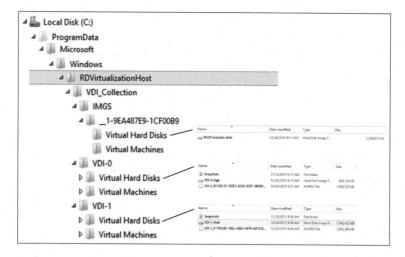

But why is the main VHDX file for each virtual machine only 1GB in size compared to the 13GB of the main image? The answer is that the RDS VDI collection is being efficient with storage and actually creates differencing disks for each virtual machine in the VDI collection instead of a complete copy of the original image. This can be seen using the Get-VHD PowerShell cmdlet on one of the VM instance VHDX files, as shown here:

```
PS C:\> get-vhd "C:\ProgramData\Microsoft\Windows\RDVirtualizationHost\VDI_
Collection\VDI-0\Virtual Hard Disks\VDI-0.vhdx"
```

```
ComputerName              : SAVDALHV01
Path                      : C:\ProgramData\Microsoft\Windows\RDVirtualizationHost\
VDI_Collection\VDI-0\Virtual Hard Disks\VDI-0.vhdx
VhdFormat                 : VHDX
VhdType                   : Differencing
FileSize                  : 970981376
Size                      : 136365211648
MinimumSize               : 136365211648
LogicalSectorSize         : 512
PhysicalSectorSize        : 4096
BlockSize                 : 2097152
ParentPath                : C:\ProgramData\Microsoft\Windows\RDVirtualizationHost\
VDI_Collection\IMGS\__1-9EA487E9-1CF00B9\Virtual Hard Disks\Win8Template.vhdx
DiskIdentifier            : 0d4018ab-5299-4511-898a-6ae821e0afc0
FragmentationPercentage   :
Alignment                 : 1
Attached                  : True
DiskNumber                :
Key                       :
IsDeleted                 : False
Number                    :
```

Notice the VHDX is a type of differencing and that its parent is the VHDX file in the IMGS subfolder. Each VM still has around 2 GB of customizations, which if you have 100 VM instances adds up to a lot of storage. This is where using data duplication will help reduce disk overhead.

The VDI collection will be available through RD Web Access, as shown in Figure 10.13; so will the other published desktops and applications. This gives a consistent experience for end users.

If you ever update the template virtual machine, you can refresh the deployment VM instances by selecting the Recreate All Virtual Desktops task for the collection and selecting the updated reference VM. This can also be done using the Update-RDVirtualDesktopCollection PowerShell cmdlet. Microsoft has a good blog on this at http://blogs.msdn.com/b/rds/archive/2012/10/29/single-image-management-for-virtual-desktop-collections-in-windows-server-2012.aspx.

As you can see, it's really quite simple to deploy VDI with Remote Desktop Services. Deploying session virtualization uses the same process, except no virtual machines are required. The same wizard is used to deploy, and the same Connection Broker can be used for multiple session virtualization collections and VDI collections. I walk through a session host deployment in the video at http://youtu.be/_dkxyr03Er4.

**FIGURE 10.13**

Seeing the VDI collection in RD Web Access

# Using RemoteFX

Windows 2008 R2 Service Pack 1 introduced two huge technologies. The first was dynamic memory, and the second was RemoteFX, which was aimed squarely at VDI environments. The goal of RemoteFX was to provide a consistent experience to end devices no matter what the capabilities of that device actually were.

Normally the Remote Desktop Protocol leverages client-side capabilities for Windows Media playback such as WMV files and for desktop composition such as Aero glass and Flip 3D (which are now gone in Windows 8). If the client device does not support media redirection, then the user experience is very basic. Additionally, because the remote operating system is in a virtual machine with no graphical hardware, many types of application technologies cannot run, such as DirectX, Silverlight, Flash, and so on. This also limited the use of many types of business applications such as videoconferencing.

RemoteFX consisted of three technologies originally: GPU virtualization, enhanced codec, and USB port-level redirection. The technologies associated with RemoteFX have grown since Windows Server 2008 R2, but together they give a great desktop experience remotely. In Windows Server 2008 R2 SP1, the RemoteFX technology was supported only in LAN environments, but this has been extended to WAN scenarios in Windows Server 2012 (there are obvious limitations to graphical fidelity if the connection is too slow).

The virtualization of the GPU in the server allows virtual GPUs to be made available to the virtual machines running on the Hyper-V server. The virtual GPUs can be leveraged by Windows 7 SP1 Enterprise/Ultimate and Windows 8/8.1 Enterprise guest operating systems running in those virtual machines. Windows 7 SP1 included the updated integration services, which allows the guest OS to see the virtualized GPU and use it without additional software installation. This means the virtual client operating system guest now sees a full-featured GPU, which allows advanced graphics to be rendered on the server side. Then the screen output is sent to the RDP client for display, which includes server-side rendering of Aero effects, multimedia, and other types of media and applications not previously possible such as Flash, Silverlight, and DirectX applications as well as enhanced capabilities in applications such as PowerPoint and Internet Explorer. Because all the rendering is performed on the Hyper-V server within the VM, the client capabilities do not matter anymore. You can connect from a full, rich client or a basic thin client; the experience and graphical fidelity will be the same because all the graphical processing can be done on the server side. The only requirement is that the end client must support RDP 8/8.1 for the best experience with Windows Server 2012 R2.

Once a client VM is RemoteFX enabled and is connected to a RemoteFX-capable client, it will appear as if the VM actually has a GPU and an amount of graphical memory based on the RemoteFX configuration for the VM. Running DXDiag on the client will show the presence of a WDDM graphics driver and the Microsoft RemoteFX Graphics Device along with support for DirectDraw, Direct3D, and AGP Texture acceleration, as shown in Figure 10.14. The actual version of DirectX 3D supported is 11.1 for Windows Server 2012 R2. While there is OpenGL support in RemoteFX, the version of OpenGL supported is very old and is essentially limited to the OpenGL provided out of the box in Windows, version 1.1. This OpenGL does not leverage the GPU but rather the CPU only, making its usage very restricted.

**FIGURE 10.14**
A RemoteFX vGPU–
enabled virtual
machine

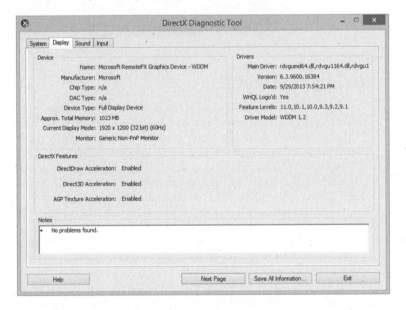

Because the GPU is virtualized, you don't need a discrete GPU for every VM that will be RemoteFX enabled. Just like CPU virtualization where a single logical CPU (such as a core) can be mapped to many virtual CPUs, a GPU can be virtualized to up to 12 virtual GPUs, allowing great scalability. One key consideration when you virtualize the GPU is the amount of graphical memory each VM will need. You can't overcommit GPU memory to achieve the 12:1 ratio. You would need to ensure the graphics card has sufficient video RAM for all the VMs.

The requirement of a GPU in the Hyper-V server in the Windows 2008 R2 SP1 implementation of RemoteFX was a challenge for many environments that traditionally did not have powerful GPUs in their servers. Windows Server 2012 introduces a basic software rasterizer that allows RemoteFX capabilities in VDI and session-based environments that do not have physical GPUs for some types of graphical capability; however, for rich graphics rendering, you will still require a physical GPU to virtualize.

To use RemoteFX vGPU, the graphics card must support DirectX 11.0 or newer and must have a WDDM 1.2 driver or newer. Microsoft has a good blog at http://blogs.msdn.com/b/rds/archive/2013/11/05/gpu-requirements-for-remotefx-on-windows-server-2012-r2.aspx that walks through some of the GPUs it has tested and recommend. The Hyper-V server must also use processors that support Secondary Level Address Translation (SLAT) because of the additional overhead of graphics drivers.

Once all the requirements are met, the GPU is enabled for RemoteFX use through the Hyper-V settings in the Physical GPUs section. Figure 10.15 shows my environment that leverages an AMD FirePro V5900 card.

**FIGURE 10.15**
Enabling a GPU for
use with RemoteFX

Virtual machines can then have a RemoteFX 3D video adapter added to it via the Add Hardware option in the virtual machine's settings. Note that a RemoteFX 3D video adapter is compatible only with generation-one virtual machines; it will not be listed as available for a generation-two virtual machine. When adding the RemoteFX 3D video adapter, you will be prompted to select the maximum number of monitors that may be connected and the maximum resolution for the monitors connected, as shown in Figure 10.16. This configuration controls the display settings when connecting and the graphic memory allocated to the virtual machine.

**FIGURE 10.16**

RemoteFX 3D video adapter options for a virtual machine

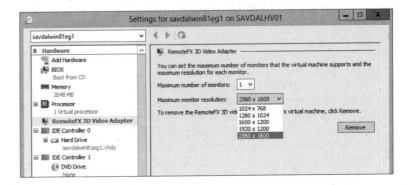

The new graphical capabilities mean a lot more screen update data and therefore bandwidth. The second part of the RemoteFX technology package is a new codec that was designed to efficiently encode and decode the display updates associated with the more intensive RemoteFX-enabled workloads. This was the only part of RemoteFX that was available to Remote Desktop Session Hosts in Windows Server 2008 R2 before RemoteFX was more widely available in Windows Server 8. The RemoteFX codec has been greatly enhanced since its original version. Consider a typical highly graphically intense workload. In Windows 7 this workload may have resulted in around 50 Mbps of network traffic. With the Windows 8 changes this same workload resulted in around 5 Mbps of traffic which was reduced a further 50 percent in Windows 8.1 to around 3 Mbps of traffic. That is a huge change and be a driving factor to migrate to the newest version of Remote Desktop Services.

The final piece of the RemoteFX technology is often overlooked; however, it really completes the ability to have a full-featured remote desktop experience by enabling the redirection of basically any USB device from the local client to the remote session. Prior to the RemoteFX USB redirection feature, there have been advancements in the type of devices that could be redirected to a remote session. We have keyboard, mouse, microphone, smartcard, disk, imaging devices with in-box functionality, and a few others that can be redirected; however, they are all redirected by abstracting the device into one of the supported high-level RDP redirection device types, which means you can access these devices on the remote session without needing any drivers on the remote OS installed. This also means you may miss device-specific functionality, and many types of USB device cannot be redirected that don't fall into these high-level types such as multifunction printers, advanced communication devices, scanners, and barcode readers.

The RemoteFX USB redirection solves this by redirecting at the USB port level in a similar way to how RDP handles the redirection of serial and parallel ports. With the RemoteFX USB redirection, the actual USB request blocks (URBs) are intercepted from the client and sent to the remote session, which means basically any type of USB device can be redirected using the RemoteFX USB redirection feature. But this does not mean you no longer want to use the RDP high-level device redirection for devices supported by the RDP high-level redirection. The RemoteFX USB redirection is designed to supplement the RDP high-level device redirection to add support for devices that don't work with the standard RDP redirections, and there are some good reasons for that.

For the RDP high-level supported device redirections such as input (keyboard/mouse), audio, drive, smart card, port, printer (Easy Print), and Plug-and-Play, optimized protocols are used for each of the redirection types to minimize bandwidth usage and ensure the best responsiveness and experience for that type of device. Additionally, the RDP high-level device redirections don't require extra drivers in the remote sessions, and multiple remote sessions can access the same local device simultaneously. Because of these optimizations, the RDP high-level device redirections can be used in both LAN and WAN environments.

Now consider the RemoteFX USB redirection where you are redirecting at the USB port level to the remote session. Because the port is being redirected, no device/load-specific optimizations can be made, and the driver for the device must be installed in the remote session since on the remote session it will look like the device has been plugged in to a virtual USB port, so it needs the driver to use the device. Also, because you are redirecting at a port level, only one session can access a device at a time, and that includes the local client, so if you redirect a device using RemoteFX USB redirection from your local client, no other session can see the device, nor can your local client. Make sure you don't try to use RemoteFX USB to redirect your keyboard. RemoteFX USB redirection is also optimized for LAN environments and cannot be used on WAN connections like the rest of RemoteFX.

Although the RemoteFX USB redirection is not using any GPU resources, it was tied to the RemoteFX experience in Windows Server 2008 R2 SP1, and the RemoteFX USB redirection could not be used with RDSH or a non-RemoteFX-enabled Windows VDI virtual machine. In Windows Server 2012, this restriction was removed, enabling the RemoteFX USB redirection to be used even when RemoteFX GPU virtualization was not used, such as in session host scenarios.

## Remote Desktop Protocol Capabilities

A protocol must be used between the client and the server for the Remote Desktop connection. That server could be an RD Session Host, a client OS running inside a virtual machine that is part of a VDI collection, or even just a regular desktop that someone wants to remotely connect to. Windows uses the Remote Desktop Protocol (RDP) that with Windows Server 2012 R2 and Windows 8.1 is currently at version 8.1. Updates for previous versions of operating systems are often available. For example, an RDP 8.0 update for Windows 7 SP1 (which natively supports RDP 7.1) is available and can easily be found by searching for RDP 8.0 and Windows 7. As RDP is updated, so too is the Remote Desktop Client (RDC) that is provided as part of Windows.

RDP has improved greatly with each new version that typically corresponds to new versions of the Windows operating system. For the best experience, the client should support the same version as the server; otherwise, the only features available will be those of the lowest common version. For example, if a Windows 7 SP1 box running RDP 7.1 connects to a Windows Server 2012 R2 session host that supports RDP 8.1, the actual usable features will be limited to those supported by RDP 7.1. It is for this reason it is a good idea to always update the RDP client to the latest possible version on your clients. To verify the RDP version supported by your Remote Desktop Client, start the client (mstsc.exe) and look at About as shown in Figure 10.17.

**FIGURE 10.17**
Showing the sup-
ported version of
RDP

Initially RDP just had to handle the sending of changes to the display as bitmap updates and passing the keyboard and mouse input. Today, the reality is that a remote desktop could be a user's primary workspace, so RDP has had to evolve to offer a lot more. As RDP has evolved, so too has the built-in Remote Desktop Client (RDC), which provides the remote connections over RDP. As enhancements to RDP are made, the RDC is updated to take advantage of the new capabilities. Often the RDC will be updated for the version of Windows that offers the new RDP features, but sometimes a new version of the RDC is created for older versions of the operating system, allowing the older operating systems to be able to connect to newer operating systems and take advantage of new features.

RDP supports a number of virtual channels, which allows different types of traffic and use scenarios for RDP to be enabled, including third parties creating additional capabilities on top of RDP. Up to 64,000 separate virtual channels are available for an RDP connection. The new RemoteFX technology takes advantage of RDP virtual channels to offer its functionality.

Looking at the RDP capabilities today, it quickly becomes apparent that a full desktop experience is possible using an entirely remote session while still accessing local devices including printers. Key capabilities include the following:

◆ Full keyboard, mouse, and touch redirection including keyboard hooking, allowing special Windows key combinations to be redirected to a remote session.

◆ Support for 32-bit color and desktop composition, enabling a full Aero Glass experience (no Aero Glass for Windows 8 and newer).

◆ True multimonitor support, enabling discrete displays to be selected for use in a remote session. Prior to RDP 7.0, while multiple monitors could be used, they were treated as a single display with a combined dimension, which meant dialog boxes would be displayed in the center of a dual display environment. Treating each display separately resolves this.

- Multimedia redirection, enabling certain types of media, such as those that typically would be played in Windows Media Player, to be redirected and played natively on the client device if the client device has the capability. This gives cleaner media playback and saves bandwidth. For example, if I played a WMV file in a remote session, the actual WMV primitive is sent over RDP to the local client and rendered locally.

- Progressive rendering of images, enabling a lower-quality version of the image to initially display and then increasing in quality as bandwidth allows. Other items on the screen such as text would still be rendered with full fidelity including font smoothing.

- Bidirectional audio, enabling sounds to be sent to the local client and from the local client. This enables capabilities such as Voice over IP applications.

- Print redirection. The RD EasyPrint functionality driverless printing is available in remote sessions (this also works for Windows 7 target machines and newer).

- Reduction of bandwidth and fully configurable experience settings to optimize the experience based on the type of connection, including a great WAN experience.

- Full encryption where required using 56- or 128-bit keys, enabling FIPS compliance where needed and Network Level Authentication (NLA) to ensure authenticity of both the server and the client.

- Clipboard, drive, port, device, and smart card redirection. Certain types of device can be redirected to a remote session in an abstracted fashion, which avoids a driver having to be installed for the specific hardware on the remote server. Devices with in-boxes such as cameras are great examples.

- Port-level USB redirection with RemoteFX, enabling any USB device to be redirected to a remote session. However, because the redirection is at a port level, the driver for the USB device must be present on the remote server, and the device is available to only one remote session at a time and is no longer available to the local client.

- RDP 8.0 added automatic network detect, removing the need to manually select the type of network in the Remote Desktop Client.

- RDP 8.0 added UDP and TCP support to provide the best possible experience over different types of networks.

- RDP 8.0 added multitouch support with up to 256 touch points (and of course RemoteFX Multi-Touch offers a richer experience where available).

- RDP 8.0 adds the ability to have nested RDP sessions.

- RDP 8.1 provides dynamic monitor and resolution changes, which supports automatic changing of the display in the remote session as the display of the local client changes, for example, rotating a table or adding a second display.

- RDP 8.1 improved transparent window and moves/resizes of RemoteApps on the local device.

To summarize, as you look at RDP, it is not a basic protocol anymore. It has a huge array of features, it works very well over WAN connections, and, even better, Microsoft now provides RDP clients not just for Windows (including the nice-to-use modern Remote Desktop application). Microsoft provides RDP clients for Mac, iOS, and Android. These clients all support RD Gateway and application publishing.

◆ iOS: `https://itunes.apple.com/us/app/microsoft-remote-desktop/id714464092`

◆ Android: `https://play.google.com/store/apps/details?id=com.microsoft.rdc` `.android`

◆ Mac: `https://itunes.apple.com/us/app/microsoft-remote-desktop/` `id715768417?mt=12`

Figure 10.18 shows the published applications from an iOS device on my network. Note that the applications are the same as those you saw in the RD Web Access site earlier in this chapter and the same ones you would see on a Windows client.

**FIGURE 10.18**
A view of published applications on an iOS device using the Microsoft client

## Choosing the Right Desktop Virtualization Technology

Earlier in this chapter I talked about how VDI was pushed by a number of vendors and is very much the "in thing" right now, but often using session-based desktops is a better solution. How do you decide where to use each type of technology? There is no right answer, and every environment is different. I will share my insights about where VDI and session virtualization work best, but there are always different opinions. In reality, most companies I work with will have a mix of session virtualization and VDI. The key is no matter what approach, or combination of approaches, is used, the same user state, data, and application virtualization can be used for all of them, and the physical desktops in the organization give the user a consistent experience across every device they will ever use—physical, session, or virtual.

I'll quickly recap the key difference between session virtualization and VDI. Figure 10.19 shows session virtualization on the left and VDI on the right. With session virtualization, each user connects to their own session on a shared server operating system such as Windows Server 2012 R2, and with VDI each user connects to their own desktop operating system such as Windows 8.1 running inside a virtual machine running on a machine virtualization platform such as Microsoft Hyper-V. As the figure shows, to the end user it looks exactly the same.

**FIGURE 10.19**
Session-based virtualization and VDI high-level overview

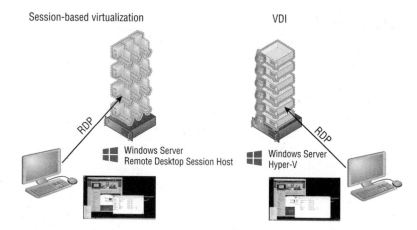

To help you make the right decision, I will cover what is the same and then what is different about using session virtualization and VDI. I want to explore both from the user's experience and from the infrastructure/management perspective. Both factors must be evaluated to help guide organizations the right way.

What is the same is the desktop environment. While with session virtualization, the user is connecting to a server operating system and with VDI the user connects to a client operating system, under the covers both the server and the client OS share a huge amount of code, so the actual desktop experience will look and feel the same. The users have the same Start screen, same capabilities, and same ability to run the same applications, and each user can still have a unique IP address (a feature of RDS that enables IP virtualization, giving each session or a specific application within the session a unique IP address, is required for some applications). The same RDP protocol is used to connect to both environments, which means the same client devices can be used. User settings and data virtualization plus application virtualization can and should be used with both session virtualization and VDI.

The key difference is that with session virtualization each user has their own session on a shared operating system, while with VDI each user has their own operating system instance. Fundamentally, the difference is in the level of isolation users have from other users. I think of session virtualization as being many people sharing an office, each having their own cubicle, but because they share a room, they have to behave, can't sing loudly, or run about changing the office because it would affect the other users sharing that office. They can do their work in the cubicle and customize their cubicle with pictures on the cubicle walls. I think of VDI as each user having their own heavily padded office; the users can run around, bouncing off the walls screaming, and they won't affect users in other offices.

This means that session virtualization is a good fit for task-based workers who run things like Internet Explorer, Office, and line-of-business applications but don't need to customize the operating system. They can still perform customizations of their desktop wallpaper, shortcuts, and applications. A user in session virtualization needs to be locked down so they can't install and uninstall applications or reboot the operating system, which would affect everyone else on the server.

VDI is a good fit for power users, for developers, or for users who run applications that will not run on a server operating system. Basically, if the user needs to modify the actual operating system or reboot the operating system, then VDI must be used. If you ever hear someone talking about using VDI but needing to heavily lock down the environment because it's being used for task workers who shouldn't change the OS, then they should probably be using session virtualization instead. If there are applications that run only on a client operating system, which is very rare, then VDI would also have to be used.

This is why often you will see a mix of session virtualization and VDI being used, specifically, session virtualization for most of the user population and VDI for those power users. The next question is "Well, wouldn't VDI work for everyone? Why use two solutions if VDI works for all?" That really brings us to the other differences between session virtualization and VDI.

Session virtualization uses a server operating system that hosts large numbers of sessions for many concurrent users. This could be hundreds of users on each session host depending on the applications being run and the amount of memory needed. Each session may use a couple of hundred megabytes of memory, assuming a fairly heavy application workload for each user. If I have a server with 64 GB of RAM, I can probably get around 300 users on that box. That's one operating system instance with 300 users.

With VDI, I take the same piece of hardware. I run a hypervisor on it and then create lots of virtual machines, and each virtual machine runs a full client operating system (which has CPU and memory requirements). Then I run the applications on that client OS. Hypervisors have some great memory technologies to get the most from the box, only assigning memory as the OS needs it. Typically a client OS will need around 700 MB of memory just to log on and then additional memory as applications run, so let's say a very low 1 GB of memory per virtual machine. Remember that realistically the actual memory needed could rise to 2 GB. On that same server, removing memory for the OS, that may be 62 virtual machines.

On the same server, with session virtualization, I get five times more users than with VDI, and in some environments I see ten times more users on a session-based environment than the same VDI environment. That's a huge difference in bang for the buck for the same hardware. There are other differences that also make VDI more expensive.

The licensing is also different because with session virtualization an RDS Client Access License is required, but with VDI there are numerous licenses needed depending on the exact solution.

So, the issue is not that session virtualization has capabilities beyond VDI but rather that VDI is more expensive, requires more hardware, and needs more management than session virtualization. This means, where possible, use more session virtualization and save VDI for where it's actually needed.

I've heard of organizations talking about moving to VDI to save money. I've never found this to be the case. If an organization has a poorly managed desktop environment, moving it to the datacenter with VDI will mean a poorly managed VDI and a bigger mess. The move to VDI normally introduces a whole new infrastructure that makes the environment more managed, which in reality could have been used to clean up the physical desktop environment without purchasing all the hardware for the VDI servers.

What is interesting is when I talk to clients who need to enable BYOD scenarios or overseas contractors, they always talk VDI; they never think of session virtualization. The reason is simply there are some companies that only have VDI solutions and don't have a session virtualization solution. Therefore, VDI is the solution for everything. If you only sell a hammer, then a hammer is the right tool for everything. Take time to understand your requirements and identify the right solution based on the factors I've discussed. To summarize, start with a normal desktop operating system that is well managed. If that is not an option, then think session virtualization. If session virtualization is not an option because the users are power users, the users are developers, or the applications will not run on a server OS or run multiple instances on one OS, then use VDI. Remember, you don't have to pick one solution. Use a well-managed desktop environment for corporate assets that can run a modern desktop OS, and use session virtualization and VDI where it fits best. You will likely have all three.

Notice many times I talk about a well-managed desktop environment. Most companies have good desktops and laptops that can run Windows 8, so just adopting session virtualization or VDI to cut down on the management of the machine is a huge waste of all the resource available on those desktops and laptops. Get the right management infrastructure in place to patch the client operating systems, set up good processes to deploy new operating systems, and use the user settings and data/application virtualization to simplify the environment, and the desktops in your environment will actually become far less of a help-desk headache.

This does not mean you should never consider using session virtualization or VDI for your desktops in the organization. What if your organization has not done a desktop refresh for six years and the machines are running Windows XP but on 128 MB of memory with a Pentium II processor? That hardware will not run Windows 7; in fact, it's probably barely running Windows X. I had an experience with a company in just this position that wanted to move to a modern OS but had nowhere near enough budget to refresh 5,000 desktop machines. They set up a farm of remote desktop session hosts and replaced Windows XP with Windows Fundamentals for Legacy PCs, which allows the machine to basically act as an RDP client, and configured the OSs to connect to the new farm of remote desktop session hosts. Each desktop got a new widescreen monitor, keyboard, and mouse, and now when the users logged on, they got a Windows 7 desktop experience (even though it was actually Windows Server 2008 R2; they couldn't tell) and thought they had new PCs. They had no idea they were using session virtualization and RDP. This is one scenario where session virtualization can really save on hardware budget.

I should once again stress that whenever I talk about session virtualization, VDI, and RDP, there are great partners such as Citrix and Quest that build on the Microsoft solutions by offering their own session virtualization and VDI solutions, so look at what Microsoft provides in the box with Windows Server 2012 R2, and if that does not meet your needs, then look at the partner offerings.

## The Bottom Line

**Explain the types of desktop virtualization provided by RDS.**   Windows Server 2012 R2 provides two main types of desktop virtualization: session-based desktops and VDI-based desktops. There are two types of VDI deployments: pooled and personal.

   **Master It**   When should VDI be used over session-based virtualization?

**Describe the benefits of RemoteFX and its requirements.**   RemoteFX brings a number of technologies such as USB port-level redirection and improved codecs that with Windows Server 2012 are available separately from GPU virtualization, which is the other primary RemoteFX technology that allows a physical GPU to be virtualized and assigned to VDI virtual machines running client operating systems. Using RemoteFX vGPU enables virtual machines to have local graphical resources, which enables the ability to run rich graphical applications, specifically those that leverage DirectX. To use RemoteFX vGPU, the graphics card must support DirectX 11 or newer and have a WDDM 1.2 driver or newer. The processor must also support SLAT.

**Master It**   Is RemoteFX vGPU a good solution for OpenGL applications?

**Articulate the other technologies required for a complete virtualized desktop solution.**   The complete user experience comprises a number of layers. The operating system provided by VDI or session virtualization is just the foundation for the user experience. The users need access to their profiles, their data, and their applications. To provide data access, the most common technology is folder redirection. For a user's profile, while historically roaming profiles were used, a better and more granular solution is UE-V, which provides application-level setting replication. For the applications, technologies such as App-V and RemoteApp can be leveraged, while specific core applications could be installed on the RD Session Host or VDI virtual machine template.

**Master It**   Why is it best to minimize the number of applications installed in the VM VDI template image?

# Chapter 11

# Windows Azure IaaS and Storage

Microsoft has long provided solutions an organization can run in its own datacenters, such as Windows Server, Exchange, SQL Server, and more. Microsoft has also long provided public solutions such as Hotmail (now Outlook.com), Windows Update, MSN, Xbox Live, Bing, and Office 365. These services are all Software as a Service (SaaS) type solutions, which means they offer a complete service online. Just as the private cloud gained momentum, so too did the public cloud, the idea of services and applications being available over the Internet. Organizations could bring their own services or entire virtual machines. Microsoft's offering in this space is Windows Azure, which has constantly been evolving, with new capabilities added regularly. This chapter will focus on a relatively new offering in Windows Azure, Infrastructure as a Service (IaaS), which allows customers' virtual machines to be hosted on Microsoft infrastructure accessed over the Internet. Additionally, we'll explore Windows Azure Storage and how it can benefit organizations in different ways.

In this chapter, you will learn to

◆ Explain the difference between Platform as a Service and Infrastructure as a Service

◆ Connect Windows Azure to your on-premises network

◆ Move data between on-premises and Windows Azure

## Understanding Public Cloud "as a Service"

I briefly introduced the core types of cloud services in Chapter 1, but Figure 11.1 shows the key types of cloud services again so we can review them as they relate to Windows Azure. The image shows the main elements of a service and the boundaries of responsibility for the different cloud service options.

As you move from on-premises to Infrastructure as a Service (IaaS) to Platform as a Service (PaaS) and finally to Software as a Service (SaaS), the elements of the solution that you, as an organization, are responsible for decrease, until with SaaS there is no infrastructure management at all. Instead, only basic administration may be required, such as deciding which accounts should have which capabilities in the service.

IaaS can be thought of as a virtual machine in the cloud. The provider has a virtual environment and you purchase virtual machine instances, and you then manage the operating system, the patching, the data, and the applications within them. The most well-known example of IaaS today is Amazon's Elastic Computing 2 (EC2), which offers organizations the ability to run operating systems inside Amazon's virtual environment, Microsoft introduced an IaaS component to Windows Azure in 2012.

**FIGURE 11.1**
The key types
of public cloud
services

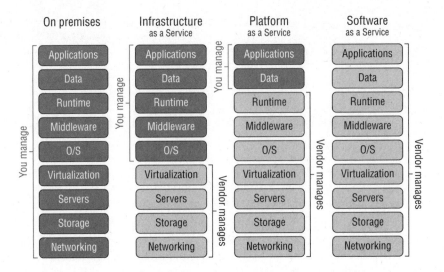

**FIGURE 11.1**
The key types
of public cloud
services

PaaS provides a framework in which custom applications can run. Organizations need to focus only on writing the very best application within the guidelines of the platform capabilities and everything else is taken care of. There are no worries about patching operating systems, updating frameworks, backing up SQL databases, or configuring high availability. The organization just writes the application and pays for the resource used. Windows Azure is the classic example of a PaaS and was the original focal point for Windows Azure.

SaaS is the ultimate in low maintenance. The complete solution is provided by the vendor. There is nothing to write or maintain by the organization other than configuring who in the organization should be allowed to use the software. Commercial examples of SaaS would be Outlook.com, which is a messaging service on the Internet. The enterprise example could be Office 365, which provides a cloud-hosted Exchange, SharePoint, and Lync service all accessed over the Internet with no application or operating system management for the organization.

The first type of cloud solution, Infrastructure as a Service, differs from an on-premises solution where you are responsible for everything because IaaS enables your focus to shift to the components within a virtual machine. This is because IaaS basically provides the ability to host virtual machines. You can see in Figure 11.1 that the IaaS provider is responsible for the networking, storage, server, and virtualization layer and then you are responsible for all aspects of the operating system within the VM, the middleware, the runtime, data, and of course the application. While it may seem like IaaS gives the most flexibility, the trade-off is that the amount of management still required is high. Many organizations, however, may first tip their toe into the cloud using IaaS and then move onto the other types to cut down on management and gain benefits offered with PaaS and SaaS.

Platform as a Service changes the amount of management for your organizations drastically. With PaaS, you only have to worry about the application you manage and the data, leaving everything else to the PaaS provider. I should point out that although you manage the data, the provider likely still provides services to actually replicate and protect the data.

Finally, with Software as a Service you are responsible for nothing. You just use the cloud-based software. Not every system can be SaaS because some organizations have their own custom code, but the goal for many organizations is a combination of PaaS and IaaS, and there will always be some systems on premises.

Unless your organization enjoys IT infrastructure management, the end goal would be SaaS for everything. With SaaS, the complete service is provided, backed up, updated, and maintained completely for you. Your only work is the basic administration, but there are only certain types of solution available as SaaS. Popular examples include solutions such as messaging, collaboration, and customer relationship management. There are times when even if a SaaS is available, there may be limitations in its flexibility because, remember, the vendor is providing this service for thousands of different customers on a shared infrastructure, which will limit the amount of customization possible. This means even if a solution is available as SaaS, it may not be a good fit for some organizations.

If a SaaS solution is not available, then the next best choice is PaaS because you can focus on just your application, providing you write the application using languages supported by the PaaS offering and stay within its guidelines. The challenge for many organizations is that they have legacy applications that don't fit within the guidelines and the developers long since left the company, leaving no documentation and no hope of making the application work in a PaaS environment. Additionally, many organizations run applications by third parties who don't follow the guidelines for the application to run in PaaS. This means that although PaaS is a great solution, many applications are simply not a fit.

Then you get to IaaS, which is just a VM in the sky essentially. Providing the operating system you wish to use is supported by the IaaS supplier, your application should be able to be moved up to the IaaS environment without modification. This is why IaaS is really the big focus for public cloud computing right now. It enables pretty much anything to run, but there are still some restrictions that may mean some services stay on premises. These restrictions could be technical, such as scalability or the type of functionality needed, or they could be legal, such as restrictions on certain types of data leaving the company's premise or leaving the country (IaaS vendors don't have datacenters in every country, which means outside of primary locations, a company's actual hosting may be provided in a datacenter geographically located in another country). It could even simply be a matter of trust. Many organizations are not comfortable with hosting some types of workloads and data off premises because of security concerns.

I think of IaaS as a great "on-ramp" to the public cloud. If an organization wants to start with public cloud services, then start with IaaS. Test specific workloads, and then work from there, such as using other types of services and more important workloads.

## When Public Cloud Services Are the Best Solution

I don't think there is a right or wrong answer for this. I know some companies want to move their entire infrastructure to public cloud services and get out of the infrastructure business completely. Other companies want to use the public cloud for disaster recovery purposes. Others want to use it for test/dev scenarios. Still others want to use it for specific projects. And some don't want to get anywhere near it! Each of these companies has specific drivers and factors that guide its public cloud strategy, and once again, they could be based on technical considerations. They can also be based on personal preference, which may not be grounded in very much fact but they are still very real factors in the decision process to leverage the public cloud.

At this point I want to take a step back and talk about a key advantage of the public cloud over on-premises solutions, and that is you pay for what you use. It's consumption-based pricing. There are various units that are used for pricing with Windows Azure, such as computer minutes (a change from the per-hour billing Windows Azure used to use), which vary in price depending on the size of the virtual machine that is running and various other configurations.

The key point is that if I run 10 four-vCPU virtual machines in Windows Azure for 4 hours a month, I pay for only those 4 hours instead of having the cost of running servers all month, which would be the case if they were run on premises.

You also pay for storage, for SQL Server storage, and for bandwidth used out of the Windows Azure datacenters. Notice that you don't pay for inbound (ingress) traffic into Windows Azure. On the compute side, you are paying for when the virtual machine is deployed. If the VM is idle or if it is running at full capacity, you pay the same unless you completely deprovision it, which I will cover in more detail later. That is why it's important that you don't create instances and forget to deprovision them.

Many organizations may have certain tasks that perhaps run only once a month but require huge amounts of compute or storage when they run. It is a waste to have all that computer and storage fabric idle for most of the month. This would be a great type of application to run on Windows Azure because you would deploy only the application and scale to many instances during those critical few days each month. There are other types of business that may get really busy on a particular day of the year, and only on that day do those organizations require thousands of instances of their website VMs and application VMs, while the rest of the year they may need only a hundredth of those instances or perhaps run on premises during that time. The sidebar "Super Bowl Sunday and the American Love of Pizza" takes a look at a great use of Windows Azure.

---

### SUPER BOWL SUNDAY AND THE AMERICAN LOVE OF PIZZA

I'll be up front; I'm English, and I don't understand the American football game. I've tried to watch it a couple of times. I even watched the 2006 Super Bowl—it seemed like it took 5 hours for 2 minutes of action, then a 5-minute commercial break, and then a different set of players coming out and moving the ball a couple of yards. It would be hard to get me to watch it again, but nonetheless, it's very popular in the United States. As Americans watch the Super Bowl, they like to eat pizza, and what's interesting is that the Super Bowl represents a perfect storm for pizza ordering peaks. During the Super Bowl, people throughout the entire United States—across all four time zones—are in sync and ordering at the same times, during breaks between the first and second quarters, at halftime, and between the third and fourth quarters.

These three spikes require 50 percent more compute power to handle the ordering and processing than a typical Friday dinner time, which is the high point for pizza ordering.

Normally systems have to be built to handle the busiest time, so our pizza company would have to provision capacity of 50 percent more than would ever be needed just for that one day. Remember also that it's 50 percent more than is needed for dinner time on Friday, which itself is much more than is needed any other time of the week. This would be a hugely expensive and wasteful exercise. Instead, Windows Azure is used.

During normal times, there could be 10 web instances and 10 application instances handling the website and processing. On Friday between 2 p.m. and midnight, this increases to 20 instances of each role, and then on Super Bowl Sunday between 12 p.m. and 5 p.m., this increases to 30 instances of each role. I'm making up the numbers of instances, but the key here is that the additional instances exist only when needed and therefore the customer is charged extra only when additional resources are needed and not at other times. This elasticity is key to public cloud services.

To be clear, I totally understand the eating pizza part!

The pizza scenario is a case of *Predictable Bursting*, which is a known period of increased utilization and is one of the scenarios that is perfect for cloud computing. Figure 11.2 shows the four main scenarios in which cloud computing is clearly the right choice. There are many other scenarios that work great in the cloud as well, but these four are uniquely suited because there are periods of utilization, and with the public cloud, you pay only for what you use.

**FIGURE 11.2**
The key types of highly variable workloads that are a great fit for consumption-based pricing

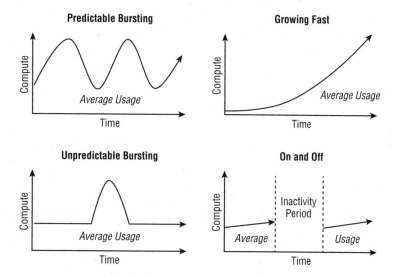

In the Growing Fast scenario, a particular service's utilization is growing very rapidly and a traditional on-premises infrastructure may not be able to scale fast enough to keep up with demand. Leveraging the "infinite" scale of the public cloud removes the danger of not being able to keep up with demand.

With Unpredictable Bursting, there may be big bursts in utilization, but the exact timing cannot be planned, and with the On and Off scenario, services are needed at certain times but completely turned off at other times. This could be in the form of monthly batch processes that run for only 8 hours a month, or it could be used by a company such as a tax return accounting service that runs for three months out of the year.

While the use of the public cloud is a no-brainer in these four cases, there are still many other scenarios (some I hinted at in the beginning of this section) in which a public cloud solution is a good option. Additionally, while these four scenarios are great for the public cloud, some are also a good fit for hybrid solutions with a mix of on-premises and public cloud services. Consider the various bursting scenarios like our pizza example. The normal baseline could be handled on premises but the bursts could be expanded out to use public cloud capacity.

For startup organizations, there is a saying, "Fail fast." This does not mean the goal of the startup is to fail but rather if it is going to fail, it's better to fail fast because less money is wasted than would be in a long drawn-out failure. The public cloud is a great option for startups because very little up-front capital expenditure is needed to buy servers and datacenter space. Instead, the startup has just operating expenses, paying for the amount of service it actually uses. This is why startups like services such as Office 365 for their messaging and collaboration. Not only do they not need infrastructure, they don't need messaging administrators to maintain it. Public cloud IaaS is a great solution for virtual machines because, once again, no up-front infrastructure is required and companies pay for what they use. As the company grows, its utilization goes up and so does its operating expenditure, but it's proportional to the business. This type of pay-as-you-go model is also attractive to potential financers because there is less initial outlay and therefore reduced risk.

If your organization needs a highly available application but you don't have the infrastructure to support the level of availability required, Windows Azure is a great fit. This can similarly apply to disaster recovery, and I've actually seen a lot of organizations interested. Some organizations have a main datacenter but not a second datacenter that can be used for disaster recovery. In this case, leveraging a public cloud IaaS can be a good option for a disaster recovery plan. There are a lot of considerations. First, for the smoothest failover, the hypervisor used on premises should match that in the public cloud, which for Windows Azure would be Hyper-V. Otherwise, there are messy conversions when moving between the hypervisors. You also need to consider the best way to keep the virtual machines in Windows Azure IaaS current.

If you have an application that has a fairly short lifetime (maybe related to a specific promotion or advertising campaign), Windows Azure is a great fit. The resources are spun up in Windows Azure for the duration of the workload and then deleted.

Another popular type of workload is development and test workloads, which are lower priority workloads but also tend to be constantly provisioned and deprovisioned, resulting in a lot of overhead for the on-premises infrastructure and IT team. By moving these workloads to the public cloud, you remove that overhead, and if the organization does not currently have private cloud solutions, then the end user experience will also be simpler, which will result in faster provisioning times. I would urge caution here though, because the point of testing is to ensure that an application works as anticipated. The operating system, application, and the data would look the same running on premises or in a public cloud IaaS, and if the same hypervisor is used, the hardware would also look the same. However, the actual underlying networking and the underlying storage is different, and so while initial development and testing can be performed in a nonproduction-like environment, the final user acceptance testing should be performed on premises to ensure that there is not some difference in storage or networking or even the compute that will affect the functionality of the application.

There are some technical limitations to Windows Azure today that relate to elements of compute, network, and storage (and I will cover them in this chapter). However, outside of those, there is really not a workload that couldn't run in Windows Azure IaaS.

The decision about whether a workload is a better fit for on premises or the public cloud really comes down to how well architected and managed an organization's on-premises resources are and what workloads it's been architected to support. If an organization has implemented an on-premises private cloud, helping to maximize resource utilization, pool all resources, ease the ongoing management, and give very fast provisioning capabilities, then many scenarios will be able to be handled efficiently using the on-premises private cloud solution, but there may be specific scenarios where the public cloud is a better fit. If, on the other hand, an organization has not implemented a good management infrastructure, has not pooled resources, and has many siloed resource islands, which has led to limited scalability and slow provisioning, then the public cloud will be a great fit for many more workloads and scenarios. In the next chapter, I will talk in more detail about architecting the right solution.

# Windows Azure 101

The focus of this chapter is on Windows Azure IaaS and storage, but Windows Azure does have other capabilities. I want to briefly cover the major ones so you at least have some basic knowledge of the breadth of Windows Azure functionality.

Figure 11.3 shows there are three main building blocks to the Windows Azure platform and then networking to enable various types of connectivity and traffic management. First is Windows Azure Compute itself. It provides the primary compute capabilities of Windows Azure, such as virtual machines, cloud services, and websites plus the Fabric Controller, which actually manages all the virtual machines and hosts that provide the Windows Azure platform. Windows Azure Data Services, as the name suggests, provides storage, backup, and SQL Server capabilities in the cloud, including relational databases, which are not available in the core Windows Azure component. Finally, Windows Azure App Services provides services such as access control and directory services, Service Bus for communication between components both within Azure and outside of Azure, and caching capabilities. There is also a Windows Azure Marketplace that allows buying and selling Windows Azure applications, components, and data sets.

**FIGURE 11.3**
The three main building blocks of the Windows Azure Platform: Windows Azure Compute, App Services, and Data Services

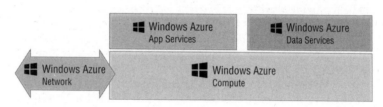

In the next sections, I'll cover servers, storage, load balancing, and all of the goodness needed to actually run applications for all of these components. Microsoft has many datacenters distributed throughout the world where Windows Azure applications can run. There are currently four datacenters in the United States and two each in Europe and Asia. When an application is deployed to Windows Azure, the customer can select where the application should be deployed. All datacenters in Windows Azure are paired to protect the data replicated between them in the event of a site failure.

In the following sections, I'll cover the main services available in Windows Azure, but keep in mind that it is a constantly changing service. For the most up-to-date list of available services and to get more details, I recommend viewing www.windowsazure.com/en-us/services/.

## Windows Azure Compute

The main building block of the Windows Azure platform is Windows Azure itself, which provides key capabilities to enable cloud-based hosting of applications and data. Windows Azure has evolved, and so have the names of the different types of services and where they sit in the hierarchy, which is why if you looked at Windows Azure a year ago, the components would have seemed different from those I describe today.

The fundamental building block of everything is the virtual machine; this is the part that actually runs the applications, which could be a website, some custom middleware code, or some legacy application. All of the compute capabilities are enabled through virtual machines that vary in size. While virtual machines are directly accessible and used with Windows Azure IaaS, other services such as PaaS, websites, networking, and so on are also built using virtual machines, although they may not be visible to you. The IaaS virtual machines are something I will be focusing on in this chapter.

There is also a Web role, with the sole purpose of acting as the web server for your web applications such as ASP.NET, Classic ASP, PHP, Python, and Node.js applications. The Web role leverages Internet Information Services (IIS) to run the web applications. If you request five instances of a Web role for your web application, behind the scenes five virtual machines running IIS are created and load balanced, all running your web code. If in the future you want additional instances, you just request additional instances and Windows Azure automatically creates new instances of the Web role, deploys your custom code, and adds those new instances to the load balancing. Separate from Web roles is the concept of Windows Azure Web Sites, which provide a fast way to deploy a web application.

For backend applications that are not IIS web applications but leverage PaaS, the Worker role is used, which can run many different types of tasks. Just as with the Web role, when you deploy your application, you just tell Windows Azure how many instances of the role you want and Windows Azure distributes your application to all instances and balances load. Using Worker roles, you could run applications such as Java Virtual Machines and Apache Tomcat, which is really where the Windows Azure flexibility can be seen.

You can have any combination of Web roles, Worker roles, and VMs for your application running inside a cloud service. Some applications may have only Web roles, some may have Web and Worker roles, some could be just VMs. The point is that the flexibility is there to create roles that meet the needs of the application you are deploying.

Windows Azure Compute also features a Mobile Services set of services that are designed to provide the backend for mobile applications running on Windows, iOS, and Android platforms. There are numerous services available, but some of the most useful allow integration into authentication services such as Microsoft and Facebook accounts plus the ability to push notifications to devices.

Windows Azure does not automatically scale instances of all roles. For example, if you had five IaaS VMs and the instances were running at full capacity, it would not add two more automatically. Because you are charged for each instance, that type of automatic scaling behavior could be a problem. Instead, through the Windows Azure website it is easy to request additional instances of a role, which are instantly deployed, or you can leverage System Center App Controller on premises, or you can programmatically request new instances, allowing you to write your own auto-scaling functionality. There are also third-party solutions such as AzureWatch from www.paraleap.com, which automatically scale based on defined thresholds. At the time of this writing, Windows Azure does feature an auto-scale capability for web applications, but this is currently in preview, although it allows scaling within defined minimum and maximum instance numbers.

Then there is the Fabric Controller itself. Windows Azure seems like magic. As a customer, I deploy my application and Windows Azure just spins up as many instances as I tell it to. I can scale up or scale down at any time. My service is always available per the Windows Azure

99.95 percent monthly service-level agreement (SLA), and the operating systems and dependent services are constantly patched and tuned. This magic is enabled by the Windows Azure Fabric Controller, which itself is a distributed application running on Windows Azure that has a fabric agent running on all the virtual machines (except for those that are IaaS VMs) and hosts that make up the Windows Azure Compute fabric. The Fabric Controller constantly monitors, and if it sees a problem, it can spin up new instances of a role. If a request is made for more instances of a role, then the Fabric Controller creates the new instances and adds them to the load balancer configuration. The Fabric Controller handles all patching and updates (again, apart from those VMs that are IaaS VMs), and this is a key reason that to be covered by the 99.95 percent SLA, you must deploy at least two instances of any role. The Fabric Controller will take down one instance to patch, and then once it's running again, it will take down the other. As you have more and more instances, more instances can be patched simultaneously based on groupings of role instances called *upgrade domains*. When patching occurs, all instances within an upgrade domain are brought down and updated at the same time, and then once the update is complete, the next upgrade domain is updated, and so on.

## Windows Azure Data Services

The ability to store data is critical to any service, and Windows Azure Data Services provides numerous types of storage that's available to Azure-based services but also to on-premises solutions.

Windows Azure provides two primary types of storage:

**Binary Large Object (BLOB)**    This is just a unstructured collection of bytes that can be used to store basically anything, including large media files. Currently BLOBs can scale up to 200 TB.

**Tables**    This can actually be confusing. These are not tables in the relational table sense. For relational database needs, SQL Database is used. A Windows Azure Table is simply a structured store based on key values that is designed to store large amounts of data for massive scale solutions and requires some basic structure but doesn't need relationships between data. Windows Azure Tables can be thought of as a NoSQL implementation, which is a growing class of database management systems that don't use Structure Query Language (SQL) or implement relational table capabilities.

**Windows Azure Drive**   I said Windows Azure provides two primary types of storage, but the Windows Azure Drive is a feature that allows a BLOB to actually be used as a virtual hard disk (VHD) and formatted as an NTFS volume. This allows applications to interact with the BLOB as an actual volume, but it's not actually a different type of storage.

Any data stored in Windows Azure is replicated three times within the same datacenter, and Windows Azure BLOB and Table contents are geo-replicated to another datacenter hundreds of miles away to provide resiliency against major site-level disasters. The geo-replication is not synchronous but is performed very quickly, which means there should not be much difference between the data content at the primary location and the geo-replicated location at any given time. Read access is available to the geo-replicated copy of the storage if required. Applications interact with storage using HTTP or HTTPS, and for the Tables, the Open Data (OData) Protocol is used, which actually builds on web technologies to provide flexible ways to interact with data.

Microsoft also provides an Import/Export capability that gives you a clean way to transport large amounts of data where transportation over the network is not practical. With the

Import/Export service, the data is copied to a 3.5 inch SATA HDD that is encrypted with BitLocker. The drive is then shipped to the Microsoft datacenter where the data is imported and available in your Azure account.

Where a relational database capability is required, Windows Azure SQL Databases should be used, which provides relational data through a subset of SQL Server capability in the cloud. This gives Windows Azure applications full access to a relational database where needed. A separate pricing model is used for SQL Azure, different than one used for the Computer and Storage components of Windows Azure. It's also priced differently than normal storage because you are really paying for the SQL service rather than raw storage. There are two types of database available: Web Edition, which has a 10 GB maximum database size, and Business Edition, which has a 150 GB maximum database size. Billing is based on database size in gigabyte increments. SQL Reporting is also available.

There are other types of services available. For insight into your big data, Windows Azure features HDInsight, which is a Hadoop-based service that bring great insight into structured and unstructured data. A shared cache service is available to provide improved storage performance. Another service that is gaining traction is Windows Azure Backup, which provides a vault hosted in Windows Azure to act as the target for backup data that is encrypted during transmission and encrypted when stored in Windows Azure. This provides an easy-to-implement cloud-based backup solution. Currently, Windows Server Backup and System Center Data Protection Manager can utilize Windows Azure Backup as a target. Hyper-V Recovery Manager also falls within the Data Services family of services.

## Windows Azure App Services

The Windows Azure App Services component encompasses various technologies that can be used to augment the Windows Azure applications. At the time of this writing, there are a number of technologies that make up the Window Azure App Services:

**Queues** These are used for a number of purposes but primarily for reliable and persistent messaging between applications within Windows Azure. A common use for Queues is for the communication between Web roles and Worker roles. Queues have very basic functionality, which makes them fast, but they don't have familiar characteristics such as First In, First Out (FIFO). Instead, the developers implement their own features on top of the Windows Azure Queue feature.

**Content Delivery Network (CDN)** There are Windows Azure datacenters all around the globe as I've already discussed, but there are certain types of data you may want available even closer to the consumer for the very best performance of high-bandwidth content. The Content Delivery Network (CDN) allows BLOB data within Windows Azure Storage to be cached at points of presence (PoPs) managed by Microsoft, which are far greater in number than the Windows Azure datacenters themselves. The first person in a region to download the content would use the CDN to pull down the data, which would obtain the data originally from the Windows Azure Storage BLOB at one of the major datacenters. This content is now stored at that CDN PoP and the data is sent to the first user. The second person to view the data in that location would now pull the data directly from the PoP cache, getting a fast response. Usage of the CDN is optional, and it has its own SLA with a pay-as-you-go pricing structure based on transactions and amount of data. Many organizations leverage the CDN for delivering their high-bandwidth data even if it's separate from an actual Windows Azure application, and it's easy to enable.

**Windows Azure Active Directory**    This provides an identity and access management solution that integrates with on premises where required and is leveraged by many Microsoft solutions (such as Office 365) in addition to your own custom solutions. Multifactor authentication is available, enabling your mobile phone to act as part of the authentication process by sending a text with a code required to complete the logon to your mobile phone or even phoning the mobile phone and requiring a key to be pressed.

**Service Bus**    This supports multiple messaging protocols and provides reliable message delivery between on-premises and cloud systems. There can typically be problems with on-premises, mobile, and other solutions to communicate with services on the Internet because of firewalls and IP address translation. Communication is enabled through the Service Bus component.

**Media Services**    These are focused on providing high-quality media experiences such as streaming of HD live video and also the various types of encoding and content protection.

**Scheduler**    As the name suggests, the scheduler enables jobs to run on a defined schedule.

### Windows Azure Network

I am going to go into a lot of detail about the Windows Azure virtual networks and the options to connect later in this chapter, so I'm going to skip that for now, but there is another component, Traffic Manager. Traffic Manager allows organizations to define how geographically distributed users should be routed to where applications have been deployed over multiple Windows Azure global datacenters and if that distribution should change based on various times of the day. It could also help redirect incoming requests if one datacenter is not available, almost like network load balancing.

## Capabilities of Azure IaaS and How It Is Purchased

I would like to start with a completely strange example of Windows Azure IaaS in action. My goal is to stress a very important point that will aid in your understanding of exactly what IaaS is: IaaS simply provides virtual machines in the cloud. What you do with those virtual machines is pretty much up to you providing the usage is within the capabilities exposed by the IaaS provider. Remember, in our private cloud it was possible to create capability profiles that defined which features were available and what a virtual machine could look like, such as, for example, how may vCPUs it could have, how much memory, how many disks. Just as with a private cloud, you can choose what storage to expose and what the networking will look like. This is exactly the same with Windows Azure IaaS, and as with any IaaS solution, you create virtual machines within the capabilities allowed and then within the virtual machines, you install operating systems that are supported by Windows Azure IaaS or use some of the provided templates in Windows Azure IaaS or even use your own. Behind the scenes, at the time of this writing, Windows Azure actually runs on Windows Server 2012 Hyper-V.

To stress this, one of the first projects I ask people to perform is to spin up a Minecraft server in Windows Azure IaaS. If you don't know what Minecraft is, go ask some kids. They'll tell you it's a popular building game. A Minecraft server allows multiple people to play together to build worlds. It's is actually a Java application and was never designed to run in a public cloud service, so it's a great example to show that you really can run almost anything in an IaaS solution and, specifically, in Windows Azure IaaS. It also helps demonstrate some of the key concepts that I will go into more detail about throughout the rest of this chapter.

Before you get started, you will need a Windows Azure account. Your organization may already have Windows Azure, but they may not want you to create a Minecraft server using their corporate account, so there are other options:

◆ If you have an MSDN subscription, depending on the subscription level, you have Windows Azure included quota. Activate this subscription via the MSDN subscription site, and under your My Account details, you will see the subscription benefits. One of these is Windows Azure, and there is a link to activate it. Once it's activated, you will have a certain amount of Windows Azure credit each month. For example, MSDN Visual Studio Ultimate subscriptions receive $150 of Windows Azure credit each month and reduced prices for the consumption of resources as detailed at www.windowsazure.com/en-us/offers/ms-azr-0049p.

To put this into perspective, at the time of this writing, it costs around $45 to run a single vCPU VM in Windows Azure for an entire month. This means I could run three small virtual machines all month in Windows Azure with the Ultimate MSDN subscription.

◆ Sign up for a one-month free trial with $200 of credit (that was the cost at the time I was writing this) at www.windowsazure.com/en-us/pricing/free-trial/. This is a great way to learn Windows Azure for free.

Once you have a subscription, you manage Windows Azure via https://manage.windows-azure.com. Through this portal you can perform nearly every aspect of Windows Azure management. At the top of the portal, your credit status is shown, as in Figure 11.4. If you click the View More Details line, you will get detailed information on your usage. Previously, you had to supply a credit card number even if you had included Windows Azure credit, but Microsoft removed this requirement and instead will now simply shut down your services if you run out of credit. If you want to remove the spending limit, this can be done via the account page by using a credit card, but it does mean you could be billed if you go over the included credit amount.

**FIGURE 11.4**
Basic credit status of your Windows Azure account

Now that you have a Windows Azure subscription, I want you to follow the step-by-step tutorial I have at http://youtu.be/KzESaLpV8l8, which walks through every step of creating a new virtual machine in Windows Azure, adding a data disk, installing Minecraft, enabling endpoints, and then connecting. It will probably take about 30 minutes, but I really recommend that you stop and do this now. Even if you don't want to play Minecraft (your kids will think you are a hero if you do this for them), the video walks you through key elements of using Windows Azure IaaS. In the next section, I will get into the details of creating virtual machines. But for now, I want to stress some key points to keep in mind:

- An extra-small Azure virtual machine (VM) would be fine for fewer than 10 users; however, consider a small VM for more than that, and unless you are very short on credit, I recommend using a small VM for even fewer than 10 users.

- Use the Windows Server 2012 Datacenter gallery image. Use the version with the latest release date, which is just a patch level.

- Create a separate data disk to store the Minecraft server executable and its data files. You will need to initialize and format this disk using Disk Management (`diskmgmt.msc`).

- Install the 64-bit version of Java. At the time of this writing, the Java Runtime Environments were available from the following location:

  `http://www.oracle.com/technetwork/java/javase/downloads/jre7-downloads-1880261.html`

- Download `Minecraft_Server.exe` from `https://minecraft.net/download` and save to the Minecraft folder you create on your data drive.

- Create a firewall exception for TCP port 25565, which is what Minecraft listens on.

- Create an endpoint for the VM in the Azure portal for public and private port 25565 to enable external communication to the port on the VM. I cover this in detail in the next section.

- Add your Minecraft account name to the `ops.txt` file to make yourself an operator on the server.

- To run the Minecraft server I use the following command, which gives Minecraft 1 GB of memory instead of 100 MB. Save this to a `start.bat` file and use it to initialize.

  ```
  "C:\Program Files\Java\jre7\bin\javaw.exe" -Xms1024m -Xmx1024m -jar "Minecraft_
  Server.exe"
  ```

You now have an up-and-running Minecraft server that you can access using the name you specified during the VM instance creation, as shown in Figure 11.5. There really was nothing special that was Windows Azure IaaS specific except creating the endpoint to allow connectivity over the Internet. (And thanks to my son for creating the likeness of me on his Windows Azure Minecraft server.) Notice also in the figure that through the Windows Azure portal I can see the various resource usage states of the virtual machine. This helps me check whether my son's playing when he should be doing homework. Notice that you have full console access to this virtual machine and can pretty much do anything you want within the capabilities of Windows Azure IaaS.

**FIGURE 11.5**

A connection to my Minecraft server running in Windows Azure

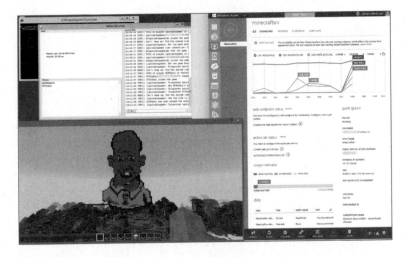

It should be noted that the Windows Azure IaaS virtual machine is not the same as the previously available VM role that was part of PaaS; that was a stateless virtual machine that had no persistent state. The Windows Azure IaaS virtual machine is a fully persistent solution.

I want to look at the capabilities of Windows Azure IaaS in more detail starting with the list of supported operating systems. Windows Azure IaaS supports only 64-bit operating systems and specifically these:

◆ Windows Server 2008 R2 SP1

◆ Windows Server 2012

◆ Windows Server 2012 R2

◆ A number of Linux distributions, which is constantly expanding but includes Oracle Linux, openSUSE, SUSE Linux Enterprise Server, Ubuntu Server, and OpenLogic (CentOS)

One easy way to check supported operating systems is to look at the templates provided in Windows Azure itself. Figure 11.6 shows the image selection screen you see when creating a new virtual machine. Note that there are categories not only for Windows but also for the various distributions of Linux. You do not have to use these templates. You can create your own sysprep'd images, but do *not* put an unattend.xml answer file in the image (Windows Azure needs to create that when deploying) and do not install the Windows Azure Integration Components. Once your image is ready, you upload them to Windows Azure and use them. The included Windows Azure templates are just there to help you get started. Microsoft has a step-by-step guide on uploading your own VHD to Windows Azure at the following location:

www.windowsazure.com/en-us/manage/windows/common-tasks/upload-a-vhd/

**FIGURE 11.6**

The template selection in Windows Azure

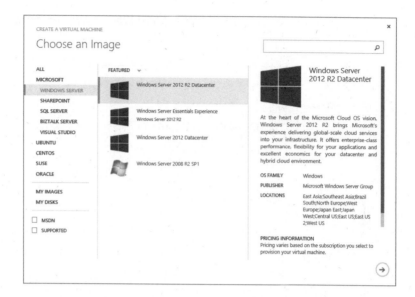

Regarding what can run in the Windows Azure IaaS virtual machine, remember, it is just a virtual machine. However, this does not mean vendors support their applications running in Windows Azure IaaS. Notice that Microsoft actually has templates in Windows Azure IaaS for SharePoint, SQL Server, Visual Studio, and BizTalk, but that does not mean that's the only Microsoft software that is supported. Microsoft has a full list at http://support.microsoft .com/kb/2721672/en-us, which also shows which components of System Center can run in Windows Azure IaaS and which roles of Windows Server run in Windows Azure. Remember, there is a difference between what is supported and what works, but do you really want to run something for production purposes that is not supported by the vendor of the application?

I want to point out that currently there is no Windows Azure management agent installed in Windows Azure IaaS virtual machines and no additional Windows Azure–specific software installed. This may change in the future, but there are no definite plans.

The virtual machines created can be one of a set of defined sizes. You cannot create custom combinations of vCPUs and memory. At the time I was writing this, the virtual machine sizes shown in Table 11.1 were available. These do change over time, though, and you can see the latest list at the following location:

http://msdn.microsoft.com/en-us/library/windowsazure/dn197896.aspx

The sizes also refer to the number of data disks that can be connected, which can be up to 1 TB in size each and have a 500 IOPs limit. The actual cores used in Windows Azure are not the highest-performing cores, but they are the more power efficient options. For example, you can view the exact type by looking in Task Manager at the processor details. The exact cores will vary based on the datacenter and generation of the servers being used, but my current virtual machine is using AMD Opteron Processor 4171 HE cores.

**TABLE 11.1:** Windows Azure IaaS virtual machine sizes

| SIZE | CPU CORES | MEMORY | OS DISK SIZE | MAXIMUM NUMBER OF DISKS |
|------|-----------|--------|--------------|-------------------------|
| ExtraSmall | Shared | 768 MB | 127 GB, 20 GB Temp | 1 |
| Small (A1) | 1 | 1.75 GB | 127 GB, 70 GB Temp | 2 |
| Medium (A2) | 2 | 3.5 GB | 127 GB, 135 GB Temp | 4 |
| Large (A3) | 4 | 7 GB | 127 GB, 285 GB Temp | 8 |
| ExtraLarge (A4) | 8 | 14 GB | 127 GB, 605 GB Temp | 16 |
| A5 | 2 | 14 GB | 127 GB, 135 GB Temp | 4 |
| A6 | 4 | 28 GB | 127 GB, 285 GB Temp | 8 |
| A7 | 8 | 56 GB | 127 GB, 605 GB Temp | 16 |

Source: http://msdn.microsoft.com/en-us/library/windowsazure/dn197896.aspx

Notice that the different-sized virtual machines have different sizes for the temporary storage disk, which can be used for any temporary data (think scratch space) that does not need to be persisted (that is, sustained).

The Windows pagefile is also stored on this temporary storage. Anytime the VM is moved, such as for patching, upgrades, or simply because of a node problem, the contents of the temporary disk will be lost. Figure 11.7 shows the view of my Minecraft Azure IaaS virtual machine, which has the standard 127 GB operating system disk, the 70 GB temporary disk, and a 100 GB data disk I added.

If you walked through the Minecraft tutorial, you will have noticed that you did not specify an IP address or a number of network adapters. A Windows Azure IaaS VM can have only a single network adapter, and its IP address is allocated by the Windows Azure fabric using DHCP. There is some control of the virtual networks in Windows Azure that I will cover later, but you can never specify a static IP address. The IP address must be allocated by Windows Azure. Additionally, the single adapter can have only a single IP address, the one set by Windows Azure. If you set the IP address statically, at some point you will lose access to your virtual machine. The good news is that using Azure Virtual Networks, you can do some clever things to make sure a virtual machine always gets the same IP address within ranges you configure. For communication, you can use TCP, UDP, and any IP-based protocol within the virtual network in Windows Azure, but you cannot perform broadcast communications.

Virtual machines and other Windows Azure constructs live within a cloud service, which can be thought of as a management, configuration, security, service model, and networking (unless you use virtual networks) boundary. In the case of IaaS virtual machines, each VM actually lives within a Virtual Machine role, and currently a Virtual Machine role can contain only one VM. Each cloud service supports up to 50 virtual machines at the time of this writing. Each cloud service has a virtual IP address (VIP), which is an Internet-routable address used to access services running in the cloud service (unless you enable site-to-site or point-to-site connectivity into virtual networks). It is using this VIP and an endpoint that allows RDP connections to virtual machines in Windows Azure and other services. Another great capability is the Windows Azure load balancer, which allows incoming traffic over the VIP to be distributed among multiple virtual machines in the cloud service; for example, port 80 could be load balanced for the VIP, which actually is directed to 10 virtual machines.

**FIGURE 11.7**
Disk view within a Windows Azure IaaS virtual machine

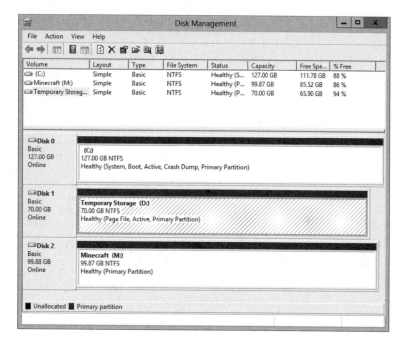

Hopefully at this point it is very clear that Windows Azure IaaS is giving you various sized virtual machines that you can pretty much do anything you wish with providing you stay within the capabilities of Windows Azure IaaS that I briefly covered earlier. The next question is, How much does it cost?

Azure is not broken into separate buckets of credit. You have a certain amount of Azure credit and you can use it however you want: for storage, VMs, websites, SQL databases, services, and so on. You are charged for the services you use under your Azure account, and different services and different sizes of service vary in their price. The easiest way to understand the cost of various services is to use the Windows Azure pricing calculator available at www.windows-azure.com/en-us/pricing/calculator/. The calculator allows you to specify the quantity you need of all the different services and then shows the monthly price. Note that discounts are available as part of various plans and agreements with Microsoft. Figure 11.8 shows part of the virtual machine section of the pricing calculator where I have requested pricing to run 10 small Windows and 10 small Linux virtual machines along with 2 medium SQL Server instances.

I also specified 203 GB of egress (outbound) traffic from Windows Azure. It shows me the estimated monthly price of the requested virtual elements.

**FIGURE 11.8**
Sample of the
Windows Azure
pricing calculator

You may wonder why the price of a Linux virtual machine is less than the price of a Windows Server virtual machine if all that is being provided is the virtual machine. You are actually getting more than that with a Windows Server virtual machine. The Windows Server license is part of the price of the VM instance, which means you don't need to separately license the Windows Server operating system running in Windows Azure. That is not the case for any paid Linux distributions or other applications such as SQL Server, which have to be separately licensed unless when creating the virtual machine you select a SQL Server or Biztalk Server image that includes the SQL Server/Biztalk Server license as part of the virtual machine price. Also note that if you want to manage virtual machines running in Windows Azure with System Center, you need to license System Center accordingly.

If you intend to host a long term SQL Server in Windows Azure it is likely cheaper to install a regular Windows Azure Windows Server virtual machine and then install SQL Server and use your own SQL license. If you need SQL Server short term, such as for a project then using the Windows Azure SQL image with included SQL Server license is likely more cost effective than buying a license.

There is an important point about virtual machines and how the billing works. Prior to June 2013, a virtual machine was charged while it existed, whether it was running or not. A big change was announced in June 2013 at TechEd related to Windows Azure—stopped virtual machines would no longer be billed and billing would be per minute instead of rounded to the nearest hour. This makes it sound like all you have to do is shut down the virtual machine and you stop paying for it, but this is not really the case.

There are actually two different types of shutdown for a Windows Azure IaaS VM. A virtual machine can be stopped and it can be deallocated. It's only when a virtual machine is deallocated that billing stops, but this also affects the IP address of the virtual machine.

If you stop a VM from within the guest OS of the VM or you use the `Stop-AzureVM` cmdlet with the `-StayProvisioned` parameter, the VM stays allocated in the Windows Azure fabric. This means the VM still has reserved resources, and it will keep the IP address it was dynamically assigned via DHCP (Dynamic IP, or DIP). A VM shut down this way is considered stopped, but not deallocated, which means it will continue to be billed. Its status in the Windows Azure portal will show as Stopped.

If you stop a VM from the Windows Azure portal by using the Shut Down button, then the VM is actually deallocated from Windows Azure resources. It no longer has resources reserved, and it loses its network configuration—and therefore its IP address lease. When you start the VM, it's reprovisioned in Windows Azure, resources are assigned, a network adapter is added, and it gets a new IP lease, which means its IP address will change. This type of deprovisioning also happens when the `Stop-AzureVM` cmdlet is used without the `-StayProvisioned` parameter. The VM will show as Stopped (Deallocated) and VMs in this status will not incur any billing.

An important point is that each cloud service has a virtual IP (VIP), which is the external IP address. If every VM in a cloud service is in a Stopped (Deallocated) state, then the cloud service might lose its VIP, and when VMs are restarted, it could get a new VIP. If consistency of the VIP is important, then ensure that at least one VM in each cloud service stays provisioned.

Here's a summary:

- Shutdown within the VM or `Stop-AzureVM -StayProvisioned`: Billing continues for the VM, and it keeps resources reserved, including keeping its leased IP address.

- Shutdown from Windows Azure Portal or `Stop-AzureVM` without `-StayProvisioned`: Billing stops for the VM, and all resources are deprovisioned, including network adapters, which means the IP address lease is lost.

I want to quickly cover one scenario that commonly comes up, and that is Desktop as a Service (DaaS), the idea of offering desktop environments in the public cloud. Windows Azure does not currently offer DaaS, but there is nothing to stop you from creating your own for your organization. Microsoft actually has guidance on the configuration of Remote Desktop Services (RDS) in Windows Azure, which will give you a session-based desktop experience. This guidance can be found at the following location:

```
http://msdn.microsoft.com/en-us/library/windowsazure/dn451351.aspx
```

What you cannot do is to run Windows client operating systems in Windows Azure and any other public cloud service for that matter. This is not a technical limitation but rather a licensing one. There is no way to license a Windows client to run in a public cloud environment. That is why any DaaS offerings you see are based around sessions running on Windows Server as opposed to connections to an actual Windows client operating system. The good news, as discussed in the previous chapter, is using session-based services actually gives the same end-user experience and a higher density of users, so it's actually a win-win.

## Creating Virtual Machines in Azure IaaS

Now that you understand the basics of Windows Azure IaaS, I want to take you through the actual creation of a virtual machine using the Windows Azure management portal, explain some of the options, and then walk through a simple creation using PowerShell.

As previously mentioned, the management of Windows Azure is performed through the Windows Azure management portal at `https://manage.windowsazure.com`. Through the portal, you have access to all the various datacenters that can host Windows Azure services, and where you wish to host your Windows Azure infrastructure is one of the first things you need to decide. You should pick the location closest to where the services will be consumed because this will result in the lowest network latencies.

There are two constructs required to create a virtual machine: a cloud service to contain the virtual machine and a storage account to host the VHD file that will be used by the virtual machine. During the creation of the virtual machine, you can create a new cloud service and an automatically generated storage account, or you can created them in advance manually. Additionally, if you have already created a virtual machine, the automatically created cloud service and storage account from the previous virtual machine can be reused. Both the cloud service and the storage account can be used by more than just the virtual machines, but they can also be used for the various other types of role available within Windows Azure. They both need to reside in the same Windows Azure region because it would not be performant to have virtual machines running in one datacenter using storage in another datacenter.

The Windows Azure management portal is very intuitive, and the only information needed to create a cloud service is to select the region (or affinity group) and a name for the cloud, which will be `<something>.cloudapp.net`. This needs to be unique for all of Windows Azure, which means TestApp is not likely to be available, so it's best to pick something that includes your company name, for example. In the example in Figure 11.9, I used the name of this book for a new cloud service and East US for the region. Creating a storage account is a similar intuitive process; simply give a unique name for the storage account URL and pick the location. You can also select the replication options for the storage account, which can be locally redundant or geo-redundant. The same name can be used for the cloud service and the storage account because the cloud service is part of `cloudapp.net` DNS domain, while the storage account is part of `core.windows.net` DNS domain.

**FIGURE 11.9**
Selecting the region and URL for a new cloud service

When creating both the cloud service and the storage account, I mentioned selecting a Windows Azure region or an affinity group. There are many times you want to ensure that different aspects of your Windows Azure service are located in the same datacenter to optimize performance. By creating an affinity group and then placing resources in it, you ensure close proximity. Additionally, you must use an affinity group when using virtual networks. It's therefore a good idea to use affinity groups from the start rather than select regions for each of your resources. To create an affinity group, perform the following steps:

1. In the Windows Azure management portal, select the Settings navigation node item.

2. Select the Affinity Groups tab.

3. Click the Add button.

4. Enter a name for the new affinity group (which must be unique in Windows Azure), a description, and the region that will host the affinity group and therefore all the resources that are placed into it (more on resources later). This is shown in Figure 11.10.

5. Click the tick icon to complete creation.

**FIGURE 11.10**
Creating a new
affinity group

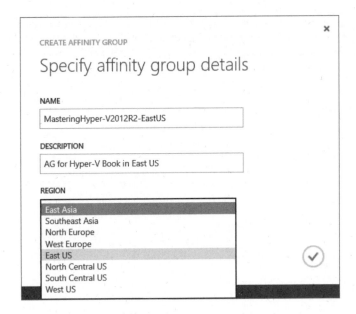

Note that once you create resources, you cannot just move them between datacenters. You would need to export out the resources and import them into the new region, so pick your regions carefully when creating new services. Once the affinity group is created, you will be able to select it when creating other types of resources, such as cloud services and storage accounts.

Notice at the bottom of the Windows Azure management portal is a status bar that has the actions related to management such as New and on the right, a number of status icons. The far right green icon shows operations that are running or recently completed such as creating and deleting objects. Click the icon to get details such as those shown in Figure 11.11. Some of the notifications can be dismissed and others will show more details via an information icon.

**FIGURE 11.11**
Viewing the
recently completed
and currently run-
ning operations in
Windows Azure

When a cloud service is empty, no VIP will be assigned and no details will appear. It is only when a cloud service contains a resource that it is actually truly provisioned and has its common properties. Likewise, the storage account has to have containers. However, when a virtual machine is created and the storage account is selected, a VHDs container will automatically be created for you. You are ready then to create a virtual machine:

1. Log in to the Windows Azure management portal.

2. Select the virtual machines navigation node.

3. Click the New action at the bottom left of the portal, which will automatically expand to Compute ➤ Virtual Machine. Select the From Gallery option.

4. The Create A Virtual Machine Wizard will start. Select the image you wish to use—for example, Windows Serve 2012 R2 Datacenter—and click the Next arrow.

5. Select the version release date required, which is basically a certain patch level. Enter a name for the virtual machine, which has to be unique only within the specific cloud service. Select a size for the new virtual machine and enter a new username and password for the administrator of the new virtual machine. You cannot use *Administrator* or common names like John. An example is shown in Figure 11.12. Click the Next arrow.

6. The next screen allows configuration of where this virtual machine will be located. By default, the option to create a new cloud service will be selected, but in the previous steps you created a new cloud service in the affinity group, so that's what you should select. When the existing cloud service is selected, the cloud service DNS name and region will automatically be selected. Select the storage account that was created and leave Availability Set as (None). See Figure 11.13 for an example. Click the Next arrow.

7. The default endpoints for the virtual machine will be displayed. Leave these as they are, but notice that there is an endpoint for the Remote Desktop Protocol (RDP) to allow remote connectivity and also for PowerShell. Click the tick arrow to complete the virtual machine creation. Figure 11.14 shows this screen.

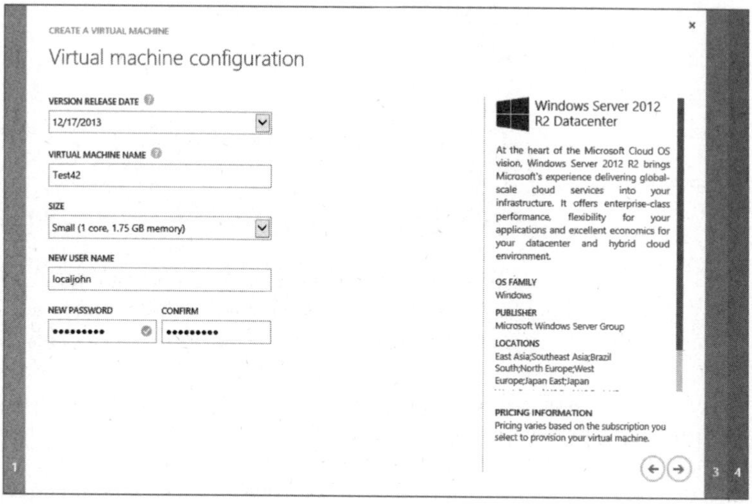

**FIGURE 11.12**
Selecting the basic information for the new virtual machine

**FIGURE 11.13**
Specifying the
cloud service and
storage details

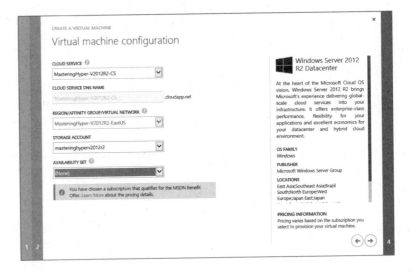

**FIGURE 11.14**
Confirming the
endpoints

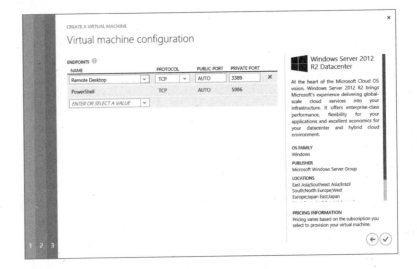

The virtual machine will now be provisioned. This will take some time as the template is copied into a BLOB in Windows Azure Storage in the specified account, specialization is performed on the copied VHD, and the virtual machine is made available. Once the provisioning process is complete, select the virtual machine in the virtual machines view of the Windows Azure management portal to get details about it and also access to actions. The Dashboard page shows performance information about the virtual machine, its status, and the internal IP and the external IP address for the cloud service it is contained within. The Monitor tab gives more detailed performance statistics, on the Configure tab, you can change the size of the virtual machine (which will require a reboot) plus define an availability set. The Endpoints tab allows the various connections available to virtual machines to be defined via the VIP of the cloud service. Both the endpoint and availability set deserve some more detail.

Consider a cloud service that has a single VIP that is available over the Internet, and may contain many virtual machines. You wish to connect various services over the Internet to the virtual machines, which are using TCP or UDP and a specific port. Consider a Remote Desktop Connection from a client computer that normally uses TCP port 3389, as shown in Figure 11.15. The problem is you may have 20 virtual machines in a single cloud service that all share the Internet IP address, the VIP, which means you cannot just connect to the VIP via port 3389 because you don't know which virtual machine the connection will be forwarded to. This is what endpoints solve. A virtual machine has endpoints defined that provide a mapping of a port offered via the cloud service's VIP and then the port it is forwarded to for a specific virtual machine in the cloud service. In the example in Figure 11.15, you can see that both virtual machines listen on port 3389. However, each has a different endpoint configured using a different public port on the VIP. Therefore, when connecting to the VIP on port 52577, the endpoints are examined and the forwarding logic knows traffic on 52577 should be forwarded to port 3389 on VM1. This means different virtual machines cannot use the same port on the VIP and the Windows Azure management portal will stop you from doing this.

**FIGURE 11.15**
Example of endpoints in action

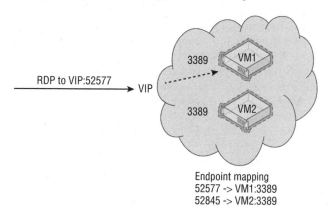

By default, when a virtual machine is created, an endpoint for Remote Desktop and PowerShell is configured automatically. Additionally, endpoints can be added via the Endpoints menu for a virtual machine, and in the Minecraft tutorial, an endpoint was added for the Minecraft service. Remember to also enable firewall exceptions within the virtual machine for the standard port to allow the traffic in, which is just a normal operational step.

In addition to standard endpoints, it possible to add an endpoint to a load-balanced set. A load-balanced set allows multiple virtual machines to be part of a single port on the VIP, and traffic is load balanced between all the virtual machines that are part of the load-balanced set. Consider three virtual machines all running web servers. A load-balanced set would be created for port 80, which would point to all three of the virtual machines and then distribute the traffic accordingly, provided the target virtual machine was available. Virtual machines must be in the same cloud service to be part of a load-balanced set. When you are adding an endpoint, you can select a load-balanced set or create a new one. The concept is shown in Figure 11.16.

**FIGURE 11.16**
Load-balanced set
in action

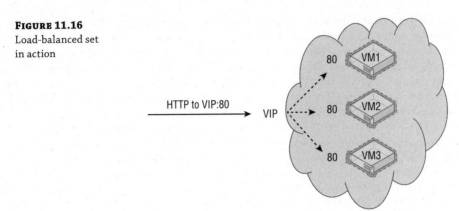

Load-balanced set
80 – VM1:80, VM2:80, VM3:80

An availability set is an important concept if you want high availability in Windows Azure. Consider that Windows Azure actually comprises many datacenters and those datacenters have many racks of servers. Each of those racks can be considered a point of failure, a fault domain, which includes the servers, power, networking, and so on. While Microsoft takes every precaution, there is the chance a rack could fail, which will cause a brief interruption of virtual machines/services running on that rack. Additionally, Microsoft does perform maintenance, which will result in virtual machines in the rack being shut down. To avoid a single point of failure, you may deploy two instances of a service (for example, deploying two domain controllers into Windows Azure), but you have no guarantee that those two instances are not running in the same rack and therefore a rack failure would affect both instances. By placing virtual machines in an availability set, you place the virtual machines into separate fault domains and therefore separate racks, and, thus prevent a single failure from affecting all the instances in the availability set. Availability sets can be created when the virtual machine is created, or a virtual machine can be added to an availability set using the Configure tab in the virtual machine's properties, where you can select an availability set or create a new one, as shown in Figure 11.17.

**FIGURE 11.17**
Adding a virtual
machine to a new
availability set

| DASHBOARD | MONITOR | ENDPOINTS | **CONFIGURE** |

settings

VIRTUAL MACHINE SIZE    Small (1 core, 1.75 GB memory)

AVAILABILITY SET    Create an availability set ∨  TestAS

The number of fault domains that the virtual machines in an availability set will be split over is not exact. The availability set guarantees that not *all* virtual machines in it will go down at the same time. This means if there were three VMs in an availability set, it might be possible that two of them are in the same fault domain. The fault domain can be viewed by looking at the Cloud Services view containing the virtual machines and looking at the Instances tab. There should be different values for the fault domains; for example, if there were two virtual machines in an availability set, one virtual machine would have a fault domain of 0 and the other a fault domain of 1. Notice in the example shown in Figure 11.18 that I have three VMs in the availability set and two of them are in the same fault domain. It's therefore important to make sure availability sets contain only virtual machines that are performing exactly the same function. If you mix the functions of virtual machines into a single availability set, then the virtual machines performing the same function could end up in the same fault domain, which would be a very bad thing. Notice there is also an Update Domain column. An update domain is a logical unit that defines how services are updated to minimize the number of instances of a service updated concurrently. Update domains don't apply to IaaS because updates are applied by the administrator manually to the virtual machines rather than automatically by Windows Azure.

**FIGURE 11.18**
Viewing the fault domain virtual machines are in

| STATUS | ROLE | SIZE | UPDATE DOMAIN | FAULT DOM... |
|--------|------|------|---------------|--------------|
| ✔ Running | MineCraftSrv | Small | 0 | 0 |
| ✔ Running | test5 | Small | 1 | 1 |
| ✱ Starting | test6 | Small | 2 | 0 |

The first action you are likely going to want to perform to your new virtual machine is to connect to it. To do so you'll use the Connect action, which will open an RDP configuration file that will launch an RDP connection to the new virtual machine. If you save the RDP file and then edit it, you will see that it's configured with the cloud service name and the endpoint port for the specific virtual machine—for example, `MasteringHyper-V2012R2-CS.cloudapp.net:52577`. You can now connect to your virtual machine using the username and password you specified during the virtual machine creation. The RDP file can also be fetched using PowerShell:

```
$mySvc = "MasteringHyper-V2012R2-CS"
$myVM = "Test42"
Get-AzureRemoteDesktopFile -ServiceName $mySvc -Name $myVM -Launch
```

Once connected, you will have full console access. If you open the Disk Management tool (`diskmgmt.msc`), you will see two disks: the 127 GB operating system disk and the temporary storage disk, which by default contains the pagefile. If you look at the Storage area in the Windows Azure portal, select the storage account of the virtual machine, and select the Containers tab, you will see the default vhds folder. Within the vhds folder, you will be able to see the operating system VHD for the new virtual machine, as shown in Figure 11.19. Note that the temporary storage drive is not shown because this VHD is stored on the local Hyper-V host storage rather than in Windows Azure Storage, which is why the temporary storage drive is only a temporary drive whose content should not be considered persistent.

**FIGURE 11.19**
Looking at the storage for a virtual machine

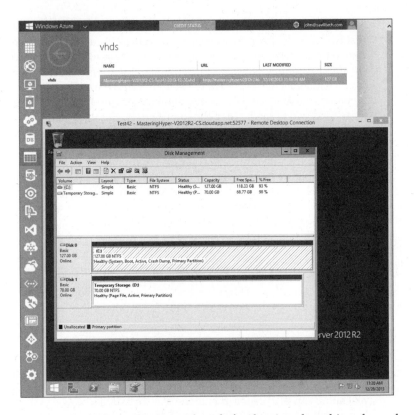

The usage of Windows Azure Storage is a great benefit for the virtual machines for multiple reasons. The Hyper-V host has a virtualized storage driver that works with a component, RDSSD, which consists of some local cache, and then it communicates to Windows Azure Storage (xStore), which has a number of BLOBs. The BLOBs are formatted as fixed VHDs and exist within specific storage accounts. Windows Azure holds an infinite lease on the BLOBs that are considered disks in the storage account to prevent them from ever being accidentally deleted. The fact that fixed VHD is used may cause concern because you pay for used storage and you may create a 1 TB VHD but initially use only a small amount of storage. The good news is that the BLOB is actually sparsely stored, which means only blocks written to it are actually stored and therefore you pay only for data written rather than the total size of the VHD. This means you can safely always use 1 TB as the size for your VHDs. Additionally, if you delete content, TRIM is supported, which means when data is deleted, the TRIM command is sent to the storage subsystem on the Hyper-V host, which then marks the blocks as no longer needed, and in Windows Azure Storage, the blocks are actually deallocated so you stop paying for the deleted data.

Windows Azure Storage ensures that every piece of data is replicated three times to provide protection from data loss, and asynchronous data replication is also available to replicate the data to another datacenter, and it's then replicated three times at that datacenter. Another advantage of using Windows Azure Storage is that all existing tools for Windows Azure Storage work without modification with the VHD-formatted BLOBs making management very simple. A great tool for working with Windows Azure Storage is CloudXplorer from ClumsyLeaf software, which you can download at http://clumsyleaf.com/products/cloudxplorer. CloudXplorer is free and easy to use. The only information needed to connect to your Windows Azure Storage account is the name of the storage account and the access key. This information is available on the Dashboard page of the storage account in the Windows Azure management portal when you click the Manage Access Keys action at the bottom of the screen. This will open a dialog containing the account name and the access key, including a copy icon to copy the data into the Clipboard and then it can easily be used in CloudXplorer. CloudXplorer actually understands the VHD formatted BLOB and will show the contents, as shown in Figure 11.20.

**FIGURE 11.20**

Browsing a Windows Azure Storage account using CloudXplorer

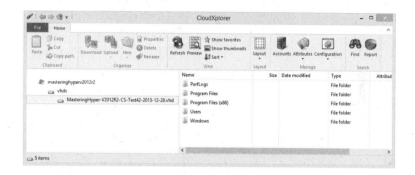

When a virtual machine is created in Windows Azure IaaS, it has the operating system VHD, but you likely don't want to store application data on this disk. Additional disks can be added to a virtual machine, and a reboot is not required because the disks are added to the virtual SCSI controller, which supports hot-adding storage.

Additional disks are added through the dashboard view of a virtual machine via the Attach action by selecting the Attach Empty Disk option. When you add a disk, it will be a data disk type. You can specify a name for the disk and a size up to 1 TB (although 1,023 GB is the maximum size, not 1,024 as would be expected). The type of caching can also be configured, as shown in Figure 11.21. Once the options are configured, click the tick icon to complete the addition, which will generate a new BLOB in Windows Azure Storage and attach the disk to the virtual machine.

There are two types of disk available: the OS disk used to store the operating system and a data disk used to store data. The caching options available differ depending on the type of disk. For an OS disk, caching can be Read/Write or Read Only (Read/Write is the default). For an operating system disk that has many small IOs using Read/Write, caching gives the best performance. For other types of disks or workloads such as a SQL database, no caching is desired and all IOs should persist to storage directly. This is why data disks have the Read/Write and Read Only cache options but also a None option, which is the default and results in no caching. Caching options can be changed with PowerShell for existing disks using Set-AzureOSDisk or Set-AzureDataDisk. Microsoft has a nice blog post on Azure Storage at the following location:

http://blogs.msdn.com/b/windowsazurestorage/archive/2012/06/28/exploring-windows-azure-drives-disks-and-images.aspx.

The number of disks that can be attached to a virtual machine varies depending on the size of the virtual machine, as shown earlier in Table 11.1. Suppose you add 16 disks 1 TB in size to a virtual machine. You will have 16 separate disks in the virtual machine. But what if you wanted an actual 16 TB volume? The Windows operating system has the ability to create striped volumes that effectively join multiple disks together. Once you have added all the disks to the Azure virtual machine, log into the virtual machine and start the disk management tool, `diskmgmt.msc`. Select one of the disks, select the Create Striped Volume action, and ensure that all disks are included in the selection. Select the Quick Format option to minimize time to format, and once it's complete, you will have a single volume of 16 TB that can be used. For Linux operating systems, you can use the MD capability or LVM to get the stripe. You don't need to use any kind of RAID, such as mirroring or parity, because each of the disks is already fault tolerant through the three copies stored in the Windows Azure datacenter.

**FIGURE 11.21**
Options for a new data disk attached to a virtual machine

At this point you have a virtual machine with numerous configurations available. If a virtual machine is no longer required, you can use the Delete option within the virtual machine's dashboard view. With the Delete option comes the option to keep or delete its associated VHD files. If you don't delete the VHDs during the virtual machine deletion, when you later want to delete them, you will need to delete them via the Disks tab under Virtual Machines because if you try to delete within the Containers view in Storage, it will notify you that a lease exists on the BLOB.

While the Windows Azure management portal is a great interface for managing Windows Azure virtual machines, if users also access virtual machines in a private cloud, remember that you can leverage System Center App Controller to give access to virtual machines both on and off premise. I go into detail on this in Chapter 9, "Implementing the Private Cloud and

SCVMM." I do want to point out that I'm often asked about more granular access control for users in Windows Azure and if App Controller adds more granular user access, and the answer is it does not. App Controller only allows the same levels as those in the Windows Azure management portal, which really is not very much. If you need more granular access, you are looking at creating a custom solution.

## Managing with PowerShell

I went into detail on the creation of virtual machines using the Windows Azure web-based management portal. Virtual machines can also be created using PowerShell, and there is even an Integration Pack for System Center Orchestrator. I want to focus on PowerShell but if you are heavily leveraging System Center Orchestrator, keep in mind that the Integration Pack is available.

The first step is to download the Windows Azure PowerShell module, which is available from the Windows Azure downloads page at www.windowsazure.com/en-us/downloads/?fb=en-us. It can be found at the bottom of the downloads page in the Command Line Tools section. Once you click the Windows Azure PowerShell link, the Web Platform Installer will launch, enabling you to click Install to complete the Windows Azure PowerShell module installation. There are a number of prerequisites, which will automatically be downloaded and installed.

The installation of the Windows Azure command-line tools adds shortcuts to the Start Screen or Start Menu (depending on your operating system) for PowerShell with the Windows Azure module loaded. These shortcuts can be found by typing **Azure** on the Start screen, or the module can be imported into existing PowerShell sessions. Depending on your PowerShell environment, configuration may require a change to the execution policy to allow the remotely signed cmdlets to execute. The following command changes the execution policy; it must be run from an elevated PowerShell prompt (right-click the PowerShell prompt on the search results and select Run As Administrator from the options, which will launch PowerShell with *Administrator*: at the start of the PowerShell window title). Run the command below, and when prompted, press **Y**:

```
Set-ExecutionPolicy RemoteSigned
```

If the PowerShell environment was not launched via the Windows Azure PowerShell program, then the first step is to actually import the Windows Azure PowerShell module, which is accomplished using the following command:

```
Import-Module "C:\Program Files (x86)\Microsoft SDKs\Windows Azure\PowerShell\
Azure\Azure.psd1"
```

Once they are imported, all the available cmdlets in the Windows Azure module can be seen using this command:

```
Get-Command -Module Azure
```

Running this command will give you an idea of the full capability of the PowerShell module for Windows Azure because you see nearly 200 cmdlets, which are not limited to just Windows Azure IaaS virtual machines. There are also cmdlets specific to web roles, storage, PHP, SQL databases, Services, and much more.

Before any actual cmdlets can be used against your Windows Azure subscription, you first have to configure your PowerShell environment to know what your Windows Azure subscription is and to provide a secure way to communicate with it. There are ways to achieve this manually, which are documented at the following location:

http://msdn.microsoft.com/en-us/library/windowsazure/jj554332.aspx

However, I recommend using the Get-AzurePublishSettingsFile cmdlet, which will open a browser window and let you sign in to your Windows Azure subscription and then automatically download the full configuration file. Once this configuration file is downloaded, it is imported using the Import-AzurePublishSettingsFile <file>.publishsettings cmdlet, as in this example:

Get-AzurePublishSettingsFile

Download the file from the site and enter your credentials in the web browser. The file will be saved in the Downloads folder, and the file name will vary based on your subscription name. For my subscription, the file name is WindowsAzureSavillTechMSDN-credentials. publishsettings.

```
Import-AzurePublishSettingsFile C:\Users\john\Downloads\
WindowsAzureSavillTechMSDN-credentials.publishsettings
```

At this point you are ready to use Windows Azure from PowerShell. The first step is to check that you are truly using the Windows Azure subscription you think you are by using the Get-AzureSubscription cmdlet:

```
PS C:\Users\john> Get-AzureSubscription

SubscriptionName           : Windows Azure MSDN - Visual Studio Ultimate
SubscriptionId             : xxxxxxxx-xxxx-xxxx-xxxx-xxxxxxxxxxxx
ServiceEndpoint            : https://management.core.windows.net/
ActiveDirectoryEndpoint    :
ActiveDirectoryTenantId    :
IsDefault                  : True
Certificate                : [Subject]
                               CN=Windows Azure Tools

                             [Issuer]
                               CN=Windows Azure Tools

                             [Serial Number]
                               XXXXXXXXXXXXXXXXXXXXXXXXXXXXX

                             [Not Before]
                               12/28/2013 1:19:05 PM

                             [Not After]
                               12/28/2014 1:19:05 PM

                             [Thumbprint]
                               XXXXXXXXXXXXXXXXXXXXXXXXXXXXXXXXXXXXXXXXXX
```

```
CurrentStorageAccountName   :
CurrentCloudStorageAccount  :
ActiveDirectoryUserId       :
```

To view your storage accounts, use the `Get-AzureStorageAccount` cmdlet because, providing you have created a virtual machine before, there will be an implicitly created storage account to use. Make a note of the value of the `StorageAccountName` attribute that will be shown. You need to configure the Azure subscription with a default storage account to make creating a virtual machine easy:

```
Set-AzureSubscription -SubscriptionName "<your subscription name from
Get-AzureSubscription SubscriptionName attribute" `
 -CurrentStorageAccountName "<storage account name from
Get-AzureStorageAccount StorageAccountName attribute>"
```

At this point I will assume you have created a virtual machine using the Windows Azure web portal and saw the nice list of virtual machine templates available in the gallery. That gallery is just scratching the surface of what is really available. Run the following command to see every template that is really available:

```
Get-AzureVMImage | ft Label,ImageName,LogicalSizeInGB -AutoSize
```

I'm going to simply create a new virtual machine using the Windows Server 2012 R2 image, and I'm going to create that in my existing cloud service (all cloud services can be found with `Get-AzureService` and all locations can be found with the `Get-AzureLocation` cmdlet) and my existing affinity group (`Get-AzureAffinityGroup` to list). In the following code, I use my existing cloud service, I set a password, and then I create the virtual machine from the template. The first command fetches all images into an array variable; then when creating the actual VM, I use the index number of the actual element I want:

```
$images = Get-AzureVMImage
$mySvc = "MasteringHyper-V2012R2-CS"
$myAG = "MasteringHyper-V2012R2-EastUS"
$myPwd = "P@ssw0rd"
New-AzureQuickVM -Windows -name "Test43" -ImageName $images[46].ImageName `
 -ServiceName $mySvc -AffinityGroup $myAG —AdminUserName AdminJohn -Password
$myPwd
```

The command will take some time, but it will be visible in the Windows Azure portal and the cmdlet will show the various actions taken and their successful completion.

Adding disks to an existing virtual machine is simple. The following command adds two data disks:

```
$mySvc = "MasteringHyper-V2012R2-CS"
$myVM = "Test43"
Get-AzureVM -Name $myVM -ServiceName $mySvc |
    Add-AzureDataDisk -CreateNew -DiskSizeInGB 1023 `
```

```
-DiskLabel 'datadisk1' -LUN 0 |
    Add-AzureDataDisk -CreateNew -DiskSizeInGB 1023 `
-DiskLabel 'datadisk2' -LUN 1 |
    Update-AzureVM
```

There are so many other commands available. Anything you can do in the management portal can be done with PowerShell and more. Here are a few more bonus ones:

```
# Get VM Details for all VMs in a specific cloud
Get-AzureVM -ServiceName $mySvc
# Restart a VM
Restart-AzureVM -ServiceName $mySvc -Name $myVM
# Shutdown a VM
Stop-AzureVM -ServiceName $mySvc -Name $myVM
# Start a VM
Start-AzureVM -ServiceName $mySvc -Name $myVM
```

## Windows Azure Virtual Networks

Previously in this chapter, when I introduced the different types of cloud services, I explained that a cloud service was a boundary for many things, including network communication between virtual machines within it. Additionally, the internal IP address given to each virtual machine (the dynamic IP, or DIP) has to be assigned via DHCP, and Windows Azure controls that IP address assignment. This means if you have multiple cloud services in Windows Azure, you will have islands of communication as shown in Figure 11.22.

**FIGURE 11.22**
Islands of communication between virtual machines

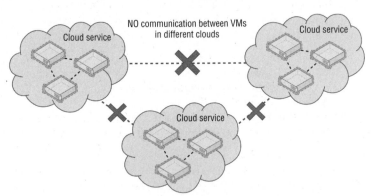

Additionally, using the default networking there is no way to add communications to your on-premises networks, nor can you use any DNS service other than the Azure-provided DNS, which provides name resolution between virtual machines in the same cloud service only. The only external connectivity available to virtual machines it out to the Internet.

Windows Azure Virtual Networks solves this by enabling networks to be defined within an affinity group that has the following benefits:

◆ You can use a private IPv4 space you specify, and different virtual subnets can be created within the virtual network.

♦ The virtual network can be connected to your on-premises network using site-to-site VPN, and it can also support point-to-site VPN connections.

♦ You have the ability to use custom DNS such as an on-premises DNS server, a DNS server deployed to Windows Azure IaaS, or even a public DNS service. This allows DNS resolution outside just those resources within a cloud service.

When you put these capabilities together, it means your on-premises network can now be extended out into Windows Azure, bringing seamless connectivity that is not using the cloud service VIP and removes the need to use the endpoints defined for the virtual machines. Figure 11.23 shows the new connectivity when using a virtual network.

**FIGURE 11.23**
Connectivity when using virtual networks

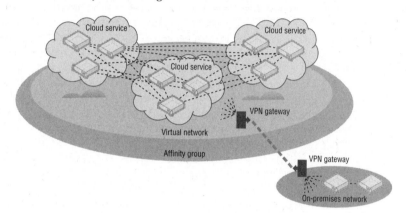

Note that multiple virtual networks can be created within an affinity group but a virtual network cannot cross affinity groups and therefore cannot cross regions. All cloud services within the affinity group can then access the same virtual networks, and when virtual machines are created, the virtual subnet they should be connected to is selected. (I will cover this in more detail later in this section.) This enables virtual machines in different cloud services to communicate provided they are connected to the same virtual network, which also means the cloud service they are part of is in the same affinity group.

The valid IP address ranges you can specify to use for a virtual network are those defined in RFC 1918 that are the private, non-Internet routable addresses. No other IP addresses can be used in Windows Azure. Those usable address ranges are as follows:

♦ 10.0.0.0 to 10.255.255.255 (10/8 prefix)

♦ 172.16.0.0 to 172.31.255.255 (172.16/12 prefix)

♦ 192.168.0.0 to 192.168.255.255 (192.168/16 prefix)

When deciding which IP network to use in Windows Azure, always consider that even if you don't want to connect Windows Azure to your on-premises network today, you may want to in the future. Therefore, use an IP network that is not used on premises so connectivity and routing will be possible in the future. If my organization used the 10.0.0.0/8 IP range on premises, I would like to use the 172.16.0.0/12 range in Windows Azure to avoid any risk of overlap. Once you decide on the IP address range you wish to use for the Windows Azure network, you can divide it into subnets for use by different types of services. For example, I like to create different subnets for my Windows Azure infrastructure servers, such as domain controllers, and another for my Windows Azure application services such as SQL servers. The Windows Azure gateway to provide VPN also requires its own IP subnet. A subnet can be as large as /8 and as small as /29 (using CIDR subnet definitions). Remember, this is showing the number of bits in the IP address that defines the network. A /8 means a subnet mask of 255.0.0.0, and I don't think you would ever have a subnet anywhere close to this size. Gateway functionality between subnets in a virtual network is provided automatically by the virtual network, but you cannot ping the gateway for each subnet, nor will tracert-type utilities work.

Within a virtual network subnet, the first and last IP addresses of a subnet are reserved as part of the protocol for network addresses (host ID all 0s) and broadcast addresses (host ID all 1s), respectively. Windows Azure also reserves the first three IP addresses in each subnet (binary 01, 10, and 11 in the host ID portion of the IP address). This can be seen in Figure 11.24, where I show an example virtual network I have defined that has three subnets. Note that in the example, my virtual network is a small address space, 10.7.115.0/24, and within it I've divided some of that space into subnets. The gateway subnet is the easiest example to understand: 10.7.115.0/29. Normally this would allow six usable IP addresses, 10.7.115.1 to 10.7.115.6. However, it shows that only three IP addresses are usable, .4 to .6. This is because Windows Azure has reserved the first three usable addresses, .1 to .3, for its own purposes. Subnets cannot overlap each other. Note that IPv6 is currently not supported.

Once you define subnets and virtual machines are added to a subnet, the virtual machine's IP address will be allocated from the IP address range from that subnet as an infinite lease. Even though DHCP is used to assign the IP address to the virtual machine, the actual IP address will never change while the virtual machine is provisioned, that is, while you are paying for it. This does mean you have to be careful to never deprovision the virtual machine, such as shutting it down from the Windows Azure management portal, because this will result in the virtual machine getting a new virtual network adapter and a new MAC when it is subsequently started, and therefore a new IP address. If you want to ensure that your virtual machine's dynamic IP address (DIP) never changes, then never deprovision it. There are some tricks to help with keeping IP addresses for virtual machines, which I'll cover shortly.

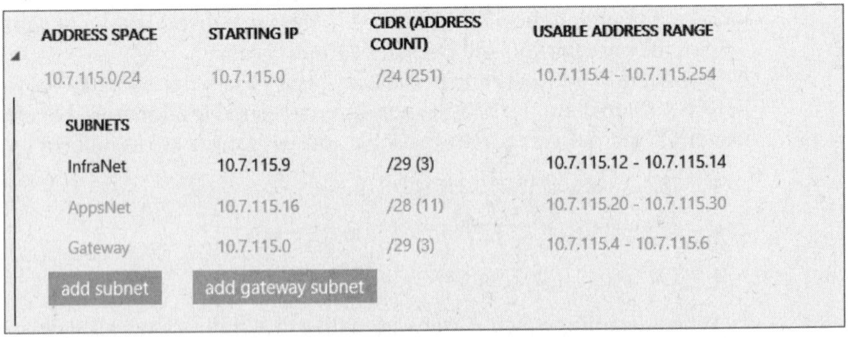

**FIGURE 11.24**
IP subnets in a virtual network

| ADDRESS SPACE | STARTING IP | CIDR (ADDRESS COUNT) | USABLE ADDRESS RANGE |
|---|---|---|---|
| 10.7.115.0/24 | 10.7.115.0 | /24 (251) | 10.7.115.4 - 10.7.115.254 |
| **SUBNETS** | | | |
| InfraNet | 10.7.115.9 | /29 (3) | 10.7.115.12 - 10.7.115.14 |
| AppsNet | 10.7.115.16 | /28 (11) | 10.7.115.20 - 10.7.115.30 |
| Gateway | 10.7.115.0 | /29 (3) | 10.7.115.4 - 10.7.115.6 |
| add subnet | add gateway subnet | | |

Within a virtual network, most IP-based protocols—such as TCP, UDP, and ICMP—will work. However, multicast, broadcast, IP-in-IP encapsulated packets, and GRE packets are blocked. The GRE blocking is logical when you consider that behind the scenes Windows Azure is leveraging Hyper-V Network Virtualization, which itself uses GRE.

If you have multiple virtual networks, there is currently no way to connect them in Windows Azure; that is, there is no way to have Windows Azure act as a network router for the different virtual networks. The only currently available solution would be to route traffic between virtual networks by connecting the Windows Azure virtual networks to your on-premises location and let the on-premises infrastructure route between them, as shown in Figure 11.25 along with an example communication between two virtual machines in different virtual networks. This is far from ideal, especially because you have to pay for egress (outbound) traffic from Windows Azure and the communication is traveling via the Internet to your datacenter and back again. I would expect at some point in the future Microsoft will add the ability to link virtual networks in Windows Azure and route accordingly, but there is no promise or timeline for that.

**FIGURE 11.25**
Routing between virtual networks using your on-premises network

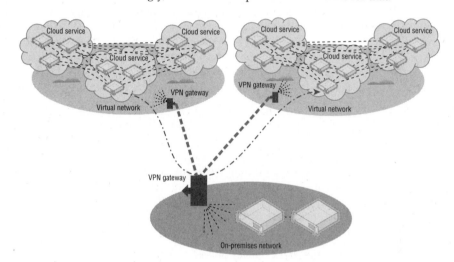

This really is all a virtual network is. You have an IP address space you define and then divide into subnets, and virtual machines are then assigned to the subnets when they are created. You cannot move existing virtual machines into a subnet or move a virtual machine out of a subnet. The configuration must be done at the time of virtual machine creation. I am referring exclusively to virtual machines, but PaaS Web and Worker roles can also leverage virtual networks.

Walking through the creation of a virtual network will help solidify your understanding, and I can also share a few hints I have found useful to optimize IP address allocation. I am assuming you already have an affinity group created that will contain the new virtual network. Follow these steps:

1. In the Windows Azure portal, select the Networks navigation item.

2. Select the New action and select the Custom Create option for Virtual Network menu item.

3. Enter a name for the new virtual network and select the affinity group. Make the name for the virtual network something that will identify the network. Click the Next arrow.

4. Specify the DNS servers the virtual network will use. If you don't have this information, leave it blank. Also select the option to configure a site-to-site VPN, as shown in

Figure 11.26. Note that the option to enable a point-to-site VPN is also available and this can be set post-creation. Click the Next arrow.

5. The next page can initially be confusing as to what it is asking, but this is where you enter the details for your on-premises infrastructure: a name for your on-premises location, the IP address for your Internet facing gateway device that will be used by Windows Azure to connect to when creating the VPN, and the IP address space used on premises in your organization so Windows Azure knows how to route accordingly. This IP address can be changed later. If I use 172.16.0.0/12 on premises, I would configure this as shown in Figure 11.27.

6. The final screen allows configuration of the subnets available in the virtual network. By default, a subnet has been added at the start of the IP address space, but I prefer to modify this because I like to have the gateway subnet at the start of the IP address space. To make this happen, you have to do a few things. Also you can change the actual address space used from the default 10.0.0.0/8 to anything you want by just clicking in the Starting IP field and changing it as required.

7. Change the name of subnet added by default to a useful name, such as InfraVMs, and change the starting IP to $x.x.x.9$ instead of $x.x.x.0$; for example, I set mine to 10.0.0.9. I will use this for my domain controllers that will also be DNS servers in Windows Azure. I use a dedicated subnet just for these servers so that even if the virtual machines get deal-located at some point in the future and lose their IP address because only my domain controllers are in this subnet, no one else will take their address and I can safely specify the IP addresses as DNS servers for the entire virtual network. Because I will have three or fewer domain controllers, I set the address count to /29, which gives me three usable IP addresses.

8. Click the Add Gateway Subnet action (shown in Figure 11.28), which will now take the start of the address space, 10.0.0.0, because it needs at least two IP addresses, and because I started at .9 for my previous subnet, the gateway can fit in the gap I left. Sneaky!

9. I would now create additional subnets for my application servers and so on. There is a bug in Windows Azure web site that limits the size of the address counts to only one more than the previous subnet, which is a pain point. Using PowerShell works around this, but be aware of this limitation (it may be fixed by the time you read this, hopefully).

10. Click the tick icon to complete the virtual network creation.

**FIGURE 11.26**
Enabling site-to-site VPN configuration for the new virtual network

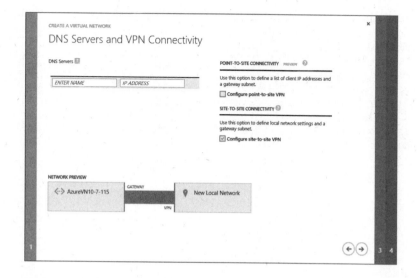

**FIGURE 11.27**
Specifying the on-premises details that will be used for a site-to-site VPN connection

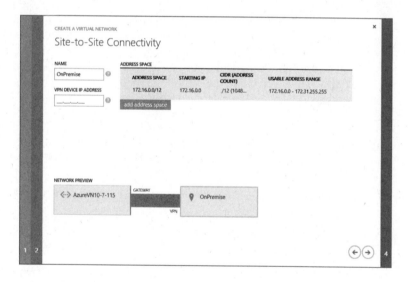

**FIGURE 11.28**
Forcing the gateway subnet to the start of the IP address range and carving out a special subnet just for my Azure DC/DNS servers to lock in their IP addresses

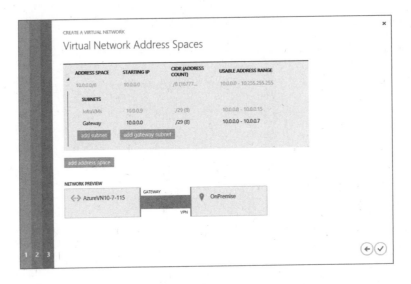

The virtual network will take a few seconds to provision and will then be ready to use. Notice on the Networks page of the management portal that by default it shows the Virtual Networks view but also available are the Local Networks view and DNS Servers view. Additional local networks can be created and existing local networks can be modified, such as changing the gateway IP address for the network and also its address space, as shown in Figure 11.29, by clicking the Edit action. If you did not select the option to configure site-to-site when creating the virtual network (which creates the local site via the wizard), then you would have to manually create the local site if you later wanted to add a site-to-site VPN to an existing virtual network. The DNS Servers view allows you to add and remove DNS servers, which can be used by the virtual networks. All of this configuration (such as creating the virtual network, creating the local network, and configuring DNS) can be done through PowerShell. For example, to add a DNS server I use the following command:

```
New-AzureDns -Name 'PremDNS' -IPAddress '192.168.1.10'
```

To dump out the entire configuration of a virtual network, use the following command, which gives a huge amount of information and can actually be used to modify and then reimport the configuration:

```
Get-AzureVNetConfig | select -ExpandProperty xmlconfiguration
```

Here is an example output:

```
PS C:\> Get-AzureVNetConfig | select -ExpandProperty xmlconfiguration
<?xml version="1.0" encoding="utf-8"?>
<NetworkConfiguration xmlns:xsd="http://www.w3.org/2001/XMLSchema"
  xmlns:xsi="http://www.w3.org/2001/XMLSchema-instance" x
mlns="http://schemas.microsoft.com/ServiceHosting/2011/07/NetworkConfiguration">
  <VirtualNetworkConfiguration>
    <Dns />
    <LocalNetworkSites>
```

```
        <LocalNetworkSite name="OnPremise">
          <AddressSpace>
            <AddressPrefix>172.16.0.0/12</AddressPrefix>
          </AddressSpace>
          <VPNGatewayAddress>99.99.99.99</VPNGatewayAddress>
        </LocalNetworkSite>
      </LocalNetworkSites>
      <VirtualNetworkSites>
        <VirtualNetworkSite name="AzureVN10-7-115"
  AffinityGroup="MasteringHyper-V2012R2-EastUS">
          <AddressSpace>
            <AddressPrefix>10.0.0.0/8</AddressPrefix>
          </AddressSpace>
          <Subnets>
            <Subnet name="InfraVMs">
              <AddressPrefix>10.0.0.9/29</AddressPrefix>
            </Subnet>
            <Subnet name="AppVMs">
              <AddressPrefix>10.0.0.16/28</AddressPrefix>
            </Subnet>
            <Subnet name="GatewaySubnet">
              <AddressPrefix>10.0.0.0/29</AddressPrefix>
            </Subnet>
          </Subnets>
          <Gateway>
            <ConnectionsToLocalNetwork>
              <LocalNetworkSiteRef name="OnPremise">
                <Connection type="IPsec" />
              </LocalNetworkSiteRef>
            </ConnectionsToLocalNetwork>
          </Gateway>
        </VirtualNetworkSite>
      </VirtualNetworkSites>
    </VirtualNetworkConfiguration>
  </NetworkConfiguration>
```

Back in the Virtual Networks view, a virtual network can be selected and further configured via the Configure tab of the virtual network. On this tab you can specify DNS servers, which will be configured to the virtual machines via the DHCP. The various types of VPN connectivity can be enabled and also the subnets can be updated, but you cannot change a subnet that has resources using it.

Creating the actual VPN connection will be covered in the next section, so the only task left is to use the virtual network, and specifically subnets, with your virtual machines. The process to create a virtual machine is exactly the same except in the Virtual Machine Configuration page of the Create A Virtual Machine Wizard, you select a virtual network instead of a region or affinity group and select the desired subnet for the VM, as shown in Figure 11.30. You would also select a storage account and cloud service as per normal.

**FIGURE 11.29**
Modifying a local
network

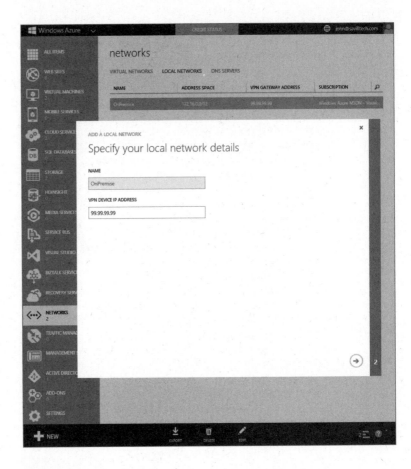

**FIGURE 11.30**
Assigning a virtual
machine to a vir-
tual network and
subnet

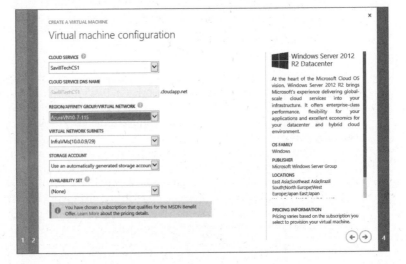

The selection of the cloud service may initially cause some confusion. When you create the virtual network, it is placed within an affinity group. You may also already have cloud services in that same affinity group. However, those cloud services will not be usable with the virtual network if they already have resources deployed to them. This is because those resources would already have IP addresses and therefore the cloud services are already using an automatically generated IP range. Only a new cloud service that does not have resources can be used with a virtual network, or you need to create a new cloud service as part of the virtual machine creation.

The virtual network is now being used, and if you look at the virtual machine's IP configuration, you will see it has an IP address from the IP range of the subnet and the DNS configuration will use the DNS servers configured for the virtual network.

# Linking On-Premises Networks with Azure IaaS

In an earlier section I discussed endpoints as a way to connect to services running in virtual machines via the cloud service's VIP. If you require a lot of connectivity between on-premises and virtual machines in Windows Azure, using the endpoints it not practical, plus the traffic is sent over the Internet and may not be encrypted, depending on the type of traffic. A better solution is to create a site-to-site (s2s) VPN connection between on-premises and Windows Azure that then avoids the endpoints completely and allows direct communication between the systems.

Once your virtual networks are created in Windows Azure, it's actually easy to enable the site-to-site VPN to bring cross-premises connectivity. If you followed the steps in the previous section, when creating the virtual network, you already configured your local on-premises network and specified the public IP address for your local network, so you are basically already done. If you did not check the option for site-to-site connectivity during the virtual network creation, you need to perform the following additional steps:

◆ Navigate to the Networks area in the Windows Azure management portal. Select Local Networks and create a new local network, configuring the IP address range used on premises and the public IP address.

◆ In the Networks area, select Virtual Networks and select your virtual network. Click the Configure tab. Check the box for site-to-site connectivity and select the local network definition from the displayed list.

You are now ready to create the actual gateway, which is achieved by clicking Create Gateway and then either Dynamic Routing or Static Routing on the Dashboard page of the virtual network in the Windows Azure management portal. Which one you choose, Dynamic Routing or Static Routing, depends on the gateway on your premises. If you are using Windows Server 2012 RRAS locally, then you would select the Dynamic Routing option. The Windows Azure gateway creation will take around 5 minutes, and behind the scenes two virtual machines that are the Windows Azure side of the VPN gateway are being created in an active-passive configuration for redundancy.

Once the configuration is completed, click the Download VPN Device Script link (see Figure 11.31), which will give a list of supported devices—such as those from Cisco and Juniper plus Microsoft's own RRAS—that will actually generate a complete configuration script that can be used to complete the configuration on your local network infrastructure.

Once your side of the VPN gateway is configured, you can click the Connect action on the virtual network Dashboard to trigger a connection and you should now have cross-premises connectivity. You can also trigger the connection from your on-premises side. If you are using RRAS, you can use the following command:

```
Connect-VpnS2SInterface -Name <Azure Gateway IP address>
```

**FIGURE 11.31**
A completed gateway connection

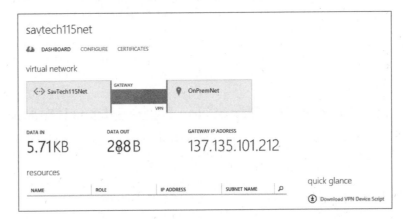

I actually walk through the entire process in a video at http://youtu.be/O8wUnt4mDUc, which I recommend if you are setting this up for the first time. You can expect bandwidth transfers over the VPN of about 80 Mbps. This is limited by the fact that IPsec is used, and on the Windows Azure side effectively one processor core is used to handle the VPN connection and the IPsec calculations.

The next question I always hear when I talk about this is how to add a second VPN connection to a Windows Azure virtual network to provide connectivity to another datacenter for normal operations or perhaps for disaster recovery if the main datacenter fails. At the time of this writing, you can't. A virtual network can have only a single gateway. I know the Windows Azure team is aware of the need to have more than one gateway, but I know of no committed time frame. If you have another datacenter that needs connectivity to the Windows Azure resources via the VPN, your primary datacenter that has the VPN connection to the virtual network will act as the routing hub, as shown in Figure 11.32, which shows an example VM in Datacenter 2 talking to a VM in Windows Azure. This is not ideal, but it works. If you need protection if the main datacenter fails, the only recommendation right now is to have the PowerShell ready to delete and re-create the gateway on the Windows Azure side to use your gateway in the second datacenter. There is nothing stopping your datacenter from having VPN connections to multiple Windows Azure virtual networks, as discussed previously in this chapter.

**FIGURE 11.32**
Multiple datacenters connecting to Windows Azure

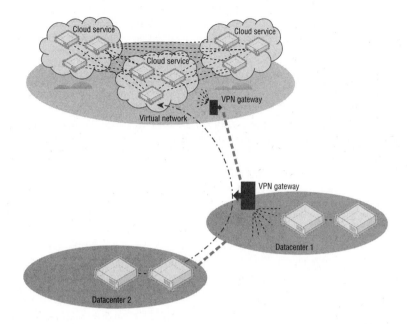

Many organizations place domain-joined resources and even place domain controllers in Windows Azure. I recommend creating a separate Active Directory site for the IP range used by Windows Azure. If you want to have a failover cluster stretch between your on-premises and Windows Azure, there are a number of complications. I wrote up how to make it work at the following location: this is especially useful if you want to leverage cross-premise SQL AlwaysOn.

http://windowsitpro.com/hybrid-cloud/extend-failover-cluster-windows-azure

At this point Windows Azure is an extension of your datacenter, and you should use it in ways that make the most sense for your organization. There is also a point-to-site VPN capability available to give specific machines connectivity to Windows Azure. It leverages a special client component that is downloaded from the Windows Azure management portal and the clients connecting using the VPN client component receive an IP address from a pool defined as part of the Windows Azure point-to-site VPN configuration. If you need this kind of point-to-site VPN, it is available as an option, and Microsoft has plenty of documentation, including a nice blog post at the following location:

http://blogs.msdn.com/b/piyushranjan/archive/2013/06/01/point-to-site-vpn-in-azure-virtual-networks.aspx

For most virtualization-type communications in the datacenter, though, you will want to use the site-to-site VPN options, which is why I'm not covering point-to-site in detail.

## Migrating Virtual Machines between Hyper-V and Azure IaaS

A huge "better together" with Windows Azure and Microsoft Hyper-V on premises is the compatibility aspect of the virtual machines enabling virtual machines to be moved between on-premises and Windows Azure and back again. There are some considerations:

◆ At the time of this writing, Windows Azure does not support VHDX, so your virtual hard disks should be VHD.

◆ At the time of this writing, Windows Azure has a 1,023 GB size limit, so keep the VHD files at 1,023 GB or less.

◆ Windows Azure only supports fixed VHD files, but dynamic VHDs are automatically converted to fixed when uploaded using Add-AzureVHD.

◆ App Controller enables a virtual machine stored in the library to be deployed to Windows Azure directly.

◆ Windows Azure virtual machines can have only a single network address and its IP must be configured using DHCP.

◆ Windows Azure is currently based on Windows Server 2012 Hyper-V and not Windows Server 2012 R2.

◆ Windows Azure does not currently support Generation 2 virtual machines which means use Generation 1 virtual machines only.

Primarily to move virtual machines, the VHD file(s) for the virtual machine will be uploaded or downloaded from Windows Azure and then a new virtual machine will be created that uses the VHD file(s). The process to perform an on-premises to Windows Azure migration is as follows:

1. Upload the VHD(s) to Windows Azure using the Add-AzureVhd cmdlet. For example, here I create a test VHD and then upload it:

```
$sourceVHD = "D:\Temp\vhdtst.vhd"
$destinationVHD = https://masteringhyperv2012r2.blob.core.windows.net/vhds/
vhdtst.vhd"
New-VHD -Path $sourceVHD -Dynamic -SizeBytes 10GB
Add-AzureVhd -LocalFilePath $sourceVHD -Destination $destinationVHD `
            -NumberOfUploaderThreads 5
```

2. Once the file is uploaded, it must be configured as an OS or data disk using Add-AzureDisk. To make a disk an OS disk, add the -OS <Windows or Linux> switch. I will make my disk a data disk:

```
Add-AzureDisk -DiskName 'vhdtst' -MediaLocation $destinationVHD `
-Label 'vhdtst'
```

3. Now the disk is added to an existing VM (or a new VM could be created using the uploaded VHD if it was an OS disk). Normally when using Add-AzureDataDisk, the

`-CreateNew` switch is used, but since I have an existing disk, I will import it by name and add it to the virtual machine:

```
$mySvc = "MasteringHyper-V2012R2-CS"
$myVM = "Test42"
Get-AzureVM -Name $myVM -ServiceName $mySvc |
    Add-AzureDataDisk -Import -DiskName vhdtst -LUN 2 |
    Update-AzureVM
```

In this example I used a data disk, but it would be exactly the same process if I used an OS disk except I would have use the `-OS <OS>` switch when performing the addition to Windows Azure, as previously mentioned.

To retrieve a VHD from Windows Azure, the process is similar. Download the VHD and then create a virtual machine locally that uses it. To download the VHD, perform the following:

```
$sourceVHD = `
"https://masteringhyperv2012r2.blob.core.windows.net/vhds/test-Test42-1228-1.vhd"
$destinationVHD = "D:\temp\test-Test42-1228-1.vhd"

Save-AzureVhd -Source $sourceVHD -LocalFilePath $destinationVHD `
            -NumberOfThreads 5
```

Hopefully this showed that it's fairly simple to move VHDs into and out of Windows Azure. PowerShell is just one option, but you can use it in pretty much any other environment, including automated processes to bulk-move virtual machines.

## Leveraging Azure Storage

This chapter has gone into a lot of detail about using Windows Azure Storage on Windows Azure IaaS virtual machines. Now I want to briefly cover other ways Windows Azure Storage can be used. Specifically, I want to tell you about two key usages that I've found to be the most interesting for my customers.

The first is backup, because with Windows Azure Storage, you effectively have a limitless amount of offsite storage and Windows Azure provides the ability to create backup vaults that can then be used by backup applications, including Windows Backup (which is built into Windows Server) and also System Center Data Protection Manager (DPM). In the case of System Center DPM, the Windows Azure backup acts as a secondary, offsite backup target that is in addition to the disk-based primary backup target.

Microsoft has detailed instructions on configuring the Windows Azure backup vault, creating the certificate required, and downloading and installing the Windows Azure backup agent at the following location:

www.windowsazure.com/en-us/manage/services/recovery-services/configure-a-backup-vault/

My goal is to ensure that you knew about the capability because it's an easy way to get offsite backups and architect a backup solution where a certain number of days' backups are kept onsite and then an additional duration kept in the public cloud.

Using Windows Azure Storage for backups is a great use case but if things go well, you will never actually use it, and it's not helping solve organizations' number 1 pain point with data, namely, that there is too much of it and it's getting harder and harder to store and manage it. Figure 11.33 shows a typical organization's amount of data over time, and as you can see, it is exponentially increasing. However, also notice that the actual working set of data that is really used is much smaller and grows much more slowly.

**FIGURE 11.33**

Typical organizational data volume over time

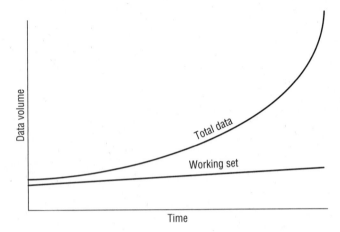

Microsoft acquired StorSimple, which is a storage appliance that has a certain amount of local storage, both HDD and SSD, but can also leverage Windows Azure Storage. The StorSimple appliance acts as an iSCSI target and then at a block level leverages tiers of storage, including using deduplication and compression to store the data. The more frequently accessed data will be stored on a higher tier; for example, the most-used data will be stored in the SSD tier, less-used data would be stored in the HDD tier, while rarely used data will be stored in Windows Azure Storage. This reorganizing of data happens automatically using algorithms built into StorSimple. What this means is that all the data that exists, but is rarely used, would be uploaded to Windows Azure Storage and then deleted from the local storage, keeping the most-used data local (plus also storing in Windows Azure for protection), which gives the highest performance while providing essentially an infinite total capacity size. To the end user all the data looks like it's available locally on the StorSimple appliance because even data moved to Windows Azure Storage keeps a local thumbprint (representing the Windows Azure stored data) on the StorSimple storage, like a stub file but at a data block level.

If data that has been offloaded to Windows Azure is accessed, then the StorSimple device will automatically download it and make it available, but obviously this would impact storage performance because the data has to be downloaded over the Internet. It is also possible to pin certain data to always be kept locally (near) or configure it to be offloaded to Windows Azure as soon as possible (far). Figure 11.34 shows a view of the local capacity of a StorSimple device. Notice that there is SSD Linear (not deduplicated), SSD Dedupe (deduplicated), and then HDD (which is deduplicated and compressed). What is not shown is the final Windows Azure Storage tier. Data stored in Windows Azure Storage is not only deduplicated and compressed, it's also encrypted using a key known only to the StorSimple appliance. Initially data is written to the SSD Linear tier and then over time deduplicated in SSD, and then, depending on its usage, it may get moved to the HDD tier or even Windows Azure Storage.

**FIGURE 11.34**
StorSimple Local
Capacity Usage
report

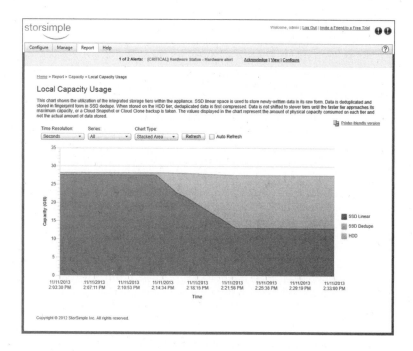

This automatic tiering may sound familiar. Storage Spaces in Windows Server 2012 R2 does something similar with its HDD and SSD tiers. Currently StorSimple is based on Linux, but I expect this to change. I also don't think it would be much of a "leap" for the StorSimple algorithms used to offload to Windows Azure to find their way into the next version of Windows Server and become part of Storage Spaces, adding the Windows Azure Storage tier to Storage Spaces. Then the StorSimple appliances could just be based on Windows Server vNext. This is all pure conjecture on my part, but it would make complete sense because Microsoft pushes Storage Spaces and it now owns StorSimple.

The StorSimple appliances come in different sizes, and to help you use Windows Azure Storage more easily, Microsoft is actually giving them away if you purchase certain amounts of Windows Azure credit. There are key scenarios in which StorSimple is a great solution. It's great as a storage for file servers and archive servers. It can be used for low- to mid-range Hyper-V VM storage and SQL workloads, including SharePoint. It should not be used for high disk IOPs Hyper-V and SQL scenarios because it will not deliver the storage performance that is required. It should also not be used as a backup target because once it hits 80 percent full of its local storage, all future writes have to basically go directly to Windows Azure, which means at that point the storage performance would be terrible during the backup. Exchange is not recommended to run on StorSimple.

Windows Azure Storage can be used in many other ways, through custom applications and more, but the backup scenario and StorSimple are powerful and easy ways to quickly get real benefits.

# The Bottom Line

**Explain the difference between Platform as a Service and Infrastructure as a Service.**   The key difference relates to who is responsible for which elements of the solution. With Platform as a Service, solutions are written for a supplied platform within certain guidelines. The platform then ensures availability and protection for the application, and there is no operating system or fabric management required. The key point is that the application must be written to work with the PaaS platform. With Infrastructure as a Service, a virtual machine is provided, which means the provider manages the compute, storage, and network fabric but the user of the virtual machine is responsible for the operating system and everything within it and also patching it. The benefit of IaaS is that you have complete access to the operating system, so normal applications can run in IaaS without requiring customization. A key principal of IaaS is that you should not have to modify the application to work on it.

**Master It**   What is Software as a Service?

**Connect Windows Azure to your on-premises network.**   To create connectivity between Windows Azure and your local network, there are a number of requirements. First, virtual networks need to be defined in Windows Azure in affinity groups. Virtual machines are created and configured at the time of creation to use a specific subnet in the virtual network. A site-to-site gateway is created between Windows Azure and your on-premises network, which permits seamless connectivity.

**Master It**   Can Windows Server 2012 RRAS be used on the local premises side of the VPN gateway?

**Move data between on-premises and Windows Azure.**   Windows Azure is built on Windows Server Hyper-V and specifically leverages the VHD format currently. A virtual machine that uses VHD can be copied to Windows Azure storage and used with a new Windows Azure virtual machine or added to an existing virtual machine. Similarly, VHD files used in Windows Azure virtual machines can be downloaded to on-premises and used with Hyper-V virtual machines.

**Master It**   What PowerShell cmdlets are used to copy VHDs to and from Windows Azure?

**Master It**   Can dynamic VHDs be used in Windows Azure?

# Chapter 12

# Bringing It All Together with a Best-of-Breed Cloud Solution

A large number of technologies have been covered in this book so far—on-premises technologies and those that are available through the public cloud. It can seem daunting to know which technology to use in different scenarios. This chapter will look at all the technologies and provide some guidelines for when to use them, and you'll also see what other companies are doing.

In this chapter, you will learn to

♦ Identify the overall best architecture for your organization

## Which Is the Right Technology To Choose?

The most important step in choosing the right technology is to have a direction for your organization. Does your organization want to focus on the public cloud first and have a minimal on-premises infrastructure? Is it investing in brand-new datacenters and servers and looking to maximize that investment by focusing its on-premises infrastructure? Or does it want to achieve best of breed with a hybrid approach?

Having a direction is important, but it's also critical to know your limits. By this I mean what can your organization realistically implement and support with its given resources, which includes budget. It's doubtful that a 50-person company with a single "IT guy" could operate a complete on-premises infrastructure and have the facilities to have a disaster recovery location. At this point, the company has to evaluate where its IT resources should be focused and for some IT services, look at external solutions. A great example I see a lot in the industry, even for the very largest organizations, is using Software as a Service (SaaS) for email and collaboration, such as the Microsoft Office 365 service. Messaging can be complex. It's considered a tier-1 application for many companies, which means it must always be available, and so rather than try to architect what can become complex messaging solutions, it's easier for organizations to effectively outsource this.

Take time to understand the types of IT services your organization needs to provide. Understand the data retention, backup, and compliance requirements and regulations for your business. Understand the criticality of the system and the services it depends upon. Then look at your resources and what you can support because this will certainly help guide your direction. You may have services on premises today that would be a good fit to move to the cloud because contracts are ending, hardware could be reused for other projects, and so on.

Many organizations today spend huge amounts of time, effort, and expense on applications and services that really consume way more than they should, especially in proportion to their benefit to the organization.

## Consider the Public Cloud

Looking at the public cloud services available, if I'm a new company I would be thinking about using them where possible. Email, collaboration, application platforms, and customer relationship management—these are all critical areas that require large initial investments to get running. Using a public cloud solution such as Software as a Service (SaaS) or Platform as a Service (PaaS) allows you to "pay as you go," which means you are paying a small amount when your company starts and the amount you pay grows as your company grows. That's perfect for a growing startup.

If I'm an established company and I'm looking at ways to cut down on my IT expenses or diversify them, moving some services off premises and to the cloud may make a lot of sense, particularly if I'm looking for new features or site disaster recovery capabilities. Using a cloud service like Office 365 instantly gives an organization enterprise email, communication, and collaboration resources that are replicated across multiple sites with a per-user, per-month fee structure. When I talk to organizations, I hear more and more the desire to move from capital expenditure (cap ex) to operational expenditure (op ex), and using a pay-as-you-go public cloud service removes the cap ex part almost completely. Keep in mind that moving services to the public cloud is not "free." Most likely you will need help from a consulting organization to enable a smooth migration process because there will likely be period of time you will have a hybrid solution, such as for email (some mailboxes may be on premises while others are in the cloud). Some services will remain hybrid services. For example, I've seen some organizations that host Exchange mailboxes on premises for office-based workers but use Office 365 for other workers, such as those in retail locations that have a higher turnover or can function with a lower quality of service. I've also seen the opposite, where the most important people in a company have their email hosted on Office 365 to ensure its availability while everyone else stays on premises.

If a new application is needed for the short term, or if high availability and growth potential are requirement, hosting it on Windows Azure would be a great choice. Development scenarios are a great fit because they have high turnover with environments constantly being created and deleted, and without a private cloud on premises, that could result in a lot of work for administrators.

Familiarize yourself with the public cloud solutions available and use them in the right way. Use them where it makes sense, but don't use them just to sidestep internal provisioning processes or their shortcomings. Some organizations I have worked with took six weeks to provision a new virtual machine. Because of this long delay, business units decided to just use public cloud instead. That is a poor reason to use the public cloud. Fix the internal process using capabilities such as self-service and the private cloud that I've talked about in detail in earlier chapters.

Moving services to the public cloud has additional advantages. Typically, those solutions will ensure the availability of the service and perform the backups. It's also easy to scale up and down as you pay for what you use, but consider that many services are consumed from anywhere. I check my email at home, on my phone, and on a laptop at a restaurant, which means my company would have to provide Internet-based access to at least a portion of the corporate infrastructure if the service was housed on premises. By leveraging a public cloud solution, the organization does not have to provide that access. The service is already being offered on the Internet.

If you are creating a new custom application, consider whether it is a fit for a Platform as a Service (PaaS) solution such as Windows Azure. Something like this will minimize the ongoing IT overhead required because the only work to do is to maintain the application. For other applications and workloads that you want to run in the public cloud, using Infrastructure as a Service (IaaS) most should work without modification, which is a key principle of IaaS.

If your organization utilizes Windows Azure for just development, testing, and stand-alone projects, then no communication may be required between Windows Azure and your on-premises network outside of the standard Internet-based communications using end points defined using the cloud service's virtual IP. What is more common is that seamless connectivity between Windows Azure and the on-premises network is required to enable cross-premises connectivity. To enable the cross-premises connectivity, you need to configure the Windows Azure VPN gateway functionality. On the on-premises side, a hardware gateway can be leveraged or a software gateway, such as, for example, Windows Server Routing and Remote Access Service (RRAS).

Before implementing the Windows Azure gateway, you need to have created a virtual network with subnets defined that will be used by virtual machines created after you create the virtual network. It is important to use an IP scheme for the virtual network in Windows Azure that does not conflict with any on-premises IP allocation. When you use a different IP address range in Windows Azure, IP traffic will be able to be routed cross premises. If the on-premises gateway device that is used to connect to Windows Azure is not the default gateway for on premises, you will need to add manual routes so on-premises traffic that is destined for Windows Azure will route correctly. Also make sure all on-premises IP scopes are defined within Windows Azure correctly to ensure correct routing of traffic from Windows Azure to the on-premises network.

At the time of this writing, only one VPN connection can be configured from Windows Azure to an on-premises location. The primary datacenter should be used to connect to Windows Azure. When Windows Azure supports multiple gateways, it would be advisable to establish at least one additional VPN connection to another site to provide redundancy from site failure in addition to more efficient routing of traffic.

Once network connectivity is established cross premises, most likely some operating system instances running in Windows Azure will need to be domain joined. This introduces a number of considerations. One requirement is name resolution via DNS. Initially, configure the virtual network in Windows Azure to use on-premises DNS servers for name resolution, which will allow machines to locate domain controllers and join the domain. Using a shared DNS infrastructure between on-premises servers and Windows Azure will also allow cross-premises name resolution.

Within Active Directory, create a separate Active Directory site for the IP ranges used in Windows Azure and create a site link to the actual on-premises location that has connectivity. Make sure to set the site link cost and replication interval to values that meet your requirements. The default replication every 3 hours is likely not fast enough.

The next decision is whether Active Directory domain controllers should be placed in Windows Azure. Initially, many organizations have security concerns about placing a domain controller in Windows Azure for fear of directory or security compromise, which would potentially expose the entire contents of the directory service. As previously discussed, the Microsoft datacenters likely have far more security than any normal company could hope for. When the domain controller in Windows Azure is configured, care is taken to make sure end points that aren't required are not exposed and to ensure that firewall services and monitoring is in place. These are the same steps you would take for an on-premises domain controller, but you need to be aware if any end points defined for the virtual machine are directly accessible on the Internet. Most likely, the domain controller would also be a global catalog, or at least one of them if you place multiple domain controllers in Windows Azure. For a small number of domain-joined machines in Windows Azure, the authentication traffic and other directory services data could be facilitated by the on-premises domain controllers and accessed using the VPN gateway, but as the number of domain-joined Windows Azure resources grows, it will become necessary to have a local domain controller.

Companies often consider using a read-only domain controller (RODC) in Windows Azure because an RODC has passwords for only a subset of the users cached and cannot make changes, which minimizes damage if the RODC is compromised. The decision depends on which services are running in Windows Azure and if they work with an RODC. If a service does not work with RODCs, then there is no point in placing an RODC in Windows Azure and you will need a regular domain controller or will need to accept that the Active Directory traffic will need to traverse cross premises. Another option is to create a child domain for Windows Azure.

Once a domain controller is running in Windows Azure and it is configured as a DNS server, the virtual network can be modified to use the domain controller(s) in Windows Azure as the primary DNS server. Remember to not deprovision the domain controller(s) because this could result in an IP address change. However, using a small, separate subnet just for domain controllers can help alleviate this problem by reducing the possible IP addresses that can be allocated to the domain controllers and stopping other VMs from using those IP addresses.

With cross-premises connectivity and Active Directory services, you can really open up the services that can be placed in Windows Azure. I see many organizations using a hybrid approach. Often they start with testing and development in Windows Azure, and once the technology is proven and trusted, it is expanded. Remember to constantly look at what new capabilities are available, and while initially you could, for example, deploy an IaaS VM running SQL Server databases, over time those databases may be able to be moved to SQL Azure instead, reducing your management overhead.

An interesting use case I have seen is to use Windows Azure as the disaster recovery site. At the time of this writing, Windows Azure cannot be the target for Hyper-V, which means you cannot replicate at a VM level the virtual machine to Windows Azure. Instead, you need to look at each service and how to replicate. Here are some approaches. Keep in mind that there is not one right answer; it will depend on the workload.

◆   For Active Directory, deploy domain controllers to Windows Azure and use Active Directory multimaster replication to keep the Windows Azure domain controllers up-to-date.

◆   For file data, one option would be to use Distributed File System Replication (DFS-R) to replicate data to a file server running in Windows Azure IaaS. Distributed File System

Namespaces (DFS-N) could be used to give users transparent access to the data. Another option is to use StorSimple, which will also store data in Windows Azure. However, at time of writing there is not a virtual StorSimple appliance that would give access to the data stored in Windows Azure from a VM running in Windows Azure. This is expected to change. Another option would be to periodically copy data using Robocopy or PowerShell.

◆ SQL databases can be replicated using SQL Server 2012 AlwaysOn, which should be used in asynchronous mode. This will require stretching a cluster between your premises and Windows Azure, which I discuss at the following location:

`http://windowsitpro.com/hybrid-cloud/extend-failover-cluster-windows-azure`

◆ SharePoint instances are mainly SQL Server data, therefore deploy SharePoint instances in Windows Azure and use SQL Server AlwaysOn to replicate the SharePoint data. For non–SQL Server stored data, use another process to replicate file system configuration periodically or as part of a change control process.

◆ Exchange and Lync are not supported to run in IaaS. If you want disaster recovery for your Exchange and Lync, the best solution is to migrate users to Office 365 if you need offsite capabilities. This type of migration will likely be a major undertaking and you will run in a hybrid mode during the migration.

◆ Other applications will need to use a combination of technologies. If the application uses a SQL database, use SQL replication to replicate the database. Use file system replication to replicate other file system assets.

◆ For replication of anything running in an operating system, one third-party solution I found is Double-Take, which you can find at the following location:

`www.visionsolutions.com/products/Virtual-Server-Protection.aspx`

It provides replication from within the OS to another OS instance. In the future, if Hyper-V Replica is supported for Windows Azure, this would be another option.

To ensure mobility between on-premise infrastructure and Windows Azure, make sure that for those workloads that need to be transportable, you use only features common to both environments, such as the following:

◆ Generation 1 virtual machines

◆ VHD disk format of 1023 GB maximum size

◆ One network adapter

◆ No requirement on IPv6 communications

There is also an interesting licensing consideration for placing workloads in Windows Azure. Your organization may already have a large number of Windows Server licenses, but they are not required when using Windows Azure because the Windows Server license is included.

It may be possible to repurpose licenses for other on-premises workloads. Your organization may have multiyear agreements for licenses, in which case you may be able to negotiate converting elements of the agreement to cloud-based services.

Ultimately, the public cloud offers many capabilities. Your organization should look at each one and decide if it is a good fit for some workloads. Then deploy in a carefully planned manner to maintain service availability and supportability.

## Decide If a Server Workload Should Be Virtualized

While the public cloud is great, there will be many workloads that you want to keep internally on your company's systems. As you read this, your company probably has some kind of server virtualization. It could be VMware ESX, it could be Microsoft Hyper-V, it could be Citrix XenServer, or it could be something else, and likely your organization is using multiple hypervisors. The most common scenario I see is ESX organizations evaluating Hyper-V so they have both in their datacenter.

The default for most organizations is virtual first for any new server workload except for servers with very high resource requirements and some specialty services, such as domain controllers that provide the Active Directory domain services for the environment. (Typically, though, only one domain controller is a physical server while all others are virtualized.)

Most of these exceptions are based on limitations of the previous generation of hypervisors.

The reality is that with Windows Server 8 and the ability to run very large virtual machines with 64 vCPUs, NUMA topology projected to VM, 1 TB of memory, direct access to network cards using SR-IOV if needed, 64 TB VHDX virtual storage, shared VHDX, and access to both iSCSI and Fibre Channel storage where necessary, there really are very few workloads that now cannot run in a virtual machine and run the same as on bare metal, including high-resource workloads such as SQL Server. Even if you had a physical server that only had one virtual machine running because it needed all the resources, virtualizing is a good idea because all the other benefits of virtualization would still apply:

♦ Abstraction from the underlying hardware, giving complete portability

♦ Ability to move the VM between physical hosts for hardware maintenance purposes

♦ Leveraging the high availability and replica features of Hyper-V where needed

♦ Consistent deployment and provisioning

There may still be some applications you cannot virtualize, either because they need more than the resource limits of a virtual machine or, more likely, because of supportability. Some application vendors will not support their applications running in a virtualized manner, sometimes because they have not had time to test it, or the vendor may have its own virtualization solution so it will support only its product on its hypervisor. For example, Oracle supported only its products on its own Oracle VM hypervisor, but this changed in 2013 and Oracle now supports its products on Hyper-V and Windows Azure. Prior to this shift in support, organizations had to make a decision at this point on how to proceed. Remember, applications don't really know they are running on a virtual operating system. To the application, the operating system looks exactly the same as if it were running on bare metal, except that certain types of devices, such as network and storage devices, will be different because they are virtual devices, so virtualizing an application should not introduce problems with today's hypervisors. Carrying on with the Oracle example, in my experience, even before the supportability update, the Oracle products worked just fine on Hyper-V, and Oracle support would even try to assist if there was a problem with it running on a non-Oracle hypervisor on a best efforts basis. However, organizations have to be prepared because if a problem cannot be fixed, the application vendor may ask for the problem to be reproduced on a supported configuration, such as on a bare-metal system without virtualization or on a supported hypervisor. Technology can help here. There are third-party solutions that normally help with physical-to-virtual conversions when organizations want to move to a virtual environment and can also take a virtual machine and deploy to bare metal. This could be an emergency backup option for organizations that want to standardize on one hypervisor and run all applications on virtual operating systems even when not officially supported.

It really comes down to an organization's appetite for some risk, however small, and how critical the application is should it hit a problem. If you have a noncritical application, then virtualizing in a nonsupported configuration that has been well tested by the organization is probably OK. If it's a critical system that would need instant support by the vendor if there was a problem, then running in an officially unsupported configuration is probably not the best option.

In the past, there were concerns about virtualizing domain controllers. That is not the case with Windows Server 2012 and Windows Server 2012 Hyper-V, which have special capabilities directly related to Active Directory, VM-GenerationID, as covered in Chapter 6, "Maintaining a Hyper-V Environment." Most companies I work with today virtualize domain controllers, and in Windows Server 2012 failover clustering, there is even protection from the cluster not being able to start if a domain controller was not available, which was a previous concern. Essentially, prior to Windows Server 2012, if all the domain controllers were running on a cluster, there was a problem if you shut down the cluster. Normally virtual machines cannot start until the cluster service starts. The cluster service could not start without contacting a domain controller. Therefore, if the domain controller was a virtual machine, nothing could start. Windows Server 2012 failover clustering removed this dependency.

I've focused on Windows workloads and how Windows can be virtualized, but many organizations have some non-Windows servers as well. Hyper-V has great support for a number of Linux distributions, and even Linux distributions that are not officially supported will likely still work and can use the Hyper-V integration services to give you a great experience. This equally applies to Windows Azure, which has a wide range of Linux support. Just because a workload is not a Windows Server workload does not mean it cannot be virtualized. There are some Linux/Unix workloads that cannot be virtualized on any x86 hypervisor because they are using a non-x86 architecture. A good example is Solaris running on SPARC, and this cannot be virtualized on a x86 hypervisor because SPARC is a different hardware architecture. If you are using the x86 version of Solaris, then it would probably run on Hyper-V. However, at the time of this writing, it's not a supported Linux distribution for Hyper-V, and if you are running this Solaris workload, it's probably pretty important, so running in a nonsupported manner may not make sense for you.

When you are using clustering within virtualized environments that require shared storage, there are a number of options. Where possible, use Shared VDHX because this maintains complete virtualization of the storage and removes direct storage fabric visibility for the virtual machines. If Shared VHDX is not an option—if you're not running Windows Server 2012 R2 Hyper-V or you have a mixed cluster of virtual and nonvirtual operating systems—then virtual Fibre Channel or iSCSI can be used and perhaps even a SMB 3 file share if the service supports it.

Remember that just because Hyper-V has a great replication technology with Hyper-V Replica, this should not be the first choice. It is always better to use an application-/service-aware replication technology such as Active Directory replication, SQL AlwaysOn, Exchange Database Availability Groups, and so on. Only if there is no native replication solution should Hyper-V Replica be used. Remember that replication is not a replacement for backups.

## Do I Want a Private Cloud?

I talk to many customers about the private cloud, and some are open to it and some just hate the idea. This is largely because of a misunderstanding about what the private cloud has to mean to the organization. Instead of asking if they want to use a private cloud, I could ask the following questions and get very different responses:

◆ Do you want easier management and deployment?

◆ Do you want better insight into networking and storage?

◆ Do you want to abstract deployment processes from the underlying fabric, enabling deployments to any datacenter without worrying about all the underlying details like which SAN, VLAN, IP subnet, and so on?

◆ Do you want to better track and even show and charge back based on usage to business units?

◆ Do you want to be able to deploy multitiered services with a single click instead of focusing on every virtual machine that is needed?

◆ Do you want to simplify the process of creating new virtual environments?

I would get yes answers from pretty much everyone. And I could take it a step further by asking, "Do you want to enable users to request their own virtual environments or service instances through a self-service portal with full-approval workflow within quotas you define that are automatically enforced, including virtual machine automatic expiration if required?"

I may start to get some head-shaking on this one. IT teams can have concerns about letting users have self-service portals even with quotas, even with approval workflows, and even will full tracking. That's OK. As with using public cloud services, when implementing end-user self-service solutions, it can take some time for IT to trust the controls and process and see that it won't result in VM sprawl and a wild west of uncontrolled VM mayhem. In reality, with the private cloud there will be better tracking and more controls than with the processes used in most organizations today.

The key point is that adopting a private cloud only brings benefit to IT departments and the organization as a whole, allowing far greater utilization of the resources the company already has, better insight into those resources, much better responsiveness to requirements of the business (such as provisioning new environments), and the ability for everyone to really focus on what they care about, the application.

Go back to those first questions I asked. If your answers to any of those are yes, then a move to the private cloud model makes sense, and remember that you don't have to expose all of its capabilities to end users. You can have self-service capabilities but let only the IT teams use them to better enable provisioning processes. It's still helping the environment.

Remember that the private cloud provides a foundation on which you can offer many types of services. You can offer basic virtual machines as an in-house Infrastructure as a Service. You can offer environments with certain runtime environments like .NET or J2E to enable Platform as a Service where business units can easily run their applications. You can even have complete services that model an entire multitiered application through service templates, thus offering Software as a Service. It's really whatever makes sense for your organization. Typically organizations will start with basic Infrastructure as a Service, offering virtual machines, and then build up from that point on as confidence and experience grows.

My recommendation is to get your organization on the latest version of Hyper-V. The new capabilities really make it the best virtualization platform out there. It adds support for far larger virtual machines and larger clusters. It has better replication and availability features and better support for direct access to network hardware and network virtualization. It has full PowerShell management and guest-level Fibre Channel access, which means more workloads can be virtualized and therefore you can have a simpler datacenter. And that's just scratching the surface.

It probably seems daunting. There seems to be a lot of change going on, and if you are currently struggling to keep things running by either not patching servers or patching them manually and always installing servers by running round with a DVD or ISO, this will seem like a huge difference, but it's a good difference. There is a large time investment to initially get these processes and solutions in place, so some organizations may need to bite the bullet and get a consulting company in to help them get running. If that's the case with your company, make sure they don't work in isolation. Work with the consultants, and be part of the decision and planning because that way, when they leave, you understand *why* things were done as they were and can carry on any best practices that were implemented.

## Enabling Single Pane of Glass Management

Virtualization does not have to change the way you manage your datacenter. It would be possible to carry on managing each operating system instance, deploying each instance by booting to an ISO, but you really are not getting the most from the technologies available and are making life far harder than it needs to be.

One of the biggest changes that virtualization introduces to the datacenter initially is how you provision new servers. Instead of installing operating systems via an ISO file, use virtual machine templates that can include customizations, join a domain automatically, and install applications and run scripts. Most likely you will have a few virtual hard disks that can be used by many different templates that can be tailored for the exact needs of the organization.

The longer-term goal is to shift from creating virtual machines to deploying instances of services that are made up of many virtual machines and service templates. Using service templates is a big change in how services and virtual machines are provisioned. The benefits they bring—such as easy deployment, updating of deployed instances by updating the template, server application virtualization, and automated configuration of network hardware—really make the use of service templates something that should be a goal. This is not to say normal virtual machines will never be deployed. Service templates are great to enable the deployment of services within an organization, but there will always be those applications that just need to be deployed once, and often the additional work in creating a service template does not make sense.

What is important, though, is that you *don't* end up with two completely different management solutions or even potentially more:

◆ One management solution for virtual machines

◆ One management solution for physical machines

◆ One management solution for the virtual infrastructure such as the hypervisor

◆ One management solution for the public cloud resources such as Window Azure IaaS virtual machines

The goal is to manage your environment as simply and with as few tools as possible. Look for management solutions that enable complete management without having to put in lots of point solutions for different aspects of your datacenter. Patching is a great example: There are a number of solutions that will patch just virtual machines, and there are different solutions to patch hypervisors, others for desktops. A solution such as System Center Configuration Manager (SCCM) 2012 R2 will provide patching for all servers, physical or virtual, and your desktops. Also, with Hyper-V, because it's part of Windows, SCCM can patch the hypervisor itself. One solution is to patch everything. SCCM can also integrate with many third parties to actually also be able to apply updates to hardware (such as firmware and BIOS) plus also deploy updates for Microsoft and non-Microsoft applications.

The same idea applies to all aspects of your datacenter. Try to stay away from point solutions. System Center Operations Manager (SCOM) can monitor your physical servers, the virtual servers, the operating system, applications, custom .NET and J2E applications, networking equipment, and even non-Windows workloads in addition to monitoring and integrating with Windows Azure. This gives a complete view, from soup to nuts as they say. The same applies for backup, for service management, and for orchestration; keep it simple and minimize the number of separate tools.

From a virtual machine management perspective, System Center App Controller provides a single view of on-premises virtual machines that are managed by System Center Virtual Machine Manager (SCVMM) and also virtual machines running in Windows Azure and even virtual machines running with hosters that leverage Service Provider Foundation (SPF). The same can apply to provisioning with more complex workflows using System Center Service Manager (SCSM) to provide a service catalog fronting many different services, including virtual machine provisioning and management.

Orchestration is where I would like to really finish because it really brings together everything about the datacenter. As organizations use more and more IT, and your organization will have more and more operating system instances to manage, technologies like service templates help to bring the focus to the application instead of the operating system. However, there will still be large numbers of operating systems that require management. To really scale, you must look at automation capabilities and working with multiple operating system instances at the same time.

PowerShell really is a key part of enabling automation. Especially in Windows Server 2012 and above, basically everything that can be done with the GUI can be done with PowerShell. Actions can be scripted, but more important, they can be executed on many machines concurrently and in an automated fashion. Building on orchestrating tasks and beyond just PowerShell, take some time to look at System Center Orchestrator. Every client I talk to gets very excited about Orchestrator in terms of its ability to really connect to any system that exists through various methods and then to graphically create runbooks, which are sets of actions that should be performed in a sequence and based on results from previous actions across all those connected systems. Start with something small, some set of actions you perform manually each day, and automate them in Orchestrator. Another good way to learn is to take a simple PowerShell script you have and model it in Orchestrator instead. Once clients I've worked with start using Orchestrator, it becomes the greatest thing since sliced bread and gets used for everything. This does not mean you won't need PowerShell. I find that with Orchestrator many tasks can be 80 percent completed with the built-in activities, but then PowerShell is called from Orchestrator to complete the final 20 percent.

For organizations taking a hybrid approach, providing a seamless experience for the users of services is vital. System Center App Controller provides the seamless pane of glass, but it's key for the IT organization to own the process of deciding if new virtual machines will be deployed on premises or in Windows Azure. I've had great success using System Center Orchestrator with runbooks that utilize PowerShell to receive a provisioning request made via System Center Service Manager. The logic of whether to deploy to on-premise or in Windows Azure is made by the logic built into the Orchestrator runbook and based on the target use for the new environment, the available capacity on premises, the predicted length of usage of the environment, and the capabilities requested. Once the logic provisions the virtual machine either on-premise or in Windows Azure, the requesting user receives an email with an RDP file to enable connectivity or the new service is added to their list of services in App Controller. The point is that the provisioning process and ongoing interaction is the same no matter where the virtual machine is actually hosted.

## The Bottom Line

**Identify the overall best architecture for your organization.** As this chapter has shown, there are a lot of thing to consider when choosing a cloud-based solution for an organization. It's important to take the time to understand the organization's strategic direction, its resources, and the needs of its workloads. Only then can an architecture be created that utilizes the strengths of the different options.

**Master It** What is the most important first step in deciding on the best architecture?

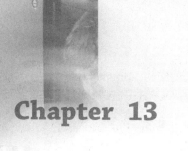

# Chapter 13

# The Hyper-V Decoder Ring for the VMware Administrator

This chapter offers a quick decoder ring for readers with VMware experience. Throughout this book I have covered Hyper-V and System Center; in this final chapter, I explain what the Hyper-V and System Center equivalents are for the VMware technologies that you may be familiar with. I also address some common misconceptions I have seen when comparing VMware to Hyper-V. My goal for this chapter is not to point out flaws in VMware; instead, I will show how Hyper-V technologies map to features you may already be using in VMware.

In this chapter, you will learn to

- ◆ Understand how System Center compares to vSphere solutions
- ◆ Convert a VMware virtual machine to Hyper-V

## Overview of the VMware Solution and Key Differences from Hyper-V

The VMware hypervisor is ESXi, which (like Hyper-V) is a type 1 hypervisor that runs directly on the hardware. Unlike ESX, ESXi does not use the ESX Service Console, which was a Linux environment used as part of the boot process and for management purposes. ESXi has a small footprint, less than 200 MB, and is a monolithic hypervisor, meaning all drivers are specifically written to be contained and used within the hypervisor.

You manage a VMware environment through the VMware vSphere Client. The client can connect directly to an ESXi host or to a VMware vCenter Server. Connecting to a vCenter server provides a higher level of management capability and enables more features of vSphere. A web client is also available for browser-based management.

While the ESXi hypervisor is a free download (like the free full-featured Microsoft Hyper-V Server), to enable the majority of features, such as migration and high availability, you need to buy a license for one of the available vSphere editions. They are licensed in one-processor increments. VMware has a detailed comparison between the different versions at `www.vmware` `.com/products/vsphere/compare`. The following are the key features enabled in the three main versions:

**Standard**   vMotion; Storage vMotion; HA; Fault Tolerance; hot-add of CPUs, memory, and devices; vSphere replication; data protection; and vShield Endpoint

**Enterprise**   Reliable memory, Hadoop support, Virtual Serial Port Concentrator, DRS and DPM, storage APIs for array integration, and multipathing

**Enterprise Plus**   Storage DRS, storage policies, Storage and Network I/O Control, SR-IOV, flash read cache, distributed switch, host profiles, and autodeploy

For details of the number of virtual processors for a virtual machine, see `http://kb.vmware.com/selfservice/microsites/search.do?language=en_US&cmd` `=displayKC&externalId=2001113`. This document shows the following (based on vSphere 5.5):

- ◆   Standard: 8 vCPUs per VM

- ◆   Enterprise: 32 vCPUs per VM

- ◆   Enterprise Plus: 64 vCPUs per VM

Many VMware enterprises struggle to convert this type of licensing to Hyper-V licensing. Remember, with Hyper-V, it is a role of Windows Server, and the Hyper-V capabilities are the same if you use Windows Server Standard, Windows Server Datacenter, or even the free Microsoft Hyper-V Server. The only difference between the versions is the number of virtual Windows Server operating system instance rights that are included, shown here:

- ◆   Microsoft Hyper-V Server: 0

- ◆   Windows Server Standard: 2

- ◆   Windows Server Datacenter: Unlimited

The number of virtual machines you want to run that will use the Windows Server operating system will guide the version of Windows Server you use. Obviously, VMware does not include license rights for Windows Server guest operating systems, and when using VMware, you will still license the Windows Server operating system where needed. This is why Hyper-V is considered "free." You likely already own Windows Server to license the virtual machines running on VMware. If you don't run Windows Server virtual machines, then you can use the free Microsoft Hyper-V Server. Windows Server licenses also cover two physical processors.

To achieve a similar level of management and to enable a small number of comparative features such as VMware's DRS, you must also use System Center. System Center is licensed the same as Windows Server, as either Standard or Datacenter. Once again, Standard includes two virtual OS instances, while Datacenter covers an unlimited number. The difference with System Center is that if the VM is being managed by System Center, it needs to be covered even if it is not running Windows Server OS. For example, Linux VMs being managed by System Center need to be licensed for System Center.

A vSphere vCenter Server is deployed to provide the enterprise management of ESXi and to enable most of the features such as vMotion and DRS. vCenter Server can be installed on Windows Server or is available as a Linux-based virtual appliance. The same vSphere client is used to connect to a vCenter Server, and the vCenter Server provides centralized management of all the ESXi hosts in the environment. A number of plug-ins are available for vCenter Server; an example is the vSphere Update Manager, which is used to patch the vCenter instance and the ESXi hosts, as well as selected virtual machines.

In recent years VMware has purchased a number of companies and has developed technologies to offer a richer management solution, enabling VMware to move beyond just the hypervisor. Currently there are a number of ways to purchase these solutions. VMware has grouped the technologies into VMware vCloud Suite, which can be thought of as the VMware version of System Center in addition to other capabilities. The suite enables, among other things, private cloud capabilities. Some key products include the following:

**vCenter Orchestrator**   Automation technologies and workflow capabilities

**vCloud Automation Center**   Enables self-service, a service delivery, and the ability to unify cloud management across different vendor clouds

**vCenter Operations Management Suite**   Monitoring and insight into the infrastructure

**vCloud Director**   Creation of virtual datacenters including computer, storage, and networking

**cSphere Data Protection Advanced**   Backup and recovery solution

There is a lot of similarity between the various VMware and Microsoft products and components. Table 13.1 maps the key areas of functionality. There are differences in exact features available, but that's not something I cover in this chapter; instead, this table highlights the corresponding Microsoft solution for those familiar with VMware.

**TABLE 13.1:**   Technology solutions for Microsoft and VMware

| TECHNOLOGY | MICROSOFT | VMWARE |
| --- | --- | --- |
| Hypervisor | Hyper-V | ESXi |
| VM management | System Center Virtual Machine Manager | vCenter Server |
| Backup and protection | System Center Data Protection Manager | vSphere Data Protection Advanced |
| Monitoring | System Center Operations Manager | vCenter Operations Management Suite |
| Automation | System Center Orchestrator | vCenter Orchestrator |
| Service manager | System Center Service Manager | vCloud Automation Center |
| Self-service | App Controller and System Center Service Manager | vCloud Director |

In the next section, I cover the Hyper-V equivalents of the most popular VMware technologies and more importantly how to achieve the desired functionality. Often I see organizations hung up on "Where is VMware feature X in Hyper-V?" when what they really want to know is

"How do I achieve this capability in Hyper-V?" Different products work in different ways; that's what gives products advantages and disadvantages compared to each other. What is important is being able to meet the needs of an organization in the way that is most efficient for a product rather than trying to force a product to behave like another.

## Translating Key VMware Technologies and Actions to Hyper-V

I've seen my fair share of requests for comment (RFCs) and requests for proposal (RFPs) from organizations looking to evaluate their virtualization needs or private cloud needs. Sometimes they have been a fair, open exercise with the focus being on how to achieve a certain requirement. Other times they looked like they were written by one of the vendors and were completely skewed to "How do you do vendor feature X?" As I've worked with a number of organizations that were evaluating or implementing Hyper-V after using VMware for many years, I've found a huge level of misunderstanding surrounding using Hyper-V in Windows Server 2008 or about Virtual Server. If you have read the rest of this book, you will have great insight into the range of capabilities of Hyper-V; in this section, I highlight the most common VMware features and also address some of the biggest misunderstandings I've seen.

### Translations

Table 13.2 shows some of the most common maximums related to hosts and virtual machines. The VMware information is based on www.vmware.com/pdf/vsphere5/r55/vsphere-55 -configuration-maximums.pdf. vSphere 5.5 increased a number of key maximums from 5.1 to match the Hyper-V values.

**TABLE 13.2:**     VMware and Hyper-V Maximums

| ITEM | VMWARE | HYPER-V |
| --- | --- | --- |
| Logical CPUs per host | 320 | 320 (640 without Hyper-V) |
| vCPUs per host | 4096 | 2048 |
| Memory per host | 4 TB | 4 TB |
| VMs per host | 512 | 1024 |
| Nodes per cluster | 32 | 64 |
| VMs per cluster | 4000 | 8000 |
| vCPUs per VM | 64 | 64 |
| RAM per VM | 1 TB | 1 TB |

| ITEM | VMWARE | HYPER-V |
|------|--------|---------|
| Virtual SCSI adapters per VM | 4 | 4 |
| Attached disks per virtual SCSI adapter | 15 | 64 |
| Virtual network adapters per VM | 10 | 8 synthetic (plus 4 legacy in generation-one VM) |
| USB devices per VM | 20 | USB not supported; use USB over IP solutions if required or map USB drives as part of an RDP connection to a VM |
| Maximum virtual hard disk | 62 TB | 64 TB |
| Number of snapshots (VMware)/ checkpoints (Hyper-V) | 32 (although 2 to 3 recommended per VM; see http://kb.vmware.com/selfservice/ microsites/search.do?language= en_US&cmd=displayKC&externalId= 1025279) | 50 |

As you can see, the maximums are similar, and both hypervisors can scale to high levels to run pretty much any workload. Next I cover specific technologies and how they compare.

## HOT-ADD OF RESOURCES

Hyper-V supports the hot-add of storage to the SCSI controller but not to the IDE controller. In generation-two virtual machines, the only type of controller is SCSI, and for generation-one virtual machines, the SCSI controller should be used for data disks, with the IDE controller used for the OS disk only.

If a virtual machine is configured to have dynamic memory, then memory is added to and removed from the virtual machine as needed. The maximum memory for a virtual machine can be increased while the virtual machine is running. If a virtual machine is configured to use static memory, then its memory cannot be increased.

The hot-add of processors is not supported by Hyper-V; however, because Hyper-V and ESX differ in how processors are scheduled, there is no downside to allocating more vCPUs than you determine you need to Hyper-V virtual machines. In other words, you can safely over-allocate vCPUs to a VM.

To restrict the number of CPUs that can be used by a virtual machine, the virtual machine limit on the processor (as shown in Figure 13.1) could be set to a lower percentage. Then, if the virtual machine needs more processor resources, the virtual machine limit value can be increased while the virtual machine is running. For example, I may give a virtual machine four vCPUs but set the virtual machine limit to 50 percent, which effectively means the virtual machine can use two vCPUs' worth of resource. At a later time while the virtual machine is running, I could change the limit to 75 percent or 100 percent to increase its processor resources. This approach is beneficial to the majority of applications because most applications don't actually support the hot-add of processors.

**FIGURE 13.1**
Setting the virtual machine limit for processors

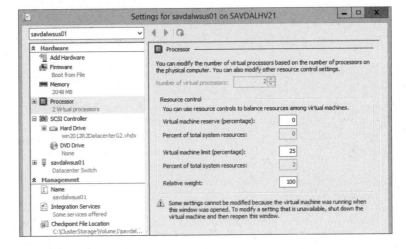

## FILE-LEVEL STORAGE USAGE

VMware can leverage NFS servers to store virtual machines. For Hyper-V SMB 3, storage can be leveraged such as from a Windows file server running Windows Server 2012 or newer or a SAN/NAS that supports SMB 3.

## VIRTUAL HARD DISK FORMAT

While VMware uses VMDK, Hyper-V uses the VHD and VHDX formats for its virtual hard disks. VHDX also supports sharing a VHDX between multiple virtual machines, which is seen as shared storage by the virtual machines and can be used as clustered shared storage.

VMware supports thick and thin VMDK files. The Hyper-V equivalents are dynamic VHDX for a thin VMDK, which allocates space as data is written, and fixed VHDX for thick VMDK, where all space is preallocated. Parent-child relationships are also supported using the differencing-type VHDX.

Both Hyper-V and VMware support mapping raw storage directly to a virtual machine.

## NETWORKING FEATURES

Both VMware and Hyper-V support a range of networking capabilities such as VLANs, PVLANs, IPv6, Jumbo Frames, offload support, network QoS, NIC teaming, and so on. VMware has VMware NSX for software-defined networking (SDN), while Hyper-V uses Hyper-V Network Virtualization.

Hyper-V supports the Cisco Nexus 1000V in addition to many other extensions for the Hyper-V Extensible switch.

## DISTRIBUTED SWITCH

To provide centralized management and configuration for virtual switches in Hyper-V, System Center Virtual Machine Manager network fabric management is used. Using a combination of logical networks, port profiles, and logical switches, a centralized network architecture is created, and connectivity is centrally managed and deployed to groups of Hyper-V hosts.

## vMotion and Storage vMotion

Hyper-V uses Live Migration (think vMotion) to provide zero-downtime migration of virtual machines between nodes in a cluster. Hyper-V also has Storage Migration (think Storage vMotion) to move storage with no impact to the availability of virtual machines. Windows Server 2012 introduced shared-nothing live migration; this enables virtual machines to be moved between hosts without any common infrastructure such as storage or cluster membership. There is no VMware equivalent. Windows Server 2012 supports multiple simultaneous live migrations with no fixed limit but rather dynamically adjusts the concurrent number based on available bandwidth and the optimal number. Windows Server 2012 R2 features compression of live migration data in addition to leveraging RDMA if available on the network adapter.

VMware leverages Enhanced vMotion Compatibility (EVC) to enable vMotion between hosts with different versions of a processor within a processor family. Hyper-V has a similar feature, processor compatibility mode, that enables the same mobility between different versions of processors within a family. Note you cannot live migrate between Intel and AMD processors.

## Distributed Resource Scheduling and Distributed Power Management

Distributed Resource Scheduling (DRS) provides the automatic vMotion of virtual machines based on processor, memory, and storage utilization to better balance workloads across hosts. SCVMM has this same capability, Dynamic Optimization, which balances workloads across hosts based on defined criteria related to CPU, memory, disk, and network, as shown in Figure 13.2, and moves the virtual machines using Live Migration.

**FIGURE 13.2**
Configuring dynamic optimization on a host group in SCVMM

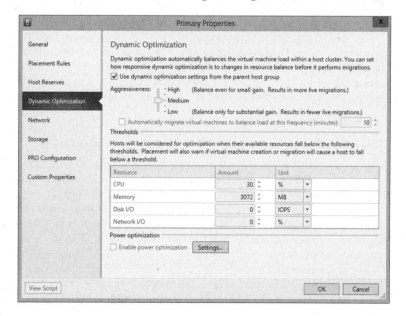

Distributed Power Management (DPM) consolidates virtual machines on hosts to minimize power utilization and enable hosts to be powered down in quiet times. SCVMM has the same feature, called Power Optimization.

Note that this is one of the few features that requires SCVMM instead of being native to Hyper-V.

### Update Manager

Update Manager provides the patching of the vSphere environment with some limited guest patching. Hyper-V is a role of Windows Server, which means existing Windows patching solutions can be used such as Windows Server Update Services and System Center Configuration Manager. Additionally, solutions exist to patch an entire Windows Server cluster with one click with no impact to the clustered resources, including virtual machines, which are automatically live migrated between hosts. SCVMM and Failover Clustering both provide this one-click patching capability.

### High Availability

Hyper-V leverages the Failover Clustering feature of Windows for its high availability and automatic restart, which is similar to the VMware clustering feature.

Failover Clustering is a proven technology, and while it had complexities related to its setup and maintenance prior to Windows Server 2008, with Windows Server 2008 the management side of Failover Clustering was rewritten. Now it provides a simple setup procedure requiring minimal information, and the maintenance is far more intuitive. Additionally, the old quorum disk is no longer required. Instead, a file share or disk witness is configured that is used only if required based on the current number of active nodes in the cluster.

### Fault Tolerance

Fault Tolerance is a VMware feature that enables a second instance of a VM to run on another VMware host and keeps them synchronized using a processor lockstep process. This requires low-latency network connections, and virtual machines are limited to a single vCPU. This feature is not available in Hyper-V. This type of fault tolerance is better implemented in the application than the hypervisor. It is possible to achieve this type of Fault Tolerance with Hyper-V with third-party software on specific hardware, but it's still better to let the application provide this type of availability.

### vSphere Replication and Site Recovery Manager

vSphere Replication provides replication of a virtual machine to another host, and Site Recovery Manager (SRM) provides an enterprise failover experience, which is used by a number of VMware customers.

Hyper-V Replica provides an asynchronous replication of virtual machines including the ability to maintain checkpoints of previous points in time with optional VSS integration. Hyper-V Replica supports planned, unplanned, and test failovers with the option of alternate IP injection as part of the failover process.

For an orchestrated complete failover with additional actions such as running scripts, Hyper-V Recovery Manager (HRM) can be used, which is a Windows Azure service that works by communicating to SCVMM instances in each datacenter.

### MEMORY OVERCOMMIT AND TRANSPARENT PAGE SHARING

VMware memory allocation for virtual machines works by having a single amount of memory defined for a virtual machine, and then the actual physical RAM is allocated as the virtual machine tries to write to the memory. This enables an "overcommit" of memory allocation by allowing, for example, four virtual machines to be configured with 4 GB of memory each, and all could start on a host with 8 GB of memory. This is assuming that each virtual machine would not try to write to all its configured memory; this assumption is flawed for modern operating systems such as Windows Server 2008, which will use all available memory if possible, even if it is for caching purposes. The logic is, why have empty memory if it could bring some benefit? Therefore, in most production environments, a modern operating system's memory overcommit is not widely used or even recommended to be used aggressively. And, if physical memory is not available, disk-based paging may be used, which results in performance degradation.

Hyper-V uses dynamic memory that uses start, minimum, and maximum values defined on the virtual machine and monitors the actual memory used by the operating system within the virtual machine. Additional memory is added to the virtual machine if needed by processes. Hyper-V, like VMware, uses ballooning to reclaim memory.

Transparent page sharing works by looking for duplicate 4 KB memory pages and, if found, the page is stored only once in memory. This can work well for hosts with many of the same OS versions running in virtual machines. The problem is that modern operating systems (Windows Server 2008 and modern Linux) use large memory pages that are 2 MB in size. The chances of finding duplicate 2 MB pages is virtually nil, and there are some other negatives (as discussed previously in this book). Therefore, TPS is not used on large memory pages by VMware. Because of the limited usefulness of TPS on modern operating systems, Hyper-V does not implement a memory deduplication feature.

## Most Common Misconceptions

The following are some common misconceptions:

**Hyper-V runs on Windows Server and is a type 2 hypervisor.**   Hyper-V is a type 1 hypervisor and runs directly on the bare-metal hardware. It requires the processor to support hardware-assisted virtualization or Ring -1. The confusion stems from the sequence of actions to install Hyper-V:

1. Install Windows Server.

2. Enable the Hyper-V role.

3. Manage it from Windows Server.

It is quite reasonable to assume Hyper-V is running on top of Windows Server and therefore is a type 2 hypervisor. The reality is when the Hyper-V role is enabled, the boot manager for Windows is modified to load the Hyper-V hypervisor first, and then the existing Windows Server operating system runs on top of Hyper-V. The Windows Server operating system acts as a management partition for Hyper-V, enabling management of the operating system and also handling resource access for networking and storage.

**Hyper-V requires far more patching than ESXi.**   This is a trickier one, and I've seen numbers from both sides. The reality is ESXi requires patching, as does Hyper-V and the

Windows Server management partition Hyper-V relies on. By using the Server Core installation of Windows Server for the management partition, the number of fixes required is greatly reduced, and therefore the frequency of reboots is reduced as well. I don't think the difference is as great as we are commonly led to believe, though, and I've seen numbers that show ESXi actually had more patches than were necessary on Hyper-V. The key point, however, is that by using SCVMM or leveraging the Failover Clustering feature's one-click patching, there is no actual administrative work to patch an entire cluster, and there is no downtime to the virtual machines, which are seamlessly moved between hosts during host patching. This means even when you do require patching and even if a reboot is required, it's not any work for you and doesn't impact the virtual machines.

**Hyper-V is a security risk because of the install size.** Size is not a good indication of security risk. The smallest paper bag is not more secure than the largest vaults made of steel. What's important is the design, testing, and processes for a solution. Strictly speaking, the Hyper-V hypervisor is actually smaller than ESXi, but Hyper-V relies on the Windows Server management partition for certain resource access and virtual machine management, which has a far larger disk footprint; however, using Server Core reduces the number of applicable patches and reduces the attack surface.

It's important to realize that Windows Server is used to run most of the application workloads used in organizations anyway, which means it's already a trusted platform from a security perspective, has great technologies built in to mitigate security risks, and is one of, if not *the*, most tested operating system in the world with huge numbers of resources ensuring its integrity. Windows is certified to the highest security standards and is used by governments, militaries, and the largest companies in the world.

**VMware supports more operating systems than Hyper-V.** This one is a fact. VMware supports more operating systems than Hyper-V; see `http://technet.microsoft.com/en-us/library/hh831531.aspx` for the list of operating systems supported on Hyper-V. It is a comprehensive list of the supported versions of Windows Server, Windows clients, and Linux distributions.

VMware supports far more operating systems, but the truth is that it supports operating systems that OS vendors no longer support. For example, VMware supports Windows Server 2000, which isn't supported by Microsoft anymore. In fact, VMware only just stopped MS-DOS and Windows NT support with ESXi 5.5 (`http://blogs.vmware.com/guestosguide/2013/09/terminated-os-releases.html`).

Microsoft takes a stricter approach to the operating systems supported with Hyper-V; it supports only those operating systems that are supported by the vendor as well. Other operating systems will work on Hyper-V. In fact, even Windows Server 2012 R2 Hyper-V still has the processor compatibility flag that enables Windows NT to run on Hyper-V, but Microsoft does not support the operating system on Hyper-V since the Windows NT operating system itself is no longer supported. I therefore think this is a nonissue because both hypervisors support modern operating systems and those that are still supported by the vendor.

From a Windows perspective, Hyper-V has better and more integrated support for newer operating system versions, and even new Linux distributions have the Hyper-V integration services built-in.

**VMware can host more VMs than Hyper-V.** This was true with older operating systems such as Windows Server 2003 because the allocate-on-first write VMware approach worked well for these operating systems and transparent page sharing worked because older operating systems used small memory pages. With Windows Server 2008 and modern Linux operating systems utilizing available memory for caching and other optimization purposes, the VMware memory optimizations are no longer as effective, and the Hyper-V dynamic memory feature actually yields a higher density of virtual machines because the memory allocation is based on the memory used by processes running within the VM rather than a static amount. Dynamic memory also works with Linux virtual machines when using the latest supported Linux distributions.

**Hyper-V works well only for Windows guests.**   Hyper-V works great for Windows virtual machines, but it, as of R2, offers almost the same set of features for virtual machines running Linux. Microsoft was actually one of the top 20 contributors to the Linux kernel in 2012, and the Hyper-V integration services are built in to the latest Linux distributions. Microsoft has a long list of supported Linux guests, as documented at http://technet.microsoft.com/en-us/library/hh831531.aspx. The following are supported with Linux guests: 64 vCPUs, 1 TB of RAM, live migration, Hyper-V Replica including IP injection during failover, and pretty much everything else. The only features I am aware of that currently do not work with Linux are Virtual Fibre Channel, RemoteFX, SR-IOV, vRSS, and generation-two virtual machines. Microsoft considers Linux a first-class operating system for Hyper-V and is looking to ensure feature parity for Windows and Linux guests as much as possible, making Hyper-V a great virtualization solution for Windows and Linux.

**Hyper-V does not have a clustered file system.**   Windows has the well-established NTFS file system that is industry proven and is well understood by most IT groups, and it has a huge set of partner tools that work with it. Microsoft has leveraged NTFS as the foundation for shared disk cluster purposes by enhancing it with Cluster Shared Volumes to create CSVFS; this enables NTFS volumes to be simultaneously used by all the nodes in the cluster. Because CSVFS is built on NTFS, the existing disk tools work without requiring modification.

**The application is supported only on VMware.**   Server virtualization provides a virtualized set of hardware for the operating system that is installed in the virtual machine. The actual application running in the virtual machine should perform the same way if it's running on physical hardware in a Hyper-V virtual machine or a VMware virtual machine. However, the application vendors do need to bless the various virtualization solutions to ensure they will support your deployment. In my experience, there are few application vendors that support VMware but don't support Hyper-V. For example, Oracle now supports its solutions on Hyper-V in addition to its own hypervisor. Check with the vendors of your applications to be 100 percent clear on their support policies.

If you have virtual appliances that are provided as OVF format, there is an import tool available (documented at http://technet.microsoft.com/en-us/library/jj158932.aspx) that will allow their conversion and import into Hyper-V.

**Hyper-V is not a proven platform.**   Hyper-V is now in its fourth major version. If you look at the Gartner magic quadrant for x86 server virtualization, Microsoft is one of only two vendors in the leaders quadrant (along with VMware). Hyper-V is used by many of the Fortune 500 organizations and powers some of the largest services in the world, including Windows Azure.

**VMware runs great, so why change it?**   Actually this one I agree with. If VMware is working exactly how you need it to work, can be managed the way you want, and works for your organization financially, then changing to Hyper-V does not make sense. In reality, however, many organizations are looking to save IT dollars by using Hyper-V and System Center because most already own them. In addition, organizations are looking to use a single management platform across operating systems, hypervisors, and the actual fabric, and organizations want compatibility with Windows Azure and other cloud solutions. There are many more reasons, but the key point is the shift to Hyper-V should be because of the benefits your organization will get from the switch.

**The migration from VMware to Hyper-V is too risky.**   This is a valid concern, but later in this chapter I will talk about the tools that provide an automated conversion of VMware virtual machines to Hyper-V, namely, the Microsoft Virtual Machine Converter Solution Accelerator (MVMC) and the Migration Automation Toolkit (MAT). The tool you use is one part of the complete migration; equally important are the discovery, planning, and preparation phases, which is why organizations often bring in a consulting organization to assist with at least some of the migration.

## Converting VMware Skills to Hyper-V and System Center

If you have administered only VMware and not Windows Server, then the move to Hyper-V and System Center will seem intimidating because you also need to be familiar with Windows Server. If you have administered Windows Server, then Hyper-V will be fairly intuitive, and all the components of System Center share a common user interface. Still, there is a lot to learn.

You should feel confident that your knowledge of VMware equates to many virtualization best practices and concepts that translate to Hyper-V and System Center functionality, and this book is a great step in becoming a master of Hyper-V and in aspects of System Center and Windows Azure. There are many other resources available, especially from Microsoft. Microsoft has made a big effort to help VMware administrators learn the Microsoft technologies and has even created some virtualization-specific certifications to help show your Microsoft virtualization skills.

Microsoft has an online training class in its virtual academy focused on Hyper-V and System Center (http://aka.ms/SvrVirt). At the time of this writing, once you complete the class, a free exam certification token is available to take exam 70-409, which gives you the Microsoft Certified Specialist: Server Virtualization with Hyper-V and System Center certification if you pass. There are also lots of other training classes available at the online academy and also great videos showing details of technologies. Microsoft also runs an annual event, TechEd, and now many of the sessions are streamed over the Internet live and available after the event for everyone to watch. This is a great way to get the latest information from the people at Microsoft who create the technologies. http://channel9.msdn.com/Events/TechEd/ is a good starting point to find the TechEd recordings.

To take certifications further, there are five exams that, once you've passed them all, give you the Microsoft Certified Solutions Expert Private Cloud certification, which is detailed at www .microsoft.com/learning/en-us/private-cloud-certification.aspx. The Private Cloud certification tests all aspects of System Center including details about monitoring and protection, which will require learning outside of that covered in this book. There are classroom training classes for each of the exams.

Personally I've never taken any classroom training related to technologies and prefer to learn by installing the products in a lab, trying different implementations, trying to solve problems and fixing things when they don't work (which is when I find you learn the most). The best way to learn Hyper-V and System Center and convert your VMware skills is to get an environment running with Hyper-V and System Center and start implementing solutions that match what you are doing in VMware today. Look for new ways to do things; this chapter outlines some of those key "mappings" of technologies. For every technology you read about, such as those in this book, try them in your environment. Every action you perform using the graphical interfaces, try doing with PowerShell. If you are using Hyper-V Manager, find where the feature is in SCVMM. This will give you the best understanding of the complete Microsoft solution.

## Migrating from VMware to Hyper-V

I want to be very clear on this: I never tell people to migrate from VMware to Hyper-V without a reason. VMware ESXi is a great hypervisor, it has a proven track record, and it offers great functionality with vSphere vCenter. Hyper-V is also a great hypervisor. It's now in its fourth major version, and the fact that it powers some of the largest services in the world such as Windows Azure and is used by the largest companies in the world shows it has a proven track record and great functionality that gets even better with System Center. There needs to be a reason to migrate; these are ones I commonly hear from customers:

- Money. You're already paying for Windows Server, so Hyper-V is effectively free.

- Your organization is using System Center and is largely Microsoft-based, so you want unified management.

- You want to use some piece of functionality that would be an additional license if using VMware.

- You're using Windows Azure and want compatibility between on- and off-premise services.

It's important for organizations to minimize the transitory risk when performing a virtualization migration. While the end state of running on Hyper-V may be trusted, the actual process of migrating virtual machines and having a period of critical services spread over multiple hypervisors can be concerning to IT organizations. The best way to manage this risk is careful planning with fallback processes in place and a good testing plan to ensure no surprises.

When planning migrations, migrate the least important systems first, fine-tune the migration process, iron out any resource access problems, and perfect the processes to identify all dependent resources before moving on to the more important and visible systems.

Make sure the IT team, the help desk, and the support staff are properly trained in the new environment, and update any processes as systems are migrated. Are changes in the DR process required? Has the backup and restore process changed? Are the monitoring systems monitoring the correct systems? How are the virtual machines provisioned? Are the Hyper-V hosts part of a patch process?

Unless your organization is in the habit of performing this type of migration, most likely the best approach is to hire an outside consulting organization to assist for at least the discovery, planning, and pilot, if not for the entire migration project. Using a consulting organization that does this type of migration every day will help you avoid the inevitable mistakes that will occur when trying this for the first time yourself.

The actual conversion of the VMware virtual machine and primarily the VMDK to a VHDX to be usable by Hyper-V is a known process, and there are a number of solutions available, the foremost being the Microsoft Virtual Machine Converter Solution Accelerator (MVMC), available at www.microsoft.com/en-us/download/details.aspx?id=34591. I discussed this and other solutions in Chapter 5. For a slightly tongue-in-cheek view of the VMware to Hyper-V migration using the MAT and a NetApp storage array to expedite the VMDK to VHD conversion, see http://aka.ms/mat4shift. NetApp has a native VMDK to VHD conversion that rewrites only the header of the virtual hard disk, resulting in conversions in seconds instead of minutes. The solution outlined in the video uses a temporary NetApp storage array at the organization just for the conversion process. For example, here are the steps:

1. Use Storage vMotion to move the virtual machine storage to the NetApp storage array, which enables the virtual machine to keep running while being moved to the NetApp array.

2. Shut down the virtual machine from VMware.

3. Perform the conversion using MVMC.

4. Start the converted virtual machine on Hyper-V that is connected to the same NetApp storage array. This allows the amount of downtime for the virtual machine to be minimal.

5. Live Storage Move is used on Hyper-V to move the running virtual machine to its permanent storage location.

Microsoft has actually announced some exciting enhancements coming to MVMC, which I've summarized here; these are accurate at the time of this writing.

**MVMC 2.0: Planned Release—Spring 2014**   The main focus for this release are updates to support various distributions of Linux, Azure VM conversion, as well as PowerShell support.

Highlights:

◆ On-Premises VM to Azure VM conversion

◆ PowerShell interface for scripting and automation support

◆ Added support for vCenter & ESX(i) 4.1, 5.0, and now 5.5

◆ VMware virtual hardware version 4–10 support

◆ Linux Guest OS support including CentOS, Debian, Oracle, Red Hat Enterprise, SuSE Linux Enterprise, and Ubuntu.

**MVMC 3.0: Planned Release—Fall 2014**   For the V3 release the focus is on P2V as well as efficiency improvements.

Highlights:

◆ Physical to virtual (Hyper-V) machine conversion (supported versions of Windows)

Take the time to fully understand your virtualization requirements, equate these to Hyper-V and System Center configurations, ensure everyone is trained accordingly, and make sure the processes are updated. Create detailed migration plans with fallback procedures, testing processes, and success criteria. With the proper preparation and planning, the migration can be smooth and invisible to the users.

# The Bottom Line

**Understand how System Center compares to vSphere solutions.**   System Center comprises a number of components that each provide different functionalities. vSphere has a similar set of solutions, and a basic mapping is shown here:

- SC Virtual Machine Manager = vCenter Server

- SC Data Protection Manager = vSphere Data Protection Advanced

- SC Operations Manager = vCenter Ops Mgmt Suite

- SC Orchestrator = vCenter Orchestrator

- SC Service Manager = vCloud Automation Center

- App Controller and SC Service Manager = vCloud Director

The levels of functionality are not exactly the same, but the mapping shows the key functional area mapping of the products.

**Master It**   How is System Center licensed?

**Convert a VMware virtual machine to Hyper-V.**   There are two aspects to converting a virtual machine; there is the virtual machine configuration, such as the number of vCPUs, memory, network connectivity, and so on, and then there are the virtual hard disks that contain the operating system and data. There are various solutions to address both parts of the conversion. The primary Microsoft VMware to Hyper-V tool is Microsoft Virtual Machine Converter, which performs migrations in an interactive fashion. Command-line tools are also available.

**Master It**   How can MVMC be used as part of a bulk conversion process?

**Master It**   How does NetApp help with VMDK to VHD conversions?

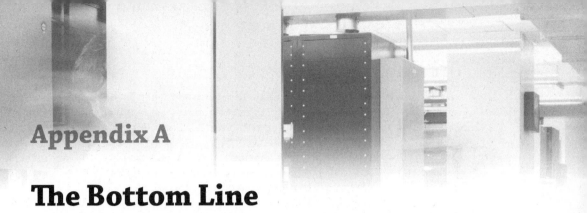

# Appendix A

# The Bottom Line

Each of The Bottom Line sections in the chapters suggests exercises to deepen skills and understanding. Sometimes there is only one possible solution, but often you are encouraged to use your skills and creativity to create something that builds on what you know and lets you explore one of many possibilities.

## Chapter 1: Introduction to Virtualization and Microsoft Solutions

**Articulate the key value propositions of virtualization.**   Virtualization solves the numerous pain points and limitations of physical server deployments today. Primary benefits of virtualization include consolidation of resources, which increases resource utilization and provides OS abstraction from hardware, allowing OS mobility; financial savings through less server hardware, less datacenter space, and simpler licensing; faster provisioning of environments; and additional backup and recovery options.

> **Master It**   How does virtualization help in service isolation in branch office situations?
>
> **Solution**   Virtualization enables the different roles required (such as domain controllers and file services) to run on different operating system instances, ensuring isolation without requiring large amounts of hardware.

**Understand the differences in functionality between the different versions of Hyper-V.**   Windows Server 2008 introduced the foundational Hyper-V capabilities, and the major new features in 2008 R2 were Live Migration and Cluster Shared Volumes (CSV). Windows 2008 R2 SP1 introduced Dynamic Memory and RemoteFX. Windows Server 2012 introduced new levels of scalability and mobility with features such as Shared Nothing Live Migration, Storage Live Migration, and Hyper-V Replica in addition to new networking and storage capabilities. Windows 2012 R2 Hyper-V enhances many of the 2012 features with generation 2 virtual machines, Live Migration compression and SMB support, new Hyper-V Replica replication granularity, and Hyper-V Replica Extended replication.

> **Master It**   What is the largest virtual machine that can be created on Windows Server 2012 Hyper-V?
>
> **Solution**   The largest virtual machine can have 64 vCPUs with 1 TB of memory.
>
> **Master It**   What features were enabled for Linux virtual machines in Windows Server 2012 R2 Hyper-V?
>
> **Solution**   Two key features enabled for Linux in Windows Server 2012 R2 Hyper-V were Dynamic Memory and file-consistent backup.

**Differentiate between the types of cloud service and when each type is best utilized.** There are three primary types of cloud services. Software as a Service (SaaS), Platform as a Service (PaaS), and Infrastructure as a Service (IaaS). SaaS provides a complete software solution that is entirely managed by the providing vendor, such as a hosted mail solution. PaaS provides a platform on which custom-written applications can run and should be used for new custom applications when possible because it minimizes maintenance by the client. IaaS allows virtual machines to be run on a provided service, but the entire OS and application must be managed by the client. IaaS is suitable where PaaS or SaaS cannot be used and in development/test environments.

# Chapter 2: Virtual Machine Resource Fundamentals

**Describe how the resources of a virtual machine are virtualized by the hypervisor.** The hypervisor directly manages the processor and memory resources with Hyper-V. Logical processors are scheduled to satisfy computer requirements of virtual processors assigned to virtual machines. Multiple virtual processors can share the same logical processor. Virtual machines are assigned memory by the hypervisor from the memory available in the physical host. Dynamic memory allows memory to be added and removed from a virtual machine based on resource need. Other types of resources, such as network and storage, are provided by the management partition through a kernel mode memory bus known as a VMBus. This allows existing Windows drivers to be used for the wide array of storage and network devices typically used.

**Master It** How is Dynamic Memory different from Memory Overcommit?

**Solution** Dynamic Memory allocates memory in an intelligent fashion to virtual machines based on how it is being used by processes running inside the virtual machine. Memory Overcommit technologies work by telling a virtual machine that it has a large amount of memory and only allocating the memory as the virtual machine writes to the it. However, this approach does not work well with modern operating systems that try to use all memory available, even if it's only for cache purposes.

**Correctly use processor and memory advanced configuration options.** The compatibility configuration of a virtual machine processor should be used when a virtual machine may be moved between hosts with different versions of the same processor family. The processor compatibility option hides higher-level features from the guest operating system, enabling migrations without downtime to the virtual machine. Processor reserve and limit options ensure that a virtual machines coexists with other virtual machines without getting too many or too few resources. Dynamic Memory configurations allow the startup, minimum, and maximum amounts of memory for a virtual machine to be configured. It's important to note that the maximum amount of memory configured is available only if sufficient memory exists within the host.

**Master It** When should the NUMA properties of a virtual machine be modified?

**Solution** Hyper-V will configure the optimal settings for virtual machines based on the physical NUMA configuration of the hosts. However, if a virtual machine will be moved between hosts with different NUMA configurations, then the NUMA configuration of the virtual machine should be changed to match the smallest NUMA configuration of all the hosts it may be moved between.

**Explain the difference between VHD/VHDX and pass-through storage.** VHD and VHDX files are virtual hard disks that are files on a file system or share accessible to the Hyper-V host. They provide abstraction of the storage seen by the virtual machine and the underlying physical storage. Pass-through storage directly maps a virtual machine to a physical disk accessible from the host, which limits Hyper-V functionality and breaks one of the key principals of virtualization: the abstraction of the virtual machine from the physical fabric.

**Master It** Why would VHD still be used with Windows Server 2012 Hyper-V?

**Solution** VHDX is superior to VHD in every way. However, if you need backward compatibility with Windows Server 2008 R2 Hyper-V or Windows Azure IaaS (at time of this writing), then VHD should still be used.

# Chapter 3: Virtual Networking

**Architect the right network design for your Hyper-V hosts and virtual machines using the options available.** There are many different networking traffic types related to a Hyper-V host, including management, virtual machine, cluster, live migration, and storage. While traditionally separate, network adapters were used with each type of traffic; a preferred approach is to create multiple vNICs in the management partition that connect to a shared virtual switch. This minimizes the number of physical NICs required while providing resiliency from a NIC failure for all workloads connected to the switch.

**Master It** Why are separate network adapters required if SMB is leveraged and the network adapters support RDMA?

**Solution** RDMA is not compatible with NIC teaming, which would have been used as the foundation for the connectivity of the virtual switch. Therefore, if RDMA needs to be leveraged for the best performance, it would be necessary to have additional network adapters that are not part of a NIC team for the RDMA optimized workloads such as Live Migration, Cluster, and SMB file traffic.

**Identify when to use the types of NVGRE Gateway.** There are three separate scenarios supported by NVGRE Gateway: S2S VPN, NAT, and Forwarder. S2S VPN should be used when a virtual network needs to communicate with another network such as a remote network. Forwarder is used when the IP scheme used in the virtual network is routable on the physical fabric, such as, for example, when the physical fabric network is expanded into the virtual network. NAT is required when the IP scheme in the virtual network is not routable on the physical network fabric and requires external connectivity, such as when tenants needed to access the Internet.

**Leverage SCVMM 2012 R2 for many networking tasks.** While Hyper-V Manager enables many networking functions to be performed, each of these configurations are limited to a single host and are hard to manage at scale. SCVMM is focused on enabling the network to be modeled at a physical level, and then the types of network required by virtual environments can be separately modeled with different classifications of connectivity defined. While the initial work may seem daunting, the long-term management and flexibility of a centralized networking environment is a huge benefit.

**Master It** Why is SCVMM required for network virtualization?

**Solution**   There are three planes to network virtualization: data, control, and management. SCVMM is the management plane and also part of the control plane. For proper routing between virtual machines in a virtual network, SCVMM is vital for populating the policies to each participating Hyper-V host.

# Chapter 4: Storage Configurations

**Explain the types of storage available to a virtual machine.**   Windows Server 2012 R2 provides a number of different types of storage to a virtual machine. VHDX files provide a completely abstracted and self-contained virtual container for file systems available to virtual machines, and 2012 R2 allows a VHDX file connected to the SCSI bus to be shared between multiple virtual machines, providing shared storage. Additionally, storage can be exposed to virtual machines that are hosted in SAN environments through the use of iSCSI running inside the guest operating system or through the new Virtual Fibre Channel capability.

**Master It**   Why is MPIO required?

**Solution**   Where multiple paths are available to storage for resiliency purposes, the storage will be seen multiple times by the operating system. MPIO makes the operating system aware of the multiple paths to the storage and consolidates the storage view to one object for each storage instance.

**Identify when to use Virtual Fibre Channel and when to use shared VHDX and the benefits of each.**   Virtual Fibre Channel allows virtual machines to be directly connected to a fibre channel SAN without the host requiring zoning to the storage, but it requires knowledge of the storage fabric. Shared VHDX provides shared storage to the virtual machine without requiring that the users of the shared VHDX have knowledge of the storage fabric, which is useful in hosting the type of scenarios where all aspects of the physical fabric should be hidden from the users.

**Articulate how SMB 3.0 can be used.**   SMB 3.0 went through a huge upgrade in Windows Server 2012, providing an enterprise-level file-based protocol that can now be used to store Hyper-V virtual machines. This includes additional storage options for Hyper-V environments, including fronting existing SANs with a Windows Server 2012 R2 scale-out file server cluster to extend the SAN's accessibility beyond hosts with direct SAN connectivity.

**Master It**   Which two SMB technologies enable virtual machines to move between nodes in a SoFS without any interruption to processing?

**Solution**   SMB Transparent Failover and SMB Scale-Out enable the movement of SMB clients between servers without the need for LUNs to be moved and with no loss of handles and locks.

# Chapter 5: Managing Hyper-V

**Identify the different ways to deploy Hyper-V.**   Windows Server 2012 R2 Hyper-V can be deployed using a number of methods. The traditional approach is to install a server from setup media, which could be a DVD, USB device, or even files obtained over the network. Enterprise systems management solutions such as System Center Configuration Manager and Windows Deployment Services can be used to customize deployments. System Center

Virtual Machine Manager can also be deployed to deploy Hyper-V hosts using Boot to VHD technology, providing a single management solution for deployment of hosts and virtual machines.

**Master It**   What other types of server can SCVMM 2012 R2 deploy?

**Solution**   In addition to deploying Hyper-V hosts, SCVMM 2012 R2 can deploy scale-out file servers to act as storage hosts for Hyper-V virtual machines.

**Explain why using Server Core is beneficial to deployments.**   Windows Server and Windows client operating systems share a lot of common code, and a typical Windows Server deployment has a graphical interface, Internet browser, and many graphical tools. These components all take up space, require patching, and may have vulnerabilities. For many types of server roles, these graphical elements are not required. Server Core provides a minimal server footprint that is managed remotely, which means less patching and therefore fewer reboots in addition to a smaller attack surface. Because a host reboot requires all virtual machines to also be rebooted, using Server Core is a big benefit for Hyper-V environments to remove as many reboots as possible.

**Master It**   What was the big change to Server Core between Windows Server 2008 R2 and Windows Server 2012?

**Solution**   In Windows Server 2008 R2, the choice to use Server Core or Full Install had to be made at installation time and could not be changed. Windows Server 2012 introduced configuration levels, which allow the graphical shell and separately management tools to be added and removed at any time, requiring only a reboot to change configuration level.

**Explain how to create and use virtual machine templates.**   While it is possible to manually create the virtual machine environment and install the operating system for each new virtual machine, it's inefficient considering the virtual machine uses a file for its virtual storage. A far more efficient and expedient approach is to create a generalized operating system template VHDX file, which can then be deployed to new virtual machines very quickly. A virtual machine template allows the virtual hardware configuration of a virtual machine to be configured, including OS properties such as domain join instructions, local administrator password, and more. The configuration is then linked to a template VHDX file. When the template is deployed, minimal interaction is required by the requesting user, typically just an optional name, and within minutes, the new virtual environment with a configured guest operating system is available.

# Chapter 6: Maintaining a Hyper-V Environment

**Explain how backup works in a Hyper-V environment.**   Windows features the VSS component that enables application-consistent backups to be taken of an operating system by calling VSS writers created by application vendors. When a backup is taken of a virtual machine at the Hyper-V host level, the VSS request is passed to the guest operating system via the backup guest service, which allows the guest OS to ensure that the disk is in a backup-ready state, allowing the virtual hard disk to be backed up at the host and be application consistent.

**Master It**   Is shared VHDX backed up when you perform a VM backup at the host level?

**Solution**   No. Shared VHDX, iSCSI, and fibre channel–connected storage are not backed up when performing a VM backup at the host level. To back up these types of storage, a backup within the virtual machine must be performed.

**Understand how to best use checkpoints and where not to use them.**   Checkpoints, previously known as snapshots, allow a point-in-time view of a virtual machine to be captured and then applied at a later time to revert the virtual machine back to the state it was in at the time the snapshot was taken. This is useful in testing scenarios but should not be used in production because the effect of moving a virtual machine back in time can cause problems for many services. It can even cause domain membership problems if the computer's AD account password changes after the checkpoint creation.

**Understand the benefits of service templates.**   Typically a virtual machine is created from a virtual machine template, which allows a single virtual machine to be deployed. A service template allows a complete, multitiered service to be designed and then deployed through a single action. Additionally, each tier can be configured to scale up and down as workloads vary, which enables additional instances of the virtual machine for a tier to be created and deleted as necessary. Deployed instances of a service template retain their relationship to the original service template, which means if the original service template is updated, the deployed instances can be refreshed and updated with the service template changes without losing application state.

# Chapter 7: Failover Clustering and Migration Technologies

**Understand the quorum model used in Windows Server 2012 R12.**   Windows Server 2012 R2 removes all the previous different models that were based on how votes were allocated and the type of quorum resource. In Windows Server 2012 R2, each node has a vote and a witness is always configured, but it's only used when required. Windows Server 2012 introduced dynamic quorum, which helps ensure that clusters stay running for as long as possible as nodes' votes are removed from quorum because the nodes are unavailable. Windows Server 2012 R2 added dynamic witness to change the vote of the witness resource based on if there are an odd or even number of nodes in the cluster.

**Identify the types of mobility available with Hyper-V.**   Mobility focuses on the ability to move virtual machines between Hyper-V hosts. Virtual machines within a cluster can be live migrated between any node very efficiently since all nodes have access to the same storage, allowing only the memory and state to be copied between the nodes. Windows Server 2012 introduced the ability to move the storage of a virtual machine with no downtime, which when combined with Live Migration enables a Shared Nothing Live Migration capability that means a virtual machine can be moved between any two Hyper-V hosts without the need for shared storage or a cluster, with no downtime to the virtual machine.

Shared Nothing Live Migration does not remove the need for failover clustering but provides the maximum flexibility possible, enabling virtual machines to be moved between stand-alone hosts, between clusters, and between stand-alone hosts and clusters.

**Master It**   Why is constrained delegation needed when using Shared Nothing Live Migration with remote management?

**Solution**   Windows does not allow a server that has been given a credential to pass that credential on to another server. Constrained delegation enables credentials to be passed from a server to another specific server for defined purposes. This enables management to be performed remotely, including migration initialization.

**Understand the best way to patch a cluster with minimal impact to workloads.**   All virtual machines in a cluster can run on any of the member nodes. That means before you patch and reboot a node, all virtual machines should be moved to other nodes using Live Migration, which removes any impact on the availability of the virtual machines. While the migration of virtual machines between nodes can be performed manually, Windows Server 2012 failover clustering provides Cluster Aware Updating, giving you a single-click ability to patch the entire cluster without any impact to virtual machines' availability. For pre–Windows Server 2012 clusters, SCVMM 2012 also provides an automated patching capability.

# Chapter 8: Hyper-V Replica and Cloud Orchestration

**Identify the best options to provide disaster recovery for the different services in your organization.**   When planning disaster recovery, an application-aware disaster recovery should be used first where possible, such as SQL AlwaysOn, Exchange DAG, Active Directory multimaster replication, and so on. If no application-aware replication and DR capability is available, another option is to look at the replication capabilities of the SAN such as synchronous replication. Additionally, replicating at the virtual machine disk level such as Hyper-V Replica provides a replication solution that has no requirements on the guest operating system or the application.

**Master It**   Why is Hyper-V Recovery Manager useful?

**Solution**   Hyper-V Replica provides the replication of the virtual machine but does not provide any enterprise management or failover orchestration. Hyper-V Recovery Manager provides a cloud-based portal to enable enterprise-level configuration, management, and execution of failover plans in a structured manner.

**Describe the types of failover for Hyper-V Replica.**   There are three types of Hyper-V Replica failover. A test failover is performed on the replica server and creates a clone of the replica virtual machine that is disconnected from the network and allows testing of the failover process without any impact to the ongoing protection of the primary workload as replication continues. A planned failover is triggered on the primary Hyper-V host and stops the virtual machine, ensures any pending changes are replicated, starts the replica virtual machine, and reverses the replication. An unplanned failover is triggered on the replica Hyper-V host and is used when an unforeseen disaster occurs and the primary datacenter is lost. This means there may be some loss of state from the primary virtual machine. When possible, a planned failover should always be used.

**Master It**   In an unplanned failover how much data could be lost?

**Solution**   The Hyper-V Replica configuration specifies a time interval to perform replication, which can be 30 seconds, 5 minutes, or 15 minutes. This relates to the recovery point objective (RPO), which is the amount of data that can be lost. A replication of 15 minutes means that potentially up to 15 minutes of data could be lost, while a replication of 30 seconds means that the maximum amount of data loss should be 30 seconds, provided there is no network bottleneck that is slowing down the transmission of replica log files.

**Explain the automated options for Hyper-V Replica failover.**   Hyper-V Replica has no automated failover capability. To automate the failover steps, PowerShell could be used, System Center Orchestrator could be used, or for a complete solution Hyper-V Recovery Manager could be used. The key point is the actual decision to failover should not be automatic because there could be many conditions such as a break in network connectivity that could trigger a false failover. The automation required should be the orchestration of the failover once a manual action is taken to decide a failover should occur.

# Chapter 9: Implementing the Private Cloud and SCVMM

**Explain the difference between virtualization and the private cloud.**   Virtualization enables multiple operating system instances to run on a single physical piece of hardware by creating multiple virtual machines that can share the resources of the physical server. This enables greater utilization of a server's resource, reduction in server hardware, and potential improvements to provisioning processes. The private cloud is fundamentally a management solution that builds on virtualization but brings additional capabilities by interfacing with the entire fabric including network and storage to provide a complete abstraction and there-fore management of the entire infrastructure. This allows a greater utilization of all available resources, which leads to greater scalability. Because of the abstraction of the actual fabric, it is possible to enable user self-service based on their assignment to various clouds.

**Master It**   Do you need to change your fabric to implement the private cloud?

**Solution**   Typically not. Providing your storage supports SMI-S to enable it to be com-municated to and from SCVMM and your compute and network resources meet your needs in terms of your desired levels of capability, there should be no need to change the actual fabric. Only the management will change.

**Describe the must-have components to create a Microsoft private cloud.**   The founda-tion of a Microsoft private cloud solution would be virtualization hosts using Hyper-V and then SCVMM and App Controller to provide the core fabric management, abstraction, cloud creation, and end-user self-service functionality. Orchestrator and Service Manager can be utilized to build on this core set of private cloud functionality to bring more advanced work-flows, authorization of requests, and charge-back functionality.

# Chapter 10: Remote Desktop Services

**Explain the types of desktop virtualization provided by RDS.**   Windows Server 2012 R2 provides two main types of desktop virtualization: session-based desktops and VDI-based desktops. There are two types of VDI deployments: pooled and personal.

**Master It**   When should VDI be used over session-based virtualization?

**Solution**   The primary difference between session-based virtualization and VDI desk-tops is one of isolation. If there are particular users who require a high level of isolation from other users such as needing to customize the operating system or reboot it, then VDI is a good fit. For other users such as task-based ones who are more locked down, then session-based virtualization is a good solution.

**Describe the benefits of RemoteFX and its requirements.**   RemoteFX brings a number of technologies such as USB port-level redirection and improved codecs that with Windows Server 2012 are available separately from GPU virtualization, which is the other primary RemoteFX technology that allows a physical GPU to be virtualized and assigned to VDI virtual machines running client operating systems. Using RemoteFX vGPU enables virtual machines to have local graphical resources, which enables the ability to run rich graphical applications, specifically those that leverage DirectX. To use RemoteFX vGPU, the graphics card must support DirectX 11 or newer and have a WDDM 1.2 driver or newer. The processor must also support SLAT.

**Master It**   Is RemoteFX vGPU a good solution for OpenGL applications?

**Solution**   No. OpenGL 1.1 is supported using CPU only and does not utilize the vGPU. RemoteFX vGPU is targeted at DirectX applications.

**Articulate the other technologies required for a complete virtualized desktop solution.**   The complete user experience comprises a number of layers. The operating system provided by VDI or session virtualization is just the foundation for the user experience. The users need access to their profiles, their data, and their applications. To provide data access, the most common technology is folder redirection. For a user's profile, while historically roaming profiles were used, a better and more granular solution is UE-V, which provides application-level setting replication. For the applications, technologies such as App-V and RemoteApp can be leveraged, while specific core applications could be installed on the RD Session Host or VDI virtual machine template.

**Master It**   Why is it best to minimize the number of applications installed in the VM VDI template image?

**Solution**   Every application installed in a reference image will eventually need to be updated, which is additional maintenance on the template. This is not a simple process because any change will require running Sysprep again, which has its own complexities. Additionally, the more applications installed in the template, the bigger the template and the more resources consumed that would be wasted unless the application is used by every single user. With App-V and RemoteApp, there are better ways to enable applications in the environment.

# Chapter 11: Windows Azure IaaS and Storage

**Explain the difference between Platform as a Service and Infrastructure as a Service.**   The key difference relates to who is responsible for which elements of the solution. With Platform as a Service, solutions are written for a supplied platform within certain guidelines. The platform then ensures availability and protection for the application, and there is no operating system or fabric management required. The key point is that the application must be written to work with the PaaS platform. With Infrastructure as a Service, a virtual machine is provided, which means the provider manages the compute, storage, and network fabric but the user of the virtual machine is responsible for the operating system and everything within it and also patching it. The benefit of IaaS is that you have complete access to the operating system, so normal applications can run in IaaS without requiring customization. A key principal of IaaS is that you should not have to modify the application to work on it.

**Master It**   What is Software as a Service?

**Solution**   Software as a Service requires no infrastructure management from the user of the service because a complete, maintained solution is provided that is accessible, typically over the Internet. The only administration relates to basic configuration and administration of users of the service. A good example of SaaS is Office 365, which is Microsoft's Exchange-, Lync-, and SharePoint-based service in the cloud.

**Connect Windows Azure to your on-premises network.**   To create connectivity between Windows Azure and your local network, there are a number of requirements. First, virtual networks need to be defined in Windows Azure in affinity groups. Virtual machines are created and configured at the time of creation to use a specific subnet in the virtual network. A site-to-site gateway is created between Windows Azure and your on-premises network, which permits seamless connectivity.

**Master It**   Can Windows Server 2012 RRAS be used on the local premises side of the VPN gateway?

**Solution**   Yes. Windows Server 2012 RRAS can be used for the on-premises side of the VPN connection and the Windows Azure management portal will generate the full configuration script required to enable automatic configuration.

**Move data between on-premises and Windows Azure.**   Windows Azure is built on Windows Server Hyper-V and specifically leverages the VHD format currently. A virtual machine that uses VHD can be copied to Windows Azure storage and used with a new Windows Azure virtual machine or added to an existing virtual machine. Similarly, VHD files used in Windows Azure virtual machines can be downloaded to on-premises and used with Hyper-V virtual machines.

**Master It**   What PowerShell cmdlets are used to copy VHDs to and from Windows Azure?

**Solution**   `Add-AzureVhd` and `Save-AzureVhd` are used.

**Master It**   Can dynamic VHDs be used in Windows Azure?

**Solution**   No. All VHDs must be fixed, and the `Add-AzureVhd` cmdlet converts dynamic VHDs to fixed VHDs during the upload. However, Windows Azure Storage stores files sparsely, which means only blocks that have data written to them are actually stored and therefore billed.

# Chapter 12: Bringing It All Together with a Best-of-Breed Cloud Solution

**Identify the overall best architecture for your organization.**   As this chapter has shown, there are a lot of things to consider when choosing a cloud-based solution for an organization. It's important to take the time to understand the organization's strategic direction, its resources, and the needs of its workloads. Only then can an architecture be created that utilizes the strengths of the different options.

**Master It**   What is the most important first step in deciding on the best architecture?

**Solution**   Have a clear direction for your IT organization. Is it cloud first? Is it to focus on best-in-class datacenters? This will guide the architecture design and final solution.

# Chapter 13: The Hyper-V Decoder Ring for the VMware Administrator

**Understand how System Center compares to vSphere solutions.**   System Center comprises a number of components that each provide different functionalities. vSphere has a similar set of solutions, and a basic mapping is shown here:

- ◆ SC Virtual Machine Manager = vCenter Server

- ◆ SC Data Protection Manager = vSphere Data Protection Advanced

- ◆ SC Operations Manager = vCenter Ops Mgmt Suite

- ◆ SC Orchestrator = vCenter Orchestrator

- ◆ SC Service Manager = vCloud Automation Center

- ◆ App Controller and SC Service Manager = vCloud Director

The levels of functionality are not exactly the same, but the mapping shows the key functional area mapping of the products.

**Master It**   How is System Center licensed?

**Solution**   System Center is a single product that is available in two versions, Standard and Datacenter. Both versions are functionally identical, with the only difference being the number of virtual OS instances that are managed as part of the license. Standard provides licensing for two virtual OS instances, while Datacenter provides licensing for an unlimited number of virtual OS instances. Both Standard and Datacenter are licensed by physical processor, and each license covers two processors.

**Convert a VMware virtual machine to Hyper-V.**   There are two aspects to converting a virtual machine: there is the virtual machine configuration, such as the number of vCPUs, memory, network connectivity, and so on; and then there are the virtual hard disks that contain the operating system and data. There are various solutions to address both parts of the conversion. The primary Microsoft VMware to Hyper-V tool is Microsoft Virtual Machine Converter, which performs migrations in an interactive fashion. Command-line tools are also available.

**Master It**   How can MVMC be used as part of a bulk conversion process?

**Solution**   The Microsoft Automation Toolkit (MAT) available at http://gallery.technet.microsoft.com/Automation-Toolkit-for-d0822a53 utilizes MVMC but adds discovery and automation to provide a larger-scale conversion solution.

**Master It**   How does NetApp help with VMDK to VHD conversions?

**Solution**   NetApp has a native VMDK to VHD conversion capability that rewrites the header of the virtual hard disk instead of having to perform a full conversion of the actual virtual hard disk data. This enables conversions in seconds instead of minutes.

# Index

## A

access control lists, 77
ACPI Static Resource Affinity Table, 57
Active Directory
    Azure, 451
    Domain Controller, 197, 257, 493
    multimaster replication, 367, 368, 494, 525
    RBAC, 209–210
    virtualization safe, 257
    VM-generationIDs, 257–258, 497
    write caching, 156
Active Directory Based Activation, 23, 217
active nodes, 274, 275, 282, 319, 510
Add Network Service Wizard, 128
Add Roles And Features Wizard, 424
Add-ClusterSharedVolume -Name "Cluster
    Disk 1", 310
Add-ClusterVMMonitoredItem -VirtualMachine
    savdaltst01 -Service spooler, 291
Address Hash, 138, 143
Add-VMHardDiskDrive, 72
Add-VMMigrationNetwork, 321
Add-VMNetworkAdapter, 270
Add-VMNetworkAdapter -ManagementOS
    -SwitchName, 145
agnostic of underlying fabric, 370–371, 405, 526
Alpha processor architecture, 1, 3
AlwaysOn technology, 341–342, 367, 368, 485, 495,
    498, 525
AMD NX bit, 196
Android, 28, 404, 436, 448
anti-affinity group, 293–294
App Controller. *See also* System Center
    defined, 28
    installation and configuration, 394–396
    user access to private cloud, 393–399
    vCloud Director, 505, 517, 529
App-V, 258, 259, 416, 417, 418, 422, 440, 527
asynchronous replication, 20, 342–343, 344, 368,
    510. *See also* Hyper-V Replica

Authorization Manager, Windows, 209
automated failover. *See* Hyper-V Recovery
    Manager
Automatic Virtual Machine Activation, 217
availability set, 466–467
AVHDX file, 254, 427
Azure
    high availability, 466–467
    management portal, 460–471
    platform, 447–451
Azure Active Directory, 451
Azure App Services, 450–451
Azure Compute, 447–449
Azure Data Services, 449–450
Azure Drive, 449
Azure IaaS
    capabilities, 451–457
    file share witness, 287
    Minecraft, 451–454, 456, 465
    purchasing, 457–460
    site-to-site VPN connection, 483–486
    supported operating systems, 454
    virtual machines
        creation, management portal, 460–471
        creation, PowerShell, 471–474
        migration, 486–487
        sizes, 455–456
Azure Storage
    BLOBs, 449, 450, 464, 468–469, 470
    CloudXplorer, 468–469
    Content Delivery Network, 450
    Media Services, 451
    Queues, 450
    Scheduler, 451
    Service Bus, 451
    StorSimple appliance, 488–489, 495
    using, 487–489
Azure Virtual Networks
    described, 474–483
    Traffic Manager, 451

## B

backup planning
    Hyper-V environment, 249–252, 271, 523–524
    Hyper-V Integration Services Backup (volume
      snapshot), 231, 250
    Linux, 251
    VSS
      coordination service, 250
      P2V migration, 233–234
      request, 13, 250, 271, 523
      VSS for SMB File Shares, 170
      writers, 234, 249–250, 251, 271, 348, 523
ballooning, 63–66, 511
bare-metal, 10, 42, 154, 199, 233, 262, 497, 511
best-of-breed cloud solution. *See* cloud solution
BIN file, checkpoint feature, 254
BIOS, 40
BitLocker, 161, 214, 273, 450
BITS, 192, 226, 385
BizTalk, 455, 459
blade systems, 2
BLOBs, 449, 450, 464, 468–469, 470
block-level access, 3–4
blue network-red network, 113, 118, 120, 121, 122,
    123, 130, 151
Boot from VHD feature, 67, 69, 202, 203
Bottom Line. *See* exercises
Bring Your Own Device, 411, 439
business units/tenants/labs, 93

## C

capability profiles, private cloud, 390–391
capacity planner, 360
checkpoints feature
    fixed VHDs, 255
    snapshots compared to, 13
    using, 254–258, 524
Checkpoint-VM, 212, 256
child partitions, 12, 36, 37, 38
ChkDsk, 18, 69, 154, 155, 188, 312–313
Cisco Nexus 1000V, 80, 81, 132, 508
Citrix XenServer, 26, 233, 333, 376, 382, 385, 390, 496
cloud services, 30–32. *See also* public cloud services
cloud solution, best-of-breed, 491–501
    choosing best architecture
      first step, 491–492, 528–529
      management solutions, 499–501

      private cloud, 498–499
      public cloud services, 492–496
      server virtualization options, 496–498
    exercises, 501, 528–529
clouds, 30–32. *See also* private clouds; public cloud
  services
CloudXplorer, 468–469
Cluster Migration Wizard, 237–238, 239, 240
Cluster Name Object, 277
cluster setup wizard, 275
Cluster Shared Volumes (CSV)
    data deduplication, 188
    defined, 14
    using, 310–313
cluster validation, 303–306
Cluster-Aware Updating, 248, 281, 291–292
clustered virtual machines, 314–316
clusters (Failover Clustering feature), 273–316
    basics, 273–275
    components, 274
    exercises, 337, 524–525
    Failover Cluster Manager
      cluster validation, 304–305
      clustered virtual machine creation,
        314–316
      Hyper-V Replica Broker, 352
      Hyper-V Replica failover, 353
      Live Migration, 319–320
      service monitoring, 290
      SMB with Hyper-V Storage, 172–173
      votes modification, 282–284
      witness configuration, 278
    forcing quorum, 285
    geographically distributed, 286–287
    Hyper-V
      configuring, 295–307
      creating with SCVMM, 307–309
      network requirements and configurations,
        296–301
      patching, 245–248
      reasons for using, 287–295
      where to implement high availability,
        292–295
    Install-WindowsFeature Failover-
      Clustering, 186, 274
    nodes, 274–316
      active, 274, 275, 282, 319, 510
      heartbeats, 276, 296, 300, 340

passive, 274, 275
vote configuration, 280–284
purpose, 273
quorum
advanced options, 284–285
basics, 276–282
disk witness, 277–279, 282, 286, 510
dynamic quorum feature, 277, 280–281, 282, 283, 337, 524
dynamic witness, 283, 284, 337, 524
file share witness, 277–279, 286, 287, 510
force quorum resiliency, 285–286
forcing, 279, 285–286
service monitoring, 288–291
Set-ClusterOwnerNode, 294
Set-ClusterParameter
CsvEnableBlockCache 1, 313
Set-ClusterQuorum -DiskOnly, 278
Set-ClusterQuorum -DiskWitness, 278
Set-ClusterQuorum -FileShareWitness, 278
Set-ClusterQuorum -NoWitness, 278
single-node, 274
Update Manager, 505, 510
virtual network adapter, 301–303
VMware clustering feature, 510
codec, RemoteFX, 16
collections, 419
COM ports, 43
community mode, PVLANs, 87–90
Compare-VM, 212
Configuration Cluster Quorum Settings, 278, 282
configuration levels, 197–198
configuration management database, 29–30, 400. *See also* Service Manager
Configuration Manager. *See* SCCM
Connection Broker, RD, 411, 412, 414–415, 425, 428
constrained delegation, 322, 324, 328–330, 337, 524–525
Content Delivery Network, Azure App Services, 450
Contig tool, 254
control plane, 116, 522
converged Hyper-V host configuration, 146–147, 300
Convert-VHD, 70, 158
coordination service, VSS, 250
Coreinfo utility, 15, 54–57, 196
corporate networks, 92

counters, performance, 263–264
Create Cloud Wizard, 387–388
Create Cluster Wizard, 304, 307
Create Collection Wizard, 425
Create Logical Network Wizard, 89, 100
Create Logical Switch Wizard, 109
Create User Role Wizard, 392
Create Virtual Machine Wizard, 316, 463, 481
CredSSP, 322, 328, 329, 330, 332
CSV. *See* Cluster Shared Volumes
CSVFS, 310, 311, 513
custom metadata, 69, 155
customer address, 97, 112, 113, 120

**D**

data deduplication, 188–189
data exchange, Hyper-V Integration Services, 230–231
Data Execution Prevention, 12, 196
data plane, 116, 522
Data Protection Manager (DPM), 29, 251, 386, 404, 450, 487, 505, 517, 529
database availability groups, Exchange, 367, 498
Datacenter, Windows Server 2012 R2, 24, 195
datacenters
evolution, 1–10
licensing, 8
memory considerations, 3
networking, 4
processors, 1–3
storage, 3–4
Debug-VM, 212
decoder ring. *See* VMware
Default Stores page, 199
defrag.exe utility, 253
defragmentation, 252–254
Delete Checkpoint, 255
deployment
Hyper-V servers, 202–203
Server Core, 241, 523
virtual machine templates, 224–229
Windows Deployment Service, 202, 241, 522
desktop. *See also* RDS
complete desktop solution requirements, 416–421
Desktop Experience configuration level, 408–409
personal desktops, 410, 412, 413, 424

Details pane, SCVMM management console, 380
Device Manager output with Task Manager,
    physical server, 5
DHCPv4 Server Switch Extension, VMM, 82
differencing VHD/VHDX, 68–69, 175, 250, 255
dinner analogy, 50–51
Direct IO, 311
disable automatic logical network creation,
    SCVMM, 98, 99
Disable-NetAdapterRss, 140
Disable-VMResourceMetering, 266
disaster recovery. *See also* Hyper-V Replica
    Active Directory multimaster replication, 367,
        368, 494, 525
    basics, 339–341
    Exchange database availability groups, 367, 498
    need for, 339–340
    options, 367–368, 525
    recovery point objective, 341, 343, 525
    recovery time objective, 341
    SQL AlwaysOn technology, 341–342, 367, 368,
        485, 495, 498, 525
disk witness, 277–279, 282, 286, 510
disk2vhd, 152, 234
Dismount-VHD, 157
Distributed File System Namespaces, 384, 495
Distributed File System Replication, 384, 494
Distributed Power Management (DPM), 509, 510.
    *See also* Power Optimization
Distributed Resource Scheduling (DRS), 509
Double-Take, 234, 495
DPM. *See* Data Protection Manager; Distributed
    Power Management
DRS. *See* Distributed Resource Scheduling
dual-parity spaces, 164
DVMQ (Dynamic Virtual Machine Queue),
    136–138
DXdiag, 430
dynamic learning, of IP addresses, 123–124
Dynamic Memory
    defined, 15
    described, 60–67
    hot-add, 507
    introduction, 429, 519
    Linux, 513, 519
    memory overcommit, 61, 63, 65, 72, 511, 520
    migrations, 236

performance counters, 264
performance tuning, 261
production environments, 378
VDI template, 423
dynamic NIC Teaming, 142
Dynamic Optimization, 332–335, 509
dynamic quorum feature, 277, 280–281, 282, 283,
    337, 524
dynamic resize, VHDX, 159–160
dynamic VHD/VHDX, 67–69
Dynamic Virtual Machine Queue. *See* DVMQ
Dynamic VMQ NIC Teaming option, 138, 143
dynamic witness, 283, 284, 337, 524

**E**

Edit Disk action, 69, 71, 157, 158, 159
Edit Virtual Disk Wizard, 69, 159
elasticity, public cloud services, 444
emulated hardware, 22, 39, 42, 44, 147
Enable-NetAdapterRss, 140
Enable-VMReplication, 348, 352
Enable-VMResourceMetering
    -ResourcePoolName, 269
Enable-VMResourceMetering -VMName, 266
endpoints, 464–465
Enhanced Session Mode, 218–219
Enhanced vMotion Compatibility (EVC), 509. *See
    also* processor compatibility mode
enlightened operating systems, 229, 233
Enterprise Software Deployment solution, 418. *See
    also* SCCM
ESX, 26, 80, 233, 234, 235, 236, 333, 376, 382, 385, 390,
    496, 503
ESXi, 503–505, 511, 512, 515
EVC. *See* Enhanced vMotion Compatibility
Exchange database availability groups, 367, 498
exercises
    best-of-breed cloud solution, 501, 528–529
    clustering, 337, 524–525
    Hyper-V Replica, 368, 525–526
    Live Migration, 337, 524–525
    private clouds, 405, 526
    RDS, 440, 526–527
    solutions, 519–529
    storage, 193, 522
    virtual machine resources, 72–73, 520–521
    virtual networks, 152, 521–522

Export-VM, 212, 213
Extend Replication Wizard, 352
Extended Page Tables, 196
extended replication, 32, 351, 352, 356, 358, 367, 519
extensible switch, 80–82, 508
external storage, 3–4
external virtual switches, 76–77

## F

Fabric workspace, 89, 100, 107, 109, 125, 128, 202, 246, 308, 381
Fail fast, 445
failover. *See also* Hyper-V Replica
    automated, HRM, 361–367, 368, 450, 510, 525, 526
    planned, 356, 357, 361, 366, 368, 525
    test, 355, 357, 366, 368, 510, 525
    unplanned, 356, 357, 366, 368, 525
Failover Cluster Manager
    cluster validation, 304–305
    clustered virtual machine creation, 314–316
    Hyper-V Replica Broker, 352
    Hyper-V Replica failover, 353
    Live Migration, 319–320
    service monitoring, 290
    SMB with Hyper-V Storage, 172–173
    votes modification, 282–284
    witness configuration, 278
Failover Clustering feature. *See* clusters
fat/thick provisioning, 161
Fault Tolerance, 504, 510
features, roles and, 273
Fibre Channel, 3, 4, 22, 160. *See also* virtual Fibre Channel
file share witness, 277–279, 286, 287, 510
file-level access, 3–4
file-level protocols, 3
file-system snapshot driver, 251
fixed VHD/VHDX, 68, 255
flexible single-master operation roles, 258
force quorum resiliency, 285–286
Force Unit Access, 156
forcing quorum, 279, 285–286
Forwarder gateway, 124, 126, 152, 521
free processor scheduling, 51

## G

gang scheduling, 50, 51, 52
gateway
    HNV Gateway
        behind the curtain, 130–131
        deploying, 125–130
        described, 124–125
        Forwarder, 124, 126, 152, 521
        NAT, 124, 125, 126, 129, 130, 152, 521
        online document, 126
        S2S, 124–125, 126, 152, 521
        TCP compartments, 125, 130–131
    NV Gateway, 124
    RD Gateway, 412, 413, 415, 436
generation 1 virtual machines
    BIOS, 40
    COM ports, 43
    defined, 39
    generation 1 to generation 2 comparison, 45
    generation 1 to generation 2 conversion, 46
    IDE controllers, 41–42, 156–157
    SCSI controllers, 42–43, 156, 157
    USB ports, 43
    virtual motherboard, 40
generation 2 virtual machines
    defined, 22
    described, 44–46
    generation 1 to generation 2 comparison, 45
    generation 1 to generation 2 conversion, 46
    SCSI controllers, 44, 46, 156–157
Generic Command Execution, 259
geographically distributed clusters, 286–287
Get-AzurePublishSettingsFile, 472
Get-ClusterSharedVolumeState, 314
Get-Command -Module AppController, 396
Get-Command -Module Azure, 471
Get-NetAdapterRss, 170
Get-NetAdapterSriov, 135
Get-NetAdapterVmq, 136
Get-NetAdapterVmqQueue, 137
Get-NetCompartment, 131
Get-NetIPAdress, 119
Get-NetVirtualizationCustomerRoute, 121
Get-NetVirtualizationLookupRecord, 120, 121
Get-NetVirtualizationProviderAddress, 119
Get-SCLogicalNetwork | ft Name, 105
Get-SMBBandwidthLimit, 191

Get-SMBConnection, 169
Get-SmbMultiChannelConnection, 170
Get-VM, 212
Get-VM | Format-Table Name, ResourceMeteringEnable, 266
Get-VMHost -ComputerNameserver | Format-List, 212
Get-vmreplicationserver -computername savdalhv24 | fl, 345
Get-VMResourcePool, 268, 270
Get-VMSnapshot, 256, 357, 358
Group Policy, 214, 245, 418
groups, private cloud, 392–393
Growing Fast scenario, 445
Guest Dynamic IP inbox virtual port profile, 95, 124
guest network adapters, 147–150
guest operating system
    activating, 217
    defined, 6
    enlightened, 229, 233
    RDP, 219
guest partitions, 12
guest services, Hyper-V Integration Services, 231–232
GUID Partition Table, 18

**H**

HAL. *See* hardware abstraction layer
hanging problems, 53
hard disk drives. *See* HDDs
hardware abstraction layer (HAL), 3
hardware load balancers, 370, 386, 388, 391
hardware-assisted virtualization, 12, 54, 196, 511
HBAs (host bus adapters), 4, 178–183. *See also* virtual Fibre Channel
HDDs (hard disk drives)
    defragmentation, 252
    HDD tiers, 164–165
    StorSimple appliance, 488–489
heartbeats
    Hyper-V Integration Services, 231
    nodes, 276, 296, 300, 340
high availability. *See also* clusters
    Azure, 466–467
    Hyper-V clustering, 292–295
HNV (Hyper-V Network Virtualization), 81, 104, 117, 118, 476, 508

HNV Gateway (Hyper-V NV Gateway)
    behind the curtain, 130–131
    deploying, 125–130
    described, 124–125
    Forwarder, 124, 126, 152, 521
    NAT, 124, 125, 126, 129, 130, 152, 521
    online document, 126
    S2S, 124–125, 126, 152, 521
    TCP compartments, 125, 130–131
host bus adapters. *See* HBAs
host groups, 97, 98
hot blocks, 165–166
HRM. *See* Hyper-V Recovery Manager
HTTP Listener, 346, 352
HTTPS Listener, 346
HVCLUS account, 172
hyperthreading
    defined, 3
    NUMA, 57
    performance, 47
    Receive Side Scaling, 139
    turning off, 49, 262
Hyper-V
    architecture, 11–12
    clusters
        configuring, 295–307
        creating with SCVMM, 307–309
        High Availability, 292–295
        network requirements and configurations, 296–301
        patching, 245–248
        reasons for using, 287–295
    control plane, 116, 522
    converting VMware skills to Hyper-V and System Center, 514–515
    data deduplication, 188–189
    data plane, 116, 522
    enable Hyper-V role, 198–200
    environment
        backup planning, 249–252, 271, 523–524
        checkpoints, 13, 254–258, 524
        defragmentation, 252–254
        malware protection, 200, 214, 236, 248–249
        monitoring, 270–271
        patching, 243–248, 511–512
        Performance Monitor, 261, 263–265
        resource metering, 22, 190, 265–270
    fault tolerance, 510

features
Windows Server 2008, 12–13
Windows Server 2008 R2, 13–15
Windows Server 2008 R2 Service Pack 1, 15–16
Windows Server 2012, 16–21
Windows Server 2012 R2, 21–23
hardware-assisted virtualization, 12, 54, 196, 511
history, 10–23
install, 195–203
iSCSI, 173–178
licensing, 23–27
management, 195–241
management environments, 204–205
microkernelized hypervisor, 36
misconceptions, 511–514
page sharing technologies, 66–67, 511, 513
post installation actions, 200–202
production-equivalent test environment, 201
servers
deploying with SCVMM, 202–203
securing, 214
SMB usage, 172–173
time synchronization integration service, 40–41, 230
type 1 hypervisor, 10–11, 36, 511
versions, 195
choosing, 26–27
functionality differences, 12–23, 32, 519
virtual Fibre Channel, 179
VLANs, 86–87
VMware compared to, 511–514
VMware compared to Hyper-V
distributed switch, 508–509
file-level disk format, 508
hot-add of resources, 507–508
maximums, 506–507
misconceptions, 511–514
networking features, 508
VMware to Hyper-V migration, 515–516
Hyper-V hosts
converged Hyper-V host configuration, 146–147, 300
deploy with SCVMM, 202–203
limits, 262
logical switches, 109–112
virtual adapters, 143–147

Hyper-V Hypervisor Logical Processor – % Total Run Time, 263
Hyper-V Hypervisor Root Virtual Processor – % Total Run Time, 263
Hyper-V Hypervisor Virtual Processor – % Total Run Time, 264
Hyper-V Integration Services, 229–233
Hyper-V Manager
checkpoints, 254–256
Edit Disk action, 69, 71, 157, 158, 159
interface, 206
Remote Server Administration Tools, 199, 204, 236
resource pools viewing, 269
using, 205–210
virtual machines, creating and managing, 214–219
virtual switch creation, 78–80
Hyper-V Network Virtualization. *See* HNV
Hyper-V NV Gateway. *See* HNV Gateway
Hyper-V Port, 138, 142, 143
Hyper-V Recovery Manager (HRM), 361–367, 368, 450, 510, 525, 526
Hyper-V Replica
asynchronous replication, 20, 342–343, 344, 368, 510
Broker, 352–353
configuring, 346–352
disaster recovery planning
Active Directory multimaster replication, 367, 368, 494, 525
basics, 339–341
Exchange database availability groups, 367, 498
need for, 339–340
options, 367–368, 525
recovery point objective, 341, 343, 525
recovery time objective, 341
SQL AlwaysOn technology, 341–342, 367, 368, 485, 495, 498, 525
enabling, 344–346
exercises, 368, 525–526
extended replication, 32, 351, 352, 356, 358, 367, 519
failover, 353–359
planned, 356, 357, 361, 366, 368, 525
test, 355, 357, 366, 368, 510, 525
unplanned, 356, 357, 366, 368, 525

HTTP Listener, 346, 352
HTTPS Listener, 346
inject IP address with PowerShell, 350
introduction, 342–344
Orchestrator, 361, 368, 526
recovery point configuration, 347–348
Replication – Remove Replication action, 352
Replication – View Replication Health
    action, 353
Replication Configuration Wizard, 346
sizing solutions, 359–361
synchronous replication, 20, 286, 341–342
vSphere Replication, 510
Hyper-V Server, 26, 195–196
hypervisors
    microkernelized, 36
    monolithic, 36, 503
    type 1
        ESXi, 503
        Hyper-V, 10–11, 36, 511
    type 2, 10–11, 511

**I**

IaaS (Infrastructure as a Service). *See also* Azure
    IaaS; public cloud services
    cloud services comparison, 30–32, 441–443
    defined, 31, 441
IDE controllers, 41–42, 156–157
IHV drivers, 35, 38
Import-AzurePublishSettingsFile <file>.
    publishsettings, 472
Import-Module Hyper-V, 204
Import-Module virtualmachinemanager, 213
Infrastructure as a Service. *See* IaaS
Initiator, iSCSI, 174, 177–178
INITSYNC requirement, 258
inject IP address outside Hyper-V Replica, 350
input/output operations per second. *See* IOPS
installation
    App Controller, 394–396
    Hyper-V, 195–203
    SCVMM, 377–379
Install-WindowsFeature Failover-
    Clustering, 186, 274
Install-WindowsFeature FS-iSCSITarget-
    Server, 175
Install-WindowsFeature FS_SMBBW, 191

Install-WindowsFeature -Name Hyper-V
    -Restart, 199
Install-WindowsFeature RSAT-Remote-Access-
    PowerShell, DirectAccess-VPN, Routing, 127
Install-WindowsFeature Server-Gui-Mgmt-
    Infra,Server-Gui-Shell –Restart, 198
integration packs, 30, 400, 471
Intel XD bit, 196
internal storage, 3–4
internal virtual switches, 76–77
Internet, logical networks and, 92
IOPS (input/output operations per second), 4,
    189–190
iOS, 28, 264, 404, 436, 448, 469
IP addresses
    dynamic learning, 123–124
    inject, outside Hyper-V Replica, 350
    ranges, 103, 104, 475, 476, 480, 483, 493
IP pools, 82, 93, 94, 98, 102, 103, 104
IP rewrite, 115
IP subnets, Azure Virtual Networks, 476
IPMI, 202
IPv6 support, 93, 297, 349, 476, 495, 508
IQNs, 176, 177, 178
iSCSI
    benefits, 160
    block-level access, 3
    considerations for use, 178
    with Hyper-V, 173–178
    Initiator, 174, 177–178
    NIC Teaming, 174
    targets, 174, 175–176
ISO files, library content, 385–386
isolated mode, PVLANs, 87–90
isolation methods, 132
isolation of services, 8–9, 32, 519
iWARP, 171

**J**

JBOD (just a bunch of disks), 161
jumbo frames, 15, 297, 508
just a bunch of disks. *See* JBOD

**K**

Kerberos, 328–330, 332, 344–347
Key Management Server, 217

# L

L1 cache, 2
L2 cache, 2
labs/business units/tenants, 93
LACP. *See* Link Aggregation Control Protocol
libraries, 382–386, 388–389
licensing
    datacenters, 8
    Hyper-V, 23–27
    System Center, 503–504, 517, 529
Link Aggregation Control Protocol
   (LACP), 142
Linux
    backups, 251
    Hyper-V Integration Services, 232–233
    Hyper-V Server, 20, 195–196
    virtual Fibre Channel, 186
    virtual machine templates, 221–222
    virtual machines capabilities, 23
    Windows Server 2012 scalability, 18
Live Migration, 316–336
    complete process, 319
    defined, 316–317
    enhancements, 320–322, 331–332
    exercises, 337, 524–525
    high-level view, 13–14
    Live Storage Move (Storage Migration)
        described, 322–326, 516
        Storage vMotion, 504, 509, 519
    Shared Nothing Live Migration
        automated NUMA configuration, 59
        constrained delegation, 322, 324, 328–330,
           337, 524–525
        defined, 19
        described, 326–328
    simultaneous migrations, 331
    stages, 317
    virtual Fibre Channel, 183
    vMotion, 333, 504, 509
Live Migration Settings, 319
Live Storage Move (Storage Migration)
    described, 322–326, 516
    Storage vMotion, 504, 509, 519
logical networks
    creating, SCVMM, 100–104
    described, 92–94
    designing, 94

    high level view, 94
    private cloud creation, 387–388
logical processors. *See also* virtual processors
    described, 47–60
    Performance Monitor, 263–264
logical switches, 94–96. *See also* port profiles
    Hyper-V host configuration, 109–112
    SCVMM network configuration steps, 107–109
logical unit numbers. *See* LUNs
lookup tables, 114, 120, 121, 123, 125
LUNs (logical unit numbers)
    CSV, 14
    defined, 13
    SMB Scale-Out, 167–168, 522
    SMB Transparent Failover, 167

# M

malware protection, 200, 214, 236, 248–249
management console. *See* SCVMM
Management network connectivity, 144
management networks, 92
management partition, 12
management plane, 116, 125, 522
management portal, Azure, 460–471
MAP (Microsoft Assessment and Planning
   Toolkit), 235
MAT (Microsoft Automation Toolkit), 235,
   514, 529
maximums
    IOPS, 189–190
    virtual processors, for each operating system,
       51–52
    VMware compared to Hyper-V, 506–507
Measure-VM, 212, 266
Measure-VM -VMName savdalfs01 | fl, 267
Measure-VMReplication, 354, 355
Media Services, Azure App Services, 451
memory
    Dynamic Memory
        defined, 15
        described, 60–67
        hot-add, 507
        introduction, 429, 519
        Linux, 513, 519
        migrations, 236
        performance counters, 264
        performance tuning, 261

production environments, 378
VDI template, 423
error-correcting code, 3
NUMA
described, 57–60
spanning, 59–60, 209, 264
vNUMA, 57, 59, 60
performance counters, 264
physical servers, 3
RDMA, 22, 146, 147, 152, 171, 299, 331, 509, 521
64 vCPUs, 1TB memory, 17, 18, 47, 48, 57, 261, 262, 390, 513, 519
virtual machines, 60–67
memory overcommit, 61, 63, 65, 72, 511, 520
Message Analyzer, 150–151
microkernelized hypervisor, 36
Microsoft Assessment and Planning Toolkit. *See* MAP
Microsoft Automation Toolkit. *See* MAT
Microsoft Consulting Services, 235
Microsoft Management Console, 379, 380
Microsoft Security Compliance Manager, 214
Microsoft Virtual Machine Converter (MVMC), 234–235, 514, 516, 517, 529
"Migrate to a physical computer with a different processor version" setting, 53
migration. *See also* Live Migration
Cluster Migration Wizard, 237–238, 239, 240
physical servers/virtual machines to Hyper-V virtual machines, 233–236
upgrading/migrating from previous versions, 236–240
virtual machines between Hyper-V and Azure Iaas, 486–487
VMware to Hyper-V, 515–516
Minecraft, 451–454, 456, 465
minimum IOPS, 189–190
MIPS, 1, 3
mirroring
port mirroring, 80, 149, 150
RAID, 161, 470
Storage Spaces, 163, 164
monitoring. *See also* performance
Hyper-V environment, 270–271
Performance Monitor, 261, 263–265
resource metering, 22, 190, 265–270
SCOM
changes, 402–403
defined, 28

described, 28–29, 270–271, 291, 500
domain service accounts, 378
Hyper-V Replica, 354
Performance Resource Optimization, 333
private cloud, 370, 386, 389, 402–404
vCenter Operations Management Suite, 505
service monitoring, clusters, 288–291
monolithic hypervisor, 36, 503
Mount-VHD, 157
Move-VM, 212, 327, 331
MPIO (Multi-Path I/O), 4, 169, 174, 179, 185, 193, 522
Multichannel, SMB, 146, 147, 169–170, 297, 323
multicore processors, 2, 7, 47
multimaster replication, Active Directory, 367, 368, 494, 525
Multi-Path I/O. *See* MPIO
Multiple Activation Key, 217
MVMC. *See* Microsoft Virtual Machine Converter

## N

NAT gateway, 124, 125, 126, 129, 130, 152, 521
Navigation pane, SCVMM management console, 380
NDISCAP, 150
NEC OpenFlow, 80, 132
Net start clussvc /ForceQuorum, 285
Net start clussvc /PQ, 285
NetBIOS, 168, 297, 307
NetFT virtual adapter, 302–303
NetMon, 150
network adapters, 147–150
virtual machines between Hyper-V and Azure
Network Device Interface Specification filter drivers, 80, 81
Network File System. *See* NFS
network forwarding, 81
Network Load Balancing, 149, 293, 367, 451
Network Monitor tool, 150
network packet filter, 80
network packet inspection, 80
network QoS, 91, 359, 508
Network Topology Generator, 297–298
network virtualization
commands, 119–124
control plane, 116, 522
data plane, 116, 522
high-level overview, 113
implementing, 117–119
introduction, 75

IP rewrite, 115
isolation methods, 132
management plane, 116, 125, 522
NVGRE, 114–115, 116, 152, 521
overview, 112–117
Network Virtualization Gateway. *See* NV Gateway
Network Virtualization Generic Routing
   Encapsulation. *See* NVGRE
New iSCSI Virtual Disk Wizard, 176
New Storage Pool Wizard, 162
New Virtual Hard Disk Wizard, 70
New Virtual Machine Wizard, 314
New-AzureDns -Name 'PremDNS' -IPAddress
   '192.168.1.10', 480
New-IscsiServerTarget, 176
New-IscsiVirtualDisk, 176
New-NetQoSPolicy, 300
New-VHD commands, 71–72
New-VHD -ParentPath D:Virtualsnewfix
   .vhdx, 71
New-VHD -Path D:Virtualsnewdyn.vhdx
   -Dynamic -SizeBytes 1TB, 71
New-VHD -Path D:Virtualsnewfix.vhdx -Fixed
   -SizeBytes 10GB, 71
New-VMReplicationAuthorizationEntry, 346
New-VMSwitch, 134
Nexus 1000V, Cisco, 80, 81, 132, 508
NFS (Network File System), 3
NIC Teaming
   described, 141–143
   iSCSI, 174
   Protected Network, 291
   RDMA-capable network adapters, 171
Node Vote Weights, 282
nodes, 274–316
   active, 274, 275, 282, 319, 510
   heartbeats, 276, 296, 300, 340
   passive, 274, 275
   vote configuration, 280–284
non-uniform memory access. *See* NUMA
Now state, 255–256, 256–257
N-Port ID Virtualization (NPIV), 179–180
NTFS. *See also* Cluster Shared Volumes
   ChkDsk problem, 155
   corruption, 14
   CSVFS, 310, 311, 513
   disk witness, 278
   GUID Partition Table, 18
   shared nothing file system, 13, 14, 167, 310

ntttcp.exe test tool, 140
NUMA (non-uniform memory access)
   described, 57–60
   spanning, 59–60, 209, 264
   vNUMA, 57, 59, 60
NV (Network Virtualization) Gateway, 124. *See also*
   HNV Gateway
NVGRE (Network Virtualization Generic Routing
   Encapsulation), 114–115, 116, 152, 521

**O**

ODX. *See* offloaded data transfer
offload support, 508
offloaded data transfer (ODX), 191–192, 226, 323
One Connected Network option, 100, 104
1TB memory, 64 vCPUs, 17, 18, 47, 48, 57, 261, 262,
   390, 513, 519
one-node cluster, 274
on-premises solution, 31, 441, 442, 443. *See also* IaaS;
   PaaS; SaaS
Opalis, 30
Open Data Protocol, 449
OpenFlow, NEC, 80, 132
OpenVMS, 1
operating systems. *See also specific operating systems*
   Azure IaaS, 454
   enlightened, 229, 233
   guest
      activating, 217
      defined, 6
      enlightened, 229, 233
      RDP, 219
   maximum virtual processors, for each
      operating system, 51–52
   shutdown, Hyper-V Integration Services, 230
   support, VMware compared to Hyper-V, 512
Operations Manager. *See* SCOM
Optimize Drives utility, 253
Optimize-VHD, 158
Orchestrator. *See also* System Center
   capabilities, 399
   described, 30
   Hyper-V Replica, 361, 368, 526
   private clouds, 399–402
   SMA, 220
   vCenter Orchestrator, 505, 517, 529
   VM templates, 223
Out Of Box Experience Wizard, 218

## P

P2V (physical to virtual), 233–234
PaaS (Platform as a Service). *See also* public cloud
   services
      cloud services comparison, 30–32, 441–443
      defined, 31, 442
page sharing technologies, 66–67, 511, 513
pain points
      physical server deployments, 5–7, 32, 519
      virtual environments
         activation, 23
         licensing of Hyper-V, 23
parity
      dual-parity spaces, 164
      Parity layout, Storage Spaces, 163
      RAID, 161, 470
      Storage Spaces, 163, 164, 165, 314
passive nodes, 274, 275
pass-through storage, 13, 17, 67, 72, 73, 154, 521
patching
      ESXi, 511, 512
      Hyper-V clusters, 245–248
      Hyper-V environment, 243–248, 511–512
      after Hyper-V install, 201
      IaaS, 31
      PaaS, 31
      SCCM, 201, 500, 510
      Server Core, 197, 198
      SMB Transparent Failover, 167
      virtual machine templates, 220–221
      WSUS, 201, 244–245, 292, 510
PEFNDIS, 150
% Total Run Time counters, 263–264
performance. *See also* monitoring
      counters, 263–264
      drop, virtualization, 261–262
      Storage Spaces, 164
Performance Monitor, 261, 263–265
Performance Resource Optimization, 333–334
personal desktops, 410, 412, 413, 424
physical servers
      bare-metal, 10, 42, 154, 199, 233, 262, 497, 511
      datacenter evolution, 1–10
      Device Manager output, with Task Manager, 5
      memory considerations, 3
      migration to Hyper-V virtual machines,
         233–236

networking, 4
      pain points, 5–7, 32, 519
      processor architectures, 1–2
      processors, 2–3
      storage, 3–4
ping -p, 122
pizza, Super Bowl Sunday, 444
planned failover, 356, 357, 361, 366, 368, 525
planned outage, 287–288
PlateSpin, 234
Platform as a Service. *See* PaaS
port classifications, 97, 107, 109, 388
port mirroring, 80, 149, 150
port profiles
      Guest Dynamic IP inbox virtual port profile,
         95, 124
      SCVMM network configuration steps, 107–109
      uplink, 95–96, 98, 107–108, 109, 110, 111
      virtual, 95, 97, 98, 107, 109, 110, 124
Power Optimization, 334–335, 510
PowerShell cmdlets
      Add-ClusterSharedVolume -Name "Cluster
         Disk 1", 310
      Add-ClusterVMMonitoredItem
         -VirtualMachine savdaltst01 -Service
         spooler, 291
      Add-VMHardDiskDrive, 72
      Add-VMMigrationNetwork, 321
      Add-VMNetworkAdapter, 270
      Add-VMNetworkAdapter -ManagementOS
         -SwitchName, 145
      Azure management portal, 471–474
      checkpoints feature, 256–257
      Checkpoint-VM, 212, 256
      Compare-VM, 212
      Debug-VM, 212
      Disable-NetAdapterRss, 140
      Disable-VMResourceMetering, 266
      Dismount-VHD, 157
      Enable-NetAdapterRss, 140
      Enable-VMReplication, 348, 352
      Enable-VMResourceMetering
         -ResourcePoolName, 269
      Enable-VMResourceMetering -VMName, 266
      Export-VM, 212, 213
      Get-AzurePublishSettingsFile, 472
      Get-ClusterSharedVolumeState, 314

Get-Command -Module AppController, 396
Get-Command -Module Azure, 471
Get-NetAdapterRss, 170
Get-NetAdapterSriov, 135
Get-NetAdapterVmq, 136
Get-NetAdapterVmqQueue, 137
Get-NetCompartment, 131
Get-NetIPAdress, 119
Get-NetVirtualizationCustomerRoute, 121
Get-NetVirtualizationLookupRecord,
   120, 121
Get-NetVirtualizationProviderAddress,
   119
Get-SCLogicalNetwork | ft Name, 105
Get-SMBBandwidthLimit, 191
Get-SMBConnection, 169
Get-SmbMultiChannelConnection, 170
Get-VM, 212
Get-VM | Format-Table Name,
   ResourceMeteringEnable, 266
Get-VMHost -ComputerNameserver |
   Format-List, 212
Get-vmreplicationserver -computername
   savdalhv24 | fl, 345
Get-VMResourcePool, 268, 270
Get-VMSnapshot, 256, 357, 358
Hyper-V, 204, 210–213
Import-AzurePublishSettingsFile <file>.
   publishsettings, 472
Import-Module Hyper-V, 204
Import-Module virtualmachinemanager, 213
inject IP address outside Hyper-V Replica, 350
Install-WindowsFeature Failover-
   Clustering, 186, 274
Install-WindowsFeature FS-iSCSITarget-
   Server, 175
Install-WindowsFeature FS_SMBBW, 191
Install-WindowsFeature -Name Hyper-V
   -Restart, 199
Install-WindowsFeature RSAT-
   RemoteAccess-PowerShell,
   DirectAccess-VPN, Routing, 127
Install-WindowsFeature Server-Gui-Mgmt-
   Infra,Server-Gui-Shell -Restart, 198
Measure-VM, 212, 266
Measure-VM -VMName savdalfs01 | fl, 267
Measure-VMReplication, 354, 355

Mount-VHD, 157
Move-VM, 212, 327, 331
Net start clussvc /ForceQuorum, 285
Net start clussvc /PQ, 285
New-AzureDns -Name 'PremDNS' -IPAddress
   '192.168.1.10', 480
New-IscsiServerTarget, 176
New-IscsiVirtualDisk, 176
New-NetQoSPolicy, 300
New-VHD commands, 71–72
New-VHD -ParentPath D:Virtualsnewfix.
   vhdx, 71
New-VHD -Path D:Virtualsnewdyn.vhdx
   -Dynamic -SizeBytes 1TB, 71
New-VHD -Path D:Virtualsnewfix.vhdx
   -Fixed -SizeBytes 10GB, 71
New-VMReplicationAuthorizationEntry, 346
New-VMSwitch, 134
Optimize-VHD, 158
Read-SCLibraryShare, 384
Remove-SMBBandwidthLimit, 191
Remove-VM, 212
Remove-VMReplication, 352, 358
Remove-VMReplication –VMName, 358
Rename-VM, 212
Repair-VM, 212
Repair-Volume -Scan <disk>, 155
Repair-Volume -SpotFix <disk>, 155
Reset-VMResourceMetering, 266
Resize-VHD, 160
Restart-VM, 212
Restore-VMSnapshot, 256
Resume-VM, 212
Resume-VMReplication, 355, 358
Save-AzureVhd, 487, 528
Save-VM, 212
SCVMM, 213
Select-NetVirtualizationNextHop, 122–123
Set-ClusterOwnerNode, 294
Set-ClusterParameter
   CsvEnableBlockCache 1, 313
Set-ClusterQuorum -DiskOnly, 278
Set-ClusterQuorum -DiskWitness, 278
Set-ClusterQuorum -FileShareWitness, 278
Set-ClusterQuorum -NoWitness, 278
Set-ExecutionPolicy RemoteSigned, 471
Set-NetAdapterRss, 140

Set-NetFirewallProfile, 127
Set-NetFirewallRule -DisplayGroup
  "Virtual Machine Monitoring", 290
Set-NetQoSPolicy, 300
Set-SCVirtualMachine, 365
Set-SMBBandwidthLimit, 191
Set-SmbPathAcl, 173
Set-VM, 212, 213
Set-VMComPort, 44
Set-VMFirmware -EnableSecureBoot Off, 44
Set-VMHardDiskDrive, 190
Set-VMHost, 212, 330
Set-VMHost -MaximumStorageMigrations,
  324
Set-VMNetworkAdapter -VMName <VM Name>
  -AllowTeaming On, 143
Set-VMNetworkAdapterVlan, 86, 88–89
Set-VMProcessor
  -CompatibilityForMigrationEnabled, 54
Set-VMProcessor -Compatibility
  ForOlderOperatingSystems
  Enabled, 54
Set-VMReplication -reverse, 357
Set-VMReplication –VMName, 358
Set-VMReplicationServer, 345
simultaneous migrations, 331
Start-ClusterNode -ForceQuorum, 285
Start-ClusterNode -PreventQuorum, 285
Start-VM, 212
Start-VMFailover, 357, 358
Start-VMInitialReplication, 348
Stop-VM, 212, 357
Suspend-VM, 212
Suspend-VMReplication, 355
System Center, 382
Test-Cluster, 306
Test-VMNetworkAdapter, 122, 123
virtual machines creation, Azure IaaS, 471–474
Predictable Bursting, 445
private clouds. *See also* public cloud services
  agnostic of underlying fabric, 370–371, 405, 526
  attributes, 369–370
  benefits, 369–374
  creation, SCVMM
    capability profiles, 390–391
    cloud capacity, 389
    configuration ready, 386–387
    library configuration, 388–389

logical networks, 387–388
    name and description, 387
    resources, 387
    storage tiers, 388
    users and groups, 392–393
  defined, 31
  exercises, 405, 526
  groups, 392–393
  Orchestrator, 399–402
  SCCM, 386–387, 404–405
  SCOM, 370, 386, 389, 402–404
  Service Manager, 399–402
  service templates, 370, 383, 386, 393, 394, 395,
    397, 398, 399
  System Center, 402–405
  user access
    App Controller, 393–399
    SCVMM management console, 392–393
  virtualization compared to, 371–373, 405, 526
  when to use, 498–499
private virtual switches, 76–77
private VLANs. *See* PVLANS
processor assignment, 52–54
processor compatibility mode, 15, 72, 233, 295, 327,
  509, 512, 520
processors. *See also* virtual processors
  hyperthreading
    defined, 3
    NUMA, 57
    performance, 47
    Receive Side Scaling, 139
    turning off, 49, 262
  multicore, 2, 7, 47
  physical servers, datacenter evolution, 1–3
  virtual machines, 47–60
production-equivalent test environment, 201
promiscuous mode, PVLANs, 87–90
Protected Network setting, 149, 291, 292
provider address, 104, 112, 113, 119, 120, 122
public cloud services. *See also* private clouds
  comparison of types, 30–32, 441–443
  defined, 31
  elasticity, 444
  reasons for using, 443–446, 492–496
purchasing Azure IaaS, 457–460
PVLANs (private VLANs)
  described, 87–90
  isolation methods, 132

# Q

Quality of Service (QoS)
  network, 91, 359, 508
  storage, 22, 189–191
  virtualization, 9
  vNICs, 145
Quest, 234, 411, 439
Queues, Azure App Services, 450
quorum
  advanced options, 284–285
  basics, 276–282
  disk witness, 277–279, 282, 286, 510
  dynamic quorum feature, 277, 280–281, 282, 283, 337, 524
  dynamic witness, 283, 284, 337, 524
  file share witness, 277–279, 286, 287, 510
  force quorum resiliency, 285–286
  forcing, 279, 285–286
  understanding, 275–287, 337, 524

# R

RAID (Redundant Array of Independent Disks), 4, 153, 161, 163–164, 411, 470
rapid context switching, 60
Rapid Virtualization Indexing, 196
RBAC. *See* role-based access control
RD Connection Broker, 411, 412, 414–415, 425, 428
RD Gateway, 412, 413, 415, 436
RD Virtualization Host, 413, 415, 425
RD Web Access, 412, 413–414, 425, 428, 429, 436
RDMA (Remote Direct Memory Access), 22, 146, 147, 152, 171, 299, 331, 509, 521
RDMA over Converged Ethernet, 171
RDP (Remote Desktop Protocol)
  capabilities, 433–436
  ESM, 218–219
  guest operating system, 219
  Management network connectivity, 144
  RemoteFX USB redirection, 16, 43
RDS (Remote Desktop Services), 407–440
  Bring Your Own Device, 411, 439
  complete desktop solution requirements, 416–421
  Desktop Experience configuration level, 408–409
  exercises, 440, 526–527
  personal desktops, 410, 412, 413, 424

RD Connection Broker, 411, 412, 414–415, 425, 428
RD Gateway, 412, 413, 415, 436
RD Virtualization Host, 413, 415, 425
RD Web Access, 412, 413–414, 425, 428, 429, 436
RemoteFX, 429–433
session virtualization
  described, 407–415
  when to use, 436–440
Terminal Services, 407
UE-V, 416–421, 440, 527
user profile disks, 419–421, 426
VDI
  collection, scenario-based deployment, 424–429
  creating template, 421–424
  full implementation, 412–413
  solution, 409–410
  when to use, 436–440
RDSH (Remote Desktop Session Host), 205, 381, 407, 408, 412, 414, 432, 433, 437, 439
read-only domain controller, 494
Read-SCLibraryShare, 384
real-time clock, 40
Receive Side Scaling. *See* RSS
recovery point configuration, 347–348
recovery point objective (RPO), 341, 343, 525
recovery time objective, 341
red network-blue network, 113, 118, 120, 121, 122, 123, 130, 151
Redundant Array of Independent Disks. *See* RAID
ReFS (Resilient File System), 188, 278, 310, 314
relative ID (RID), 257, 258
Relative Weight, 52–53
remote capture, 150–151
Remote Desktop Protocol. *See* RDP
Remote Desktop Services. *See* RDS
Remote Desktop Session Host. *See* RDSH
Remote Direct Memory Access. *See* RDMA
Remote Server Administration Tools (RSAT), 127, 199, 204, 205, 236
Remote Shared Virtual Hard Disk Protocol, 188
RemoteFX. *See also* RDS
  codec, 16
  defined, 15–16
  USB redirection, 16, 432–433, 435
  using, 429–433
Remove-SMBBandwidthLimit, 191

Remove-VM, 212
Remove-VMReplication, 352, 358
Remove-VMReplication -VMName, 358
Rename-VM, 212
Repair-VM, 212
Repair-Volume -Scan <disk>, 155
Repair-Volume -SpotFix <disk>, 155
replicates mailboxes, 367
replicating library content, 384
Replication, vSphere, 504, 510. *See also* Hyper-V
    Replica
Replication – Remove Replication action, 352
Replication – View Replication Health action, 353
Replication Configuration Wizard, 346
request, VSS, 13, 250, 271, 523
Reset-VMResourceMetering, 266
Resilient File System. *See* ReFS
Resize-VHD, 160
resource balancing, 332–336. *See also* Dynamic
    Optimization
resource metering, 22, 190, 265–270
resource pools, 268–270
Restart-VM, 212
Restore-VMSnapshot, 256
Results pane, SCVMM management console, 380
Resume-VM, 212
Resume-VMReplication, 355, 358
ribbon, SCVMM management console, 379
RID. *See* relative ID
Robust File Copy tool, 384
role-based access control (RBAC), 209–210, 376, 380
roles, features and, 273
Routing and Remote Access Service. *See* RRAS
routing domains, 116, 121. *See also* virtual networks
routing tables, 114, 120, 121, 123, 125
RPO. *See* recovery point objective
RRAS (Routing and Remote Access Service), 125,
    483–484, 490, 493, 528
RSAT. *See* Remote Server Administration Tools
RSS (Receive Side Scaling), 138–141
Run As accounts, 98, 128, 308, 393

**S**

S2S gateway, 124–125, 126, 152, 521
SaaS (Software as a Service). *See also* public cloud
    services
    cloud services comparison, 30–32, 441–443
    defined, 32, 442

SANs (storage area networks)
    defined, 3
    ODX, 191–192, 226, 323
    SCVMM, 191–193
Save-AzureVhd, 487, 528
Save-VM, 212
scalability
    Windows Server 2012, 17–18
Scale-Out File Server option, 168, 307
SCCM (System Center Configuration Manager)
    defined, 28
    domain service account, 378
    Enterprise Software Deployment solution, 418
    integration packs, 400
    patching operations, 201, 500, 510
    private cloud considerations, 386–387, 404–405
    UE-V, 418
    Windows Deployment Services, 202, 241, 522
    WSUS, 245, 246
Scheduler, Azure App Services, 451
SCOM (System Center Operations Manager)
    changes, 402–403
    defined, 28
    described, 28–29, 270–271, 291, 500
    domain service accounts, 378
    Hyper-V Replica, 354
    Performance Resource Optimization, 333
    private cloud, 370, 386, 389, 402–404
    vCenter Operations Management Suite, 505,
        517, 529
SCSI controllers, 42–43, 44, 46, 156–157
SCVMM (System Center Virtual Machine
    Manager)
    cluster creation, 307–309
    Cluster-Aware Updating, 248, 281, 291–292
    control plane, 116, 522
    defined, 28
    deploying Hyper-V servers, 202–203
    Dynamic Optimization, 332–335, 509
    fundamentals, 376–386
    installation, 377–379
    libraries, 382–386, 388–389
    management console, 379–382
    management plane, 116, 125, 522
    network configuration steps
        disable automatic logical network creation,
            98–99
        high level view, 99

host groups, 97, 98
Hyper-V host configuration, logical switch, 109–112
logical networks creation, 100–104
logical switches creation, 107–109
port profiles creation, 107–109
Run As accounts, 97, 98
virtual networks creation, 104–107
networking architectural components
design and planning, 91–92
logical networks, 92–94
logical switches, 94–96
poster diagram, 97
VM networks, 96–97
ODX, 191–192, 226, 323
Power Optimization, 334–335, 510
PowerShell cmdlets, 213
private cloud creation
capability profiles, 390–391
cloud capacity, 389
configuration ready, 386–387
library configuration, 388–389
logical networks, 387–388
name and description, 387
resources, 387
storage tiers, 388
users and groups, 392–393
PVLAN configuration, 89
SAN storage, 191–193
Update Manager, 505, 510
vCenter Server, 503, 504, 505, 517, 529
VMs And Services workspace, 104, 110, 117, 129, 221, 224, 260, 335, 379, 385, 387
Second Level Address Translation. *See* SLAT
Select-NetVirtualizationNextHop, 122–123
Server App-V, 258, 259
Server Core
benefits to deployments, 241, 523
changes, 523
configuration levels, 197–198
goals, 197
patching, 197, 198
remote capture, 150–151
Server Manager, 142
Server Message Block. *See* SMB
Server Roles screen, 199
Server-Gui-Mgmt-Infra, 197, 198
Server-Gui-Shell, 197, 198

Service Bus, Azure App Services, 451
service catalog, 30, 371, 400, 401, 500
Service Designer, 260, 261
Service Manager. *See also* System Center
configuration management database, 29–30, 400
defined, 29–30
private clouds, 399–402
vCloud Automation Center, 505, 517, 529
service monitoring, 288–291
service templates
benefits, 271–272, 524
four-stage life cycle, 259–260
private clouds, 370, 383, 386, 393, 394, 395, 397, 398, 399
tiering, 258–260, 272, 370, 383, 524
using, 258–261
services. *See* cloud services
SES protocol, 161
session virtualization. *See also* RDS
described, 407–415
when to use, 436–440
Set-ClusterOwnerNode, 294
Set-ClusterParameter CsvEnableBlockCache 1, 313
Set-ClusterQuorum -DiskOnly, 278
Set-ClusterQuorum -DiskWitness, 278
Set-ClusterQuorum -FileShareWitness, 278
Set-ClusterQuorum -NoWitness, 278
Set-ExecutionPolicy RemoteSigned, 471
Set-NetAdapterRss, 140
Set-NetFirewallProfile, 127
Set-NetFirewallRule -DisplayGroup "Virtual Machine Monitoring", 290
Set-NetQoSPolicy, 300
Set-SCVirtualMachine, 365
Set-SMBBandwidthLimit, 191
Set-SmbPathAcl, 173
Set-VM, 212, 213
Set-VMComPort, 44
Set-VMFirmware -EnableSecureBoot Off, 44
Set-VMHardDiskDrive, 190
Set-VMHost, 212, 330
Set-VMHost -MaximumStorageMigrations, 324
Set-VMNetworkAdapter -VMName <VM Name> -AllowTeaming On, 143
Set-VMNetworkAdapterVlan, 86, 88–89
Set-VMProcessor -Compatibility ForMigrationEnabled, 54

`Set-VMProcessor -Compatibility`
`ForOlderOperatingSystemsEnabled`, 54
`Set-VMReplication -reverse`, 357
`Set-VMReplication -VMName`, 358
`Set-VMReplicationServer`, 345
sFlow Traffic Monitoring, 80, 82
shared nothing file system. *See* NTFS
Shared Nothing Live Migration
    automated NUMA configuration, 59
    constrained delegation, 322, 324, 328–330, 337,
      524–525
    defined, 19
    described, 326–328
shared VHDX
    backups, 271, 524
    benefits, 193, 522
    described, 186–189
    requirements, 186
    when to use, 193, 522
Silverlight, 16, 28, 30, 393, 396, 400, 401, 429, 430
Simple, Storage Spaces layout, 163
simultaneous migrations, 331
single root I/O virtualization. *See* SR-IOV
single-node cluster, 274
Site Recovery Manager (SRM), 510
site-to-site VPN connection, 483–486
64 TB VHDX scalability, 17, 69, 154, 160, 175, 262,
    322, 496, 507
64 vCPUs, 1TB memory, 17, 18, 47, 48, 57, 261, 262,
    390, 513, 519
SLAT (Second Level Address Translation), 15, 196,
    431, 440, 527
Smart Paging feature, 65–66
SMASH, 202
SMB 3.0 (Server Message Block), 166–173
    file share witness, 277–279, 286, 287, 510
    file-level protocol, 3
    how to use, 193, 522
    Hyper-V storage, 172–173
    leveraging, 171–172
    Multichannel, 146, 147, 169–170, 297, 323
    RDMA, 171
    Remote Shared Virtual Hard Disk Protocol, 188
    Scale-Out, 167–168, 522
    storage QoS, 191
    technologies, 166–167
    Transparent Failover, 167, 522

SMB Direct, 22, 146, 170–171, 323, 331
SMI-S. *See* Storage Management Initiative
    Specification
SMP (symmetric multiprocessing), 12, 50
snapshots, 13. *See also* checkpoints
Software as a Service. *See* SaaS
solid-state drives. *See* SSDs
SPARC, 1, 497
special networks, 92–93
SQL AlwaysOn technology, 341–342, 367, 368, 485,
    495, 498, 525
SQL DAC, 258, 259
SR-IOV (single root I/O virtualization), 132–136
SRM. *See* Site Recovery Manager
SSDs (solid-state drives)
    datacenter storage solution, 4
    defragmentation, 252
    SSD tier, 164–166, 189
    StorSimple appliance, 488–489
    trim support, 155
Standard, Windows Server 2012 R2, 24, 196
`Start-ClusterNode -ForceQuorum`, 285
`Start-ClusterNode -PreventQuorum`, 285
`Start-VM`, 212
`Start-VMFailover`, 357, 358
`Start-VMInitialReplication`, 348
static NIC Teaming, 142
Static Resource Affinity Table, 57
`Stop-VM`, 212, 357
storage, 153–193
    Azure Storage
      BLOBs, 449, 450, 464, 468–469, 470
      CloudXplorer, 468–469
      Content Delivery Network, 450
      Media Services, 451
      Queues, 450
      Scheduler, 451
      Service Bus, 451
      StorSimple appliance, 488–489, 495
      using, 487–489
    block-level access, 3–4
    exercises, 193, 522
    external, 3–4
    file-level access, 3–4
    internal, 3–4
    MPIO, 4, 169, 174, 179, 185, 193, 522
    pass-through, 13, 17, 67, 72, 73, 154, 521

performance counters, 264
physical servers, 3–4
RAID, 4, 153, 161, 163–164, 411, 470
types, 193, 522
VHDs
    Boot from VHD feature, 67, 69, 202, 203
    creating, 70–72
    described, 67–69
    differencing VHD/VHDX, 68–69, 175, 250, 255
    dynamic VHD/VHDX, 67–69
    fixed VHD/VHDX, 68, 255
    pass-through storage, 13, 17, 67, 72, 73, 154, 521
    types, 67–68
VHDX, 153–160
    AVHDX file, 254, 427
    described, 69–70
    differencing VHD/VHDX, 68–69, 175, 250, 255
    dynamic resize, 159–160
    dynamic VHD/VHDX, 67–69
    fixed VHD/VHDX, 68, 255
    maintenance actions, 157–159
    pass-through storage, 13, 17, 67, 72, 73, 154, 521
    VHD compared to, 154–155
storage area networks. *See* SANs
Storage Live Migration, 19, 32, 519. *See also* Live Migration
Storage Management Initiative Specification (SMI-S), 192, 375, 386, 526
storage pool
    creating, 162
    defined, 161
    supported disk types, 161
storage QoS, 22, 189–191
Storage Spaces
    architecture, 165
    Control Panel applet, 163
    dual-parity spaces, 164
    improvements, 164
    introduction, 161
    mirroring, 163, 164
    parity, 163, 164, 165, 314
    performance, 164
    SES protocol, 161

thin provisioning, 161, 162, 188
tiering feature, 164, 165, 166, 314, 489
virtual disks, 162–163
write-back cache, 164, 314
Storage vMotion, 504, 509, 519. *See also* Live Storage Move
StorSimple appliance, 488–489, 495
striping, 161
Super Bowl Sunday, pizza and, 444
Suspend-VM, 212
Suspend-VMReplication, 355
switch independent NIC Teaming, 142
symmetric multiprocessing. *See* SMP
synchronous replication, 20, 286, 341–342. *See also* Hyper-V Replica
SysInternals
    Contig tool, 254
    Coreinfo utility, 15, 54–57, 196
    disk2vhd, 152, 234
System Center. *See also* SCVMM
    App Controller
        defined, 28
        installation and configuration, 394–396
        user access to private cloud, 393–399
        vCloud Director, 505, 517, 529
    components, 27–30
    converting VMware skills to Hyper-V and System Center, 514–515
    Data Protection Manager, 29, 251, 386, 404, 450, 487, 505, 517, 529
    licensing, 503–504, 517, 529
    Orchestrator
        capabilities, 399
        described, 30
        Hyper-V Replica, 361, 368, 526
        private clouds, 399–402
        SMA, 220
        vCenter Orchestrator, 505, 517, 529
        VM templates, 223
    PowerShell usage, 382
    private cloud architecture, 402–405
    RBAC, 380
    role, 27–30
    SCCM
        defined, 28
        domain service account, 378
        Enterprise Software Deployment solution, 418

integration packs, 400
patching operations, 201, 500, 510
private cloud considerations, 386–387,
    404–405
UE-V, 418
Windows Deployment Services, 202, 241,
    522
WSUS, 245, 246
SCOM
changes, 402–403
defined, 28
described, 28–29, 270–271, 291, 500
domain service accounts, 378
Hyper-V Replica, 354
Performance Resource Optimization, 333
private cloud, 370, 386, 389, 402–404
vCenter Operations Management Suite, 505,
    517, 529
Service Manager
configuration management database, 29–30,
    400
defined, 29–30
private clouds, 399–402
vCloud Automation Center, 505, 517, 529
System Center Configuration Manager. *See* SCCM
System Center Operations Manager. *See* SCOM
System Center Virtual Machine Manager. *See*
    SCVMM

**T**

Tables, Azure Data Services, 449
tagged ports, 85
Take No Action, 289, 290
targets, iSCSI, 174, 175–176
Task Manager
with Device Manager output, physical server, 5
Performance Monitor compared to, 263
TCP 3343, 296, 302
TCP compartments, 125, 130–131
templates
service templates
benefits, 271–272, 524
four-stage life cycle, 259–260
private clouds, 370, 383, 386, 393, 394, 395,
    397, 398, 399
tiering, 258–260, 272, 370, 383, 524
using, 258–261

virtual machine templates, 219–229
application configurations, 223
defined, 219
deploying, 224–229
features, 223
Linux-based, 221–222
patches, 220–221
roles, 223
SQL configuration, 223
tenants/labs/business units, 93
Terminal Services, 407. *See also* RDS
test failover, 355, 357, 366, 368, 510, 525
Test-Cluster, 306
Test-VMNetworkAdapter, 122, 123
thick VMDK, 508
thick/fat provisioning, 161
thin provisioning, 161, 162, 188
tiering
service templates, 258–260, 272, 370, 383, 524
Storage Spaces, 164, 165, 166, 314, 489
time synchronization integration service, 40–41, 230
Traffic Manager, 451. *See also* Azure Virtual
    Networks
Transparent Failover, SMB, 167, 522
transparent page sharing, 511, 513
trim support, 155
type 1 hypervisors
ESXi, 503
Hyper-V, 10–11, 36, 511
type 2 hypervisors, 10–11, 511

**U**

UDP 3343, 296, 302
UE-V. *See* User Experience Virtualization
unattend.xml, 227, 454
Unified Extensible Firmware Interface (UEFI), 22,
    44, 46, 49
Uninstall-WindowsFeature Server-Gui-Mgmt-
    Infra -Restart, 198
unplanned failover, 356, 357, 366, 368, 525
unplanned outage, 287–288
Unpredictable Bursting, 445
untagged ports, 85
Update Manager, 505, 510
update sequencer numbers (USNs), 257–258
Update Services, Windows Server, 201, 244–245,
    292, 510

upgrade domains, 449
upgrading/migrating from previous versions, 236–240
uplink port profiles, 95–96, 98, 107–108, 109, 110, 111
USB ports, 43
USB redirection, 16, 432–433, 435
user access, private cloud
    App Controller, 393–399
    SCVMM management console, 392–393
User Experience Virtualization (UE-V), 416–421, 440, 527
user profile disks, 419–421, 426
USNs. *See* update sequencer numbers

# V

V2V (virtual to virtual), 233, 234–236
Validate a Configuration Wizard, 304
vCenter Operations Management Suite, 505, 517, 529. *See also* SCOM
vCenter Orchestrator, 505, 517, 529. *See also* Orchestrator
vCenter Server, 503, 504, 505, 517, 529
vCloud Automation Center, 505, 517, 529
vCloud Director, 505, 517, 529
VDI (Virtual Desktop Infrastructure). *See also* RDS
    data deduplication, 188–189
    Hyper-V Server, 195–196
    RDS
        collection, scenario-based deployment, 424–429
        creating template, 421–424
        full implementation, 412–413
        solution, 409–410
        when to use, 436–440
    RemoteFX, 15
    template, 421–424
vFCAs (virtual fibre channel adapters), 181–184, 186
VHDs (virtual hard disks)
    Boot from VHD feature, 67, 69, 202, 203
    creating, 70–72
    described, 67–69
    differencing VHD/VHDX, 68–69, 175, 250, 255
    dynamic VHD/VHDX, 67–69
    fixed VHD/VHDX, 68, 255
    pass-through storage, 13, 17, 67, 72, 73, 154, 521
    types, 67–68

VHDX, 153–160
    AVHDX file, 254, 427
    described, 69–70
    differencing VHD/VHDX, 68–69, 175, 250, 255
    dynamic resize, 159–160
    dynamic VHD/VHDX, 67–69
    fixed VHD/VHDX, 68, 255
    maintenance actions, 157–159
    pass-through storage, 13, 17, 67, 72, 73, 154, 521
    VHD compared to, 154–155
View Script button, 101, 103, 213, 226, 336, 382, 391
Virtual Desktop Infrastructure. *See* VDI
virtual disks, Storage Spaces, 162–163
virtual Fibre Channel
    benefits, 193, 522
    described, 178–186
    with Hyper-V, 179
    Linux, 186
    NPIV supportability, 179–180
    when to use, 193, 522
virtual fibre channel adapters. *See* vFCAs
virtual hard disks. *See* VHDs
Virtual Machine Limit (Percentage), 52, 53, 507, 508
Virtual Machine Management Service. *See* VMMS
Virtual Machine Manager. *See* SCVMM
Virtual Machine Reserve (Percentage), 52, 53
Virtual Machine Servicing Tool, 220
virtual machine templates, 219–229
    application configurations, 223
    defined, 219
    deploying, 224–229
    features, 223
    Linux-based, 221–222
    patches, 220–221
    roles, 223
    SQL configuration, 223
Virtual Machine Worker processes. *See* VMWPs
virtual machines
    anatomy, 38–46
    child partitions, 12, 36, 37, 38
    clustered, 314–316
    creation
        Azure IaaS, 460–474
        Hyper-V, 214–219
    generation 1
        BIOS, 40
        COM ports, 43

defined, 39
generation 1 to generation 2 comparison, 45
generation 1 to generation 2 conversion, 46
IDE controllers, 41–42, 156–157
SCSI controllers, 42–43, 156, 157
USB ports, 43
virtual motherboard, 40
generation 2
defined, 22
described, 44–46
generation 1 to generation 2 comparison, 45
generation 1 to generation 2 conversion, 46
SCSI controllers, 44, 46, 156–157
hanging problems, 52
limits, 262–263
memory, 60–67
migration to, 233–236
NIC Teaming, 143
Now state, 255, 256–257
objectives, 38
processors, 47–60
resources, 35–73, 520–521
sizes, Azure Iaas, 455–456
VMware, conversion to Hyper-V, 517, 529
virtual motherboard, 40
virtual network adapter, cluster, 301–303
virtual networks, 75–152. *See also* Azure Virtual
Networks; PVLANs; SCVMM; VLANs; VM
networks
exercises, 152, 521–522
names, 116
network configuration steps, SCVMM
disable automatic logical network creation,
98–99
high level view, 99
host groups, 97, 98
Hyper-V host configuration, logical switch,
109–112
logical networks creation, 100–104
logical switches creation, 107–109
port profiles creation, 107–109
Run As accounts, 97, 98
virtual networks creation, 104–107
networking architectural components,
SCVMM
design and planning, 91–92
logical networks, 92–94

logical switches, 94–96
poster diagram, 97
VM networks, 96–97
virtual operating environments, 195
virtual port profiles, 95, 97, 98, 107, 109, 110, 124
virtual processors, 47–60
maximum numbers, for each operating system,
51–52
virtual processor to logical processor
scheduling, 49–52
virtual Receive Side Scaling. *See* vRSS
virtual service clients (VSCs), 37, 38, 42, 63
virtual service providers (VSPs), 37–38, 42, 63, 323
virtual storage. *See* storage
virtual subnet ID (VSID), 114, 115, 116, 120
Virtual Switch Manager, 78–79, 81
virtual switches, 75–82
creating, 78–80
extensible, 80–82, 508
external, 76–77
internal, 76–77
private, 76–77
virtual to virtual. *See* V2V
virtualization
benefits, 9–10
datacenter evolution, 1–10
enlightened, 6, 42, 44, 229, 233
goal, 96
hardware-assisted, 12, 54, 196, 511
high-level view, 5–7
introduction, 1–33
isolation of services, 8–9, 32, 519
key value propositions, 5–10, 32, 519
network virtualization
commands, 119–124
control plane, 116, 522
data plane, 116, 522
high-level overview, 113
implementing, 117–119
introduction, 75
IP rewrite, 115
isolation methods, 132
management plane, 116, 125, 522
NVGRE, 114–115, 116, 152, 521
overview, 112–117
objectives, 38
performance drop, 261–262

private clouds compared to, 371–373, 405, 526
session virtualization
    described, 407–415
    when to use, 436–440
    User Experience Virtualization, 416–421, 440, 527
Virtualization Host, RD, 413, 415, 425
virtualization infrastructure driver, 38
virtualization safe Active Directory, 257
virus protection. *See* malware protection
VLANs (virtual LANS)
    configuration problems, 84–85
    drawbacks, 84–86
    features, 83
    Hyper-V usage, 86–87
    isolation methods, 132
    PVLANs
        described, 87–90
        isolation methods, 132
    tagged ports, 85
    untagged ports, 85
VM networks, 96–97. *See also* virtual networks
VMBus
    architecture, 38
    understanding, 35–38
vmconnect.exe, 217–218, 229
VM-FEX, 136
VM-generationIDs, 257–258, 497
vmguest.iso, 229
VMM DHCPv4 Server Switch Extension, 82
VMMS (Virtual Machine Management Service), 36, 37, 38, 189, 323, 378
vmms.exe, 36–37, 38, 200, 248
vMotion, 333, 504, 509. *See also* Live Migration
VMQ. *See* DVMQ
VMs And Services workspace, 104, 110, 117, 129, 221, 224, 260, 335, 379, 385, 387
VMware
    Cisco Nexus 1000V, 80, 81, 132, 508
    clustering feature, 510
    converting VMware skills to Hyper-V and System Center, 514–515
    ESX, 26, 80, 233, 234, 235, 236, 333, 376, 382, 385, 390, 496, 503
    ESXi, 503–505, 511, 512, 515
    Fault Tolerance, 504, 510
    Hyper-V compared to VMware, 503–506

distributed switch, 508–509
file-level disk format, 508
hot-add of resources, 507–508
maximums, 506–507
misconceptions, 511–514
networking features, 508
overview, 503–506
SRM, 510
transparent page sharing, 511
vCenter Operations Management Suite, 505
vCenter Orchestrator, 505, 517, 529
vCenter Server, 503, 504, 505, 517, 529
vCloud Automation Center, 505, 517, 529
vCloud Director, 505, 517, 529
virtual machine conversion, 517, 529
VMware to Hyper-V migration, 515–516
vSphere Data Protection Advanced, 505, 517, 529
vSphere Replication, 504, 510
vSphere Update Manager, 505, 510
vmwp.exe, 36–37, 38, 39, 42, 248
VMWPs (Virtual Machine Worker processes), 36, 38
vNICs, 145–147, 152, 521
vNUMA, 57, 59, 60
Volume Shadow Copy Service. *See* VSS
vote configuration, 280–284
vRSS (virtual Receive Side Scaling), 140–141, 149
VSCs. *See* virtual service clients
VSID. *See* virtual subnet ID
vSphere Data Protection Advanced, 505, 517, 529
vSphere Replication, 504, 510
vSphere Update Manager, 505, 510
VSPs. *See* virtual service providers
VSS (Volume Shadow Copy Service)
    coordination service, 250
    P2V migration, 233–234
    request, 13, 250, 271, 523
    VSS for SMB File Shares, 170
    writers, 234, 249–250, 251, 271, 348, 523
VSV file, checkpoint feature, 254

# W

Web Access, RD, 412, 413–414, 425, 428, 429, 436
Web Deploy, 258, 259
Web roles, 448

Windows 8.1
  Enhanced Session Mode, 218–219
  Hyper-V, 196
  Hyper-V management tools, 204
Windows Authorization Manager, 209
Windows Azure. *See* Azure
Windows Deployment Service, 202, 241, 522
Windows Filtering Platform callout driver, 80, 81
Windows Hypervisor Interface Library, 38
Windows Server 2012 R2 Datacenter, 24, 195
Windows Server 2012 R2 Standard, 24, 196
Windows Server Hyper-V features. *See also*
  Hyper-V
    Windows Server 2008, 12–13
    Windows Server 2008 R2, 13–15
    Windows Server 2008 R2 Service Pack 1, 15–16
    Windows Server 2012, 16–21
    Windows Server 2012 R2, 21–23
Windows Server Update Services (WSUS), 201,
  244–245, 292, 510
witness
  disk witness, 277–279, 282, 286, 510
  dynamic witness, 283, 284, 337, 524
  file share witness, 277–279, 286, 287, 510
  witness service capability, 167, 169
witness service capability, 167, 169
wizards
  Add Network Service Wizard, 128
  Add Roles And Features Wizard, 424
  Cluster Migration Wizard, 237–238, 239,
    240
  cluster setup, 275
  Create Cloud Wizard, 387–388
  Create Cluster Wizard, 304, 307
  Create Collection Wizard, 425
  Create Logical Network Wizard, 89, 100
  Create Logical Switch Wizard, 109
  Create User Role Wizard, 392
  Create Virtual Machine Wizard, 316, 463, 481
  Edit Virtual Disk Wizard, 69, 159
  Extend Replication Wizard, 352
  New iSCSI Virtual Disk Wizard, 176
  New Storage Pool Wizard, 162
  New Virtual Hard Disk Wizard, 70
  New Virtual Machine Wizard, 314
  Out Of Box Experience Wizard, 218
  Replication Configuration Wizard, 346
  Validate a Configuration Wizard, 304
Worker roles, 448
workspaces
  Fabric workspace, 89, 100, 107, 109, 125, 128, 202,
    246, 308, 381
  SCVMM management console, 379
  VMs And Services workspace, 104, 110, 117, 129,
    221, 224, 260, 335, 379, 385, 387
World Wide Node Name. *See* WWNN
World Wide Port Names. *See* WWPNs
write caching, 156–157
write-back cache, 164, 314
writers, VSS, 234, 249–250, 251, 271, 348, 523
WS-MAN, 144
WSUS. *See* Windows Server Update Services
wunderbars, 379. *See also* workspaces
WWNN (World Wide Node Name), 181
WWPNs (World Wide Port Names), 181–184

# X

x86 architecture, 2
XenServer, 26, 233, 333, 376, 382, 385, 390, 496
XML file, checkpoint feature, 254